TOWARD A THEORY OF LIBRARIANSHIP

Papers in Honor of
JESSE HAUK SHERA

edited by
Conrad H. Rawski

The Scarecrow Press, Inc.
Metuchen, N. J.   1973

Library of Congress Cataloging in Publication Data
Main entry under title:

Toward a theory of librarianship.

    CONTENTS: Foreword, by V. W. Clapp.--A bibliography
of Jesse Hauk Shera, by G. M. Isard (p.   )--Intro-
duction, by C. H. Rawski. [etc.]
    1. Library science--Addresses, essays, lectures.
I. Shera, Jesse Hauk, 1903-   II. Rawski, Conrad H.,
ed.
Z674.T68   020   72-5764
ISBN 0-8108-0535-9

Frontispiece by Margaret Partington

ACKNOWLEDGMENTS

The editor of a collective volume such as this is indebted to many people. I would like to tender my thanks to all who, directly or indirectly, helped make this book: my students, faculty colleagues, fellow librarians, and friends.

Miss Margaret Kaltenbach and Richard K. Gardner consulted with me during the initial phases of the project. Miss Ruth A. Frear served as a reliable, ever cheerful editorial assistant and general amanuensis. Ryan Hoover and the secretarial staff of the School of Library Science, Case Western Reserve University, coped with sundry and often difficult typing and reprographic chores.

I am deeply grateful to the contributors, whose work and patience made the book possible. I am indebted to artists George Constant, for permission to reproduce his woodcut "The Kiss," and Margaret Partington, who did the pen and ink portrait of Dr. Shera; to Merald E. Wrolstad and his thought-provoking missives, some of which I used without citing the source; and to Mrs. Phyllis A. Richmond and Thomas J. Galvin, who listened to my editorial quandaries and made helpful suggestions. And, last but not least, I do thank my wife, Helen, who forgave the piles of copy on her oriental rug.

It should be noted that many of the papers contained in this volume were written in 1969 and early in 1970, hence do not consider the most recent publications that may pertain.

C. H. R.
Chagrin Falls, Ohio
June 1971

"Yet one inescapable conclusion emerges. Despite the fact that the topography of the future is obscured by yet undispelled fog, as the contours of Martha's Vineyard are shrouded by the mists of early morning, unquestionably there are tides running, and currents moving beneath the surface, that can dramatically reshape the coastline of librarianship so familiar to us today. The librarian can blind himself to these changes in his environment and follow the sabre-toothed tiger to extinction; or he can see in them the vision of a new heaven and a new earth with boundless opportunities for extended and more effective service, and with them, almost unlimited enrichment of the intellectual content of his professional practice."

J. H. Shera, Documentation and ..., p. 121.

CONTENTS

Foreword   (Verner W. Clapp)   7

A Bibliography of Jesse Hauk Shera
        (Gretchen M. Isard)   11

Introduction   (Conrad H. Rawski)   41

I.   THE PERTINENCE OF HISTORY   55

The Research and Writing of Library History
        (Sidney Ditzion)   55
Growth Patterns of Public Libraries
        (Dorothy M. Sinclair)   70
Origins of the Mouseion of Alexandria
        (H. J. de Vleeschauwer and H. Curtis Wright)   87

II.   BASIC ISSUES   115

The Interdisciplinarity of Librarianship
        (Conrad H. Rawski)   116
The Nature of Information Science (B. C. Vickery)   147
The Contribution of Classification to a Theory of
        Librarianship (D. J. Foskett)   169
Referential Consulting Networks (Manfred Kochen)   187
The World Encyclopedia Concept (Glynn Harmon)   221

III.   INFORMATION RETRIEVAL   233

On Information Retrieval Systems (William Goffman)   234
On a Fallacy in the Use of Computing Machines for
        Automated Dictionary Retrieval
        (Andrew D. Booth)   243
Browsing and Search Theory (Philip M. Morse)   246
The Symmetries of Ignorance (Robert A. Fairthorne)   262
A Thesaurus Within a Thesaurus: A Study in
        Ambiguity (Phyllis A. Richmond)   268

IV.   CATALOG TOPICS   303

When Is a Subject Not a Subject? (John Metcalfe)   303
From Pig to Man (Paul S. Dunkin)   339
Book Catalogs (Maurice F. Tauber and Hilda Feinberg)   350

V.   CONTEXTS   379

Historiographs, Librarianship, and the History of
      Science (Eugene Garfield)   380
Informal Communication in Science: Its Advantages
      and Its Formal Analogues (Herbert Menzel)   403
Writing-System: A Datum in Bibliographical
      Description (John Mountford)   415

VI.   FORECAST   451

Innovation in Libraries: Effect on Function and
      Organization (Robert S. Taylor)   451
The Library in the Future of Higher Education
      (Neal Harlow)   463

VII.   LIBRARY EDUCATION   471

The Library as a Complex Organization: Impli-
      cations for Library Education
      (Patricia B. Knapp)   472
What and How of Documentation Training
      (S. R. Ranganathan)   495
On the Professional Image and the Education of
      the Librarian (Horst Kunze)   515

The Contributors   523

Index   529

FOREWORD: Toward a Theory of Jesse Shera

As the editor will explain in his Introduction, in the very earliest discussion of plans for a collection of papers with which to honor Jesse Shera, it was agreed that the topic most consonant with the Dean's own life-long preoccupation and at the same time of significance for library work was the theory of librarianship. It would be difficult to contest, with any chance of success, the justice of this choice. In consequence, we have in the present volume, from the pens of some of the most distinguished of the Dean's contemporaries both here and abroad, a series of contributions assembled about this topic. It may be expected that future discussions of the philosophy of librarianship will be compelled to refer to the present work as necessarily as they will be compelled to refer to the work of the cheerful philosopher to whom it is dedicated. Librarianship will owe a debt to Professor Rawski and his colleagues, while owing a still greater debt to Jesse Shera.

It may, I think, be admitted that the philosophy of librarianship, no more than a theory of the cosmos or a system of ethics, can never be final and complete. The work of the human philosopher Jesse Shera, however, is by contrast sufficiently complete that it has assumed a form and shape the future will not greatly alter. It is not too early, in consequence, to devise a theory of Jesse Shera. But this is one thing that the present volume does not afford.

To most of us Jesse Shera is a phenomenon, like the universe itself, or--to take an example closer at hand--like the fire-works on a Fourth of July celebration. Out there in the gloom and the smoke we see a shadowy figure at work. Suddenly we hear a hiss and a roar, and the night is suddenly stabbed by a brilliant flash which reveals our surroundings in a strange new light. Jesse Shera has done it again! Another flash! We get an entirely different view! Sometimes whimsical little ideas whirl and wriggle around in the black sky, uttering squeals of mischievous glee. Then again, there is no light at all, but only a loud detonation--

bang! ... bang-bang! ... bang!--followed by silence pro-
founder than before.

And this, of course, has been going on for 30 years
or more. What does go on? Only someone who has lived
close to the source can know enough of the facts even to
hazard conjectures toward an explanation. Margaret Egan
could perhaps have told us, but her absence in this matter
is only one of the ways in which we suffer from her loss.

Gretchen Isard's bibliography of the writings of Dean
Shera which follows this Foreword provides some clues that
would undoubtedly contribute to any theory of Jesse Shera.
Here we find that, from January 1931 to December 1971,
Dean Shera was the author of 381 separate publications--
books, articles, contributions, reports, editorials, columns,
and reviews. The average for the entire period was over
nine per year. In 14 of the years he had over ten publications a year, and in seven he had over 20. In his (numeri-
cally) most productive year he had 26 publications (four contributions, six articles, ten columns and six reviews). His
prodigious range attests the liveliness of his mind--he goes
from book-binding to Thomas Jefferson to epistemology with
no loss of pace or assurance. Liveliness, indeed, a sure
self-confidence, and felicity of expression are the hall-marks
of his manner. These are displayed in his titles--"Automation without Fear," "Little Girls Don't Play Librarian," "On
Keeping Up with Keeping Up," "Librarians' Pugwash," "O!
Medium, O! Media." But he is also a confirmed balloon-
pricker: "Yes, Virginia, There Is a Verner Clapp."

And, of course, all the time that he was shooting off
all these sparks, he was holding down a series of important
full-time jobs.

Now no one claims, I think, that with all his pyro-
technics Jesse Shera invariably hits his target. If he has
scored more bull's eyes than most of us, he has also had
his share of missing wide the mark, of Homeric nodding,
and of simple error. But here, too, appears a function of
his mystique. The fact is that Jesse Shera has been too
many for us; we could not keep up with him; and while we
were heavily preparing to confront him on one front, he was
gaily firing off on another. If we had really wanted to contain him, we should have had to appoint a "truth squad" (as
the Republicans used to call it) to camp on his trail.

But for this we lacked the incentive; Jesse Shera was

much too engaging, much too lovable, to motivate the appointment of a "truth squad." And this has been an essential element in the theory. To introduce a personal note, although I do not feel myself to be eye-to-eye with Dean Shera on many matters of library doctrine, I shall always count as among the most enjoyable hours of my life the day I spent in his company, plodding in a cold November rain through the French countryside, together with the British documentalist, D. J. Urquhart.

Here are a few of the makings. Will someone now please give us a complete theory of Jesse Shera?

Verner W. Clapp
Washington, D. C.

A BIBLIOGRAPHY OF JESSE HAUK SHERA

Compiled by Gretchen M. Isard; through December 1971

BOOKS

1. Foundations of the Public Library: The Origins of the
   Public Library Movement in New England, 1629-1855.
   Chicago: University of Chicago Press, 1949.

2. ed. with Margaret E. Egan. Bibliographic Organization: Papers Presented Before the Fifteenth Annual
   Conference of the Graduate Library School, July 24-29,
   1950. Chicago: University of Chicago Press, 1951.

3. Historians, Books, and Libraries. Cleveland: Western Reserve University Press, 1953.

4. with Margaret E. Egan. The Classified Catalog:
   Basic Principles and Practices. Chicago: American
   Library Association, 1956.

5. ed. with Allen Kent and James W. Perry. Documentation in Action. New York: Reinhold Publishing Co.,
   1956.

6. ed. with Allen Kent and James W. Perry. Information Systems in Documentation New York: Interscience
   Publishers, Inc., 1957.

7. ed. with Allen Kent and James W. Perry. Informa-
   tion Resources: A Challenge to American Science and
   Industry. Cleveland: Western Reserve University
   Press, 1958.

8. Libraries and the Organization of Knowledge. D. J.
   Foskett, ed. London: Crosby Lockwood & Son,
   Ltd.; Hamden, Conn.: Archon Books, 1965.

9. Documentation and the Organization of Knowledge.

D. J. Foskett, ed. London: Crosby Lockwood & Son
Ltd.; Hamden, Conn.: Archon Books, 1966.

10. The Compleat Librarian. Cleveland: Press of Case
Western Reserve University, 1971.

11. The Sociological Foundations of Librarianship. New
York: Asia Publishing House, 1970. (Sarada Ranganathan Lectures, no. 3, 1967).

CHAPTERS IN BOOKS

12. "Libraries and Museums" in Seba Eldridge, ed.,
Development of Collective Enterprise: Dynamics of an
Emergent Economy. Lawrence: University of Kansas
Press, 1943, p. 183-207.

13. "The Center of Documentation--A Regional Approach"
in Philadelphia Biographical Center and Union Library
Catalogue. Documentation on a Regional Basis. Symposium on Post-War Activities. Philadelphia: The
Center, 1944, p. vi-ix (mimeographed).

14. "Administration of the Library--Technical Operations"
in Margaret E. Egan, Survey of the Saginaw Library
System. Chicago: The Author, 1948, p. 103-127.

15. "A Summary of the Historical Background of Classification Theory" in U.S. Research and Development
Board. Special Committee on Technical Information.
Symposium on Special Classification Systems. Washington, D.C.: U.S. Research and Development Board,
1949, p. 1-6 (mimeographed).

16. with Margaret E. Egan. "The Training of Librarians
and Documentalists in the United States" in Suzanne
Briet Enquiry Concerning the Professional Education
of Librarians and Documentalists; Report to the Joint
Committee of the International Federation of Library
Associations and of the International Federation for
Documentation. Paris: United Nations Educational,
Scientific, and Cultural Organization, 1951.

17. "The Beginnings of Systematic Bibliography in Amer-
ica, 1642-1799" in Frederick R. Goff, ed., Essays
Honoring Lawrence C. Wroth. Portland, Maine:
[Anthoensen Press] 1951, p. 263-278.

18. "Classification: Current Functions and Applications to
     the Subject Analysis of Library Materials" in Maurice
     F. Tauber, ed., The Subject Analysis of Library Ma-
     terials. New York: Columbia University School of
     Library Service, 1953, p. 29-42.

19. with Margaret E. Egan. "A Review of the Present
     State of Librarianship and Documentation" in S. C.
     Bradford Documentation. 2nd ed. London: Crosby
     Lockwood & Son Ltd., 1953, p. 11-45.
        Spanish translation: "Examen del Estado Actuel de
     la Biblioteconomia y de la Documentacion." Santa Fe,
     Argentina: Centro de Documentacion e Informacion de
     Asuntos Municipales, 1965, 45p.

20. "The Role of the College Library--A Reappraisal" in
     Library-Instructional Integration on the College Level.
     Chicago: Association of College and Reference Li-
     braries, April 1955 (A.C.R.L. Monographs No. 13),
     p. 6-13.

21. Preface to Eunice Keen. Manual for Use in the Cata-
     loging of Audio-Visual Materials for a High School
     Library. Lakeland, Fla.: The Author, 1965, p. iii.

22. Foreword to James W. Perry, Allen Kent, and
     Madeline M. Berry. Machine Literature Searching.
     New York: Western Reserve University Press and
     Interscience Publishers, 1956, p. v-vi.

23. Foreword to James W. Perry and Allen Kent.
     Documentation and Information Retrieval. Cleveland:
     Western Reserve University Press and Interscience
     Publishers, 1957, p. iii-v.

24. "Patterns, Structure, and Conceptualization in Classi-
     fication" in Proceedings of the International Study
     Conference on Classification for Information Retrieval.
     London: Aslib, 1957, p. 15-27.

25. "What Lies Ahead in Classification" in Thelma Eaton
     and Donald E. Strout, eds., The Role of Classification
     in the Modern American Library. Champaign, Ill.:
     Illini Union Bookstore, 1959, p. 116-128.

26. "Communicating Office of Education Statistics" in
     U.S. Office of Education, Advisory Committee of
     Users of Educational Statistics Report. Washington,

D.C.: U.S. Department of Health, Education and Welfare, 1960, p. 33-41.

27. "Present Day Methods for the Storage and Retrieval of Information" in Margaret I. Rufsvold and Carolyn Guss, eds., Proceedings of the Work Conference on Bibliographic Control of Newer Educational Media. Bloomington: Indiana University, 1960, p. 42-55.

28. "Common Languages in Librarianship and Documentation" in Allen Kent, ed., Information Retrieval and Machine Translation. Part II. New York: Interscience Publishers, Inc., 1961, p. 1051-1060.

29. "Developments in Machine Literature Searching" in Edward A. Tomeski, Richard W. Wescott, and Mary Covington, eds., The Clarification, Unification, and Integration of Information Storage and Retrieval. Proceedings of February 23, 1961 Symposium. New York: Management Dynamics; Lincoln Square Chapter, Systems and Procedures Association, Science Technology Division; New York Chapter, Special Libraries Association, 1961, p. 22-34.

30. "Automation Without Fear" in D. J. Foskett and B. I. Palmer, eds., The Sayers Memorial Volume: Essays in Librarianship in Memory of William Charles Berwick Sayers. London: The Library Association, 1961, p. 168-181 [see also no. 124].

31. "Objectives of the School of Library Science." Western Reserve University, School of Library Science, Academic Year 1961-62. Cleveland: The School, p. 1-5.

32. with Barbara Denison. "College and University Libraries" in article on "Libraries," Encyclopedia Americana. New York: Americana Corporation, 1962, p. 385-388.

33. "The Propaedeutic of the New Librarianship" in Wesley Simonton, ed., Information Retrieval Today: Papers Presented at the Institute Conducted by the Library School and the Center for Continuation Study, University of Minnesota, September 19-22, 1962. Minneapolis: Center for Continuation Study, University of Minnesota, 1963, p. 5-19.

34.   "The Book Catalog and the Scholar--A Reexamination
       of an Old Partnership" in Robert E. Kingery and
       Maurice F. Tauber Book Catalogs. New York: Scare-
       crow Press, 1963, p. 1-12 [see also no. 129].

35.   "Libraries, History of" in article on "Libraries,"
       Encyclopedia International. New York: Grolier, Inc.,
       1964, p. 521-522.

36.   "Librarianship as a Career." World Topics Yearbook.
       Lake Bluff, Ill.: United Educators, Inc., 1964, p.
       207-217.

37.   "Staffing Library Service to Meet Student Needs--
       Library Education" in American Library Association,
       Student Use of Libraries: An Inquiry Into the Needs of
       Students, Libraries, and the Educational Process.
       Papers of the Conference Within a Conference, July
       16-18, 1963. Chicago: American Library Association,
       1964, p. 122-133.

38.   with Barbara Denison. "Library" in American Edu-
       cators Encyclopedia. v. 9. Lake Bluff, Ill.: United
       Educators, Inc., 1964, p. L-124--L-151.

39.   "Introduction and Welcome" in A. J. Goldwyn and
       Alan M. Rees, eds., The Education of Science In-
       formation Personnel--1964. Proceedings of an Invi-
       tational Conference. Cleveland: Center for Docu-
       mentation and Communication Research, School of
       Library Science, Western Reserve University, 1965,
       p. 1-5.

40.   "Changing Concepts of Classification, Philosophical
       and Educational Implications" in P. N. Kaula, ed., Li-
       brary Science Today: Ranganathan Festschrift. v. 1.
       New York: Asia Publishing House, 1965, p. 37-48.

41.   "The Problem of Finance. Working Paper No. 4"
       in Sarah R. Reed, ed., Problems of Library School
       Administration. Report of an Institute, April 14-15,
       1965. Washington, D.C.: U.S. Department of
       Health, Education and Welfare. Office of Education,
       1965, p. 33-45.

42.   "The Present State of Education and Training in
       Documentation, Information Science, and Special
       Librarianship in the United States" in Proceedings of

the 31st Meeting and Congress of the International Federation for Documentation in Cooperation with the American Documentation Institute. Washington, D.C. October 7-16, 1965. Washington, D.C.: Spartan Books, 1966, p. 27-37.

43. "Automated Information Exchange for Business and Industry" in Report of a Rochester Area Conference on Technology Transfer and Innovation in Business and Industry. Rochester: University of Rochester and the State Technical Services Administration, New York State Department of Commerce, 1967, p. 21-24.

44. "Comments" in Barbara Denison, Robert G. Cheshier, and Alan M. Rees, eds., Proceedings of a Conference on Regional Medical Library Service. Cleveland: Cleveland Medical Society Library and School of Library Science, Western Reserve University, 1967, p. 38-52.

45. "The Library Profession." Introduction to Peterson's Career and Adviser's Booklet to Librarianship and Information Science. Princeton, N.J.: Peterson's Guides, Inc., 1967.

46. "Information Storage and Retrieval—Libraries" in David L. Sills, ed., International Encyclopedia of the Social Sciences. v. 7. New York: Macmillan-Free Press, 1968, p. 314-318.

47. "Libraries" in George D. Stoddard, ed., Living History of the World. 1968 Yearbook. New York: Stravon Publishers, 1968, p. 318-319.

48. "Federal Support for Income and Expenditures of Library Education Programs" in Frank L. Schick, ed., North American Library Education: Directory and Statistics, 1966-1968. Chicago: American Library Association, 1968, p. 1-4.

49. "An Epistemological Foundation for Library Science" in Edward B. Montgomery, ed., The Foundations of Access to Knowledge. A Symposium. Syracuse, N.Y.: Syracuse University Press, 1968, p. 7-25.

50. "Preface" in Gorgonio D. Siega, ed., Librarianship as a Profession in the Philippines: Proceedings of the First Regional Seminar of College and University

Librarians; Bisayas and Mindanao Areas. Nov. 11-13, 1968. Dumaguete City, P.I.: Silliman University Library, 1969, p. iii-v.

51. "Libraries" in George D. Stoddard, ed., Living History of the World Yearbook, 1969. New York: Stravon Educational Press and Parents' Magazine, 1969, p. 314-315.

52. with Anne Southworth McFarland. "Professional Aspects of Information Science and Technology" in Carlos A. Cuadra, ed., Annual Review of Information Science, v. 4. Chicago: Encyclopaedia Britannica Inc., 1969, p. 439-471.

53. "The Library and Social Change." in World Topics Yearbook, 1970. Lake Bluff, Illinois: United Educators, Inc., 1970, p. 257-263.

54. "Case Western Reserve University. School of Library Science" in Allen Kent and Harold Lancour eds. Encyclopedia of Library and Information Science. New York: Marcel Dekker, 1971, v. 4 p. 220-228.

55. "Research Needs Relating to the Aims and Needs of Graduate Library Education. in Harold Borko, ed. A Study of the Research Needs of Library and Information Science Education. Final Report. Los Angeles: Institute of Library Research, University of California at Los Angeles, 1970, p. 21-46.

56. "Libraries" in World Topics Yearbook, 1971. Lake Bluff, Ill.: United Educators, 1971, p. 299-302.

REPORTS

57. with Margaret E. Egan. The United States Report on National and International Bibliographic Problems. Chicago: Graduate Library School, University of Chicago, 1950, 14p. (mimeographed).

58. Report of the United States Delegate to the UNESCO Conference on the Improvement of Bibliographic Services: Paris, France, November 7-10, 1950. Chicago: Graduate Library School, University of Chicago, 1951, 15+, 16+, 14+.

59. Program for the Stimulation of National Bibliography

in the Critical Areas.   Chicago: American Library Association, 1953, 4p. (mimeographed).

60. Proposal for a Study of the Curriculum of the School of
    Library Science, Western Reserve University.   Cleve-
    land: Western Reserve University, 1953, 10p.

61. with Barbara Denison.   "Documentation in Action."
    American Scientist, v. 44, no. 2 (April 1956), p. 94A-
    104A.

62. "Report of the Publications Committee."   Special Li-
    braries.   v. 47, no. 6 (July-August 1956), p. 270-274.

63. with Allen Kent.   Resolution of the Literature Crisis
    in the Decade 1960-1970.   Cleveland: Western Reserve
    University, School of Library Science, Center for
    Documentation and Communication Research, 1958, 21p.

64. with Theodore C. Hines.   Report of Consultants to the
    Ad Hoc Committee on the Establishment of a School of
    Library Studies at the State University of New York at
    Buffalo.   Buffalo: State University of New York at
    Buffalo, 1965, 51p. (mimeographed).

65. "Special Libraries, Why 'Special'?"   in Robert J.
    Havlik, Bill M. Woods, and Leona A. Vogt, eds.
    Special Libraries: Problems and Cooperative Potentials.
    (Prepared for the President's National Advisory Com-
    mission on Libraries) Washington, D.C.: American
    Documentation Institute, 1967, p. 5-16.

66. "Report on the Proposed Doctoral Program in the De-
    partment of Library Science, School of Graduate
    Studies, University of Toronto."   October 31, 1970
    (unpublished), 7p.

ARTICLES

67. "Handmaidens of the Learned World."   Library Journal.
    v. 56, no. 1 (January 1931), p. 21-22.

68. "The Age Factor in Employment--a Bibliography."
    Bulletin of Bibliography.   v. 14, no. 5 (May-August
    1931), p. 100-101; no. 6 (September-December 1931),
    p. 128-129; no. 7 (January-April 1932), p. 154-155;
    no. 8 (May-August 1932), p. 175-177; no. 9 (September-

December 1932), p. 193-195.

69. "The Place of Library Service in Research: A Suggestion." Libraries. v. 36, no. 9 (November 1931), p. 387-390.

70. "The Librarian's 'Changing World.' " Library Journal. v. 58, no. 4 (February 15, 1933), p. 149-152.

71. "Recent Social Trends and Future Library Policy." Library Quarterly. v. 3, no. 4 (October 1933), p. 339-353.

72. " 'Viewpoint Shift in Reference Work' " Special Libraries. v. 25, no. 9 (November 1934), p. 235-237.

73. "An Eddy in the Western Flow of American Culture: the History of Printing and Publishing in Oxford, Ohio, 1827-1841." Ohio State Archaeological and Historical Quarterly, v. 44, no. 1 (January 1935), p. 103-137.

74. "The 'Unaffiliated' Member and the S. L. A." Special Libraries. v. 26, no. 5 (May-June 1935), p. 124-125.

75. "The College Library of the Future." American Library Association Bulletin. v. 30, no. 6 (June 1936), p. 494-501.

76. "Richmond--and Beyond!" Wilson Bulletin, v. 10, no. 10 (June 1936), p. 648-649.

77. "College Librarianship and Educational Reform." American Library Association Bulletin. v. 31, no. 3 (March 1937), p. 141-146.

78. "Training for 'Specials'; a Prologue to Revision." Special Libraries. v. 28, no. 5 (May-June 1937), p. 139-144.

79. "Barred Gates: a Librarian's Plea for Freedom." P. N. L. A. Quarterly. v. 1, no. 4 (July 1937), p. 54-55.

80. "Training for 'Specials': The Status of the Library Schools." Special Libraries. v. 28, no. 9 (Nov. 1937), p. 317-321.

81. "Swan-song of a Junior." American Library Associa-

tion Bulletin. v. 32, no. 3 (March 1938), p. 181-184.

82.   "The Strength of the Pack." Cincinnati Chapter,
       Special Libraries Association, Newsletter, (Dec. 1938),
       p. 2-3.

83.   "Accent on Youth; the Significance of A. L. A. Reorgani-
       zation for the Young Librarian." Wilson Bulletin. v.
       13, no. 5 (Jan. 1939), p. 312-313; 324.

84.   "Special Library Objectives and Their Relation to Ad-
       ministration." Special Libraries. v. 35, no. 3 (March
       1944), p. 91-94.

85.   "The Literature of American Library History."
       Library Quarterly. v. 15, no. 1 (Jan. 1945), p. 1-24.

86.   with Margaret E. Egan. "Prolegomena to Bibliographic
       Control." Journal of Cataloging and Classification.
       v. 5, no. 2 (Winter 1949), p. 17-19.

87.   with Margaret E. Egan. "Documentation in the United
       States." American Documentation. v. 1, no. 1
       (Jan. 1950), p. 8-12.

88.   "The UNESCO Conference on the Improvement of Bib-
       liographic Services: A Preliminary Report." Amer-
       ican Documentation. v. 1, no. 3 (Aug. 1950), p. 144-
       146 [see also no. 92].

89.   with Margaret E. Egan. "The United States Report on
       National and International Bibliographic Problems."
       American Documentation. v. 1., no. 3 (Aug. 1950),
       p. 146-151.

90.   "Documentation; Its Scope and Limitations." Library
       Quarterly. v. 21, no. 1 (Jan. 1951), p. 13-26.

91.   with Margaret E. Egan. "The Present State of Bib-
       liography in the United States; a Condensation of the
       U. S. Report on National and International Bibliographic
       Problems." ALA Bulletin. v. 45, no. 2 (Feb. 1951),
       p. 52-55.

92.   "The UNESCO Conference on the Improvement of Bib-
       liographic Services." U. S. Department of State Bul-
       letin. v. 24, no. 617 (April 30, 1951), p. 707-709

[see also no. 88].

93. "Bibliographic Management." American Documentation. v. 2, no. 1 (Winter 1951), p. 47-54.

94. "Effect of Machine Methods on the Organization of Knowledge." American Documentation. v. 3, no. 1 (Winter 1952), p. 15-20.

95. "The Preservation of Local Illinois Newspapers. A Report of the Committee on Local Illinois Newspapers." I.L.A. Record. v. 5, no. 3 (March 1952), p. 49-52.

96. with Margaret E. Egan. "Foundations of a Theory of Bibliography." Library Quarterly. v. 22, no. 2 (April 1952), p. 125-137.

97. "On the Value of Library History." Library Quarterly, v. 22, no. 3 (July 1952), p. 240-251.

98. "Special Librarianship and Documentation." Library Trends. v. 1, no. 2 (Oct. 1952), p. 189-199.

99. "Emergence of a New Institutional Structure for the Dissemination of Specialized Information." American Documentation. v. 4, no. 4 (Fall 1953), p. 163-173.

100. "Education for Librarianship--An Integrated Approach." ALA Bulletin. v. 38, no. 3 (March 1954), p. 129-130; 169-173.

101. with Barbara Denison. "Preliminary Planning Conference on Information Processing and Correlation." American Documentation. v. 6, no. 3 (July 1955), p. 162-166.

102. "Training the Chemical Librarian: a Challenge and an Opportunity." Special Libraries. v. 47, no. 1 (Jan. 1956), p. 8-16.

103. "Librarianship in a High Key." ALA Bulletin. v. 50, no. 2 (Feb. 1956), p. 103-105.

104. "Research and Training in Documentation at Western Reserve University." Microcosm. v. 2, no. 1 (Spring 1956), p. 3.

105. "Mirror for Documentalists." D.C. Libraries. v. 27, no. 2 (April 1956), p. 2-4.

106. "On the Teaching of Cataloging." Journal of Cataloging and Classification. v. 12, no. 3 (July 1956), p. 130-132.

107. "Putting Knowledge to Work--The Reaffirmation of a Credo, A Rededication to the Faith." Special Libraries. v. 47, no. 7 (Sept. 1956), p. 322-325.

108. "Knowledge Goes Berserk." Saturday Review. Dec. 1, 1956, p. 69-71.

109. "The Librarians' New Frontier." Library Journal. v. 82, no. 1 (Jan. 1, 1957), p. 26-28.

110. "Research and Development in Documentation." Library Trends. v. 6, no. 2 (Oct. 1957), p. 187-206.

111. "Classification at Dorking; the International Study Conference on Classification for Information Retrieval." Library Resources and Technical Services. v. 2, no. 1 (Jan. 1958), p. 33-43.

112. "Background Courses in Education for Librarianship." Association of American Library Schools Bulletin. June 1958, p. 20-22.

113. "Education for Documentation." Special Libraries. v. 49, no. 8 (Oct. 1958), p. 389-390.

114. "The Place of Bookbinding in the Library School Curriculum." The Rub-Off. v. 10, no. 1 (Jan. -Feb. 1959), p. 1-3.

115. "Isis and the Librarian's Quest for Unity." OLA Bulletin. v. 29, no. 2 (April 1959), p. 19;21.

116. "New Tools for Easing the Burden of Historical Research." American Documentation. v. 10, no. 4 (Oct. 1959), p. 274-277.

117. "Theory and Technique in Library Education." Library Journal. v. 85, no. 9 (May 1, 1960), p. 1736-1739.

118.   "The Changing Philosophy of Bibliographic Classifica-
       tion." Revue de la Documentation. v. 27, no. 4 (Nov.
       1960), p. 139-140.

119.   "Social Epistemology, General Semantics, and Librar-
       ies." Yearbook of the Institute of General Semantics.
       Nos. 26 & 27 (1960), p. 19-21 [see also no. 121].

120.   "An Educational Program for Special Librarians."
       Journal of Education for Librarianship. v. 1, no. 3
       (Winter 1961), p. 121-128.

121.   "Social Epistemology, General Semantics, and Librar-
       ies." Wilson Library Bulletin. v. 35, no. 10 (June
       1961), p. 767-770 [see also no. 119].

122.   "The Librarian and the Machine." Library Journal.
       v. 86, no. 12 (June 15, 1961) p. 2250-2254.

123.   "How Much is a Physicist's Inertia Worth?" Physics
       Today. v. 14, no. 8 (Aug. 1961), p. 42-63.

124.   "Automation Without Fear." ALA Bulletin. v. 55, no.
       9 (Oct. 1961), p. 787-794 [see also no. 30].

125.   "What is Librarianship?" Louisiana Library Associa-
       tion. v. 24, no. 3 (Fall 1961) p. 95-97.

126.   "The Dignity and Advancement of Bacon." College and
       Research Libraries. v. 23, no. 1 (Jan. 1962), p. 18-
       23.

127.   "On Keeping Up with Keeping Up." UNESCO Bulletin
       for Libraries. v. 16, no. 2 (March-April 1962), p.
       64-72.

128.   "How Engineers Can Keep Abreast of Professional and
       Technical Literature." ASME Design Engineering
       Conference. 1962, p. 49-53.

129.   "The Book Catalog and the Scholar--A Reexamination
       of an Old Partnership." Library Resources and Tech-
       nical Services. v. 6, no. 3 (Summer 1962), p. 210-
       216 [see also no. 34].

130.   "Little Girls Don't Play Librarian." Library Journal.
       v. 87, no. 22 (Dec. 15, 1962), p. 4483-4487.

131. "The Library of the Future." UNESCO Courrier. v.
      16 (Jan. 1963), p. 11-13 (also translated into French,
      Spanish, German, Russian, Japanese, Portuguese)
      [see also no. 134].

132. "Toward a Program for Ohio Librarians." The Rub-
      Off. v. 14, no. 2 (March-April 1963), p. 1-3.

133. "Toward a New Dimension for Library Education."
      ALA Bulletin. v. 57, no. 4 (April 1963), p. 313-317.

134. "Library of the Future." Indian Librarian. v. 18
      (June 1963), p. 20-24 [see also no. 131].

135. "Staffing Library Services to Meet Student Needs--Li-
      brary Education." An Inquiry Into the Needs of Stu-
      dents, Libraries, and the Educational Process. ALA
      Conference Within a Conference. 1963, 7p.

136. "S. R. Ranganathan--One American View." Pakistan
      Library Review. v. 4, nos. 3 & 4 (Nov.-Dec. 1962),
      p. 6-8 [see also no. 191].

137. "O! Medium, O! Media." Library Journal. v. 88,
      no. 19 (Nov. 1, 1963), p. 4149-4151.

138. "In Defense of Diversity." Journal of Education for
      Librarianship. v. 4, no. 3 (Winter 1964), p. 137-142.

139. Introduction (to special issue on documentation and
      automation). Wilson Library Bulletin. v. 38, no. 9
      (May 1964), p. 741-742.

140. "Dimensions of the Master's Program." ALA Bulletin.
      v. 35, no. 6 (June 1964), p. 519-522.

141. "Automation and the Reference Librarian." RQ. v. 3,
      no. 6 (July 1964), p. 3-7.

142. "Darwin, Bacon, and Research in Librarianship."
      Library Trends. v. 13, no. 1 (July 1964), p. 141-149.

143. "Western Reserve University Library School."
      Ohioana: of Ohio and Ohioans. v. 7, no. 4 (Winter
      1964), p. 131-133.

144. "Machine Retrieval Systems and Automated Procedures.
      Part A. Use of Automated Systems." Journal of

Medical Education. v. 40, no. 1 (January 1965) p. 46-
49.

145.   "Librarian's Pugwash, or Intrex on the Cape."
        Wilson Library Bulletin. v. 40, no. 4 (December
        1965), p. 359-362.

146.   "The Library as an Agency of Social Communication."
        Journal of Documentation. v. 21, no. 4 (December
        1965), p. 241-243.

147.   Introduction (to special issue on bibliographic organiza-
        tion) Wilson Library Bulletin. v. 40, no. 8 (April
        1966), p. 703-705.

148.   "The Library: Institutional Deep-Freeze or Intellec-
        tual Accelerator?" Outlook (Western Reserve Uni-
        versity). v. 3, no. 4 (Summer 1966) p. 6-9 [see
        also no. 152].

149.   "The Beginning of a Great Career." SOLTAS News
        (Florida State University Library School). v. 21, no. 4
        (Sept. 1966) p. 3-4.

150.   "Foundations of a Theory of Reference Service."
        Reference, Research and Regionalist. 1966, p. 13-20.

151.   "The Changing Role of the Reference Librarian."
        Reference, Research and Regionalist. 1966, p. 21-34.

152.   "The Library: Institutional Deep-Freeze or Intellec-
        tual Accelerator?" The Library Binder, v. 14, no. 2
        (December 1966), p. 25-32 [see also no. 148].

153.   "Beyond 1984: What Is Past Is Prologue." ALA
        Bulletin. v. 61, no. 1 (Jan. 1967), p. 35-47.

154.   "Librarians Against Machines." Science. v. 156,
        no. 3776, p. 746-750 [see also no. 155].

155.   "Librarians Against Machines." (revised version)
        Wilson Library Bulletin. v. 42, no. 1 (Sept. 1967),
        p. 65-73 [see also no. 154].

156.   "More Library Schools," Ohio Library Association
        Bulletin. Oct. 1967, p. 5-9.

157.   with Conrad H. Rawski. "The Diagram Is the

Message." Library Resources and Technical Services. v. 11, no. 4 (Fall 1967), p. 487-498
[see also no. 159].

158.   "What Librarianship Is of Most Worth?" Ohio Association of School Librarians Bulletin. v. 20, no. 1
(Jan. 1968), p. 4-9.

159.   with Conrad H. Rawski. "The Diagram is the Message." Journal of Typographic Research. v. 2, no.
2 (April 1968), p. 171-188 [see also no. 157].

160.   "On the Importance of Theory." The Rub-Off. v. 19,
no. 3 (May-June 1968), p. 2-4.

161.   "Of Librarianship, Documentation, and Information
Science." UNESCO Bulletin for Libraries. v. 22, no.
2 (March-April 1968), p. 58-65.
        Reprinted in Arthur W. Elias, ed., Key Papers
in Information Science. Washington, D.C.: American
Society for Information Science, 1971, p. 4-11.

162.   "The Cerebral Foundations of Library Science."
Library School Review. (Kansas State Teachers College) Oct. 1968, p. 3-6.

163.   "The Quiet Stir of Thought, or What the Computer Cannot Do." Library Journal v. 94, no. 15 (September
1, 1969), p. 2875-2880.
        First issued as a separate by the State University
of New York at Geneseo, as the Richardson Lecture
for 1969, at the School of Library Science. Geneseo,
New York: School of Library Science, College of
Arts and Sciences, State University of New York,
1969. iv.+22p.
        Also reprinted in Library Association Record. v.
72, no. 2 (February 1970), p. 37-42.

164.   "Twelve Apostles and a Few Heretics." (Short
version.) American Library Association. Library
Education Division. News Letter. no. 68 (February
1969), p. 24-26.
        Same (full version), Journal of Education for Li-
brarianship. v. 10, no. 1 (Summer 1969), p. 3-10.

165.   " 'The Hungry Sheep Look Up'; A Prolegomena to a
Theory of Education for Librarianship." Library
School Review (Department of Librarianship. Kansas

State Teachers College, Emporia, Kansas), 1969.
p. 3-7.

166.   "The New Constituency and Library Education in the
        '70s." Florida Libraries. v. 20, no. 4 (December
        1969), p. 185-192.

167.   "The School of Library Science at Case Western Uni-
        versity." The Library Binder. v. 17, no. 2
        (December 1969), p. 20-24.

168.   "Plus ça Change." Library Journal. v. 95, no. 6
        (March 15, 1970), p. 979-986.

169.   "The Readiness Is All." Ohio Library Association
        Bulletin. v. 40, no. 2 (April 1970), p. 4-9.

170.   "What Is a Book That a Man May Know It?" Bulletin
        of the Cleveland Medical Library. v. 17, no. 2 (April
        1970), p. 32-43.

171.   "The Library School and its Dean." The Rub-Off. v.
        21, no. 3 (May-June 1970), p. 30-33.

172.   "President's Message." Beta Phi Mu Newsletter.
        no. 30 (November 1970), p. 1-2.

173.   "The Sociological Relationships of Information Science."
        Journal of The American Society for Information Sci-
        ence. v. 22 (March-April 1971), p. 76-80.

174.   "President's Message." Beta Phi Mu Newsletter. no.
        31 (April 1971), p. 1-3.

WILSON LIBRARY BULLETIN COLUMNS

Volume 36

175.   "Cloudland Revisited." Sept. 1961, p. 69.
176.   "Of Red Carpets and Pruning Shears." Oct. 1961,
        p. 170; 175.
177.   "Cult of the Audio-Visual." Nov. 1961, p. 251.
178.   "A Curriculum for Mr. Ciardi." Dec. 1961, p. 330.
179.   "The 'Dismal Science' and Librarianship." Jan. 1962, p.
        382.
180.   "Officer, Arrest That Book!" Feb. 1962, p. 488.
181.   "Cards Is Cards." March 1962, p. 586; 588.

28 Toward a Theory of Librarianship

182. "The Bad-Humor Man." April 1962, p. 682.
183. "On the Permanence of the Invisible." May 1962, p. 764.
184. "Only Low Conversation." June 1962, p. 846.

Volume 37

185. "Fremont Rides Through the Dewey Dewey Fog." Sept. 1962, p. 69-72; 81
186. "What Is a Book?" Oct. 1962, p. 176.
187. "Discipline, Dissent, and Documentation." Nov. 1962, p. 290-291.
188. "Yes, Virginia, There Is a Verner Clapp." Dec. 1962, p. 358-359.
189. "In Defense of Miss Groby." Jan. 1963, p. 430.
190. "Libraries Are for Growing." Feb. 1963, p. 498-499.
191. "S. R. Ranganathan--An American View." March 1963, p. 581-582 [see also no. 136].
192. "D.R.Ś. to the G.L.S." April 1963, p. 687; 715.
193. "A Book for Burning." May 1963, p. 790.
194. "Bamboo and Silk and the Art of Talking Back." June 1963, p. 870.

Volume 38

195. "Far Above Cayuga's Waters." Sept. 1963, p. 73; 93.
196. "Where Is Today's 'Brother Keppel'?" Oct. 1963, p. 185; 190.
197. "The 'Guide' Stands First." Nov. 1963, p. 285; 295.
198. "Trusteeship--Trust or Bust?" Dec. 1963, p. 354; 356.
199. "A Warm Puppy Is Not Happiness." Jan. 1964, p. 409.
200. "The Epistle of Paul to the Pedants." Feb. 1964, p. 485.
201. "Backward to Normalcy." March 1964, p. 561.
202. "William to Tucker to Jess." April 1964, p. 677.
203. "Of Librarians and Other Aborigines." May 1964, p. 781.
204. "The Compleat Librarian." June 1964, p. 867; 878.

Volume 39

205. "The Turning of the Worm." Sept. 1964, p. 73; 84.
206. "On the Encouragement of Reading." Oct. 1964, p. 169; 191.
207. "The Future, Too, Is Prologue." Nov. 1964, p. 253; 280.

208.   "Daedalus, Icarus, and the Technological Revolution."
         Dec. 1964, p. 335.
209.   "The Age of Paradox." Jan. 1965, p. 409; 414.
210.   "Is Youth Rejecting Science?"   Feb. 1965, p. 489;
         509.
211.   "Daddy Warbucks and the School Librarian." March
         1965, p. 573; 595.
212.   "A Better Class of Mouse." April 1965, p. 677.
213.   "The Lifeblood of the Profession." May 1965, p. 785.
214.   "Of Wine, Waiters, and Librarians." June 1965, p.
         903; 909.

Volume 40

215.   "This Could Be the Start." Sept. 1965, p. 89.
216.   "As You Wished You Were." Oct. 1965, p. 179.
217.   "A Renaissance in Library History?" Nov. 1965, p.
         281.
218.   "Kinder, Küche, und Bibliotheken." Dec. 1965, p. 365.
219.   "The Sheepskin Syndrome." Jan. 1966, p. 461; 465.
220.   "Equus Donatus and the IRS." Feb. 1966, p. 545-552.
221.   "What the Historian Has Been Missing." March 1966,
         p. 639; 650.
222.   "NLW and the Cult of Reading." April 1966, p. 767.
223.   "Of Comforts and Amenities." May 1966, p. 859.
224.   "Caveat Venditor." June 1966, p. 955; 973.

Volume 41

225.   "The Librarian as Anthologist." Sept. 1966, p. 89;
         106.
226.   "Je Crois Qu'elle Osé Regarder Mon Nez." Oct.
         1966, p. 215; 242.
227.   "The Golden Egg of Federal Support." Nov. 1966;
         p. 327; 348.
228.   "Cherchez l'Homme." Dec. 1966, p. 423; 435.
229.   "The 'Trickster' in Library Research." Jan. 1967,
         p. 521; 533.
230.   "Standard Lists: An Unstandardized View." Feb.
         1967, p. 615; 630.
231.   "You're Going on a Spree in 1973." March 1967,
         p. 723; 738.
232.   "The Computer and the Chancellor." April 1967,
         p. 837; 856.
233.   "What's Wrong with Educational Excellence?" May
         1967, p. 969; 985.
234.   "An Aslib For America." June 1967, p. 1063-1064.

Volume 42

235.   "The Phronemophobic ALA." Sept. 1967, p. 85; 104-
        105.
236.   "Try to Remember ..." Oct. 1967, p. 215; 235.
237.   "Intellectual Freedom--Intellectual? Free?" Nov.
        1967, p. 323; 344.
238.   "For a New Theory of the Leisure Class." Dec.
        1967, p. 423; 436-437.
239.   "Playgirl of the Western World." Jan. 1967, p. 529;
        540.
240.   "Is Documentation 'Camp'?" Feb. 1968, p. 621; 634.
241.   "The People, Yes." March 1968, p. 727; 754.
242.   "The Forty-First Chair." April 1968, p. 837; 862.
243.   "An Ombudsman for ALA?" May 1968, p. 937; 950.
244.   "Of Parting, Umbrellas, and Prepositions." June
        1968, p. 1037; 1054.

Volume 43

245.   "A Good Five-Page Report." Sept. 1968, p. 71-72.
246.   "On the Importance of Theory." Oct. 1968, p. 171;
        174.
247.   "Dichtung und Wahrheit." Nov. 1968, p. 281-282.
248.   "Isis and the Librarian's Quest for Unity." Dec.
        1968, p. 373.

AMERICAN DOCUMENTATION EDITORIALS

Volume 4

249.   Editorial. April 1953.
250.   Editorial. Oct. 1953.

Volume 5

251.   Editorial. Jan. 1954.
252.   Editorial. April 1954.
253.   Editorial. Aug. 1954.
254.   Editorial. Oct. 1954.

Volume 6

255.   "Ralph A. Beals and Jack C. Morris." Jan. 1955.
256.   "The Truth, the Whole Truth..." April 1955.
257.   "A House Divided." July 1955.
258.   "Toward the Formation of a Library Editors' Council."
        Oct. 1955.

Volume 7

259. Editorial. Jan. 1956.
260. "Needed--'Creative Documentation.' " April 1956.
261. "Fundamental Research--A Few Fundamentals."
        July 1956.
262. "UNESCO--Ten Years After." Oct. 1956.

Volume 8

263. "Loue par Ceux-ci..." Jan. 1957.
264. "Thoughts on New Year's Eve." April 1957.
265. Editorial. July 1957.
266. "Home Thoughts from Abroad." Oct. 1957.

Volume 9

267. "Of Mountains, and Coffee, and Documentation." Jan.
        1958.
268. "Librarians and the Sputnik." April 1958.
269. "The Parlement of Foules." July 1958.
270. "The New World's Debt to the Old." Oct. 1958.

Volume 10

271. "Antidote for Tranquilizers." Jan. 1959.
272. "The Renaissance of Classification." April 1959.
273. "A Science Full of Living Problems." July 1959.
274. "The Historian and Documentation." Oct. 1959.

Volume 11

275. "The Solitary Esophagus." Jan. 1960.
276. "A New High at Lehigh." April 1960.
277. "A Mandate for Documentation." Oct. 1960.

REVIEWS

278. The Cures in the Colophon, by Edgar J. Goodspeed.
      Library Journal, v. 61, no. 1 (Jan. 1, 1936), p. 24.

279. Social Change and Education. Thirteenth Yearbook,
      prepared by the Commission on Education for the New
      Social and Economic Relationships. Library Quarter-
      ly, v. 6, no. 2 (April 1936), p. 203-204.

280. "Tomorrow, and Tomorrow, and Tomorrow." Review
      of The Library of Tomorrow, by Emily V. Danton.

ALA Bulletin, v. 33, no. 4 (April 1939), p. 249; 278.

281.   The New England Mind, by Perry Miller. Library
       Quarterly, v. 10, no. 2 (April 1940), p. 302-306.

282.   Business and the Public Library, by Marian C. Man-
       ley. Library Quarterly, v. 10, no. 4 (Oct. 1940),
       p. 603-605.

283.   The Feminine Fifties, by Fred Lewis Pattee.
       Library Quarterly, v. 10, no. 4 (Oct. 1940), p. 618-
       621.

284.   Cotton Mather, A Bibliography of His Works, by
       Thomas J. Holmes. Library Quarterly, v. 11, no. 2
       (April 1941), p. 232-234.

285.   The Sentimental Novel in America, 1789-1860, by
       Herbert Ross Brown. Library Quarterly, v. 12, no.
       1 (Jan. 1942), p. 133-136.

286.   Seventh Annual Report of the Archivist of the United
       States for the Fiscal Year Ending June 30, 1941, by
       the National Archives. Library Quarterly, v. 12, no.
       4 (Oct. 1942), p. 851-853.

287.   The Growth of the American Republic, by Samuel
       Eliot Morison and Henry Steele Commager.
       Mississippi Valley Historical Review, v. 29, no. 4
       (March 1943), p. 580-581.

288.   The Growth of American Nationality, by Fred W.
       Wellborn. Mississippi Valley Historical Review, v. 30,
       no. 2 (Sept. 1949), p. 249-250.

289.   The Growth of American Thought, by Merle Curi.
       Library Quarterly, v. 14, no. 3 (July 1944), p. 250-
       252.

290.   Land of the Free, by Homer C. Hockett and Arthur
       M. Schlesinger. Mississippi Valley Historical Re-
       view, no. 4, v. 31 (March 1945), p. 588-589.

291.   The Idea of Progress in America. by Arthur A.
       Ekrich. Library Quarterly, v. 15, no. 3 (July 1945),
       p. 252-254.

292.   Eleventh Catalogers' and Classifiers' Yearbook, 1945,

by the Division of Cataloging and Classification, American Library Association. College and Research Libraries, v. 6, no. 4 (Sept. 1945), p. 371-372.

293.   "Influence on American Culture." Review of Foreign Influences in American Life: Essays and Critical Bibliographies, by David F. Bowers, ed. College and Research Libraries, v. 7, no. 1 (Jan. 1946), p. 95-96.

294.   The House of Macmillan, by Charles Morgan. Library Quarterly, v. 16, no. 2 (April 1946), p. 173-175.

295.   The Cambridge Press, 1638-1692, by George Parker Winship. Mississippi Valley Historical Review, v. 33, no. 1 (June 1946), p. 158-159.

296.   Harvard Library Bulletin, v. 1, no. 1, Winter 1947. Library Quarterly, v. 18, no. 2 (April 1948), p. 130.

297.   A History of Libraries in Great Britain and North America, by Albert Predeek. Library Quarterly, v. 18, no. 3 (July 1948), p. 226-228.

298.   Vatican Library. Rules for the Catalog of Printed Books, by Wyllis E. Wright, ed. Library Quarterly, v. 18, no. 4 (Oct. 1948), p. 299-302.

299.   Documentation, by S. C. Bradford. College and Research Libraries, v. 10, no. 3 (July 1949), p. 276-277.

300.   Library and Reference Facilities in the Area of the District of Columbia, used by the Loan Division, U.S. Library of Congress. Library Quarterly, v. 19, no. 3 (July 1949), p. 216-217.

301.   Cataloguing: a Textbook for Use in Libraries, by Henry A. Sharp. Library Quarterly, v. 19, no. 4 (Oct. 1949), p. 304-305.

302.   Fundamentals of Practical Cataloguing, by Margaret S. Taylor. Library Quarterly, v. 19, no. 4 (Oct. 1949), p. 304-305.

303.   A. L. A. Cataloging Rules for Author and Title Entries, prepared by the Division of Cataloging and Classification of the American Library Association, Clare

Beetle, ed. Library Quarterly, v. 20, no. 2 (April 1950), p. 147-150.

304.   Rules for Descriptive Cataloging in the Library of Congress, issued by the Descriptive Cataloging Division, Library of Congress. Library Quarterly, v. 20, no. 2 (April 1950), p. 147-150.

305.   The Story of Illinois, by Theodore Calvin Pease. Ohio State Archaeological and Historical Quarterly, v. 59, no. 2 (April 1950), p. 217-219.

306.   This is Illinois, a Pictorial History, by Jay Monaghan. Ohio State Archaeological and Historical Quarterly, p. 59, no. 2 (April 1950), p. 217-219.

307.   with Margaret E. Egan. Review of Standards of Bibliographical Description, by Curt F. Buhler, James G. McManaway, and Lawrence C. Wroth. College and Research Libraries, v. 11, no. 4 (October 1950), p. 399-401.

308.   with Margaret E. Egan. Review of Principles of Bibliographical Description, by Fredson Bowers. College and Research Libraries, v. 11, no. 4 (Oct. 1950), p. 399-401.

309.   The Papers of Thomas Jefferson, ed. by Julian P. Boyd and others. Minnesota History, v. 31 (1950), p. 179-180.

310.   A History of Libraries, by Alfred Hessel. Library Quarterly, v. 21, no. 1 (Jan. 1951), p. 46-48.

311.   Catalogue of United States Census Publications, 1790-1945, by Henry J. Dubester. Library Quarterly, v. 21, no. 2 (April 1951), p. 144-145.

312.   The H. W. Wilson Company, by John Lawler. College and Research Libraries, v. 12, no. 3 (July 1951), p. 299-300.

313.   The Papers of Thomas Jefferson, vols. 2, 3, 4. ed. Julian P. Boyd. Minnesota History, v. 32, no. 4 (Dec. 1951), p. 248-249.

314.   Colon Classification, 3rd ed., by S. R. Ranganathan. Library Quarterly, v. 22, no. 1 (Jan. 1952), p. 59-61.

315.   The Librarians' Conference of 1853, by George B.
        Utley. Library Quarterly, v. 22, no. 2 (April 1952),
        p. 145-147.

316.   The Fundamentals of Library Classification, by Ber-
        nard I. Palmer and A. J. Wells. Library Quarterly,
        v. 22, no. 4 (Oct. 1952), p. 354-356.

317.   The Alexandrian Library, by Edward A. Parsons.
        Library Quarterly, v. 23, no. 2 (April 1953), p. 137-
        138.

318.   R. R. Bowker: Militant Liberal, by E. McClung
        Fleming. Mississippi Valley Historical Review, v.
        40, no. 1 (June 1953), p. 155-156.

319.   The Papers of Thomas Jefferson, vols. 5 and 6, ed. by
        Julian P. Boyd. Minnesota History, v. 3 (Summer
        1953), p. 260-261.

320.   Scholar's Workshop: Evolving Concepts of Library
        Service, by Kenneth J. Brough. College and Research
        Libraries, v. 15, no. 2 (April 1954), p. 243-244.

321.   Social Education Literature for Authors, Artists, Pub-
        lishers, Teachers, Librarians, and Governments, by
        S. R. Ranganathan. Library Quarterly, v. 24, no. 3
        (July 1954), p. 255-257.

322.   Library Book Selection, by S. R. Ranganathan.
        Library Quarterly, v. 24, no. 3 (July 1954), p. 255-
        257.

323.   Social Bibliography or Physical Bibliography for Li-
        brarians, by S. R. Ranganathan. Library Quarterly,
        v. 24, no. 3 (July 1954), p. 255-257.

324.   The Core of Education for Librarianship, ed. by
        Lester Asheim. College and Research Libraries,
        v. 15, no. 3 (July 1954), p. 348-352.

325.   The Papers of Thomas Jefferson, vols. 7 and 8, ed.
        Julian P. Boyd. Minnesota History, 1954, p. 118-119.

326.   The University of Virginia Library, 1825-1950: Story
        of a Jefferson Foundation, by Harry Clemons. Mis-
        sissippi Valley Historical Review, v. 41, no. 4
        (March 1955), p. 722-723.

327.   The Technical Report, by B. H. Weil, ed. American
        Documentation, v. 6, no. 2 (April 1955), p. 104-105.

328.   The Papers of Thomas Jefferson, vols. 9 and 10, ed.
        Julian P. Boyd. Minnesota History, 1955, p. 252-253.

329.   Standards in the Domain of Documentation, issued by
        Technical Committee 46--Documentation, International
        Organization for Standardization. Journal of Catalog-
        ing and Classification, v. 11, no. 4 (Oct. 1955), p.
        252-254.

330.   The University Library, by Louis Round Wilson and
        Maurice F. Tauber. American Documentation, v. 7,
        no. 2 (April 1956), p. 137.

331.   The Papers of Thomas Jefferson, vols. 11, 12, ed. J. P.
        Boyd. Minnesota History (September 1956), p. 144-145.

332.   The Boston Public Library: a Centennial History, by
        Walter Muir Whitehill. Mississippi Valley Historical
        Review (September 1956), p. 339-340.

333.   Man on his Past, by Herbert Butterfield. College and
        Research Libraries, v. 18, no. 1 (Jan. 1957), p. 82-
        84.

334.   Essays in the History of Ideas, by Arthur O. Lovejoy.
        College and Research Libraries, v. 18, no. 1 (Jan.
        (1957), p. 82-84.

335.   The Papers of Thomas Jefferson, v. 13, ed. Julian
        P. Boyd. Minnesota History (June 1957), p. 285-286.

336.   "Selection," Chapter 7 in FID Manual of Document Re-
        production and Selection. Review of Documentation,
        v. 24, no. 3 (1957), p. 121.

337.   Imprints on History: Book Publishers and American
        Frontiers, by Madeline B. Stern. Mississippi Valley
        Historical Review, v. 44, no. 3 (Dec. 1957), p. 576-
        577.

338.   The Papers of Thomas Jefferson, vols. 14, 15, ed.
        J. P. Boyd. Minnesota History, (June 1959), p. 231-232.

339.   "A Passion for Books," by Lawrence Powell. Bulletin

of the Ohio Library Association, v. 30, no. 1 (Jan. 1960), p. 6-7.

340. The Making of an American Community, by Merle Curti and others. The Ohio Historical Quarterly, v. 69, no. 1 (Jan. 1960), p. 86-89.

341. Borrowings from the Bristol Library, 1773-1874, by Paul Kaufman. College and Research Libraries, v. 22, no. 1 (Jan. 1961), p. 80-82.

342. Cataloging and Classification by Maurice F. Tauber, and Subject Headings by Carlyle J. Frarey. Library Resources and Technical Services, v. 5, no. 2 (Spring 1961), p. 162-163.

343. The National Library of Medicine Index Medicus Project. Library Quarterly, v. 32, no. 1 (Jan. 1962), p. 85-86.

344. Papers of Thomas Jefferson, v. 16, ed. Julian P. Boyd. Minnesota History (June 1962), p. 90-91.

345. Research Opportunities in American Cultural History, by John Francis McDermott, ed. Library Quarterly, v. 32 (July 1962), p. 236-238.

346. The Western Book Trade: Cincinnati as a Nineteenth Century Publishing and Book Trade Center, by Walter Sutton. Ohio History, v. 71, no. 3 (Oct. 1962), p. 267-269.

347. Scientific Books, Libraries, and Collections, by John L. Thornton and R. I. J. Tully. Library Journal, v. 88, no. 3 (Feb. 1, 1963), p. 547-548.

348. The Scarlet Letter, by Nathaniel Hawthorne. American Notes and Queries, v. 1, no. 10 (June 1963), p. 159-160.

349. Itself an Education, by Bernard I. Palmer. Library Quarterly, v. 33, no. 3 (July 1963), p. 289-291.

350. Enlarged Prints from Library Microfilms, by William R. Hawken. Library Journal, v. 88, no. 13 (July 1963), p. 2670.

351. Directory of Special Libraries and Information Centers,

by Anthony T. Kruzas, comp. Library Journal, v. 88, no. 16 (Sept. 1963), p. 3194-3195.

352.   Nonconventional Technical Information Retrieval Systems in Current Use, by the National Science Foundation. College and Research Libraries, v. 24, no. 5 (Sept. 1963), p. 435-437.

353.   Charles Evans, American Bibliographer, by Edward G. Holley. Library Journal, v. 88, no. 21 (Dec. 1963), p. 4614.

354.   Readings in Special Librarianship, by Harold S. Sharp. Special Libraries, v. 44, no. 2 (Feb. 1964), p. 121-122.

355.   Classification and Indexing in the Social Sciences, by D. J. Foskett. Revue Internationale de Documentation, v. 31, no. 1 (1964), p. 31-32.

356.   William Frederick Poole and the Modern Library Movement, by William L. Williamson. Wisconsin Magazine of History, v. 47, no. 3 (Spring 1964), p. 272-273.

357.   Henry Stevens of Vermont: American Rare Book Dealer in London, 1845-1886, by Wyman Parker. Library Quarterly, v. 34, no. 3 (July 1964), p. 272-273.

358.   The Printed Book Catalog in American Libraries, 1723-1900, by Joseph Ranz. Library Journal, v. 89 (May 1964), p. 1940-1941.

359.   Some Problems of a General Classification Scheme. Report of a Conference Held in London, June 1963, by the Library Association. Journal of Documentation, v. 20 (Dec. 1964), p. 238-240.

360.   Parnassus on Main Street, by Frank B. Woodford. Library Journal, v. 90, no. 15 (Sept. 1965), p. 3424-3425.

361.   The Papers of Thomas Jefferson, v. 17, ed. Julian P. Boyd. Minnesota History (Fall 1965), p. 295-296.

362.   Science, Humanism, and Libraries, by D. J. Fockett.

Library Quarterly, v. 36, no. 1 (Jan. 1966), p. 67-69.

363. Focus on Information and Communication, by Barbara Kyle, ed. College and Research Libraries, v. 27, no. 2 (March 1966), p. 244-245.

364. New England Transplanted, by Kenneth V. Lottich. Ohio History, v. 74, no. 4 (Autumn 1965), p. 275-276.

365. Early Public Libraries: A History of Public Libraries in Great Britain Before 1850, by Thomas Kelly. Library Journal, v. 91, no. 15 (Sept. 1966), p. 3912.

366. Approaches to Library History: Proceedings of the Second Library History Seminar, Florida State University Library School, March 4-6, 1965, by John David Marshall, ed. Library Journal, v. 91, no. 17 (Oct. 1966), p. 4627.

367. Classification Research: Proceedings of the Second International Study Conference Held at Hotel Prins Hamlet, Elsinore, Denmark, September 14-18, 1964, by Pauline Atherton, ed. Library Quarterly, v. 36, no. 4 (Oct. 1966), p. 356-358.

368. Who's Who in Library Service, 4th ed., by Lee Ash and others. Library Journal, v. 92, no. 1 (Jan. 1967), p. 87.

369. Selected Readings in the History of Librarianship, by John L. Thornton, ed. Library Journal, v. 92, no. 6 (March 1967), p. 1132.

370. Aslib Conference 1964. American Documentation, v. 18, no. 2 (April 1967), p. 115-116.

371. Move the Information: a Kind of Missionary Spirit, by Rowena W. Swanson. Library Journal, v. 92, no. 19 (Nov. 1967), p. 3975.

372. Raking the Coals of History: The ALA Scrapbook of 1876, by Edward G. Holley. Library Quarterly, v. 38, no. 2 (April 1968), p. 207-209.

373. A Chronology of Librarianship, by Josephine Metcalf Smith. Library Journal, v. 93, no. 11 (June 1968), p. 2219.

374.   Manual of Public Libraries, Institutions and Societies
        in the United States and the British Provinces of North
        America, by William J. Rhees. Library Journal, v.
        93, no. 17 (Oct. 1968), p. 3522.

375.   World Guide to Libraries, 2nd ed., by Klaus G. Saur,
        comp. Library Journal, v. 94, no. 15 (September 1,
        1969), p. 2893.

376.   A History of Library Education, by Gerald Bramley.
        Library Journal v. 94, no. 18 (October 15, 1969), p.
        3628.

377.   Libraries and Their Users, by Paul Kaufman. Library
        Journal, v. 95, no. 7 (April 1, 1970), p. 1299.

378.   Advances in Librarianship, by Melvin J. Voigt, ed.
        Library Journal, v. 95, no. 9 (May 1, 1970), p.
        1717.

379.   The Case for Faculty Status of Academic Librarians,
        by Lewis C. Branscomb, ed. Educational Studies,
        v. 1 (Winter 1970), p. 100.

380.   Library History; and Examination Guidebook, by James
        G. Olle. Library Journal, v. 96 (May 15, 1971),
        p. 1668.

381.   "One Man's Humor." Review of Library Humor:
        A Bibliothecal Miscellany, by Norman D. Stevens,
        comp. Library Journal, v. 96 (September 1, 1971),
        p. 2606.

INTRODUCTION

Conrad H. Rawski

"The first responsibility of a profession is to know itself, which means, first, knowing what a profession is;
second, knowing what kind of a profession it is; and
third, knowing what differentiates it from all other professions. There is in every profession a quintessential
element that distinguishes it from other human activities
and which may derive from the intellectual content of
its discipline, the technology of its practice, the responsibilities which society has placed upon it. It may
be defined in terms of all or any combination of these.
But librarianship, unfortunately, has been little given
to professional introspection. For generations, librarians have accepted the social responsibility for custody
of mankind's graphic records, hammered out empirical
procedures for the organization and servicing of those
records, and argued indifferently the right of their technology to qualify as a science. ... The conventional
response of librarianship, already burdened with the
stigma of technological vocationalism, to the growing
importance of graphic records to society has been to
introduce new technologies and skills derived from the
applied sciences. ... There is nothing inherently
wrong with this search for increased efficiency in the
engineering aspects of librarianship. That librarians
are, with the aid of the engineer, developing a highly
efficient technology, and that the proliferation of
knowledge necessitates a revolution in that technology
are scarcely debatable. But a technology is a means,
not an end. Lacking theory to give it direction and
purpose, it drifts aimlessly. If it reaches its goal it
does so only by fortuitous circumstance."[1]

These sentences by Jesse H. Shera motivate our book.

When plans for a collection of papers in honor of Dr.
Shera were first discussed late in 1967, it was agreed that
the kind of cento-volume which, recently, evoked Bohannan's

macaronic outburst "Fest Me No Schriften."[2] did not serve
the purpose. We decided "to produce a book which would
bring together original papers on theoretic concerns attendant
upon librarianship."[3] This is a topic of significance. It holds
a conspicuous place in Shera's work, and thus seemed appropriate for an offering dedicated to him.

Theory has been called "the x factor in librarianship."[4] For some of us the very word "theory" holds a dis-
paraging connotation. Many more use it as what (with
apology to A. A. Milne) may be called a woozle-word, designating anything which in some fashion seems to be removed
from the factual specifics of how-to-do-it. The "new outlook"
Butler hoped for in 1933 did not materialize. When it comes
to reflective inquiry, librarianship still has to grasp the full
meaning of Butler's lesson that "there can be no search until
the searcher has decided what he shall look for. And this
must have a scientific importance."[5] Scientific importance
relates to savoir, not to savoir faire.[6]

As a professional activity, librarianship comprises
the sum total of actions directed toward goals desired by
others who themselves are not engaged in performing these
actions, although they may be involved in them. The professional assists those who are literally patients toward what
they desire, by doing, i.e., making true, what he believes
to be true. This involves knowledge and not superstition or
habit, if we are agreed that the actions performed are
rational ones. In order to obtain a reliable base for this
professional knowledge and its gradual improvement we need
reasonably accurate data and founded and tested assumptions
which skilled know-how and its uncritical tradition cannot
supply.[7] Also, professional performance tries to "get things
right" within real-life, highly complex situations requiring the
application of whole sets of practical measures and rules. It
cannot neatly discriminate between variables, and even were
this possible, still has to consider its cognitive data in terms
of normative factors before effecting policy.

Practical success, unfortunately, is not a criterion of
truth. No matter how careful and methodologically sophisticated our reconstructions of past professional action may be,
they cannot furnish a reliable knowledge base for future professional action. Even ad hoc problems, satisfied by what
Hempel calls the tool-for-optimal-action model,[8] require
more than the "empirical riches of descriptive work" can
offer. Common sense knowledge[9] establishes familiarity in
the sense of credibility and the taxonomic ordering and

diagnostic use of data based on credibility. But, though precisely formulated and arranged, data can only be catalogued
and re-catalogued.[10] They do not add up to the kind of
knowledge serious professional activity needs. Professional
knowledge is sought as a means to attain and to continue to
attain what we desire to be true. Hence, professional knowledge must strive for more than after-the-fact assurance. It
must seek explanatory relevance and predictive power. Both
explanation and prediction depend on conceptual reconstruction of the objective patterns of events (i.e., facts subsumed
under general principles), and thus link the quest for action
knowledge to scientific inquiry.[11] Stated narrowly, the
knowledge situation here involves a schema which leads from
data described in observables to grounds for expectation in
terms of observables via interpretive connectives[12] and
theoretical statements permitting argument, and requires concepts, propositions, and theorems which the diagnostic vocabulary of records of past experience alone cannot provide.[13] To avoid Shera's fallacy: "the librarian means to
do good, and by dint of self-sacrifice and hard work he does
what he means to do, and therefore that which he does is
good,"[14] we need theory.

It is important to note the propositional character of
such theory in support of the goals, principal concerns, activities, and basic properties and relationships characteristic
of librarianship. Data hunting, methodology, and taxonomic
efforts are instrumentally involved in providing an appropriate base of inquiry.[15] The target, however, is scientific
theory, i.e., theory that supports explanations of facts and
their patterns by means of a deductive system, and thus allows us to address meaningfully the realities, both actual and
possible, of the librarian's world. Inquiry, so directed,
views librarianship in its totality, from above as it were, as
a problem area of scientific study, and engages in systematic
efforts to produce a body of reliable knowledge on and about
librarianship--which involves conjectures, hypotheses, laws,
theories, and tests. Argument about what to call such efforts
remains trivial as long as we clearly keep in mind the kind
of knowledge our professional commitments require.

> What is it to supply a theory? It is at least this:
> to offer an intelligible, systematic, conceptual pat-
> tern for the observed data. The value of such a
> pattern lies in its capacity to unite phenomena
> which, without the theory, are either surprising,
> anomalous, or left wholly unnoticed.[16]

Such a pattern, even if very limited in scope, involves assumptions which in some respect (and to some extent) are general, relate of necessity to the pattern, and are empirically corroborated--in short, law-like statements which permit interpretation of empirical data by deduction. Hanson's theoretical pattern is not a map portraying reality, but "rather what makes it possible to observe phenomena as being of a certain sort, and as related to other phenomena."[17] This explanatory function is illustrated by George Constant's woodcut, reproduced as Figure 1. A first look at the print may suggest the image of a single person, male or female, which in terms of this image (or, rather, in terms of the assumptions supporting our belief) could be described as long-haired, squat, etc. As soon as we discover that Constant's work bears the title "The Kiss," we revise our judgment and, consequently, our observation statements (now two "lovers" are "seen" to be "embracing," etc.). The conceptual framework has changed and thus each factual interpretation that follows. We give a new explanation based on the same evidence which, it turns out, was not evident after all.[18] The different pattern has not only rearranged our knowledge (as distinct from aesthetic feeling, appreciative enjoyment, approval, disapproval, etc.). It has altered its content.[19]

A schematic representation of the nature and function of theory based on Margenau is shown in Figure 2.[20] The continuum of cognitive experience, i.e., that vaguely definable part of experience associated with knowledge, can be divided, again vaguely, into two fields: one, dominated by sensory elements, and another, dominated by rational elements. The "protocol data" in the former include raw sensation (whatever it may be), its memories, observation in the sense of Northrop's natural history data, records of observations, etc., all of which contain certain conceptualizations (e.g., "greater than"), but are accepted as "incontrovertibly true" within the context of a problem area, discipline, science, etc. The heavy P-plane line indicates this boundary of given P-facts, the contingent protocol experience which varies from problem area to problem area. The C-field so bounded, contains concepts and conceptual constructions invented in order to deal rationally with the protocol data. These minor unobservable "constructs" correspond to the protocol data, but are not identical with them. They possess logical connectivity, allow for formal reasoning, analysis, calculation, etc., and hence, can be extended into theoretical patterns, which in turn allow us to transcend the discreteness of P-facts given in everyday acquaintance, to

Figure 1.   Original woodcut by George Constant.

Cognitive Experience

CONSTRUCTS	PROTOCOL DATA
rational elements; concepts	sensory of elements; acts and results of seeing, hearing, etc.
INVENTED	GIVEN
have logical connectivity	discrete
C-field	P-plane

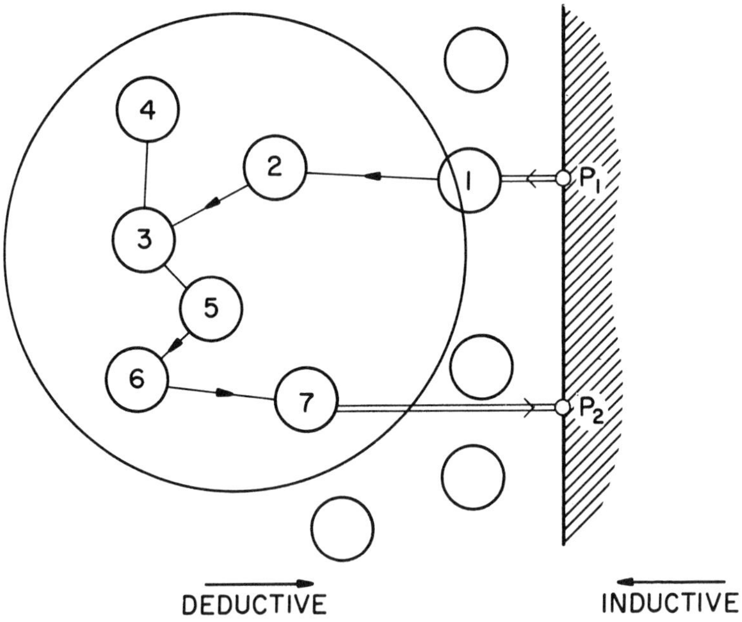
4
2
1
P_1
3
5
6
7
P_2
DEDUCTIVE
INDUCTIVE

A theory is a complex of circles (constructs) connected by single lines (logical and mathematical relations), together with the double lines (rules of correspondence), which connect the complex (C-field) with the protocol data (P-plane).

Figure 2. (After Margenau)

attempt coherent interpretations in terms of actual and possible situations, and thus help us understand and control the
events under study.[21] Some constructs are very close to
the P-plane, others are more abstract and lie some distance
away. But they all are interconnected and thus form a much
stronger knowledge base than incoherent protocol experience.
This requires "good" constructs. It also requires empirical
confirmation in terms of "rules of correspondence," in order
to define operationally our theoretical network. In Figure 2
double lines designate rules of correspondence, circles denote constructs, and single lines, logical and mathematical
relations between constructs. A theory is depicted as a
complex of circles connected by single lines together with
the double lines which connect the complex with the protocol
data.

Establishing a theory begins at some point P_1, the
problem, and proceeds[22] by conjecture and refutation to
the constructs of rational knowledge (1 - 7) as indicated by
the directed lines.[23] The theory remains tentative until it
is confirmed by the passage to P_2, the theory's "challenge
to Nature."[24] Confirmation reflects upon the constructs
themselves, permits re-evaluation and re-ordering (which,
e.g., may discard as uninteresting construct 4), and,
eventually, leads to an objective pattern of a part of reality. Once established the theory enables us to enter at P_1
and, without further inspection, predict P_2. This prediction
is based on both our empirical diagnosis (P_1) and our
rational knowledge (constructs 1 - 7), which stresses the
need for error control in both fields.

Without further discussion, Figure 2 offers only a
rough approximation. Yet it drives home the basic points of
theoretical knowledge, which (1) deals primarily with unobservable and often wholly unfamiliar events; (2) invents and
applies conjectures beyond common knowledge and regardless
of empirical probability; and (3) tests them with the help of
special techniques. Theories systematize by establishing
logical and mathematical relations among the disconnected
data of perception and action; they explain the data by seeking propositions from which these data follow, hence, after
critical confirmation, can be predicted; they try to enhance
testability and error control. This built-in process of critical
evaluation has important consequences. It leads to more inclusive, more powerful rational constructions in terms of
which we identify basic principles (representing, if you will,
the knowledge most worth having[25] of a subject or discipline),

be it now as they obtain for a certain point in time, or, as
in the "hard" sciences, for any given time. It also suggests
new lines of inquiry, new data searches and investigations
unthought of heretofore--it allows us to ask new questions as
well as to provide answers to old ones.

Where does all this leave us librarians? We have at
our disposal a sizable body of data and, probably, also of
workable concepts and propositions, produced in various fields.
But how are we to decide their significance? We do not possess an ordered corpus of empirical properties and relations
and have to make do with "as many independent assumptions
and propositions ... as there are naively observed facts."[26]
Our growing literature of specific data, and ad hoc classifications and interpretations of these specific data, more often
than not equates that which is analyzed with the recorded observations,[27] and ignores epistemic questions (which, in
fact, we are not equipped to answer). Thus it obstructs
rather than facilitates theory formation, which Ryle compares
to the work of making a path, "marking the ground, digging,
fetching loads of gravel, rolling and draining ... where there
was yet no path," so that in the end we might have a path.[27]
How does one go about making a path that leads out of the
clutter of natural history data and toward a theory of librarianship?

This brings us back to Shera's "quintessential element"
and professional introspection.

Introspection is reflective self-examination. Professional introspection begins with the professional situation,
its goals, concerns, activities, properties, and relationships.
Using what knowledge we have of the essentials of librarianship, we must set out "from where are are"[29] and examine
the territory as it is, not as it has been represented to be.[30]
We must attempt a synoptic mapping of the large areas of
professional concern and their interrelationships, and explore
the logical implications of the map in order to describe our
findings as unambiguously as possible. The map may be ill-
plotted and our map language inadequate. But as we explore
we test certain basic notions, we look for quintessential characteristics fundamental to the professional situation of librarianship. We seek out data, concepts, expressions, designa-
tions, and statements that are needed because they are entailed by these quintessential characteristics. We begin to
theorize; but to theorize about librarianship as the problem,
and not about parochial bibliothecal predicaments, pressing
as they may be, which we do not (and, at present, cannot)

view coherently within the larger contexts required for their anticipation and solution.   Efforts toward a synoptic model and a syntactically and semantically less naive language,[31] are the first tasks of professional introspection.   Subsequent steps include (1) the search for primitive concepts from which all other concepts of the subject matter are derived by definition, and propositions from which all other propositions are deduced by logical implication; (2) a sufficient scientific language base (which does not mean more mathematics, but more functional use of mathematics); and (3) operational measures for reliable testing.   Thus the speculative thrusts and epistemological awareness of our first efforts lead to the patterns of deductively formulated and operationally verifiable theory. [32]

Many important details are missing from this crude sketch.   This may well reflect the ignorance of this writer, but has no bearing on the subject.   Librarianship has yet to take the first step toward discovering the quintessential elements of the profession, has yet to map its native grounds, distinguishing geomorphic surface properties from gopher holes, and to conjecture about needs and fruitful solutions, about meanings and about truths, and how to state them. Questions must be formulated and answers undertaken in a scientific manner concerning the fundamental problems of librarianship, how to attain its accepted goals, under varying circumstances, now and in the future, how to control its destinies.   To seek knowledge is one thing, to seek the right kind of knowledge quite another.

* * * *

The papers contained in this book should be considered in terms of this situation.   This is not an attempt to remove them from critical evaluation as independent individual statements, or to apologize for our concerted effort and its obvious limitations--but rather an invitation to the reader to ponder the state of things documented here and the generic problem which, in various ways and to various extent, these papers address.   In this respect, both our accomplishment and our failure are clearly symptomatic.

Common to all papers is the earnest professional concern with the responsibilities of the task.   They all seek viable grounds for that which librarians are dedicated to do and, it seems to me, demonstrate a consensus that many of the answers we seek lie beyond observation and description in two-termed subject-predicate syntax, and cannot be found without critical analysis, empirically and formally valid theories, and epistemically sound evaluative applications. Such reflective theoretic work may not be enough to attain Shera's "vision of a new heaven and a new earth" and what he has to say about it, but it may help us get a little closer.

Notes

1. J. H. Shera, Libraries..., 162-163.
2. Science, 166 (1969), 819.
3. First letter of invitation to contribute papers to a Festschrift for J. H. Shera, November 1967.
4. B. G. Petrof, "Theory: The X Factor in Librarianship," College and Research Libraries, 26 (1965), 316 f.
5. P. Butler, An Introduction to Library Science (1933), Chicago, University of Chicago Press, 1961, 26; 110. Emphasis added.
6. N. R. Hanson, Patterns of Discovery, Cambridge, University Press, 1961, 26.
7. Cf. G. Ryle, The Concept of Mind, London, Hutchinson, 1949, and later, chap. ii.
8. C. G. Hempel, "Deductive-Nomological vs. Statistical Explanation" in Minnesota Studies in the Philosophy of Science, vol. iii, ed. H. Feigl and G. Maxwell, Minneapolis, Minn., University of Minnesota Press, 1962, 160.
9. "... [C]ommon sense--that repository of ancient error." N. Goodman, Languages of Art, Indianapolis, Ind., Bobbs-Merrill, 1968, xii.
10. On this, e.g., H. L. Zetterberg, On Theory and Verification in Sociology, 3rd ed., Totowa, N.J., Bedminster Press, 1965, chaps. i, ii; R. Brown, Explanation in Social Science, Chicago, Aldine, 1963, espec. chap. 11; L. S. King, "What Is a Diagnosis?" Journal of the American Medical Association, 202 (November 20, 1967), 714-717.
11. Thus, many professions rely on supportive disciplines such as the life and health sciences, jurisprudence, the engineering sciences, criminology, etc.
12. Margenau's "rules of correspondence." See below, Figure 2. Cf. also P. Caws, The Philosophy of Science, Princeton, N.J., D. Van Nostrand, 1965, chap. 17.
13. Cf. C. G. Hempel, Aspects of Scientific Explanation, New York, Free Press, 1965, 182-185.

14. J. H. Shera, op. cit., 212.
15. G. C. Homans refers to such necessities of theory formation as "theoretical work; but ... not theory per se." ("Contemporary Theory in Sociology" in Handbook of Modern Sociology, ed. E. E. L. Faris, Chicago, Rand McNally, 1964, 957a.)
16. N. R. Hanson, op. cit., 121; The Concept of the Positron, Cambridge, England, University Press, 1963, 44.
17. N. R. Hanson, Patterns..., 90. Cf. also N. Goodman, op. cit., chaps. I, IV, V.
18. I. Levi, Gambling with Truth, New York, A. A. Knopf, 1967, 15. The iconographic implications of these circumstances have been explored by E. N. Gombrich (e. g., Meditations on a Hobby Horse and Other Essays on the Theory of Art, London, Phaidon, 1963, espec. 45-69). Cf. also J. H. Shera and C. H. Rawski, "The Diagram Is the Message," Journal of Typographic Research, 2 (1968), 171-188.
19. Thus Nadel's often quoted "Facts are safer than theory and more solid than explanation, as observation is safer and more solid than thinking about observation," which, it should be noted, sounds far less rigid within his context (The Foundations of Social Anthropology, Glencoe, Ill., Free Press, 1951, 24), invokes feelings to which all humans tend instinctively, but leads nowhere. Nor is there a real issue. As soon as we cease to "observe" "facts" and want to know why the facts and our observations concerning them should be as they are, we will have to refer to some kind of testable logically coordinated pattern-allowing subsumption, i.e., engage precisely in those abstract intellectual operations which according to Nadel are less safe and less solid. This involves clearly the very grounds required to make facts and observation "safe" and "solid." As, I think, Mario Bunge observed: "No theory, no science."
20. Figure 2 is based on diagrams and commentary in three publications by H. Margenau: The Nature of Physical Reality, New York, McGraw-Hill, 1950, chaps. 6 and 21; Open Vistas, New Haven, Conn., Yale University Press, 1961, chap. 1; and "What Is a Theory?" in The Structure of Economic Science, ed. S. R. Krupp, Englewood Cliffs, N.J., Prentice Hall, 1966, 25-38. The responsibility for the composite figure and an interpretation which differs somewhat from Professor Margenau's is mine.

21.   Thus it is possible "to accept a theory that vastly out-
      reaches its evidential basis if that theory promises
      to exhibit an underlying order, a system of deep and
      simple systematic connections among what had pre-
      viously been a mass of disparate and multifarious
      facts." C. G. Hempel, "Recent Problems of Induc-
      tion" in Mind and Cosmos, ed. R. G. Colodny,
      Pittsburgh, University of Pittsburgh Press, 1966,
      132. Cf. K. R. Popper, Conjectures and Refutations,
      New York, Basic Books, 1965, 55-59; and P. Frank,
      Philosophy of Science, Englewood Cliffs, N.J.,
      Prentice Hall, 1957, espec. chaps. 14, 15.
22.   The phrase is K. R. Popper's.
23.   Harary, Norman, and Cartwright, Structural Models,
      New York, J. Wiley, 1965, chap. 1.
24.   H. Margenau, The Nature..., 105. H. Selye sum-
      marizes as follows: "The importance of facts and
      theories is interdependent; if a woman wants to wear
      a string of pearls, it is hardly possible to single out
      the thread or the beads as more essential. The
      reason why this problem has so often led to misunder-
      standing is that the construction of a theory appears
      to be a more creative accomplishment than mere
      observation of facts, while a tangible fact appears
      to have some inherent value, quite apart from its
      interpretation. This is erroneous. A theory is a
      bond between facts; it holds them together and guides
      us to more facts." (From Dream to Discovery, New
      York, McGraw-Hill, 1964, 279.)
25.   The paraphrase of Herbert Spencer's title "What Knowl-
      edge Is of Most Worth?" is by W. C. Booth.
26.   F. S. C. Northrop, "Toward a Deductively Formulated
      and Operationally Verifiable Comparative Cultural
      Anthropology" in Cross-Cultural Understanding, ed.
      F. S. C. Northrop and H. H. Livingston, New York,
      Harper & Row, 1964, 195.
27.   C. H. Coombs, A Theory of Data, New York, J. Wiley,
      1964, 4.
28.   G. Ryle, op. cit., 289.
29.   Charles Sanders Peirce, as quoted in A. Kaplan, The
      Conduct of Inquiry, San Francisco, Chandler, 1964,
      86.
30.   That is, in the terms of the problem situation and its
      goal intentions, which must not be confused with
      specific aspects as construed by professional action.
      Cf. G. Ryle, who uses a "bibliothecal" example in
      Dilemmas, Cambridge, University Press, 1954, 75-
      77; and N. Goodman, "The Way the World Is,"

Review of Metaphysics, 14 (1960), 48-56.

31. Cf. C. H. Rawski, "Subject Literatures and Librarianship in Library School Teaching Methods: Courses in
the Selection of Adult Materials, ed. L. E. Bone,
Urbana, University of Illinois, 1969, 100; and his
paper "The Scientific Study of Subject Literatures,"
Cleveland Medical Library Association, 1969.

32. F. S. C. Northrop, op. cit., 194-215.

I. THE PERTINENCE OF HISTORY

"From history comes a better understanding of the present as the result of past forces, a true sense of historicity that may eventually take shape in the search for universal laws or philosophical principles that may have prognostic value. ... Similarly, one may turn to history for a rationale for a desired course of action in the present, and though caution may warn that historical analogy is beset by pitfalls, the argument is convincing. ... From historical consciousness derives also adaptability to change, an acute realisation that life has not always been as it is today, and that it will not forever remain as it is at present. Thus one arrives at a proper perspective upon contemporary events, an ability to relate each to its appropriate antecedents and to project, at least to some extent, its possible consequences. History properly comprehended enriches and deepens the understanding of contemporary society."

J. H. Shera, <u>Historians...</u>, 110-112.

THE RESEARCH AND WRITING OF LIBRARY HISTORY

Sidney Ditzion

Libraries, broadly defined, have almost always been with us. Societies and their leaders, it would seem, have exhibited an inherent wish to preserve some sort of record of cultural accomplishment if only to symbolize and justify claims to pride, power, and social continuity. When language took on its visual aspect of writing--and later of printing--library repositories, if only of one or two textual items, assumed the elementary function of preserving the record for use or for show.

Most societies have, in addition, developed specialists in the art of collecting materials concerning the traditions and deeds of the community for the purpose of implementing the

recollection of past accomplishments. These priestly, political,
or intellectual functionaries, called historians, have had to call
upon this record (as preserved in library repositories) so as
to recapture, in limited ways, the historical substance of
things thought and felt, said and done, in this irretrievable
past. No wonder then that there should have been an historical line of keepers of books and others who felt impelled
to tell of the history of historical repositories. No surprise
to find a tradition in which reporters, chroniclers, document
producers, interpreters, and historians of libraries have
come forth to help complete the tales of their story-telling
institutions.

The very stirrings of the 1930's and onward in the field
of public library history is in itself a notable historical occurrence. There had been numerous sallies into this territory
long before. But, as Shera has pointed out,[1] in one way or
another the "historians" were either fact-gatherers, chroniclers of libraries, reminiscers and celebrators of libraries and
librarians, or propagandizers for the movement and the profession. This is not to minimize the contributions made by
these writers who sometimes did a magnificent job of compiling scattered data. They performed a fair part of the task of
establishing the basis for factual coherence, later to be employed by more disciplined historians. The user of these materials, of course, must keep in mind their incompleteness,
weakness in the selection of data, the assumptions of their
writers, and lack of criteria in interpretation. In short,
these authors, not always trained in history and much given
to personal enthusiasms, too frequently saw only what they
wanted to see. They rarely wanted to see the historical picture, stark and entire.

The new library history represents the coming together
of a trend in American historical writing with the sharpening
of social consciousness in the New Deal period. New modes
of thought are rarely entirely new to specific times and places.
The new trend in American history refers to the somewhat innovative methodology and content introduced into the discipline
around the beginning of the century by men like James Harvey Robinson and Charles A. Beard. If forced to make a
brief definition of the change, one could say that history
began to embrace more than the older emphases on generals,
politicians, personalities, and pleaders. Forces of economic
and social significance, of enormous human interest in themselves, began to be seen as driving elements in history.
Along with social and sociological factors, ideas (especially
those which had strong operational significance) began to play

stronger parts in the drama of history.   Perhaps the economic role was overplayed, as doubtless, more recently,
historians have given too many lines to the vagaries of the
human psyche.

What is significant is that the story of the American
past began to take on a fullness and a richness that came
closer than ever before to the ideal of reproducing what actually had happened.   More and more factors of life were in-
troduced--the work of Arthur M. Schlesinger and his Harvard
graduate students deserves special kudos in this regard--not
as discrete lines in history but as interacting processes.
The experience of mankind was recognized as being far more
complicated, and more interesting, than politico-military power and a perennial concern with geographic boundary lines.
Added were the meaning of life in rural and urban places,
the exteriors and interiors of man's dwelling places, the
pots, pans, and plumbing that conditioned man's life and
were reciprocally created by him.   Also into the accounting
came his religion, recreation, family life, and education;
also his literature, art, and music.

"The new historians," as Shera has observed, "were
laying a foundation of sound scholarship upon which ... an
objective consideration of library origins might rest; but in
this reappraisal itself the library was neglected."[2]   One
could indeed also say that, despite the vast output of excellent American educational history, the new historians had not
gotten around to an interweaving of schools with the total culture.   This was not soundly done until the year 1935, when
Professor Merle Curti (a former student of A.M. Schlesinger) published his The Social Ideas of American Educators.
It is notable that this volume appeared in a series[3] wherein
elsewhere Charles Beard searched for a new frame of historical reference which should be more relevant to current
consumers of works of history.

This frame of reference turned out to be the broad
one of collective participation, that is, the dynamics of group
give-and-take among all classes of the population.   Such was
the context of historical thinking, in which the University of
Chicago's Graduate Library School and its Library Quarterly
began a fresh interest in the new library history.   This,
joined with a pervasive preoccupation with the decade's depression, produced students who would hypothesize concerning the social forces which supported libraries, and then research the relevant sources of history toward testing their

speculations.[4] These students doubtless turned their attention to public library history because this was where the social nexus was most visible and appealing.* Besides, the
school at Chicago was developing in a sociologically obsessed
household.

What others sensed, Shera expressed: The public library was not an institution which had an insulated life of its
own, one which evolved in splendored isolation. It was an
"agency" of society which was "where things were at." Quite
different from other library types, which performed as commanded for the specialized purposes of specialized groups,
the public library was the institutional invention of a reasonably organized population aggregate. Hence, its evolution
would be quite distinct from that of college,[5] school, and a
host of special libraries, functional to goals established by
the organizations which they serve. This insistence on the
term "agency" (which caught reviewers' attention both because Shera announced the conception at the very beginning
of his book[6] and because it was intellectually attractive) as
against "institution" would seem to be a matter of taste and
training. Other institutions, after all, are also inextricably
bound in with total community behavior. They have separate
lives as well as combined lives. But, beyond the unimportant matter of words, it helped considerably to dramatize the
nature of library history as it had to be written.

The history of the American public library began to be
seen, then, as being thoroughly intermeshed with the history
of American life in many intricate ways, as being folded in
with residues of intellectual and social behavior of the past
as well as with social impacts of the present, i.e. at any
point in time. Ideas that were generally operational in American society were examined for their relevance to library
history. Students also looked for a certain amount of cross-
pollenization in the Atlantic community, along with manifestations of cultural imperialism in the United States in the form
of idea and people migrations from New England and New
York.[7] Library historians, a handful to be sure, felt called
upon to examine aspects of their frame of reference and historical assumptions in the manner appropriate to general social historians.

---

*For this reason, and for reasons of the interests of
Jesse Shera and the present writer, this paper will be confined
to public library history.

A few students, fascinated by the generalizations of modern sociology about institutions and their development, have transplanted these uncritically into the library context. In a case or two, there has been an attempt to impose the mould of some prestigious sociological text on a smattering of historical knowledge, and then to make the knowledge fit. Elsewhere one senses, or sees, the marks of slick social evolutionary patterns, such as followed in the wake of America's love affair with Herbert Spencer. However illuminating such discussions may be, and they often are, they encourage the illusion that definitions of library function in stages one, two, and three of evolution can replace the laborious excavating of solid historical data.

Substituting the word "library," where other social phenomena appear in an unrelated but imposing professional formulation, cannot take the place of that approximation of truth that goes by the name of history. Recent sociologists seem, on the whole, to prefer building historical theory for one kind of institution, or social agency, whose special social functions can readily be isolated for purpose of study. This is closer to feasible historical approaches which operate, to a great extent, inductively from a body of primary and secondary sources.

Fortunately, the predominant output of library history has followed this last approach. Moreover, the intelligent use of this more or less conventional methodology has helped both to produce a sensible definition for the "public" library and to delineate a true evolutionary pattern which fits both American library history and social history comfortably. One of the early problems of defining the substantive and chronological boundaries of the field derived from the fact that interest had developed mostly out of life problems of the tax-supported library, vintage circa 1850. Even the perspicacious Jesse Shera seems to have had a mild case of definitional virus which led him to research the Foundations of the Public Library through a period of over two centuries. What Shera revealed was correct, except that the foundations had been erected about halfway through his time period.

Our American ancestors, from the very beginning, drove toward the socialization of books and other reading materials through private, semi-private, and public roadways. They arrived on these shores led by book-bound leaders of late Elizabethan England. For a time, in early New England, folks tried to live by The Book and its explications. They

invented agencies for collecting and making books available
as the circle of literacy competence widened, and people
lived close enough to each other to buy (pecuniary competence
was of course always a factor), borrow, and lend.   Wealthy
individuals might cater to narrow circles of friends or endow
book collections for wider communities.   Private enterprise
might service localities on a public market basis.   Large
corporate membership groups served themselves on a propri-
etary or subscription basis.   And so on.   Any one of the
above could, and many did, offer the use of their library
property freely or in limited ways to the larger public.   The
general point is that American communities tended to evolve
some aspects of their cultural life in ways that resembled
the development of non-cultural services: from individual and
joint private arrangements to tax-supported public arrangements.   At each stage, the manner of monetary support followed customary ways of handling problems in the United
States; from middle-class exclusiveness to middle-class in-
clusiveness, to classless ideals with public responsibility and
responsiveness.

But this is a gross historical picture which can only
provide a clue for searching out factors of institutional development.   Unfortunately, the bulk of these local histories
have been written by local library employees untrained in the
art of asking the past to answer the right and important questions.   The histories, therefore, feature leading men and
women on the local scene as prime movers and "causers" of
library formulation and development.   These histories convey
much too much of the feeling that the history of public libraries is the biography of librarians and philanthropists great
and small.   No one would wish to counsel students of the
subject to neglect these articulators and activists in the business of cultural progress.   But surely it must be clear that
the real contributions of such people lie not in the inspiration to create, but in the ability to seize upon significant so-
cial-cultural pressures, and, as catalysts and accelerators,
to move them on to institutional realization.

The real roots of institutional impetus must be pulled
up out of the soil of social circumstances and operational
ideas.   The sources of movement must be sought in the ways
of thinking that pervade communities and permeate the civic
and social actions of both the leaders and the led.   This
would seem to be true even when, as a few stories go, the
library movement seemed to be a one man job.   For, without widespread public conviction and acceptance, even the off-

spring of the gods do not endure.   V. I. P. 's and chief librarians do contribute heavily by perceiving powerful needs and
by shrewdly promoting lines of development toward fulfilling
these needs; but they do not account for the existence of the
"agency" itself.

Nor is it intellectually tolerable to imply, as individual
historians often do, that each community mystically strikes up
its own library movement out of the creative spirit of leading
citizens.   We must remind ourselves, despite the obviousness
of the phenomenon, that once an institution comes to successful maturity in one town, one city, one state, or one county,
the idea and the process migrate--by word or in the minds
of people who migrate--to other places.   As the message is
transported from one place to another, it carries with it elements of justification which help advance cultural interests in
new host environments.   Modifications will be added in the
framework of new places and fresh minds.   The New Eng-
landers and New Yorkers, who moved westward to seek their
fortunes in mid-western towns, were neither uninformed nor
suffering from mass amnesia.   Hence, it is somewhat surprising to find the excellent historian of the Chicago Public
Library[8] laboring so extensively (and effectively) at a research which discovers the draft of an Illinois library law to
be entirely novel and apparently independent of what happened
in Massachusetts some two decades earlier.   Doubtless there
would be refinements and novelties; and what if the new
framer never read the wording of the old law?   The ideas
were in the air.

There have been in the "air" of American life many
ideas, including residues of ideas more appropriate to former
times, which influence cultural behavior.   One recalls that
reading was related to salvation in Massachusetts Bay Colony; that part of the foundation of Harvard College was a book
collection; that the 1640's saw the enactment of public education laws that announced religious, practical, and civic goals
rolled into one.   The spirit of onetime Protestantism had
weakened, but had remained very much alive during ensuing
centuries.   It is documentable.   The American Enlightenment
of the eighteenth century filled the atmosphere with a faith
in science and education, with an optimism about progress
and the indefinite perfectibility of man and his institutions.
Surely Benjamin Franklin and his contemporaries in and out
of Philadelphia were infused with this idea, along with their
more mundane purposes, when they banded together to form
common book collections, academies, and colleges.   Surely

the confidence bred by a successful revolution, by a new nation, by territorial expansion and the enlargement of economic opportunity helped push cultural institutions on their way.
With libraries, as with like projects, the prosperous led the
way. When asked what factors seemed most important in
the library movement of the last quarter of the nineteenth
century, some librarians, active at the time, spoke of the
centennial spirit of 1876. And what of the ideas of self-im-
provement and the self-made man? Could not books and libraries implement these even better than schools? Were
not public libraries the high schools of the people? The best
of our library history has firmly attached the public library
to the public school. Systematic tax support appeared in its
earliest forms for school-district libraries, that well-meant
but ultimately misguided attempt to supply books to readers
of all ages. [9] The two movements have shared citizen leaders and political sponsors, although it is something of a distortion to trace library history along one-sided lines of educational purpose. [10] They have even shared in the great
American ambivalence: that abiding faith in education accompanied by a negativism toward adequate moral and financial support. [11]

A good deal may be said in behalf of cultural nationalism as a force favorable to public library interests despite
the difficulty of documenting this point profusely. It is true
that Ticknor, Everett, and others who had spent time abroad
in European universities, were indeed envious of the great
continental scholars' libraries. It is also true that they
looked upon their Boston public library project as something
of an answer to the scholar's dream. But it can never be
gainsaid that their major interests and motivation to support
the project lay in educational and humanitarian considerations
of a broadly democratic nature. Cultural rivalry played a
minor part here, as did intermunicipal rivalry among cities
within the United States. Also to be mentioned is the vague
tension set up by a desire after 1800 to produce an American
national literature. Here too a significant role seems to have
been played by our cosmopolitan literati. [12] Nor were the
grounds selfish. The argument was based on the premise
that if American authorship were to be encouraged, American
discriminating readers had to be bred. Libraries, according
to a scattering of contemporary writers, would do the job.

What then of the insistent question of what caused
what in history? What are the main motivations that spur
on prime movers? What, for example, caused the rash of

debating societies and subscription libraries around Houston, Texas, in the late 1830's and early 1840's?[13]   In all likelihood an airborne bacillus.   There must be forgiveness for a flippant evasion of a serious question.   Political historians step in where social historians fear to tread.   Cultural inventions occur as a result of the flowing together of many tributaries of human behavior.   We can estimate the time when they became mainstreams and institutional rivers, but the hows and whys are a different matter.   We gather up our sources, organize them into some rational pattern, and then state our approximated truth.   That is about it.

The successful study of American library history requires a probing of the same kinds of primary material as are used by historians in general.   Some are more applicable than others.   Things like theoretical treatises and contemporary histories have little if any value.   The writers of both are sufficiently conscious of the instrumental value of libraries so as to make frequent acknowledgement to libraries and librarians for valued assistance.   But this tells little of how communities and societies hold libraries in their psyche.

Personal documents of large numbers of citizens are a possibility; but this would limit us to the letters, diaries, and autobiographies of peculiarly self-conscious and articulate people.   The problem here has to do with how large and how good a sampling the historian would find.   And where does he start?   The unpublished documentation of American librarianship would be extremely useful, despite some weaknesses, as historical material.   But neither libraries nor library associations, paradoxically, have systematically done for themselves that which they occupationally do for others--organize and maintain their own unprinted thoughts and reports.   As Stanley Pargellis has so aptly remarked, librarians are and have been interested in population clusters, processes, and facilities, rather than in blood-and-guts citizens.   They have shared with sociologists the penchant for aggregates rather than people.   This has apparently been the American way of life since antebellum days, when Emerson declared sadly that things are in the saddle and ride mankind.   Social historians must first take stock of human aspirations and later of the "things" which are used to satisfy them.

Another conventional source for the life of a people and its institutions are creative expressions like literature, art, and music.   Frequently one finds herein the historic images of behaviors, relationships, and general public re-

sponses. Of the three, art seems least promising, because
it is a form of discourse distant from that world of the
printed word with which libraries are identified.   Public library architecture and its variations in time and place may
tell us something. Someone ought to try his hand at it.
Popular music has often told us a good deal through lyric
and song title.   But popular music directs itself to a mass
heart wherein public libraries do not occupy more than a tiny
space.   The "compleat" student, nevertheless, ought to look
here too.   The theatre has shown some interest and must be
included in the accounting as should motion pictures and television.   Fiction which aims at middle-cult audiences has done
well.

In recent times a breed of cliometricians has been
making profitable magic with historical statistics and meth-
odized quantifications.   All to the good, when one makes discounts for the limitations of compiling.   Even when the compilers observe all of the cautions they should, it must be remembered that statistics are but inferences from or about
reality.   However, from what we know of subconscious self-
serving by the professions, one ought to be very careful in
using statistical reports on collections, circulation, membership registration, and the rest.   The statistical manipulations
of careful scholars like Jesse Shera and Haynes McMullen
are of considerable help in reconstructing certain aspects of
library history.[14]   They correlate the founding of libraries
with questions of population concentration, economic vicissi-
tudes, and migration patterns.   It is gratifying to note that
these historians observe appropriate caveats about the careful
consideration of assumptions, the creation of categories that
approximate reality, the necessity of studying the individual
life stories of libraries, and the extensive checking against
other forms of documentation.   It is well to be aware that
subscription libraries may die years after the starvation period in an economic depression; or that tax-supported public
libraries may be born years after the popular pressures built
up in days of unemployment.

Such matters are often confirmable by the printed
word.   The managing boards of subscription libraries in large
numbers of instances begged to be converted into tax-supported public libraries during hardship years.   Economic re-
covery rarely stemmed the momentum.   Sooner or later the
conversion occurred.   The tragic contradiction of lessened
library appropriations and increased clientele pressure during
lean years found frequent expression in library reporting.[15]

This truism, that "the rediscovery of the Public Library is
a by-product of the depression," turned up in the 1934 report
of the Examining Committee of the Boston Public Library.[16]
During depressions libraries have been for some a refuge,
for others a source of solace, or a place to retool occupationally toward better times.   They have been adult education
centers and a place to compensate for the general drain of
energies.   They have provided the means of inquiry into the
causes of social ills and the possible ways of curing them.

The storehouse of printed documentation, then, is still
the major hope of library history, provided it is used with
historical intelligence.   The printed record tells us much of
what was on the public mind and how libraries fitted into the
social behavior of communities.   An accumulation of references to a given need as expressed in the writings of trustees
and librarians can say a good deal for the historical record,
provided we apply a variety of "discounts."   Some of these
would be for self-deception and other-deception.   There would
be exaggerated claims for the social contributions of libraries.
There would be a multiplication of fashion followers, who argue the case for their institutions in terms that seemed to
work for other librarians at some other time.   How many
promoters simply cribbed the fine rationale contained in the
1852 preliminary report of the trustees of the Boston Public
Library?   On the other hand, the picture we take away from
the collective evidence docs tell us about the kind of social
movements and ideas which in one way or another assisted
in the birth and raising of public libraries.   We find out what
sort of persuasion loosened the purses of town fathers and
philanthropists.   We discover what people thought libraries
were for; and, after all, history is more what people think
happened than what actually happened.

If one accepts at face value the full gamut of nineteenth century documentation from "interested" sources, the
American public library held the promise of repairing all social and cultural maladjustments and the kitchen sink (vocational or do-it-yourself training) to boot.   From early days,
libraries were an adjunct of the temperance movement and
remained so until the prohibition era.   The partnership was
perhaps most vividly dramatized at the very beginning of the
century by Jesse Torrey, of Ballston Spa, New York.   Torrey,
asserting the principle "of extracting the greatest good from
the worst evil," proposed that "sufficient funds may be raised,
by a liberal system of duties on ARDENT SPIRITS, for the
universal establishment of Free Lancasterian Schools, and

Free Public Libraries."[17]   The anti-drink argument worked
for a century, as did the anti-crime and delinquency promise
of public libraries, despite the fact that someone should have
noticed that the graphs of social evil and library establishment took about the same direction.   All rose as cities rose.

Onward marched the parade of library promoters beating their drums in attractive rhythm patterns.   Privileged
groups responded to conscience, to religious sense of duty,
to promise of public acclaim, to threats of new ideas, and
to implied threats of organized movements from below.   Reading would make workers more efficient, intelligent voters,
self-improving units of the great transcendental thrust toward
union with the Oversoul.   Libraries were instruments of up-
ward mobility in a society that was still believed to be offering such mobility to those who would read, attend lectures,
and lift themselves.   In the latter decades of the nineteenth
century, a most important assist to the movement in mid-
western towns and cities was the spread of women's clubs
(most of them having a vague feminist leaning), study classes,
and coteries of both men and women.   Such activities were
symptomatic of the progressive movement in general, a middle class drive which pressed government to take greater responsibility for social and educational services.

Which brings us back to one of the early hypotheses
of library historianship of the 1930's: that the public library
movement was somehow led from below, possibly from working class impetus.   This turns out to be true in a sense, although the working class showed little interest in cultural
agencies of this type.   In fact, there were occasions on which
labor tried to persuade municipalities to turn down a Carnegie
grant, on grounds of anti-labor policies at Homestead, Pennsylvania, as well as for reasons of Carnegie's general ex-
ploitative position in American society.   The impetus that
came from below was somewhat in the form of a stimulus to
those in power positions to satisfy the needs of the less fortunate so as to avoid social disharmony.   This is not to say
that democratic-humanitarian impulses did not play an even
stronger role than the conservative defense phenomenon.
Evidence of concern for the poor and the disadvantaged im-
migrant occurs frequently, genuinely, and strongly.

Such obvious evidence of the public library's involvement in community interests and problems has occasionally
led an historian to extravagent claims for the centrality of
the institution in the life of society.   Woodford's work on the

Detroit Public Library[18] has led him to believe that powerful
influences on the community have radiated from its public library.   Citing the responses of the library to a variety of
events, crises, social and economic changes in Detroit, he
makes the library out to be the mirrored center of a civic
merry-go-round about which all revolves.   The point is rather that good public library administrations make admirable
responses to community needs.   This is their agency function
in Jesse Shera's sense.   A quick perusal of Library Literature for the 1960's under subject headings like "Libraries
and Social and Economic Problems," "Public Libraries--Ne-
groes, Civil Rights, etc.," "Public Libraries--Urban Problems," and the like turns up well over a hundred items.   The
Peace Movement has not as yet taken its turn; the explanation doubtless lies in community negativism (as of March
1968), or in the historic reticence of librarians.

It would seem, then, that the work of public library
historians is never done.   A handful of rich histories of single libraries are wholesome and helpful, but generally want-
ing in interpretation and synthesis.   The broadly conceived
works of the 1940's, those of Spencer, Shera, and Ditzion,
serve to bring us to 1900.   Their geographic limits need to
be extended and, in the normal course of things, their assumptions and inferences could use further scrutiny.   It is
the twentieth century--already three score and ten years
gone--that begs attention.   Lee has made a start albeit a
"unilateral" one.[19]   Our century has many rich fields available for plowing.   The sources are closer, the professional
and lay interests more developed, and communities as self-
conscious as before.   An important drawback most somehow
be overcome.   The rewards of historianship in the library
profession are meager.   This is a matter for schools of librarianship and professional organizations to ponder.

Notes

1.   J. H. Shera, "The Literature of Library History," Li-
       brary Quarterly XV (1945), 1-24.
2.   Shera, op. cit., 17.
3.   Report of the Commission on Social Studies of the Amer-
       ican Historical Association.
4.   As recollection has it, Dean Louis Round Wilson en-
       couraged and/or nourished Gwladys Spencer and
       Jesse Shera in Chicago, and Sidney Ditzion in New
       York.   The latter happily had his research directed by
       Merle Curti.

5. This despite the evidence that the American college li-
    braries were partly goaded to maturity by student
    literary societies.
6. Jesse H. Shera, Foundations of the Public Library...,
    Chicago, University of Chicago Press, 1949, V.
7. Cf. Elizabeth M. Richards, "Alexandre Vattemare and
    His System of International Exchanges," Bulletin on
    the Medical Library Association, XXXII (1944), pas-
    sim; Walter Muir Whitehill, Boston Public Library;
    A Centennial History, Cambridge, Mass., Harvard
    University Press, 1956, 3-9; Sidney Ditzion, "The
    Anglo-American Library Scene...," Library Quarter-
    ly XVI (1946), 281-301.
8. Gwladys Spencer, The Chicago Public Library, Origins
    and Backgrounds, Chicago, University of Chicago
    Press, 1943, 239ff.
9. Sidney Ditzion, "The District-School Library, 1835-55,"
    Library Quarterly X (1940), 545-77.
10. See Robert Ellis Lee, Continuing Education for Adults
    through the American Public Library, 1833-1964,
    Chicago, American Library Association, 1966.
11. Merle Curti, American Paradox: The Conflict of
    Thought and Action, New Brunswick, N.J., Rutgers
    University Press, 1956.
12. Ray W. Frantz, Jr., "A Re-Examination of the Influence
    of Literary Nationalism on the Public Library,"
    Journal of Library History, I (1966), 182-86.
13. A phenomenon noted in Orin W. Hatch, Lyceum to Li-
    brary: A Chapter in the Cultural History of Houston,
    Houston, Texas Gulf Coast Historical Association,
    1965.
14. Shera, Foundations, esp. List of Tables, p. XV, and
    plates IV-VI; Haynes McMullen, "The Founding of
    Social and Public Libraries in Ohio, Indiana, and
    Illinois through 1850," University of Illinois Library
    School. Occasional Papers, 51, March 1958; McMul-
    len, "Through Library History with Punch and Nee-
    dle...," in J.D. Marshall, ed., Approaches to Li-
    brary History, Tallahassee, Fla., Journal of Library
    History, 1966, 81-90.
15. Sidney Ditzion, Arsenals of a Democratic Culture...,
    Chicago, A.L.A., 1947, 115-117.
16. Cited in Whitehill, Boston Public Library, 221; see also
    chap. XI on "Depression and Consolidation."
17. Jesse Torrey, The Intellectual Torch (1815), reprint
    Woodstock, Vt., Elm Tree Press, 1912, 8, 12-13,
    27.

18. Frank Woodford, "Second Thoughts on Writing Library
         History," _Journal of Library History_, I (1966), 34-
         42.
19. Lee, _Continuing Education for Adults_..., _loc. cit._

GROWTH PATTERNS OF PUBLIC LIBRARIES

Dorothy M. Sinclair

In a period of change it is ironic that history, a
discipline whose chief concern is change, should often be
dismissed as irrelevant. To the unhistorically minded, the
past is either gone (and good riddance!) or quaint, romantic,
faintly amusing costume drama to be viewed with the sentimental patronage of the antiquarian. The fact that every age
that has ever existed or will exist is, in its own terms,
modern, seems to occur only to those who, temporarily,
partially, and for purposes of investigation, live and move
in another era. This simple and self-evident concept yields
a more realistic assessment of the achievements and failures
of the past, and a sounder grasp of the present. It is profoundly aware of the transitory nature of its own proudest accomplishments. It knows the roots of today's difficulties and
paradoxically combines an understanding of anachronisms with
the basis for a shrewd guess at the manner in which they
may be dealt with.

The library world would gain from attention to history, not to foster a feeling of complacent superiority to our
predecessors, but rather to throw light on the continuum of
which we represent a part. History does not claim the pre-
dictability which characterizes the hard sciences; its subject
matter--mankind in time--is too complex and impossible to
control. But it can illuminate the present and provide at
least clues to the future. Surely librarianship, in this day
of perplexity and transition, cannot afford to ignore it.

The following text is part of a dissertation undertaken
at a library school whose dean long ago called on librarians
to be aware of their own past, and who set a notable example
which has been followed by too few successors. It attempts
to discern and describe a pattern in recent American public
library development, one which will not only help to account
for today's multi-library systems, but also make some contribution toward the approach to problems of the future.

For a number of reasons, the movement in American public librarianship toward multi-library systems is over-ripe for the attention of the historian. It represents a change of major significance. In 1900, most public libraries served cities, towns (in the New England sense as well as the more usual meaning) or, in rare cases, counties. Except for the limited activities of a few state libraries which took care of the needs of the otherwise unserved or eked out the inadequate resources of the smaller public libraries with travelling collections and interlibrary loans, library service was a local affair. Rural America was largely unserved. A handful of large cities maintained public libraries of importance; these were objects of awe but not envy to those in charge of their smaller counterparts, who no more aspired to attainment of comparable stature than owners of rural general stores hoped to reach the heights attained by Macy's or Gimbel's.

Today the user of the small local library outlet, in a large and increasing proportion of the nation, can command the resources of the Macys and Gimbels of the library world. His own library has connections with larger neighbors whose collections he can call upon, and groups of libraries jointly offer services and specializations formerly out of the reach of the individual unit. Through teletype, a WATS line, or other device, he is linked with an increasingly complex network of libraries.

While this development is one of importance for library history, and for social history in general, it is little known by those outside its immediate influence. The library profession itself is only partially and dimly aware of the movement.[1]

From a practical viewpoint, also, a systematic study is desirable. The movement is still progressing, but has proceeded at different rates of speed in different geographic areas. Despite the confirmed belief among local librarians, officials, and publics that each locality's situation and problems are significantly different from those elsewhere, the same problems do, in fact, turn up in east and west, north and south. While it is true that regional differences exist, a comparison of public library systems throughout the nation reveals many more similarities. States and localities can, if they will, learn from the experiences of each other.

Important as the topic is, however, it presents dif-

ficulties as a subject for historical investigation.   The uneven
development in geographic regions, and in time, rule out a
simple chronological account.   The pattern of development,
the significance of innovative efforts, would be obscured by
such a treatment.   The usual methods of abridgment adopted
by historians are not open.   To study only a brief time-seg-
ment, or to slice off and investigate a geographic region,
would defeat the purpose of this inquiry.   An initial problem,
therefore, is to design an approach which will preserve the
broad scope of the topic, moving about in time and space
while at the same time focussing attention on the process of
change.   To put the matter in another way, since the topic
cannot be curtailed chronologically or regionally, it must be
curtailed substantively.   Some of the meat of it (the rich regional background, the connections with other social and political movements) must be sacrificed in order that the skeleton may be revealed, for closer inspection of the articulation of its bones.

Figures 1 to 5 represent an effort to diagram such
a study as a series of triangles, each of which represents a
phase in the development of public library systems.   Each
triangle begins with a Point A, representing the situation at
the beginning of the phase.   Point B, at the right of each
triangle's base, represents the problems inherent in Situation
A, and Point C, at the apex, the solution (almost always a
partial one) to the problems in the light of the situation.
Solution C of a phase becomes Situation A of the next phase.*

The sequence begins with the small independent public
library (Figure 1).   It is a fascinating fact that the development begins with, and proceeds from weakness rather than
strength, that--for a long time--this is a story of pygmies
rather than giants, and that the giants of the library world
enter the picture relatively late, drawn into a movement initiated by the needs of weaklings.   There were, at the movement's beginning, and still are, many small, isolated public
libraries in the United States.   As Figure 1 indicates, they
are indeed limited -- in resources, services, funds, and
especially in conception of what public library service should
be.   Despite these inadequacies, per capita costs may be

---

*The triangles may appear, at first glance, to rep-
resent in crude form a kind of decision-making model.   It
should become clear, as the paper progresses, that they are
quite different.   They do, however, bear some relationship to
Hegel's dialectical model.

Phase I: From Small, Independent Local Unit
to County or Multi-County Public Library

C.[1] "Solution"
   County or multi-county service
   Larger tax base
   Larger service area
   Larger collection
   Professional staff (small)
     Centralized professional services
       Processing
       Requests and reference
       In service training
   Coordinated service pattern
     Local stations, local personnel
     Bookmobiles
     Delivery service
     Newsletters
     Fluid collections

A.[1] Situation
   Small, independent,
   local library unit

B.[1] Problems
   Difficulties
     High per capita costs
     Low tax base
     Many gaps in service-
       many unserved
   Inadequacies
     Limited resources
     Little reference or
       subject material
     Limited conception,
       among public, officials,
       staff

Figure 1.

relatively high.

As shown in Figure 1, the immediate solution most frequently reached for the problems of the small community library has traditionally been the county library, which also has had the advantage of bringing service to previously unserved rural populations. Whether the town library expanded into or cooperated with the new county library, or whether it served the unincorporated area by contract, it commanded a larger resource, sometimes a professional staff, and a broader tax base. Of these three organizational patterns -- consolidated library, cooperation between city and county libraries, and city library serving the unincorporated area -- only the second was truly multi-library. Another type, belonging to this phase and developing almost simultaneously was the multi-county library, which might be also a multi-library system. Regardless of the organization, these early county and multi-county libraries developed coordinated methods of reaching the entire service area which, for their day, were innovative and effective.[2]

The rural county library was not, however, without its own problems and difficulties (Figure 2). Centralized professional staff and resources gave service at second hand to rural library users, whose quality of service was too dependent on partially-trained local personnel. The fluid collection, while clearly the best way yet devised to distribute materials in small and isolated communities unsuited to bookmobile service, tended to dissipate resources and necessitated cumbersome bookkeeping. Where several political jurisdictions besides the county itself were concerned, sharing of costs became a problem. All these difficulties encountered by the county libraries of the early decades of this century are forerunners of those met by today's more sophisticated systems: service at a distance; distribution of resources over a large geographic area; sharing of costs. While the partial solutions reached were adequate for their time, better solutions to the same problems were to be needed later.*

_____

*The question might be raised, whether municipal libraries with branches did not meet and solve the same problems. This is true only in part. City branches serve concentrations of population large enough to warrant sizable permanent collections and staffs; main city libraries are within reach of most residents; administration is centralized; there are no problems of cost sharing.

Phase II: From Local Plus County or Multi-County Service
to Local/County/Multi-County Service Supplemented by
State Service

C.[2] "Solution"
    State library assistance to public libraries
     Consultant service
     Backstop request service
      Union catalogs
     Workshops--in service training programs
     Publications
     Travelling and supplementary collections
     Regional service centers (to aid libraries)
    State library service to officials and local
     lay groups
     Encouragement of establishment of libraries
     Work with library boards
    State library service to individuals
     Mail service to unserved readers

A.[2] Situation
    County or
    multi-county
    service devel-
    oped as "Solu-
    tion" in Phase I

B.[2] Problems
    Difficulties
    Costs - Problems of dividing
     costs in multi-county service
     Variations in local ability
     to support
    Access - Centralized request
     service slow
    Structure - Cumbersome record-
     keeping
     Problems of dealing with several
     groups of officials
    Inadequacies
     Usually no direct professional
     service
     Quality of service too dependent
     on quality of local personnel
    Resources - Scattered through
     fluid collection
     Limited attention to special
     local needs
    Conception continues limited

Figure 2.

Phase II represents a new dimension and an improvement in service. For this reason it is given a separate triangle and is called a distinct phase. It does not, however, represent a direct response to the problems of the county or multi-county library as shown at Point B^2, but is rather a response to the problems the county library still shared with the small library of Situation A^1--the need for greater resources than the local (or county) jurisdiction could be expected to support. In some states, Phases I and II developed simultaneously, but in many an expansion of the services of the state extension agency developed in response to the needs of the small county and town libraries. Along with the continuing effort to persuade localities to initiate library service, State Libraries increased their supplementary book and interlibrary loan activities, and their consultant services. State Library branches, or regional service centers operated by the state, began to appear, bringing the services formerly offered only from the capital closer to the regions. In this phase, at its height, the State Library supplemented local service in whatever way was appropriate--by direct service to the unserved, by providing what was lacking in local resources, by offering workshops and institutes for local librarians, and--in a number of states--by making available centralized processing.

The supplementary role of the State Library is a familiar one in most states, and constitutes the major state service in a good many today. Its problems are, to some extent, identical with those of the county library serving its local outlets, but raised from the county level to that of the state. In Phase III, we find once again problems of service at second hand--delays, misinterpretations, dependence on local personnel for initiation of service with consequent failure to use it to the fullest extent. But a new problem is perhaps even more serious. When the resources and consultants of the State Library are readily available, it is easy for localities to rely on the state without feeling the need to build up local resources. State agency personnel, in their supplementary role, feel an uneasiness and wonder whether, in improving their services to local libraries, setting up service centers, etc., they may not be inhibiting the growth of on-the-spot service supported by local funds. A personal dependency on the part of local librarians also causes concern. State agency staff finds itself on the horns of a dilemma: the better its service, the greater the disservice it may possibly be doing the local library.

Phase III: From State Supplemented Local Service
to Limited State Coordination of Local Service

C.[3] "Solution"
   State Aid programs (money grants)
      Standards for eligibility
   Federal aid (limited) available through states
      Limited to rural areas
   Demonstration programs to encourage improvement
   of local service
   Encouragement of formal or informal cooperation
   among local libraries
   Surveys of regional or statewide service

A.[3] Situation
   State supplemented
   local service devel-
   oped as "Solution" in
   Phase II

B.[3] Problems
   Difficulties
      Costs - Proper balance of
      costs between state and
      local governments
      Access - State service slow
      Problems of misinterpre-
      tation of user needs
      Resources - Difficulty in
      deciding on appropriate
      extent of state supplemen-
      tary resource, to supple-
      ment but not inhibit de-
      velopment of local re-
      sources
      Conception - Tendency of
      local libraries to depend
      on state
   Inadequacies
      Resources - Extent not ful-
      ly known, and thus not
      used
      Conception - Continues
      limited, resulting in lim-
      ited use of available
      service

Figure 3.

Some states found Solution C^3 before 1956, when the
first federal funds under the Library Services Act became
available to all states willing and able to use them. These
pioneer states had been able, previously, to obtain state
funds for grants-in-aid to individual libraries and used a variety of incentive arrangements in the effort to upgrade the
quality of direct local service. Many states, however, had
to wait for the Library Services Act to provide such funds.
Although their use was, by law, limited to rural areas, the
federal funds enabled a number of states to embark upon
such projects for the improvement of direct local service as
demonstrations for a limited period, after which local support was to be provided; grants to assist in the formation of
county, multi-county, city-county or even more complex systems. During the years of LSA operation, these projects
were small, partly because of the rural limitation, partly
because funds themselves were limited, and partly because
almost every state had to use a goodly proportion of the federal money to catch up with Phase II. Nevertheless, Phase
III represents a landmark in public library system development, a shift on the part of state agencies from major emphasis on supplementary service, on the one hand, to grants
to enable localities to improve local resources and decrease
dependency on those of the state itself, on the other. As is
true of every phase, this one has come at different times to
different states and regions; a number of states are still, for
a variety of geographic and historic reasons, emphasizing the
Phase II type of service.

The problems of Phase IV have already been fore-
shadowed: inadequate funds for grants, the rural limitation
where federal funds were used, weaknesses and inadequacies
in the local libraries and in the state agencies themselves. [3]
New problems arise, however, which are to continue and in-
tensify to the end of our cycle. When state and federal
funds begin to assist local libraries to band together in systems, we begin to see new problems of structure. A new
type of organization arises, in which autonomous libraries
share services and jointly expend funds made available to
the state. Here, for the first time, we find the multi-library system in its fully developed form. In Situation A^4
problems of the new type are modest, involving perhaps
swapping of services or sharing of staff and materials. Even
at this elementary level, however, we meet problems of
cost (Who pays for what? Who gets how much and on what
basis?) and problems of control (Who supervises the joint
services? Who decides how the state money is to be spent?

Phase IV: From Limited to Full State Coordination
of Public Library Services

C.[4] "Solution"
 Increased State Aid programs aimed primarily
 at system development
 Federal fund limitation to rural areas
 removed
 Large libraries designated (and compensated) as regional or statewide resource
 centers
 Large multi-library systems, including
 larger libraries, with special collections,
 consultants, services
 Developing contract services among local
 libraries
 Statewide communications networks, using
 Teletype, etc.

A.[4] Situation
 Limited state co-
 ordination of local
 services as developed
 as "Solution" in Phase
 III

B.[4] Problems
 Difficulties
 Costs - Inadequate state/fed-
 eral funds to assist development or provide incentives
 Funds limited to rural areas
 when only federal available
 Structure - Problems of government in formal cooperative programs among independent libraries
 Conception - Fear of state or
 federal control
 Inadequacies
 Resources - Inadequate to
 meet more sophisticated
 needs
 Access - Collection of larger
 libraries still not available
 Conception - Complacency
 over limited accomplish-
 ments

Figure 4.

Who legally owns the bookmobiles and other expensive equipment purchased with the state money?). Tentative contracts, various formulas for measuring costs and expenditures, first steps toward formation of multi-jurisdictional boards, all developed during Phase IV. Their unresolved difficulties provide some of the problems of Phase V. As state and federal support increases, another problem appears--the fear of state and federal control.

A major frustration of Situation A[4], a combination of increasingly sophisticated needs and the ineligibility for federal funds of non-rural libraries, was happily removed when the Library Services and Construction Act removed the rural limitation. Public library systems were now able, as only a handful with sizable State Aid grants had formerly been, to build on existing strength, to draw the large libraries into the systems and to compensate them for their contributions to their smaller neighbors. Happily, too, LSCA provided considerably larger sums needed for the more sophisticated services required, for the more expensive technological devices used to connect systems growing larger geographically, and for the commissioning of more, and more specialized, surveys of state and regional needs.

The drawing into the system picture of the larger and stronger public libraries, at long last, occurred in different ways in different states. In general, there are two patterns: local option or state designation. In a few states, new laws for the development of systems and the distribution of state and/or federal funds permitted groups of local libraries to form their own combinations. Under this pattern, the large and small libraries might together be active partners in system development. The local option pattern has been successful in populous states where strong local libraries and professional leadership are found. In other cases, large libraries have been assigned by the states to the role of "major resource library" or some similar designation, with already delineated regions to be served. In the latter cases, the large library has often been expected to take the lead in developing a variety of cooperative and system-type services in the assigned area.[4] Some states have developed several levels or layers of service, with regularly assigned channels through which the user's request should go. Some have combined the two patterns.

Regardless of the pattern adopted, Phase IV's solution brought for the first time to some libraries' users access to

reasonably good resources and services. The small library
no longer had to depend on infrequent visits of the state consultant for advice; the system had its own group of consultant-
specialists. Audiovisual service, teletype communication,
coordinated public relations, processing centers, etc., along
with a much stronger collection of books, available both on
loan to local libraries and directly to all the system's users,
became the rule of Phase IV's "Solution." If Phase III marks
the turning point in the state agency's role, Phase IV is the
one in which it begins to appear more than a wild dream that
every library user may have access to good library service.
To return to our earlier metaphor, the library equivalents of
Macy's and Gimbel's are now accessible to the local user.

While the situation at the close of Phase IV is far in
advance of the present situation of many libraries and the accomplishments of many state agencies, it does not constitute
Utopian public library service. It is true that some libraries
and systems seem content to rest here. Complacency has
been an enemy of progress in each of our phases, a fact
which explains in part why leaders in successive phases tend
to appear in different states. It is thus reassuring to find
in some of the presently most advanced areas that Phase IV
is beginning to give way to Phase V. Problems encountered
in Phase IV reflect the fact that difficulties multiply as organizations become complex. The introduction of larger and
more highly organized government jurisdictions requires more
formal structuring. Methods of determining compensation for
imbalance of services rendered over services received, call
for expertise in cost accounting. The inclusion of larger libraries raises the question of proportional representation on
system boards and administrative councils. "One library,
one vote," may satisfy a group of libraries of approximately
the same size, but the large municipal or metropolitan county
library, representing perhaps populations close to the million
figure, may rebel if it is to have no more voice in the system's councils than its smallest neighbor. This problem is
complicated by the fears of the small libraries, only too
ready to believe that their large neighbor is scheming to
"welcome little fishes in with gently smiling jaws."

The "happy family" of the system of smaller libraries
thus undergoes a change when the large library enters. Adjustments on both sides are necessary. The large library's
representatives must carefully avoid patronizing, the small
ones a fiercely defensive attitude. These adjustments take
time. Similarly adjustments are required at this stage of

Phase V: From Statewide Coordination of Public Library Service
Toward Interstate and Inter-[type of] Library Cooperation

C.[5] "Solution"
Planning programs, involving cooperation among
types of libraries, under Title III, LSCA
Networks involving academic, special, and
school libraries, along with public libraries
Three R's program in New York State
Interstate compacts beginning to be utilized
for interstate service
Experiments with more sophisticated technology,
e.g., facsimile transmission

A.[5] Situation
Full state coordina-
tion of public library
service, as developed
as "Solution" in Phase
IV

B.[5] Problems
Difficulties
Costs - Determination of
equitable compensation for
system services given by
larger libraries
High cost of some devices
used
Access - Reluctance of some
libraries to share resources,
even when compensated
Structure - Appropriate representation of libraries in a
large system (e.g., 1/1
per library, or some type
of proportional representation)
Conception - Lack of mutual
understanding among large
and small libraries
Changing role of State agency
Difference in relationships
Extent of appropriate
"oversight"
Resources - Pressure from
federal government to co-
ordinate with other federal-
ly-supported programs

Figure 5.

the state agency staff, especially consultants who no longer deal with the small library and the untrained librarian but work with system consultant-specialists and system administrators of a high level of competence.

Phase V represents another milestone in that its "solution" begins to look more frequently outside the public library ranks. Partly because of pressures from the federal sector for the coordination of federally-assisted library programs, and partly from the logic of the case, Phase V brings another swing toward attention to local library resources. In Phase III states had ceased to stress supplementary service and begun more actively to encourage improvement of local resources. Now, in Phase V, we have librarians and officials at every level asking why it is necessary to send a hundred miles for a book from another public library, when a college or university library near at hand can supply it. When both are receiving federal and/or state support, the question is especially hard to answer. The cooperation of school libraries, both as local resources and as beneficiaries of the system's resources, is also a matter of concern in Phase V. Encouraged by Title III of the Library Services and Construction Act, local cooperatives among libraries of different types are being developed to utilize local resources, establish ground-rules, arrange for communication and delivery, etc. Plugging in to a research library component, for the benefit of public library systems' users with specialized needs, is a reasonable next step already under way in New York State's Three R's program and in a few other places. [5]

Phase V has only barely approached another logical step, that of crossing state lines in developing library cooperation. Just as certain regions within the states make natural groupings, so do many interstate regions. Interstate Compact legislation has been passed by a number of states, removing formidable legal barriers to interstate library cooperative ventures. A few rather modest interstate activities, in the public library sector, have been in existence for some years[6] and, of course, interstate interlibrary loan activity has always been brisk. Regional associations and regional bibliographic centers are also familiar. More recently, such interstate partnerships as academic library consortia and "Metro" in the New York area have appeared and may be forerunners of further interstate cooperation of a more formal type than the earlier loose arrangements.

We depart from history and enter the realm of specu-

Phase VI: From Interstate and Inter-[type of] Library
Cooperation Toward Unknown Future Developments

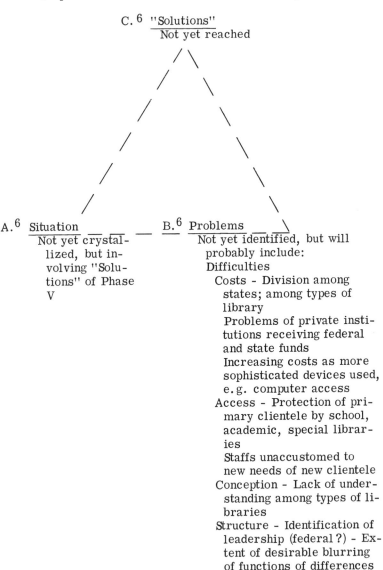

C.[6] "Solutions"
Not yet reached

A.[6] Situation
Not yet crystal-
lized, but in-
volving "Solu-
tions" of Phase
V

B.[6] Problems
Not yet identified, but will
probably include:
Difficulties
Costs - Division among
states; among types of
library
Problems of private institutions receiving federal
and state funds
Increasing costs as more
sophisticated devices used,
e.g. computer access
Access - Protection of primary clientele by school,
academic, special librar-
ies
Staffs unaccustomed to
new needs of new clientele
Conception - Lack of understanding among types of libraries
Structure - Identification of
leadership (federal ?) - Extent of desirable blurring
of functions of differences
among types of libraries

Figure 6

lation when we attempt to predict Phase VI.   But already the
problems inherent in the "solution" to Phase V can be anticipated.   The complexities of government and cost-sharing
among multi-library systems made up only of public libraries
were formidable, but those of systems involving libraries of
all types, public and private, will require increased wisdom
and expertise.   The whole question of structure may require
a new look: Shall each type of library continue to retain its
special characteristics and protect the needs of its primary
clientele, or will there be a merging of functions and a blurring of boundaries, with all types of libraries freely serving
all comers, for appropriate compensation?   Overall supervision and coordination in Phase VI might well move to a new
level, beyond that of the state.   Just as, within a state, the
concern has been to bring to bear its library strengths for
the benefit of weaker libraries and poorer regions, so the
next step may well be a similar movement toward equaliza-
tion among states.   If so, the federal role may increase.
Another possibility, in metropolitan areas which cross state
lines, might be library authorities, supported by all jurisdictions and agencies needing library service within the region,
and charged with providing total library service to the region.

It is hazardous, and no part of the historian's business, to attempt to arrive at solutions to problems which are
themselves only dimly framed.   Nevertheless, if the pattern
of triangular sequences has any practical utility, it should
assist states and individual libraries and systems, which
have now reached one of the phases already outlined, to anticipate problems, and to be aided in their solution by ob-
serving the outcomes of their forerunners' efforts.   Some
phases may be speeded up, others perhaps combined.   Some
problems may be avoided.   Special attention might be given
by the profession to recurring problems.   One, the ultimate
dependence on the local librarian of the success of all the
efforts, recurs in almost every phase.   This potentially weak
link must not be overlooked while sophisticated networks and
communications systems are developed. [7]   Another, increasing
in difficulty from phase to phase, is that of administrative
structure.   Librarians have, almost by chance, created what
appears to be a distinctive type of organization, in which
autonomous units band together to set up machinery which
performs services for all, under the supervision of councils
representing members and without loss of the members' autonomy.   One can think of multi-unit organizations which perform peripheral functions, but it is hard to think of a precedent for a multi-unit organization whose activities are central

to each unit's goals. The United Nations, in its much more exalted sphere, does appear to share some characteristics, and like this illustrious prototype, library organizations may be vulnerable. Already one hears of rumblings of disagreement in an occasional system, and even a withdrawal or two. At this stage, library systems may require the assistance of experts in management and organizational behavior, as well as sophisticated studies of interlibrary operations as such. [8]

Notes

1. The first study of the genre appeared in 1969: Nelson
    Associates, Public Library Systems in the United States:
    A Survey of Multijurisdictional Systems, Chicago,
    American Library Association, 1969. As defined in
    this study, "multijurisdictional systems" is a term
    which includes, but is not confined to, what we are
    here designating as "Multi-library systems." The
    Nelson study includes, for example, libraries under
    one administration serving a city and a county.
2. A detailed, now dated, description of some of the tech-
    niques devised may be found in Gretchen Knief Schenk,
    County and Regional Library Development, Chicago,
    American Library Association, 1954.
3. Phillip Monypenny, The Library Functions of the States,
    Chicago, American Library Association, 1966, 90ff.
4. Nelson Associates. Public Library Systems in the United
    States, 22.
5. The New York program has been described frequently in
    professional literature. An early summary, by the
    Deputy Commissioner of Education of New York State
    is: E. B. Nyquist, "The Three R's in New York,"
    ALA Bulletin, 60 (December, 1966), 1134-1138.
6. Michelle R. Vale, "The Interstate Library Compact,"
    Library Journal, 91 (May 15, 1966), 2419-2422.
7. "The Training of Village Librarians," Major Problems
    in the Education of Librarians, ed. Robert D. Leigh,
    New York, Columbia University Press, 1954, 47-64,
    is an early instance of recognition of this problem.
8. Maryann Duggan, "Library Network Analysis and Planning
    (Lib-NAT), Journal of Library Automation, 2 (Septem-
    ber, 1969), 157-175, is a good example.

ORIGINS OF THE MOUSEION OF ALEXANDRIA

H. J. de Vleeschauwer and H. Curtis Wright*

> The museum is also part of the palace precincts. It consists of a philosophical school with a covered walkway, an auditorium, and a large dining hall where the literati associated with the museum share a common mess. They also have their goods in common, and one of their number (presently assigned by Caesar, but formerly appointed by the kings) is a priest who presides over the museum.[1]

Fifteen years ago I began a collection called Mousaion, a serial which I have continued for 100 issues or more. It grew out of a study of the Alexandrian Mouseion from which, incidentally, I derived the name of the collection. In a statement too brief to be satisfactory, yet too provocative to avoid opposition, I objected to the commonly held view of the origin of the Mouseion.[2] The opinio communis of both classical philology and library science is reflected in Milkau's statement that "the purely Greek character of the library of Alexandria cannot be called into doubt."[3] In contrast to this view I argued that the Mouseion cannot be explained adequately without accounting for its Oriental antecedents. Classical philology is not likely to accept this apparent expropriation, although in petto I desire neither to deprive the Greeks of this Hellenistic monument, nor to bestow it on the ancient Orient. I am merely proposing a kind of Zweistrombegriff for the establishment of the Mouseion, as there are two streams which flow into its underlying reservoir of causes. It might be mentioned that Milkau's "Greek thesis" is also defended by Parsons;[4] but--and this is the point I am stressing--the reasons for their arguments seem unconvincing. I shall, therefore, retain my own views in the matter. This controversy about one of the famous facets of our library

---

*Professor de Vleeschauwer is the author of this paper. Professor Wright has edited the English version and supplied the scholarly apparatus.

Marble bust of King Ptolemy I. Soter, 323-285 B.C.
Courtesy of Ny Carlsberg Glyptotek, Copenhagen.

past is here brought out by way of paying my tribute of respect and admiration to Dr. J. H. Shera.

   The Greek thesis amounts to saying (1) that the actual
creator of the Mouseion was Demetrius of Phalerum who, in
response to an appeal by Ptolemy, created at Alexandria an
Aristotelian Lyceum of gigantic proportions which became the
Mouseion proper, a kind of university dedicated to educational
excellence in the fields of literature and science; and (2) that
Demetrius, relying on the quasi boundless munificience of
his king, endowed this institution with a massive library of
equally universal character.   Ptolemy, it is true, favored
this twofold creation, as he had long been familiar with Aristotelian concepts.   He was descended from the Lagides and
related to the royal family of Macedon--he was even said,
albeit clandestinely, to be the son of Arsinoe and Philip, and
thus half-brother to Alexander.   Ptolemy, ten years older
than Alexander, had indeed frequented the court where he
had, in fact, been educated; but all of this was prior to Philip's appointment of Aristotle as the tutor of Alexander.   From
this association an assured friendship developed between
Ptolemy and Alexander, a friendship that remained unbroken
during the entire Asian campaign.   They surely would have
spoken of Aristotle on occasion, and of his school enterprises
at Athens for which the State treasury had provided generous
pecuniary support.

   Ptolemy, following the unexpected death of Alexander
and the ensuing disorder caused by the problem of succession
and the dislocation of the empire, lived with his souvenirs
and secrets.   He intended all along to establish in the capitol
of his new Egyptian kingdom a university and library on the
pattern of Aristotle's Athenian models; but he was obliged to
await patiently the realization of this idea, for the situation
in Egypt, while flourishing economically, was politically men-
acing and unstable.   More than 20 years went by until finally,
about 295 B. C., Ptolemy approached Theophrastus, Aristotle's
successor in the Athenian Peripatos, with this object in view.

   Theophrastus, however, declined his proposal and suggested that he consider Demetrius of Phalerum, one of the
victims of a crazed Athenian democracy.   Demetrius, sus-
pected of collaboration with the Macedonian power, was living
in exile at Thebes following his ten-year reign over the tur-
bulent and unsettled capital of Attica.   Ptolemy agreed, and
Demetrius, aided by the staff of the Peripatos, began at once
to set up the university as a center of research and instruc-

tion. It became immediately obvious that the work of this institution called for the resources of a library commensurate
with the universality of its aims. Demetrius, therefore, un-
dertook the successful collection of some 200, 000 rolls, but
not before he had incurred the displeasure of the second
Ptolemy, ironically called Philadelphos, and was relegated
to the provinces. The Mouseion of Alexandria, in this view,
must be considered an entirely Greek achievement, conceived
after the manner of the Athenian Peripatos, and owing its
origin to the indefatigable efforts of Demetrius. The universal, Panhellenic tendency of the Mouseion thus took shape in
the New Macedonian asylum of hellenistic science and asserted itself with renewed vigor only when Demetrius decided
to collect the most important literature of African, Oriental,
and other non-Greek peoples in Greek translation. The so-
called Septuagint, for instance, a Greek translation of the
Pentateuch, may be cited as one of the examples of this tendency. These, in outline, are the basic features of the Greek
thesis.

    To this Greek or Aristotelian thesis I should like to
oppose another, namely, the Ptolemaic thesis. While this
theory attributes the Mouseion proper to the inspiration of
Aristotle's Lyceum it nevertheless regards the library itself
as derived from Ptolemy and his recollections of Oriental
library institutions. If the Greek thesis tends to make Demetrius the mastermind behind both the Mouseion and its library, I, for my part, tend to view them as the work of both
Ptolemy and Demetrius in their respective roles as initiator
and executor. If my thesis is at all plausible we may expect
to find a greater Macedonian participation in the organization
and policy of the library than is ordinarily supposed. We
must rely on merely circumstantial evidence for an explanation of the Mouseion and its library, however, as authentic
documents relating to this problem are few and far between.
In view of this circumstance historical reconstruction often
boils down to feats of deduction and interpretation. Parsons,
the latest defender of the Greek thesis, proves prudent and
circumspect in this regard. He represents the opinions he
wishes to defend as plausible and reasonable in every instance. I shall, therefore, avail myself of this same privi-
lege. It should also be observed that our opinions do in fact
coincide in some respects, and that a certain amount of par-
allelism is therefore unavoidable in the exposition of these
two theses.

    The Greek thesis, it seems to me, exaggerates the

influence of Demetrius and underestimates that of the Lagide.
It should be obvious that the initiative was taken by the latter,
as it is most presumptious to assume that Demetrius pres-
sured the king into founding the Mouseion.   The problem
must also be resolved in favor of Ptolemy I, Soter, and not
in favor of Philadelphos, his successor, as some have maintained.   It is essential that these institutions be referred to
the first Ptolemy if the role of Demetrius is to be taken seriously.   If it could be shown that Philadelphos founded the
Mouseion it would also prove that Demetrius had no part
whatever in its establishment.   We know that Demetrius incurred the disfavor of the second Ptolemy who, on acceding
to the throne, lost no time in removing him from the capitol
to Busiris, a town on the outskirts of Memphis.   It is probably no mere coincidence, on the other hand, that Ptolemy I
invited Demetrius to Alexandria at the approximate time of
his actual departure from Thebes.

Throughout Cassander's rule at Athens Demetrius had
felt safe in Greece, secure in the knowledge that he could
devote himself fully to literary activity with ample provision
for his subsistence.   But this sense of security faded with
Cassander's death in 297.   Calculations of ancient historians
which date Demetrius' arrival at Alexandria between 305-301
cannot be confirmed, but 297-96 tallies perfectly with Ptolemy's decision to implement, after so long a delay, his
Kulturpolitik, a policy that had been held in abeyance since
323.   This was due to the rivalries between the Diadochi and
Epigones, as well as to the pressing need of effecting an internal and external consolidation of his satrapy which he intended to establish as an independent kingdom.

Now if we assign the initiative for founding the Mouseion to the son of Lagus another question arises: what
might persuade a head of State, like Ptolemy, to change into
a devotee of literature and science?   The answer, surely,
is the influence of Alexander the Great.   We have already
noted that Ptolemy belonged to the royal family and had
gained admission to the court; but prior to Aristotle's tuition
of the young nobles he had been exiled by Philip for his involvement in a noisome situation prevailing in the royal family.   Aristotle's tuition did not last long, however, as the
young Alexander secured temporary regency in 340-39 during
his father's military actions against Byzantium.   A few years
later, when Philip was assassinated in 336, Alexander assumed the throne at the age of 20 and recalled Ptolemy from
exile.   An old friendship was thus renewed, a friendship that

would henceforth prove unalterable. The policy that Ptolemy
will pursue in Egypt, moreover, is the perfect antitype of
Alexander's policies regarding the numerous peoples he sub-
dued. After the accession, on the other hand, Aristotle's
relationship with Alexander is seemingly diminished. He has
not the slightest influence on his former pupil who, in fact,
contemplates and implements the very Asian campaign most
feared by the old general-minister Antipater and his Stagirite
confidant.

But Ptolemy, now intimate with the king, is entrusted
with an important command. He could not fail to observe,
once the expedition was under way, that his chief had included books from the royal library in the campaign baggage,
and scholars, historians, geographers, physicians, etc., in
the train of his army. Why? Alexander had not only brought
the Iliad (which had always claimed his reverent attention),
but, generally speaking, books and scholars were mobilized
as political and administrative instruments of his Hellenizing
policy. He may actually have spoken to Ptolemy of his Pan-
hellenistic dreams--of a Hellenism henceforth destined to extend the Greek oikoumene, to force the Persians back a re-
spectable distance from Macedonia and Greece, to seize the
Mediterranean coast with a view toward subduing the Near and
Middle East, and, finally, to insure the Greek spiritual unity
of all the conquered peoples, but having due regard for their
ethnic institutions and their religious and administrative traditions.

The Macedonian pantheon would include the local gods;
he would substitute, but without oppression and violence, the
Greek language for the universal Semitic idiom of the Orient;
he would also seek the support of priestly, intellectual, and
economically influential classes, for he wanted to appear,
not in the role of conqueror, but as a liberator who would
deliver the people from Persian bondage. His staff of scholars had been provided to assist the various satraps who
would be allowed to retain their administrative positions. It
was to be an administration that took account of the individual
characteristics of each region. The book, too, was to become an instrument of government.

All of Alexander's energies, in short, were poured into the creation of a rational administrative policy for an ever-
growing empire. After the final push to the borders of the
Indus every center of importance was to experience his new
style of government, a style which favorably distinguished it-

self from the ancient despotism of the Babylonian, Hittite,
Assyrian, and Persian rules.

It is reasonable to assume that throughout the campaign Alexander discussed important matters of military
strategy with his general staff and immediate collaborators.
Is it rash, then, to further suppose that such discussions included his political designs for organizing this vast empire
following the cessation of hostilities? It was only after his
death that the notion of plural independent states under Macedonian rule arose in the minds of the Diadochi--a notion,
incidentally, that became the principal cause of their domestic wars. Alexander's political ideas had crystallized under
the daily pressure of events and experience. Among them
we perceive one of profound significance for librarianship:
the idea of a universal syncretism, a Hellenism taking root
everywhere without uprooting the autochthons and their cultures. There is abundant evidence to show that governing
a mosaic of different peoples is always a doubtful enterprise
in which mere armed force rarely succeeds, since a policy
which commands prestige can only develop in a climate of
peace. It is probably for this reason that Alexander's benev-
olent rule over a network of quasi-independencies was projected as the most suitable instrument for the attainment of
his aims.

Alexander and most of his commanders were intellectuals, and some had even become authors in their spare
time. They witnessed for the first time the usefulness of
scholarship in the execution of their policies and the discharge of their military duties. On the whole, their expedition was one of the most daring in all recorded history.
During those incessant marches and countermarches along
the Mediterranean coast and throughout the vast reaches of
the Asian inland they encountered many cities with highly
educated populations. Everywhere, it seemed, they met
graphomania: in the palace, the temple, the administration,
in commerce and in farming; the whole world seemed able
to read and write, and literacy was well-nigh universally esteemed. The Semites, perhaps, were not so morbidly smitten
with the methods of statistics as the Egyptians, but Alexander
and his scholarly entourage could see for themselves that
virtually every public body maintained archives and collected
books.

The originators of this craze for the written word
have, alas, disappeared from view. The libraries of Hattusa

and Nineveh remain the most noteworthy collections surviving
from the imposing mountain of ancient documents victimized
by the military predecessors of the Persian satraps. The
Persians themselves, on the other hand, did not scruple to
press the written word into the service of their policy and
the governance of their occupied territories. The Babylonians, Hittites and Assyrians, moreover, had transmitted their
modus vivendi to the entire oriental world, including every
important center whither the accident of arms or alliances
had led the Macedonians. It thus happened that Alexander
and his generals encountered everywhere among the upper
classes a veneration of writing and the book, which seemingly appeared as the natural manifestation of the political, religious, intellectual and economic life of a society destined to
become part of Alexander's empire. His amiable relations
with the conquered cities provided sufficient testimony of
their esteem for the book, a fact the Greek world seems not
to have appreciated fully until then.

This exaltation of the written word would have im-
pressed the Macedonians in still another way as regards the
form and material of the oriental book, for they were accustomed to the papyrus rolls of Greece and the Mediterranean. Our present-day libraries of printed books are awe-
some enough to those who view them for the first time. But
let us imagine, for example, a university library that preserved a million volumes in the form of rolls by providing
an immense number of alveoli specially constructed for that
purpose. Our first exposure to such a library would be a
wondrous and baffling experience to say the least. Let us
further suppose that the same library had been designed to
house the small but bulky clay tablets of the ancient Orient.
Our ordinary volumes in octavo would occupy several papyrus
rolls and many of these small tablets. It is not difficult,
then, to imagine the vividity of the foreign impression left
by a library composed of yellow and reddish lumps inscribed
with writing, together with everything necessary for their
order arrangements and material preservation.

This, then, is precisely the kind of lasting impression
an oriental library would make upon its Macedonian spectators.
These "charnel houses" of colored clay would have been imposing, especially in their massiveness; indeed, the impression of mass must have become familiar to them. They
probably learned, too, that Assurbanipal had actually essayed
to gather the whole of oriental literature into his library,
and may have sensed their own documental inferiority in rela-

tion to these "barbarians"--their subjects of tomorrow.

It may be conjectured that among those who had opportunity to learn de visu et auditu about the oriental world
of books was Ptolemy, habitual guest and future historian of
Alexander.   Family loyalties, military talents, diplomatic
finesse, political sagacity, a flair for cultural and literary
pursuits--all these qualities combined to make him the confidant of the conqueror.   The Asian campaign offered Ptolemy
everything he needed for the Alexandrian adventure when,
after the death of his chief, Egypt fell to him.   In view of
these circumstances the Greek thesis seems utterly inadequate, for Ptolemy was much better acquainted with library
matters than were Aristotle and the Greeks.

A second weakness of the Greek thesis consists in
overestimating the influence of Greek libraries generally, and
that of Aristotle in particular.   The Greeks of the Hellenic
period did not have large libraries.   There were libraries
under the tyrants, to be sure, although this is disputed--
without convincing evidence--by classical philologists.   From
the time of the Sophists small quasi-scholastic libraries are
known in the gymnasia and ephebea.   There were also private
libraries of various philosophers and writers, and a library
was incorporated into the temple at Delphi. [5]   It is clear,
however, that the Greek was neither bibliomaniac nor bibli-
ophile; his was not a scribal culture.

The only truly compact and well organized library of
importance seems to be that of Aristotle in the Lyceum.
We do not know the exact extent of its holdings, but no historian has gone beyond an estimate of a thousand rolls, and
most of them have been content to guess at 700 or so.   The
collection was undoubtedly universal in character, since it
included all of the known intellectual disciplines.   It is important to realize that, while the intention was not lacking,
it remained only an intention.   The reality of Aristotle's library was disappointing and would have seemed ridiculous
when compared with the libraries of the Orient.   Ptolemy had
seen both and, unlike Athenians such as Demetrius, could
view the small collections of the Greeks and Aristotle in true
perspective.   Moreover, he must have told Demetrius of end-
less corridors where, as far as the eye could see, there
were tablets arranged in piles, baskets strewn up and down
the halls, and rectangular chambers stuffed with tablets written in enigmatic cuneiform.   The idea of a massive library
containing hundreds of thousands of rolls could not have aris-

en from Demetrius' contemplation of the modest library of
Aristotle.   The grandeur and magnificence later associated
with the Alexandrian library retained an oriental flavor of
which Ptolemy, enlightened by the Orient itself, could speak
with authority.

A third failing of the Greek thesis lies in its inability
to grasp the true meaning of the Alexandrian Museum.   Its
deference to humanistic presuppositions makes it stress the
intellectual factors of this institution and ignore other important factors.   Political considerations are often excluded, for
example, when the library activities of Ptolemy and the other
Diadochi are treated separately.   These activities, as a matter of fact, are always parts of a larger political structure
even though they seldom get top billing among the affairs of
state.   A new regime, especially when it cannot count on
spontaneous adhesion for its constitutional character, usually
tends to win the allegiance of its subjects by impressing them
with the magic of its policy.   Demetrius surely understood
this, for he had personally employed similar methods during
his ten-year reign at Athens.

The Macedonians, generally speaking, began building
new cities everywhere in the East, cities modelled on the
styles of Alexander's successors.   One could count these
magnificient new cities by the dozens.   The Greek tyrants,
let it be said with due regard for classical philology, were
somewhat restricted in their operations and were therefore
content to alter the appearance of their capitols by means of
new and sumptuous constructions, to introduce national and
popular festivities, and to provide for literary courts, the
predecessors of our academies.   If one traces the cultural
ancestors of Ptolemy as founder of the Mouseion, he is inevitably led to Peisistratos or Polycrates rather than to Aristotle.

It must be noted also that this prestigious element of
culture is but one of the factors to be accounted for.   It is
one of many that derives its inspiration directly from the
policy of Alexander, for he attached great political importance
to it.   He planned, before his death, to make his way to the
Occident, and, at the same time, organized the famous mari-
time expedition of Nearchos with a view toward finding a
route to India from Egypt.   If these plans had materialized,
Alexandria would have become the new center of his vast
world empire.   Ptolemy had no such plans in mind, but he
clearly understood that Egypt was that part of the empire

where Alexander intended to establish his political residence
and possibly his capitol.

We are also wrong in a different way, I fear, when
we separate the Mouseion from the library.   The intellectual
movement created by Ptolemy in Egypt is not an isolated
event, nor is it his only accomplishment.   Alexander's military chieftains were all intellectuals, Seleukos no less than
Ptolemy, and each one of them promoted the growth of Greek
literary culture.   They all appreciated the importance of the
book, not only as a means of public and private enlightenment,
but also as an instrument of governmental policy.   All of
them, too, had gone to school with Alexander, and Ptolemy
had even served a "probation" as librarian.   Most of the
Diadochi and Epigoni associated with scholars and men of letters and followed one or another of the Greek schools; they
were not all Peripatetics by any means.   Pella, for example,
identified with the Stoics whose origin and inspiration are
distinctively Semitic.   Pergamus, too, behaves in distinct and
eclectic ways.

It appears, then, that the intellectual policies of these
founders and promoters of Hellenism responded to common
needs and derived from a common source.   This is confirmed
by the perfect identity of the instruments they devised.   The
Diadochi gathered about them erudite scholars entrusted with
the redaction of standard texts of Homer and the poets, as
well as with the exposition and cultivation of the most varied
specialized sciences among which grammar always occupied
an honored place.   The status of philosophy, on the other
hand, was seemingly very low--a circumstance, incidentally,
which tends to belie the assumption that these men were bent
on perpetuating the institutions of Aristotle.   It is difficult
to resist the inference that the Aristotelian concept of the
Mouseion is the result of Athenian propaganda and not at all
the work of the Diadochi.

Another mistake in the Greek thesis may be seen, I
think, in the questionable interpretation of the Mouseion as a
scholastic institution.   Milkau and Parsons both regarded it
as a kind of university, similar to and derived from the
Aristotelian Lyceum.   This interpretation, however, raises
an important question: Was the Mouseion really given to the
transmission of science and letters, or did it focus on scientific research?   The evidence so far seems to suggest the
latter, for nowhere in any of the surviving sources is it described as an instructional institution: all of the documents

make us think, not of schools of higher learning, but of academies where, thanks to the munificence of the state, established scholars can pursue their studies free from worries
about their livelihood. The scholars admittedly introduced
certain innovations into their research, but there is nothing
to suggest that the Mouseion functioned as an organized school
or university committed by its founders to a formal program
of instruction. Criticism and research predominate throughout, but there is no educational traditio.

The impact of the Mouseion upon Hellenistic culture,
moreover, is not due to the teaching of its scholars, but to
their vigorous research. It organized conferences and public
recitations, but it is nowhere evident that it made possible a
cooperative relationship between teacher and students. One
must stretch the facts, I think, in order to see the macro-
cosm of a peripatos or a lyceum in the Mouseion. It resembles rather a kind of learned academy whose internal organization reminds us more of the activities of Peisistratos than
of Aristotle. 6

During the seventh to third centuries B. C. there was
throughout the entire ancient world a general tendency to set
down in writing the religious and historical traditions then
accumulating in great numbers. It was Peisistratos who, in
the seventh century, gathered around his throne a company
of literati appointed precisely for that purpose. In the Levant,
Ezra began constituting the Jewish biblical canon, a work that
was not completed until the second century. Essentially the
same thing happened at the court of Assurbanipal. Greek
civilization, of course, underwent profound transformations
in the centuries after Peisistratos. The Sophists invaded
Greece, for example, introducing an impressionable enlightenment which left its mark in all those provinces of thought
against which the Academy of Plato (this time a real school)
and its Socratic myth revolted. I am not arguing here for a
direct connection between the work of the Mouseion and the
literary labors of Peisistratos, but this should not prevent
us from acknowledging the fundamental identity of the concept
underlying both of these movements.

There are still other considerations that prevent us
from seeing the Mouseion as a purely Greek creation. Among
its many activities are those related to the incorporation of
the non-Greek literatures into the framework of its library.
This work was basically a matter of translating the literary
monuments of the Babylonians, the Phoenicians, the Egyptians,

and the Hebrews--in short, of the entire Orient. The question now arises: did translations of this kind exist before the
advent of the Mouseion, or were they undertaken in the wake
of its foundation? These translations cannot be adequately
explained by pointing to Rhodes' desire to become an important center in the ancient book trade. Nor was Attica responsible for them--Athens' contempt for the barbarian is too
well known to allow the imputation of these international cu-
riosities to the Acropolis; and Demetrius, certainly, could
not have succeeded by pouring his energies into channels
which threatened to divert the mighty headwaters of Aristotle
and Theophrastos. Oriental experience and Diadochian policy
are the only things that can explain the awakening of this new
cultural exoticism.

The Lyceum of Aristotle was universal in that it em-
braced all of the Greek sciences, but not in the new and
wider meaning of the term, for it did not include the sciences of all nations. Athens showed precious little respect
for the literary monuments of the barbarians, but these
achievements were prominent in the thinking of Alexander.
His military chiefs, too--all of them founders of dynasties,
bent on culture, and full of sympathy for the Orient--promoted
the intellectual advantages and political necessity of incorpo-
rating the alien literatures into this ongoing work of Hellenistic acculturation.

This much-praised Hellenization, unless we permit
ourselves to be deceived by appearances, consisted in making
the Greek language (but not the Greek spirit) universal. The
immediate effects of this policy, moreover, prove this point.
The Greek paid for promoting his language as a universal
idiom by becoming oriental in his thought. The Greeks in
general, and particularly the schools of Plato and Aristotle,
were quite unable to resist this powerful movement of
Überfremdung, and from then on Greek thought became more
and more Semitic. The idea of royal or state initiative in
matters of literature, the sciences, and libraries, while not
conforming to Greek models, answers very well to oriental
antecedents.

Greece, like England in this respect, had never regarded the state as the proper agent of culture and education,
and, by extension, of intellectual life and library policy.
This aversion, however, cannot be pressed too far, as the
polis did organize the palaestrae, ephebea, and gymnasia,
for instance, and we also meet occasional examples of librar-

ies that are more or less demotic in character.   In contrast
with the general Hellenic tradition, however, the Hellenistic
library institution is strictly the concern of the state, and not
that of the schoolmaster, for it has an ulterior political objective in addition to its cultural aims.

We see this very clearly in the creation of the Serapeion.   Ptolemy, following Alexander's lead, avoided appearing in the role of conqueror by posing as Pharaoh.   He then
exploited an old Pharaonic custom which allowed a new dynasty to promote its own tutelary divinity and elevated the
god Serapis to this dignity. [7]   The Serapeion, residence of
the new official cult, was a temple on the Egyptian and Oriental style.   It housed a large consortium of priests entrusted with the new cult and charged with organizing an educational traditio that would perpetuate the priestly caste.
This school provided both formal instruction and a library
whose book stock was selected in accordance with the aims
of the priests and financed by the good offices of the Mouseion.
The Serapeion was a state institution, and Demetrius, apparently, had very little to do with it.   Its involvements were
purely and simply political and included only Ptolemy and the
priestly class.

The foregoing discussion has shown, I think, that the
influence of continental Greece did not play a decisive role
in the libraries of Alexandria.   The Greek thesis suggests,
without expressly saying it, that Aristotle dominated Macedonian cultural policy with all his weight.   Personally, I do
not think that we should be taken in by such a suggestion.
There is no need, on the one hand, to exaggerate Macedonian
sympathy for Aristotle, or, on the other, to deny him any
influence whatsoever.   What is certain, though, particularly
in view of subsequent events, is that his star was in decline.
He, like Antipater, had dreaded Alexander's passion for the
Asian campaign; but his counsels went unheeded although,
seemingly, his relationship with Alexander remained intact.
That relationship had been strained, however, and it finally
snapped in 327 when Alexander executed Callisthenes, Aristotle's nephew, for his alleged involvement in the conspiracy
of the pages.

Tradition has it that Ptolemy, who knew all about the
swelling antipathy between Alexander and Aristotle, tried to
assuage the hostility of Athens and Macedon by inviting Theophrastos to direct the cultural policy of Alexandria.   But
was such an appeal ever actually made?   I rather doubt it

in view of Theophrastos' age, for he was over 80 at the time. A consultation with the venerated rector of the Lyceum would have been more likely, in my opinion, than a formal invitation to an old and aging man. This accords very well, moreover, with a proposition made to Demetrius, who was only barely acceptable to the Macedonians, and whose authority rested entirely on the presence of Cassander. His only strong point, other than his ten-year dictatorship of Athens, had been his aloofness from an Athenian plot to depose the next Macedonian ruler of the city.

One often hears another argument in favor of Aristotle, namely, that Neleus, supposed ill-fated successor of Theophrastos, sold his library containing the books of both Aristotle and Theophrastos to the Mouseion in execution of their testamentary dispositions. It must be said, first of all, that such a purchase is not necessarily a manifestation of sympathy, for it was a transaction of such importance that Ptolemy would have negotiated even with his worst enemy for it. Secondly, it should be remembered that Neleus acted in this instance on an impulse of spiteful anger against the Peripatos. And thirdly, if the sale actually did take place, it could only have occurred in 288-87 or thereabouts, toward the end of Soter's reign, for Philadelphos succeeded him in 283; all this would have transpired after the establishment of the library. There was, incidentally no apparent reason why the transaction could not have been deferred until after Neleus' departure for Skepsis, his birthplace in the Troad. And finally, the sale of this library is recorded in only one version of the sources. It is, perhaps, the most likely version, but, for what it is worth, the other one is completely silent on the subject of this transaction.

It is a very difficult thing, even long after the establishment of the Mouseion, to descry Aristotle's influence at work in Egypt. It strikes one as odd indeed, if he really was the prime mover in the intellectual life of Alexandria, that his philosophy was so poorly represented at the Mouseion, an institution, I must add, that later became the seat of a Platonism which gradually assimilated the distinctively oriental characteristics of its environment. The antagonism which developed between Neleus and Straton is revealing in this connection. Straton, the philosophical enemy of Neleus, had broken with the Peripatos and come to Egypt for the purpose of educating the children of King Philadelphos.

The fact that the King called upon him for this job is

not without significance. After the death of Theophrastos
there had been a lawsuit at Athens that threatened the very
existence of the Peripatos, a litigation revealing deep animos-
ities between Neleus and Straton, the chief representatives of
polarized opposite concepts regarding the proper business of
the Lyceum. Neleus, conscrvative to the core, wanted to
continue the Aristotelian line of teaching as advocated by his
famous predecessors, whereas Straton advocated the surrender
of its universal character in favor of a progressive scientific
specialization. Now it just so happens that the sum total of
the Mouseion's interests, the entire gamut of its activities
from first to last, was grounded on the bedrock principle of
scientific specialization; and it is precisely for this reason
that Aristotelian philosophy never felt at home in Alexandria.
One cannot bank too heavily, it seems to me, on Demetrius'
ability to make the Mouseion an institution for perpetuating
the spirit and work of Aristotle.

Whatever the combined strength of all these considerations, I have reserved till last the most decisive and telling
evidence against the Greek thesis. My case so far relies
more heavily on circumstantial evidence than on the scientific
examination of documents, and I must now turn to facts that
derive, not from ancient Greece, but from the oriental libraries themselves. I refer, of course, to the library methods
which are known to have been used at the Mouseion. We
see them in actual practice in the Orient and they conform
remarkably well to those employed at Alexandria. These
methods, as far as we know, are at least as old as the
Hittites; they are already operative at Hattusa, for instance,
and were later put to work in the Assyrian royal library of
Assurbanipal. It is asking too much, even if we strain our
credulity, to assume that they were thrice invented independently in unrelated circumstances; and, since the despoiling
of the Hittites by Assyrian expansionism is an historic fact,
we are justified in postulating the direct appropriation of
bibliothecal policy by a capitol on the rise from a capitol in
decline.

Hattusa and Nineveh, furthermore, since the latter
came to rule virtually the whole of Asia Minor, were in a
remarkable position for the creation and dissemination of
their library traditions. The later Persian occupation did
not effect substantial changes in these institutions, so that
the Macedonian armies, on inheriting the libraries of the
Orient, came into possession of procedures and policies unlike anything in their own metropolitan culture. When the

Greeks called on Ptolemy to preside over the Mouseion they could have had no inkling of such proceedings, but he, like the other Diadochi, had already been exposed to them. The massive oriental library and its methodoligical devices had been impressive, and the problems resolved by them were hardly less so. What, then, did he actually see and hear in the East?

He came to understand, first of all, that at least one oriental ruler, Assurbanipal, had inaugurated an Assyrian cultural policy that attempted to gather into the palace library all of the literature of Mesopotamia, a policy universal in both the content and the origin of the documents it sought to collect. The library was to include the literary, religious, historical, political, and scientific writings of the entire Orient, where, in the course of two millenia, the most diverse political and military dynasties had relentlessly succeeded one another. Ptolemy was later to incorporate this same twofold universality into his cultural policy. I should admit, I suppose, that this same universal dualism could also have been derived from Aristotle. There are, to be sure, certain difficulties associated with this admission, but it, too, as we shall see, can only strengthen my Ptolmaic thesis in the end.

Secondly, the attainment of this universality in the Orient was essentially a matter of the systematic purchasing and copying of documents on a large scale. Virtually all of the temples of Sumer, Babylonia, and Assyria, like their Egyptian counterparts, commanded an atelier of copyists who worked for the state; the 20 thousand tablets of Assurbanipal are a good example of their labors. In addition, copyists were often drafted on the spot to transcribe texts in remote corners of the empire, as it was not always possible to have this done at Nineveh. Ptolemy follows these same procedures, but with this difference: Assurbanipal, apparently, did not resort to violence in the acquisition of documents, whereas the Diadochi do not shrink from the use of force in order to achieve their ends. We must note here, of course, that the Greeks also purchased and copied documents in order to build their book collections, but on a much smaller scale than in the East. The grand scale on which oriental libraries operated was only possible because they were always regarded as an official concern of the state, while Greek libraries were a private matter without sufficient support for indulging in far-reaching operations.

These oriental copyists, thirdly, were supported by groups of experts and even by erudite scholars on occasion. Their task was neither personal research nor the exegetical study and interpretation of documents, but the accurate establishment of the texts themselves. This presupposed a certain aptitude on their part for textual criticism, and included the collation, emendation, and restoration of corrupt and defective texts and the translation of foreign originals. All this was likewise the normal business of the Mouseion, whose work, however, was also expanded to subsume exegesis and all kinds of research including grammatical, scientific, and historical studies. The oriental libraries had been mere libraries, whereas the Mouseion was primarily a research institution that valued and utilized its library in the pursuit of its objectives. There was nothing like this in ancient Greece, where the libraries were too tiny and insignificant to justify the wholesale copying of manuscripts. The Greeks never aimed at the procuration of massive collections, and transcription was usually accomplished by the library itself or by the private industry of individual copyists. It also seems that textual criticism was never a strong point with the Greeks, [8] as may be seen, for example, in the Athenian attempt to preserve under lock and key the Urtexte of its national tragedies.

One of the principal activities of any organized library is the incorporation of bibliographical units into its general stock and the designation of catalog entries for their description and location. Such entries are actually found in the Orient and at the Mouseion, but there is not the slightest indication of their presence in Greece. At Hattusa and Nineveh, for example, these catalogica indicate the author, title, and provenance of autographs and copies, and, for the latter, add the name and residence of the original's owner. The origins of documents seem to have been especially important, and, whenever a manuscript was corrected or reconstituted, the names of its redactor and/or copyist were carefully supplied. Identical procedures are found at Alexandria, but the modest libraries of Greece required nothing as meticulous as this. The large library, however, in order to adequately support scientific research, must pay attention to details of this kind. In view of the large scale bibliographic needs of Alexandria, even Milkau must point to the Orient for precedents. [9]

Oriental bibliography always pursued a double goal: first of all, to provide a basis for locating and procuring texts, and secondly, to insure the rational classification of

those texts in the library.   This means, then, that for a library of universal character there must be an accurate bibliographical account of the literature actually existing in its
collection.   This bibliographic account did in fact comprise
an author and title catalog and was the basis for designing
the library with a view toward the rational arrangement of
its book stock on the tables along the walls.   We know that
the pinakes of Callimachus, if we may trust tradition, were
drawn up in the reign of Philadelphos when the library contained at least 200, 000 volumes.   These pinakes were probably duplicates of the Mouseion's catalog; they cannot, at any
rate, be regarded as the original catalogic bibliographies
drawn up in the time of Demetrius.   Lists of available documents must also have been prepared locally and sent to Alexandria for use by the travelling emissaries who went to Athens, Rhodes, and dozens of other places in search of manuscripts.   These various lists constituted the catalogs of the
library and facilitated the scholarly consideration of documents not yet owned by the Mouseion.

One looks in vain for this kind of bibliographical activity in Greece and discovers, for example, why Aristotle
had such difficulty in locating the politeias of 150 city-states
as the documental basis of an ideal polis-constitution.   This
feat, incidentally, has been lauded to the skies, but it is
completely overshadowed by the extensive bibliographical activities that went on as a matter of course in the Mouseion.

It remains for me, finally, to show the parallels between Alexandria and the Orient in this matter of creating
and maintaining the order relations of huge libraries.   They
answer to one another amazingly well, and, surprisingly
enough, for almost identical reasons.   The form and material of ancient books underlie the difficulties besetting the use
of such enormous collections.   The oriental book is made up
of small clay tablets which, at least after Mycenaean times,
are seldom if ever found in the West.   Now clay tablets are
considerably bulkier and less readily conjoined than papyrus
leaves or sheets of paper, and these facts give rise to twin
ordinal difficulties in their use: how to create and maintain
order (a) in a series of tablets that together constitute one
work; and (b) among the various works housed in the library.
How, then, did oriental librarianship attempt to insure these
two kinds of order?

In pursuance of the first aim the Orient invented a
series of procedures some of which remain in use even today.

Before reviewing those procedures, however, let us observe
that, generally speaking, the preservation of the tablets in
their proper inter-relating order demanded a rigorous standardization in their forms and sizes, coupled with some sort
of insurance against the constant threat of disorder due to
spillage, etc. Now as to the procedures themselves. The
book, first of all, was identified by its author, title, and
subject, and described both at the beginning of the book and
in a final colophon which added complete information about
copies and copyists. As further devices of identification the
following may be added: (1) the numbering of tablets (corresponding to our foliation, pagination, etc.); (2) the repetition of a tablet's last line atop the following tablet (like the
reclamantes, or catch-words, of medieval manuscripts); (3)
the isolation of piles of tablets constituting single works, or,
wherever that was impossible (for economic and other reasons), the insertion of indicator tablets separating individual
works;[10] and (4) the housing of longer works (requiring a lot
of tablets) in specially reserved jars provided with their own
indicator tablets.

Once again, we do not hear of these procedures in
Greece where the smaller collections required no such measures. They are found mutatis mutandis, however, in the library institutions of Alexandria. The papyrus book starts
with a leaf marking the title and providing the same bibliographical information as in the Orient, and often ends with
an identical colophon. Since the Alexandrian "book" was
rolled up in such a way that the title ended up inside--a pre-
caution, incidentally, against losing this essential informa-
tion--the Mouseion avoided needless unrollings and rerollings
by inventing the titulus, a papyrus wrapper containing the
bibliographical information required for identification. Pagination and the reclamantes were not employed, however, because the sequence of columns in a roll was fixed. Let us
note, though, that the Mouseion did impose standardized formats on its copyists in order to facilitate the storage of rolls
in the alveoli of armaria. It was probably not Demetrius
who thought up all of these devices, for the Greeks had never faced the necessity of arranging their small papyrus collections in this manner.

The second kind of order pertains to the over-all bibliographical organization of titles throughout the book collection itself and in the corresponding catalog of entries. It
presupposes the existence of workable filing arrangements
and classification devices constructed with a view to daily

use. We know that the library of the Hittites had an author
catalog, for example, and that a shelf list was employed at
Nineveh showing a perfect correspondence between enumerated
series and locations in the collection. The Mouseion arranged
its thousands of rolls in precisely this same manner, and the
pinakes of Callimachus reproduced the order of the general
catalog. We have, unfortunately no exact information regarding the details of actual book stock arrangement in the Mouseion, but it seems likely that oriental patterns were followed by Ptolemy here, for without reliable correspondence
between catalog entries and the locations of books in the collection the library could not have fulfilled its purposes.

What actually distinguishes the total activity of the
Mouseion from the oriental library is its double function, for
in addition to gathering and preserving books and preparing
them for use, it had to support the rigorous special inquiries
of scientific research. This scientific function was lacking
in the oriental library. It was strictly and solely a library,
and its order requirements, therefore, were not as stringent
as those required by the Mouseion. The former is a purely
conventional, the latter a highly specialized, type of library.

The twofold nature of the Mouseion permits us, finally,
to assign equally to Greece and the Orient the double genesis
of this superb and unique Macedonian achievement. Its scientific policy and activity are traceable to Greek sources and
initiatives, for Peisistratos and Aristotle, each in his own
way, made contributions to it. Its library policies and activities, however, are borrowed directly from the Orient.
The idea of an academy in Egypt was Aristotle's spiritual
grandchild, but the notion of a splendid library on a grand
scale was born of Ptolemy's experiences in the Near and Middle East. It was this happy conjunction of influences which
produced the Zweistrombegriff that became the Mouseion.
This, indeed, is the Ptolemaic thesis which I propose as an
alternative to the too-strictly-Greek thesis of Milkau and
Parsons.

I find it impossible to believe that Ptolemy merely
placed unlimited financial resources at the disposal of Demetrius, who revived in Alexandria a kind of peripatos on the
grand style. No, the Mouseion was, above all else, a political work long since brought to maturity, a work of peace
and stability, symbol of Macedonian progress. Ptolemy,
thanks to his association with Alexander, believed himself
called upon by fate to perpetuate and immortalize the cult of

the soma, a cult he had brought from Syria to Egypt in the
most extraordinary funeral procession of all history. It was
for the sake of this cult that he had erected the mausoleum
within the Mouseion, constituting at once an homage and a
lasting memorial to the spirit of his unforgettable chief. He
found himself fulfilling the political designs of Alexander that
presupposed a policy appealing to culture rather than to arms.
The Mouseion thus became a work of realistic piety dedicated
to the immortal "Son of Zeus" in whose shadows Ptolemy and
his peers had lived through a glorious epoch. A quarter
century of trivial quarrels had indeed cast a blight on the
glory and somewhat diminished the grandeur of this era, but
it had not succeeded in obliterating from memory the experience of an extraordinary adventure which had given sense
and meaning to the lives of the Diadochi.

Bibliographical Note [H. C. W.]

    De Vleeschauwer's attempt to derive the libraries of
Alexandria from oriental antecendents is enlightening in many
ways. Interpretations of this sort are not entirely new, but
have often been avoided because their evidential structures,
as De Vleeschauwer recognizes, are characterized by indirec-
tion. The whole problem is discussed by Hessel,[11] for example, and his reluctance to speculate in the absence of solid
evidence has been shared by many.

> There were undeniably remarkable resemblances bet-
> ween the libraries of Nineveh and Alexandria. Both
> were institutions of a universal character brought into
> being by reigning princes. It is also proper to
> point out that in more than one respect the inner
> organization of the Hellenistic library calls to mind
> the Assyrian library, and that there are even many
> similarities in the treatment of the individual liter-
> ary work in both places despite the difference in
> writing material .... Nevertheless it seems to me
> at present still too risky to insist upon establishing
> a direct connection of Alexandria with Nineveh.
> Between them lie four centuries; between them lies
> the reign of the Medo-Persian kings, who, so far
> as in known, paid no attention to library matters.
> It must be left to the future to disclose lines of
> connection which at present are obscure.[12]

The bibliographical sources for a critical study of the

governmental and cultural policies of the Diadochi are numerous, and, furthermore, must be evaluated against the larger
context of the ancient Orient.   For those interested in approaching the Alexandrian libraries by this method the civilizations of the Sumerians, Babylonians, Hittites, Assyrians,
Hebrews, Medes, Persians, Arabs, etc., may be studied by
the systematic evaluation of materials listed in such sophisticated instruments as the "Keilschriftbibliographie"[13] and
Elenchus Bibliographicus Biblicus.[14]   The scholarly literature
on the on the Diadochi and Ptolemaic Egypt is presented in
the appropriate subsections of A and C under "Histoire" in
S. Lambrino, Bibliographie de l'Antiquité Classique 1896-
1914;[15] J. Marouzeau, Dix Années de Bibliographie Classique
... pour la Period 1914-1924;[16] and L'anée Philologique,
1924 to the present.[17]   The Journal of Egyptian Archaeology
provides extensive bibliographical coverage of Graeco-Roman
Egypt, especially for the pre-World War II era.[18]   The
Archäologische Bibliographie, supplement to the Jahrbuch des
Deutschen Archäeologischen Instituts, also lists a wide variety
of archaeological publications.

        The lemmata and observations of scholiasts, especially
on such authors as Homer and Aristophanes, deserve careful
study, as they often throw much light on Ptolemaic institutions.   There are some useful items in the rambling bibliography of Parsons.[19]

        The following list, in addition to the sources men-
tioned in this note and cited by de Vleeschauwer, should constitute a convenient starting point in the study of Alexandria's
ancient library institutions.

Awad, Mohamed. "A note on the Alleged Destruction of the
        Alexandria Library by the Arabs," Journal of World
        History, 8 (1964), 213-14.
Bell, Harold Idris. Egypt from Alexander the Great to the
        Arab Conquest: A Study in the Diffusion and Decay of
        Hellenism.   ("Gregynog Lectures for 1946.")   Oxford:
        Clarendon Press, 1948.   Has a valuable bibliography,
        pp. 151-62.
_____. "Alexandria," Journal of Egyptian Archaeology,
        13 (1927), 171-84.
_____. Cults and Creeds in Graeco-Roman Egypt.
        ("Forwood Lectures," 1952.) Liverpool, Eng.: Uni-
        versity Press, 1957.
_____. "The Custody of Records in Roman Egypt," Indian

Archives, 4 (1950), 116-25.

___. "Hellenic Culture in Egypt," Journal of Egyptian Archaeology, 8 (1922), 139-55.

Bernand, André. Alexandrie le Grande. "Collection Signes des Temps," 19. Paris: Arthaud, 1966.

Bevan, Edwyn. The House of Ptolemy: A History of Egypt under the Ptolemaic Dynasty. Chicago: Argonaut, 1968. This first American edition is a revised reissue of the 1927 edition.

Binns, N. E. An Introduction to Historical Bibliography. 2d ed. rev. and enl. London: Association of Assistant librarians, 1962.

Bouché-Leclercq, Auguste. Histoire des Lagides. Bruxelles: Culture et Civilization, 1963. A reprint of the original Paris edition of 1903-1907.

Breccia, Evaristo. Alexandrea ad Aegyptum: A Guide to the Ancient and Modern Town, and to its Graeco-Roman Museum. Bergamo: Instituto Italiano d'Arti Grafichi, 1922.

Bushnell, George H. "The Alexandrian Library," Antiquity, 2 (1928), 196-204.

Callmer, C. "Antike Bibliotheken," Opuscula Archaeologica, 3 (1944), 145-93.

Cary, Max. A History of the Greek World from 323 to 146 B.C. (New York: Barnes and Noble, 1963), 321-22, and notes 1-4, p. 322.

Cerny, J. Paper and Books in Ancient Egypt. London: Lewis, 1952.

Davis, Harold T. Alexandria, the Golden City. Evanston, Ill.: Principia Press, 1957. 2 vols.

Dunlap, Leslie Whitaker. Alexandria, the Capital of Memory: A Lecture. Emporia: Kansas State Teachers College, 1963. This lecture is vol. 43, no. 3 of the Bulletin of Information of the Kansas State Teachers College at Emporia.

Forster, Edward Morgan. Alexandria: A History and a Guide. Gloucester, Mass.: P. Smith, 1968.

Fraser, Peter Marshall. "Some Alexandrian Forgeries," Proceedings of the British Academy, 47 (1962), 243-50.

Gardthausen, Viktor Emil. Die Alexandrinische Bibliothek, ihr Vorbild, Katalog und Betrieb. Leipzig: Deutsches Museum für Buch and Schrift, 1922.

Holmes, T. Rice. The Roman Republic and the Founder of the Empire (3 vols.; Oxford: Clarendon Press, 1923), III, 487-89. This brief appendix presents most of the evidence pertaining to the alleged destruction of the Alexandrian library by Caesar.

Jondet, Gaston. Atlas Historique de la Ville et des Ports
d'Alexandrie. Le Caire: Impr. de l'Institut Français
d'Archéologie Orientale, 1921.

Leyh, G. "Vorbemerkugen zu einer Geschichte der Bibliotheken," Forschungen und Fortschritte, 1940, 232-34.

Peremans, W. "Bibliotheek en Bibliothecarissen te Alex-
andrië," in Étienne van Cauwenbergh, Scrinium Lovaniense;
Historische Opstellen ("Université de Louvain. Recueil
de Travaux d'histoire et de la philologie," sér. 4, fasc.
24; Louvain: 1961), 79-88.

Pfeiffer, Rudolf, ed. Callimachus. Oxford: The Clarendon
Press, 1949-1953. 2 vols.

Roemer, A. Die Homerexegese Aristarchs in ihren Grundzü-
gen dargestellt. Bear. u. hrsg. v. E. Bilzner.
"Studien für Geschichte und Kultur des Altertums,"
XIII, 2-3. Paderborn: Schöningh, 1924. See also his
Studien zu Aristophanes. 1902.

Savile, Leopold Halliday. "Ancient Harbours," Antiquity,
15 (1941), 209-232. The first portion of this article
treats the Great Harbour at Alexandria.

Schubart, W. Die Griechen in Aegypten. Leipzig: Hinrichs,
1927.

Skeat, Theodore Cressy. The Reigns of the Ptolemies.
"Münchener Beiträge zur Papyrusforschung und antiken
Rechtsgeschichte," Heft 39; München: Beck, 1954.

Staquet, J. "César à Alexandrie. L'incendie de la Bibliothèque," Nova et Vetera, 12 (1928), 157-77.

Turner, E.G. "L'érudition alexandrine et les papyrus,"
Chronique d'Egypte, 37 (1962), 135-152.

Wendel, C. "Die bauliche Entwicklung der antiken Bibliothek,"
Zentralblatt für Bibliothekswesen, 63 (1949), 407-428.

Westermann, William Linn. "The Library of Ancient Alexandria"; lecture delivered at the University Reception
Hall, December 21, 1953. Alexandria, Egypt: University of Alexandria Press, 1954.

Wyss, Wilhelm von. Die Bibliotheken des Altertums und
ihre Aufgabe. Zürich: Beer, 1923.

Notes

1. H.C. Wright's translation of Strabo, Geographica XVII.1.
8: τῶν δὲ βασιλείων μέρος ἐστὶ καὶ τὸ Μουσεῖον, ἔχον περίπατον καὶ
ἐξέδραν καὶ οἶκον μέγαν, ἐν ᾧ τὸ συσσίτιον τῶν μετεχόντων τοῦ Μουσείου
φιλολόγων ἀνδρῶν. ἔστι δὲ τῇ συνόδῳ ταύτῃ καὶ χρήματα κοινὰ καὶ ἱερεὺς
ὁ ἐπὶ τῷ Μουσείῳ, τεταγμένος τότε μὲν ὑπὸ τῶν βασιλέων, νῦν δ' ὑπὸ
Καίσαρος.

2. Herman Jean de Vleeschauwer, Les bibliothèques pto-
leméenes d'Alexandrie ("Mousaion," no. 1; Pretoria,
S. Africa: H.J. de Vleeschauwer, 1955).
3. Fritz Milkau, ed., Handbuch der Bibliothekswissenschaft
(2. verm. und verb. Aufl., hrsg. von Georg Leyh;
Wiesbaden: O. Harrassowitz, 1952), v.3, pt.1, 17.
4. Edward Alexander Parsons, The Alexandrian Library,
Glory of the Hellenic World: Its Rise, Antiquities,
and Destructions (New York: Elsevier Press, 1952).
5. For these and other Greek libraries see Jenö Platthy,
Sources on the Earliest Greek Libraries, with the
Testimonia (Amsterdam: Adolf M. Hakkert, 1968),
passim.
6. The Serapeion, on the other hand, resembled an educational institution in many ways, for the temple of
Serapis included both a school and a theological training center in order to perpetuate the official cult of
its god and coordinate the Greek and Egyptian elements of the population.
7. Milkau, op. cit., v.3, pt.1, 65. See also note 6 above.
8. The so-called Peistratean recension of Homer may be
an exception here, however.
9. Milkau, op. cit., v.3, pt.1, 73.
10. The ancients did not attach much importance to these
indicator tablets, although they often repeated bibliographical information for the works they separated and
frequently identified their libraries. They were called
girganacki in Assyrian, and the librarian was Rab
girganacki, "master of the tablets." This suggests,
incidentally, that the librarian may also have been
identified by his code tablets. These tablets served
precisely the same function as the tituli in collections
of papyrus rolls.
11. Alfred Hessel, A History of Libraries, trans. Reuben
Peiss (New Brunswick, N.J.: Scarecrow Press, 1955),
chapters 1-5, and notes 1-5, 129.
12. Ibid., 2.
13. Issued since 1940 as a bibliographical section of Orien-
talia, it provides extremely broad coverage of many
ancient civilizations.
14. Volumes 1-48 (1920-1967) were issued as a bibliographical supplement to Biblica, but beginning with vol. 49
(1968) it has become a journal in its own right. It
rarely misses anything of importance to biblical
studies. Other important bibliographical controls for
Near Eastern studies may be found in the American
Historical Association's latest Guide to Historical Lit-

erature, section F.
15.   Paris, Sociéte d'Edition "Les Belles Lettres," 1951- .
      Two volumes were projected, but vol. 1 carried this
      note: "La seconde partie: Matières et Disciplines,
      sera publiée dès que le permettront les ressources de
      la Société de bibliographie classique." It is apparent-
      ly not yet published.
16.   Paris, Société d'Edition "Les Belles Lettres," 1957.
      2 volumes.
17.   The latest volume of APh, alas, is two or three years
      old, and may be brought to within one or two months
      of the present by searching the appropriate sections
      of the bibliographical "Beilagen" of Gnomon.
18.   See the individual indexes of the JEA under "Bibliog-
      raphy: Graeco-Roman Egypt" for volumes 1-3, 6-27,
      31, 34, 36, 40-48. These bibliographies cover 1914-
      1962 so far, and where individual volumes are not in-
      dexed their respective tables of contents must be con-
      sulted. Papyrological coverage, unfortunately, was
      interrupted by World War II and not resumed after
      vol. 26 (1940), but the epigraphical coverage continues
      until 1962. It will be unfortunate if the JEA discon-
      tinues these bibliographies altogether.
19.   Parsons, op. cit., 433-61. Parsons' treatment of the
      Alexandrian library is ganz unwissenschaftlich, how-
      ever, and must be used with caution.

II. BASIC ISSUES

"If librarianship is to be concerned--as it must be--
with the epistemological problem in society, it must
also be interdisciplinary. It must bring to its practitioners the methods of any number of sciences. The
term "library science" is, then, not a verbal obfusca-
tion invented to conceal the flimsy foundations of the
scholarship of the field. The real question that librarians must ask themselves is not "Is librarianship a
science?" but rather "What kind of science does librarianship represent?" Few will deny, we believe, that
the human use of the graphic records of society (the
"social transcript," to borrow Kenneth Boulding's term)
is a scientifically based study to which all branches of
human knowledge can contribute. Because librarianship
is primarily concerned with the utilization of the social
transcript by human beings both individually and collectively, it is fundamentally a behavioristic science, but
because the methods and findings of the physical and
biological sciences are being increasingly applied to the
study of human behavior, librarianship must be "scientific" even in the classical use of the term. A librarian, therefore, must be a scientist, not because he
may be doling out scientific literature to scientists and
will perforce need to communicate intelligibly with his
patrons, but because science, in its broadest sense, is
the foundation of the librarian's scholarship."

J. H. Shera, The Foundations of Access..., 24.

"Information science, then, is not antithetical to librarianship; on the contrary, the two are natural allies, and
librarians should not reject this new intellectual relative,
nor should the information scientist discredit the librarian. Both have made and will continue to make mistakes, and if the librarian is the more guilty it is only
because he has had more time in which to err. The
laws of chance prohibit innovation without error. For
the moment at least the librarian and the information

scientist may speak with different tongues--new concepts require a new terminology--but eventually a consensus and a common understanding will be achieved."

J. H. Shera, UNESCO Bulletin for Libraries,
22 (1968), 65.

THE INTERDISCIPLINARITY OF LIBRARIANSHIP

Conrad H. Rawski

1.   Interdisciplinarity

1.1.   The Inward Structure.[1]

"And out of the ground the Lord God formed every beast of the field, and every fowl of the air ... and whatsoever Adam called every living creature that was the name thereof." (Genesis ii, 19.) Man has been naming, identifying, ordering, and categorizing ever since.[2]

In order to know we structure. There is no conscious beginning or end to this process, which, Shera reminds us, plays a crucial part in the origin and the development of the sciences and the arts.[3] The notion of the realm of knowledge as a set of subjects, areas, fields, disciplines, and, if you will, attendant axiomatic systems, which exhibit some kind of order, is age-old. Cicero spoke of this order:

> Almost all things now included in the arts were once dispersed and disordered. So in music, ... in geometry, ... in astronomy, ... in grammar, ... all these things seemed fragmentary and without coherence. A certain art, of a different sort and claimed in its entirety by the philosophers, was therefore imposed on them from without to tie together the disconnected and scattered material and delimit it in some kind of rational order.[4]

For the medieval scholar the logical order "imposed from without" had become the property of the system:

> It is in the seven liberal arts, however, that the foundation of all learning is to be found. ... These, indeed, so hang together and so depend upon one an-

> other in their ideas that if only one of the arts be
> lacking, all the rest cannot make a man into a
> philosopher. Therefore, those persons seem to
> me to be in error who, not appreciating the coher-
> ence among the arts, select certain of them for
> study, and, leaving the rest untouched, think they
> can become perfect in these alone. 5

Hugh of St. Victor stressed the interdependence of the liberal
arts at a time when burgeoning inquiry within special areas
had begun to strain severely the framework of the ancient
disciplinary structure. 6

Today the map of knowledge, as it were, has drasti-
cally changed. In certain respects the cartographic methods
have changed too. And we have, perhaps, become more conscious of the assumptions upon which these methods rest.
But the "faith in the division of intelligibility,"7 and with it
the disciplinary network, survives. Edmund Husserl summarized in our time:

> The notion of the objectives of a scientific disci-
> pline is expressed in the definition of that disci-
> pline. This, of course, does not imply that suc-
> cessful work in a discipline must be preceded by
> an adequate definition of the field. Such definitions
> are in fact reflections of developmental stages: the
> growth of knowledge within a discipline is followed
> by insights into the conceptual character of its sub-
> jects and its position and delimitation in respect to
> other disciplines. Yet, the degree of appropriate-
> ness of the definition or, rather, of the notions
> concerning the nature of the discipline behind that
> definition, influences in turn the course of inquiry
> within the discipline. Depending upon the kind of
> error involved, an inappropriate definition may
> have minor or major consequences in regard to
> scientific progress in the discipline. Objectively,
> the area of a scientific discipline is an intrinsically
> determined unit. We cannot arbitrarily decide
> where and how to delimit a field. The realm of
> truth has its compartments, and these objective
> units have to be heeded when a discipline is being
> organized. There are disciplines of numbers, of
> geometrical figures, and of living beings; but there
> is no discipline of prime numbers, or trapezoids,
> or lions, not to speak of a discipline combining

these three.   Whenever a set of insights and problems exhibits relationships which justify grouping
as a discipline, the delimitation of the field can be
inappropriate only in the sense that the field has
been too narrowly conceived; that the concatenation
of determining factors leads eventually beyond the
original area and requires further contexts in order
to attain systematic unity.   Such a limited horizon
does not necessarily inhibit scientific progress.   It
may be that at the outset theoretical interests are
satisfied within a narrow circle and that the work
undertaken without considering deeper and more
complex logical ramifications constitutes what, in
fact, is needed at this point.

Much more dangerous is a different kind of
inappropriateness in delimiting a field, namely,
disciplinary sortcrossing, which fuses disparate
ingredients into spurious unity, particularly so,
when it basically misinterprets the subject matter
the envisioned discipline is supposed to study. Such
an unintentional "substitution of a different kind"[8]
can have the most noxious consequences: articulation of unwarranted objectives; use of methods in-
commensurate with the true subject matter of the
discipline; and jumbling of logical levels, with the
result that basic propositions and theories make
their appearance in strange disguises, wedged between totally alien trends of thought, as if they
were accidental or just of marginal significance,
etc. [9]

Within a conjectural discipline Husserl distinguishes between
subject matter and our notion of objectives, i. e., between given
objects, events and processes and the aspects of these objects, events and processes we propose to study.   As we do
what we proposed to do, we learn: a new body of knowledge
interprets the subject matter and we are able to triangulate
the position of our field in terms of these interpretations.
From a logical point of view we operate within an abstractive
continuum.   "Inappropriateness" can occur only in the sense
of "initial limitation" of the field.   Yet the ever present human factor necessitates constant critical analysis, not only
of our results, but of the methods, and the fundamental issues.   What we first set out to study may be revised in
terms of later findings.   But it may also be sideswiped, mis-
construed, or dissipated by improper interpretations, or
methods, or both.   This is Husserl's disciplinary sortcross-

ing, where subject matter, inquiry, and critical evaluation
are no longer meaningfully related.

One further point merits consideration. Husserl refers to diachronic aspects, the from-to of the process of inquiry. The subject matter which "justifies" the discipline,
and the aggregate knowledge concerning this subject matter
have been established by this process. They represent the
state of the discipline--Kuhn's normal science.[10] But the
process goes on. It may follow directions within the discipline, or it may in one way or another go beyond the original area. In either case, the intellectual armamentarium of
the inquiry will reflect the state of the discipline. If the old
tools fail, new concepts, theories, methods, and instruments
will have to be sought in order to obtain results.[11] The ap-
propriateness of these new tools is determined by the problem at hand, and not by the disciplinary armamentarium.
Strictly speaking, i.e., without regard to purposes of established procedural implementation or the basic education of
students, there is no such thing as "disciplinary" research.
The logical thus-and-so of Husserl's compartments of truth
does not necessarily coincide with the here-and-now of the
state of the discipline.[12] It will take further steps to incorporate the work in progress into the "systematic unity" of
the discipline. All of which should not obscure that history
is full of instances when the state of the discipline effectively inhibited "appropriate" solutions or recognition of a need
for them; and that the new tools and even the new interests
generating them, may be misconceived because of carry-over
from the established framework of thought.[13]

1.2.   The Interdisciplinary Situation.

1.2.1.   Interdependence. Thus the problem situation
of reflective inquiry becomes the immediate locus of interdisciplinarity. This is implied by John Dewey's principle of
autonomy of inquiry. A scientist may use whatever he finds
relevant in terms of his problem.

> In the one world of ideas there are no barriers to
> trade or travel. Each discipline may take from
> others techniques, concepts, laws, data, models,
> theories, or explanations--in short, whatever it
> finds useful in its own inquiries. And it is a meas-
> ure of its success in these inquiries that it is asked
> in turn to give of its riches to other disciplines.

> Even more, it may find itself unexpectedly in an
> area conventionally identified as "belonging to" an-
> other science. Some of the most exciting encoun-
> ters in the history of science are those between
> workers in what appears to be quite distinct fields
> who are suddenly brought face to face as a result
> of their independent investigations. The autonomy
> of inquiry is in no way incompatible with the mature
> dependency of several sciences on one another.[14]

Kaplan's "mature dependency" obtains in such diverse areas
as the study of the origin of life, of the properties of the
atmosphere, creative processes in the arts, the classics, or
the nature and growth of knowledge. The face to face confrontation may be dramatic-as in the case of Clausius' entropy[15]-or in form of a gradually unfolding structure-as the
great confrontation of geometry and physics in the last 100
years,[16] or the remarkable fusion of philological word history and ideational analysis and interpretation of literature
emerging in the work of scholars like Friedrich Maurer,
Erich Auerbach, and Leo Spitzer. The results may assume
the form of trends--Parsons speaks of movements toward
synthesis[17] as we find them in linguistics[18] and organization
studies,[19] or of new fields (Boulding's "multisexual interdisciplines"[20]), such as geophysics (which, the exasperated lex-
icographer informs us, "is very broad in scope, and its
boundaries are undefinable"[21]); ecology; cybernetics; and,
most recently, Piaget's genetic epistemology.[22] And then
there are the supportive structures of the professions, ranging from biomedical engineering and the management sciences
to criminology and musical therapy. These are the faits
accomplis of interdisciplinarity, brought about by the processes of disciplinary interdependence.

As we look closer we discover easily that there are
various kinds of interdependence. It is one thing for the
historian to make use of infra-red photography, astronomical
tables, or text-critical applications of historical grammar,
and quite another to write a history of mathematics, or to
seek laws of causality in the historical process. The first
instance is one of use for historical purposes of a device and
knowledge developed in another discipline. This discipline
may be essentially unknown to the historian who uses its
product. Writing a history of a discipline requires a deeper
connection between the historian's task and the nature of the
discipline.[23] Exploring the compatibility of logical structures
and historical factuality and sequence involves interaction to
the point of translation.[24]

The relationship function clearly entails questions of degree, level, locus, and compatibility. Yet it is not easy to isolate and to assess the specific instances in this floating world of interdependencies.

1. 2. 2.   Piaget's System of the Sciences.   In his system of the sciences Jean Piaget employs the following ordering relations. [25]

The cycle of scientific disciplines is divided into the quadrants of logico-mathematical; physical; biological; and psycho-sociological sciences[26] I - II - III - IV.

In each quadrant four domains or levels, [27] A, B, C, and D are distinguished. [28]

A	subject matter and materials	(numbers and functions; bodies; energies; organs; mental operations, etc.)
B	conceptual structure	(descriptions, interpretations, theories)
C	endemic epistemology	(critical evaluation of the main body of the discipline, A and B, in terms of the sources and methods of obtaining knowledge within the discipline)
D	derived epistemology	(a broader inquiry involving comparison of the endemic sources and methods of obtaining knowledge C with those developed in other fields of knowledge)

The structure of a single discipline as well as interdependence between disciplines can be expressed in terms of these domains or levels.

Piaget distinguishes further between sciences which depend essentially on causative relationships, namely those dealing with material objects, such as the physical and biological sciences, quadrants II and III, including the behavioral areas of psychology; and sciences which depend essentially on implication in a general sense, "of which the various forms of logical implication ... are particular instances."[29] Here belong the logico-mathematical and the psycho-sociological sciences, quadrants I and IV. Interdependence between these causative and implicative disciplines, abbreviated here as

C-systems and I-systems, can occur (a) between C-systems; (b) between C- and I-systems; (c) between I-systems, and will have to be grasped in terms of these C-systems and I-systems, i.e., in terms of their structural characteristics as, e.g., expressed through levels A, B, C, D and their compatibilities and incompatibilities. Piaget attempts to accomplish this by an ingenious cyclic system connecting the sciences I, II, III, IV on levels A, B, C, D and six "essential modes of dependency," which express relationship functions conceivable between C- and I-systems.

The details and intricacies of Piaget's system of the sciences do not concern us here. Our rough outline in Figure 1, for which the present author alone is responsible, suffices to map the interdisciplinary situation. It involves (1) subject matter and knowledge of various kinds in the disciplines concerned; (2) the epistemic processes basic to these disciplines; and (3) essential modes of dependency. [30]

Interdisciplinarity may occur in varying degrees, symmetrically, as it were, involving interdependence between disciplines, or, asymmetrically, within one discipline utilizing results developed in another. From a diachronic viewpoint, symmetric situations bring about formation of a new discipline by fusion (e.g., astrophysics, or oceanography), asymmetric situations, by fission (witness the growing independence from the parent discipline of fields such as crystallography, meteorology, ethnomusicology, etc.). This, of course, does not necessarily determine the disciplinary loyalties and affinities professed by or demanded of the newly established disciplines. [31]

1.3.   The Interdisciplinary Encounter.

Piaget's system maps fundamental entities and relations pertaining to the situation of interdependence between disciplines. It shows us the ingredient complexities, the "points," as bookman say, of the interdisciplinary situation, as it has occurred or might be expected to occur. Yet "the confluence and interlocking of previously separate departments of knowledge"[32] is enacted on the grounds of a problem and its recognized requirements. It is in terms of these requirements that confrontation between disciplines is initiated. Thus we must distinguish between the interdisciplinary encounter and the interdisciplinary situation, which is its result. The interdisciplinary encounter is part of the inquiry

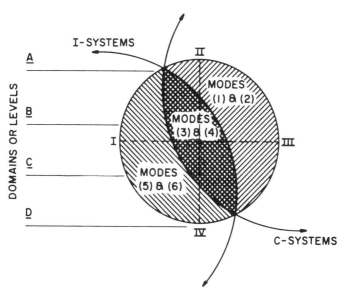

Quadrants:
  I   logico-mathematical ⎤   ⎧ Implicative
  II   physical   ⎬ sciences ⎨ Causative
  III biological   ⎪   ⎨ Causative
  IV   psycho-sociological ⎦   ⎩ Implicative

Domains or Levels:
  A subject matter and materials
  B̄ conceptual structure
  C̄ endemic epistemology
  D̄ derived epistemology

Modes of Dependency:[33]

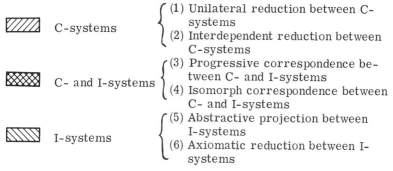

▨ C-systems   ⎧ (1) Unilateral reduction between C-systems
                   ⎩ (2) Interdependent reduction between C-systems

▩ C- and I-systems ⎧ (3) Progressive correspondence between C- and I-systems
                   ⎩ (4) Isomorph correspondence between C- and I-systems

▧ I-systems   ⎧ (5) Abstractive projection between I-systems
                   ⎩ (6) Axiomatic reduction between I-systems

Figure 1. Piaget's System of the Sciences (graphic representation and English terminology by C. H. R.).

into the problem. Consequently, its "points" are altogether different from those characterizing the interdisciplinary situation.

Any interdisciplinary encounter requires a knowledge of relevant facts in the two disciplinary areas involved, and certain connective notions, supported by these relevant facts. In order to use radioactive carbon 14 in dating events the historian must know what carbon 14 analysis can do, and have reason to believe that his problem is likely to benefit from this technique. If the use of carbon 14 in similar instances is well established, and the problem in hand is indeed in the nature of these instances, our historian will proceed routinely within an interdisciplinary situation that has become part of the professional know-how. If this is not the case, he will have to test with some care the connective notions which lead him to expect that carbon 14 analysis might be appropriate, lest his assumptions may turn out to be false.

Figure 2 attempts to sketch schematically the sequence involved. Let P denote a problem situation and C the possible connective notions concerning a specific aspect of the problem (diagram 1). In diagram 2, the specific problem aspect has been expressed in terms of connective notions, which relate to an area in another discipline E (diagram 3). If the encounter is found significant an interdisciplinary situation (PE) results, which does not require further support by connective notions C (diagram 4).

The four diagrams in Figure 2 show precise interlocking between P, C, and E as circumstances creating the interdisciplinary situation (PE), and (PE) as stable in terms of these circumstances. If (PE) is to serve in connection with a new problem P1, it can do so only if the specific aspects of P1 in question do, in fact, warrant P, C, and E. It is important to note that failure to recognize this may lead to Husserl's error of disciplinary sortcrossing. [34]

The interdisciplinary encounter, then, is to be understood as a problem-generated interface between areas and aspects of various disciplines. Its success or failure depends on the conduct of inquiry: the grasp of the problem through careful analysis; and the use of appropriate procedures and an appropriate course of action. We need good concepts, theories, laws, explanatory patterns, and values; astute critical observations; and accurate experiments, measurements, and models. And we need also a methodology which helps us

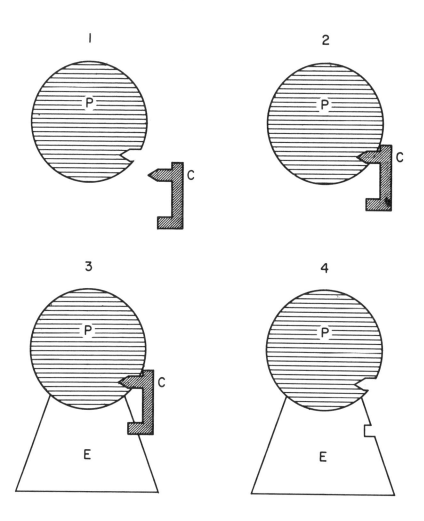

Figure 2. The Interdisciplinary Encounter (adapted from a diagram by L'Heritier of Szilard's model of regulative processes in the synthesis of enzymes).

to evaluate or, in Popper's words, to conjecture and to re-
fute.[35] The interdisciplinary encounter requires us, quite
literally, to know what we are doing in terms of where we
are; what is needed; and where (if anywhere) it is to be had.
It is in these terms, and not by way of analogies or outward
proximities,[36] that meaningful interdisciplinary situations
come into being. And even when an interdisciplinary situation has been properly established, reflective examination in
these terms must enter into its applications within other contexts, although they may appear to be related.[37] The validity of the new application and the implicit connective notions
cannot be determined on the basis of an existing interdisciplinary situation as it presents itself to us. It is not enough
to know that such and such is the case. In order to control
the interdisciplinary encounter in terms of our problem
(which is the reason for the encounter), we must know why
this is so.[38]

When it comes to specific instances, all this is clearly a matter of degree. Simple asymmetric situations, such
as the use of radioactive carbon 14 or the electron micro-
analyzer in archeology, will, as a rule, not require repeated
scrutiny. But we have not overstated the essential nature of
our subject. The locus of the interdisciplinary situation is
the event of interdisciplinarity. The locus of the interdisciplinary encounter is the problem. And we must not con-
fuse the two. An interdisciplinary situation, no matter how
familiar, remains indeterminate as far as a problem is concerned until an equivalence relationship is established in
terms of an interdisciplinary encounter or, if you will, in
terms of the connective notions operative in such an encounter. Only the interdisciplinary encounter can attain the explanatory relevance without which our "tests" (based upon
situations assumed, but not proven, to be pertinent) remain
construals that may or may not apply.[39]

Are models of doctor-patient relationship[40] appropriate
in situations involving other professionals and their clients?
The answer to this question depends not on an inventory of
known ("obvious") similarities exhibited by the models, but
rather on an analysis of the specific situation under scrutiny,
on a critical sorting out of relevant facts which enable us to
state why applicability does or does not obtain. The conversational gesture "why shouldn't it be so?" beclouds the real
issue, namely, that in order to know we must "grasp" in the
full sense of the word and ascertain grounds supporting an
explanation.

2.   The Interdisciplinarity of Librarianship

2.1.   The Librarian's Business.

Interdisciplinarity in the field of librarianship may thus be approached in terms of what librarians do when they are doing well as librarians. [41]

According to Shera, the "librarian's business" is "effective access to recorded knowledge."[42]   This includes Butler's "transmission of the accumulated experience of society to its individual members through the instrumentality of the book."[43]   Librarians engage in an activity, which has as its goal effective access to recorded knowledge[44] as a service to those seeking, or expected to need, such access.   This constitutes an organic system of activities involving knowledge records and services to people; and the intellectual and material equipment and know-how necessary in order to create conditions which promise to support, if not to optimize, effective access to recorded knowledge for those with a purpose of gaining such access.   These fundamental relations are suggested by the Venn diagram in Figure 3.

We note right here that librarianship implies a compound situation, the kind of broad problem area Weinberg described as "extrinsically motivated."[45]   This problem area is (1) the staging area for the librarian's daily course of action: it fixes the tasks with which the librarian has to cope by "(a) answering questions, (b) solving problems, and (c) developing more effective procedures for answering questions and solving problems";[46] (2) It furnishes also the framework for less immediate efforts to discover and grasp epistemically disciplinary aspects and properties relevant to librarianship; and (3) constitutes the ultimate locus for all research in librarianship in the sense that reflective inquiry is initiated and must seek its confirmations within these domains. [47]

Charged with furnishing to users knowledge records and knowledge based on knowledge records appropriate to the users' "notions,"[48] the librarian undertakes the acquisition (which in most instances includes selection); preservation; organization and housing as a collection; and making available of documents, i.e., objects made to record, store, display, and transmit knowledge.   When engaging in these bibliothecal activities the librarian encounters the structural and function-

"From above:"   L as a field of study

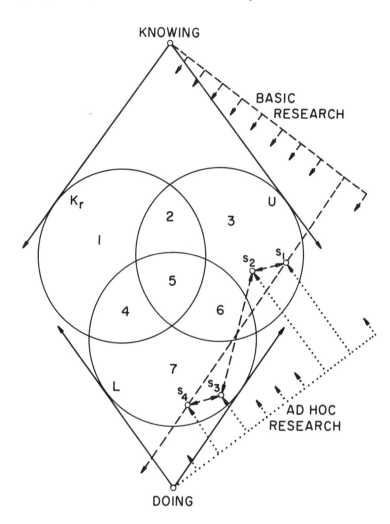

"From below:"   L as a professional acitivity

K_r Recorded Knowledge s_1, s_2, s_3, s_4 Problem
                                                    situations
L   Librarianship

U   Use

Figure 3. The Principal Concerns of Librarianship

al properties of these objects, and the need to control them. Documents exist in terms of object, content, and (intended and not intended) use potential: They all exhibit certain physical characteristics (O), the price of admission to their content (C); and lend themselves to uses (U) determined by content (C) and/or physical characteristics (O). Maintenance of a library collection clearly requires control of these circumstances, internally (c_1), pertaining to the documents available within the collection, and externally (c_2), pertaining to documents available elsewhere. These ingredients of the bibliothecal situation are sketched in Figure 4. The bibliothecal situation permits access to the documents it controls in terms of these documents, i.e., in terms of the O-C-U syndrome symptomatic of the documents. Its indigenous concept of use is that generated in and by the documents. Effectiveness of access is attempted in these same terms.

It is up to the librarian to understand the properties of the bibliothecal situation and to translate them into a functioning system; to negotiate the mission-discipline duality;[49] to meld the requirements of each user with the state of things in the collection, and to adjust the prevailing use concept to new requirements that are judged significant in terms of actual or anticipated use of the collection. This is roughly the core situation of bibliothecal activity one may wish to associate with segments 4 (K_r and L, but not U), 6 (U and L, but not K_r), and 5 (K_r and U and L) in Figure 3.

Segment 6 reminds us of the service activities involved. Here belong requirements of human communication, face-to-face interaction, social and even clinical contexts, which have a bearing on the transactual as well as the contractual aspects of library service.[50] Behavioral patterns and attitudes play an important and often perplexing part, perhaps not wholly unlike the paradox of disease and patient treatment that bedevils the doctor's role.[51] Goal-intended activities[52] are judged successful or unsuccessful in terms of the "goal-object,"[53] while other areas remain indeterminate. The goal of effective access to recorded knowledge can be viewed primarily in terms of the "information" (segment 4); as well as in terms of human factors (segment 6). Obviously, these two approaches are not mutually exclusive. But they are not of the same order. Though often argued as conflicting opposites, their nature and degree of interdependence remain problems of librarianship to which the librarian (in segment 5) has to address himself in his daily activities as best he can, as he judges effectiveness in ac-

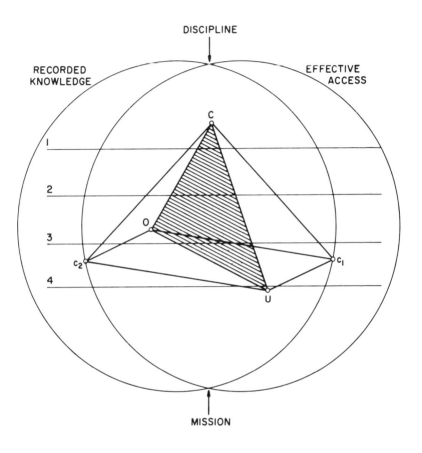

DISCIPLINE

RECORDED
KNOWLEDGE

EFFECTIVE
ACCESS

C

O

c_2

c_1

U

1

2

3

4

MISSION

BIBLIOTHECAL ACTIVITIES:
1 Acquisition
2 Preservation
3 Organization and Housing
4 Making Available

BASIC PROPERTIES:
C Content
O Object
U Use

CONTROLS:
c_1 internal
c_2 external

Figure 4.   The Bibliothecal Situation

cordance with personal, professional, and institutional pre-
cepts.

Here arise socio-psychological, educational, and also
economical and ethical questions, and with them the subject
of essential professional knowledge. It is not difficult to see
that, regardless of its specific concerns, this knowledge cannot be limited to observation and sundry reconstructions based
or believed to be based on observation often referred to as
"experience." "Observational knowledge is restricted to the
past and the present; knowledge of the future is not of the
observational type."[54] Yet it is precisely Reichenbach's
"knowledge of the future," i. e., knowledge that truly permits
us to conclude, to explain, to modify, and, if you will, to
predict and postdict,[55] which is needed, if the librarian is to
address himself efficiently to his tasks. The point at issue
here is not that it may often be difficult to obtain such knowledge for the various concerns of librarianship, but, rather,
that such knowledge is basic for all decisions that demand
more than after-the-fact assurance; or an accurate interpretation of observed facts as a basis for logical derivation.

Bibliothecal and service activities require a variety of
supportive activities and attendant competencies, ranging from
top level administration, management and planning to maintenance and receiving and shipping. Here belongs the entire
armamentarium entailed by the goals the librarian serves, including the professional hierarchies and organizational systems and patterns.

Educational programs and procedures intended to serve
librarianship will have to produce the competencies needed
for the bibliothecal, service, and supportive activities, and
supply the necessary foundations and perspectives for research
in librarianship. They may come from many sources. But
like the activities they seek to serve, they derive relevance
from the business of librarianship. If this business, somehow, remains unclear in its areas, educational effort concerning these areas is not likely to rise above mere guess-
work--which raises a problem of educational objectives and
returns us to the locus classicus of interdisciplinarity.

2. 2.   Interdisciplinary Concerns.

The librarian's business entails a twofold concern with
interdisciplinarity, i. e., with interdisciplinary situations and

encounters as they obtain for (1) librarianship as such, and
(2) the subject fields, their literatures and research interests,
served by the librarian.   These two concerns are related by
the fact that the librarian is not only concerned with interdisciplinarity as exhibited by (2), but also with appropriate ac-
tion--Shera's "efficient and effective management"[56]--in regard to this interdisciplinarity.   This is a professional concern.   It constitutes itself a condition of interdisciplinarity,
in which the librarian acts according to his purpose.   This
purpose determines the nature of his concern with interdisciplinarity.

Implicit here are the matters of subject and craft,
often debated as "theory" versus "practice," because we fail
to remember that "theory is of practice, and must stand and
fall with its practicality, provided only that the mode and
context of its application are suitably specified."[57]   Figure
3 suggests that librarianship can be approached from below
as a professional activity, from above as a field of study.

In a professional activity the essential motive is doing.
The immediate objective is to gain and maintain control by
means of whatever competence is required for the making of
decisions that permit effective manipulation of resources,
men, and machines.   The immediacy of the task demands
the pragmatic search for what does the job, concern with
how best to answer the question posed by the incidence of
the situation (s_1, s_2, s_3, or s_4).   The literature produced
by such inquiries (ad hoc research in Figure 3), will strive
to bring together the largest number of facts bearing on the
problem situation under consideration.   H. M. Sheffer speaks
of the quest for maximal implicational consequents, generated
in terms of each problem situation.[58]   This quest may produce considerable expertise and an explosion of specific and,
possibly, sophisticated information concerning a host of tasks
and techniques.   It may also de-emphasize, if not inhibit, an
inclusive overview of the entire field and its boundaries, as
well as systematic endeavors to grasp its states, structures,
and functions.   For the view from below the primary effort
concerns the How of each task--with which goes often the
immanent empiricism of the "hard look at the facts" approach.
Accurate mapping and critical analysis and understanding of
the total professional situation and its assumptions is secondary.   It is not required for prediction based on speculative
extrapolation of empirical data from past events, or for the
encyclopedic compilation of the improvements accomplished
by ad hoc research.

In scientific inquiry from above the essential motive is <u>knowing</u>. The immediate objective is to avoid self-deception, meaning the kind of error which prevents us from laying the groundwork of knowledge "hard" enough to support "systematic explanation and dependable prediction."[59] Here, the pragmatic search includes all activities of librarianship, as well as the epistemic bases of these activities and the pragmatic searches they engage in. Problems of topology and its language are explored; the questions <u>and</u> the answers within the professional activity of librarianship become significant in terms of systematic relatedness, of structure and function, rather than in terms of a given incidental situation. The issue now is not to answer the questions asked concerning specific and, possibly, urgent tasks and their wherewithal within the domains of professional activity and decisionmaking, but to assess these questions as such and in regard to the totality of the professional situation. For such basic research situations $s_1, \ldots s_4$ (Figure 3) pose the questions of explanation, hence, the search for basic concepts and propositions--Sheffer's minimal theoretical antecedents,[60] which hold true for the entire situation and thus may furnish terms of interconnection for the situations $s_1, \ldots s_4$, viewed heretofore as unrelated and studied by discrete <u>ad hoc</u> efforts (as indicated in Figure 3). Unhampered by sets of objectives specified by and for the purpose of this or that professional task, or, if you will, espousing as its only objective solid subject knowledge and the corollaries of Peirce's "Do not block the way of inquiry,"[61] the view from above strives for synoptic grasp and description, analysis, and explanation based on it. These concerns may lead to results which are abstract and, perhaps, operationally infeasible at the time, but demonstrably true as materials for a theoretic statics (and, conceivably, even a theoretic dynamics);[62] and systematic efforts to develop valid formal statements.

Thus, the problem situations $s_1, \ldots s_4$ acquire different dimension as we approach them motivated "by curiosity" or "by a desire to obtain practical objectives."[63] Whether we deal with the subject of a library code of ethics or "a torpedo with a target-seeking mechanism," the <u>ad hoc</u> inquiry will primarily render specifics concerning matters of immediate significance for the criteria to be satisfied, while reflective analysis of the basic notions involved in seach of explanation may lead to occupation with generic aspects of "purposefulness as a concept necessary for the understanding of certain modes of behavior," as discussed by Rosenblueth, Wiener, and Bigelow.[64] We note that, regardless of popular and

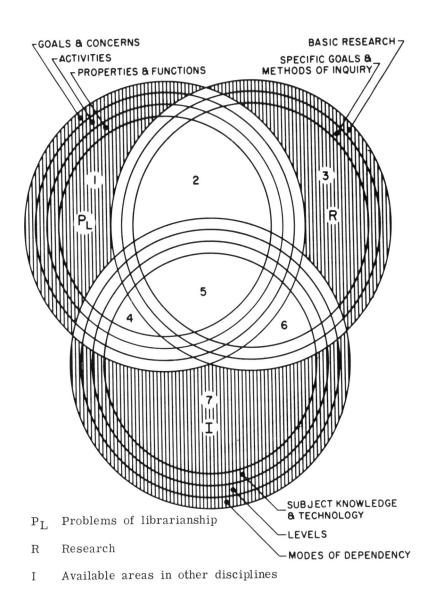

GOALS & CONCERNS
ACTIVITIES
PROPERTIES & FUNCTIONS

BASIC RESEARCH
SPECIFIC GOALS &
METHODS OF INQUIRY

SUBJECT KNOWLEDGE
& TECHNOLOGY

LEVELS

MODES OF DEPENDENCY

P$_L$ Problems of librarianship

R   Research

I   Available areas in other disciplines

Figure 5.   The Interdisciplinarity of Librarianship.

mostly pointless arguments pro and con, these two approaches
are not necessarily orthogonal, and that they both determine
the purposive continuum of librarianship and, hence, its interdisciplinary concerns. [65]

2.3.   Conclusions.

The interdisciplinarity of librarianship, therefore,
must be stated within the problem area of librarianship and
in terms of these approaches: Specific problems involving
the goals and principal concerns; activities; and basic properties and functions, outlined above (2.1), are being grasped
and studied from characteristic vantage points (2.2) judged
appropriate at the time.   Answers and decisions utilizing other disciplines and their technologies are based on interdisciplinary situations resulting from the conduct of inquiry into
the problem.   These interdisciplinary situations, in turn, exhibit the features discussed heretofore, i.e., subject matter
and knowledge of various kinds, and attendant epistemic levels and modes of dependency (1.2.2).

Figure 5 shows the relationships that obtain.   It suggests also the consequences of imbalance among these relationships.   An interdisciplinary solution requires knowledge
of the nature and grounds of both the problem (segment 2)
and the disciplinary area in question (segment 4).   The interdisciplinary encounter is determined by the connective notions
(1.3) held by the inquirer in his approach to and analysis of
the problem as well as of the subject of his interest within
the other discipline.   If these notions rest on erroneous assumptions concerning P_L or I, the most sophisticated methods of inquiry in R will not prevent inapplicable outcomes.
There is no room for "naive bandwagon feeling:"[66]   The proposed interdisciplinary adoption has to be significant in terms
of the problem.   This requires reasons which permit us to
expect a solution of this particular, interdisciplinary, nature.
Segment 5 represents the required elements of any valid condition of interdisciplinarity.

In order to establish an interdisciplinary situation in
the field of librarianship we must have properly recognized
and analyzed a problem as a problem of librarianship; asked
relevant questions based upon relevant facts pertaining to the
problem; and have discovered reasons on which to base an
expectation concerning the applicability of subject matter from
another discipline.   This requires (1) knowledge of the prob-

lem as a problem of librarianship adequate to allow us to
seek out a solution in another discipline, the topology of
which must be sufficiently known to us for this purpose; and
(2) research approaches and methods commensurate with the
undertaking. It is possible that the cycle of inquiry actually
originates in I, as, e.g., was the case with the mathematical
treatment of indifference-curve analysis in economics. However, this use of mathematics turned out to be of value only,
because it drew attention to the "limited penetration into the
underlying economic problem,"[67] i.e., precisely in terms of
the problem area as ultimate locus of significant interdisciplinarity.

3.   Postscript.   "To know: To grasp and to explain."[68]

    In its pertinent traits and requirements the interdisci-
plinarity of librarianship stated here differs sharply from the
notions and practices often indicated in the literature of librarianship, where interdisciplinarity (e.g., as desirable in
a library and information science curriculum) appears as a
promising condition for certain outcomes (e.g., better educated, more effective graduates). The desired result is
hoped for in terms of circumstances which are believed to
be capable of producing it. One feels it "stands to reason"
that interdependence (e.g., with the social sciences) will have
positive effects. At this point, however, the nature and
modes of interdependence are indeterminate and so, of course,
are the chances for occurrence of desired results. In fact,
the essential terms we seek to satisfy have not been stated.
Conversely, "tools" from other disciplines are recommended
as useful to librarianship on similar grounds, and are accepted with the same naive confidence. When it comes to
research approaches we are assured that "traditionally library
research has been concerned both with knowing for the sake
of knowing and with knowledge that helps in a practical way,"[69]
but promptly fail to address ourselves to the characteristics of
these perspectives and their functional relations to the structure
and boundaries of problems in librarianship.

    In terms of reflective inquiry we have failed to accept
Shera's proposition that "the first responsibility of a profession
is to know itself..."[70] Consequently, we are uneasy when it
comes to problem articulation in our field. Ever busy answering the questions asked by our clientele, we neglect to
initiate inquiries allowing us to identify and study fundamental
questions that need to be posed in our field in order that we

should pursue our business with appropriate effectiveness.
Thus, critical analysis and evaluation based upon critical
analysis are often replaced by gratuitous action or repentant
breast-beating. Obscurity and vagueness in the field spawn
proneness to nostrums: the theories, methods, devices, gim-
micks, and fancy terminology, which may be "the thing" at
the moment, but do not relieve the basic circumstances of
our helplessness. As a profession we have never grasped
that "we can write satisfying programs for computers when,
and only when, we have learned to write satisfying programs
for ourselves."[71]

   The same insufficiency speaks from the (predominantly
asymmetric) interdisciplinary situations that exist as unrelated
enclaves, by accident as it were, within the domains of librarianship. Some are valid and promise genuine results.
(Here belong efforts in the field of classification, and a growing number of inquiries and systems applications in information storage and retrieval.) Some, like the enthusiastic manipulation of new statistical tools, require further careful
study. Others are pseudoapplications, viz., meaningless use
of mathematical symbols, confusion of nomenclature with discovery of principles or problem solutions, and homespun
"applications" of information theory and other scientific subject matter--all intellectually embarrassing and professionally unimportant. There is little sorting out of this motley
cluster and even less knowledgeable systematic search for
warranted dialogue with other subject areas. At present, librarianship is simply not equipped to designate the interdisciplinary "spillins" and "spillouts"[72] proper to its native
grounds.

   As the ultimate locus of all possible interdisciplinary
encounters these native grounds are quite literally our problem. They pose Bridgman's two-fold aspect of the problem
of understanding--"the problem of understanding the world
around us, and ... the problem of understanding the nature
of the intellectual tools with which we attempt to understand
the world around us."[73] As long as we do not find the time
to explore methodically this two-fold problem of synoptic
grasp (Piaget's levels A and B) and epistemic analysis (Piaget's levels C and D; above, 1.2.2. and Figure 1), our professional efforts, no matter how dedicated, remain haphazard.
We will have to go on guessing, because we do not know.

   A meaningful interdisciplinarity of librarianship depends upon our willingness to address and our capacity to

answer correctly questions concerning credibility and intelligibility, in short, on the soundness of our reasons and our
explanations.[74] This involves the explicit logical analysis of
concepts and methods which Northrop and others have demonstrated as a first requirement for the growth of any empirical discipline. Without being able to state the fundamental
entities and fundamental relations of our field we lack the
wherewithal for concepts, propositions, and theorems. And
without the latter we cannot deductively formulate, test, or
confirm, let alone evaluate and predict. There is no scientific discourse--only after-the-fact adjustment. We cannot
grasp and cannot explain. And thus we remain wide open to
the implicit risk of the interdisciplinary condition: that we
credulously accept as compatible Husserl's disciplinary sortcrossing, which effectively inhibits inquiry and progress in
the profession we hope to serve.

Notes

1. "The subjective reason explains outer frequency by in-
    ward structure, not inward structure by outer fre-
    quency." W. James, The Principles of Psychology,
    New York, H. Holt, 1890, ii, 643.
2. On the use of names cf. John Stuart Mill's Philosophy
    of Scientific Method, ed. E. Nagel, New York, Hafner,
    1950, I, ii and iii; B. Blanshard, The Nature of
    Thought, London, Allen & Unwin, 1939, i, 537-545.
3. J. H. Shera, Libraries and the Organization of Knowl-
    edge, Hamden, Conn., Archon Books, 1965, 116f.,
    130-133.
4. Cicero, De Oratore i, 42, 187-183.
5. Transl. J. Taylor, The Didascalicon of Hugh of St.
    Victor, New York, Columbia University Press, 1961,
    89. Hugh echoes Vitruvius, De architectura i, 1, 12:
    "... they easily believe it possible that all disciplines
    are linked together in subject matter and have a com-
    mon bond. The curriculum of the disciplines (encyclios
    disciplina), like a single body, is composed of the dis-
    ciplines as so many numbers." Taylor, op. cit., 212,
    n. 46.
6. Hugh's own system admits new disciplines and new dis-
    ciplinary interpretations. Cf. G. Paré, La Renais-
    sance du xiie Siècle, Paris, Vrin, 1933, 100. Two
    centuries later, Petrarch thought that "it is enough
    for one man's mind to attain distinction in one field
    of study." (C. H. Rawski, Petrarch: Four Dialogues

for Scholars, Cleveland, Press of Western Reserve University, 1967, 187.)

7. W. J. Ong, Ramus: Method, and the Decay of Dialogue, Cambridge, Mass., Harvard University Press, 1958, 165.

8. Husserl has μετάβασις εἰς ἀλλο γένός.

9. E. Husserl, Logische Untersuchungen, vol. i, Halle, M. Niemeyer, 1928, 5 f. English version by C. H. R.

10. T. S. Kuhn, The Structure of Scientific Revolutions, Chicago, University of Chicago Press, 1962, 10.

11. "The greatest changes of all come not as the thief in the night, but as the oak-tree from the acorn. The most radical of thinkers is soaked in tradition; he spends a lifetime bending ancient ideas to a slightly different use, and his followers soon revert to the familiar pattern while still mumbling the novel terms. And it is so: men can work only upon what they have inherited. Fresh experience and novel problems they must understand with the instruments they have learned from those who came before them. New ideas they must grasp in the concepts they already know, for they have no others; new habits they must work slowly into the accepted patterns of their lives." J. H. Randall, The Career of Philosophy, vol. i, New York, Columbia University Press, 1962, 9. Note also the remarks on immanence and extramanence in P. Frankl, The Gothic, Princeton, Princeton University Press, 1960, 223.

12. Cf. M. Black, "The Definition of Scientific Method," in his Problems of Analysis, Ithaca, N. Y., Cornell University Press, 1954, 3-23. Scheler noted that "the factual interconnections traced by reflective inquiry lead in directions altogether different from those required for the pragmatic summation of a field of knowledge for the purposes of a discipline or a profession." M. Scheler, Die Wissensformen und die Gesellschaft (1925), Gesammelte Werke, vol. 8, Bern, Francke, 1960, 391.

13. On the relationship of state of knowledge and process of inquiry in a scientific discipline cf., e. g., T. S. Kuhn, op. cit., and the discussions of Kuhn's views in A. C. Crombie, Scientific Change, New York, Basic Books, 1963, 370-394; I. Scheffler, Science and Subjectivity, Indianapolis, Bobbs-Merrill, 1967, 15-19, 74-89; and in Criticism and the Growth of Knowledge, ed. I. Lakatos and A. Musgrave, Cambridge, Eng., University Press, 1970.

14. A. Kaplan, The Conduct of Inquiry, San Francisco,
     Chandler, 1964, 4.
15. C.C. Gillispie, The Edge of Objectivity, Princeton,
     Princeton University Press, 1960, chap. ix.   Note
     also Kuhn, op. cit., 50 f.
16. P. Frank, Philosophy of Science, Englewood Cliffs,
     N.J., Prentice-Hall, 1957, chap. 3.
17. T. Parsons, "Unity and Diversity in the Modern Intel-
     lectual Disciplines: The Role of the Social Sciences,"
     in G. Holton, Science and Culture, Boston, Houghton
     Mifflin, 1965, 49.
18. For an interesting echo in clinical medicine cf. R.M.
     Magraw, Ferment in Medicine, Philadelphia, Saunders,
     1966, chap. 2.
19. J.G. March, ed., Handbook of Organizations, Chicago,
     Rand-McNally, 1965, xiv f.
20. K. Boulding, "General Systems Theory," Management
     Science, 2 (1956), 199.
21. The Columbia Encyclopedia, 3rd edition, New York,
     Columbia University Press, 1963, 809b.
22. Cf. D. Elkind's introduction in J. Piaget, Six Psycho-
     logical Studies (1964), New York, Random House,
     1967.
23. "The scholar who studies the history of science, for ex-
     ample, must combine a knowledge of languages, his-
     tory, and philosophy with the knowledge of a scientist."
     R. Schlatter in C.A. Holbrook, Religion, a Humanistic
     Field, Englewood Cliffs, N.J., Prentice-Hall, 1963,
     vii f.
24. Cf. e.g., the discussion in A.C. Danto, Analytical
     Philosophy of History, Cambridge, University Press,
     1965, chap. x; and M. White, Foundations of Histori-
     cal Knowledge, New York, Harper & Row, 1965,
     chaps. ii, iii.
25. Piaget discusses the system in "Les Deux Directions de
     la Pensée Scientifique," Archives des Sciences Phy-
     siques et Naturelles, 11 (1929), 145-162; Introduction
     à l'Épistémologie Génétique, vol. iii, Paris, Presses
     Universitaires de France, 1950; and Logique et Con-
     naissance Scientifique, Paris, Gallimard, 1967, 1172-
     1224.
26. Included within the latter are the areas of scientific in-
     quiry in the humanities.
27. Piaget uses the term niveaux in the sense of specific
     kinds rather than of ordering or rank patterns.
28. A domaines materiels; B domaines conceptuels; C do-
     maines épistémologiques internes; D domaines épisté-

mologiques dérivés.

29. According to Piaget, the phenomena of consciousness do not depend on causality. They are essentially characterized by the capacity to establish "significations," and one cannot say that one signification is the "cause" of another; it rather entails or implies the other. The mathematical and logical sciences also ignore causality. They rely entirely on relations of implication. Piaget refers here also to Kelsen's concept of imputation (e.g., H. Kelsen, Pure Theory of Law [1960], trans. M. Knight, Berkeley, University of California Press, 1967, 75-81). On the relationship between the natural sciences which "explain" and the human sciences which "understand," cf. Danto, op. cit., 20 f., and A. Nevins, The Gateway to History, Garden City, N.Y., Doubleday Anchor, 1962, chap. viii.

30. For an illustration of modes of dependency see the chapter on "Theoretical Reduction" in C.G. Hempel, Philosophy of Natural Science, Englewood Cliffs, N.J., Prentice Hall, 1966, 101-110.

31. Similarly, we must consider our own position as initiators of an interdisciplinary situation; users of results produced by an interdisciplinary situation; or students of this situation itself, when trying to sort out our notions concerning the subject. J.D. Watson, The Double Helix, New York, Atheneum, 1968, offers a noteworthy case study of interdisciplinarity.

32. D. de Solla Price, Science Since Babylon, New Haven, Yale, University Press, 1961, 22.

33. (1) Réduction unilatérale d'une science ou théorie causale à une autre.
    (2) Réduction par interdependance de sciences ou théories causales.
    (3) Mise en correspondance d'un système causal avec un système implicatif jusq'à assimilation du premier au second.
    (4) Mise en correspondance d'un système causal avec un système implicatif avec recherche d' "isomorphisme."
    (5) Interdependance entre deux systèmes implicatifs par abstraction réfléchissante.
    (6) Réduction entre deux systèmes implicatifs par axiomatisation.

34. Cf. e.g., the questions of applicability discussed in A. Kaplan, "Sociology Learns the Language of Mathematics," The World of Mathematics, ed. J.R. New-

man, New York, Simon & Schuster, 1956, ii, 1294-
1313. A subtle hazard of interdependence is mentioned
by J. H. Woodger, who finds "that when one science
(e. g., physics) is applied in another (e. g., biology)
the applied science will automatically impose its modes
of abstraction on the science in which it is applied,
and this will inhibit the independent discovery of new
modes of abstraction suitable to the latter science."
(Logic, Methodology and Philosophy of Science, ed.
Nagel, Suppes, and Tarski, Stanford, Stanford University Press, 1962, 293.) On this, note also E. Nagel,
The Structure of Science, New York, Harcourt, Brace,
World, 1961, chap. 11.

35. K. R. Popper, Conjectures and Refutations, New York,
Basic Books, 1965, chap. 1, R. L. Ackoff refers to
"the procedures which characterize science" as tools,
techniques, and methods. "By a scientific tool we
mean a physical or conceptual instrument that is used
in scientific inquiry ... by a scientific technique we
refer to a way of accomplishing a ... scientific course
of action. Techniques, therefore, are ways of using
scientific tools.... By a scientific method we refer
to the ways techniques are selected in science....
Methods are rules of choice; techniques are the choices
themselves.... The study of scientific methods is
frequently referred to as methodology." Ackoff, Gupta,
and Minas, Scientific Method: Optimizing Applied Research Decisions, New York, Wiley, 1962, 5 f. (Emphasis in original.)

36. Cf. J. G. Miller's remarks on formal identities in The
State of the Social Sciences, ed. L. D. White, Chicago,
University of Chicago Press, 1956, 41 f.

37. A. G. Oettinger discusses the consequences of a failure
to do this in the application of information technology
in schools. "The Myths of Educational Technology,"
Saturday Review, May 18, 1968, 76-77; 91.

38. C. G. Hempel distinguishes between reason-seeking why
questions aimed at credibility ("Why should it be believed that p?"), and explanation-seeking why questions
aimed at intelligibility ("Why is it the case that p?").
Both these questions are addressed here, although the
sense of familiarity created by answers to reason seeking why questions must eventually give way to questions seeking "to provide a systematic understanding
of empirical phenomena by showing that they fit into
a nomic nexus." (Aspects of Scientific Explanation,
New York, Free Press, 1965, 334 f., 488.)

39. In short: "We must look for techniques that fit the
    problem and not for problems that fit the technique."
    (H. Selye, From Dream to Discovery, New York,
    McGraw Hill, 1964, 94. Emphasis in original.) Cf.
    also W.H. Starbuck, on the effects of "cookbook"
    mathematics, in Handbook of Organizations, ed. J.G.
    March, Chicago, Rand McNally, 1965, 345 b.
40. Cf. the convenient summary in A.B. Ford, The Doctor's
    Perspective, Cleveland, Case Western Reserve Univer-
    sity Press, 1967, chap. 1.
41. Adapted from Kaplan's "Logic, in short, deals with what
    scientists do when they are doing well as scientists."
    A. Kaplan, op. cit., 8.
42. J.H. Shera, Libraries..., 161.
43. P. Butler, An Introduction to Library Science (1933),
    Chicago, University of Chicago Press, 1961, 29, 84.
    -- Other statements of purpose range from stress on
    bibliographic control (R. Irwin, Librarianship, Lon-
    don, Grafton, 1949; recently also E. Smith in Library
    Journal, 94 [Feb. 1, 1969], 503) to formulations with-
    in socio-cultural contexts (e.g., A. Broadfield, A
    Philosophy of Librarianship, London, Grafton, 1949;
    L.R. Wilson, Education and Libraries, ed. M.F.
    Tauber & J.Orne, n.p., Shoestring Press, 1966).
    C.M. White speaks of librarianship as standing "for
    the accumulated power over the works of the mind."
    (Bases of Librarianship, New York, Pergamon Press
    and Macmillan, 1964, 12.) A careful discussion of
    the goals of librarianship in our times is badly needed,
    but does not concern us when dealing with the situation
    of librarianship and its constitutive states and factors.
    On definitions cf. M. Black, op. cit., 24-45; G. Ryle,
    The Concept of Mind, London, Hutchinson, 1949, 118f.
44. The term recorded knowledge denotes all available,
    i.e., socially transmitted knowledge. (Cf. F. Machlup,
    The Production and Distribution of Knowledge in the
    United States, Princeton, Princeton University Press,
    1962, 14f.) The knowledge record may be of diverse
    provenance. It may, in fact, have been made by the
    librarian aware of a need for a document of this kind.
45. A. Weinberg, Reflections on Big Science, Cambridge,
    Mass., M.I.T. Press, 1967, 147-152.
46. Ackoff, Gupta, and Minas, op. cit., 1.
47. Cf. H. Margenan, Open Vistas, New Haven, Yale Uni-
    versity Press, 1961, chap. 1.
48. R.A. Fairthorne, "'Use' and 'Mention' in the Informa-
    tion Sciences," Proceedings of the Symposium on Edu-

cation for Information Science, Warrenton, Va., ed.
L. B. Heilprin, Washington, D. C., Spartan Books,
1965, 11.

49.   A. Weinberg, "Science, Government, and Information,"
in The Growth of Knowledge, ed. M. Kochen, New
York, J. Wiley, 1967, 42 f.

50.   K. Menninger, Theory of Psychoanalytic Technique
(Menninger Clinic Monograph Series No. 12), New
York, Basic Books, 1958, 17.

51.   R. M. Magraw, op. cit., chaps. 2, 6, 7.

52.   The phrase indicates purposive goal-directed behavior.
Cf. A. B. Braithwaite, Scientific Explanation, Cambridge, University Press, 1955, 325.

53.   Cf. I. Scheffler, The Anatomy of Inquiry, New York,
A. A. Knopf, 1963, 113.

54.   H. Reichenbach, The Rise of Scientific Philosophy,
Berkeley, University of California Press, 1951, 91.

55.   C. G. Hempel, Aspects..., 173, n. 1.

56.   The Foundations of Access to Knowledge, ed. E. B.
Montgomery, Syracuse, Syracuse University Press,
1968, 25.

57.   A. Kaplan, The Conduct..., 296.

58.   Quoted in F. S. C. Northrop and H. H. Livingston, Cross-
Cultural Understanding, New York, Harper & Row,
1964, 195.

59.   E. Nagel, The Structure..., 450.

60.   Northrop and Livingston, ibid.

61.   Philosophical Writings of Peirce, ed. J. Buchler, New
York, Dover, 1956, 54.

62.   Scientific theory requires an empirically verified deductive system. When its basic concepts and propositions
(and the definitions and theorems derived from them)
are sufficient to designate (i. e., determine without
further observation) the specific state of the system
at a particular moment of time, we may speak of
theoretical statics. "A theory of dynamics exists for
a given science when its concepts are sufficient to
designate the specific state of a system at a given
time and its postulates permit the deduction of a specific state for any future time." (F. S. C. Northrop,
The Logic of the Sciences and the Humanities, New
York, Macmillan, 1947, 235.) Common to both, a
deductively formulated statics and dynamics, are not
only the basic concepts and propositions and their
formally deduced derivates, but also the state function
and its independent variables and their "correlated
operational definitions which specify how one experi-

mentally, or observationally, determines the empirical
values of the independent variables of the state function of the system in question at any present moment
of time." (Northrop and Livingston, op. cit., 199.)

63. G. Tullock, The Organization of Inquiry, Durham, N.C.,
Duke University Press, 1966, 12. "In all studies
Peirce recognized two branches: 'Theoretical, whose
purpose is simply and solely knowledge of God's truth;
and Practical, for the uses of Life'." (J.K. Feibleman, An Introduction to the Philosophy of Charles S.
Peirce, Cambridge, Mass., M.I.T. Press, 1969,
288).

64. A. Rosenblueth, N. Wiener, and J. Bigelow, "Behavior,
Purpose, and Teleology," Philosophy of Science, 10
(1943), 23. For this classical paper and the ensuing
discussion by Taylor, Churchman and Ackoff, and
Moore and Lewis, see Modern Systems Research for
the Behavioral Scientists, ed. W. Buckly, Chicago,
Aldine, 1968, 221-255.

65. On this, Tullock, op. cit., chaps. i; ii; Ackoff, Gupta,
and Minas, op. cit., chap. 1; also, the essays by
M. Bronfenbrenner and J.M. Buchanan in The Structure of Economic Science, ed. S.R. Krupp, Englewood
Cliffs, N.J., Prentice Hall, 1966, 5-24, 166-183;
C.W. Churchman, Prediction and Optimal Decision,
1961, chap 1; and also G. Ryle, op. cit., 25-61.

66. R.D. Luce and H. Raiffa, Games and Decisions, New
York, J. Wiley, 1957, 10.

67. O. Morgenstern, "Limits to the Uses of Mathematics
in Economics," in Mathematics and the Social Sciences,
ed. J.C. Charlesworth, Philadelphia, Am. Acad. of
Pol. and Soc. Sci., 1963, 20.

68. The sentence "Connaître: comprendre et expliquer."
is by Henri-Irenée Marrou.

69. R.D. Walker, "Research Methods--A Selected Bibliography," Journal of Education for Librarianship, 7
(1967), 211.

70. J.H. Shera, Libraries..., 162. Note also his remarks
on the scientific bases of librarianship in The Foundations of Access to Knowledge..., 24.

71. E.E. Morison, Men, Machines, and Modern Times,
Cambridge, Mass., M.I.T. Press, 1966, 84. Cf.
also J.H. Shera, "Darwin, Bacon, and Research in
Librarianship," in his Libraries..., 208-216.

72. Burton Weisbrod, as quoted in J.M. Buchanan, op. cit.,
171.

73. P.W. Bridgman, The Way Things Are, Cambridge,

Mass., Harvard University Press, 1959, 1.
74. See above, note 38.

THE NATURE OF INFORMATION SCIENCE

B. C. Vickery

Librarianship and documentation are developing into, or being absorbed by, a new discipline called "information science and technology." Carlos Cuadra, cautiously declining to define the discipline, identifies it as having "a shared deep concern with information--its generation, transformation, communication, storage, retrieval, and use." The core audience for a review publication in the field "is interested, first, in the processes by which individuals communicate with other individuals over time and distance by means of records, and second, in new computer technologies, particularly in the ways these technologies support and enhance communication (information transfer) and our understanding of communication processes."

In the same annual review, Robert Taylor points to information science and technology as pertaining to "the theoretical, experimental, and operational study of the interface between man and organized knowledge." The technology is concerned with "the development, design, and operation of information systems," the science "explicates systems and their components and is concerned with the basic sciences underlying system development: neurophysiology, linguistics, mathematics, logic, psychology, sociology, epistemology."

To my mind, these definitions or descriptions claim both too much and too little. We know very well that the discipline does not study all aspects of information--for example, laboratory research (which generates information) and academic instruction (which communicates it) are not part of the field. On the other hand, too little is claimed if the discipline is called a science only because it is concerned with other sciences such as neurophysiology and the rest. Every technology is "concerned with" a science, some (like electrical or nuclear engineering) are very much based on sciences. But this does not make the technology itself a science.

If we are to claim the emergence of an information

science, we must demonstrate that it has itself the characteristics of a science, and indicate its place in the system of
sciences.   In this paper I wish to explore our right to make
this claim.

Let us first remind ourselves of the characteristic
features of those bodies of knowledge that are considered to
be sciences.   First, like all human thinking, science uses
concepts--for classes of entity (e.g., animal, molecule), for
qualities (e.g., vertebrate, gaseous), and for classes of
process (e.g., reproduction, diffusion).   Second, these concepts are often variables, that can exist in more than one
state (e.g., the different types of animal or molecule).   The
states of a variable may simply differ among themselves
(e.g., an element is either a metal or a non-metal), or it
may be possible to arrange them on a scale (e.g., gas, liquid, solid) or in a quantitative series (e.g., densities).

Third, each science amasses a large number of reliably established descriptive statements linking entities, qualities and processes.   These start as qualitative statements
about individual entities and processes (e.g., nitrogen is a
colorless gas, the specific gravity of lead is 11, the gesta-
tion period for humans is nine months), and are generalized
to statements about classes of entity and process (e.g., all
gases can be condensed into liquids, all mammals are vivip-
arous).   Based upon these statements, entities may be arranged in a structured hierarchy (e.g., a biological classification, the periodic table of chemical elements).   Fourth, the
descriptive statements shade into relational propositions concerning interactions between concepts (e.g., the process of
lowering the temperature of a chemical entity results in a
change of quality successively from gaseous to liquid to solid).

Fifth--and this is accepted as the real hallmark of
science--the concepts, statements, and propositions are woven into a postulational system, a deductive hierarchy in
which certain broad propositions are taken as axiomatic, and
the rest of the system is derived from them.   The axiomatic
basis may consist of firmly established propositions, or of
propositions concerning hypothetical entities (as in the initial
stages of the atomic theory).

Sixth, such postulational systems or theories are constantly being tested by their ability (a) to incorporate and explain new propositions and (b) to predict new propositions

whose validity is then sought for and established.   Finally,
to derive descriptions and relations, and to test predictions,
each science builds up a set of methods and tools, experimental and mental procedures.

Not every field of knowledge accepted as a science
can display the whole range of characteristics briefly noted
above.   In particular, the social sciences have little in the
way of theory from which testable predictions can be made--
in this field, says W. J. H. Sprott, "theory is a specialist
study to which actual research makes only incidental contributions, while the research itself is to a very large extent carried on without reference to theory, finding its validation at
the court of sophisticated common sense."   Consequently, social concepts are ill-defined, few qualities are quantifiable,
much research is concerned only with fact-finding and establishing descriptive statements, and the range of relational
propositions is still limited.

The reasons for this underdevelopment of the social
sciences are well known.   The field of study is so wide and
varied, relative to the research resources devoted to it; research is necessarily restricted to accessible areas--we
know more about students than about engineers because the
former are so much more accessible to investigators; and
research often (and rightly) has the practical aim of providing guidance on which policy decisions can be based.   The
net result is a widely dispersed and unintegrated medley of
empirical investigations.   To this must be added the difficulties of social research--the complexity of social life, our
inability to isolate variables for investigation, the rare occasions on which confirmatory experiments can be undertaken,
and the fact that an investigation into human behavior may
itself change that behavior.

A fully-fledged science has all the characteristics
noted earlier.   But a discipline can be recognized as becoming scientific if it begins to display them.   Our task must
be to examine the discipline called information science to
see if its characteristics justify the name.

The first concept that needs examination is the name
itself--can it be defined so as to point to a relatively self-
contained field of knowledge that we can conceive as capable
of being organized, one day, into a postulational system ?

If one thing is clear from the descriptions and definitions provided by Cuadra and Taylor, it is that our field is concerned with human interaction ("the processes by which individuals communicate"; "the interface between man and organized knowledge"). But we are not concerned with all types of communication. Russel Ackoff suggests three types, distinguished according to purpose: to inform, to instruct, and to motivate (persuade); we might perhaps add a fourth--to amuse (entertain). The first two are both concerned with altering the receiver's concepts, the others with changing his preferences or feelings.

The emerging discipline of information science does not study communication to motivate or amuse, and communicating to instruct (education) is only of marginal interest. Although instructional communication is a closely related field, that may for certain purposes be combined with ours, yet the center of our study is informative communication. Librarianship and documentation have been traditionally concerned with informative communication that, as Cuadra puts it, takes place "over time and distance by means of records." However, we know very well that not all information transfer is via records--a great part of it is personal, face-to-face--and a new science would be unwise to restrict its scope to documentary transfer.

An act of communication has been analysed by Yehoshua Bar-Hillel into the following technical stages, which I have expanded at each end:

G: the operation of formulating a new concept, statement, proposition, or postulate in the natural language of the information source
F: the operation of putting natural language into a standardized, functional form
C: the operation of encoding the functional language into a symbol sequence
S: the operation of transforming a symbol into a signal sequence
R: the operation of transmitting--and, in the process, perhaps distorting--a signal sequence
S*: the operation of transforming a signal sequence into a symbol sequence
C*: the operation of decoding a symbol sequence into functional language
F*: the operation of putting functional language into natural form
U: the operation of using the new concept, statement,

proposition, or postulate in some further human action.

The middle operation--R, transmission--is a physical one, and involves technology. Transmission by telecommunication involves electrotechnology, documentary transmission involves printing technology, transmission mediated by retrieval operations may involve computer technology, and so on. The signals into which and from which symbols are transformed, in operations S and S*, are types of machine code, and their study is again a matter for communication technology. But the symbols encoded and decoded in operations C and C* are for human use--examples are any form of written script, telegraphese or notation. Operations F and F* involve the standardization of language. Operation G concerns the manner in which information is generated by human interaction with the environment, and U concerns the use of information in the interaction--and both these therefore involve both (a) the nature of human cognition and (b) the subject fields of the information transferred.

Now it cannot be doubted that information technology must be concerned with all these operations. We cannot develop, design and operate an effective information system without taking into account the nature of the subject field, the ways in which information is generated and used, its standard representation and symbolization, and signal transmission. Consequently, information technology will lean on any science that contributes to any of these operations--and it is for this reason that Taylor mentions such sciences as neurophysiology, linguistics, mathematics, logic, psychology, and epistemology.

However, the question I am asking here is whether there is an independent information science, making a contribution to information technology that is distinct from the contributions of linguistics, logic and the rest. Our analysis of the single act of communication has revealed one field to which librarianship and documentation have made distinctive contributions--in operations F, the use of standardized functional language, and C, its encoding in symbol sequences. But we must still ask, is this part of a wider science?

In repeating, just above, Taylor's list of underlying sciences, I deliberately omitted sociology, for it is in looking at informative communication as a social act, rather than just a technical one, that we may find a clue to its scientific

status.   Information transfer only takes place if information
is both transmitted and received.   Even in a single act, both
transmitter and receiver must be active, the one verbalizing
and encoding, the other decoding and understanding.   When
we look at information transfer as a whole, we see both
sides engaged in search--sources of information seeking potential users, users seeking potential sources.   This interactive process occurs in all forms of communication--whether
to inform, instruct, persuade, or entertain.   The search for
an audience is more marked in persuasive communication
(publicity, propaganda).   In informative communication, the
search for a source is equally prominent.

The search for an audience by primary information
sources takes the form of spreading the information abroad
in multiple copies; intermediary sources receive this information, and spread it still further; both primary and intermediary sources also spread abroad secondary guides--keys,
clues or leads to the existence of information.   In scientific
documentation, for example, we have the pattern shown in
Figure 1.

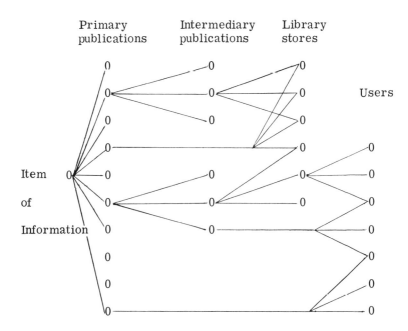

Figure 1.

In this Figure, primary publications are articles, reports, patents, and so on; intermediary are textbooks, handbooks, encyclopedias, and so on; secondary are indexes, abstracts, bibliographies, reviews, catalogs, and so on. The multiple links illustrate the spreading abroad of multiple copies in search of users.

The whole pattern can be reversed to show the search for a source: see Figure 2. The user seeks through many libraries, secondary guides, and intermediary and primary publications for needed information.

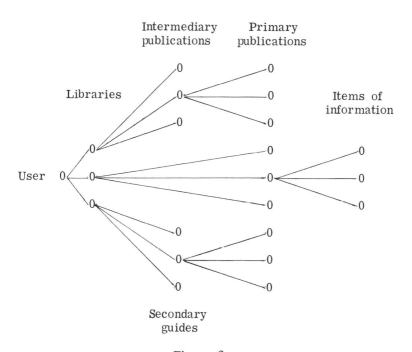

Figure 2.

We can now, perhaps, attempt a definition of the field in which information science lies. It is concerned with that aspect of human communication the purpose of which is to inform; which is rarely a single act, direct from source to receiver, but is usually mediated, a chain of acts through intermediary sources; and which involves search activities by all parties concerned. The technical aspects of commu-

nication are, as we have seen, largely though not entirely
based on other sciences. Information science is also concerned with the social aspect of this field of communication.

A fairly persistent search in sociological texts over
the last few years reveals only modest contributions to the
scientific understanding of informative communication. Strip-
ping the process down to its simplest terms, H. D. Lasswell
recognizes five key aspects to communication: who, says
what, in which channel, to whom, with what effect. These
aspects can be rephrased as the concepts of source, message, channel or medium, receiver, and response. All the
factors that can interfere with or distort information transfer
are classed as noise, and the attempt to allow for this leads
to repetition of content or redundancy. Another variable is
direction of transfer: it can be one-way, from A to B, or
interactive, with feedback from B to A. All communication
takes place within a given environment, the main types recognized being the small group, the organization, and the
community. The receiver has certain predispositions, prior
information, attitudes--in sum, a certain orientation.

An inventory of scientific findings in the field of human behavior, compiled by Berelson and Steiner, cites some
descriptive statements and relational propositions linking
these concepts. For example, one-way communication is
faster than interactive, but less accurate, the information
being more easily distorted. Orientation affects what information is received--attention is selective, people receive
more readily communications on subjects in which they are
interested. In particular, anticipating a subsequent use for
information increases receptivity. Information received ac-
cidentally, rather than deliberately sought, is more liable
to be distorted.

Within a small group, the volume of communication
will vary with the rank of the member: it will be greater
between equals and from higher to lower rank, less from
lower to higher. In total, high-ranking members interact
more than low. Communication increases with physical proximity. The communication structure of a group affects its
performance--centralized communication makes for efficiency
on a task requiring coordination of individual contributions,
but has a greater chance of falling into errors and less
chance of correcting them.

Scientific findings on communication within organiza-

tions have been reviewed by March and Simon. Any activity
(individual or organizational) can usually be traced back to
an environmental stimulus, that may be the receipt of some
information. There are two broad kinds of response to
stimuli. At one extreme, the evoked response has previously
been learned and routinized into a "program." At the other
extreme, a stimulus evokes problem-solving activity to develop an appropriate programatic response. Problem-solving
generally involves search, that may be (a) physical--e.g.,
finding correspondence in a file, (b) perceptual--e.g., scanning a journal for relevant articles, (c) cognitive--e.g., using associative processes to locate relevant information in
the memory.

    The "focus of attention" or orientation of the receiver
is itself influenced by several factors--by the "span of attention," or range of communication channels to which attention
is paid; by the "focus of information," or range of content
in which the receiver is interested; and by the communication
structure of the organization. The span of attention is itself
influenced by this structure (what channels are available to
the receiver) and by "time pressure," and the focus of information is affected by the receiver's work activity and by his
professional specialization. We get a chain of influence relations:

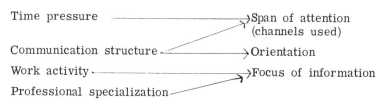

Time pressure ————————————→Span of attention
                                   (channels used)

Communication structure ————————→Orientation

Work activity ————————————→Focus of information

Professional specialization

    Information received by an organization does not get
transmitted unchanged--it is condensed, summarized, standardized, classed; in a word, categorized. The more that
this takes place--the more that information is standardized,
represented in one of a small number of categories--the
more easily will it be related to a routinized program, and
the less will it be seen as novel, giving rise to problem-
solving and search. Categorization takes place by the representation of information in an organization's own technical
vocabulary and classification scheme. The more complex
the data received, and the less adequate the organization's
language, the closer to the original source will categorization take place, and the greater will be the degree of sum-

marization. When categorization and the use of a routine
program is not possible, a problem may be recognized, and
a search activity then begins. The initial search is through
an organization's collective memory for possible programs
to handle the novel information. Both the rate of problem-
solving and the type of solution found will thus be influenced
by the communication structure of the organization.

Studies on the diffusion of information through a com-
munity--as signaled by the acceptance of practical innovations
--have been reviewed by Everett Rogers. He distinguishes
five stages of the acceptance process--awareness, interest,
evaluation, trial, adoption. Information sources are divided
according to proximity into cosmopolitan and local, and according to channel into impersonal and personal. Cosmopolitan sources are most important at the awareness stage, local sources at evaluation. Personal sources are most important at the evaluation stage. The rate of adoption is influenced by the content of the innovation--in particular, by
its complexity and communicability.

This brief look at some results of sociological research indicates that not many relational propositions have
yet been established in this field, but a number of useful
concepts have been developed. We will see these reappearing
in studies undertaken by those engaged in information work.

A good many such studies of (mainly scientific and
technical) information transfer have been carried out during
the last 20 years (conveniently summarized by William Paisley
and by Herbert Menzel). Several dozen concepts--including
or derived from those mentioned above--have been examined
as potentially useful variables in exploring aspects of informative communication. A summary of the concepts used is
presented in the Appendix: characteristics of the information
environment, the receiver, the message, the channel, and
the source.

Evidence has been obtained giving some support to the
following relational propositions. Each relation has been established only in one or a few disparate environments, and
rarely has the observed variation been shown to be statisti-
cally significant. Nevertheless, we can accept them cautiously as probably established.

As far as the receiver is concerned:

1. the volume of search (concept B9), measured in various ways, is related to:
    A1 - the nature of the institution in which he works
    A3 - the size of his work-team
    A4 - the duration of his work project
    A5 - his rank in the institution
    B1 - his age
    B2 - his education
    B4 - the nature of his job
    B5 - the subject field of his job
    D3 - the bibliographic form of medium used
2. his search purpose (B10), distinguished in various ways, is related to:
    A1 - the nature of the institution in which he works
    A5 - his rank
    A6 - the communication structure of his institution
    B4 - the nature of his job
    C3 - the message type sought
    D3 - the bibliographic form of medium used
3. his subject scan (B6), or degree of concentration on his "own field," is related to:
    A5 - his rank
    A6 - the communication structure of his institution
    B4 - the nature of his job
    B5 - the subject field of his job
    C3 - the message type sought

    As for messages:

4. the message type sought (C3) is related to:
    A1 - the nature of the institution in which the receiver works
    A5 - his rank
    B4 - the nature of his job
    B5 - the subject field of his job
    B12 - the state his research has reached
    C1 - the subject field of the message
5. the age of message used (C2) is related to:
    A1 - the nature of the institution in which the receiver works
    C1 - the subject field of the message
    C3 - its type
    D32 - the form of secondary medium used

    As for channels used:

6. the type of channel (personal/impersonal, D1) is related to:

A1 - the nature of the institution in which the receiver
      works
A6 - the communication structure of the institution
B1 - the receiver's age
B4 - the nature of his job
B14 - the allowable time for search
C3 - the message type sought
7. the form of primary medium used (D31) is related to:
A1 - the nature of the institution in which the receiver
      works
B4 - the nature of his job
B5 - its subject field
B10 - his search purpose
C3 - the message type sought
D32 - the secondary medium used
8. the form of secondary medium used (D32) is related to:
A1 - the nature of the institution in which the receiver
      works
A5 - his rank
B4 - the nature of his job
B10 - his search purpose
C3 - the type of message sought
9. the language of the channel (D8) is related to:
B3 - the linguistic ability of the receiver

Work has also been done on the success of the search,
variously measured (e.g., by Cyril Cleverdon, Margaret
Slater, John Martyn). It is related to:

A1 - the nature of the institution in which the receiver
      works
B4 - the nature of his job
C5 - characteristics of the index record
D32 - the secondary medium used

Relations such as these make an obvious contribution
to information technology. Even if some of them do little
more than confirm common observation, they may help to
guide the design of information services. For example,
from the relations shown in 1, above, we can predict that the
highest volume of search is likely to be undertaken by the
older, more highly qualified pure scientist, of a medium-
high rank in his organization (rather than high or low), working on a long-term project in a team of six to eight (rather
than smaller or larger). In contrast, the least search is
likely to be undertaken by the younger, less qualified applied
scientist, of low rank, working on a short-term project in a
team of two to four.

The concepts used in this example are all relatively well defined and scalar--ages, qualifications, ranks, project durations, and team sizes can each be arranged in a sequence. But the predictive value of many relations is lessened, or even annulled, because there is no agreement as to the breakdown of the classes used, and because the entities within a class cannot be arranged on a scale. Examples of this are the concepts A1 (e.g., type of industry), A6 (communication structure), B4 (nature of job), B5, C1, D76 (all subject field), B10 (search purpose), B11 (purposiveness of search), C3 (message type), and D3 (bibliographic form).

The effect of these deficiencies may be illustrated by Table 1 relating message-type (C3) to primary channel used (D1 and D31), from a survey of informative communication among mechanical engineers that was carried out by Wood and Hamilton (numbers are percentages of information received).

TABLE 1

Channel

Message type	Oral	Books	Science journals	Commercial journals	Advertisements Brochures
Competitive products	22.0	0.7	7.4	43.2	22.2
Improvements in technical performance	20.4	6.6	32.2	29.6	6.4
New technical ideas	15.5	3.2	39.0	29.8	8.1

We can see that, among U.K. mechanical engineers, commercial journals were most used for information on competitive products, science journals for improvements in performance and for new ideas. But suppose we want to predict the use of patents for information on improvements, or the use of books for information on mathematical techniques? The tabulation is no help, because data on patents and math-

ematical techniques have not been collected, and because it
is not possible to interpolate either of these entities in a
scalar arrangement of channels or message types.

In short, if the relational propositions established by
research studies are to have real predictive value, then (a)
agreement must be reached on the range of entities to be included within each class concept, and either (b) the full range
must be included in each study made, or (c) if possible, the
entities must be arranged in an agreed scale into which inter-
polation can be made.

The main relations set out in this section, together
with a few other relations reported in the previous section,
are summarized in Table 2.

The subject of information science is informative communication, usually mediated and involving search on the part
of both sources and receivers. Information received can
lead to the operation of a routinized program, or to problem-solving activities. There are thus two forms of informative communication--the transfer of routine information; and
the transfer of new information.

Traditionally, the first form has been studied mostly
as an aspect of management and administration, the second
as the province of the information worker. It is true that
the information technologist is beginning to be interested in
the first form. With the coming prospect of mechanizing
large libraries, the flow of routine information (concerning
document input, output, and processing) is being considered
by information workers. There may be a case for regarding
both forms as part of the same discipline, but I prefer the
present practice of restricting the field of information science to the communication of new information.

This field can be viewed as a system--sketched in the
briefest outline in diagrams earlier in this paper. From
many sources, many messages are transferred, via many
channels, to many intermediaries, and thence to many receivers. In order to optimize this system, information technology needs to understand the following:

(a) the structure of the system in detail--for examples,
at different levels, see Carter and others, Orr, and
Murdock and Liston.
(b) a quantification of the system--how much information

TABLE 2.

| | | Factor Influenced | | | | | |
Influencing Factor	B10: search purpose	B6: subject scan	C3: message type	B9: volume of search	D1: channel type	D31: primary medium	D32: secondary medium
A1: institution	X		X	X	X	X	X
A6: communication structure	X	X			X	X	X
A5: receiver rank	X	X	X	X			X
B4: receiver job	X	X	X	X	X	X	X
B5: subject of job		X	X	X		X	
B12: stage of job			X				
C3: message type	X	X			X	X	X
D32: secondary medium						X	
A4, B14: time pressure					X		

of different kinds flows through each channel and at
what rates.

(c) what variable factors affect the volumes and rates
of information transfer.

(d) how the volume and rate of information transfer affect different types of receiver.

Understanding these, the information technologist can
plan to manipulate the system to give an optimum service to
users. What demands does he make of the information scientist?

The information technologist cannot manipulate any
and every variable in the system. Let us look at those
listed in the Appendix. In section A, only A6, the communication structure of the institution, can be regarded as ma-
nipulable, and even here we can only alter part of the formal
communication structure--much of it is inherent in the general organizational structure--and we can have only a minor
influence on informal communication. In section B, we may
hope to modify B2, receiver education (e.g., by training in
information search). In section C, we can alter the extent
and characteristics of messages. In section D, the information technologist can really come into his own, to manipulate
the directness, bibliographic form, characteristics and language of channels.

Such manipulations will affect the behavior of receiv-
ers--in particular, their subject scan (B6), volume of search
activity (B9), search purpose (B10), and search purposiveness (B11)--and of course, will effect search success. The
technologist needs criteria for the effectiveness of an information system, and for the efficiency with which a given
level of effectiveness is achieved. He needs to learn three
things from the information scientist:

(1) Of the variables that he cannot manipulate, which
are the most important? In the last section the most frequently mentioned influencing variables are the nature of the
institution in which the receiver works, his rank, the nature
of his job, and its subject field. These influences need to
be more precisely established so that a series of relatively
distinct "information environments" can be defined.

(2) How do the variables that he can manipulate affect receiver behavior in each such environment? The effects of variations in communication structure (that may include variations in the volume of search by the source), in

message extent and characteristics, and in channels, need more investigation.

(3) How is receiver behavior related to the effectiveness of informative communication? This is the nub of the whole problem, for unless it can be stated, we cannot demonstrate that any change in the system is an improvement. It is the most difficult question, but the most necessary to answer.

Appendix

The concepts have largely been extracted from the surveys by Herbert Menzel and by William Paisley. Other specific sources are mentioned below.

A. Environment. At least seven aspects of the information environment have been used:

(A1) Nature of the institution at which the receiver works. The most frequent breakdown is academic /industrial. Wood and Hamilton, in the United Kingdom, have used a more detailed breakdown, distinguishing between private and nationalized industry, between university and college, and adding other types of research establishment; and have also analyzed by type of industry (metals, mining, aircraft, etc.)

(A2) Size of the institution, in terms of employees.

(A3) Size of the team in which the receiver is working (2 to 4/6 to 8/9 to 11).

(A4) Duration of the project on which the receiver is working (1 to 5 days/6 to 22/22 to 132/over).

(A5) Rank of the receiver within the institution. This may be broken down into senior/junior; high/medium high/medium low/low; supervisors/professionals/assistants.

(A6) Communication structure of the institution--e.g., existence of a library, circulation of periodicals, of bulletins (Wood and Hamilton).

(A7) Nationality of the receiver.

B. Receiver. Many more characteristics of the receiver have been used in analysis.

(B1) Age.

(B2)   Education--e.g., higher degree/first degree/tech-
        nical qualification/none; also subject of qualifica-
        tion.

(B3)   Linguistic ability.

(B4)   Nature of job, work activity--e.g., management/
        research/production supervision. Wood and Ham-
        ilton break down jobs into general management/
        engineering/research/development/production/de-
        sign/testing/sales/maintenance/teaching. Berul
        uses detailed science or engineering/technical
        evaluation/technical administration. Another
        broad breakdown is pure/applied.

(B5)   Subject field of job. Mote has recognized three
        types of subject, according to degree of develop-
        ment, organization and definition.

(B6)   Subject scan of the receiver (degree of concentra-
        tion on "own field"), focus of information.

(B7)   Length of experience in the job (under 1 year/
        1 to 5/over).

(B8)   Scientific type. Hagstrom has attempted a typol-
        ogy--scientific statesmen/highly involved leaders/
        informal leaders/student-oriented leaders/student-
        oriented scientists/intradepartmentally-oriented
        scientists/productive isolates/nonproductive iso-
        lates/marginal scientists.

(B9)   Volume of search activity-inquiries per month,
        reading hours per week, papers read per week,
        journals seen regularly.

(B10)   Purpose of search. This topic has been reviewed
        by Menzel (Vol. 1, Chapter II B). Breakdowns
        used have been for publication, lecturing or teach-
        ing/research/transmittal to a colleague/general
        interest; general information/specific interest;
        current awareness/back search; current aware-
        ness/everyday information/exhaustive search.
        Menzel proposes more purposes including:
        seeking answers to specific questions/keeping
        abreast of current developments/brushing up/
        certifying the reliability of a source/broadening
        the area of attention/assessing position of a
        research topic.

(B11)   Purposiveness of search--Rosenbloom and Wolek
        distinguish between information obtained because
        deliberately sought/because provided by source
        knowing receiver's interest/because found acci-
        dentally while searching for something else/be-
        cause found during general current or retrospec-
        tive search.

(B12)   Research stage.   Egan and Henkle suggest that
        information search will be affected by the research
        stage reached--perception of a problem/definition
        of problem/formulation of hypothesis/choice of
        method/choice of techniques/search for data/
        drawing of conclusions/discussion of consequences.

(B13)   Acceptance stage.   Rogers finds information trans-
        fer to vary with the stage of acceptance of an in-
        novation--awareness/interest/evaluation/trial/
        adoption.

(B14)   Allowable time for search--no limit/under 1 day/
        under 1 week/under 1 month/over.

C.   Message.   Several features of the message have
been considered as variables.

(C1)   Subject field.

(C2)   Date of publication.

(C3)   Type of message.   Breakdowns used include the-
        oretical statements/results and data/methods and
        procedures; account of apparatus/standard or
        specification/physical or chemical constant/meth-
        od of procedure/theory.   Wood and Hamilton dis-
        tinguish between information on competitive prod-
        uct/improvement in technical performance/new
        idea, and Berul between concept/cost and funding/
        technique, process, procedure/mathematical aid
        or formula/performance, characteristics, speci-
        fication/raw data/technical status.

(C4)   Extent of message--full text/summary (abstract)/
        extract (data)/index record.

(C5)   Characteristics of index records have been ana-
        lyzed: (C51) Nature of vocabulary used, (C52)
        Syntactic devices used, (C53) Number of search
        keys per record.

D.   Channel.   Various ways of analyzing channels
have been developed.

(D1)   Type of channel--personal (oral, correspondence)/
        impersonal media (documentary).

(D2)   Directness of channel--distinguishing between pri-
        mary (carrying an information message) and sec-
        ondary (carrying a lead, clue or key to informa-
        tion).

(D3)   Bibliographic form of impersonal media including
        (D31) forms of primary media--e.g., book/jour-
        nal/report/patent, and (D32) forms of secondary
        media--e.g., abstracts journal/index/catalogue/
        bibliography/review.

(D4)   Purpose--any medium may be designed to meet a
        special search requirement, such as those listed
        in (B10).

(D5)   Sections of journal--Wood and Hamilton list pro-
        fessional news/editorial comment/review of prog-
        ress/historical article/summary of original paper/
        correspondence/original research report/adver-
        tisement/design feature/operational article/mate-
        rials article/new plant, equipment, product/train-
        ing and education/situations vacant. This mixture
        includes message types (C3) and extents (C4).

(D6)   Form of personal channel--Rosenbloom and Wolek
        distinguish between engineer or scientist in indus-
        trial institutions of receiver/nontechnical employee
        in institution/engineer or scientist from another
        institution/sales representative of another institu-
        tion/employee of a university/employee of govern-
        ment agency.

(D7)   Characteristics of secondary media, such as (D71)
        number of index records, (D72) growth rate of
        records file, (D73) mode of file organization,
        (D74) size of index vocabulary, (D75) growth rate
        of vocabulary, (D76) subject field, (D77) storage
        medium, etc.--see NSF surveys.

(D8)   Language of medium.

        E. Source. The ultimate source of information could
be analyzed in the same way as receivers, but this has rarely been attempted. Institutional sources are recognized by
Wood and Hamilton: government department/research organ-
ization/professional society/consultant/private industry/na-
tionalized industry/university, college/local authority.

Notes

Ackoff, R. "Systems, Organizations and Interdisciplinary
        Research." General Systems, 5 (1960), 6.
Bar-Hillel, Y. Language and Communication. Cambridge,
        Mass., Addison Wesley, 1964.
Berelson, B., and Steiner, G.A. Human Behavior. New

York, Harcourt Brace, 1964.

Berul, L. H., et. al. DOD User Needs Study, phase 1. Auerbach Corporation, 1965.

Carter, L. F., et. al. National Document-Handling Systems for Science and Technology. New York, Wiley, 1967.

Cleverdon, C. W., et. al. Reports from Aslib Cranfield Projects during 1960-67.

Cuadra, C. A., in Annual Review of Information Science and Technology, vol. 1. New York, Interscience, 1966.

Egan, M., and Henkle, H. H. "Ways and Means in Which Research Workers, Executives and Others Use Information." Documentation in Action. J. H. Shera, et. al. New York, Reinhold, 1956.

Hagstrom, W. The Scientific Community. New York, Basic Books, 1965.

Lasswell, H. D., in The Communication of Ideas. Edited by L. Bryson. New York, Harper, 1948.

March, J. G. and Simon, H. A. Organizations. New York, Wiley, 1958.

Martyn, J. Report of an Investigation on Literature Searching by Research Scientists. London, Aslib, 1964.

Martyn, J., and Slater, M. "Tests on Abstracts Journals." Journal of Documentation, 20 (1964), 212-35 and 23 (1967), 45-70.

Menzel, H., et. al. Review of Studies in the Flow of Information among Scientists. New York, Columbia University, Bureau of Applied Social Research, 1960.

Mote, L. J. B. "Reasons for the Variations in the Information Needs of Scientists." Journal of Documentation, 18 (1962), 169-75.

Murdock, J. W., and Liston, D. M. "A General Model of Information Transfer," American Documentation, 18 (1967), 197-208.

National Science Foundation. Nonconventional Scientific and Technical Information Systems in Current Use. No. 4, 1966.

Orr, R. H., et. al. "The Biomedical Information Complex Viewed as a System." Federation Proceedings, 23 (1964), 1133-45.

Paisley, W. J. The Flow of (Behavioral) Science Information. Stanford, Calif., Stanford University, Institute for Communication Research, 1965.

Rogers, E. M. Diffusion of Innovations. New York, Free Press, 1962.

Rosenbloom, R. S., and Wolek, F. W. Studies of the Flow of Technical Information. Cambridge, Mass., Harvard University Press, 1966.

Slater, M.   Technical Libraries: Users and Their Demands.
          London, Aslib, 1964.
Sprott, W. J. H.   Science and Social Action.   London, Watts,
          1954
Taylor, R. S. , in Annual Review of Information Science and
          Technology, vol. 1.   New York, Interscience, 1966.
Vickery, B. C.   "The Present State of Research into the
          Communication of Information."   Aslib Proceedings,
          16 (1964), 79-88.
Wood, D. N. , and Hamilton, D. R. L.   The Information Re-
          quirements of Mechanical Engineers.   London, Library
          Association, 1967.

Methods used in information science have mainly been
taken from social survey and operations research--see M. B.
Line, Library Surveys (London, Bingley, 1967).   Techniques
particular to information science include the evaluation of
search success, as developed by Cleverdon and others, and
the use of citations as a measure of information diffusion,
as developed by workers such as D. J. Price.

THE CONTRIBUTION OF CLASSIFICATION TO A THEORY OF LIBRARIANSHIP

D. J. Foskett

Librarianship exhibits many of the features which contribute to the maturity of a field of study, or activity; but in one particular it makes a poor showing indeed. Few attempts at a general theory have appeared, and the effects of this lack are all around us, from the most complacent of branch librarians who serves only his committee, to the most richly funded erector of systems, procognitive and other, who solves all the problems of libraries by a masterful flick of his computer switch. No simple prescription will unravel so complex a labyrinth of false starts, blind alleys and loose ends, but here I wish to comment on two factors that have helped to bring about and exaggerate the confusion. These are, on the one hand, the absence of a philosophical approach to professional matters, and, on the other, the inevitable concomitant, a willing but foolish acquiescence in the reduction of librarianship to a technology.

Now it is demonstrably true that librarianship depends on technology; the simplest card catalog must have cards and cabinets manufactured to fine tolerances if it is to work smoothly. We may feel safe, as J.H. Shera has said, in welcoming automation without fear, and we need such assistance in the task of handling the vast quantities of information that are produced daily. (Whether all, or even most, of this "information" is worth the trouble is another question that will have to be answered some time). But even the most exciting and intricate technology is not, and can never be, an end in itself. We have always to remember that the primary motive for establishing a technology is not to provide work for machines to do, but to meet some human need.

The actual human need that libraries are supposed to meet is the need for information, and before discussing the appropriate technology, we must make clear what we mean by this. Several studies by philosophers and psychologists have appeared, but their impact on librarians and informa-

tion scientists has been small; S. R. Ranganathan's "Five
Laws of Library Science" and Shera's "Social Epistemology"
are contributions from librarians, and we can warmly welcome the reprinting of Pierce Butler's Introduction to Library Science, which doubtless helped to formulate Shera's
views.   But the fundamental issues raised by these writers
have hardly received the attention they deserve, and all too
often nowadays what passes for theory is no more than a
facile manipulation of mathematical and other symbols without
any truly general significance.

Man needs information in order to cope with his en-
vironment--a trite enough remark, which no one would dis-
pute; so much so, in fact, that unless we say what it means,
it has hardly any meaning at all.   I do not mean simply the
mastering of nature to the extent that we can control our
physical well being by providing food, warmth and shelter;
I do not even mean the improvement of such control to provide seaside holiday resorts, motor cars to get to them,
roads, petrol, yachts and all the other household gods of this
century.   Man is what he is, and distinct from the apes, because he has developed a mind that can reason about the environment, make abstractions, and predict the course of
events.   He does not have to be perpetually surprised by
what the passage of time brings, he can anticipate and prepare for events.   As J. Bronowski has said, Man has the
unique capacity for constantly enlarging his own "self" by
integrating his experiences into it through the use of the
imagination, "that is, the human faculty of operating in the
mind with images of things which are not present to the
senses."   He has also, over the centuries, learned to put a
value on things, and to arrive at the concept of "desirable"
courses of action.   Not all agree on the desirability of all
courses of action, but Man has even been able to deal with
this by constructing rules and laws for regulating his own
behavior.   There has developed a social sense, a public acceptance of certain opinions and practices, and the purpose
of this is to give a quality to life, as Whitehead remarked,
beyond the mere fact of life.   One aspect of this quality is
that it widens the gap between Man and the apes, by improving the scope and refinement of the mind through education--
education conceived in the sense of R. S. Peters, as "initiation" into a public tradition, a body of knowledge and code
of conduct hammered out and elaborated over the centuries,
a process which Pierce Butler called "the social accumulation of knowledge."   Man has been able to do this because
he has learned to exercise control over communication, and

the tradition can be handed on efficiently and economically.
Each child does not have to learn everything by experience,
like the young animal; and thanks to technological advances,
we no longer have to rely on the fortunate chance of being
able to hear the wise men relating their stories of wisdom.

By the growth of these powers, Man has acquired the
ability, not only to understand the world, but to change it for
the better.   This is, and must inevitably be, a social ambi-
tion, for it depends on public agreement on what is meant by
"the better," and public co-operation in shaping the tools
that will effect the change.   We still have a long way to go
toward a completely democratic process of obtaining this
public agreement, but at least we are not now subject to the
whims of hereditary despots.   We progress, there is a fair
measure of public agreement that we progress, and such
progress is partly due to the performance of libraries and
information services in preserving and transmitting the record of human acitivity and achievement.

Now, if we accept that the methods of making records
have often changed and will continue to change, and that the
printed book is not necessarily the last word in perfection
of form, we can agree that there is little to argue about
over the concept of preservation.   Transmission, however,
is quite another matter, not only because it involves questions of value ("Is this document worth preserving at all?"),
but also because the form of transmission, which ought to
be of paramount concern, has come to be relegated to a
quite minor position.   This does not mean that form ought
to take precedence over content; it means precisely the opposite because lack of attention to form cannot help but result in some degradation of content.   What is happening at
the moment is that technology is in danger of being used in
the wrong way, so that the form suffers and the content
along with it.   Research on information transmission now
takes the paths imposed on it by the capabilities of machines,
and not vice versa.   This is, of course, a radical departure
from the normal procedure, in which Man first decides what
he wants to do, and then fashions a tool to do it; and the
situation in information science, where the end result is determined by the tool (often designed for some other purpose),
means that the art and science have themselves been reduced to a technology.   Librarians are partly to blame, because they were slow to see the possibilities of using machines to produce desirable results, and furthermore they
were inadequately prepared to state what these desirable re-

sults were and how they should be protected.

Classification and indexing have suffered from this reductionism, and the contrast between what is and what might be can be shown by an analysis of their contribution to a theory of librarianship.

The need to increase one's store of information arises directly from the process of learning--that is, of acquiring the body of knowledge that has been socially accumulated. Those engaged in experimental research are attempting to enlarge the body of knowledge by adding their new discoveries to it, but it is not the function of a library to make discoveries, and in so far as research workers use libraries, they want access to knowledge already discovered and recorded. It is the function of a library, however, to make that access as easy as possible, and, if possible, to offer positive help to the enquirer in formulating his ideas about his work.

One's object in acquiring knowledge is to form a rational idea of the world, that is, to arrange information in an ordered and consistent system of concepts. We examine instances and phenomena, observe the relationships between them, and try to understand them by bringing them into a further relationship with what we have in our mind already. We give structure to our systems of concepts, and we try to make this structure correspond to the real relationships we are studying. We do not simply add item after item to our store of information, and leave all these items lying around in a disordered heap, "like peas in a bag," as L. S. Vygotsky put it in his seminal work on the relation between thought and language. If we did not attempt to structure our thoughts, we should be unable to form patterns of concepts and there would then be no way of relating new experiences to old, and no control over life. We should never know what to expect. The whole of science is built upon the assumption that there is pattern and order in nature, and that patterns repeat themselves so that we can construct hypotheses to account for them and to predict their recurrence. We can land objects on the moon because we know from past experiences where the moon will be when those objects reach it.

An author writes about his own experience. Whether his treatment be scientific or artistic, factual or inspirational, he tries to convey his sense of the world, or of some corner of it, so as to increase the understanding of his readers. A library collects materials on different subjects and by different authors, but it must arrange them so that the conceptual structures of the authors may be brought into relationship with those of the readers. It is simply not enough to add new documents to the collection and to leave them lying around in unrelated heaps. The arrangement of documents, and of their proxies (such as index entries), must exhibit a helpful structure if it is to play any positive role in ordering a reader's thoughts and helping him to think further. If, as the editor of a certain KWIC index remarked, there is no structure in the index because the reader is expected to have it in his head already, then the system has in fact turned its back on the notion of a positive role; it has been reduced to a mere exercise in technology, and the convenience of the reader has been sacrificed to the convenience of the machine. Means have been turned into ends.

On this view of indexing (in its widest sense) there is no future for librarianship; all those involved with records will be either custodians or machine operators. They will treat their charges either as objects to be cared for, or as marks on tallies which have to be translated into machine readable form so that the machines can make the same marks on different tallies. Neither functionary will need to concern himself with the intellectual content of the literature, and he will have no use for any system of concept co-ordination. It is also unlikely that any library user will feel disposed to regard him as of any assistance in the search for knowledge.

I do not myself hold this view, and I am certain that there will be more, not less, need for structured schemes in the information systems of the future. But what sort of schemes? The advance of the natural sciences over the last two centuries has been greatly aided by the use of hierarchic, or genus-species, classifications. One cannot make generalizations or predictions without first studying sufficient instances, but one does not have to examine every instance. Most of the foundation papers in the classificatory sciences are concerned with taxonomy: the identification of species and genera by enumerating their essential characteristics, features shared by all of the entities in a given group. Such descriptions are the necessary building blocks of a science, but they are not the whole science, which aims at describing the relations between entities as well as the entities themselves. In applying the method of generic classification to books, Melvil Dewey made the mistake of regarding subjects as objects, and of trying to fit all types of phenomena into one particular mould. Not until the 17th edition of the DC

did "Storytelling" cease to appear as a "species" of "Kinder-
garten and nursery schools."

The aim of a writer is not limited by the idea of a
universe of static entities, and by no means all writings are
mere descriptions. We must therefore revise our ideas of
classification if we are to provide an arrangement that fits
with the multiform pattern of reality as written about in documents. Modern work on learning theory and concept formation has thrown considerable light on techniques of classifying and utilizing sense data to form structured systems.
Shera drew attention to the writings of J. S. Bruner, David
Rapaport and others at the Dorking Conference in 1957, in
particular to the role of categorization as an aid to the identification and understanding of objects. In further development os some of these ideas (for example, the value of hierarchies within categories) by Wingfield, Pollack and Johnson,
among others, it has been shown that hierarchical structuring
is of particular use in ordering unfamiliar concepts--the usual situation when a reader poses an inquiry to an information
service.

At the same time, one cannot remain within the confines of one generic hierarchy. This has long been the theme
of criticisms based on "common sense," and the "Storytelling"
example above could be multiplied manifold from the older
general schemes. An experimental basis for rejecting single
hierarchies has been built up over many years by Jean Piaget,
Bärbel Inhelder and their colleagues in Geneva, who have
shown that we learn by translating sense data, given by ob-
serving and doing, into concepts of objects assigned to
classes. If we take a certain object which is round and
reddish-yellow in color, and strip off the peel, we find inside a sweet juicy edible substance, and we conclude, by
reference to past experience, that this is an orange. There
are two ways of forming a system, or class of such things.
One is by analysis (the descending method); or, the separation
of objects from a collection by identifying their specific properties; and the other is by synthesis (the ascending method);
or, the collecting together into a group of objects which have
certain properties in common. Now it soon becomes evident
that such collection and separation can be made on the basis
of more than one property, or set of properties: thus the
processes of forming concepts involve multiplicative classifications, or lattices, and not just single hierarchies. Mastery
of these processes brings the ability not only to form classes,
but also to identify the relations between objects that exist in

the real, material world--to increase understanding of that world.

The other major factor involved is, of course, language. The study of language has been transformed during this century, and the role of structure has been emphasized by such writers as de Saussure, Louis Hjelmslev, and the Russian L. S. Vygotsky. Language is a system of terms, a signalling system of which the units are not simply the words, but combinations of the words and what they refer to--"word meanings." A system of word-meanings--a language--enables us to move from "spontaneous concepts," single notions unrelated to any others, to "scientific concepts," notions with multiplicative class relations established within a structured scheme of ideas. The process of disciplining concepts into such a scheme itself aids further thinking and understanding. In so far as a writer understands what he writes, it is because he has fitted his various concepts into a system which he has grasped and can explain; it makes sense to him precisely because it corresponds to the system of real relations learned by experience. He has arrived at generalizations, he has progressed beyond instances.

Now when a writer communicates, he does more than hand on a message. A parrot, properly trained, can hand on a message, but we do not say that a parrot communicates. A message can be passed along a wire, in Morse code, but the wire does not communicate. Here lies the danger of confusing information theory with "information science." Communication means the conveying of information (a message) and of understanding (of what the message means); that is, of conveying the notions of system into the mind of the reader, building knowledge of relations into a network of entities. When a librarian sets out to organize documents in a helpful scheme, therefore, he must avoid interposing an artificial formal barrier between writer's concepts and reader's; he should try to find a scheme that can be brought into reasonable correspondence with real phenomena, because the reader is seeking to enlarge his pattern of concepts so that it corresponds more closely with reality. This is in fact the crucial operation in library and information service: helping the reader to form a match between his own conceptual scheme (which is lacking something or he would not be making the inquiry) and those of the writers who may be able to supply what is lacking. Even though they in turn may not have given complete descriptions, they may still provide what is required in a particular inquiry. The concept of relevance

enters here, and it hardly need be said that most discussions
of it so far do little more than skim the surface, mainly because those who take part are unwilling to deal in terms of
structured systems.

Now those who equate "classification" with the 19th-
century schemes of Dewey and the Library of Congress will
claim, not without justification, that such classification cannot hope to match the multi-dimensional continuum of real
phenomena. Such claims ignore completely all the advances
in the theory and practice of classification over the last forty
years, but in spite of this the view is still quite prevalent,
particularly in the United States. It mars, for example, the
otherwise valuable account given by Barbara A. Montague to
the 1964 meeting of the American Documentation Institute, in
which "classification scheme" appears to mean an alphabetical
subject index with the barest minimum of cross references.
Such a description would not be recognized by anyone who had
participated in any classification research, and it is vital for
the success of future developments that such confusions should
be cleared up.

In papers given at the 1964 Conference of the Chicago
Graduate Library School and in the issue of the Journal of
Documentation presented to Barbara Kyle, I have tried to
show how modern classification schemes based on the facet
analysis technique fashioned by Ranganathan are quite able to
produce schedules that are lattices and not simple hierarchies, and are indeed based on the same approach to knowledge
as that of the research workers in psychology and linguistics.
In working out the notion that classification should aim to be
an artificial language of ordinal numbers, Ranganathan has
introduced the concepts of modern mathematics and logic
without discarding altogether those aspects of traditional,
Aristotelian logic that have proved to be of value. This,
incidentally, is in contrast to some of the wilder contemporary critics who, because classification cannot do everything,
including original research, reject it utterly, all oblivious of
the fact that they themselves must use it frequently in their
own daily lives if they wish to survive.

Of course, there is still plenty of room for argument
on the theoretical basis of classification schemes. Ranganathan's notion that all facets of any subject may be related
to one or another of five fundamental abstract categories,
Personality, Matter, Energy, Space, and Time, has not won
universal acceptance; in the Colon Classification itself, he

does not always keep to his own rules, since some Main
Classes are first divided into "canonical" divisions, including
arithmetic, algebra, geometry in Mathematics; heat, light
and sound in Physics; logic, epistemology, ethics in Philosophy; and so on. It is easy enough to relate the sciences and
technologies to P, M, E, S, T, but not so easy in some
fields of the humanities; and Ranganathan has always preferred to postulate certain features such as the choice of
Main Classes, rather than to spend time on discussing their
derivation from any theory of knowledge. But there can be
no doubt about the importance of Ranganathan's work in clarifying the theoretical basis for classification schemes,
and although acknowledgment is rarely made to him, it is interesting to note how some of his ideas have been incorporated
into the most recent attempt to evade the issue, the "thesaurus," a term which first made its mark in the information
retrieval world around 1957, to denote the controlled vocabulary used in association with electronic sorting devices.

The original Thesaurus of English Words and Phrases
compiled by Peter Mark Roget was an attempt to classify
concepts into a series of categories based on abstract notions
like Existence, Relation, Quantity, Order, Number, and so
on; similar to but not exactly like the categories of Aristotle.
Any term with several meanings or nuances of meaning could
appear in more than one category, according to the several
groups of concepts to which it might belong. An alphabetical
index listed under each word a reference to every place in
which it appeared--as in Dewey's Relative Index to the Decimal Classification. The thesaurus comprised the analysis
into categories, to which there was an index; most modern
so-called thesauri are alphabetical lists of subject headings,
however, without such a categorical analysis, and since they
resemble the traditional subject headings lists in most, if
not all, particulars, it is hard to see what justification there
is for using the word "thesaurus." One of the most important of such lists does not call itself such: the Medical Subject Headings used in the MEDLARS scheme at the U. S. National Library of Medicine. MESH does, however, include
an analysis into categories as well as the alphabetical list,
and the practical help that this can give to a searcher can
easily be illustrated. The article "A Diabetic Detection Program at Work," Amer. Ass. Industr. Nurses, 14 (June 66)
27-8, is indexed in Index Medicus under the heading MASS
SCREENING TECHNICS but not under DIAGNOSIS, though it
would clearly be useful to a researcher on mass methods of
diagnosis. On the other hand, the article "Computer-Aided

Diagnostic Screening for 100 Common Diseases," JAMA,
197 (12 Sep 66) 901-5, is indexed under DIAGNOSIS but not
under MASS SCREENING TECHNICS, to which again it clearly relates. (An article on "Multi-Phasic Screening as a
Diagnostic Method in Preventive Medicine" is under both
headings). There are no cross-references between the two,
but a searcher would be helped by the listing in Category E1
of many related terms under DIAGNOSIS, including Mass
Screening Technics; this listing provides a guide to all the
terms that may be involved with diagnosis, including methods,
diseases, symptoms and so on. The route for the searcher
is somewhat circuitous, but it exists, thanks to the categories, and can be found without much trouble; without the
categories, however, the searcher would have no such pointer
from one of these related terms to the other.

The multiplicative classificatory approach, therefore,
can offer help to the thesaurus, not only by categorical analysis, but also by introducing system into the references to
Broader and Narrower Terms, which nearly always correspond to the hierarchies one would find within a facet. The
Related Terms are not so easy, of course, but a good start
could be made by examining the other facets of the main
class within which a term appears. Thus we might take an
extract from, say, Class J, Agriculture, in the Colon Classification:

[P] facet		[E] facet	
3	Food	7	Harvesting
37	Fruit	78	Storing
371	Apple		
372	Orange		

This could be transformed into these thesaurus entries:

Apple			Fruit (Cont.)	
BT	Fruit		RT	Harvesting
RT	Harvesting			
			Harvesting	
Food			NT	Storing
NT	Fruit		RT	Food
RT	Harvesting			
			Orange	
Fruit			BT	Fruit
BT	Food		RT	Harvesting
NT	Apple			
	Orange			

Storing
    BT   Harvesting
    RT   Food

As is obvious, the classification scheme is likely to be more economical in layout than the thesaurus, since its index entries are specific, and point to class numbers, not to other sets of words.

One thesaurus that has taken advantage of facet analysis is the Education thesaurus developed for the Educational Research Information Center of the U. S. Office of Education. A progress report from the Western Reserve University team involved with this project points out another advantage of the systematic structure. In order to test the ease of updating and modifying the system, it was applied to a different but related field, that of unemployment. Out of 1799 terms in that field, only 219 were already present in the ERIC thesaurus, but of the other 1560, 1426 were successfully inserted into the existing facets. In other words, new terms could easily be accommodated because the system's conceptual framework corresponded to a helpful ordering of the related field as well as of the original field. This emphasizes the fact that where the constructs of a classification scheme are made to match the real phenomena they represent, they will also fit in with the publicly accepted class schemes and will provide a helpful ordering of the documentation. The scheme thus makes a positive contribution to social epistemology, because, as G. A. Kelly says, "constructs are the channels along which one's mental processes run," and man's mental processes are developed by, and reflect, his unique nature as a social being.

The examples of MESH and ERIC bring to the fore a further problem. Although MESH was designed for medical literature, its list of categories covers a far wider range-- virtually the whole of knowledge, even if not in detail. Western Reserve University has proved that a faceted structure allows the scope of a specialized system to be extended without too much difficulty. But both of these systems, like most other thesauri, begin from a known field, one that purports to be bounded by stated limits. Most of the recent schemes of classification have been similarly limited. But the whole trend of modern research is away from the concept of "disciplines," or main classes, and towards a more realistic assessment of the interrelations between fields. As with MESH, the makers of special schemes invariably find that they have to go beyond the stated boundaries if they are to cope with the actual literature.

One of the main reasons for the crop of specialized schemes has been that each of them has actually been produced, not so much for a stated field as for a stated group of users. The Western Reserve University teams, indeed, have introduced the concept of User Groups into their methodology of constructing and testing. One can readily accept the validity of this, for it not only introduces a certain control over vocabulary from the start, but also defines to some extent the social purpose of the system; it is terribly hard to identify the 'general' reader and his purposes. But to concentrate on special fields and reject the idea of a general classification is both cumbersome in method and wasteful of effort, in a realm where all too little effort is available.

After several years experience of making special schemes for defined subject fields, the Classification Research Group turned its attention towards the construction of a new general scheme. In spite of some feeling of urgency, its members did not feel happy with the prospect of postulating Main Classes, because (as Ranganathan's own subsequent work shows) one can never be certain which Main Classes to postulate. Barbara Kyle's scheme for the social sciences had used facet analysis to make two long lists of personalities (individuals and groups of various kinds) and activities, but she too ran into difficulties, because some ordering of the lists was necessary and no clear-cut principles were available.

About 15 years ago, in 1957, the CRG began to discuss the theory of integrative levels as a basis for the identification and ordering of entities. The theory has appeared in several forms over the years, notably in the writings of J. K. Feibleman and Oliver Reiser, and it has become clear that it, or something very like it, now forms an important part of the theory of knowledge of many modern scientists and philosophers. Several papers have been circulated and discussed among CRG members, and the first part of the research should have been completed by the middle of 1968. An important stage in the work was marked by the presentation of a critical review by Phyllis Richmond to the Second International Study Conference on Classification Research, held at Elsinore in 1964, which provoked a valuable exchange of views.

My original attempt to formulate this theory in relation to classification dealt primarily with the classification
of entities. Supposing that, in Ranganathan's terms, we
could collect together all Personality isolates into one long
list, what principle could we use to order it? In mathematical terms, suppose we take the set of all "entities," on
what basis can we form well-ordered subsets? We wish to
demonstrate the correspondence between our constructs and
the real world which gives rise to other people's constructs:
therefore many orders, including an all-through alphabetical
order, are irrelevant. Aluminum and Altruism are not related terms, but Aluminum and Zinc are. The integrative
levels, in the Richmond modification, are groups of entities
which evolve from the simple towards the complex by an accumulation of properties and relations; at a succession of
levels, these aggregations reach new degrees of complexity
and become new wholes, with individual and unique identities.
Each whole is greater than the sum of its parts, acts as a
unit, and ceases to possess its identity if broken down again.
In other words, the process is not reversible without loss of
identity. Applying this theory to the ordering of entity terms
results in a set of groupings, beginning with fundamental
particles, proceeding through atoms and molecules to cells
and human beings; I would myself maintain that the series
could continue, with aggregations of human beings engaged in
different activities, such as the biological, producing families; the economic, producing business firms; the political,
producing states and governments; and so on. I do not anticipate any special problems in applying the series to form
a classification schedule.

If we next turn to what Ranganathan names the Energy
facet, we face two possibilities which overlap and are not
alternatives. One is to form a schedule of Energy terms
appropriate to each schedule of Entity terms, to contain
those activities (behavior, properties) characteristic of that
level of Entity. This should not be too difficult, either.
The second is to try to formulate a series of levels of Energy terms, as described, for example, by Reiser. This,
we have found a much more troublesome exercise and indeed
Reiser himself does not actually dismiss entities altogether,
since he sees the generalized notion of energy levels as represented by the increasing complexity of the structure of
matter, passing from nuclear to atomic and so on, with the
"energy spectra" correlated to the various levels of organization.

One other factor, however, suggests that the levels of energy should be further investigated. In the entity series, each level is distinguishable by the context in which its entities are discussed, and by their irrelevance in other contexts. We do not, for example, speak of the color of atoms or committees (except metaphorically); it is purposeless to speak of chemical elements in relation to voting in elections. But certain process or activity terms, such as "motion," can be seen to have the widest possible relevance, and, like Ranganathan's fundamental categories, can be identified in terms appropriate to any or every context. This suggests that it should be possible to draw up a schedule of such generalized energy terms, which would, in expressing relationships, come close to the thinking of, for instance, Ludwig von Bertalanffy in the General System Theory--"a logico-mathematical field, the subject matter of which is the formulation and deduction of those principles which are valid for 'systems' in general." Once these principles have been identified and named, they might very well form the starting point of a new general scheme of classification that would embody the results of modern scientific and philosophical thought.

Dan Bergen has already drawn attention to the importance of general systems theory for librarians, but I must emphasize that this would be a "starting-point." While we would hope, with Ernest Nagel, that "patterns of relations may be discovered that are pervasive in vast ranges of fact, so that with the help of a small number of explanatory principles an indefinitely large number of propositions about these facts can be shown to constitute a logically unified body of knowledge," yet we must guard all the time against the evil of reductionism. Nagel himself has a long discussion of the conditions under which the reduction of theories is admissible, and maintains that social organizations may be regarded as entities which cannot be explained without residue in terms of the psychology of their individual human members. In his simple but convincing paper on "Science and Reality," Michael Polanyi attacks the positivist position that "a reality underlying mathematical relations between observed facts was a metaphysical conception, without tangible content." Mathematics is a useful tool for dealing with phenomena, but it is not the phenomena themselves, contrary to much modern thinking--confused thinking which is only too manifest in some writing on information science also.

From such a starting point, we should be able to

build a scheme of terms, based on the enumeration of a series of integrated "wholes" or entities, their properties, the processes they engage in, and so on, which would be readily recognizable by experts in the different fields of knowledge. We should then explode once for all the fallacy that many experts believe in, that because "classification schemes" (meaning DC and LC) are so demonstrably unhelpful in their sequences and rules of use, there must be some special librarians' reasons for preserving them in libraries. Of course there are not.

It seems to me to be of the utmost importance that serious consideration should be given to the theoretical foundations of classification, and their implications for the design of all forms of information handling systems. It is the case that we deal in realities, partly because the literature itself deals with realities which its users hope to understand, and partly because the relation between the literature and its users is a real relation, and not reducible without loss to a set of mathematical formulae. I do not, for this very reason, advance the absurd claim that classification schemes can do everything by themselves. Any tool, even a computer, is inert until it is picked up and used. What distinguishes the tools of librarianship from the tools of engineering, though, is the fact that the raw material of a librarian is information, and this is not a series of static, limited objects, as are bars of steel. Information has to be assessed in two different contexts, that of the writer and that of the reader, and a third, neutral scheme of terms can play a unique role in setting up correspondences between the two. But the scheme will not do this by itself, any more than a computer fed only on mathematics will build a rocket. Even Baron Münchhausen does not travel to the moon on x's and y's. Moreover, it is not an unlucky accident that those who maintain that books and libraries are finished do so by writing books which they insist should be added to libraries.

Classification consists of that part of the theory of librarianship which deals with the organization of knowledge-- a basic operation in the advancement of learning. In its modern form, it relates to the philosophical and psychological foundations of human communication, and so has relevance to any subject. This includes librarianship itself. A taxonomy of librarianship might be a useful exercise, though it would provide only a partial basis; the Classification Research Group's Classification of Library Science has caused us to think very hard about the scope and terminology of the profession, but we would not propose it as a substitute for thinking. It seems clear that the force of inter-disciplinary relations affects us too; there are more important contributions to our foundations than there were, and our Russian colleagues under A.I. Mikhailov at VINITI have suggested that the whole complex of library and information studies should be given the new name of "Informatics." The acceptance of such a proposal should never be based on mere personal whim, but on a study in depth of the field, which cannot be done without adopting a classificatory approach. The importance of deciding the question can hardly be exaggerated, for the future of the professional activity depends on it. If we are to play in the future a role in human communication as important as that which librarians have played in the preservation of our cultural heritage, we shall have to reach what Nagel calls "the organization and classification of knowledge on the basis of explanatory principles that is the distinctive goal of the sciences." In seeking this goal, we have to remember above all that librarianship is not a technology, but one of the social sciences, that it is social epistemology that forms the characteristic feature of our professional philosophy. Many disciplines and techniques will be laid under contribution in constructing a theory of librarianship that can stand up, not only to the test of practical efficiency, but also to examination as a consistent body of knowledge. If our theory is to succeed in the second of these trials, it must rest securely on a proper understanding of the nature and use of classification, perhaps more than of any other aspect of the profession.

Notes

Atherton, P., ed. Classification Research. Proceedings of the Second International Study Conference. Copenhagen, Munksgaard, 1965.

Bronowski, J. The Identity of Man. London, Heinemann, 1966.

Bergen, D. "Implications of General Systems Theory for Librarianship and Higher Education." College and Research Libraries, 27 (1966), 358-388.

Butler, P. An Introduction to Library Science. 1933. Chicago, Phoenix Books, 1961.

Feibleman, J.K. "The Integrative Levels in Nature," in: Kyle, Barbara, ed., Focus on Information and Communication. London, Aslib, 1965.

Foskett, D.J. "Classification and Integrative Levels," in:

Foskett, D. J. and Palmer, B. I., The Sayers Memorial Volume. London, Library Association, 1961.

Foskett, D. J. "Language and Classification." Journal of Documentation, 21 (1965), 275-8.

Foskett, D. J. "Library Education: The Role of Classification, Indexing and Subject Analysis." Library Quarterly, 34 (1964), 362-373.

Inhelder, B. and Piaget, J. The Early Growth of Logic in the Child: Classification and Seriation. London, Routledge and Kegan Paul, 1964.

Johnson, S. C. "Hierarchical Clustering Schemes." Psychometrika, 32 (1967), 241-254.

Kelly, G. A. The Psychology of Personal Constructs. New York, W. W. Norton, 1955.

Mikhailov, A. I. "Informatics--a New Name for the Theory of Scientific Information." Scientific and Technical Information (Moscow), No. 12, 1966, 25-28.

Montague, Barbara A. "Testing, Comparison and Evaluation of Recall, Relevance, and Cost of Co-ordinate Indexing with Links and Roles." Proceedings of the American Documentation Institute Meeting 1964, vol. i, 357-367.

Nagel, E. The Structure of Science. New York, Harcourt, Brace and World, 1961.

Peters, R. S. "Education as Initiation," in: Archambault, R. D., ed., Philosophical Analysis and Education. London, Routledge and Kegan Paul, 1965.

Polanyi, Michael. "Science and Reality." British Journal for the Philosophy of Science, 18 (1967), 177-196.

Pollack, L. "Speed of Classification of Words into Superordinate Categories." Journal of Verbal Learning and Verbal Behavior, 2 (1963), 159-165.

Ranganathan, S. R. Five Laws of Library Science. 2nd ed., London, Blunt, 1957.

Ranganathan, S. R. Prolegomena to Library Classification. 3d ed., New York, Asia Publishing House, 1967.

Reiser, Oliver L. The Integration of Human Knowledge. Boston, Sargent, 1958.

Richmond, Phyllis A. "Contribution Toward a New Generalized Theory of Classification," in: Atherton, Pauline, ed., Classification Research. Copenhagen, Munksgaard, 1965.

Shera, J. H. "Automation Without Fear," in: Foskett, D. J. and Palmer, B. I., eds., The Sayers Memorial Volume. London, Library Association, 1961.

Shera, J. H. "Foundations of a Theory of Bibliography," in: Shera, J. H., Libraries and the Organization of Knowl-

edge. London, Crosby, Lockwood, 1965.
Shera, J. H. "Pattern, Structure and Conceptualization in
    Classification," in: Proceedings of the International
    Study Conference on Classification for Information Re-
    trieval. London, Aslib, 1957.
Vygotsky, L. S. Thought and Language. New York, M. I. T.
    Press, (1962), 1969.
Wingfield, Arthur. "Perceptual and Response Hierarchies in
    Object Identification." Acta Psychologika, 26 (1967),
    216-226.

REFERENTIAL CONSULTING NETWORKS*

Manfred Kochen

Who has not discovered treasure in a library? An exquisite, bewildering variety of treasures. A few come in the form of answers to riddles or urgent questions, explicitly stated or covert. Most forms take the shape of books, and traditional libraries as well as their users value the physical form alongside the content it embodies. But how can we better think of the use of libraries as analagous to treasure hunting? We discuss this question by helping to explicate "reference service" as a theoretical concept, and by seeking conditions for excellence of such service. Few of us expect libraries to help solve our most common or most urgent day to day problems. Seldom does a voter who just moved into a community, for example, think of the local librarian as his most promising source of help in evaluating the candidates or the issues in an impending election.[1] But, it is conceivable that the local reference librarian--or rather his modernized counterpart, the community's professional information-please officer, for whose existence we argue in this paper--could help the newcomer, perhaps better than any other source to which he, on his own, would think to turn. Certainly the library contains copies of at least the local newspaper which might have sketched the qualifications of the candidates and summarized the pros and cons of the issues; it might also contain more detailed readings on the issues as well as biographies.

The traditional definition of a library is: a "collection of books organized for use." But the word "use" is explained no further. To maintain a collection organized for use, the library performs three traditional functions: (a) book selection, (b) bibliographic control, (c) reference.

It is also traditional to complain that library resources are under-utilized. De Sola Pool (ref. 17, end of paper)

_____
*The author's work on this paper was partially supported by grant NSF-GN-T16.

estimated that less than one-quarter of Americans, when in
need of information, regularly use libraries. Of these reg-
ular university and college library users, the majority do
known-item searches, and less than 30% do subject searches,
according to Brooks and Kilgour (2), Lipetz and Stangl (13)
Palmer (15), and a catalog use study by us (21).   A
study directed by Swanson (20) also showed that experimental subjects recall the title or author of a book with
sufficient accuracy to locate the book through the catalog only
one quarter of the time.   Finally, even if a book is located
in the catalog--in either a known-item or a subject search--
it is likely to be found in the stacks in slightly less than
half of the cases for a number of large libraries where such
studies were made.

     It has been said that library sources are under-uti-
lized because potential users have dismal expectations.
These figures do little to help those who argue that such expectations are unjustified.   If we use libraries rarely to acquire knowledge, understanding, or wisdom when we can't
specify a book likely to help us, then we are under-utilizing
library resources even more than is traditionally supposed.

     These depressed conditions may be due to an overly
narrow and outdated conception of libraries and librarianship
rather than to poor performance of the three library functions.   Shera and Egan (5) challenged the traditional concept
of a library when they proposed that its function should be
"to maximize the effective social utilization of the graphic
records of civilization."   This redefinition is a vast step
forward, because it did not confine the librarians' responsibility to books, nor to a specific collection usually delimited
by funds and space.   Above all, it replaced the vague term
"use" by the more meaningful term "maximize the effective
social utilization."

     The Shera-Egan proposal, however, implies that if a
member of the U.S. Congress acts on an important social
issue on the basis of wrong or missing knowledge when the
correct information exists in the Library of Congress, then
the Librarian of Congress is responsible.   He should have
seen to it that the legislator was given the option of using,
not using, or misusing, relevant knowledge in the Library.

     But the Librarian can hardly be expected to share the
entire responsibility for the legislator's misuse or failure to
use such knowledge.   Misuse of relevant knowledge does not

maximize its "effective social utilization."[2]   The Librarian
is only <u>partially</u> responsible.   Perhaps the Shera-Egan definition should be revised to: "to maximize the <u>greatest potentially attainable</u> effective and efficient social <u>utilization</u> of
<u>documented knowledge</u>."   Note that we also substituted the
more abstract term "documented knowledge" for the "graphic
records of civilization," to include non-graphic embodiments
of documented -- i.e., validated -- truths, such as magnetic
tape recordings.   Note also the insertion of "and efficient"
to suggest that this is to be done with a reasonable or minimum expenditure of necessary resources; in particular, the
cost of information overload on the user due to lack of fine
selectivity is to be kept within bounds.

How can librarianship change to fulfill most effectively
the new demands of such a revised definition?   Some thought
has already been given to this question.   At a conference on
reference and information services held at Columbia University in 1966, Kilgour (9) stressed the need for a more intellectual approach to librarianship.   The development of the
"knowledge industry" has placed libraries in a much more
central and responsible position in our society, which demands recognition of new, more viable techniques in librarianship.

Because of these increased responsibilities to the
community of users, the reference function has become especially important.   Thus far, however, reference librarians
have no established definition of the scope and method of
their work.[3]   Wynar has defined reference service as "any
activity related to providing information as well as guidance
and instruction in the use of library resources (a necessary
compromise)" (25).   Unless one recognizes, however, that
"information" and "library resources" have become vastly
broader in scope, such a definition could easily be applied
to a very conservative exercise of the reference function.
The vastness and variety of resources available to the reference librarian make necessary the development and use of
a real information and referral network if libraries are to
achieve "the greatest potentially attainable effective social
utilization of documented knowledge."

In this paper we stress such an expanded scope and
depth for reference librarianship.   If mathematical library
scientists can be stimulated to explore and develop the various lines of investigations opened up by the models sketched
later in this paper, perhaps the concept of indirect referral

will come to be recognized as a very important part of any good theory of reference service.

The Reference Function

The concept of "reference" is probably the most basic in library science. Although the word "refer" has several meanings (e.g. , the librarian referred him to an encyclopedia, or to a consultant; the book referred to baseball scores; the user referred to an encyclopedia), they all involve the action of pointing, directing, "passing the buck. "

In order to perform this referral function well, the reference librarian must be a generalist. While he does not have to know where to look up the latest and most reliable measurement of the velocity of light, he should at least know whom to ask, or whom to ask for a name of someone to ask. Like an executive, he needs more to know to which source to assign the responsibility for solving a problem than to solve the problem himself.

Consider the following sample of possible information needs on the part of average people in their daily lives, at work or at home.

P1.   What is the address of the Bolger Laboratory, in the vicinity of Boston? (The client may be a doctor and, on questioning, reveal that Bolger is a drug testing lab.).

P2.   A herpaterium attendant is showing symptoms of snake poisoning, though he hasn't recently been bitten. [4] Has anyone ever published reports of delayed snake poisoning? (The client may be a local physician or the afflicted patient; he might even settle for unpublished reports or the names of experts, or the names of people who have encountered this).

P3.   We just moved into the city of Jonesville which has no local hospital, and our child seems to have heart trouble from eating too much animal fat. What kind of physician should we call? And how can I get reliable help in selecting one? (The client might wish a "non-obsolete cardiologist, hematologist or internist, " though he may not realize how to ask for or spot one.)

P4.   I need a light, strong, rust-resistant material for a toy I wish to produce and market. What should I con-

sider? (The client may be happy to learn of the existence of a materials information center, or even of
a directory which informs him of its existence.)

P5.   Mr. Green is being considered for a very responsible
public position, and I must decide whether or not to
endorse this appointment. Where can I get pertinent
information about him?

P6.   Gross sales and morale in our company have been
declining steadily since last January. What should we
do?

P7.   Lately everyone seems to be taking advantage of me
and I feel very uncomfortable with other people. It
has reached the point that I can't even show my face
to my fellow workers anymore. I need help desper-
ately.

P8.   Our university is considering increasing its investment
in computers to $10 million/year by 1972. How can
we make sure of getting an optimal return on this investment, especially so as not to aggravate our key
problems?

P9.   What would be the economic consequences of establishing and enforcing national standards in the metric
system, to be in effect by 1975?

P10.   How have the attitudes of Southern whites toward integration changed from 1900 to 1968?

Consider next the following sample of "answers" for
which the questions may have to be found, sought out, motivated:

A1.   A new serum which is extremely effective against
many kinds of snake poisoning was recently tested by
the Bolger Labs. (The author of P2 may be interested).

A2.   Dr. Jones, who has been practicing cardiology in
Jonesville for the past 30 years, was found guilty in
a malpractice suit in 1950; after one year in jail, he
returned to his practice. (The author of P3 may be
interested).

A3.   Action is urgently needed on the long-delayed discussions about U.S. arms aid for Israel.

A4.   The second law of thermodynamics implies the impos-
sibility of perpetual motion machines. (The inventor
of a perpetual motion machine ought to be interested).

A5.   Task forces in which the members' personalities are
most alike on their need to give and get affection have
higher morale and productivity than do task forces in

which the members' personalities are dissimilar in
this respect, regardless of other personality factors.
(The author of P6 may be interested).

Statements such as A1-A5 usually appear in newspapers and journals. Libraries, at best, publish a periodic
accession list of book titles, and regard anything beyond this
as the responsibility of information centers. [5]

Few users would think of using a library for an answer to P1, when they could ask a telephone operator or a
colleague to help them. While many librarians may not consider themselves responsible for helping a user with such a
problem, most librarians could with great facility find the
answers while the user is still on the telephone; if they could,
they would probably be eager to do so.

No one in the public library of the small town receiving query P2 may have the materials, the time or the expertise to do the search, but he should give the user the
telephone number of, or better yet, switch the call directly
to the nearest MEDLARS search center.

There is hardly any source to which a person can
turn with P3 except simply picking a hospital or physician
from the classified telephone directory. A person with problems like P4 or P6 would normally seek the services of a
consultant rather than a librarian; for P4 a consultant might
consult literature and look up a material with specified properties, though some librarians could do this, too. If he
cannot handle P4, and certainly for P6, the information officer could reasonably be expected to refer the client to an
appropriate consultant.

A personnel investigation such as called for in P5 is
usually started by personal contacts who know people who
know people ..., etc. The librarian does not now expect,
or is not now expected, to contribute vitally to such an investigation, but his 1980 counterpart will have the opportunity
to do so. [6]

Suppose that, in addition to "socially acceptable or
neutral" questions like P1 through P10, the information officer receives questions that lead him to suspect antisocial,
criminal, revolutionary or otherwise destructive intent by
the questioner. Of course, the information officer, as an
individual, employs his personal value system in judging these

questions and interests.   If his value system is not consistent with that of his supporters and the general social group
in which it is embedded, he is likely to be replaced, or the
information service will not remain viable.   Conflicting social groups might develop competitive information systems,
and through a natural system of checks and balances, a larger information system emerges.

This important question requires separate discussion,
which was already partly begun by H. G. Wells (23).   It
should be kept in mind that, in general, there exists more
than one referential consulting network.   This gives a user
options about where to turn first.

A person who can give a useful first lead to a patron
with a question resembling any of the above would be a most
important professional in the community.   Is it suggested
that librarians of the future be expected to discharge these
great responsibilities?   Yes, though they should perhaps, no
longer be called librarians to dispel any association with
users' and librarians' own past images of the profession.
They might be called "information officers," "general community advisors" or something like that.   To discharge such
responsibilities at a high level and standard, they would have
to be selected and educated to possess adequate qualifications,
mainly an advanced liberal arts background; they would have
prestige and pay scales comparable to those of other professional consultants in law, medicine, engineering, etc.

Just what, however, is the nature of this referential
consulting task?   How can its performance be evaluated?
What resources are necessary to perform it well?   In what
follows we try to answer the first two questions, deferring
the last to other papers.

Let us simplify our discussion by restricting the referential consultant's role entirely to question-answering.
This includes question-negotiation.   But we postpone for another study the even more significant role of helping selected
people seek the questions to which he can provide answers.
The referential consultant, henceforth denoted by R, can
draw on three main resources in answering questions:

  (I) his own understanding and memory
  (II) his auxiliary memories and means of ac-
         cess to them
  (III) his colleagues who are themselves referential
          consultants.

To fix ideas, imagine a community, such as all residents of a township on a given date, from which arises a
stream of questions of unlimited variety. Select any question from this stream at random. Call it q. Suppose that
it is forwarded to R. If q falls into R's expertise, he may
try to answer it directly, drawing on resource (I). In this
regard R acts not only as a referential consultant but as an
expert consultant. In other words, every R is also an expert consultant to some degree for some class of questions. [7]

If R cannot rely on resource (I) alone but believes
that he can find (or check) the answer with the help of resource (II), he does so. By auxiliary memories we mean
an abstraction of the resources consisting of what is now his
filing cabinet, a collection of reference books at his finger-
tips, his personal library including old notes, address books,
all kinds of directories, tests, papers, etc.; also included
is the nearest non-personal library, such as the departmental
library (in a university, research center or other organization) located within 100 yards of his office; the next larger
"regional" library (of which his departmental library may be
a branch). Indeed the entire international network of library
resources to which he has access (at least through conventional inter-library loans) is indirectly part of the resource
(II). For any particular R, the Library of Congress, of
course, can hardly be called his auxiliary memory; he shares
it with millions of others. And we are justified in calling it
an aid to memory only to the extent that he recalls enough
of the title, author, or subject-headings of a book he remem-
bers to contain the answer to q. In other words, viewing
the use of a library as an aid to memory is consonant with
a large number of uses to which libraries are put: known-
item searching for items other than those recommended by
colleagues or cited in other documents. Even the latter can
often be interpreted as an aid in recall. So, every R is to
some degree also a reference librarian as well as a literature searcher/analyst for some class of questions. It is
this use of resource (II) that we stress most in this paper.

If it takes R too long, too much effort, or if R judges
it unlikely that he will answer q with the help of resources
(I), or (II), he resorts to "buck-passing." This is most
important. It is not meant to have any negative connotation
this colloquialism may imply. It takes considerable wisdom
by R to exercise good judgment about whether and just when
he ought to refer the question to someone else. [8] Thus,
every R is also to some degree a buck-passer for some

class of questions.

We assume that no R engages in research. If the answer to q is "not known" either in the recorded literature or within the community of R's, then q may be referred to an outside community of researchers. By saying that the answer to q is known we mean that it can be looked up, recalled, retrieved--that q has previously been answered--and that it need not be deduced or inferred.

What about questions asking for advice, opinion, stimulation, education, decisions, or service, like P6? Or questions revealing (or concealing) illness, confusion, ignorance, malice, or need, like P7? Responses to such questions differ sharply from "answers" in the sense meant above. Let us suppose, as in the case of questions requiring research, that such questions are referred by any R in the community of referential consultants to someone in an outside professional community of doctors, lawyers, teachers, ministers, public servants, social workers, businessmen, etc. The important qualification required of an R is the ability to recognize when to refer a question and good judgment about where to refer it.

This means that the referential consultant is a very responsible professional. Though he may also be a specialist he must be, first and foremost, a generalist. He should be broadly and deeply educated in "advanced liberal arts," experienced in and dedicated to public service with mature, sound judgment concerning the wise use of resources (I) - (III). He need not be a scholar, researcher, innovator, teacher, nor what is now a professional librarian. He would constitute a new breed of professional, a pillar of his community, a highly valued (and paid), esteemed and essential leader of that community.

A First Mathematical Model[9] for an Idealized Referential Consulting System: A Chain Organization

Consider a community of n referential consultants. Label them R_1, R_2, ..., R_n. Suppose that the randomly selected question q always reaches R_1 first. This assumption is weakened in more refined models. To reduce verbiage, let K_i denote the event that R_i knows the answer to q, using resources (I) or (II). Let A_i denote the event that R_i produces an answer to q within a certain time after q reaches him, having used resources (I) or (II). Also, $\bar{K}_i$ and $\bar{A}_i$ stand, respectively for the events of R_i not knowing and not answering q.

Next, we characterize R_i by the following variables: a_i is the probability of K_i; $b_i = 1 - a_i = \text{Prob}(\bar{K}_i)$; p_i is the conditional probability of A_i given K_i, and

$$q_i = 1 - p_i = \text{Prob}(\bar{A}_i | K_i)$$
$$p'_i = \text{Prob}(\bar{A}_i | \bar{K}_i)$$
$$q'_i = \text{Prob}(\bar{A}_i | \bar{K}_i).$$

We characterize the system as follows: v is the utility of an acceptable answer to q, averaged over all q; c is the cost to the querist of an unacceptable[10] answer to q, averaged over all q; V is the total net utility of the system per question, averaged over all questions.

Assumption 1. $a_i = a + (i-1)e$, $i = 1, \ldots n$. If R_i does not
    answer q, he refers it to R_{i+1} for $i = 1, \ldots, n-1$.
Assumption 2. $p_i = p'_i = p$ for $i = 1, \ldots n$.
Assumption 3.   The conditional events $A_1 | K_1$, $A_2 | K_2$, $\ldots$
    $A_n | K_n$ are statistically independent.

The first assumption implies a linear chain organization shown in figure 1.

$$q \longrightarrow \boxed{R_1} \longrightarrow \boxed{R_2} \longrightarrow \boxed{R_3} \longrightarrow \cdots \longrightarrow \boxed{R_n}$$

Figure 1.   A Chain Network

If R_1 "passes the buck," it is only to R_2, who is more likely by amount e to know the answer to q than is R_1. Similarly, R_2 passes the buck to R_3, and R_n, the smartest of the group, is at the end of the line.

	A_i	$\bar{A}_i$
K_i	P_i	$1 - p_i$
$\bar{K}_i$	$1 - p'_i$	p'_i

Figure 2.   The Contingency Table.
"Knowing" and "Responding" to Questions

The assumption is best seen in the contingency table of fig. 2. The top left cell is the event that R_i answers q {using resources (I) and (II)}, given that he "knows" the answer.[11] Its probability should be fairly high, .90 perhaps. The bottom right cell is the event that R_i doesn't answer q, given that he doesn't know the answer. Its probability should also be quite high, and setting it equal to p_i is not implausible. This assumption simplifies the mathematics.

The third assumption states that $R_1, \ldots R_n$ do not influence one another in their abilities to answer questions and in their referral judgments.

Let k be the number of times the "buck has been passed" before the querist gets a response, $k = 0, 1, 2, \ldots,$ n-1. Thus if R_1 answers q, $k=0$. If he does not, but R_2 does, then $k=1$. Let t be the total average time (say in hours) elapsed between R_1's receipt of q and the delivery of an answer. If T is the average time it takes R_i, for any i, to consult resources (I) and (II) until he provides an answer or "passes the buck" to R_{i+1}, then $t = (k+1)T$. It would be eminently reasonable to assume that the utility of the answer decreases with t, perhaps as v/t, or as shown in fig. 3; and the cost may increase with t, perhaps as ct.

Utility of answer with delay of t

Figure 3.
A Possible Relation between Utility and Response Time

To make a first analysis mathematically tractable however, we make the following assumption.

Assumption 4: The utility of an acceptable answer and the cost of an unacceptable answer does not vary with t, the time it takes to deliver it.

We can now derive a simple expression for V. The expected net utility of an answer from R_1, with $k=0$, is

$a_1pv - b_1(1-p)c$, because a_1p is the joint probability of A_1 and K_1, being $P(K_1)P(A_1|K_1)$, and $b_1(1-p) = P(\bar{K}_1)P(A_1|\bar{K}_1)$. Note that if R_1 does not know the answer and responds, the answer is taken to be unacceptable to the querist, with penalty c.

The events A_1K_1 and $A_1\bar{K}_1$ thus terminate buckpassing, while either event $\bar{A}_1K_1$ or $\bar{A}_1\bar{K}_1$ means that R_1 refers the question to R_2. The probability of $\bar{A}K_1$ or $\bar{A}_1\bar{K}_1$ is:

$$P(K_1)P(\bar{A}_1|K_1) + P(\bar{K}_1)P(\bar{A}_1|K_1) = a_1(1-p) + (1-a_1)p = a_1(1-p) + b_1p$$

This probability, or something like it, occurs so often that we call it P_1, the probability of passing the buck, with k=1. If the buckpassing sequence terminates with no answer, the utility of that state is taken to be 0, with V=0.

Figure 4 shows the general calculation procedure. The solid circles stand for terminal states and the hollow circles for "pass the buck" or referral states. The probability P_i of R_i being in a referral state, meaning that R_i "passes the buck" to R_{i+1}, is $P_i = a_i(1-p) + b_ip$. Hence, the probability of R_{i+1} being the first to answer q acceptably, without passing the buck, is

$$\prod_{j=1}^{i} P_j P(A_{i+1}, K_{i+1}) = \prod_{j=1}^{i} P_j P(A_{i+1}|K_{i+1})P(K_{i+1}) =$$

$$\prod_{j=1}^{i} P_j Pa_{i+1}, \text{ since } p_{i+1} = p.$$

The (positive) expected utility is therefore,

$$a_1pv + a_2pP_1v + a_3pP_1P_2v + \ldots = pv \sum_{i-1}^{n} a_i \prod_{j=0}^{i-1} P_j,$$

with $P_0 = 1$.

Consequently,

$$V = pv \sum_{i=1}^{n} a_i \prod_{j=0}^{i-1} P_j - (1-p)c \sum_{i=1}^{n} b_i \prod_{j=0}^{i-1} P_j =$$

Figure 4.   Diagram for the Buck-Passing Process

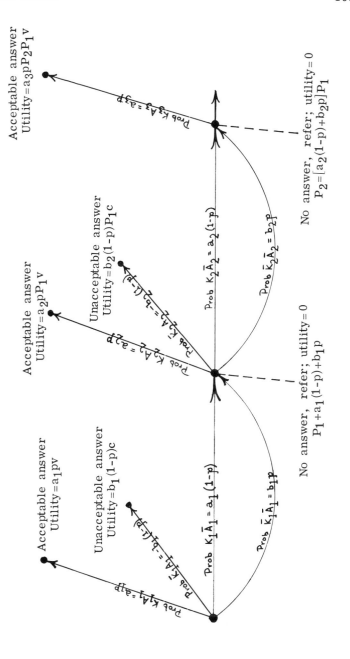

Acceptable answer
Utility = $a_3pP_2P_1v$

Prob $K_3A_3 = a_3p$

No answer, refer; utility = 0
$P_2 = [a_2(1-p) + b_2p]P_1$

Prob $K_2\bar{A}_2 = a_2(1-p)$

Prob $\bar{K}_2\bar{A}_2 = b_2p$

Acceptable answer
Utility = a_2pP_1v

Unacceptable answer
Utility = $b_2(1-p)P_1c$

Prob $\bar{K}_2A_2 = b_2(1-p)$

Prob $K_2A_2 = a_2p$

No answer, refer; utility = 0
$P_1 + a_1(1-p) + b_1p$

Prob $K_1\bar{A}_1 = a_1(1-p)$

Prob $\bar{K}_1\bar{A}_1 = b_1p$

Acceptable answer
Utility = a_1pv

Unacceptable answer
Utility = $b_1(1-p)c$

Prob $\bar{K}_1A_1 = b_1(1-p)$

Prob $K_1A_1 = a_1p$

$$= pv \sum_{i=1}^{n} [a_i - (1-p)(c/pv)b_i] \prod_{j=0}^{i-1} P_j$$

From assumption (1) we have

$$P_j = [a + (j-1)e](1-p) + [1-a-(j-1)e]p$$
$$= a(1-p) + p(1-a) + (e-2ep)(j-1)$$
$$= P_1 \{1 + [e(1-2p)/P_1](j-1)\}$$

This formula was evaluated with the help of a computer program. The results are plotted in Figures 5 and 6.

The results show that for small values of a and e, the coefficient of v increases slowly with p up to about p = .5, then rises sharply; the coefficient of c decreases slowly with p up to about .5, then drops sharply. For a value of p sufficiently close to 1, therefore, the coefficient of v exceeds the coefficient c by enough to make V positive. That is, in a larger network of referential consultants, under the conditions of this first model, the expected net utility is favorable if each consultant, though he may have a very small chance of answering questions, can very reliably refer it to a colleague whose chances are a little larger.

We express V, for any given values of p, a, and e as $V = (CV) \cdot v - (CC)c$. Here CV and CC denote the entire expressions which act as coefficients for v and c, respectively. It is instructive to examine the ratio $\dfrac{V}{(CC)c} = \dfrac{CV}{CC} \cdot \dfrac{v}{c} - 1$. Clearly, V is positive (and large) to the extent that $\dfrac{V}{(CC)c}$ is positive and large: i.e., to the extent that $\dfrac{CV}{CC}$ exceeds $\dfrac{c}{v}$. Let us therefore plot the ratio $\dfrac{CV}{CC}$ as a function of p for a few values of a and e. Note that the $\ln \dfrac{c}{v}$ is usually a positive quantity, because c, the penalty of a wrong answer, generally exceeds v, the utility of an acceptable answer. We can denote $\ln \dfrac{c}{v}$ by the dotted line in Figure 7. The condition that the network results in useful service translates in Figure 7 into the condition that the curve representing the network must be above the dotted line. This can only happen when both a and p are sufficiently large. To satisfy this condition, the larger a, the less p has to be, and the larger p, the smaller a has to be.

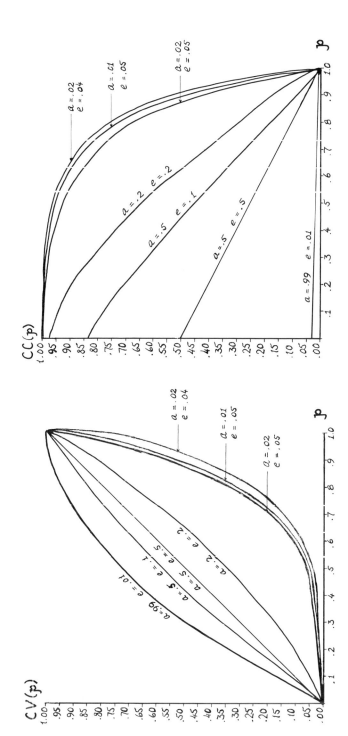

Figure 5

The coefficient of utility vs. probability of providing acceptable service.

Figure 6

The coefficient of penalty vs. probability of providing acceptable service.

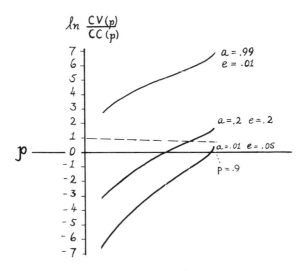

Figure 7.

A Second Mathematical Model:
A Network of Referential Consultants

Even so simple a model as sketched in the previous section gives rise to some moderately complex formulas. These are more easily evaluated by computer than by analytic approximations, although the latter has been done for the formula of section 3. But the model is more interesting for the extensions to which it can easily lead than for its own sake.

The simplest and most interesting extension is to drop assumption 1. In its place we introduce a matrix of n^2-n variables. Let c_{ij} be the probability that if R_i does not answer q, then he refers q to R_j. In other words, instead of passing q to a specific R, the choice of R is now random. Clearly $c_{ii}=0$, for all i, and $\sum_{j=1}^{n} c_{ij}=1$. The query still goes to R_1 initially. The probability, Q_1, that it is answered acceptably after one referral, at k=1, is

$$[c_{12}P(K_2)P(A_2|K_2) + c_{13}P(K_3)P(A_3|K_3) + \cdots +$$

$$c_{1n}P(K_n)(A_n|K_n)]P_1, \text{ where } P_1 \text{ is the probability that}$$

R_1 refers q; it is $a_1(1-p) + (1-a_1)p$.   This is

$$P_1 \sum_{j=2}^{n} c_{1j}a_jp_j = P_1p \sum_{j=1}^{n} c_{1j}a_j$$

under the remaining assumptions, namely that $p_j = p$ for $j=1$, ..., n.   The probability that it is answered unacceptably after one referral is $Q'_1 = P_1(1-p) \sum_{j=1}^{n} c_{1j}b_j$, where $b_j = 1 - a_j$.

The probability, Q_2, that q is acceptably answered only after two referrals, with $k=2$, is the probability that R_1 refers it to R_i for some i, which is P_1c_{1i} and that i refers it on to R_j for some j, who answers it.   The resulting probability is $\sum_i P_1c_{1i}P_i\sum_j c_{ij}p_ja_j$, where $P_i = a_i(1-p_i) + b_ip_i$.

Thus,

$$Q_2 = P_1p \sum_i c_{1i}p_i \sum_j c_{ij}a_j; \quad Q'_2$$

$$= P_1(1-p) \sum_i c_{1i}P_i \sum_j c_{ij}b_j$$

Next,

$$Q_3 = P_1p \sum_i c_{1i}P_i \sum_j c_{ij}P_j \sum_k c_{jk}a_k;$$

$$Q'_3 = P_1(1-p) \sum_i c_{ij}P_j \sum_k c_{jk}b_k$$

The probabilities that q is acceptably and unacceptably answered after k referrals are, respectively, Q_k and Q'_k, $k=0, 1, 2, \ldots, n-1$.

and

$$V = v \sum_{k=0}^{n-1} Q_k - c \sum_{k=0}^{n-1} Q'_k$$

With the help of a simple computer program it is now easy to study the effect of different referral matrices, C.   Be-

```
>
>    1.01    DEMAND N
>    1.02    TYPE "ENTER A(I) I=1 TO N"
>    1.021   FOR I=1 TO N:  DEMAND IN FREE FORM A(I)
>    1.03    TYPE "ENTER C(I,J) I=1 TO N:    J=1 TO N"
>    1.031   FOR I=1 TO N:  FOR J=1 TO N: DEMAND IN FREE FORM C(I,J)
>    1.04    DEMAND P
>    1.1     FOR I=1 TO N:  SET R(I)=A(I)*(1-P)+(1-A(I))*P
>    1.11    SET CV(0)=P*A(1)
>    1.115   SET CC(0)=(1-P)*(1-A(1))
>    1.12    TYPE CV(0), CC(0)
>    1.13    SET S=0
>    1.14    SET T=0
>    1.2     FOR K=1 TO N:  SET S=S+C(1,K)*A(K)
>    1.21    FOR K=1 TO N:  SET T=T+C(1,K)*(1-A(K))
>    1.22    SET CV(1)=CV(0)+R(1)*P*S
>    1.225   SET CC(1)=CC(0)+R(1)*(1-P)*T
>    1.23    TYPE CV(1), CC(1)
>    1.3     SET BP=2
>    1.4     SET I=BP
>    1.5     FOR K=1 TO N:  SET M(K)=A(K)
>    1.55    FOR K=1 TO N:  SET U(K)=1-A(K)
>    1.6     FOR J=1 TO N:  SET D(J)=0
>    1.65    FOR J=1 TO N:  SET E(J)=0
>    1.7     FOR J=1 TO N:  FOR K=1 TO N:  SET D(J)=D(J)+C(J,K)*M(K)
>    1.71    FOR J=1 TO N:  FOR K=1 TO N: SET E(J)=E(J)+C(J,K)*U(K)
>    1.75    IF I=1, TO STEP 1.9
>    1.8     FOR K=1 TO N:  SET M(K)=R(K)*D(K)
>    1.81    FOR K=1 TO N:  SET U(K)=R(K)*E(K)
>    1.85    SET I=I-1
>    1.86    TO STEP 1.6
>    1.9     SET CV(BP)=CV(BP-1)+R(1)*P*D(1)
>    1.91    SET CC(BP)=CC(BP-1)+R(1)*(1-P)*E(1)
>    1.92    TYPE CV(BP), CC(BP)
>    1.93    IF BP=N-1, TO STEP 1.01
>    1.94    SET BP=BP+1
>    1.95    TO STEP 1.4
>    1.99    DONE
>
```

Figure 8 [see key to symbology below].

Listing of PIL program for computing the coefficient
of utility, CV, and the coefficient of penalty, CC, as a function
of the number of times the buck is passed, BP = 0, 1, ...,
N-1, in any network of N referential consultants.

Symbol Used Here	Corresponding Symbol in Text	Meaning
N	n	Nr. of referential consultants
A(I)	a_i	Prob. (R_i knows answer to q)
C(I, J)	c_{ij}	Prob. (R_i refers q to $R_j | R_i$ doesn't answer)
P	p	Prob. (R_i answers $q | R_i$ knows answer) = Prob. (R_i doesn't answer $| R_i$ doesn't know answer) $i = 1, \ldots, N$.
R(I)	P_i	Prob. (R_i doesn't answer, refers)

cause the computer program is simpler than the mathematical formulas which explicitly express Q_k and Q'_k, we present the listing of a PIL program. This is the "Pittsburgh Interpretive Language" available on the Michigan Time-Sharing System, and its commands are self-explanatory. There is, of course, no need, with the use of a computer program, to assume that $a_i = a + ie$, and $a_1, \ldots a_n$ can be arbitrarily specified. The effects of different vectors $\underline{a}$ can thus also be investigated.

The program whose print-out is shown in Figure 8 was run for a number of networks with N= 5 and N= 7. The ratio of the value coefficient CV to the cost coefficient CC was calculated in relation to C/V. The results are presented in Figure 9. They supported the following general remarks:

1) High ratios are achieved only with relatively high a_i's. Thus the vector $\underline{a}$ = (.2, .4, .6, .8, 1) yielded consistently high ratios. It proved to be the most flexible for all networks.

2) The arrangement of the R_i's in the organization seems to be very important. When the "smartest" R_i was placed first in the network and was supported by a number of 'less smart' consultants, a substantially higher ratio is achieved than if he were placed further along, thus receiving q at a latter stage [e.g., (.8, .03, .03, .03, .03) is better than (.03, .03, .8, .03, .03)].

3) Although [as stated in (1)] high a_i's seem to indicate greater ratios, even low ratios can be increased by increasing the size of the network.

4) Note that in many cases, for example, in the case where $a_1 = .8$, $a_i = .03$ for i= 2, 3, 4, V = .743v - .104c, which is less than $V_0 = .72v - .02c$ the net value for a network with the same R_1 but no one else to whom to refer. Here $V - V_0 = .023v - .084c$, which is positive if $\dfrac{v}{c} \mathbin{\rangle} \dfrac{.084}{.023} \mathbin{\rangle} 3.$

This shows that if the benefit of an acceptable answer is more than three times the penalty of an unacceptable answer, then the network of referential consultants gives greater net utility than would the smartest consultant standing alone. Of course, the utilities and penalties of an answer can hardly ever be quantitatively estimated, so that these results are to be used only as qualitative indications of the relations among key variables.

It is quite possible that in an organization, the people R_j with higher values of a_j also rank higher. An R_i of a
[text cont. p. 208]

Figure 9.
Tabulation by Network

I.   The situation in which each R_i refers q to R_{i+1}, i=1, ..., n with the exception of R_r who can refer it to R_{n-1}. No R_i may refer to himself.   Two networks, one with 5 R_i's and the other with 7, are considered.

Values of a_i							CV(p) - CC(p)	Ratio $\frac{CV(p)}{CC(p)}$
.8,	.03,	.03,	.03,	.03			.743v - .104c	7.14
.2,	.4,	.6,	.8,	1			.851v - .145c	5.86
.03,	.03,	.8,	.03,	.03			.613v - .234c	2.62
.01,	.01,	.02,	.03,	1			.605v - .334c	1.81
.01,	.01,	.05,	.05,	.4,	.4,	.8	.561v - .388c	1.44
.01,	.01,	.01,	.02,	.02,	.03,	1	.500v - .451c	1.11
.01,	.01,	.02,	.02,	.03,	.03,	.04	.093v - .493c	.188
.01,	.02,	.03,	.02,	.01			.064v - .391c	.164
.01,	.01,	.02,	.02,	.03			.061v - .395v	.159
.01,	.01,	.01,	.01,	.01			.036v - .399c	.090

II.   The situation in which R_1 passes q directly to R_n.

Values of a_i					CV(p) - CC(p)	Ratio $\frac{CV(p)}{CC(p)}$
.01,	.01,	.02,	.02,	.03	.033v - .186c	.177
.2,	.4,	.6,	.8,	1	.918v - .082c	11.20

   B.   In this variation of (A) n=7, and q is passed with probability .7 to R_6 and with probability .3 to R_7.   The only exceptions are that R_6 always passed to R_7, and R_7 always passes to R_6.

Values of a_i							CV(p) - CC(p)	Ratio $\frac{CV(p)}{CC(p)}$
.01,	.01,	.01,	.02,	.02,	.03,	1	.831v - .168c	4.93

III.   Random buck-passing networks:

   A.   There is an equal chance of any R_i receiving q.

Values of a_i					CV(p) - CC(p)	Ratio $\frac{CV(p)}{CC(p)}$
.2,	.4,	.6,	.8,	1	.8675 - .118c	7.40

Table 9 (cont.)

III. B. There is an almost equal chance of any R_j receiving q, but top R_i's have slightly increased probability.

Values of a_i	CV(p) - CC(p)	Ratio $\dfrac{CV(p)}{CC(p)}$
.01 .01, .01, .02, .03	.526 - .328	1.59
.01, .005, .005, .005, .005, .005	.029 - .510	.057
.005, .005, .005, .01, .005, .005	.026 - .513	.051

C. This is a non-uniform random referral situation according to the following given matrices:

1.

$$\begin{bmatrix} 0 & .3 & .2 & .2 & .3 \\ .3 & 0 & .3 & .2 & .2 \\ .2 & .3 & 0 & .3 & .2 \\ .2 & .2 & .3 & 0 & .3 \\ .3 & .2 & .2 & .3 & 0 \end{bmatrix}$$

Values of a_i	CV(p) - CC(p)	Ratio $\dfrac{CV(p)}{CC(p)}$
.2, .4, .6, .8, 1	.865v - .188c	7.33

2.

$$\begin{bmatrix} 0 & 1 & 0 & 0 & 0 \\ 1 & 0 & 0 & 0 & 0 \\ 0 & 0 & 0 & 1 & 0 \\ 0 & 0 & 1 & 0 & 0 \end{bmatrix}$$

Values of a_i	CV(p) - CC(p)	Ratio $\dfrac{CV(p)}{CC(p)}$
2., 4., .6, .8, 1	.671v - .193c	3.49

3.

$$\begin{bmatrix} 0 & 0 & 0 & 0 & 0 \\ 1 & 0 & 0 & 0 & 0 \\ .6 & .4 & 0 & 0 & 0 \\ .5 & .3 & .2 & 0 & 0 \\ .4 & .3 & .2 & 1 & 0 \end{bmatrix}$$

Values of a_i	CV(p) - CC(p)	Ratio $\dfrac{CV(p)}{CC(p)}$
.2, .4, .6, .8, 1	.18v - .08c	2.2

IV. In this situation there is no buck passing at all.

Values of a_i	CC(p) - CC(p)	Ratio $\dfrac{CV(p)}{CC(p)}$
.01, .02, .03, .02, 1	.009v - .099c	.091

given rank in some organizations is more likely to pass the buck on certain questions to an R_j of lower rank than to a superior. In this case, c_{ij} would increase as a_j decreases. This is quite unfavorable.

The model studied in the previous section is a special case of this model with $c_{i, i+1} = 1$, for $i = 1, 2, \ldots, n-1$, but $c_{nj} = 0$ for all j. (R_n could never refer, violating the condition $\sum_j c_{ij} = 1$). In the present model, the question can get trapped in a bureaucratic cycle, and we can calculate the probability of this happening. For example, it is possible for R_1 to refer q to R_5; R_5 could refer it to R_9, R_9 to R_3 and R_3 back to R_1, with R_1 referring it this time to R_2, etc. The question could eventually traverse through all the R_i in all possible paths and stay in the network for an infinitely long time.

Toward Greater Realism
_____

Some severe limitations of the models considered so far, beyond those formally stated before, are described next:

(a) The question was taken to be unchanged, as first presented by the querist. No provision for conversing with the querist has been made. Suppose now that any R_i to whom q is referred can converse with the querist. Indeed, we might include the querist -- let us call him R_0 -- in the network: R_0, R_1, $\ldots$, R_n. The question can occasionally be referred back to him. This would make sense only if we permitted each R_i a fourth resource beyond (I) his memory, (II) his auxiliary memories (library items), (III) access to other R_j: namely, (IV) his ability to reinterpret, reformulate, substitute for q or to ask R_0 questions in place of either providing an answer or "passing the buck." The latter would permit R_0 to reformulate, reinterpret or substitute for q. This process may improve the quality of the question.[12] Of course, we would need to characterize R_i by an additional variable: $d_i = \text{Prob.}(R_i \text{ converses with } R_0 | \bar{A}_i)$.

(b) The variables characterizing R_i, namely a_i, p_i, p'_i, d_i, were taken to be independent of the question q, and unchanging in time. Suppose that questions can be classified and graded, a job that R_1 might do. Suppose that R_1 works with m categories $C_1, \ldots, C_m$, such as specialties in which various R_i have expertise. Then, in place of a_i, we have a_{ij}, the probability that R_i can answer a question in category

C_j. If R_i is an expert only in specialty C_j, then a_{ij} is high and a_{ik} for $k \neq j$ is low. These question categories could not only aggregate questions by common subject matter, but by quality as well. Thus, a_{ij} may be low for all j if C_j is a category of poorly formulated questions, while a_{ik} may be higher for all k were C_k is a category of well-formulated questions.

We could now further specify the system by giving the a priori probabilities of a randomly chosen question falling into C_1, C_2, ..., C_m; call these r_1, ..., r_m. Let $s_{ijk} =$ Prob [q is reformulated so that it is transferred from C_j to C_k, given that R_i converses with R_0]. Hence, $d_i s_{ijk} \cdot a_{ik}$ is the probability of R_i's conversations with R_0 resulting in an answer to the revised question, given that R_i did not answer it previously. Of course, there is a price for delay.

This permits us to compute the probability with which "buck passing" can upgrade the question. This tool must be deferred for future investigations.

(c) The matrix C embodies a referral strategy and organization. This might, however, change for questions in certain categories. The categories C_1, ..., C_m could reflect priorities assigned to questions. A high-priority question might always immediately be referred to the R_1 with the highest a_i, and he might refer it, or fragments of it formed by him, down the line.

(d) The discussions so far have assumed only person-to-person messages (questions and answers), but no "to whom it may concern" messages. Certain questions reaching R_1, could be broadcast by R_1, with an instruction that whichever R_i could readily answer q should speak up. The motivation in such a system for "speaking up" would have to be at least that of the R_i to whom a question was referred in the "buck passing" organization. If time is a very important factor, then this inherently parallel system may be preferable.

The models for analyzing such a system would be based primarily on a reinforcement function which: greatly rewards the R_i who spoke up, i.e. supplied the answer for a q such that his a_{ij} is very high; moderately rewards the R_i whose a_{ij} is low and who does not speak up or the R_i whose a_{ij} is reasonable, but who converses with R_0; punishes the R_i whose a_{ij} is high and who does not speak up or the R_i whose a_{ij} is low and who does speak up. If no one speaks up, some reward might go to the R_i who refers q to an R_k for whom $p_k a_{kj}$ is high.

The use of such a reinforcement schedule should result in learning, and the values of the p_i, p'_i would change with time.

(e) Finally, there is the question of organizational design. We assume that requests originate randomly at various geographic locations in a community. The average time to forward a question to the nearest R_i may therefore vary depending on where he is located. Perhaps there should be more than just one R_1, to each of whom all requests in his service area are initially forwarded (11). Or, perhaps having the service "areas" arranged by topic, rather than geographically, with the querist deciding upon the nearest topically specialized R_i to whom to forward q has high utility.[13]

Within the community of the R_i, similar questions arise. There is an additional question involving the number of R_i with the same a_{ij} to use redundantly, so as to handle expected loads. This is a problem in the analysis of querying networks such as studied by R. Disney (4), and an aim of organizational design is to balance idleness and congestion.

Some Problems for Further Research

(a) Even in the simplest model above (p. 195-202), what is the best point to enter a chain of R_i's? If there is no basis for assigning questions to R_i's, and if a_n is largest, then why should not all questions go initially to R_n? This would certainly be optimal from the user's viewpoint. Too, the smaller the x, where R_x is the one to whom q is initially submitted, the greater the probability of an unacceptable answer. The probability of the first acceptable answer occurring after the kth referral since R_x received q, is

$$p \sum_{i=x}^{x+k} a_i \prod_{j=0}^{i-1} P_j$$

The average net utility, if q is initially received by R_x is

$$V(x) - pv \sum_{i=x}^{n} [a+(i-1)e] \prod_{j=0}^{i-1} P_j -$$

$$(1-p)c \sum_{i=x}^{n} [1-(a+(i-1)e] \prod_{j=0}^{i-1} P_j$$

We can now seek the value of x which maximizes this expression.

(b) Suppose that a querist R_0 poses several questions to R_1, each belonging to a subject category C_j, and each was referred by R_1 to R_i, and in each case R_i provided an eminently satisfactory response. R_0 will soon learn to pose any future questions in C_j directly and initially to R_i.

In practice, much more than half of all questions posed by R_0 may fit into no more than a dozen categories, for each of which there may be an R_i whom R_0 has learned to contact initially, once he has classified the question himself. What advantages, then, does a referral network offer?

First, not all querists will have questions fitting into the same dozen categories. It may still be the case that well over half of the questions posed by anyone fall into a few dozen categories, and users may have learned to contact experts on these categories directly. The referral network then serves to teach users where to turn. This is important when the user population is constantly expanding, with an overwhelming and growing fraction of all users at any time being untrained, young newcomers.

Secondly, users may be less able to usefully categorize their own questions than could R_1. This too, can be learned, but such learning is a continuing process for the less than half of the questions that do not fall into less than a dozen categories. Any system which will be able to handle these very many relatively rare and, hence unusual, questions is bound to be expensive, because it has to be customized. This is a very important area in need of investigation.

Third, and perhaps most important, knowledge, and, perhaps wisdom also (10), are constantly growing. This means that the categories constantly change and that the set of questions that could be answered is continually expanding. Conversations between R_0 and the R_i he contacts, which can and should serve to teach R_0 which questions he might ask that he had not thought of or known to ask, play an increasingly important role. Here, a referral network offers the advantage of a multiplicity of potential teachers, and, therefore, a greater opportunity of finding treasure.

(c) The models (i.e., mathematical problems sketched

and suggested here) are useful for clarifying essential concepts. They stimulate precise new ideas. They also serve
as vehicles for developing methods of, and experience with,
mathematical analysis. But they cannot lead to theories until they are connected with empirical or experimental data.
A whole class of research problems suggested by this kind
of mathematical thinking involves data acquisition.

To some extent, special libraries already perform an
expanding reference function. By monitoring samples of the
memoranda, [14] telephone, and personal calls from R_i to R_j
in such an organization, crude estimates of the matrix C
can be obtained. A far better study, however, would be a
controlled experiment in which a sample of questions is
planted, i.e., submitted to an existing question-answering
network of referential consultants $R_1, \ldots, R_n$, such that the
consultants cannot distinguish these planted questions from
the ones they normally encounter. All the planted questions
have definite answers. The experimenter may even know
whether or not the answer to a given question is known to
R_i via library resources (II) [aids to memory]. That is, the
experimenter may have chosen the question because he has
seen the answer in the reference collection which is within
R_i's reach. Such an experiment may then permit us to estimate p_i, p'_i, a_i, c_{ij} and d_i for $i=1, \ldots$, n, and to test
certain key predictions of one or another set of assumptions.

(d) Another important line of experimental investigation involves categorization of the queries and specialization
of the referential consultants. In our models, we have mixed
three different bases for categorization: by specialty; by
priority; and by question quality. There are undoubtedly
more. Categorization by specialty is traditional (this is the
sense of "special" in special libraries) and superficially the
simplest, but it rests on a very weak theoretical foundation.

It is today no longer so important that R_i get only
questions to which his library resources are specialized, because he has access to an apparatus for bibliographic control
over resources beyond those which are literally within walk-
ing distance. The limitation lies in R_i's ability to use this
apparatus after the limits of his own expertise about the
question are exceeded.

What probably matters most in a categorization of
questions and R_i's is the quality and priority of questions.
In comparing two categorizations of a corpus of 100 ques-

tions, say $[C_1, \ldots, C_m]$ and $[C'_1, \ldots, C'_m]$, we might well ask which gives the greater value for

$$\text{Max} \ \text{Max} \ p_i a_{ij} \ \text{or} \ \Sigma_i \ \text{Max} \ p_i a_{ij}$$
$$\quad i \quad \ \ j \qquad\qquad\qquad\quad j$$

where a_{ij} is the probability of an acceptable answer from R_i to a question in category C_j or C'_j. This can be decided by data. One possible experiment to do this would be to categorize a sample of planted questions in two different ways and to broadcast with each question an appeal to all the R_1, ..., R_n for volunteers (to be rewarded) who can most easily and expertly answer it. The sample of questions is carefully chosen so as to fit into a priori designed categories by definition; data about who responds to these questions, and how successfully, is then used to determine how consistently the same R_i picks questions in C_j and is characterized by very high $p_i a_{ij}$. (e) Another very important line of experimental investigation involves the utility and cost measures. Basically v is the amount a querist is willing to pay per question for an acceptable response delivered in the minimum possible time. This value was taken to be averaged over all questions and querists. In a categorization of questions by priority, however, each question class is characterized by a different value of v. Questions of the class with highest v are of top priority.

Each question which enters the system is part of a submitted form with at least 3 parts:

    (i) The initial formulation of the question, including at least some background and hints for the referential consultant as to what kind of answer is wanted

    (ii) some indication of how much the querist values the answer, including how his utility for the answer decays with response time

    (iii) data about himself, such as would relate to estimating a_{oj}, $j = 1, \ldots, m$

This may be done by experimenting with a sample of querists, asking them to allocate a certain sum of money given them by the experimenter over a given list of possible question-answering sources. The list might include elements like: (i) act as your own referential consultant, using (1) and (2) for a particular library resource (II); (ii) same as (i) except for a different library resource (II); (iii) refer to R_1; (iv) refer to R_2; etc.

It is important to bear in mind that R_0 can always choose between many competitive sources in getting an answer to his question. By going to R_1 he ought to be assured that R_1 could point him to at least those sources he would have known about himself. I R_0 can do R_1's job better by himself, he should, of course, do so.

(f) The cost of maintaining a referral network is likely to be high. The practicality of such a serive hinges critically on the rate at which gross revenue grows relative to operating costs. Both will increase, though the service cannot be viable unless revenues grow faster than do costs. If they grow at the same rate, there must be a sizable constant difference of revenues over costs. This state can hardly be claimed to exist for current reference services. Budgets for library services are generally a small part of overhead and are the first to be cut if the total budget is reduced.[15]

Beyond the cost of maintaining the services of n referential consultants in a network are costs generated by the existence of the network itself. According to Parkinson's Law (16), the $R_1, \ldots, R_n$ will generate and send questions and answers to one another. Such messages would not have been generated if there were no network. The volume of such message traffic may vary as n^2. This limits each R_i's capacity to answer client-generated questions and may necessitate larger n to handle a specified load.

Such internally generated communications are often considered unproductive. Many consider it unprofessional to "pass the buck." Yet, "buck passing" can be a sign of both very irresponsible or very responsible professional behavior. Referring a question is professionally very responsible when it reflects the professional's understanding of his own limitations; such a professional is much more valuable than one who never refers, unless the latter is omniscient. The very irresponsible buck passing professional can be easily discriminated from his opposite by noting that he answers very few questions adequately, and is valued so low as to be dropped.

The communications generated inside the network could be productive. They could help upgrade the organization by helping the R_i teach, and learn from, one another. The measure of learning is the number of good questions R_i can ask that he could not have known to ask before. Conditions for such learning to occur could be derived; a cost-effectiveness model, backed by data, can readily be set up and used to contribute to arguments for the economic feasibility of referential consulting.

Conclusions

We have argued, in this paper, for the significance of "referential consulting." This is a new type of service to be performed by a new breed of reference librarian. It resembles expanding reference functions now practiced to an extent in some special libraries. But it goes as much beyond contemporary reference service concepts as these go beyond book delivery service concepts. In essence, referential consulting is a means of providing some kind of useful response to almost any question of importance to people in their daily lives, either by having a member of an organization of referential consultants rely on his expertise, on the library resources at his command, or on his ability to refer the question to a colleague in the organization or outside. The response may be either a direct answer, a document likely to contain the answer, or advice to go to a document or another source. A referential consultant is a very mature, learned, responsible "information officer," an essential, highly valued professional in the community.

Some investigators (1) claim that today's reference librarians already have the status of professionals like doctors, engineers, lawyers, etc. The fact that some librarians already believe this, is a hopeful sign that referential consulting is feasible. A small number of practicing librarians who were casually interviewed stated that questions such as the ten examples above (p. 190f.), reach them frequently. Though they were not prepared in library schools to answer them, on the ground that such questions are outside a reference librarian's responsibility, they rarely turn them down. Indeed, they can often give the user acceptable answers.

The very fact that libraries do contain the necessary resources to provide such services reaffirms the need for expanded referential consulting in order to utilize these library resources more effectively and to perform library functions more satisfactorily. We have redefined the function of a library to be:

to maximize the greatest potentially attainable effec-

tive and efficient social utilization of documented
knowledge.

Hopefully the models of referential networks presented here
will stimulate ideas and actions to be more nearly consonant
with this definition.

We have assumed that there is a latent need for such
a referential consulting service. This need will be made
manifest if people will use, request and pay for the referential consulting service if it is offered. We therefore recom-
mend -- urge -- the creation of such a service. We predict
that it will create demand and, in time, pay for itself. Part
of this recommendation is addressed to library science educators, to educate some of the high-level professionals capable of serving as referential consulting services, to educate
innovators, scholars and scientists who can advance and develop the concept and the underlying rationale and discipline.

We have begun an explication of the "referential consulting" concept. Though crude, it has proved capable of
clarification, of leading to further ideas and of providing
some results. We have derived conditions under which various forms of the referential consulting organization lead to
maximum or specified expected net utility.

Even our first step toward an explication of the concept of referential consulting service reveals a number of exciting intellectual puzzles. To investigators inclined toward
mathematical thinking, they can be a challenge inviting further
exploration. To investigators inclined toward observation,
they can suggest useful, empirical or experimental studies.
One study, if done well, can lead to another and, in time,
toward a theory of an important aspect of librarianship.

Acknowledgment: Many of the ideas in this paper benefited
from stimulating discussions with members of our information
science research team: C. Drott, D. Koson, R. Palmer, H.
Quenemoen, B. Segur, R. Tagliacozzo, M. Thall, Wm. vanLoo,
H. Hamburger, and T. Slavens, a colleague in the Library Science Department. Special thanks go to W. Lehmann for her assistance in the preparation of the paper and in checking the calculations, and to A. Tars for his valuable assistance in running
the computer programs.

Notes

1. For some typical questions with which libraries deal see the excellent compilation: Case Studies in Reference Work by Grogan (Ref. no. 7).

2. For example, when Stalin ignored the well-documented, encyclopedic compilation of Soviet intelligence by Richard Sorge, which showed that the Germans would attack Russia on June 22, 1941, Sorge was in no way to blame for such minimizing of the effective social utilization of graphic records.

3. This is not meant to imply that there are no definitions at all. The A.L.A. Glossary, for example, has defined reference work as "that phase of library work which is directly concerned with assistance to the readers in securing information and in using the resources of the library in study and research."

4. This example is due to D. Dennis, then head of the Health Sciences Library at the University of Michigan, now at the National Library of Medicine (private communication). This request was forwarded from a small town to the regional MEDLARS post in Ann Arbor, thence to NLM in Washington. The MEDLARS search revealed one relevant paper which was supplied a day later (rather than the usual two weeks) because of the possible urgency of the case.

5. Eloquent refutations of this viewpoint have been made by Lorenz (14), Freiser (6), and Rees (18).

6. A unique, early experiment in using libraries as community information centers is the Sheffield Free Public Library System, Sheffield, England. For details see (19).

7. Although the problem of expertise might raise several interesting questions, we do not stress it in this paper. We treat R as a specialist only secondarily.

8. For more comments on the effectiveness of question referral, see (3).

9. We use the term "model" not to describe more simply an observed entity, nor to depict an ideal way of performing a function, but to formulate and analyze designs for the referential consulting function. The virtues and limitations of mathematical thinking are well known: clarity at the cost of oversimplification, insight at the price of exact applicability, stimulation for all kinds of further investigation, experimental and theoretical, in place of minutely cataloged observations and data describing existing reality. Theories can be

better analyzed and compared if expressed mathematically, though existing mathematics imposes limitations on the complexity of theories. Sometimes mathematics is inappropriately used in a merely decorative manner. Candidly, we create and analyze models because it is exciting; models are the breeding ground of intellectual problems.

10. An unacceptable answer is one which is either false or insufficient. Answers which are made unacceptable due to extensive delay are not dealt with here.

11. Recall that this means his being able to answer the question from memory or by looking in the library at resources available to him. We stress, of course, the latter in this paper.

12. For an interesting analysis of the structure of the negotiating process, see Taylor (22).

13. This is currently the case for many of the questions cited earlier in this paper.

14. At least one origin-destination study of inter-office memoranda was done at IBM by Resnick et al., but of course the content was not examined, nor were many of the memoranda questions, such as may be transmitted to a referential network.

15. The cost factor is one reason why industrial libraries have achieved such success. Not only do they have sufficient funds, but they are able to assign a definite monetary value to correct information.

References

1. Aspnes, Grieg, Librarian for Cargill, Inc., Minneapolis, Minnesota. Private conversation with W. Lehmann, March 12, 1969.

2. Brooks, B. and Kilgour, F., "Catalog Subject Searches in the Yale Medical Library," College and Research Libraries, 25 (1964), 483-487.

3. Bundy, M. and Wasserman, P., "Professionalism Reconsidered," College and Research Libraries, 29 (1968), 9.

4. Disney, R. and Solberg, J.J., "The Effect of Three Switching Rules on Queuing Networks," Journal of Industrial Engineering, 19:12 (December 1968), 584-590.

5. Egan, M.E., "Education for Librarianship of the Future," in: Documentation in Action, Shera, J., Kent, A., and Perry, J. (eds.). Based on 1956 Conference on Documentation at Western Reserve University; New York, Reinhold, 1956.

6. Freiser, L., "Reconstruction of Library Services," in: The Present Status and Future Prospects of Reference / Information Service, Linderman, W. B. (ed). Proceedings of the Conference held at the School of Library Service, Columbia University, March 30-April 1, 1966. Chicago, ALA, 1967; 48-56.

7. Grogan, D., Case Studies in Reference Work. London, Archon Books and Clive Bingley, 1967.

8. Kahn, A., Neighborhood Information Centers: A Study and Some Proposals. New York, Columbia University School of Social Work, 1966.

9. Kilgour, F., "Implications for the Future of Reference / Information Service," in: Linderman, op. cit., 172-184.

10. Kochen, M., "Stability in the Growth of Knowledge," American Documentation, 20 (1969), 186-197.

11. Kochen, M. and Deutsch, K., "Toward a Theory of Decentralization," American Political Science Review, 63 (1969), 734-749.

12. Linderman, W., The Present Status and Future Prospects of Reference /Information Service. Proceedings of the Conference held at the School of Library Service, Columbia University, March 30 to April 1, 1966. Chicago, ALA, 1967.

13. Lipetz, B., and Stangl, P., User Clues in Initiating Searches in a Large Library Catalog. Proceedings of American Society of Information Science, Vol. 5, Columbus, Ohio, October 20-26, 1968.

14. Lorenz, J., "Regional and State Systems," in: Linderman, op. cit., 73-82.

15. Palmer, R., "User Requirements of a University Library Card Catalog." Survey conducted in the University of Michigan General Library, in the fall of 1967 for the data for the author's Ph.D. thesis in the Department of Library Science, University of Michigan.

16. Parkinson, C., "Parkinson's Law, or the Rising Pyramid," in: The Growth of Knowledge, Kochen, M. (ed.), New York; Wiley, 1967.

17. Pool, de Sola I., The People Look at Educational Television. Stanford, Calif., Stanford University Press, 1963.

18. Rees, A. M., "Broadening the Spectrum," in: Linderman, op. cit., 57-65.

19. Sheffield, England, The City Libraries of Sheffield, 1856-1956. Art Galleries and Museums Committee, 1956.

20. Swanson, D., Requirements Study for Future Catalogs.
    Progress Report No. 2, March 1968, 54.
21. Tagliacozzo, R., and Kochen, M., Catalog Use Study.
    [In preparation.]
22. Taylor, R., "Question-Negotiation and Information Seek-
    ing in Libraries," College and Research Libraries,
    28 (1967), 178-194.
23. Wells, H.G., "World Encyclopedia," in: The Growth
    of Knowledge, Kochen, M. (ed.), New York, Wiley,
    1967.
24. Vavrek, B., "The Theory of Reference Service," Col-
    lege and Research Libraries, 29 (1968), 508-510.
25. Wynar, B., "Reference Theory: Situation Hopeless but
    Not Impossible," College and Research Libraries, 28
    (1967), 339.

THE WORLD ENCYCLOPEDIA CONCEPT*

Glynn Harmon

In 1936, the historian H. G. Wells announced his uneasiness over the ignorance surrounding the tenuous settle-
ment of World War I. He argued that statesmen knew hardly
anything about the consequences of their acts; nor did they
even know what was to be known:

> Possibly all the knowledge ... needed to establish a
> wise and stable settlement of the world's affairs in
> 1919 existed in bits and fragments ... but practically
> nothing had been done to draw that knowledge and
> these ideas together into a comprehensive concep-
> tion of the world ... without a World Encyclopaedia
> to hold men's minds together in something like a
> common interpretation of reality, there is no hope
> whatever of anything but an accidental and transi-
> tory alleviation of any of our world troubles. 1

Wells envisioned a World Encyclopedia that would re-
organize the world's education and information, through the
dynamic growth, extension, revision and replacement of its
content. It would provide for the testing of statements and
verification of facts, serving the role of a politically and
economically disinterested, "undogmatic Bible" to all of hu-
manity. It would

> bring together into close juxtaposition and under
> critical scrutiny many apparently conflicting sys-
> tems of statement ... an organ of adjustment and
> adjudication, a clearing house of misunderstandings;
> it would be deliberately a synthesis and so act as
> a filter for a very great quantity of human misap-
> prehension... [A] World Encyclopaedia must have
> a perennial life ... with a progressive, adaptable
> and recuperative quality.... 2

*Work partially supported by USOE grant OEG-6-95-
45-0620-0015, Case Western Reserve University.

The problem posed by Wells has persisted, and several variations of the World Encyclopedia have been proposed
by different men in the last few years. For example, Boulding proposed in 1956 a new science of "eiconics," or theoretical imagery to serve as a basic form for the coherent unification of empirical data. Such images would consist of
"minimum knowledge," not the maximum, serving as a "general theory" of the empirical world: something which lies
between the extreme generality of mathematics and the par-
ticularity of particular disciplines."[3] In 1959, Lasswell proposed a "Social Planetarium" -- a series of research or
seminar rooms equipped to present vivid simulatory environments of natural or cultural phenomena during time segments
in the past or future. Such presentations could assist research and social policy determination by making apparent
various knowledge gaps.[4]

In 1960, Weiss cogently demonstrated that bodies of
knowledge tend to grow in a manner analogous to the growth
of organisms; that is, through the assimilation rather than
the accretion of nutrients.[5] Churchman proposed in 1961 the
establishment of a "World Information Center," which would
assess new research findings against accumulated findings in
order to identify new findings as either redundant, not properly derived from the evidence, inconsistent with previous
findings, or more supportive of certain theses and less supportive of others.[6] In 1965, de Grazia announced operation
of the "World Reference System" for the social and behavioral sciences, and Watson Davis proposed the idea of a universal or world brain, much on the order of that proposed
by Wells in 1936, but with an emphasis on utilization of computer technology.[7] More recently, Deutsch has suggested
the large scale use of theories and models as dynamic con-
figurations for the evaluation, organization, and communication of knowledge.[8]

Kochen has suggested, as one plausible goal for information science, the development of tutorial information
systems. Tutorial systems would enable a user to acquire
the degree of sophistication needed for appropriate decision
making. Such systems would be of an encyclopedic nature,
and the functions of evaluation and synthesis of knowledge
would be assigned priority over the function of retrieval.

> This alternative is to assimilate and weld newly
> generated knowledge into a coherent overall image
> at sufficient speed, so as to counteract the tend-

ency of knowledge to scatter centrifugally into isolated fragments; to impart understanding rather than
dispense information; and to aim to serve primarily
the interested non-specialist and only secondarily
the skilled specialist. [9]

If the concept of a World Encyclopedia has been per-
petuated, why has not traditional library classification been
adequate for the large scale encyclopedic organization of
knowledge? Shera summarizes one frequently disadvantageous
aspect of library classification--its linearity:

> A classification that is linear must perforce be
> mono-dimensional. Yet the relationships among
> books are poly-dimensional and can not be repre-
> sented as the projection of a straight line, or by
> the position of a specific point; i.e., a particular
> book, on that line. Thus the classifier is com-
> pelled to select a single relationship from all the
> possible relationships which any given title might
> have to its user, and to disregard the remainder,
> however important these may have been to the
> users of the collection. [10]

> Bibliographic Classification must be completely in-
> dependent of physical objects (books), for no ar-
> rangement of such objects can reveal the complex
> of relationships that may exist among the many
> separate thought-units that make up the subject con-
> tent of these books. [11]

If traditional library or book classification is inadequate for a viable and useful organization of knowledge, what
alternatives exist? Further clarification of the problem, and
the relative efficacy of existing alternatives are topics for
advanced theoretical and technological research. This paper
is devoted to one promising alternative -- the systematic exploitation of models.

Since at least the seventeenth century, the term "model" has been used broadly and loosely in the English language
to denote a type of imitative structure, a summary or abstract of ideas or written works, an exemplar or object of
imitation, a design, or the resemblance of a person, place
or thing. [12] Such broad usage of the term continues, but
there has been a rapidly growing awareness of the specialized epistemological values of models since the start of this
century, and particularly in the last ten years.

The actual use of models, however, is not a recent development. From Babylonian mythology to modern science, man has employed analogy and metaphor, which are normally essential features of models. Aristotle made frequent use of mechanical and organismic analogies. Descartes and La Mettrie used mechanical analogies to describe how organisms function, and Harvey used the analogies of pipes, pumps and valves to describe the circulation of blood. Newton used a mechanical analogy to contrive his physical system as a "world machine." Rutherford and Bohr used the planetary image to formulate atomic theory. The names of Maxwell, Kelvin and Planck are also associated with physical models. The road of history is littered with wrecks of once useful or useless models.[13]

The value of models became a topic of debate around the turn of the century. Debate is reflected in works published by two physicists, Pierre Duhem and N. R. Campbell.[14] In 1905, Duhem argued against the logical necessity of models and considered them to be a prop for feeble minds or, at the most, a psychological aid useful for suggesting theories. In contrast, Campbell wrote in 1920 that models are utterly essential to effective inquiry and can best fulfill the functions traditionally assigned to theories. While the debate continues, it appears that Campbell's arguments are more appropriate in the present era of rapid knowledge proliferation.

A significant growth in the use--or, at least, in the awareness--of models has occurred since 1960. This growth is reflected in major indexing sources, as illustrated in Figure 1 by counts of entries under the term "model" or "mathematical model" in recent years:[15]

	1963	1964	1965	1966	1967	1968
Biological Abstracts	230	240	350	400	410	634
Index Medicus	0	0	0	185	412	730
Psychological Abstracts	65	34	144	203	281	392
App. Sci. & Tech. Index	86	94	110	130	253	276
Int. Aerospace Abstracts	5	26	42	93	225	253

Figure 1.   Index Entries under the Term "Model."

A notable but less spectacular growth trend may be observed in Business Periodicals Index, Social Science and Humanities Index, Sociological Abstracts, and Education Index. Surprisingly few, if any, entries are indexed in Social Work Abstracts, Library Science Abstracts, Accounting Index, or Index to Legal Periodicals. In short, these are indications that the social sciences and the professions, with the exception of engineering and medicine, have lagged in the use of models and, possibly, in the formalization of their knowledge. In chemistry and physics, where a high proportion of expressions are of a formal, model-like nature, the use of the term "model" does not appear so frequently, probably because it would be too general as an entry term.

A general definition of the term model is difficult. The term is used loosely from context to context with a wide variety of connotations and denotations. A wide diversity of models exists. Specialists speak of models in terms of their own dialects and proffer general definitions based on the particular set of models to which they have been exposed.

Because of the wide and flexible deployability of models, and because models share properties of theories, hypotheses or descriptions, many people equate "model" with theory, hypothesis, or description. But models do possess unique features, and the use of the term model as a synonym for theory or the like can be misleading.

Writing on the formal study of models, Apostel "hints" at a general definition of model:

> Any subject using a system A that is neither directly nor indirectly interacting with a system B to obtain information about the system B is using A as a model for B.[16]

The functions of models, Apostel states, include the formation, completion, reduction, simplification, extension, and presentation of theories. Further, models are used for the indirect representation of phenomena which are too far away, too big or small, or too dangerous to be observed. Models serve as intermediaries between theories and theories, experiments and theories, experiments and experiments, and between new and old findings. Last, models can be used simply to establish relations.

The relation of models to the empirical world and the manner in which models are evaluated can be represented diagrammatically in Figure 2.[17] A longer sequence of model

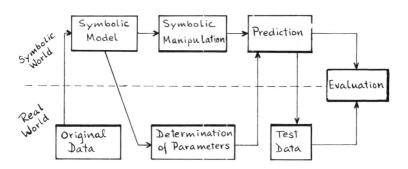

Figure 2.   A symbolic model is arbitrarily created
from empirical data, symbolic manipulation is conducted on
measurable parameters or variables, a prediction made, and
an outcome evaluated.

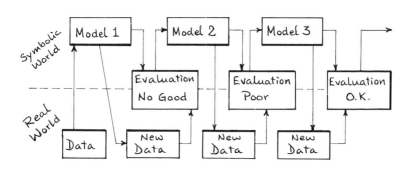

Figure 3.   Model revised against successive collections of data.

development is illustrated in Figure 3, wherein the model is revised against successive collections of data until results are deemed satisfactory.[18] The sequence in Figure 3 is illustrated by the development of the planetary model of the atom in microphysics. The atomic nucleus was first represented as Rutherford's planetary model of the atom, wherein a nucleus held electron satellites in orbit by means of electrostatic force, which was analogous to Newton's concept of gravity. When the laws of electromagnetism contradicted Rutherford's model, the planetary image was retained and the laws of electromagnetism and mechanics were modified to accord with experimental laws of spectra, resulting in the Bohr model of the atom. Further observations necessitated the invention of more complicated vectorial models. The refinement of wave mechanics necessitated the abandonment of vectorial models in favor of algebraic, hydrodynamic models. Finally, a series of more sophisticated models have been developed taking account of more recent findings in electronic spin and relativity.[19]

Models and a World Encyclopedia

Philosophers have noted the tendency of various fields of knowledge to become increasingly abstract during their approach to maturity. F. S. C. Northrop, for example, sketches the progressive growth of disciplines from their initial classification and definitional stage, to a second stage of empirically based theory, and finally to a third stage characterized by abstract deductive and postulational systems.[20] Kaplan sees the use of models as a mark of maturity of any particular discipline.[21] Boulding views the growth of knowledge as a process of progressive subordination of older theories and models to newer, more abstract ones. "The old is almost invariably seen as a special case of the new."[22]

Weinberg emphasizes a "well recognized fragmentation of science" and the danger that branches of science will cease to communicate, fertilize, and be consistent with each other. But, "as science fragments, it seeks to reintegrate itself by moving to a higher level of abstraction...the Watson-Crick model unifies many parts of biology."[23] It is this attribute of models--their integrative power particularly at higher levels of abstraction--that makes them candidates for a basic role in the encyclopedic organization of knowledge.

A host of general advantages and disadvantages in the

use of models can be obtained from literature on modeling.[24]
With regard to the encyclopedic organization of knowledge,
models possess the advantages of compactness, flexibility of
structure and purpose, general or special deployability, and
adaptability to new facts.   Further, models can be flexibly
classified by their subject origin or subject applicability, purpose, degree of abstractness, or by structural and functional
characteristics.

As time passes, the idea of a World Encyclopedia
seems to be increasingly less grandiose and utopian.   It can
be argued that the rudiments of a world encyclopedia exists
today.   According to von Bertalanffy, the chief founder of
general systems theory, "a unitary conception of the world
may be based ... on the isomorphy of laws in different
fields."[25]   Boulding has defined general systems theory as
"the skeleton of science in the sense that it aims to provide
a framework or structure of systems on which to hang the
flesh and blood of particular disciplines ... in an orderly and
coherent corpus of knowledge."[26]

In biology it has been demonstrated that different clusters of models, as sub-systems of a general system, can be
related in different ways for various types of problems:

1. as a set of individual models applied simultaneously to the same problem;
2. as complementary or overlapping models;
3. as conflicting models which stimulate events in
   mutually incompatible ways;
4. as alternative models applicable to the same
   problem;
5. as a group of nested models to explain correlated
   phenomena; or
6. as a representation of different degrees of realism,
   generalism, and precision.   Unrealistic models,
   for example, can serve to reduce uncertainty.[27]

An existing information retrieval system called
"SYNTOL" (Syntagmatic Organization Language), could be
further developed to incorporate new concepts and findings
into a model of the structure of a given subject.   "In this
way the 'culture' of the computer would continually be extended, reorganized, updated, under the impact of the recent
scientific data found in the newly processed literature."[28]

Other existing practices, which are suggested as rudiments of a World Encyclopedia, relate to the input or selection component of this hypothetical world encyclopedia. Today's "gatekeepers" or functionaries in various "clearing house" activities decide what research is feasible or what new ideas and findings are significant enough to be incorporated into a larger body of knowledge. Examples of such gatekeepers include federal research and development fund administrators, the editorial staff of journals, the "continuous revision" staff of encyclopedias, and the authors of annual reviews. The collective explicit and implicit selection criteria or "models" of these gatekeepers could suggest a set of criteria applicable to the input function of a World Encyclopedia.

Rudiments of an output or retrieval component of a World Encyclopedia are suggested by the operation of research services offered by encyclopedias, and by larger information or reference networks which have developed, or will develop. The International Federation for Documentation (FID), for example, plans a "World Science Information System," available to subscribers the world over.[29] Other rudiments of a world encyclopedia can be seen in the development of such works as the International Encyclopedia of Unified Science[30] and the International Encyclopedia of the Social Sciences, as well as in such advances as communications satellites, computer technology and miniaturization. Operation of a "world brain," predicted for the year 2095 by A.C. Clarke in Profiles of the Future,[31] may become a reality much sooner.

Notes

1. H.G. Wells "World Encyclopaedia," reprinted in M. Kochen (ed.), The Growth of Knowledge, New York, Wiley, 1967; 12-22.
2. Ibid., 18-21.
3. K.E. Boulding, The Image, Ann Arbor, University of Michigan Press, 1956; 163. See also J.R. Royce, The Encapsulated Man, New York, Van Nostrand, 1964.
4. H.D. Lasswell, "Strategies of Inquiry: The Rational Use of Observation," in D. Lerner (ed.), The Human Meaning of the Social Sciences, Cleveland, World Publishing Company, 1959; 89-113.
5. P. Weiss, "Knowledge: A Growth Process," in M. Kochen (ed.), op. cit., 209-215.
6. C.W. Churchman, "Toward a Mathematics of Social Science," in F. Massarik and P. Ratoosh, Mathematical Explorations in Behavioral Science, Homewood, Ill., Irwin, 1965; 29-36.

7. A. deGrazia, "The Universal Reference System," The American Behavioral Scientist, 8 (April, 1965), 3-14; W. Davis, "The Universal Brain: Is Centralized Storage and Retrieval of All Knowledge Possible, Feasible or Desirable?" In M. Kochen (ed.), op. cit., 60-65.
8. K. W. Deutsch, "On Theories, Taxonomies, And Models As Communication Codes for Organizing Information," Behavioral Science, 11 (January, 1966), 1-17.
9. M. Kochen (ed.) op. cit., xi.
10. J. H. Shera, Libraries and the Organization of Knowledge, Hamden, Conn.: Archon Books, 1965; 99-100.
11. Ibid., 105.
12. J. A. H. Murray (ed.), New English Dictionary on Historical Principles, Oxford, Clarendon Press, 1884-1933.
13. A. Chapanis, "Men, Machines and Models," American Psychologist, 16 (February, 1961), 113-131.
14. P. Duhem The Aim and Structure of Physical Theory, translated by P. P. Wiener, Princeton, N. J., Princeton University Press, 1954. First published as La Théorie Physique (Paris, 1905); N. R. Campbell, Physics: The Elements, Cambridge, Eng., Cambridge University Press, 1920.
15. Because of scattered entries, counts are crude. Nevertheless, the number of entries under "Models" or "Mathematical Models" was, with few exceptions, increasing rapidly relative to the total number of entries indexed in each source and relative to the entries under "Theory." In the original Encyclopedia of the Social Sciences (1933), the term "model" is difficult if not almost impossible to find; in the 1967 International Encyclopedia of the Social Sciences, models are discussed under at least 25 topics. The total population of models in all fields is probably doubling every two to five years.
16. L. Apostel, "Towards the Formal Study of Models in the Non-Formal Sciences," in H. Freudenthal (ed.), The Concept and the Role of the Model in Mathematics and Natural and Social Sciences, Dordrecht, The Netherlands, Reidel, 1961; 36.
17. I. D. J. Bross, Design for Decision, New York, Macmillan, 1953; 174.
18. Ibid., p. 177.
19. J. L. Destouches, Sur la Notion de Modèle en Microphysique," in H. Freudenthal (ed.), op. cit., 52.
20. F. S. C. Northrop, The Logic of the Sciences and the Humanities, New York, Macmillan, 1947.

21. A. Kaplan, The Conduct of Inquiry, San Francisco, Chandler, 1964; 262-263.

22. K. E. Boulding, op. cit., 78.

23. A. M. Weinberg, Reflections on Big Science, Cambridge, Mass., MIT Press, 1967; 42-44

24. See H. Freudenthal, op. cit.; A. Kaplan, op. cit., Chapter VII; M. B. Hesse, Models and Analogies in Science, Notre Dame, Ind., University of Notre Dame Press, 1966; Symposia of the Society for Experimental Biology, Models and Analogues in Biology, New York, Academic Press, 1960.

25. L. von Bertalanffy, "General Systems Theory," General Systems, First Yearbook of the Society for General Systems Research, 1956; 8.

26. K. Boulding, "General Systems Theory: The Skeleton of Science," Ibid., 17. See also D. Bergen "Implications of General Systems Theory for Librarianship and Higher Education," College and Research Libraries, 27 (September, 1966), 384.

27. R. Levins, "Mathematical Models," McGraw-Hill Yearbook of Science and Technology, New York, McGraw-Hill, 1967; 62-65.

28. J. C. Gardin, SYNTOL, New Brunswick, N.J., Graduate School of Library Service, Rutgers University, 1965; 96.

29. Library of Congress Information Bulletin (October 17, 1968), 636.

30. Cf. Neurath, Carnap, and Morris (eds.), Foundations of the Unity of Science, 2 vols., Chicago, University of Chicago Press, 1971.

31. New York, Harper & Row, 1962.

III. INFORMATION RETRIEVAL

"The great virtue of these new information retrieval
systems lies not in the speeds with which the mechanisms that many of them employ can operate. Of far
greater importance is the degree to which the design
of these systems compels an intensive analysis of the
total problem of search strategy and the extent to which
these systems can simulate the thought processes of
the human being. We think, we conceptualize, in terms
of patterns. It was Sir Charles Sherrington who
likened the brain to 'a magic loom', and the competent
reference librarian also weaves a pattern, and sometimes a very intricate pattern, in the prosecution of
his search. But the pattern of the organization of
graphic records does not always coincide with the con-
figuration of our thought processes and the pattern of
our recourse to the library's store. Nor can one always anticipate the pattern of future demands. Nevertheless, the degree to which all of those patterns coincide will determine the extent to which the reference
librarian succeeds in his search. We can learn much
from the epistemologists about the origin and nature of
knowledge, and from the brain physiologists about the
operation of the nervous system, and as our knowledge
increases we can build better systems and machines for
improving the efficiency of information retrieval. Conversely, as we work with these new machines, our understanding of the human brain should improve. There
is a reciprocity here that may be expected to yield big
dividends in the years ahead. No one can really tell
what the future holds, but I suggest that there are at
least two areas in which spectacular achievements may
be anticipated. The first is in mechanized, or automated, character recognition which will make possible
machines that will be able to 'read', respond to, and
act upon the text that is assimilated by the machine.
The second is the development of random access memories which will eliminate the necessity for sequential
search, thus freeing the machine from the magnetic
tape as the human reader was freed from the papyrus

scroll by the parchment codex.   When these two possibilities
are a reality the revolution in librarianship will really have
begun."

J. H. Shera, Documentation..., 81 f.

ON INFORMATION RETRIEVAL SYSTEMS

William Goffman

Information science is essentially concerned with the
study of the principles underlying communication processes
and information systems.   In general, a process is a time
dependent phenomenon, i. e., a sequence of actions leading
to some result.   Thus, a communication process is a sequence of events resulting in the transmission of something
called information from one object to another.   The first
object is called a source and the latter a target or destination.   The mechanism by means of which a process is realized is called a system.*   Systems whose function is the
carrying out of communication processes are referred to as
information systems.   Since a given process may be realized
by a variety of means, such systems need not be unique.
Thus, with every communication process there is associated
a set of information systems, namely those systems which
can carry out the given process.

The largest body of knowledge in the field of information science at the present time deals with the problem of
information retrieval.   An information retrieval process can
be thought of as an instrument for providing effective contact
between the source and destination within a communication
process.   That is, a process which, when properly carried
out, assures that the information transmitted from the source
to the target is relevant, i. e., results in the accumulation
of knowledge at the destination.   Since processes are realized
by systems, information retrieval processes are carried out
by information retrieval systems.   In this discussion we shall
be concerned with such systems particularly with those features which relate to their design and to the evaluation of
their performance.

---

*It is very important to distinguish between a process
and a system, since failure to make this distinction can lead
to a great deal of confusion.

Systems may be either natural or artificial. For example, biological processes are generally carried out by natural systems. Artificial systems are usually developed for the purpose of producing a process when the desired results are not obtainable by natural means. Thus artificial systems are designed to simulate natural ones. Such systems may be very complex or relatively simple and may attempt to generate a complete process or only a small part of one. To illustrate, an artificial system may be introduced in order to activate a natural system in the realization of some process. Such is the case when a vaccine is used to instigate a natural biological system to carry out an immunization process. Similarly, a telephone system places its users in a position for a natural flow of information to occur between them. In each case the system activates the development of a natural process. On the other hand, an artificial system may serve to eliminate a bottleneck somewhere along the course of development of a process. Such is the case when insulin injections are used in the treatment of diabetes. Naturally, in any given physical situation the desired results may be obtained in various ways. Finding the optimal way constitutes the fundamental problem of systems theory.

A system can be loosely defined as a collection of elements interacting in the performance of some function for some purpose. The elements of a system are called its components and may be either things or operations: that is, the elements may consist of tangible objects such as gears or relays or intangibles such as arithmetic operations or chemical reactions. The purpose of a system is associated with the requirements placed upon it by its users, while its function deals with procedure employed by the system for satisfying these requirements. It is essential that a system have both a purpose and a function, for evaluation of its performance depends upon both. The reason for this is that a system is intended to optimize a certain performance function of its inputs and outputs as related to its user's requirements. For example, the function of a vaccine is the prevention of the occurrence of some disease. Its purpose, let us say, is the betterment of mankind. Clearly, the vaccine cannot be adequately evaluated without considering both its purpose and function.

It should be noted that the purpose of a system need not be constructive nor need its users necessarily desire to avail themselves of its services. Optimization of such a system from the users' point of view would consist of mini-

mizing rather than maximizing the performance function of
its inputs and outputs.

        The function of an information retrieval system is to
carry out an information retrieval process, i.e., to put
members of a given population (its users) and information
from a certain source into effective contact with each other.
The fact that an information system puts a user in contact
with information does not guarantee a specific outcome, namely the accumulation of knowledge, just as the exposure of an
individual to infectious material need not result in a case of
disease.   In fact the system's users may not require that
this occur.   Such is the case with users of a telephone system.   They do not hold the system responsible for any particular piece of information which may be conveyed; they expect only that a contact take place.   The user of an information retrieval system, on the other hand, requires that the
contact effected by the system lead to a specific result,
namely the transmission of relevant information.   We call
such a contact an effective contact.   An effective contact,
thus, leads to the acquisition of the desired knowledge.   It
is by no means necessary that the system be activated at
the request of its users, for it may wish to volunteer or dis-
seminate information.   In this event, since its purpose is
only served by satisfying certain requirements of its users,
it is essential that the system not transmit information out
of self-satisfaction.   Thus a system which disseminates information voluntarily can be said to be enacting for the user
by formulating a query which appropriately corresponds to
his requirement.   Hence, the voluntary system is theoretically equivalent to the system activated directly by the user.
Therefore, the output of an information retrieval system consists of a collection of agents conveying relevant information
in response to a query as input.   That is, the function of an
information retrieval system is the establishment of effective
contact between its information source and its users.

        The first step in the design of any system is the def-
inition of its purpose and function.   Once it has been decided
what functions must be performed by the system in order to
satisfy its users' requirements, trial solutions can be attempted.   The system can consist of many components which
contribute to its performance.   The designer's task is to organize these components in such a way that the inputs will
optimally produce the desired outputs.   In this endeavor he
may have a choice of a number of alternative combinations
of components.

The first set of trial solutions involves the so-called single thread performance. By this is meant the solution of the engineering problem of performing the function at all, considering the requirements which must be satisfied. Usually there are techniques available from former experience for accomplishing this task. Often, however, it is necessary for new methods to be devised.

The second set of trial solutions takes into consideration the fact that some of the system's functions must be performed many times. This step is sometimes called the solution for high traffic density. Here the designer may encounter problems which do not exist in the single thread solution. Typical high traffic density problems are concerned with such things as waiting time and occupancy. Solution of such problems is very important, for example in the operation of a telephone system. Often the single thread solution must be scrapped in order to accommodate high traffic.

The third set of solutions is that of competitive design. This phase is necessary only if the system is to operate in an hostile environment. The design of an immunization system, for example, requires that the competitive nature of its environment be taken into account. For it may be that the system performs very well when in an isolated surrounding but breaks down completely when confronted with the real environment in which it must perform.

An extremely important concept in the design of systems is the notion of trade-offs. Basically trade-offs consist of a series of decisions in which the system designer gives up something in return for something else. The basis underlying the necessity of having trade-offs is that a system generally must serve many users, and a given system cannot satisfy the requirements of every one of its potential users.

As an illustration, consider an airline ticketing system which provides satisfaction to the airline's customers 98 percent of the time. Suppose that in order to accommodate the remaining 2 percent the cost of operation and maintenance is tripled. The designer must decide whether to trade off 2 percent of unhappy customers for an increased economy and decreased efficiency in the system's operation.

•

Another example which is more pertinent to our subject is concerned with the development of an artificial immunization system. As is well known there are two types of vaccines which may be used, namely, the inactive and the attenuated virus types. Assuming that it is physically possible to arrive at a solution with either system, the researcher must decide, for example, whether the greater antibody concentration achieved by the attenuated virus vaccine is worth the risk of inducing the disease.

Since information retrieval is a communication process, information retrieval systems are concerned with identification, recognition, and transmission of information. This communication is accomplished by means of a language.

Although it is beyond the scope of this short paper to launch into any detailed discussion of language, it is expedient to point out certain of its more prominent features. First of all, it is not necessary to describe the language employed by an information retrieval system. All that is needed is that it contain certain conventions which are generally understood. Secondly, the language must be specific, i.e., given a choice of languages, at most one is used. This language should contain the technical terminology and linguistic devices which are required by the members of the population for understanding. Thus the language employed by an information system may be a natural language, as, in the communication of ideas, language of chemistry as in the communication of a disease or a genetic property, or some artificial language as in the communication between man and machine, or among machines.

In its most general sense a language is defined in terms of a certain set of objects called its alphabet and a set of rules for specifying how to form certain combinations of these objects, called letters, into meaningful expressions called words and sentences. A language is not static but is in a continuous process of development. In this way it becomes more precise. The problems of languages are well-known and there is an enormous literature dealing with them from many different points of view.

A given language may be represented in any one of a number of different symbolic forms or codes. Thus, once the system designer has selected a language, he must decide upon an appropriate means for representing it. The problem of coding in information systems is basic and there exists a very elaborate theory dealing with it. This is of course the information theory initiated by Shannon and already developed into a highly specialized discipline. For an excellent treatment of the fundamentals of this theory see Khinchin (ref. 1, end of paper) or Wolfowitz (2).

An information retrieval system must provide effective contact between its information source (its file) and its users. Therefore it is not sufficient for it to provide the user with "any old" information. It must provide relevant information. Hence the system must have built into it a selection procedure for recognizing the relevant material contained in the file. Moreover, it must be able to select this material in a very efficient manner. That is, the system must have its information source organized in a fashion which allows for the location of the desired material in minimum time. This operation is called a searching procedure.

It should be noted that sources of information, as well as user requirements, are not static but in constant flux. This is true of the members of any population, whether they be cells, human beings or machines. Thus an information retrieval system should have the property of being self-organizing and error-adjusting. This property requires that the system possess certain automatic feedback loops in order to maintain optimal functioning under varying circumstances. We shall not go into this property here, except simply to point out that the design of an information retrieval system requires the consideration of the problem.

In summary, the essential components of an information retrieval system, given an information source, are: a language, a code, a searching procedure, and a series of automatic feedback loops. Each of these components may themselves be made up of other components and so-forth. There are various ways in which a set of components can be organized into a system for the purpose of carrying out a given process. The designer must determine which set of components should be assembled in order to perform the assigned task. That is, given certain classes of components, which assembly of these into a system will provide the optimum performance relative to the specified purpose and function? The answer to this question requires a means of evaluating a system's performance.

The performance M of an information retrieval system can be measured in terms of a function of two variables -- $M = f(u, v)$ -- where u is a measure of the system's effectiveness and v is a measure of the system's efficiency.

Informally, effectiveness u is defined as a measure of the system's ability to perform the task for which it was designed, while efficiency v is a measure of the cost or speed of performing this task.

Effectiveness of a system is measured by a function u which should behave in accordance with the requirements imposed upon the system's performance. The system is expected to transmit that information contained in the file and only that information which is relevant to the user's query. In other words, the system is expected to provide the user with that part of the informative source at its disposal which will result in an effective contact when transmitted to a user.

The effectiveness of an information retrieval system can be measured in the same way as the effectiveness of a diagnostic test. A diagnosis is an evaluation of the result of a communication process. Thus a diagnostic test is simply a method for determining whether an effective contact has occurred. Hence the evaluation of a diagnostic test is a special case of the evaluation of an information retrieval system. In the diagnostic case the problem is to determine whether a screening test can correctly identify an effective contact between a susceptible and the infectious material of a given disease. In the general case the problem is to determine whether an information retrieval system can correctly select the relevant material namely those information agents and only those agents which will lead to an effective contact when transmitted to the user.

In the evaluation of a screening test for a given disease, the physician is concerned with two measures which are called sensitivity and specificity. Sensitivity is defined as the "ability of the test to classify as positive those who have the condition being screened for." In other words, sensitivity is a measure of how well a test correctly identifies those individuals who have a certain disease. Specificity is defined as "the ability of the test to classify as negative those who do not have the condition." Thus specificity is a measure of how well a test correctly identifies those persons who do not have the disease. Failure of the test to identify a case of disease is called a false negative. If the test incorrectly identifies an individual as a case of the disease, this is labeled a false positive.

Just as a diagnostic test is expected to identify every case of disease within a given population, so an information retrieval system is expected to retrieve that material and only that material contained in its file (information source) which is relevant to the user's request, i.e., that will result in an effective contact. Borrowing the terminology from medicine we define effectiveness as a function of sensitivity and specificity, where sensitivity measures the system's ability to transmit to the user the relevant members of the file and specificity measures the system's ability not to transmit the non-relevant members.

Hence sensitivity S_e can be represented by the conditional probability that a member x of the file I will be transmitted to the user s given that x is relevant to s. Thus-- (1) $S_e = P_A(X)$ --where X represents the system output and A the set of relevant members contained in I.

The measure of specificity S_p can be represented as the conditional probability that a member y of I will not be transmitted by the system given that y is not relevant to s. Thus-- (2) $S_p = P_{A'}(X')$ --where X' is the complement of the system's output X and A' is the set of non-relevant members of I.

We shall define the measure of effectiveness of an information retrieval system as-- (3) $u = P_A(X) + P_{A'}(X') - 1$ -- and show that this function possesses the essential properties expected of such a measure.

First, we observe that the values of the function u can range from -1 to +1. The maximum value of +1 is attained if and only if-- $P_A(X) = 1$ and $P_{A'}(X') = 1$. This is precisely the case where the system transmits all members and only those members of the file which are relevant.

On the other hand u achieves its minimum value of -1 if and only if-- $P_A(X) = 0$ and $P_{A'}(X') = 0$. This is exactly the case where the system transmits all members and only those members of the file which are non-relevant.

Since-- $P_{A'}(X') = 1 - P_{A'}(X)$ -- (3) can be expressed as-- (3') $u = P_A(X) - P_{A'}(X)$. From (3') it can be seen that u = 0 if and only if the conditional probability that information will be transmitted by the system given that it is relevant is equal to the conditional probability that information will be transmitted given that it is non-relevant. In this event the system is operating in a random fashion. Positive values of u indicate that the system's chances of transmitting information which leads to an effective contact are better then not, while negative values of u indicate the converse.

The random performance is the worst possible, since the system under such circumstances is making no contribution to the communication process. A negative contribution in certain instances may be very desirable, i.e., in those cases where the results of a communication process are to be minimized rather than maximized, e.g., in the transmission of a disease.

The efficiency v is measured by some function which can be considered as a function of time-- $v = C(t)$. Thus the performance of an information system may in general be measured in terms of its effectiveness per unit of time-- $M = u(t)$.

Clearly the performance of an information retrieval system can provide a control over the outcome of a communication process. General methods for dealing with this problem can be found in (3) in which a general theory of communication is developed.

Notes

1. Khinchin, A.I.   The Mathematical Foundations of Information Theory, New York, Dover, 1957.
2. Wolfowitz, J.   Coding Theorems of Information Theory, Englewood Cliffs, N.J., Prentice Hall, 1961.
3. Goffman, W. & Newill, V.A. "Communication and Epidemic Processes," Proc. Roy. Soc. A, v. 298, 316-334.

ON A FALLACY IN THE USE OF COMPUTING MACHINES FOR AUTOMATED DICTIONARY RETRIEVAL

Andrew D. Booth

1. Introduction

As the use of computing machines for the storage of information has developed, the techniques proposed have tended to structure themselves to the format of the low speed storage of the machine concerned. Historically, and even at the present time, this structuring divides itself along two distinct lines: first, for magnetic tape storage, in which information becomes available only after a period of hunting to find the required spot where it is recorded on the serial medium which constitutes the tape; and second, random access storage, for example discs or large volume core stores, in which the time required to locate a particular item of information is effectively independent of the location of the stored item on the medium.

It has been regarded as "obvious" that, when a <u>single</u> item of information is to be located, random access storage will always be more rapid and, therefore, more efficient in some sense, since the hunting time on even the fastest tape units is of the order of tens of seconds, compared with times which range from a few microseconds to a few milliseconds for a random access store. Of the intermediate area nothing has been said, and it is clear that the efficiency will depend largely on the type of retrieval operation involved.

For very large scale storage and retrieval operations however, some workers, for example at the National Physical Laboratory in England, have reasoned as follows: looking up items taken in sequence, from a list in a random access store, will "obviously" take a searching time which is directly proportional to the number of items to be located. With a serial store of the magnetic tape variety however, the following process can be used: first, sort the incident questions into order so that all identical items come together, and will be looked up but once in the medium. Second, during a single pass of the tape, or other serial medium, locate all of the entries required, and associate the stored data with the request items, and third, re-sort the questions with the appropriate answers into their original order for use. The argument then runs that, using this last procedure, the number of items searched on the tape can never exceed the number of items stored on the tape, and therefore must have some upper limit. There follows the statement: "Therefore, at some question-list length, serial storage used in this mode will always be more efficient than random access storage."

2.   Mathematical Analysis

The following is an analysis of the two situations discussed above.

Let: - text length be N words
       - dictionary length be D words
       - time of access operation to the random-access store be T_r
       - time of passage of one word on tape past the reading station be T_t
       - time of one access operation to the store used for sorting be T_s.

It follows that the time to look up the N words in the random access store, using the binary or logarithmic search technique is-- (1) $NT_r\log_2 D$. In using the tape it is necessary:

1) To sort the text into an alphabetical sequence in which identical words are brought together.
2) To compare each distinct word in the text with the dictionary tape and to record the dictionary entry alongside that word.
3) To re-sort the text words into their original order.

The times for items 1) and 3) are of order $KN^2 T_s$, where K is a constant of order unity depending on the method chosen.

The time for item 2) is DT_t. Thus the operation time using tape is-- (2) $2KN^2 T_s + DT_t$ --and the condition for tape to be more efficient than random access is simply-- $2KN^2 T_s + DT_t < NT_r\log_2 D$. Since $N^2 > CN$ for all C, and for sufficiently large N, it is clear that tape is <u>not</u> more efficient than random access storage for large text sizes.

As a typical set of values we can take:

$$D = 10^6 \text{ words } \log_2 D = 20$$
$$T_r = 110 \text{ m.s.} \quad \text{(IBM disc worst case)}$$
$$T_s = 110 \text{ m.s.} \quad \text{(Assuming text cannot be sorted in high-speed store)}$$
$$T_t = 200 \, \mu \text{ sec.} \quad \text{(Typical of a 60 k.c. tape unit)}$$
$$K = 1/2$$

We then require-- $N^2.110 - 200.10^3 < N.110.20$ --i.e.,
$$N^2 - 20N + \frac{20 \times 10^3}{11} < 0$$ which is not valid for any real N

since the minimum value occurs for $N = 10$ and is

$$+ \frac{189}{11} . 10^2.$$

3. Conclusion

We have thus demonstrated the fallacy of the State-ment made in 1. This is a matter of considerable impor-tance in large scale retrieval and, whilst the details of ma-chine and storage characteristics given above will undoubted-ly vary with time, the general principle is still true, and should be taken as a guidepost to optimum procedures for the future.

[This work forms part of a program on the machine-aided translation sponsored by the National Research Council of Canada, to whom the author expresses his gratitude for continued support.]

BROWSING AND SEARCH THEORY

Philip M. Morse

The act of browsing is an important one for most library users; it is the way they search out, and often find,
the books they borrow and read. They may browse through
the display of recent books to see what is new, or through
a portion of the library shelves in the hope of finding a text
which could contribute the fact or idea needed to solve some
intellectual problem, or they might scan quickly through the
fiction collection to see whether some title might strike their
fancy. The browser is not certain just what he will find,
but past rewards have been sufficient for thim to continue
the practice. As Shera has indicated, in his columns and
talks, it would be useful to analyze the operation of browsing,
so the librarian can determine how his policies may help or
hinder browsers, and by how much.

Search and Probability

Browsing is a type of search, in many ways similar
to the search, by an observer in a plane, for an enemy ship
or submarine on the ocean surface.[1] The observer is not
sure the target is there, or that he will see it if it is there,
but he flies a search pattern in the hope of success. This
search operation was studied in some detail, both experimen-
tally and theoretically, during World War II; today most aircraft search doctrine is worked out by use of the theory of
search then developed.[2] Much of this theory can assist us
in quantifying our understanding of browsing in a library.

Experiments carried out during World War II by the
late Selig Hecht (unfortunately never published in the open
literature) cast light on the process of visual search, the
basis of browsing as well as of looking for submarines. The
eye does not move steadily along a shelf of books (or a line
of print) absorbing steadily everything as it goes. It skips
around, stopping a moment here, then jumping elsewhere.
We pick up information in glimpses, as the eyes momentarily

come to focus on a rather small area, subtending the fovea. Usually, before everything in this area is completely perceived, the glance moves elsewhere, perhaps later to come back again, to take in more detail.

Thus our perception comes to us in a sequence of glimpses, each glimpse conveying its pittance of information. If these glimpses are part of a search for a book, somewhere among a shelf-full of other books, there is a probability that one of the glimpses will reveal it. If we have no foreknowledge of just where the book we want happens to be, this probability is a product of two factors; the chance that this glimpse happens to cover the part of the shelf where the book is, and the chance that we would actually perceive the book if we were looking at it in this glimpse. The first factor is inversely proportional to the number N of books on the shelf; if there are hundreds of them the chance that a particular glimpse is pointed at the wanted book is less than if the wanted book is one of only ten. Thus this factor has the form α/N, where the value of α is related to the foveal area. The second factor, the chance μ of actually recognizing the book when the glimpse is pointed right, varies with the illumination, the size of the wanted book and with the degree of alertness of the browser. It too can be measured and a rough, average value can be found for it.

Therefore the probability of spotting the wanted book, among N others, in one particular glimpse, is equal to a constant β (which combines the α of the first factor and the second factor μ) divided by N. This quantity--
(1) $\underline{g} = \beta/\underline{N} = \alpha\mu/\underline{N}$ --is appropriately called the glimpse probability.

In browsing, of course, we would spend a lot of glimpses, not just one. In this kind of visual search there seems to be a natural "rate of glimpsing" (ω glimpses per minute, say) so the total number of glimpses spent in searching for the book would be the glimpse rate ω times the number of minutes t spent searching. By the laws of probability the chance of success, P_s, of finding the book among N others if time t is spent looking for it, is 1 minus the chance of not finding it. And this in turn is the chance $1-g$ of not finding the book in one glimpse, multiplied by itself to the power ωt of glimpses spent in the search--
(2) $\underline{P}_s = 1 - (1-\underline{g})^{\omega\underline{t}} = 1 - (1-\frac{\beta}{N})^{\omega\underline{t}}$

Usually the number of glimpses spent, $\omega\,\underline{t}$, is a large

number, several hundred or more. And usually the individual glimpse probability g is quite small, particularly if N is 100 or more. In such cases the second term in the formula can be approximated by the exponential $e^{-\beta\omega t/N}$, and we reach the basic formula for visual search, when written in terms appropriate for browsing. The probability of finding a book placed at random among N others, in time t, is--
(3) $P_S = 1 - e^{-\rho t/N}$ --where ρ (which equals $\beta\omega = \alpha\mu\omega$) may be called the search rate of the browser. Quantity $\rho t/N$ is called the search coverage. If it is large the area has been thoroughly searched; if it is small the search has been cursory. If $\rho t/N$ equals 0.7 the chance of success P_S is $1/2$; if $\rho t/N = 1.4$ then $P_S = 3/4$; if $\rho t/N$ is smaller than 0.2, P_S is roughly equal to $\rho t/N$.

We now can disregard the psycho-physiological basis of the results, as revealed by the factors α, μ and ω, and measure the search rate ρ directly, for the particular case of book browsing. Search rate, for a particular browser and set of book shelves, can be measured as follows. A particular book is placed at random among 200 to 500 other books and the person is asked to search for it for 3 minutes, say. This trial is repeated some 20 to 50 times, with a different book, in a different location, being the target each trial. The searcher should not know the size or color of the book, sometimes he should be told only the author's name, sometimes just the title. The fraction of times the trial is successful is an approximation to P_S; $\rho t/N$ can be read off Figure 1 (or from tables of the exponential) and, knowing t and N, ρ can be found. Since none of the analysis to follow requires great accuracy, it is not necessary to determine ρ very precisely and it is not usually necessary to take into account the fact that ρ changes with illumination and degree of accessibility of the shelf. The writer has determined, by trials of the sort just described, that his own search rate for books lies between 100 and 200 books per minute.

Figure 1 shows clearly that search is subject to the law of diminishing return. If $\rho t/N$ is less than $1/4$, then doubling it will roughly double the chance of success. But if the coverage $\rho t/N$ is 2, doubling it hardly increases P_S by ten percent. A good rule of thumb is that increasing search coverage $\rho t/N$ beyond unit value is hardly a paying activity; it would be better to go search in virgin territory.

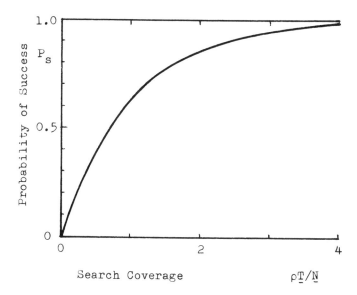

Figure 1.   Chance of spotting one book in $\underline{N}$, as function of ratio of search effort $\rho\underline{T}$ to number $\underline{N}$ of books.

Allocation of Search Effort

We still have to translate this formula into terms specifically applicable to browsing.   For the browser usually is not seeking a specific book; he is looking through the shelves to see "what catches his eye."   Nevertheless he does not allocate his search effort purely at random; he goes to that section of the library that he estimates has the highest probability of containing a book or books his immediate interests would find to be worth borrowing.   He doesn't quantify this estimate, but decision theorists[3] have indicated how it could be quantified.

The prospective browser picks a specific section of the library, containing $\underline{N}$ books, in which to browse, because he has estimated that the section contains a few books which might be of immediate interest to him.   The section may be all books on European history (for example) or it may be all books on French medieval history, depending on the narrowness of his interests just then.   In any case it is the section

within which he has no idea where the book might be, over
all of which his search must extend if he hopes to spot it.
If put to it he could probably arrive at a number E (1 or 2
or 3) as his a priori estimate of the possible number of such
books (of immediate interest to him) in the section.   Since
he has no idea where in the section these E books might be,
he has instinctively decided that each book in the section has
interest potential $V = E/N$, and deserves equal coverage
until one or more of the desired books are spotted.   In view
of his action at that moment he evidently has decided that the
interest potential of that section is higher than the interest
potential of other sections of the library, for he spends some
of his available browsing time there.

Of course there is no need for the prospective browser
to work out his actions quite so quantitatively; he could spend
the time more profitably in browsing.   But in operations
where the stakes are higher (as in antisubmarine search)
search theory[2] has worked out the optimum allocation of
search effort.   It is useful to review this theory here, to
gain understanding of the principles involved, and to see
whether and how the librarian may improve the browser's
chances.

Assume that the prospective browser had evaluated
each subject section of the library in advance, allocating to
the N'th section, which has N_n books, an a priori estimate
E_n of the number of books in that section which might be of
immediate interest to him this time.   Each of his "subject
sections" are just small enough so that the browser is completely uncertain where in the section the books of interest
might be, and just large enough so that he can distinguish
his degree of interest (his value of $V = E/N$) from one section to the next.   He also decides he has a total of T_1 minutes to spend browsing this time.   One can then plot a block
diagram like Figure 2, corresponding to his interests at the
moment.   The width of the n'th block, representing section
n, is equal to the number of books N_n in the section; the
height of the n'th block is the natural logarithm $\ln(V_n)$ of the
browser's estimated interest potential $V_n = E_n/N_n$ of this
section.

To find the optimal allocation of his T_1 minutes one
finds the horizontal line, of height $\ln \lambda_1$, such that the area
above the line (cross-hatched in Figure 2) is just equal to
ρT_1, where ρ is the browser's search rate in books per minute.   In the example shown only two blocks rise above the

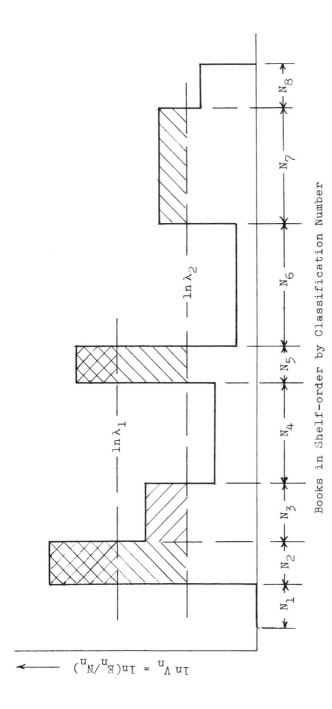

Figure 2. Illustrating procedure for optimizing browsing time among sections with different interest potentials $\underline{E}/\underline{N}$.

line $\ln\lambda_1$, so the browser should spend all his T_1 minutes in
sections 2 and 5, ignoring all the other sections. This will
be the optimal allocation of his time. The optimal division
of time between the two sections is proportional to the areas:

$$\text{Time in section 2} = (N_2/\rho) \, [\ln(E_2/N_2) - \ln(\lambda_1)]$$

$$\text{Time in section 5} = (N_5/\rho) \, [\ln(E_5/N_5) - \ln(\lambda_1)]$$

Each section should be covered uniformly in the time
allotted since, by the way we have defined each section, he
doesn't know where the books of interest are in the section.
Since, in the example, the two sections are about equal in
size, the division of time is proportional to the heights above
$\ln\lambda_1$ (roughly 5/8 of the time in section 2 and 3/8 in section 5), the search in section 2 should be nearly twice as
meticulous as that in section 5.

If the browser has time T_2 to spend, greater than T_1,
then the horizontal line $\ln\lambda_2$ is lower, to encompass the
larger area ρT_2 above it (that cross-hatched plus that shaded).
In the case shown in Figure 2, sections 2, 3, 5 and 7 should
now be included in the search. Though sections 2 and 5 still
claim the greatest density of search, section 7 claims a fair
amount of time, because of its large size. Sections 4, 6
and 9 are still to be ignored.

The major points to be drawn from this illustration
are: 1) that sections of the library which have the same a
priori interest potential V should receive the same density
of search (i.e., about the same number of glimpses per 100
books) and 2) that allocation of browsing time to sections of
differing V should exaggerate the high-potential ones, in a
quite non-linear way, even to the extent of neglecting entirely
those sections with V less than some value in $\ln\lambda$, depending
on the total time to be spent.

The Librarian's Problem

The problem is relatively simple for each individual
library user. Though his interests may change from visit
to visit, he needs only to estimate the interest potential of
books in various parts of the library, in accord with his immediate interests, and then allocate his search efforts as indicated, concentrating heavily on the highest potential sections. It is quite otherwise for the librarian, for the inter-

ests of different browsers differ widely; indeed the interests
of the same browser vary widely from visit to visit. Is
there anything the librarian can do to improve the success of
all browsers, or at least to improve the success of the average browser?

One thing is apparent immediately; the librarian should
arrange his collections so as to be obviously differentiable,
in interest potential, to the majority of library users. The
worst possible library, for a browser, would be one in which
he could not differentiate at all between the interest potentials
of different sections, where he would have to treat all shelves
as being equally likely (or, rather, equally unlikely) to produce what he might want. That library which makes it possible for the average browser to pick quickly a relatively
few, relatively small sections of high interest potential for
his present desires, so he can ignore the rest, is the library
which is most efficient for the browser to use. 9 The subdivision is not easy; too fine division requires the browser to
scan too many sections to cover his range of immediate interest; too broad divisions of equal interest preclude a meticulous search.

Parenthetically, this is the reason why card catalogs
are absurdly ineffective for browsing. Aside from the very
small search rate, every drawer is more or less equally
sparse in interest potential; very few interest spans go according to the alphabet, even in subject catalogs. It is important for the designers of computerized catalogs to realize
that they also will be spurned by the browser if they do not
have a quick and simple means of assembling sub-catalogs of
high interest potential, no matter what the interest span of
the potential browser may be. If the computer can assemble,
in a minute or so, a sub-catalog of a few thousand items,
all of interest potential high for the present browser, of combinations of disparate subjects corresponding to his present
interest span, with the browser then able to flick through the
collection in five or ten minutes; only then will the computerized catalog begin to replace the simple roaming through
the stacks, which has always been (and may always be) the
effective way of finding the book one wants. 4

But to return to the librarian's present problem. He
will (and does) help the browser immensely by arranging the
books on the shelves, not alphabetically or at random, but
by subject class, so if the user knows his Dewey or LC code
he can quickly pick out the regions of high interest potential

for his present predilections.   The librarian can further help
if he can estimate the interest potential $\overline{V}$ of each section
for the average browser.

He does have a fairly good estimate of the likelihood
that a particular book will be picked by a browser; he has
the circulation history of the book, a measure of how many
persons picked the book previously.   Thus the mean interest
potential $\overline{V}$ of a section, for the average browser, should be
roughly proportional to the mean circulation rate $\overline{R}$ of the
books in a subject section.   The actual magnitude of the
proportionality constant C does not matter here; it can be
set equal to 0. 001 for convenience.

Likewise the best estimate the librarian can have regarding the chance that a browser will pick a particular book
is $v = CR$, where R is the circulation of the book during the
previous year.   Probability v might be called its book poten-
tial.   We thus have (4) $v = CR$; $\overline{V} = C\overline{R}$; $C = 0.001$ where
$\overline{V}$ and $\overline{R}$ are the average values of v and $\overline{R}$, respectively, for
the whole section.

Given sufficient data on book circulation and on interconnections between circulations (i. e., what books are taken
out simultaneously by a given borrower) one could, in theory,
devise a book classification which would group books optimally by user interest; but this is beyond the scope of the present paper.   After all, libraries now have a classification
scheme, which browsers have come to be familiar with.
And there are approximate formulas[5] for the distribution in
circulation of books in various subject classes, so the present scheme can be analyzed in regard to browsing.

The problem of deciding just what is the size of one
of the "subject sections" we have been discussing is illustrated in Figure 3.   Here we have plotted a sample of the
circulation rates R of the books in some range of Dewey classification (for example, the biological sciences from 570 to
619).   Each bar represents a book in the sequence of Dewey
numbers in the shelf list; its height measures the book's
last year's circulation.   We note that the left-hand part of the
plot has an average height (shown by the dashed line) which
is roughly half the average height of the bars on the right-
hand side.   Obviously the right-hand portion (Dewey 600 to
619, for example) is more popular than the left.   But it is
difficult to subdivide these portions further into subsections
with appreciable differences in average circulation.

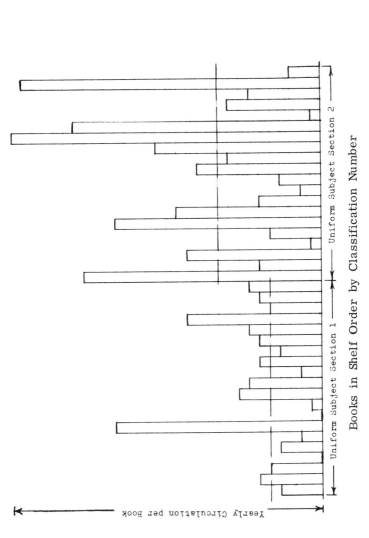

Figure 3. Sample book circulation plots for shelves from two, adjacent, uniform subject sections.

Thus, as the example has suggested, we can separate the library into sections of a hundred to several thousand books, covering ranges of classification numbers, within which mean circulation is roughly constant, differentiated from their neighbors by a noticeable change in average circulation. In most cases the separation will come at obvious places, where subject matter changes radically. Each of these sections, more or less internally uniform in regard to mean circulation, differentiated from their neighbors, can be called uniform subject sections. In the telescoped example of Figure 3, Dewey 570-599 would be one uniform subject section and 600-619 another. In some other library the whole range from 550 to 619 may be constant enough in mean circulation that it all would have to be considered as a single uniform subject section.

This does not mean that such a section is uniform in potential interest to all browsers. For example, one who is interested, just then, only in genetics does not need to scan the whole range from Dewey 570 to 619. However if the section is fairly uniform with respect to mean circulation we can be certain that only a small percentage of browsers will strongly prefer one subsection over the rest, that equal numbers of others will prefer other subsections, and that a fair fraction of the browsers will have no strong preference of one portion of the whole section over another, thus tending to scan the whole section more or less uniformly.

But these matters are not actionable unless the uniform subject section is larger than a few thousand volumes, more than can be scanned effectively in the 10 to 30 minutes the average browser can devote. The size will not handicap the specialist browser, who still can scan the small subsection, of interest to him, in a short time. But for the "generalist" browser, who has no idea where in the section the book may be, which he wants, the section is so large that his search coverage can only be superficial. He would have a much greater chance of finding a book of interest to him if the section were a quarter or a tenth of its size, with all or most of the low-interest-potential books removed to some other location.

From the point of view of the generalist browser, for whom the whole section of N books has a more or less uniform interest potential, the result of such a division into high-circulation and low-circulation portions is governed by two opposing effects. If the section is divided into a "con-

centrated" fraction xN of high-circulation books and a "retired" fraction $(1-x)\overline{N}$ of the rest (those with book potential
less than v_0, for example) the smaller, concentrated section
will be easier to search effectively.   The opposing effect
comes because there is always the chance that some of the
books he might be interested in have been withdrawn from
the fraction x and placed in the retired portion.

The average chance of finding a book in xN books by
browsers with a range of browsing times is the average of
the expression of Eq. (3) over the distribution of browsing
times.   If one assumes an exponential distribution[6] with mean
browsing time T, this factor is $\gamma/(x+\gamma)$, where $\gamma = \mathcal{S}T/N$ is
the search coverage of the undivided section, supposedly much
smaller than 1.   This factor goes to unity as $x = 0$ (as the
browsing fraction x is made smaller, it gets easier to find
one book out of $x\overline{N}$ books).   It drops to a small value at
$x = 1$ if γ is small (if the undivided section is so large that
it cannot be effectively searched in time T).

However a counter effect also acts; as x is made
smaller the chance, that the book of immediate interest is
still left in the browsing fraction, diminishes, going to zero
as x goes to zero.   It has been shown elsewhere[7] that, if
one assumes a reasonable distribution[5] of circulation rates,
the chance that a book of immediate interest still is in the
fraction x is $x[1 + \ln(1/x)]$ ($\ln y$ is the natural logarithm
of y), a formula not very sensitive to the exact form of the
circulation distribution.   This depletion factor is unity when
$x = 1$ (all of the books are present) and goes to zero as
$x \to 0$ (no books left).   The product of the two factors is the
chance of success.   The generalist browser, who has estimated that there might be E books of immediate interest
somewhere in the undivided section, would expect to find S
books during a search of average duration T, where--

$$(5) \quad S = Ex\left[1 + \ln\left(\frac{1}{x}\right)\right]\frac{\gamma}{x+\gamma} ; \quad \gamma = \frac{\mathcal{S}T}{N}$$

The expected success S has a maximum value for x
somewhere between 0 and 1; the smaller γ is the nearer to
$x = 0$ is this maximum.   For the undivided section ($x = 1$)
S has the value $S_u = \gamma/(1+\gamma)$.   For the optimal value x_0,
S has its maximum value S_0; the ratio S_0/S_u can be called
the search advantage of the browsing section over the undivided section for the generalist browser.   Formulas for
x_0 and S_0/S_u are-- $(6) \quad x_0 = \gamma \ln(1/x_0)$; S_0/S_u
$= x_0[1 + (1/\gamma)]$.   These are plotted in Figures 4 and 5.

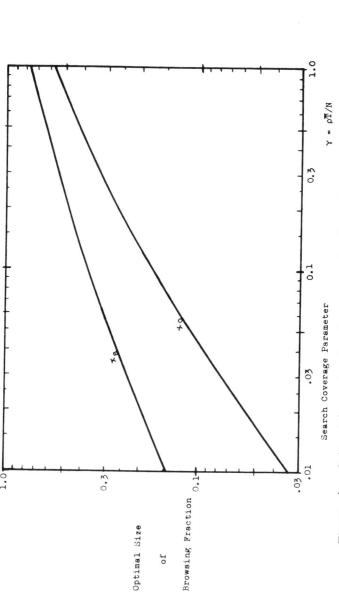

Figure 4. Optimal browsing fractions x as function of mean coverage γ; x_o for when generalist browsers predominate, x_s for when specialist browsers predominate. See note 8.

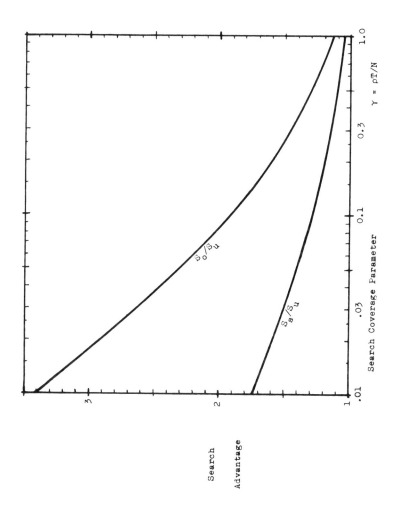

Figure 5. Search advantages S_O/S_u and S_S/S_u as functions of γ for the two limiting values of optimal browsing fractions shown in Figure 4.

If we take as a rough rule of thumb that a search advantage of at least 1.4 is needed before any concentration of a section should be contemplated, we see that search coverage should be less than about 1/3 or 1/4 for this to be the case. For a browser with search rate about 100 books a minute and an average time $T \approx 15$ minutes to spend browsing in this section, $\overline{T}$ would be about 1500. Therefore if the section contains more than about 1500 volumes, would be less than 0.3 and it should benefit the generalist browser to have all but the fraction x_0 of the highest-circulation books to be retired from the "browsing shelves."

Of course this kind of a separation would be somewhat detrimental to some specialist browsers, who can differentiate between different parts of the section and who would tend to search only a small part of the full section, a fraction y, say. If y is small enough they could have searched all $y\overline{N}$ books in time T. Retiring a fraction $1 - x_0$ means they will have to divide T between the "browsing" and the "retired" portions. Some of these, of course, those with interest in the older or more specialized books, need now only search in the retired portion; thus the division may have been a slight advantage to them also. The librarian will have to decide how many of the users of his library are generalist browsers, and whether it is desirable to separate out high-interest-potential, browsing sections for their benefit, [9] or whether the specialist users so predominate that the needs of the generalist browsers must be ignored.

To assist in this evaluation we can plot a second set of curves, for which we assume that the browsers of the section are evenly divided in degree of specialization, as many desiring to scan the whole range of subject matter as those desiring to scan only 1/3 or 1/5, or any other fraction of the range. [8] In this case we set N equal to $y\overline{N}$ in Eq. (5) and average over all values of y from 0 to 1. The resulting curve for $\overline{S}$ has a much flatter maximum; its optimal fraction $\overline{x_s}$ and search advantage $\overline{S_s}/\overline{S_u}$ are also plotted in Figures 4 and 5. We see that if the specialist user is dominant [8] then the section should be divided only when   is less than 0.05, i.e., when the undivided section is larger than about 30,000 volumes.

Presumably some intermediate choice is appropriate for most libraries. Those that serve the general public (or undergraduates in a university) will use a curve fairly close to the ones marked $\underline{x_0}$ and $\underline{S_0}/\underline{S_u}$ in Figures 4 and 5. Those libraries serving mostly specialists, who tend to browse in narrow subject ranges, would use a curve nearer the ones marked $\underline{x}_S$ and $\underline{S}_S/\underline{S}_u$. In any case, the decisions will be made on the basis of some knowledge, rather than on intuition.

Notes

1. P. M. Morse and G. E. Kimball, Methods of Operations Research, New York, MIT Press and John Wiley, 1951, Chapter 3.
2. B. O. Koopman in Operations Research, 4 (1956), 503, and 5 (1957), 613.
3. See, for example, H. Chernoff and L. Moses, Elementary Decision Theory, New York, John Wiley, 1959.
4. J. H. Shera, The Silent Stir of Thought, 12th Annual M. C. Richardson Lecture. Geneseo, N. Y., State University of New York, 1969.
5. P. M. Morse, Library Effectiveness, Cambridge, Mass., MIT Press, 1968, 101f.
6. P. M. Morse, op. cit., 39.
7. P. M. Morse, "Search Theory and Browsing," Library Quarterly, 40 (1970), 391-408.
8. Of course, if the section is uniform in regard to circulation, as we have defined a section, there must be as many specialists interested in one portion of the section as there are interested in another, which makes it rather unlikely that the generalist browsers are in the minority, as is assumed for the curves $\underline{x}_S$ and $\underline{S}_S/\underline{S}_u$.
9. See, for example, the discussion by W. S. Dix in College and Research Libraries, 25 (1964), 85-90.

THE SYMMETRIES OF IGNORANCE

Robert A. Fairthorne

Ignorance has taken many hard knocks at the hands of Jesse Shera. So not surprisingly it sometimes changes sides. This note outlines some instances where ignorance of one kind cancels ignorance of another kind. General, wilful, and invincible, ignorances remain, of course, unscathed.

The helpful kinds of ignorance are those specialized kinds that can be interpreted as indifference. These lead to applications of what may be called Gallio's Principle: we care not for certain things.

Take a very simple, though important, example: that of economical coding. In the days when superimposed coding was widely used to economize in capacity on notched and punched cards, much convoluted and usually unsound mathematics endeavored to prove that, on the average, half the sites should be punched or otherwise marked. No mathematics is needed. It suffices to note that the pack is separated into the same parts, whether we turn notches into no notches and conversely, or call 1's 0's and 0's 1's. For the system cannot know which part we are interested in, nor what we call the marks. We note also that the least efficient coding is to fill all the sites or to leave all of them blank. It follows that the most efficient coding leaves half the sites marked and half unmarked.

We have exploited here ignorance of the system about which part of the pack is which, which is rejected and much accepted, and what we choose to call these parts. The system can differentiate, but not recognize (match). Still less can it identify (put a name to). The same principle applies at higher levels of sorting and matching problems. Here we use the fact that sorters continue to dispatch items to the same destinations, even if we change the names of the destinations. This is because they can match different kinds of items, but are indifferent to what they are called. That is, they cannot identify them.

Even devices, such as human beings adequately
trained, that can identify as well as recognize and differentiate, have ignorances that librarians can exploit. To see
this, consider why people use libraries at all. Some go to
read about the melting point of aluminum, some to find dec-
larations of intent on the part of airlines and bus services,
some to look at illustrated fairy stories, some even to read
books for the fun of it, some to seek comfort and advice,
some this, some that, some the other. But all go to the library for one, and only one, proximate cause. That is, to
find out what people have to say. If they knew what people
had to say about the matter at issue, or what certain people
had to say about anything or nothing, they would not go to
find out. The approach is through ignorance, as Plato pointed
out a long time ago, and information scientists and suchlike
rediscover to this day.

This ignorance makes the librarians' task possible,
for the librarians' task is to help the reader to find out what
people have to say; not to expound to the reader what has
been said, as a substitute for the author; not to make use of
what has been said, as a substitute for the reader; not to
tell the reader what he ought to read, as a substitute for
God.

In order to help people find out what people have said,
the librarian must be knowledgeable about discourse, not
what the discourse may be about, if anything. He must
therefore know who writes about what, what he has written,
where and when, how to get hold of it, the sort of people
who read it, what they think about it, what sort of words
and language are used, and so forth. But he no more takes
part in the discourse than does or should the telegraphist,
printer, or computer programmer. If he does, he is no
longer acting as a librarian, nor can he act as a librarian.

The reader who wishes to find out what someone has
said about something, naturally does not give an exact account of what has been said: that is what he is trying to
find out. Therefore if, for instance, the reader wanted to
find out what people had written concerning the folly of Fairthorne, he would expect to be supplied with all written assertions from "Fairthorne is a blithering idiot" to "Fairthorne is not a blithering idiot," with all intermediate senti-
ments. Also he would expect to receive any published expressions of opinion that contained both or all these assertions, however inconsistent or illogical they might be within

one document. Satisfaction of the readers' demands, therefore, does not depend on truth or consistency. These matters are for the readers to decide after the librarian has
done his job, or the information retrieval system its.

What the competent librarian, or retrieval system,
then does is to forget about things he cannot do, such as
telling whether a statement is true just by looking at it or
computing upon it. He looks for the matters unaffected by
his and the readers' ignorances. In the example, he would
look for documents that mentioned the folly of Fairthorne,
whether to affirm, deny, or dither about it. This is quite
a task, because the folly of Fairthorne might be mentioned
in terms that did not involve either the word "Fairthorne"
or the word "folly." Fairthorne might have taken another
name upon entering holy orders, or for less worthy reasons,
and all languages abound in expressions for folly in all its
variety. Then there is the task of finding out where such
expressions occur. But all these tasks are fairly well defined. They raise great difficulties, but linguistic and bibliographic difficulties only. If they raised more, they would
lie outside any possible library solution. Indeed, they would
lie outside the scope and powers of the information sciences,
if the activities so denoted are defined by the activities of
those who use the term.

The problem of helping those who are ignorant, in
detail, of what people have said about things, is therefore
solved by defining "aboutness" in extension. That is by listing the things that are mentioned in a document. (A document is here defined as a unit of recorded discourse natural
to the discursive environment of the reader making the request.) From this point of view "Moby Dick" is about a
whale, which is true enough so far as it goes. In fact it
goes a long way for many purposes. Newspaper indexes are
largely of the proper names mentioned in the issues, not of
what is said about them. Chemical indexes are also largely
of proper names, but deal also with attributive statements
by using the names of classes also. In other applications
efforts are made to pick out substantival clauses as being
the entities mentioned. But always what is said about the
entities mentioned is irrelevant, because the reader is necessarily ignorant about what is said. All he knows is what it
is said about.

Extensional aboutness is not the only kind of aboutness, quite apart from the fact that the aboutness of a docu-

ment depends upon the environment of its use as well as its production, and is therefore a relation, not an attribute. The Encyclopaedia Britannica, for instance, is about the various matters its several articles are about. Also it is about many of the things that most educated English-speaking people want to read about sometime or other. That is why it was compiled, and that is why it is purchased. This is its intensional aboutness. Intensional aboutness clearly cannot be determined from study of the text alone. It entails knowledge of how it is going to be used by what class of readers.

For instance, we have shown that on behalf of a reader seeking expressions of opinion as to the folly of Fairthorne, we must give him all published and accessible statements from "Fairthorne is a fool" to "Fairthorne is not a fool," and all semantic equivalents to these that have been published. From the point of view of retrieval of opinions about Fairthorne's Folly all these are equivalent. Whether they are true or consistent or congenial are matters for the reader to decide, if he wishes. These are no business of the librarian, who has his own business, which does not include the simulation of readers' personalities, mentation, emotions, and motivation, because no one can do that except the readers themselves.

Suppose now that one finds, for a certain class of readers, equivalent statements of opinion, from the standpoint of retrieval, are "Fairthorne is a fool," "Members of ASIS are not asses," "Mary is not a fool," "Mary is a fool," "Drs. X, Y, and Z are probably fools," and similar statements. Clearly these are not about the folly of Fairthorne, but about the folly or otherwise of a certain subset of mankind. They are equivalent when retrieving documents, because the reader is necessarily ignorant of what has been said about the folly of this subset, so initially he or his delegate must be indifferent to what is said, for or against. Indifference is due not to unimportance, but to equal importance. Whether the thesis is affirmed or denied, both denial and affirmation are initially of equal interest.

This simple consideration leads to some practical points in the design of the semantic side of joint-attribute ("coordinate indexing") retrieval systems. When allotting attributes for use over the field of interest dealt with, one must do so on the basis of intensional aboutness; that is, upon the matters basic to the discourse. Extensional aboutness, what the documents mention and in what terms, cannot be determined without this intensional framework. Documents mention many things, from dictionary words and what they may stand for, to complex linguistic expressions, and what they may stand for. Considerations of why the document is being read are essential, for in social situations the word "why" has the central importance of the word "how" in physical situations.

Therefore, to find intensional aboutness appropriate to a particular class of readers, we must find what ignorances (about what people have had to say, not about the workings of the universe as such) this class need to resolve, and cannot resolve until they look at the documents they have requested. By Gallio's Principle that means eliminating those attributes about which the readers could not care less, and substituting attributes which are of equal importance whether affirmed or denied. Only in this way can we defy the initial ignorance of whether it is an affirmation or a denial. Put otherwise, both the presence and the absence of an attribute should be equally important. For the mathematically inclined, there is a sound information-theoretic proof of this, which I will omit. From the linguistic aspects of the discourse favored by the class of readers considered, we can get useful clues as to these complementary attributes or descriptors, using the last word in its original sense. The clue here is what I have called Hume's Principle.

In a footnote to his essay, "Concerning the Populousness of Ancient Nations," David Hume remarks:

> It is an universal observation which we may form
> upon language, that where two related parts of a
> whole bear any proportion to each other, in numbers, rank, or consideration, there are always
> correlative terms invented, which answer to both
> the parts, and express their mutual relation. If
> they bear no proportion to each other the term is
> only invented for the less, and marks its distinction from the whole. Thus man and woman, master and servant, father and son ... are correlative
> terms. But the words, seaman, carpenter, smith,
> tailor, etc. have no correspondent terms, which
> express those who are no seamen, or carpenters,
> etc. Languages differ very much with regard to
> the particular words where this distinction obtains;
> and may thence afford very strong inferences, concerning the manner and customs of different nations. ... "[1]

They afford very strong instances concerning also the manners, customs, and interests of specialist groups. As Hume remarks, in general speech seaman has no corresponding word to designate those who are not seamen. It is a "keyword" in the retrieval sense; a quasi-proper name that you must know else you cannot retrieve. But in the language of mariners, for whom being or not being a seaman is important, there is such a word; to wit, landlubber. Thus a joint attribute coordinate system that dealt with discourse concerning relations between mariners and the general population could well employ the concepts corresponding to "seaman" and "landlubber" as a complementary pair of retrieval attributes. Each item of the collection would be either one or the other from some defined point of view. Absence of one of these attributes is as important as its presence. Because we don't know before retrieval whether it is present or absent, we must give each equal weight. No such thing as a negative, in the sense of privative, attribute should be used in a joint attribute system. Thus the joint attribute system does not mix with the "keyword" or "telephone directory with cross reference" type of retrieval, which works on different principles.

These points were made by Calvin Mooers 21 years ago, but have been forgotten or ignored. My part here is to unify them under Gallio's Principle. If your reader is ignorant of what he wants to know, the retrieval system must be unaffected by his ignorance. Formally this means that, if we write down the incidence matrices of the system from semantic to lexical, each should be effectively unaltered, if we turn 0's into 1's and 1's into 0's.

One must be clear, however, that the ignorances we consider are those of the reader, and then only ignorance about what people have said and how to get hold of it. The librarian's job is to help him get hold of it, and there is neither excuse nor remedy for ignorance of that basic fact. For to do it one must become an expert on discourse and its management. This is a full time job that takes one's life to learn, without being under the misapprehension that the librarian's job is to teach other people theirs.

Note

1. David Hume, Essays; Moral, Political, and Literary, ed. T.H. Green and T.H. Gorse, London, Longmans, Green, 1875, vol. I., 389, note 4.

A THESAURUS WITHIN A THESAURUS:
A STUDY IN AMBIGUITY*

Phyllis A. Richmond

In recent years, there has been increasing concern about the compatibility or inter-convertibility of indexing systems. An excellent literature survey has been made by Madeline M. Henderson and associates.[1] The cost of putting the bibliographic tools needed for computerized information retrieval into machine readable form is so great that cooperation and uniform standards are virtually mandatory.

But what about indexing systems that are too compatible? Here is an interesting possibility that has not been studied. A too-compatible system is one where the index terms are so broad that they are ambiguous and create noise when added to or used with other systems. In a single system, noise is easily possible when making combinations via coordinate indexing methods, so much so that steps have been taken to avoid obvious errors of the "food fish"--"fish food" variety. When two or more systems are combined, however, a much more subtle and serious error is possible due to the fact that very few words in the English language have only one meaning. A glance at an unabridged dictionary is highly educational in case one has any illusions on this score. Thus the problem is two-fold: first, it is necessary to avoid semantic confusion in a single system. Second, it is necessary to avoid semantic confusion when two or more systems are merged.

The breadth or narrowness of the subject covered also

_____

*Definitions used in this paper: "Indexing": a systematic arrangement of terms, presented in alphabetical format. "Classification": a systematic arrangement of terms, presented in a spatial format showing relationships among the terms. "Index Terms": single or multiple words used for indexing; subject headings. "Thesaurus": a systematic arrangement of terms, presented in alphabetical format but with hierarchy and relationships indicated by sub-indexing.

is a factor. An index made for a relatively narrow field
and not designed to be used outside that field can be quite
effective with terms that would cause no end of difficulty in
combination with similar indexes for other fields. It is this
aspect of the situation which will be investigated in the present study. A thesaurus effective for one field can be less
appropriate in combination with other thesauri for reasons
entirely due to its internal structure and development.

The Engineers Joint Council's Thesaurus of Engineering Terms[2] has been used for an example. Although there
have been advances in thesaurus-making since the EJC Thesaurus was published, few of its basic weaknesses have been
recognized and guarded against in the recent draft Guidelines
circulated by the Committee on Scientific and Technical Information (COSATI).[3] The Thesaurus itself has been worked
over and improved, and a revised edition is soon to be published.

The EJC Thesaurus uses, for the most part, specific
rather than general terminology, and it employs a limited
hierarchical classification system to show relationship between terms. Four relationships are made: UF (use for),
which is a direct ("see") cross-reference, NT (narrower
term), BT (broader term) and RT (related term), which are
indirect cross-references of the "see also" type. Terms
may be single words or multiple ones, as in subject heading
lists of the type used in libraries.

The following references are made for the term LI-
BRARIES:

> RT   DOCUMENTATION
>   DOCUMENTS
>   FILING SYSTEMS
>   INDEXES (LOCATORS)
>   INFORMATION RETRIEVAL
>   LIBRARY SCIENCES

Even a cursory glance at the Thesaurus reveals that there
are many more terms which are as closely related to the
term LIBRARIES as the six listed. This made it possible
to derive another, "inner" thesaurus from the EJC one (see
Appendix A).[4] This list is not comprehensive; a more extensive list for LIBRARIES could have been made if greater
pains had been taken. The present list does cover the major
areas of the library field, other than library education.

Ten years ago it might have seemed ridiculous to even attempt to look for library terminology in an engineering subject heading collection, but now, with computers being adopted for research in various kinds of information retrieval, and with library automation in the offing, more and more non-librarians are delving into areas which used to be the exclusive preserve of the librarians, notably catalogers. Library terms or souped-up versions of them are appearing more frequently in certain areas of electrical engineering. In another ten years, it may be commonplace to expect library terminology to occur in an engineering subject heading list.

The inner thesaurus was made by collecting terms which have a meaning in library science. No word in the new list is not in the Thesaurus, although the same term may have an entirely different interpretation when used in engineering context. Existing parenthetical expressions in the EJC list have been scrupulously observed because these define the head word, and no such clearly defined word has been taken over into another context. The same is true of scope notes when they are found. [5] In some cases, the cross-reference (UF) was preferred and it has been given instead of or as well as the EJC choice. Many of the terms carried the instruction "USE MORE SPECIFIC TERM IF POSSIBLE," reflecting realization of their potential ambiguity. In two cases (MAINTENANCE, PROCEDURES), parenthetical expressions had to be added for the inner thesaurus because the hierarchy (BT or NT) changed the meaning of the head word.

The structural hierarchy from which the inner thesaurus was made is given in Appendix B. The same subterm has been used more than once if it had more than one application. Strictly speaking, these different uses should have been differentiated, but this was actually done only in the cases of the words MAINTENANCE AND PROCEDURES which were impossibly vague otherwise. A hierarchy gives relationships to words and helps define them, but this alone is not sufficient when the words have to stand by themselves, as in the alphabetical arrangement of a thesaurus.

Related terms (RT) have been omitted completely. In the EJC Thesaurus, very often the related term has been used in such a way that it changes the meaning of the head word and turns it into a synonym of itself. [6] The term CLASSIFICATION is a good example of this:

CLASSIFICATION
(USE MORE SPECIFIC TERM IF POSSIBLE)
    UF   CLASSIFYING
             SORTING
    RT   BENEFICIATION
             CLASSIFIERS (SEDIMENTATION)
             CONCENTRATORS
             ELUTRIATION
             EVALUATION
             FLOTATION
             INDEXING
             JOB ANALYSIS
             PARTICLE SIZE DISTRIBUTION
             POSITION (TITLE)
             RATES (COSTS)
             RATING
             SALARY ADMINISTRATION
             SCREENING (SIZING)
             SEPARATION
             SIEVE ANALYSIS
             SIZE DETERMINATION

According to the related terms, the head word here has at least seven distinct meanings:

CLASSIFICATION (EVALUATION)
CLASSIFICATION (INDEXING)
CLASSIFICATION (PARTICLES)
CLASSIFICATION (PERSONNEL MANAGE-
    MENT)
CLASSIFICATION (RATES--NON-PERSON-
    NEL USAGE)
CLASSIFICATION (SEPARATION)
CLASSIFICATION (SIZE DETERMINATION)

One can think of at least two more that are not here. If the Thesaurus user asks for CLASSIFICATION as an undefined term, he should expect many false drops.

The relationships of the RT (related terms) are so haphazard that they are scarcely worth including, though, as mentioned above, the terms themselves give an indication of what meanings the head word was supposed to have had. The lack of systematization is easily illustrated in the related terms given for SIGNAL GENERATORS and RADIO RECEIV-ERS:

Main term A SIGNAL GEN-ERATORS	Related terms (common to both A and B in real life. "Yes" indicates term appeared as an RT, "no" that it was absent)	Main term B RADIO RE-CEIVERS
yes	AMPLIFIERS	no
yes	ELECTRIC CIRCUITS	no
yes	ELECTRIC FILTERS	no
no	NOISE (SPURIOUS SIGNALS)	yes
yes	OSCILLATORS	no
yes	SEMICONDUCTOR DEVICES	no
yes	SOLID STATE DEVICES	no
yes	TUBES (ELECTRONIC)	yes
no	TUNERS*	yes

*use for TUNED CIRCUIT

No related term RADIO TRANSMITTERS has been given under RADIO TRANSMISSION, though an equivalent is given for RADIO RECEIVERS. For the most part, assignment of related terms appears to have been largely hit or miss.

The problems with related terms are partly a matter of poor structure and partly a lack of semantic analysis. There are also places in the EJC Thesaurus where a special, undefined meaning has been given to a term.[7] In this case, the meaning is only apparent through the related terms. Here a user could get 100% false drops if he did not use the word in the sense the Thesaurus implied. LIFE, for example, is listed as follows:

```
LIFE
   NT    FATIGUE LIFE
         HALF LIFE
         SHELF LIFE
   RT    ABANDONMENT
         AGE
         AMORTIZATION
         DEPLETION
         DEPRECIATION
         DURABILITY
         LIFE TESTING
         OBSOLESCENCE
         RESISTANCE
         VULNERABILITY
```

Biomedical engineers must find the definitions implied here somewhat shattering.

The structure of the EJC Thesaurus is such that one may trace a great many small hierarchies of a few levels by following the trails created by the BT (broader term) and NT (narrower term) distinctions. An example of one such hierarchy is given in Appendix C. There are gaps, presumably because the classification made through such hierarchies was not done systematically. Apparently the trails were not illustrated for working purposes with visual aids, such as arrowgraphs or even connecting lines (as in Appendix C). One is hard put to explain the relationships that appear if TRANSPONDERS or RADIO REPEATERS, for example, are mapped out.

Apart from structure and systematization, there are at least three main types of problem terms in the Thesaurus: (1) synonyms, which are well handled internally by UF (use for) direct cross-references. There would be additional external synonyms if the engineering list were joined with any other. (2) homographs, of which CLASSIFICATION is a good internal example; BUNDLING and RELAXATION would be ambiguous externally. (3) mataphors, which by definition, carry guaranteed, built-in confusion in meaning if taken literally, though in context they are picturesque and often clarify better than a paragraph of description. AIR CURTAINS, CASCADED NETWORKS, CLOUD CHAMBERS, BUTTERFLY VALVES, COLD TRAPS are examples. Of the three, the greatest problem is with the homographs.

The fact that the same terms in the inner and outer thesauri are used with entirely different meanings in engineering and in libraries (and some of the words which are synonyms for engineering are not so for libraries) shows that homographs abound from subject field to subject field. Indexes based on alphabetical arrangement of undefined or semi-defined words lead to ambiguity in usage. Undefined words are words in limbo and can mean anything the user wants to make them mean. We have had many examples of this in information science. In a living language, one should expect redefinition by new usage, though it makes great confusion in indexing in the interim before the new usage is established.

Since identical words have such different meanings in different subject fields, in different contexts and when used with different viewpoints, an alphabetically-arranged term index or subject heading list can scarcely be expected to function well outside a limited, homogeneous subject field. Unfortunately, limited fields have a nasty way of not staying

limited and eclectic collection of "related" terms from other
fields leads to blurring of terminological distinctness.   When,
as in the case of the EJC Thesaurus, more general terms
or terms from other fields are introduced to cover fringe
areas, there is a great need to define each term much more
exactly than is done now.

     That a fairly good inner thesaurus could be made for
LIBRARIES by using terms in the Thesaurus of Engineering
Terms indicates a serious problem in compatibility of word
indexes for retrieval of source data from storage.   Also the
variant meanings of words explain how it is possible to get
non-pertinent material with apparently pertinent index terms.
The EJC Thesaurus has many instances where the index
terms have been used with multiple meanings which have not
been defined, perhaps not even recognized.

     The inescapable conclusion to be drawn from all these
difficulties is that all index terms have to be defined precisely if they are to be fully effective as retrieval aids, and especially if there is to be any kind of compatibility between
systems.   All of which merely reinforces what Calvin Mooers
has been saying all along: "a descriptor must have a proper
description.   This definition should be a carefully drawn verbal statement, based on the scientific and intellectual nature
of the concept being dealt with."[8]   The matter of making a
good verbal definition, however, is not an easy one.   Attempts to define every word in the inner list by means of
various abridged and unabridged dictionaries were not successful because of the tendency of lexicographers to define
by means of sentences or phrases.   This would practically
make every thesaurus a little dictionary.   In fact, one might
do better by using a dictionary for a thesaurus and making
coordinate index terms like this: cloud (def. #3) chamber
(def. #5).   This could be very cumbersome, especially in
cases where one word was defined in terms of another, itself defined in terms of a third or (horrors!) in terms of
the first word.

     One cannot emphasize too strongly that index terms
need some kind of context definition or indication to have a
distinct meaning.   Mulvihill and Brenner, of the American
Petroleum Institute, have attempted to solve the problem by
"auto-posting" -- every word is defined by being added to
the list as a sub-term of its generic term.[9]   Thus every
word is posted on some higher word, and, since there is
always a higher word, no word goes undefined.   Relationships

are derived by means of a faceting procedure which indicates
multiple hierarchies rather precisely and with considerably
more sophistication than was the case with the more traditional
type of hierarchy used in the present study.   The method of
Mulvihill and Brenner should make it difficult, if not impossible, to construct a thesaurus within a thesaurus.

Finally, one cannot help being reminded that the les-
sons taught by Julia Pettee have not been learned yet.   Miss
Pettee demonstrated classification concealed in the cross-reference structure of subject headings. [10] The same can quite
easily be unearthed in thesauri.   There can be no sensible
discussion of classification vs. subject headings or classification vs. thesauri.   These two main forms of intellectual organization are inevitably and immutably intertwined.   Indexing
without careful attention to the meaning of the terms involved
produces retrieval of unsatisfactory nature because the input
itself has not been defined clearly.   With mergers, cooperation, and similar broadening of the base for information
transfer, the fundamental foundations must be broader than
heretofore, reaching once more toward the elusive goal of
universality.   Ambiguity can only be avoided by taking account of all the semantic possibilities inherent in the choice
of index terms.   Ultimately this requires spatial representation, as in classification, before even parenthetical definition
of individual terms can be made with confidence.

POSTSCRIPT

Since this paper was written, a revised and vastly enlarged edition of the Thesaurus has appeared: Thesaurus of
Engineering and Scientific Terms; A List of Engineering and
Related Scientific Terms and Their Relationships for Use as
a Vocabulary Reference in Indexing and Retrieving Technical
Information, 1st ed., New York, Engineers Joint Council,
1967 [published in early 1968].

Of the specific criticisms made in this paper, examination of the new Thesaurus reveals the following:

1)   The terms under LIBRARIES have been changed complete-
     ly, but the new version still has enough of the older
     terms so that one can still make an inner thesaurus.
     In fact, it is possible to add to it because of the en-
     larged scope of the new edition.
2)   The number of meanings for the head word CLASSIFICA-

TION has been reduced from seven to four.
3) The possible overlap in relationships among related terms common to SIGNAL GENERATORS and RADIO RE-CEIVERS appears to be unimproved. These two now have eight common terms, of which only one is actually present in both.
4) LIFE is redefined as LIFE (DURABILITY) and AMORTI-ZATION and RESISTANCE deleted. LIFE (of interest in biomedical engineering) is absent.
5) The tracing of small hierarchies remains the same and probably holds true for all thesauri because of the cross-reference structure.

Notes

1. Henderson, Madeline M. & others. Cooperation, Con-vertibility and Compatibility among Information Sys-tems; a Literature Review. Washington, Government Printing Office, 1966. (National Bureau of Standards Misc. Publications 276)
2. Engineers Joint Council. Thesaurus of Engineering Terms; a List of Engineering Terms and their Rela-tionships for Use in Vocabulary Control in Indexing and Retrieving Engineering Information. 1st ed. New York, Engineers Joint Council, 1964.
3. Federal Council for Science and Technology. Commit-tee on Scientific and Technical Information. Guide-lines for the Development of Information Retrieval Thesauri. 9 November 1966. Draft. (Multigraphed, Office of Science and Technology, Executive Office of the President, iif, 7pp.)
4. An even more extensive inner thesaurus can be made for HISTORY. Any reader who wants to make such a listing may have a beginning collection of 518 per-tinent index terms taken from the Thesaurus. Write to the author at School of Library Science, Case Western Reserve University, Cleveland, Ohio, 44106. Similar lists may be made for social sciences (eco-nomics, political science, sociology, psychology), but it is more difficult for the humanities.
5. Example of scope note: CONTROL EQUIPMENT (LIM-ITED TO AUTOMATIC CONTROL APPLICATIONS), 54. Example of a parenthetical definition: LIGHT (ILLUMINATION), 148.
6. See APPRAISALS (p.15), BLOWOUTS (26), CONTAIN-MENT (53), HISTORY (125), LANGUAGES (146), etc.

7. See LIFE (p. 148), NOMENCLATURE (175), PAINTING (185), READERS (218), SPOILERS (251), etc.
8. Mooers, Calvin. "The Indexing Language of an Information Retrieval System," Information Retrieval Today; Papers Presented at the Institute Conducted by the Library School and the Center for Continuation Study, University of Minnesota, September 19-22, 1963, ed. by Wesley Simonton. Minneapolis, Center for Continuation Study, University of Minnesota, 1963, 34.
9. Mulvihill, John G. and Everett H. Brenner. "Faceted Organization of a Thesaurus Vocabulary," Progress in Information Science and Technology. Proceedings of the American Documentation Institute Annual Meeting ... 1966. [Santa Monica, Calif.] Adrianne Press [1966] 175-183.
10. Pettee, Julia. Subject Headings: The History and Theory of the Alphabetical Subject Approach in Books. New York, H.W. Wilson, 1946, 3-4, 57-60, 73-80.

APPENDIX A

Thesaurus for the subject LIBRARIES. The list is indicative rather than exhaustive, since many more terms could have been added. The structural pattern of the Thesaurus of Engineering Terms has been followed, except UF (Use for) and RT (Related term) have been omitted in the interest of brevity and clarity respectively. There are no terms in limbo; all are tied to at least one other term, which gives some indication of their meaning, though this would be better if no constraints had been placed in the construction of the classification base (Appendix B) used for the thesaurus.

A

ABBREVIATIONS
BT   RECORDS

ABSTRACTING
BT   SERVICES

ABSTRACTS
BT   TOOLS

ACCEPTABILITY
BT   CATALOGS(INDEXES)

ACCURACY
BT   REVISING

ACQUISITION
NT   BOOKS
        DOCUMENTS
        EXCHANGING
        MAPS
        PAYMENT
        PERIODICALS
        RECOMMENDATIONS

ADDING MACHINES
BT   OFFICE EQUIPMENT

ADDITIONS(ENLARGEMENT)
BT   CLASSIFICATION
         SUBJECT HEADINGS

ADJUSTMENT
BT   WORKING CONDITIONS

AIR CONDITIONING
NT   DUCTS
         VENTS

AIR MAIL
BT   POSTAL SERVICE

AISLES
BT   DESIGN

ALLOCATIONS
BT   APPROPRIATIONS

APPRAISALS
BT   REQUIREMENTS

APPROPRIATIONS
BT   MANAGEMENT
NT   ALLOCATING
         BUDGETING
         COSTS

ARCHITECTURE
BT   FACILITIES
NT   BUILDINGS

ASSIGNMENTS
BT   PERSONNEL MANAGE-
         MENT

AUTOMATION
NT   DATA SYSTEMS
         INFORMATION SYS-
           TEMS
         MECHANIZATION
         SYSTEMS ENGINEER-
           ING

AVAILABILITY
BT   CIRCULATION
NT   DAY
         NIGHT

B

BAGS
BT   SHIPPING CONTAIN-
         ERS

BARRIERS
BT   CONTROL EQUIP-
         MENT

BIBLIOGRAPHIES
BT   SEARCHING
         TOOLS

BINDING
BT   PERIODICALS
NT   BOOKBINDING
         COVERS
         DRILLS
         GLUE
         RUBBING

BOOKBINDING
BT   BINDING

BOOKS
BT   ACQUISITION
         MATERIALS
         STORAGE
NT   CUTTING
         EMBOSSING
         JACKETS
         MARKING
         PLATING
         SLITTING
         STAMPING

BOXES
BT   SHIPPING CONTAIN-
         ERS

BRACING
BT   STACKING

BRACKETS
BT   STACKING

BUDGET ESTIMATES
BT   BUDGETING

BUDGETING
BT   APPROPRIATIONS
NT   BUDGET ESTIMATES

BUILDING CODES
BT   LAWS

BUILDINGS
BT   ARCHITECTURE
NT   CLEANING
        DESIGN
        FUMIGATION
        HEATING
        LIGHTING
        NOISE CONTROL
        PLUMBING
        PROTECTION
        REFUSE DISPOSAL
        TELEPHONE SYSTEMS
        VENTILATION

                    C

CARD REPRODUCERS
BT   PUNCHED CARD
            EQUIPMENT
        REPRODUCIBILITY

CARD SORTERS
BT   PUNCHED CARD
            EQUIPMENT

CARPETS
BT   OFFICE EQUIPMENT

CARTONS
BT   SHIPPING CONTAINERS

CATALOGING
BT   PROCESSING
NT   CODES(STANDARDS)
        PROCEDURES(CAT-
            ALOGING)
        UNIT COSTS

CATALOGS(INDEXES)
BT   PROCESSING
        SEARCHING
        TOOLS
NT   ACCEPTABILITY
        FILING SYSTEMS
        MAINTENANCE
        REVISING

CATALOGS(PUBLICATIONS)
BT   TOOLS

CENTRALIZED CONTROL
BT   CONSOLIDATION

CHARGING
BT   CIRCULATION

CHARTS
BT   STORAGE

CHECKOUT
BT   CONTROL EQUIP-
            MENT

CIRCULATION
BT   OUTPUT
NT   AVAILABILITY
        CHARGING
        CONTROL EQUIP-
            MENT
        DELIVERY
        FINES
        REGULATIONS
        STORAGE
        TIME
        USAGE

CLASSIFICATION
BT   CODES(STANDARDS)

NT   ADDITIONS(ENLARGE-
         MENT)
         CORRECTION
         EXPANSION
         NOTATION
         SUBJECT CLASSES

CLEANING
BT   BUILDINGS
         MAINTENANCE
NT   DUST

CLEARANCES
BT   DOCUMENT

CLIPS
BT   SUPPLIES

CODES(STANDARDS)
BT   CATALOGING
NT   CLASSIFICATION
         CONFORMITY
         RELIABILITY
         SUBJECT HEADINGS
         VARIATIONS

COLLATORS
BT   PUNCHED CARD
         EQUIPMENT

COLLECTING
BT   PERIODICALS

COMMUNICATION
BT   UTILIZATION

COMPACTIBILITY
BT   RECORD STORAGE
NT   MICROFILM

COMPENSATION
BT   FRINGE BENEFITS

COMPUTER STORAGE
BT   COMPUTERS

COMPUTERS
BT   DATA PROCESSING

NT   COMPUTER STOR-
         AGE
         DIGITAL COMPUT-
         ERS
         DISKS(STORAGE)
         INPUT-OUTPUT
         DEVICES
         PROGRAMS(COMPU-
         TERS)
         TAPES(DATA MEDIA)

CONFORMITY
BT   CODES(STANDARDS)

CONSOLIDATION
BT   OBJECTIVES
NT   CENTRALIZED CON-
         TROL

CONSTRUCTION
BT   FACILITIES
NT   CONSTRUCTION
         COSTS

CONSTRUCTION COSTS
BT   CONSTRUCTION

CONSULTANTS
BT   PUBLIC RELATIONS
         TRENDS

CONTROL EQUIPMENT
BT   CIRCULATION
NT   BARRIERS
         CHECKOUT
         INSPECTION

CONTROL SYSTEMS
BT   SYSTEMS

COORDINATION
BT   PERSONNEL MAN-
         AGEMENT
         PROCEDURES(MAN-
         AGEMENT
         UNIFORM FLOW

COPY RIGHTS
BT   DUPLICATING

COPYING
BT   SERVICES
NT   DUPLICATING

CORRECTION
BT   CLASSIFICATION
      ERRORS
      SUBJECT HEADINGS

COSTS
BT   APPROPRIATIONS
NT   FIXED COSTS
      OPERATING COSTS

COUNTERS
BT   FURNITURE

COUNTING
BT   UNIT COSTS

COVERS
BT   BINDING

CUTTING
BT   BOOKS

D

DAMAGE
BT   PROTECTION
      USAGE

DATA
BT   TRANSFER FUNCTION

DATA ACQUISITION
BT   DATA SYSTEMS

DATA PROCESSING
BT   DATA SYSTEMS
NT   COMPUTERS
      PUNCHED CARD
        EQUIPMENT

DATA STORAGE
BT   DATA SYSTEMS

DATA SYSTEMS
BT   AUTOMATION
      SYSTEMS
NT   DATA ACQUISITION
      DATA PROCESSING
      DATA STORAGE
      DATA TRANSMIS-
        SION

DATA TRANSMISSION
BT   DATA SYSTEMS

DATING
BT   RECORDS
      TIME

DAY
BT   AVAILABILITY

DECIMALS
BT   NOTATION

DECISION MAKING
BT   PROCEDURES(MAN-
        AGEMENT)

DELIVERY
BT   CIRCULATION
NT   HOISTS
      HOLDING(RETAIN-
        ERS)
      PNEUMATIC CON-
        VEYORS
      TRACERS
      WAITING TIME

DEPTH
BT   INDEX TERMS

DESIGN
BT   BUILDINGS
NT   AISLES
      ELEVATORS(LIFTS)
      FLOORS

               SKYLIGHTS
               WALLS
               WINDOWS

DESKS
BT   OFFICE EQUIPMENT

DICTIONARIES
BT   SEARCHING
      TOOLS

DIGITAL COMPUTERS
BT   COMPUTERS

DIRECTORIES
BT   TOOLS

DISKS(STORAGE)
BT   COMPUTERS

DIURNAL VARIATION
BT   STATISTICS

DOCUMENTS
BT   ACQUISITION
      MATERIALS
      STORAGE
NT   CLEARANCES

DRILLS
BT   BINDING

DUCTS
BT   AIR CONDITIONING

DUPLICATING
BT   COPYING
NT   COPY RIGHTS
      XEROGRAPHY

DUST
BT   CLEANING

               E

EDITING ROUTINES
BT   PUBLICATIONS

EDUCATION
BT   UTILIZATION

EFFICIENCY
BT   PROCEDURES(MAN-
         AGEMENT)

ELECTRIC POWER DISTRI-
   BUTION
BT   LIGHTING

ELEVATORS(LIFTS)
BT   DESIGN

EMPLOYMENT
BT   PERSONNEL
NT   INTERVIEWS
      OPENINGS

ENCYCLOPEDIAS
BT   TOOLS

ENTRANCES
BT   PROTECTION

EQUIPMENT
NT   FILM READERS
      FURNITURE
      HOISTS
      OFFICE EQUIPMENT
      PURCHASING
      STACKING
      SUPPLIES
      TAPE RECORDERS
      TRUCKS

ERRORS
BT   REVISING
NT   CORRECTION

ESTIMATES
BT   PURCHASING
      REQUIREMENTS

ETHICS
BT   HUMAN FACTORS

EXAMINATION
BT   PROCEDURES(CATA-
        LOGING)

EXCHANGING
BT   ACQUISITION

EXITS
BT   PROTECTION

EXPANSION
BT   CLASSIFICATION
        TRENDS

F

FACILITIES
BT   MANAGEMENT
NT   ARCHITECTURE
        CONSTRUCTION
        MAINTENANCE
        PARKING FACILITIES
        PLANNING

FANS
BT   VENTILATION

FILING SYSTEMS
BT   CATALOGS(INDEXES)
NT   ORDER(SEQUENCE)
        SORTING

FILM READERS
BT   EQUIPMENT

FINES
BT   CIRCULATION

FIRE ALARM SYSTEMS
BT   FIRE PROTECTION

FIRE EXTINGUISHERS
BT   FIRE PROTECTION

FIRE PROTECTION
BT   PROTECTION

NT   FIRE ALARM SYS-
        TEMS
        FIRE EXTINGUISH-
        ERS
        FIREWALLS

FIREWALLS
BT   FIRE PROTECTION

FIXED COSTS
BT   COSTS

FLOORS
BT   DESIGN

FORMS(PAPER)
BT   SUPPLIES

FREIGHT TRANSPORTA-
    TION
BT   SHIPPING

FRICTION
BT   HUMAN FACTORS

FRINGE BENEFITS
BT   PERSONNEL
NT   COMPENSATION
        INSURANCE
        PENSIONS

FUMIGATION
BT   BUILDINGS
NT   PEST CONTROL

FURNITURE
BT   EQUIPMENT
NT   COUNTERS
        SEATS
        TABLES(FURNITURE)

G

GLOSSARIES
BT   TOOLS

GLUE
BT   BINDING
        SUPPLIES

GROWTH
BT   TRENDS
NT   GROWTH CURVES

GROWTH CURVES
BT   GROWTH

GUARDS(PERSONNEL)
BT   PROTECTION

H

HANDBOOKS
BT   TOOLS

HEATING
BT   BUILDINGS
NT   RADIATORS
        STEAM PIPES
        TEMPERATURE CON-
            TROL

HOISTS
BT   DELIVERY
        EQUIPMENT

HOLDERS
BT   STACKING

HOLDING(RETAINING)
BT   DELIVERY

HUMAN FACTORS
BT   PUBLIC RELATIONS
NT   ETHICS
        FRICTION

I

IDENTIFICATION
BT   RECORDS
        REGULATION

INDENTATION
BT   REVISING

INDEX TERMS
BT   SUBJECT HEADINGS
NT   DEPTH

INDEXES(LOCATORS)
BT   RECORDS
        TOOLS

INDEXING
BT   SERVICES

INFORMATION RETRIEVAL
BT   AUTOMATION

INFORMATION SYSTEMS
BT   SYSTEMS
        SYSTEMS ENGINEER-
            ING
        TRANSFER FUNC-
            TIONS

INPUT
NT   PROCESSING

INPUT-OUTPUT DEVICES
BT   COMPUTERS

INSPECTION
BT   CONTROL EQUIP-
        MENT

INSURANCE
BT   FRINGE BENEFITS

INTERPRETERS
BT   PUNCHED CARD
        EQUIPMENT

INTERVIEWS
BT   EMPLOYMENT

J

JACKETS

BT   BOOKS

JOB ANALYSIS
BT   PERFORMANCE

JOB DESCRIPTION
BT   PERFORMANCE

K

KEYBOARDS
BT   TYPEWRITERS

KEY-PUNCHES
BT   PUNCHED CARD
        EQUIPMENT

L

LAMINATING
BT   MAPS

LAWS
BT   MANAGEMENT
NT   BUILDING CODES

LIGHT (ILLUMINATION)
BT   LIGHTING

LIGHTING
BT   BUILDINGS
NT   ELECTRIC POWER
        DISTRIBUTION
        LIGHT
        WIRING

LOCATING
BT   PERIODICALS

LOSSES
BT   USAGE

M

MACHINE TIME

BT   OPERATIONS

MAINTENANCE (BUILDING)
BT   FACILITIES
NT   CLEANING
        PAINTING
        RENOVATING
        REPAIRING

MAINTENANCE (CATALOGS)
BT   CATALOGS (INDEXES)

MAN-MACHINE SYSTEMS
BT   SYSTEMS
        SYSTEMS ENGINEER-
            ING

MANAGEMENT
NT   APPROPRIATIONS
        FACILITIES
        LAWS
        OBJECTIVES
        PERSONNEL MAN-
            AGEMENT
        PROCEDURES
        PUBLIC RELATIONS
        SYSTEMS
        TRENDS

MANUALS
BT   TOOLS

MAPS
BT   ACQUISITION
        MATERIALS
        STORAGE
NT   LAMINATING
        TRIMMING

MARKING
BT   BOOKS

MATERIALS
BT   PROCESSING
        TRANSFER FUNC-
            TION
NT   BOOKS
        DOCUMENTS

MAPS
PERIODICALS
RECORDS
SERIES

MECHANIZATION
BT   AUTOMATION

MICROFILM
BT   COMPACTIBILITY

MORALE
BT   WORKING CONDITIONS

N

NIGHT
BT   AVAILABILITY

NOISE CONTROL
BT   BUILDINGS
NT   NOISE ELIMINATION

NOISE ELIMINATION
BT   NOISE CONTROL

NOTATION
BT   CLASSIFICATION
NT   DECIMALS
        NUMBERS

NUMBERING SYSTEMS
BT   SYSTEMS

NUMBERS
BT   NOTATION

O

OBJECTIVES
BT   MANAGEMENT
NT   CONSOLIDATION
        PLANNING
        STANDARDS

OFFICE EQUIPMENT
BT   EQUIPMENT
NT   ADDING MACHINES
        CARPETS
        DESKS
        TYPEWRITERS

OPENINGS
BT   EMPLOYMENT

OPERATING COSTS
BT   COSTS

OPERATIONS
BT   SYSTEMS ENGINEER-
        ING
NT   MACHINE TIME

ORDER(SEQUENCE)
BT   FILING SYSTEMS

ORDERS(COMMITMENTS)
BT   PURCHASING
        RECOMMENDATIONS

OUTPUT
NT   CIRCULATION
        SERVICES
        TOOLS

P

PAINTING
BT   MAINTENANCE

PAPER PRODUCTS
BT   SUPPLIES

PARCEL POST
BT   POSTAL SERVICE

PARKING FACILITIES
BT   FACILITIES

PAYMENT
BT   ACQUISITION
        PURCHASING

PENSIONS
BT   FRINGE BENEFITS

PERFORMANCE
BT   PERSONNEL
NT   JOB ANALYSIS
        JOB DESCRIPTION
        RATING
        SKILLS
        TIME STANDARDS
          (WORK)
        UPGRADING

PERIODICAL VARIATION
BT   STATISTICS

PERIODICALS
BT   ACQUISITION
        MATERIALS
NT   BINDING
        COLLECTING
        LOCATING
        RECORDS

PERSONNEL
BT   PERSONNEL MANAGE-
          MENT
NT   EMPLOYMENT
        FRINGE BENEFITS
        PERFORMANCE
        POSITION(TITLE)
        SALARIES
        SHORTAGES
        TRAINING
        WORKING CONDITIONS

PERSONNEL MANAGEMENT
BT   MANAGEMENT
NT   ASSIGNMENTS
        COORDINATION
        PERSONNEL
        SUPERVISION

PEST CONTROL
BT   FUMIGATION

PHONOGRAPH RECORDS
BT   STORAGE

PHOTOGRAPHS
BT   STORAGE

PICTURES
BT   STORAGE

PLANNING
BT   FACILITIES
        OBJECTIVES

PLATENS
BT   TYPEWRITERS

PLATING
BT   BOOKS
NT   PLATES

PLUMBING
BT   BUILDINGS
NT   SEWER PIPELINES
        WATER PIPELINES

PNEUMATIC CONVEYORS
BT   DELIVERY

POSTAL SERVICES
BT   SHIPPING
NT   AIR MAIL
        PARCEL POST

POSITION(TITLE)
BT   PERSONNEL
NT   QUALIFICATIONS

PREDICTIONS
BT   TRENDS

PRICES
BT   PURCHASING
        REQUIREMENTS
NT   RATES
        REDUCTION

PRINTERS(FOR COMPUT-
  ERS)
BT   PUNCIIED CARD
          EQUIPMENT

PRINTING
BT   REPRODUCIBILITY

PROCEDURES(CATALOGING)
BT   CATALOGING
NT   EXAMINATION
        PRODUCTION
        SEARCHING

PROCEDURES(MANAGEMENT)
BT   MANAGEMENT
        SYSTEMS ENGINEER-
           ING
NT   COORDINATION
        DECISION MAKING
        EFFICIENCY
        WORK SIMPLIFICATION

PROCESSING
BT   INPUT
NT   CATALOGING
        CATALOGS(INDEXES)
        MATERIALS

PRODUCTION
BT   PROCEDURES(CATA-
           LOGING)
NT   REPRODUCIBILITY
        RESTORING
        REVISING
        TRANSFERRING
        UNIFORM FLOW

PROGRAMS(COMPUTERS)
BT   COMPUTERS

PROJECTIONS
BT   TRENDS

PROTECTION
BT   BUILDINGS
NT   DAMAGE
        ENTRANCES
        EXITS
        FIRE PROTECTION
        GUARDS(PERSONNEL)
        SAFETY MEASURES

PUBLIC RELATIONS
BT   MANAGEMENT
NT   CONSULTANTS
        HUMAN FACTORS
        PUBLICATIONS
        PUBLICITY

PUBLICATIONS
BT   PUBLIC RELATIONS
NT   EDITING ROUTINES

PUBLICITY
BT   PUBLIC RELATIONS

PUNCHED CARD EQUIP-
    MENT
BT   DATA PROCESSING
NT   CARD REPRODUC-
           ERS
        CARD SORTERS
        COLLATORS
        INTERPRETERS
        KEY-PUNCHES
        PRINTERS(FOR
           COMPUTERS)
        PUNCHED CARDS
        TABULATORS

PUNCHED CARDS
BT   PUNCHED CARD
        EQUIPMENT

PURCHASING
BT   EQUIPMENT
NT   ESTIMATES
        ORDERS(COMMIT-
           MENTS)
        PAYMENT
        PRICES
        QUALITY
        QUOTATIONS
        RECEIVING
        SPECIFICATIONS

Q

QUALIFICATIONS

BT   POSITION(TITLE)

QUALITY
BT   PURCHASING

QUESTIONNAIRES
BT   SURVEYS(DATA COL-
         LECTION)

QUOTATIONS
BT   PURCHASING
         REQUIREMENTS

R

RADIATORS
BT   HEATING

RANGE FINDERS
BT   STACKING

RATES
BT   PRICES

RATING
BT   PERFORMANCE

READING
BT   UTILIZATION

RECEIVING
BT   PURCHASING

RECOMMENDATIONS
BT   ACQUISITION
NT   ORDERS(COMMIT-
         MENTS)
         REJECTION
         SEARCHING
         SELECTION

RECORD STORAGE
BT   RECORDS
NT   COMPACTIBILITY

RECORDS

BT   PERIODICALS
         STORAGE

RECORDS
NT   ABBREVIATIONS
         DATING
         IDENTIFICATION
         INDEXES(LOCATORS)
         RECORD STORAGE
         SUPPLEMENTS

REDUCTION
BT   PRICES

REFUSE DISPOSAL
BT   BUILDINGS

REGULATIONS
BT   CIRCULATION
NT   IDENTIFICATION

REJECTION
BT   RECOMMENDATIONS

RELIABILITY
BT   CODES(STANDARDS)

RENOVATING
BT   MAINTENANCE

REPAIRING
BT   MAINTENANCE

REPORTS
BT   STORAGE

REPRODUCIBILITY
BT   PRODUCTION
NT   CARD REPRODUC-
         ERS
         PRINTING
         XEROGRAPHY

REQUIREMENTS
BT   ACQUISITION
NT   APPRAISALS
         ESTIMATES

QUOTATIONS
PRICES
SPECIFICATIONS

RESEARCH
BT   UTILIZATION

RESTORING
BT   PRODUCTION

REVISING
BT   CATALOGS(INDEXES)
         PRODUCTION
NT   ACCURACY
         ERRORS
         INDENTATION
         SPACING

ROUTING
BT   UNIFORM FLOW

RUBBING
BT   BINDING

S

SAFETY DEVICES
BT   SAFETY MEASURES

SAFETY MEASURES
BT   PROTECTION
NT   SAFETY DEVICES

SALARIES
BT   PERSONNEL

SCHEDULING
BT   TIME

SEARCHING
BT   PROCEDURES(CATA-
         LOGING)
         RECOMMENDATIONS
NT   BIBLIOGRAPHIES
         CATALOGS(INDEXES)
         DICTIONARIES

SEATS
BT   FURNITURE

SELECTION
BT   RECOMMENDATIONS

SERIES
BT   MATERIALS

SERVICES
BT   OUTPUT
NT   ABSTRACTING
         COPYING
         INDEXING
         SUMMARIZING
         TRANSLATING
         TRANSMISSION

SEWER PIPELINES
BT   PLUMBING

SHIPPING
BT   TRANSMISSION
NT   FREIGHT TRANS-
         PORTATION
         POSTAL SERVICE
         SHIPPING CON-
         TAINERS
         WRAPPING(PACK-
         AGING)

SHIPPING CONTAINERS
BT   SHIPPING
NT   BAGS
         BOXES
         CARTONS

SHORTAGES
BT   PERSONNEL

SKILLS
BT   PERFORMANCE

SKYLIGHTS
BT   DESIGN

SLITTING
BT   BOOKS

SORTING
BT   FILING SYSTEMS

SPACING
BT   REVISING

SPECIFICATIONS
BT   PURCHASING
      REQUIREMENTS

STACKING
BT   EQUIPMENT
NT   BRACING
      BRACKETS
      HOLDERS
      RANGE FINDERS

STAIRS
BT   DESIGN

STAMPING
BT   BOOKS

STANDARDS
BT   OBJECTIVES

STAPLES
BT   SUPPLIES

STATISTICS
BT   UNIT COSTS
      USAGE
      TRENDS
NT   DIURNAL VARIATION
      PERIODICAL VARIA-
         TION

STEAM PIPES
BT   HEATING

STORAGE
BT   CIRCULATION
NT   BOOKS
      CHARTS
      DOCUMENTS
      MAPS
      PHONOGRAPH REC-
         ORDS

      PHOTOGRAPHS
      PICTURES
      RECORDS
      REPORTS

STRESSES
BT   WORKING CONDI-
         TIONS

SUBJECT CLASSES
BT   CLASSIFICATION

SUBJECT HEADINGS
BT   CODES(STANDARDS)
NT   ADDITIONS(EN-
         LARGEMENT)
      CORRECTION
      INDEX TERMS

SUMMARIZING
BT   SERVICES

SUPERVISION
BT   PERSONNEL MAN-
         AGEMENT

SUPPLEMENTS
BT   RECORDS

SUPPLIES
BT   EQUIPMENT
NT   CLIPS
      FORMS(PAPER)
      GLUE
      PAPER PRODUCTS
      STAPLES

SURVEYS(DATA COLLEC-
   TION
BT   TRENDS
NT   QUESTIONNAIRES

SYSTEMS
BT   MANAGEMENT
NT   CONTROL SYSTEMS
      DATA SYSTEMS
      INFORMATION SYS-
         TEMS

MAN-MACHINE SYS-
TEMS
NUMBERING SYSTEMS

SYSTEMS ENGINEERING
BT   AUTOMATION
NT   INFORMATION SYS-
TEMS
MAN-MACHINE SYS-
TEMS
OPERATIONS
PROCEDURES

T

TABLES(DATA)
BT   TOOLS

TABLES(FURNITURE)
BT   FURNITURE

TABULATORS
BT   PUNCHED CARD
EQUIPMENT

TAPE RECORDERS
BT   EQUIPMENT

TELEPHONE SYSTEMS
BT   BUILDINGS

TEMPERATURE CONTROLS
BT   HEATING
NT   THERMOSTATS

THERMOSTATS
BT   TEMPERATURE CON-
TROL

TIME
BT   CIRCULATION
NT   DATING
SCHEDULING

TIME STANDARDS(WORK)
BT   PERFORMANCE

TOOLS
BT   OUTPUT
NT   ABSTRACTS
BIBLIOGRAPHIES
CATALOGS(INDEXES)
CATALOGS(PUBLI-
CATIONS)
DICTIONARIES
DIRECTORIES
ENCYCLOPEDIAS
GLOSSARIES
HANDBOOKS
INDEXES(LOCATORS)
MANUALS
TABLES(DATA)
TRANSLATIONS

TRACERS
BT   DELIVERY

TRAINING
BT   PERSONNEL

TRANSFER FUNCTIONS
BT   UTILIZATION
NT   DATA
INFORMATION SYS-
TEMS
MATERIALS

TRANSFERRING
BT   PRODUCTION

TRANSLATING
BT   SERVICES

TRANSLATIONS
BT   TOOLS

TRANSMISSION
BT   SERVICES
NT   SHIPPING

TRENDS
BT   MANAGEMENT
NT   CONSULTANTS
EXPANSION

GROWTH
PREDICTIONS
PROJECTIONS
STATISTICS
SURVEYS(DATA COL-
　　LECTION)

TRIMMING
BT   MAPS

TRUCKS
BT   EQUIPMENT

TYPEWRITERS
BT   OFFICE EQUIPMENT
NT   KEYBOARDS
　　　PLATENS

U

UNIFORM FLOW
BT   PRODUCTION
NT   COORDINATION
　　　ROUTING

UNIT COSTS
BT   CATALOGING
NT   COUNTING
　　　STATISTICS

UPGRADING
BT   PERFORMANCE

USAGE
BT   CIRCULATION
NT   DAMAGE
　　　LOSSES
　　　STATISTICS

UTILIZATION
NT   COMMUNICATION
　　　EDUCATION
　　　READING
　　　RESEARCH
　　　TRANSFER FUNCTIONS

V

VARIATIONS
BT   CODES(STANDARDS)

VENTILATIONS
BT   BINDINGS
NT   AIR CONDITIONING
　　　FANS
　　　VENTILATORS

VENTS
BT   AIR CONDITIONING

W

WALLS
BT   DESIGN

WAITING TIME
BT   DELIVERY

WATER PIPELINES
BT   PLUMBING

WINDOWS
BT   DESIGN

WIRING
BT   LIGHTING

WORK SIMPLIFICATION
BT   PROCEDURES(MAN-
　　　AGEMENT)

WORKING CONDITIONS
BT   PERSONNEL
NT   ADJUSTMENT
　　　MORALE
　　　STRESSES

WRAPPING(PACKAGING)
BT   SHIPPING
NT   SHIPPING CON-
　　　TAINERS

X

XEROGRAPHY
BT   DUPLICATING
        REPRODUCIBILITY

APPENDIX B

Rough hierarchical classification of LIBRARIES made from non-defined index terms in the Thesaurus of Engineering Terms. Used as a basis for assigning BT-NT relationships in inner thesaurus, Appendix A.

ACQUISITION

   Books
   Periodicals
   Maps
   Documents
      Clearances

   Recommendations
      Searching
      Selection
      Rejection
      Orders(Commitments)

   Exchanging

   Requirements
      Specifications
      Quotations
      Estimates
      Appraisals
      Prices
         Rates
         Reduction

   Payment

AUTOMATION

   Mechanization

   Data systems
      Data acquisition
      Data transmission
      Data storage

   Data processing
      Punched card equipment
         Punched cards
         Key-punches
         Card sorters
         Card reproducers
         Interpreters
         Collators
         Printers (for computers)
         Tabulators
      Computers
         Digital computers
         Programs (Computers)
         Computer storage
         Disks (Storage)
         Tapes (Data media)
         Input-Output devices (for computers)

   Systems engineering
      Information systems
      Man-machine systems
      Operations
         Machine time
      Procedures (Management)

   Information retrieval

BUILDINGS

   Design

Walls
Floors
Aisles
Stairs
Elevators (Lifts)
Windows
Skylights

Noise control
Noise elimination

Heating
Steam pipes
Radiators
Temperature control
Thermostats

Ventilation
Ventilators
Fans
Air conditioning
Ducts
Vents

Lighting
Light (Illumination)
Wiring
Electric power distribu-
tion

Telephone systems

Plumbing
Water pipelines
Sewer pipelines

Protection
Safety measures
Safety devices
Fire protection
Firewalls
Fire alarm systems
Fire extinguishers
Damage
Exits
Entrances
Guards (Personnel)

Cleaning
Dust

Fumigation
Pest control

Refuse disposal

EQUIPMENT

Office equipment
Adding machines
Typewriters
Keyboards
Platens
Desks
Carpets

Furniture
Tables (Furniture)
Seats
Counters

Supplies
Forms (Paper)
Paper products
Glue
Staples
Clips

Stacking
Brackets
Range finders
Holders
Bracing

Hoists

Trucks

Film readers

Tape recorders

Purchasing
Specifications

Quality
Estimates
Quotations
Prices
Reduction
Orders (Commitments)
Receiving
Payment

INPUT

Processing

Cataloging

Procedures (Cataloging)
Examination
Searching
Bibliographies
Catalogs (Indexes)
Dictionaries
Production
Reproducibility
Card repro-
ducers
Printing
Xerography
Revising
Accuracy
Errors
Correction
Spacing
Indentation
Transferring
Restoring
Uniform flow
Coordination
Routing

Codes (Standards)
Conformity
Reliability
Variations
Subject headings
Index terms
Depth

Additions
(Enlarge-
ment)
Correction
Classification
Subject
classes
Notation
Decimals
Numbers
Expansion
Additions
(Enlarge-
ment)
Correction

Unit costs
Counting
Statistics

Materials

Books
Cutting
Slitting
Embossing
Marking
Stamping
Plating
Plates
Jackets
Series
Periodicals
Records
Identification
Dating
Supplements
Indexes (Lo-
cators)
Abbreviations
Collecting
Locating
Binding
Bookbinding
Covers
Drills
Glue
Rubbing

Maps
  Laminating
  Trimming
Documents

Catalogs (Indexes)

  Maintenance
  Filing systems
    Order (Sequence)
    Sorting
  Revising
  Acceptability

MANAGEMENT

Appropriations
  Costs
    Fixed costs
    Operating costs
  Budgeting
    Budget estimates
  Allocations

Facilities
  Architecture
    Buildings
      Design
  Construction
    Construction costs
  Maintenance
    Repairing
    Renovating
    Painting
    Cleaning
  Planning
  Parking facilities

Laws
  Building codes

Public relations
  Publicity
  Consultants
  Human factors
    Ethics

Friction
Publications
  Editing routines

Personnel management
  Coordination
  Supervision
  Assignments
  Personnel
    Employment
      Openings
      Interviews
    Position (Title)
      Qualifications
    Training
    Performance
      Rating
      Skills
      Job analysis
      Job description
      Upgrading
      Time standards
        (Work)
    Salaries
    Working conditions
      Stresses
      Morale
      Adjustment
    Fringe benefits
      Compensation
      Pensions
      Insurance
    Shortages

Procedures (Management)
  Coordination
  Decision making
  Efficiency
  Work simplification

Systems
  Control systems
  Data systems
  Information systems
  Man-machine systems
  Numbering systems

Objectives
  Planning
  Standards
  Consolidation
    Centralized control

Trends
  Statistics
  Growth
    Growth curves
  Expansion
  Surveys (Data collection)
    Questionnaires
  Projections
  Predictions
  Consultants

OUTPUT

Circulation

  Storage
    Books
    Documents
    Reports
    Records
      Record storage
        Compactibility
          Microfilm
    Maps
    Charts
    Pictures
    Phonograph records
    Photographs
  Availability
    Day
    Night
  Delivery
    Waiting time
    Tracers
    Holding (Retaining)
    Pneumatic conveyors
    Hoists
  Charging
  Regulations
    Identification

Control equipment
  Barriers
  Checkout
  Inspection
Fines
Time
  Dating
  Scheduling
Usage
  Statistics
    Periodic variations
    Diurnal variations
  Losses
  Damage

Tools

  Abstracts
  Bibliographies
  Catalogs (Indexes)
  Catalogs (Publications)
  Dictionaries
  Directories
  Encyclopedias
  Glossaries
  Handbooks
  Indexes (Locators)
  Manuals
  Tables (Data)
  Translations

Services

  Abstracting
  Copying
    Duplicating
      Copyrights
      Xerography
  Indexing
  Summarizing
  Translating
  Transmission
    Shipping
      Wrapping (Pack-
        aging)
    Postal service
      Parcel post

Air mail
Freight transportation
Shipping containers
Bags
Boxes
Cartons

UTILIZATION

Communication
Education
Reading
Research
Transfer functions
Information systems
Materials
Data

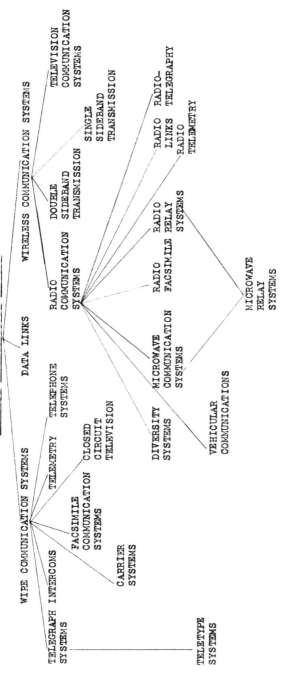

APPENDIX C. Sample of classification in the Thesaurus of Engineering Terms. Based on BT (Broader term) and NT (Narrower term) relationships.

IV.   CATALOG TOPICS

"The first, last, and most important fact about the catalog is that it is not a machine.   It is, rather, an instrumentality for objectifying and making permanent an
intellectual process of analysis and synthesis.   The
success of any catalog depends ultimately upon the disciplined intelligence of those who plan and maintain it."

Shera & Egan, The Classified..., x.

"Forty years ago it would have been safe to bet that
the book catalog was for ever buried under a mountain
of 3 x 5 cards, but modern techniques of reproduction
have made the book catalog thoroughly practicable in
certain types of bibliographical situations.   There is
even a growing tendency today to look with favor, or
at least with decreasing disapproval, on the old practice
of arranging books according to a system of fixed location.   The classified catalog is no longer regarded as
being so inferior to its dictionary counterpart as we
once believed, and the antecedents of even the modern
documentalist can be traced at least as far back as
Cassiodorus and his rules for ordering the monastic
scriptorium and library."

J. H. Shera, Documentation..., 84.

WHEN IS A SUBJECT NOT A SUBJECT?

John Metcalfe

When is a subject not a subject?   This may sound like
the conundrum, when is a door not a door, and the answer
may be, when it is alone.   But to be straightforward at the
outset, the subject of this paper is the meaning of subject,
its technical or terminological meaning, in systems of information retrieval (IR), and its understood or assumed mean-

ing for those who have to consult these oracles, on a self help or do it yourself principle. Information retrieval, or more fully storage and retrieval of information, or leads to information, implies information on subjects distinguished in some way from each other; and this seems to imply that a definition of subject for information retrieval must be a definition of subjects in the plural in some way differentiated from each other.

The question is a terminological or nomenclatural one, and its consideration may involve other terms besides subject. So to begin with something may be usefully said about terms and terminologies or glossaries of terms. There are technical terms or words with special meanings which are also words in common use, though they may have begun with special meanings. Examples are terms long since taken from logic, such as class and classification, specific and specification, dilemma and predicament. Subject may have come into IR use from its use in logic and grammar, but through common use. Other technical terms are words not in common use, at least in quite the same form; isolate as a noun in IR seems to be an example; others are words in common use but with an acquired meaning which can be contradictory; noise is a recent example, meaning any interference or interruption in communication with or without sound; and it has passed into IR for what have also been called false drops and slop.

Contemporary IR can be said to date from 1876, from Dewey's Decimal Classification and Relative Index, and Cutter's Rules for a dictionary catalog, including rules for his specific entry, with the much later introduction of coordinate indexing and mechanization. Dewey used few words in special senses, but form, mnemonic, and relative may be taken as three; by the last one he meant using his expansible or extensible class numbers to index relative locations, instead of press marks or page numbers to index fixed locations. But as this became commonplace and familiarity almost bred contempt, and as he introduced including class names in his second, 1885 edition, this is now taken to be the meaning of relative indexing; for example in his first edition index he had Teeth 611, 617, which are class numbers on page 19, and although he called this index a subject index this was what he meant by relative indexing; in the second edition he called this index relative but also added including class names, as in Teeth anatomy 611, surgery and dentistry 617, and as this could be taken to mean indexing of subject relations, this is what the term relative index was taken to mean, and is now used to mean.

Cutter in his Rules, 1876, gave definitions in alphabetical order with this preliminary note:

> There is such confusion in the use of terms in the various prefaces to catalogs--a confusion that at once springs from and leads to confusion of thought and practice--that it is worth while to propose a systematic nomenclature.

Under the same heading and note in his latest edition, the fourth, 1904, there are 115 definitions, some with long notes. Of these, 27 are more or less on subject cataloging and subject shelf arrangement; and some of these have the longest small print notes; class is defined simply as "a collection of objects having characteristics in common," but the note is three pages long; another of more than a page is under a three-line definition of classed catalogs; another 14-line note is under dictionary and other alphabetical catalogs. These notes and the long ones to his subject rules have been called a shadow land, but they have more substance in them, still of relevance to IR, than the definitions and rules themselves.

In his Definitions Cutter had

> Subject, the theme or themes of the book whether stated in the title or not.

This does little more than give theme as a synonym for subject. And under

> Polytopical, treating of several topics,

the word topic seems to be more or less a synonym for subject, as it is in its common use. But there are also his rules 340, 343:

> 340. Under subject headings group titles topically when it can be done, otherwise arrange by the authors' names.
> 343. When the titles are numerous under a subject heading divide them, but avoid subdivision.

These are rules of arrangement, 42 pages after his subject entry rules; but with their notes and examples they imply subject or object aspects as the meaning of topic and topical. In his examples, under rule 343, he gave

[Country] Ornithology.

In his rule 165, under Subject entry, he preferred New England ornithology to Ornithology of America ... of New England ... of Scotland, on the ground that these are "in effect class-entry," whereas "New England botany, New England history, New England ornithology are not parts of New England, but simply the individual New England considered in various aspects." And he then concluded:

> Of course the dictionary catalog in choosing be-
> tween a class and an individual prefers the latter.
> Its object is to show at one view all the sides of
> each object; the classed catalog shows together the
> same side of many objects.

This is hardly a shadow lead of IR generally or of specific entry in particular, that Dunkin called it.[1]

What was unfortunate was that Cutter in his distinction of object and aspect, or topic, hardly got beyond his opposition of specific and class or general entry, and subdivision merely as an arrangement device. But the immediate interest here is his distinction of object and aspect in a subject. And this is the immediate interest of a statement by Haykin in his Subject Headings: A Practical Guide (1951):

> Aspects or topics comprehended within it are likely
> to be sought under names of their own, hence, as
> a rule, require entry under independent headings,
> rather than subdivisions under a broad subject
> [p. 27].

In this context Haykin meant by a broad subject not an including class, in the sense in which Birds includes Canaries, but a subject not subdivided by aspects. His argument for multiple entry can be questioned, especially when he goes on to argue that subdivision by topic "is contrary to the principle of specific entry, since it would, in practice, result in an alphabetico-classed catalog." Clearly Cutter didn't think that it would, if topic meant aspect. But the point here is the ambiguous use of topic to mean both a subject and an aspect of a subject.

In another of his "shadow land" notes, to his rule
175, Cutter justified Ancient and Medieval history, as analogous with Europe--History, on the ground that the adjec-
tives "ancient" and "medieval" implied periods, which could
be named by the nouns "Antiquity" and "Middle Ages." And
he was a member of the three-man committee which finally
prepared for publication by the A. L. A. a List of Subject
Headings for use in dictionary catalogs, 1895, and "to be
considered as an appendix to Cutter's rules for a dictionary
catalog, ed. 3." In a "minority report" quoted in the Preface, he opposed History, Ancient and History, Medieval,
and a note is as follows,

> Minority report. C. A. Cutter prefers Ancient art,
> Ancient geography, Ancient history.... In this
> he follows the principle of concrete cataloging,
> which brings together what relates to a thing, a
> country, a period, rather than all works belonging
> to a class or form such as Geography, History
> [p. iii].

An interest in this is the use of the word "concrete,"
now associated with Julius Otto Kaiser and his systematic
indexing. He did not publish his book, Systematic Indexing,
until 1911, in London (Pitman), but according to his Introduction "the first draft was worked out in Philadelphia in 1896-
7," when he was employed in the Philadelphia Commercial
Museum. In it he got what seems to have been his first
indexing job, after emigration from Germany to Australia,
then to South and then to North America. In his 1911 book
he considered Cutter's Expansive Classification, and others,
in rejecting classified in favor of alphabetical indexing, but
there is no evidence that he knew anything of Cutter, or
Cutter of him in 1896-7, or that he read Cutter's rules for
a dictionary catalog. Like others he sharply distinguished
cataloging from indexing; he extended the former to the cataloging of periodical articles, but only as wholes, without
any breakdown to specific information, and also identified it
with what he called the catchword method [para. 10-14, 649,
652].

Kaiser's concretes were not necessarily concrete in
the usual sense; he dealt mainly with the physical objects of
commerce but said:

> The subjects of our observation and reasoning are
> things in general, real or imaginary, and the con-

> ditions attaching to them.   We shall call them con-
> cretes and processes respectively [para. 52].

His concretes could also be abstract things such as Labor
[para. 299-303].   And it was to these that he related his
units of information.

> We shall take literature to pieces and rearrange
> the pieces systematically [para. 16].   We must try
> to dissociate INFORMATION from literature, we
> do not want books, we want information, and al-
> though this information is contained in books, it
> should be looked upon as quite a different material
> and it must be treated differently from books [para.
> 48, 83].

He was insistent on concrete and process in the headings he
called Statements [para. 302]:

> It should be noted particularly that we are not
> dealing with isolated terms each conveying inde-
> pendent information, but with connected terms all
> having reference to the same pieces of informa-
> tion.   The concrete is the main term, the process
> gives the action stated of the concrete ... the
> process is always contained in the action, it is nev-
> er absent ... [para. 302, 344].

But his processes are often very general, for example Electric crane--Management, and Cotton gin roller--Description
[para. 462].   He gave the name Statement to what he systematically expressed as Concrete and Process or sometimes
as Concrete--Country--Process, and Country--Concrete--
Process, which he regarded as "two essential permutations"
out of a possible six of three terms, for example

> Nitrate--Chile--Trade
> Chile--Nitrate--Trade [para. 302, 383-5]

There could of course be Concrete and Process without
Country, but hardly Country and Concrete without Process,
because of his insistence on a Process, subordinate to every
Concrete even though the Process might be so general as to
have little or no indexing significance.   What he opposed and
would only admit as very exceptional was the reverse Proc-
ess--Concrete order of his terms, or Process, alone [para.
653-5].   But in his later presentation he was inclined to be
more flexible. [2]

Like others, Kaiser used the word subject as a medium of explanation, as in,

> Given our indexes and registers we may focus ...
> the information available on any given subject in
> a summary. Our indexes give an analytical statement of the information, for it has been cut into
> pieces ... rearranged in more suitable form....
> Too large pieces will preclude us altogether from
> reporting on smaller pieces [para. 48].

So when he used as an example an article on How paper affects metals, he said,

> Taking the whole article as one item, the information treats on wrapping paper and ... we may
> formulate our statement with little difficulty as follows: Wrapping paper--Chemical action [para.
> 458-9].

The subject of the article as a whole, and even though it was only one page in length was, however, of little interest to him. He continued,

> In addition we may formulate statements by splitting
> up the article into separate items: Metallic Article--Corrosion, or Silverware--Corrosion etc.,
> etc.... We see therefore the indexable information is successively narrowed down by the standpoint from which we regard it, and by the use to
> which we may put it [para. 459].

And although he began by using the word subject as a medium of explanation of his system, it is clear that for him subjects were what he called statements, and not subjects of documents in the usual sense. They are the subjects of his "pieces," selected according to interest and possibly less than a line in length. He began by summarizing them in his Concrete--process, or object-aspect heading which was his statement, and then if necessary added an extension in what he called an amplification, including the document reference [para. 305].

In this approach the core or nucleus or starting point is always a concrete, distinguished almost absolutely from a process. And a converse of this seems to be that if there is more than one concrete in a distinguished piece or item of information, then there should be more than one statement, which means in conventional terms more than one, and therefore multiple entry for the item.

> When two concretes appear in the same item, they must be separated into two statements. For instance the use of water power to generate electricity
>> 1st statement: Water power--Application
>> 2nd statement: Electricity--generation,
> each statement being completed in the amplification [para. 327].

He did however qualify this to allow as one alternative the collection of several concretes "into a few class terms"; and as another, the mention of several concretes implied in a process under a country in the amplification [para. 328]. An example of the first might be: fertilizers such as a, b, c, are all good for X, for which fertilizers could be used as a concrete; an example of the second might be, the trade of New Zealand is mainly butter, mutton, wool ... then the statement could be New Zealand--Trade, with the stated articles of trade listed in the amplification.

If Kaiser used the term concrete in his first draft in 1896-7 [para. 20] then he and Cutter at the same time, though apparently quite independently, used the same term, with important likeness of meaning, but also with important differences in system. For both a concrete was an object of information, or in later terminology an isolate, and for both a concrete was an unsubordinated heading in an alphabetical system of IR. But whereas Kaiser formally and consistently distinguished Concrete and Process, or in more general terms, object and aspect, as heading and subheading, Cutter thought almost exclusively of compound words such as bookbinding, or bookkeeping, or agriculture, in which an object name was the first element, or of phrases to the same effect, such as Flower fertilization, Ancient history and Medieval history, New England ornithology. Cutter's only exception was his topical grouping or division of numerous titles under subject heading or entry word.[3]

Kaiser went so far in the opposite direction as to split up compound names.

> Deal with names as you find them and provide what is missing by references. The alphabetical

> arrangement of names is so frequently resorted to,
> because it disregards definition of the terms and
> bases their sequence on the form of the terms, i.e.
> letters [para. 114].

He also said "for obvious reasons the indexer is not at liberty to change names" [para. 417]. But:

> Names of concrete and process combined should
> be resolved into concrete and process. In this
> way we shall make it easier to connect our related
> terms, for they will now be confined to the names
> of concretes [para. 184].

Examples he gave were

> bibliography   book description
> agriculture   land cultivation

But bibliography in any of its several meanings is not just
description of books, and agriculture is no longer just cultivation of land.

He seems to have contradicted himself and the principle of usage as basic to the operation of an alphabetically arranged index. A user must know a name, and the alphabetical order of the letters with which it is written; this requirement may be called known names in a known order.
Cutter did not state this explicitly, but it is at least partly
implied in the head note to his rules on Choice between different names:

> General rules always applicable ... can no more
> be given than rules without exception in grammar.
> Usage in both cases is the supreme arbiter--the
> usage in the present case, not of the cataloger but
> of the public in speaking of subjects.

There could be references such as Bibliography see Books--
Description; Kaiser did not say so, but as shown just above
he did say the opposite, "deal with names as you find them,
and provide what is missing by references." He believed
that rules meant no exception, and a basic rule or principle
of his system seems to have produced a dilemma. If concretes and processes were always to be formally distinguished,
then names of concrete and process combined had to be resolved, as he said.

Cutter's basic principle was what he called specific entry as opposed to what he called class entry, but, except to clear himself of class entry, he did not resolve combinations of object and aspect names, and even then did not do so formally, by turning an adjectival phrase such as New England ornithology into heading and subheading. He only did this as a matter of subarrangement under a heading, to "group titles topically when it can be done, and when titles are numerous under a subject heading." This limitation may have been out of respect for usage, the usage of the public in speaking of subjects, that is syntactical usage, not indicative usage, not modified even to the extent of converting beekeeping into Bees--Keeping, or even so far as to do no more than put a dash between Sheep and shearing in Sheep shearing. It seems more likely that the thinking of himself and his contemporaries was not as explicit as this on this point, and that as has been argued, more or less systematic subheading was not forced as it was later by complexity and multiplicity of subjects compounded of object and aspect.

Whatever the explanation, he did accept names as he found them in use to such an extent that he did not see subheadings as a solution of what in effect he called the no name problem:

> Some subjects have no name; they are spoken of only by a phrase or by several phrases not definite enough to be used as a heading.... There are thousands of possible matters of investigation, some of which are ... discussed, but before the catalog can profitably follow its "specific" rule ... they must ... be given some sort of name, otherwise we must assign them class entry.

Accordingly, for his example, "the movements of fluids in plants," he assigned the class heading Botany (Physiological).[5]

Clearly he regarded the relation of plants, their fluids, and their movement or circulation as a subject, to which his specific entry rule could be applied; if, he said,

> it was called, let us say, Phythydraulics, it would be seen that, under this rule, it no more ought to be under Botany than Circulation of the blood under Zoology.

But his Greek Phythydraulics is near enough to Plant fluids circulation in English.   Plants--Fluids--Circulation could be used and Plants--Circulation, though ambiguous, has been used.   The unfortunate effect of the limitations of thought of Cutter and his contemporaries may be seen in the cumbersome Library of Congress heading, Plants, Motion of fluids in, and hundreds and even thousands like it in its subject headings list.   Established compounds such as thermometer have been broken down in other systems for other reasons, for example Heat--Measurement--Instruments, and this has been called semantic factoring.   It was earlier developed as a solution of Cutter's no name problem, but not one universally or uniformly applied with his specific entry.

After the establishment of the dictionary catalog with specific entry there was, and has continued, renewal of faith and hope in the classified catalog for all points and pursuits, with consequent thinking on the subject of subject from different angles.   Dewey had used subject as a convenient but not closely defined term; at the same time he did, with consequences, establish the idea of what he called form division, with its 01-09 notation for some aspects of subjects.   Photography--Chemistry, for example, is 771.5 and Rubber--Vulcanization, 678.24, but Photography--Competitions is 770.79 and Rubber--Research, 678.072.   Cutter developed this a little in his Expansive Classification, 1891-93, but added nothing as influential as his specific entry for alphabetical cataloging.   And Brown's now equally dead Subject Classification of 1906, while radical in its single place theory and practice, did not introduce anything more exact about subject.   Specific subjects were still subordinated in a class, though only one.

A noteworthy development in theory by Dewey's editor is a statement by Custer in his Introduction to the 17th Edition of DDC,

> 2.21 DISCIPLINE.   The concept of "discipline," a field of specialization, is basic to an understanding of Dewey's system.   The primary basis for DDC arrangement and development is by discipline, while subject, strictly speaking, is secondary. There is no one place for any subject in itself; a subject may appear in any or all of the disciplines. No class can be said to cover the scope of marriage, or water, or tomatoes, or Brazil ... there is no single number for any of these concepts or subjects. [6]

All the classifications, with the exception of Brown's single place subject classification and any others like it, are like DDC in its subordination in more than one aspect, class or discipline of a thing or object, as in the case of Marriage in Religion, Law, and Customs. The interest is in the explicit limitation of the sense or use of the word. There had however already been development going further in this direction before DDC ed. 17, (1965).

Otlet in developing UDC from DC about 1895 introduced synthetic classification or the use of a classificatory subject notation to express in a combination of numbers what he called "toutes les nuances de l'analyse idéologico-bibliographique" of a document. [7] And his British disciple, S. C. Bradford, in his articles on documentation, introduced the use of notion and concept as synonymous for subject in English, but usually meaning what he called the complex notions of contemporary scientific documentation. In the flood tide of documentation identified with UDC and FID the significance of Kaiser's dissociation of information from literature, and his breaking up of the document was not realized, for example at the ASLIB Conference in 1926, at which he read a paper on his systematic indexing. [8]

Bliss, who was born in 1870, was from way back in his thinking about classification, mainly about the "order of the sciences," introduced by E. C. Richardson in his lectures in 1899 on classification theoretical and practical. Bliss stayed behind the field, and began by calling documentation a term not now suffering from unemployment. [9] But finally he hurried after the field with his now dead Bibliographic Classification "developed as a systematic and synthetic classification." He finally listed 75 "relevant definitions" of terms in his Introduction, but did not define his basic term "consensus," which has been generally misunderstood, or subject. [9] He first welcomed the Ranganathanites as minor allies, but then was overwhelmed by them. He did his best with Ranganathan's phrases and facets before he said of focus, it is "out of focus for this classifier's old eyes." But like the original documentation school he had done much to create his own nemesis and, in part at least, the Ranganathanite school has done this for itself with its prolific terminologies and metaphysics.

In his Prolegomena to Library Classification, 2nd ed. (1957), Ranganathan said,

A vast specialized terminology has already come into vogue. More will be coming in future in spite of phlegmatic and rhetorical protests from old guard take-it-easy librarians. These come from those with little experience of the exacting demands of intensive reference service. These also come from those holding classification to be little more than shelf-marking. Thought on the discipline of classification must march on in spite of them. New terminology will continue to precipitate in its wake [p. 165].

The only appropriate comment may be, and how! But what has happened may be exemplified by a controversy in the Library Association Record in 1967 as to whether Ranganathan's "facets" are mutually exclusive or not. This raged among the disciples through three issues, February, April, May, until it was mercifully closed by the editor; as it has been said that man might be suffocated in a plethora of his own print, so there are signs that interest in Ranganathan's theory and practice has been suffocated by the plethora of his terminology.

In his Colon Classification, 6th ed. (reprinted with amendments, 1963), Ranganathan said,

> ... an (IF) cannot by itself constitute a Subject. On the other hand, a (BC) can by itself constitute a Subject.

An (IF) is a division in a Facet called an Isolate Focus, or simply an Isolate (I). A (BC) is a Basic Class or Basic subject. A Subject made up of a (BC) and one or more Isolates is said to be a Compound Class (Cd C), and so on.[10] This may seem the answer first suggested to the question, when is a subject not a subject; when it is alone or an isolate. But there may still be the question, when a subject is a subject, what is it?

In Depth Classification ... Papers for discussion at the 10th All India Library Conference ... 1953, edited by S.R. Ranganathan, Vickery presented a glossary of current terminology ... a glossary of the technical terms currently in use in the development of thought on classification. About 148 terms in 320 were attributed to Ranganathan. Subject by itself was not listed; "subject device" was defined as division of formation of an isolate (Ranganathan), and "isolate,"

as any object, process, abstract term or class of these
(Farradane); as any notational symbol the component digits
of which are marks devoid of meaning (Vickery); as a generic term to denote isolate idea, isolate term or isolate number (Ranganathan).

Another glossary was published in Ranganathan's
Annals of Library Science 5:65-112, 1958.   It had in it,

211   Universe of knowledge--Assumed term; its
      entities are subject and isolates
212   Subject--Assumed term
213   Knowledge item--Subject
217   Isolate--Entity in the universe of knowledge
      which is not a subject by itself but whose
      combination with a subject (book subject) gives
      rise to a subject of smaller extension than the
      host subject....   Example "gold" is an isolate
      not a subject.   But "Chemistry of gold" is a
      subject of smaller extension than the host
      subject, Chemistry....

The Indian Standard Glossary of Classification Terms
(1963) was the work of a panel with Dr. S. R. Ranganathan
as its convener.   This glossary occupies 98 pages exclusive
of an index and is of course classified.   In Chapter C, Universe of Knowledge, Subject is stated to be an assumed term
with Knowledge mass as an "alternate term."   Isolate seems
to have no basic definition in relation to subject, and seems
on its way to being an assumed term.

In 1964, Ranganathan defined sixteen terms, including:

11   Subject.   Thought content of a document
12   Basic subject.   Assumed term.
13   Isolate.   Assumed term.

In a sense, it is not a subject by itself.   But if
it is attached to an appropriate basic subject, the
result is a subject of smaller extension.   For example 'Gold' is an isolate.

...   .

A number of isolates also may be attached to one
and the same subject.

Prospecting for Gold
Prospecting for Gold in India
Prospecting for Gold in India in 1964,

are all subjects derived from the basic subject
'Economic Geology' by attaching the isolate 'Gold'
and some other isolates to it.[11]

Explanation according to his theory and terminology
is not easy or certain, because of changes in emphasis and
terminology. There are his five fundamental categories of
facets: Personality, Matter, Energy, Space, Time, with the
notation [P] [M] [E] [S] [T]. As late as his Prolegomena,
2nd ed. (1957), little is made of Matter [p. 178]; but in the
Indian Standard Glossary (1963), much is made of it [p. 48];
things such as Gold, Prospecting, India, 1964 are "manifestations" of the fundamental categories. In his H7 Economic
Geology class, minerals such as gold seem to be manifestations of Personality, and isolates in its [P] facet; Prospecting is an isolate in its [E] or Energy facet; India is a Space
manifestation and isolate; and 1964 a Time manifestation and
isolate. And in his E class, Chemistry, Gold is a focus or
focus isolate or isolate in [P]. So gold and other things as
[M] seem to be squeezed out; but the basic or main classes
are also [P], so Economic geology might be regarded as [P],
and Gold as [M], but this does not seem likely and in any
subject whilst [P] has to be manifested in some form, not
all the other categories need be manifested; they remain pri-
mordial.

He wrote in 1949 of

... The fundamental categories at the bottom of
facet analysis. The stable rock-bottom which is
struck by the roots of facet-analysis ... the traditional categories: time, space, energy, matter,
and personality--the last being used to denote whatever is unanalysable and highly organized, though
intensely complex.[12]

This pseudo-science imposed itself on British disciples
from about 1950 on, but the terminology is used for what in
other classificatory systems are presented simply as auxiliary
tables of processes, place and date. Personality and Matter
are categories of objects or entities not clearly distinguished;
as Energy, Space and Time are categories of aspects. A
source of unintended deception is a kind of it's all done with

mirrors trick.   An appearance of science, of laws of nature
is imposed on the usual devices of hierarchical classification,
and then the system is presented as, and may appear to be,
derived from this seeming science and these seeming laws
of nature.   In this way what are obviously subjects in common uses of the word become isolates and are then said not
to be subjects, whereas the simple fact is that they are subjects in the ordinary subordination of the hierarchical classifications.

Ranganathan then attempted to meet the difficulty of
the "all about" kind of book, not very convincingly.

> A book embodying every possible subject derivable
> by attaching the isolate 'Gold' to every possible
> basic subject cannot obviously be written by a spe-
> cialist in a single subject.   It is likely to be only
> a Composite Book, consisting of several contribu-
> tions by different specialists.   And readers for the
> whole of such a book will be very few.   It is in this
> sense that an Isolate cannot be a subject by itself.

But whether a book is by one or more specialists or
not is hardly relevant; a popular "all about" book on Gold,
even though for children, is a book on an object; the book
has to be placed in a classified or alphabetico-classed catalog; there is the classifying problem of the comprehensive
book which he doesn't solve.   All he seems to have done is
to describe what is done with comprehensively specific subjects in any aspect classification; but this hardly means that
they are not subjects.

However there is also Farradane to be considered.
Ranganathan took many of his terms from where he found
them, perhaps not realizing some were hardly in the public
domain.   An example is Bliss's Anterior classes, to which
he added posterior classes.   And Farradane seems to have
introduced isolate as a technical term.   In 1950 he presented
what he called a scientific theory of classification and its
practical applications.[14]   And in a summary he said,

> ... Items of knowledge are divided into uniquely
> definable terms, called isolates, and the relations
> between them, called operators.   It is shown that
> only four basic operators exist, expressing appur-
> tenance, equivalence, reaction and causation; using
> symbols for these operators, all subjects can be
> analysed in a linear form called an analet.

His isolates were items of knowledge but something
less than subjects; explaining and developing his theory he
said,

> An item of knowledge will thus be an object or
> class of objects, a process or class of processes,
> or an abstract term or class of such terms, which
> is clearly and, at its own level of complexity,
> uniquely definable, as far as may be possible.
> Any other item would in reality be composed of
> two or more concepts, leading to logical confusions.
> Let us call these items, as defined, isolates [p.
> 87].

He then went on to what he called analysis of statements, in a formal and symbolic way. Giving examples he
said, "the action of morphine on the respiratory center of
rabbits becomes Morphine/--Respiratory Centre)/Rabbit."
In this the symbol /-- represents his reaction operator; the
symbol)/ represents his appurtenance operator, and read
back again this means an isolate morphine acting on an isolate respiratory center, in an isolate rabbit. It is one of
his analets or analyses of what would ordinarily be called
the subject of a document stated in a title or abstract, and
he himself used the term subject for his analets when he
went on to say, "let us examine the nature of these analysed
subjects more closely" [p. 89-90].

Two years later, he found it necessary to increase
his operators to eight. But his theory of classification and
indexing can hardly be pursued here beyond a point at which
it provides some food for thought on what is a subject, or
when such subject-objects as morphine and rabbits are not
subjects but isolates, which become subjects by relation.
His and Ranganathan's theory and practice certainly diverged;
for him such a relation as that given, of morphine, respiratory center, and rabbit, is a subject in the sense of the
subject of a document briefly stated, and his main interest
was his isolate relations; Ranganathan's interest was hierarchical classification. But in both there is some equivalence
of what is meant by isolates as elements in what are distinguished as subjects of different extension. And in different
terms there is Custer's idea related to DDC of "discipline"
as primary, while subject, strictly speaking, is secondary;
this too relates to hierarchical classification. [15] But Ranganathan's classified cataloging was single entry with the supplementary indexing he called chain indexing or procedure.

In the Indian Standard Glossary there is

> A41 Chain--The sequence of the classes of a uni-
> verse and of its universes of successive removes,
> carried backwards to any point desired
> 42 Link--A class in a chain
> X51 Chain procedure--Procedure for determining
> the class index entries, the specific subject entries,
> and the see also subject entries of a document
> from its class number and the class number of the
> cross reference entries provided for it.

More simply his British disciple Coates said,

> Chain is a hierarchy of terms in a classification
> scheme, each term containing or including all
> those which follow it.   Chain procedure is a method
> ... of constructing subject index entries, without
> permutation of components, by citing terms con-
> tained in a particular chain.[16]

But it is to be noted that in the Glossary chain procedure is
said to be one for determing the class index entries, specific
subject entries and some kind of see also references.

For a long time Ranganathan maintained that Cutter's
specific entry heading should be, had to be the last term in
a chain with a hierarchy of downward cross reference to it,
and then ridiculed the ridiculous result, and Cutter, for
something Cutter never even imagined.   In 1938 he asserted
that,

> The determination of Specific Subject of a book
> is ultimately in the hands of the scheme of classi-
> fication adopted.   We shall see presently how this
> shifting of the burden of determining the Specific
> Subject ... from the cataloguer to the scheme of
> classification will resolve all the nightmare diffi-
> culties in framing rules for the Specific Subject
> Entry in a Dictionary catalogue.[17]

There seems an implied assumption of a library catalog related to a shelf classification, without consideration of alphabetical bibliography apart from library cataloging.   There
is also an assumption of single entry.   His relation of hierarchical classification and alphabetico-specific entry he called
symbiosis by chain procedure.[18]

An example which he gave of this symbiosis was based on his Colon Classification number JAT : 4 K 83: G12 : 438, for Systematic study of the entomological diseases of the teakwood forest in Burma, which he called a specific subject. The hierarchy represented by the class number is reversed for his chain procedure indexing of a classified catalog entry and so runs backwards from Burma with the place number : 438 to Forestry with the class number JA. So he meant Burma by the first heading when he said,

> The Dictionary catalogue will be asked by the chain procedure to use the first of the above-mentioned headings as the heading of the specific subject entry and all the others as headings for See also subject entries.... [Apparently references, these] will send the reader from one region of the catalogue to another like a shuttlecock and tire him out at a very early stage. And at no stage will it be able to give him a connected conspectus of all his material so that he may be able to enumerate his exact requirement whatever be the first word which he presented to the catalogue [p. 240].

In his Theory of Library Catalogue (1938), Ranga-nathan made some play with Cutter's subdivision of country by some topics, whereas now the subdivision would be the reverse. But Cutter's specific entry heading for Systematic study of the entomological diseases of the teakwood forests of Burma would be Teakwood, and could be this without any extension. In his Classified Catalogue Code (1958), he spoke of conference with British National Bibliography staff, in June 1953, and said BNB represented

> ... the first large scale, systematic and continued general application of the procedure.... Though the BNB is a Classified Catalogue, its staff had been observing also the reaction of those accustomed to the Dictionary catalogue. When I visited the office of the BNB in June 1953, A.J. Wells, the Editor, and his colleague E.J. Coates, told me that those who use the Dictionary Catalogue would like to have the benefit of deriving the Subject Headings mechanically and consistently from Class numbers but would like to retain some kinds of entries they had been accustomed to when they depended on Dictionaries of Subject Headings [p. 315-16].

He was prepared to consider whether there could be alternative rules to allow what he called Classified Pockets in the Dictionary Catalogue, and his answer in 1958 was yes. But there was still to be symbiosis with classification. Taking as a subject Statistics of rural education in India brought up to the 1930's, with the Colon Classification number T9 (Y31) . 44. N3 s, this could be divided into three parts:

T9 (Y31)	Rural education
T9 (Y31) . 44	Rural education in India
T9 (Y31) . 44. N3 s	Statistics of rural education in India brought up to 1930's

And by the application of rules for the selection of links the specific entry heading would be Rural Education, India, Statistics with cross references

> Statistics, India, Rural Education
>   See also Rural Education, India, Statistics
> India, Rural Education
>   See also Rural Education, India, Statistics
> Asia, Rural Education
>   See also Rural Education, India, Statistics
> Education
>   See also Rural Education, India, Statistics [p. 314-328].

A simple way of dealing with this may be to say that there is a chain of class, subclasses, or genus, species, as in T Education ... T9 (Y31) Rural Community, or Rural education, and then aspects as in T9 (Y31) . 44, Rural education--India; T9 (Y31) . 44. N3, Rural education--India--1930s; and T9 (Y31) . 44. N3 s, Rural education--India--1930s--Statistics. Rural education is then the specific subject or object of information, and what follows are aspects. But Ranganathan was preoccupied by a hierarchy or chain in which the terminal link is most specific, and so he said in effect, all right Mr. Cutter, you want specific entry, you shall have it, the most specific term is the last in the chain, it must be your specific heading, now see what a clown you are. But if Cutter's specific entry is to be found in chains, then his specific subject is the last subdivision of an object class, though this may be followed by further aspect subdivisions. Ranganathan and his British disciples have made little or nothing of the crucial change in characteristics of division from object to aspect. And this resulted in more than one admitted difficulty in his chain procedure indexing.

In 1960 Coates in considering chain procedure for subject indexes to classified catalogs used as an example the measurement of railroad gradients, with Ranganathan's Colon Classification number D415, 4 :78 which is D Engineering, 415 Railroad, 4 Gradient :7 Construction, 8 Measurement. His index entries for this were

>   Measurements : Gradients : Railroads D415, 4 :78
>   Construction : Gradients : Railroads   D415, 4 :7
>   Gradients : Railroads : Engineering   D415, 4
>   Railroads : Engineering   D415

He then admitted that "the specific entry for the subject ... is likely to be formulated by the enquirer as Railroads, Gradients, Measurements," which the reversed chain procedure does not give, and after admitting other difficulties in "the rationale of the system" for the non-professional or uninstructed user, he concluded "This is the price which chain procedure exacts for its solution of the problem of permutation of components."[19] This is something like saying of an automobile unable to go forward, that this is the price paid for its ability to go backwards. And this finally led to a reaction from chain to rotated or cyclic permuted indexing, even among the disciples.

In 1957 Coates, who was chief cataloger for BNB, outlined, even detailed, a scheme for the derivation of dictionary catalog entry headings and see also reference headings from BNB. He took the link in a chain representing a specific subject in Cutter's sense, as a heading, with any following aspect links as subheadings, for example in 622. 344 09 4272, the digits up to 622.344 gave him Lead, 622 gave him a "qualifier" and so Lead, Mining, then he went to the end of the chain to 09 4272 for Lancashire to arrive at a Dictionary catalog chain:

>   Lead, Mining--Lancashire
>   Metals, Mining see also Lead, Mining
>   Mining see also Metals, Mining
>   Engineering see also Mining
>   Technology see also Engineering

But in discussing Sequence of subheadings, he said of Hospitals, Finance and Bridges, Suspension:

It is suggested that both varieties are in reality
inverted phrases, the only difference being that
subheadings omit a connecting preposition which is
taken as understood (e.g., HOSPITALS, Finance
[of].[20]

But this misses the logical distinction of inverted object
specification, and aspect subheading, formally expressed by
Hospitals--Finance and Hospitals, Military in Library of
Congress headings.[20]

In 1960, in his book Subject Catalogues Headings and
Structure, Coates treated Dewey, Cutter, and even Kaiser
as all stumbling forerunners of Ranganathan, and of his own
"alternative conception of specific entry," alternative that is
to Cutter's.   He saw Kaiser as contributing to the solution
of "the problem of the relative importance of the components
of a compound subject at the point at which Cutter had left
it."   But he made nothing of Cutter's distinction of object and
aspect or of Kaiser's concrete and process as a special use
of this distinction.   And going straight from Kaiser to Ranganathan and endeavoring to explain the latter's facets he
said,

> ... a schedule for Metal Manufacturers would in-
> clude on the one hand a list of products such as
> bars, plates, tubes ... and on the other hand a
> list of processes such as casting, welding, press-
> ing.... Each of these two lists represents a par-
> ticular exclusive mental angle on the topic Metal
> manufactures and are therefore facets, aspects
> would have done just as well [p. 39-44].

But use of aspect for both Ranganathan's Personality facet
and his Energy facet obscures the distinction which both
Cutter and Kaiser in their different ways made fundamental,
that between object and aspect; it even obscures Ranganathan's
own distinction of his Personality and Energy categories.

In his exposition and deposition of Cutter, Coates
dealt with Cutter's doubtfully expressed rule, "161.   Enter
a work under its subject-heading not under the heading of a
class which includes that subject."   But he did not quote the
examples immediately under it, or Cutter's clearer specific
entry definition and its examples.   He said of the rule above,

This sounds simple and straightforward especially

against our later background of detailed bibliography classification. But if we understand the rule
to mean that the subject heading is to fit the individual case, we are speedily disillusioned by the
comment which follows the rule [p. 32].

He then went straight into Cutter's note on the no name
problems and concluded:

Briefly there are two possible conceptions of specific subject entry. The one favoured by Cutter
envisages a set of stock subjects, under one of
which each book had to be accommodated. If the
subject matter of a book is more restricted in
scope than any of the stock terms, then the book
must be placed under the most restricted stock
term which contains it just as the purchaser of
ready made clothing buys the nearest larger stock
size to his actual size [p. 32-33].

The analogy of clothing may be called a travesty. It
leaves out of account the evidence of Cutter's own Boston
Athenaeum catalog in which, for example, Hitchcock, E.,
Separation of butter from cream by catalysis, is under Butter, without any extension, and Fibrilia, a substitute for cotton, is under Cotton, not Cotton--Substitutes; but an item on
Shetland wool is under that, not Wool, and one on Cotton,
Wool and Silk manufacture has multiple entries under all
three, not one entry under the class or generic heading Textiles, or Fibers. In a chain such as Textiles--Cotton--
Bleaching--Hydrogen peroxide, Cutter's specific entry is
under Cotton as opposed to class or generic entry under Textiles, as his examples under his rule and his definition made
clear. But Coates first used the prejudicial term stock subject, and then treated such a term as Cotton as a class or
generic term in relation to following aspect terms. On Library of Congress practice he said,

One suspects that the accumulation of a large
amount of material on a generically entered subject often leads to a change to specific entry.
Such a policy would be closely in line with Cutter's
use of subdivisions to break up large numbers of
aspects under the same heading [p. 69].

This however confuses Cutter's specific entry with his own
alternative conception. This alternative conception, is ac-

cording to Coates

> ... that of the subject heading made to measure,
> the subject heading co-extensive with the subject of
> the book. By devising the subject heading to fit
> the subject of the book precisely, we by-pass all
> questions of whether the subject is established, and
> how specific should headings be. The question of
> 'grouping titles topically' which Cutter advocates in
> Rule 340, does not arise.... He was being con-
> sistent with his own caveat against specific entry
> for subjects 'without a definite name' [p. 33].

But Cutter did not enter this supposed "caveat," he just
didn't realize the possibility of such headings and subheadings as Plants--Fluids--Circulation as a way round the no
name problem, which he exemplified by the movement of
fluids in plants as a specific subject. And there were and
are plenty of subjects with names allowing his specific entry,
which means the specific entry of what Coates went on to
distinguish as "the American type of dictionary catalogue"
[p. 69]. This is its direct entry under specific object names
with or without aspect subdivision, as opposed to the indirect
entry of the alphabetico-classed catalog, for example, As-
tronomy--Stars, or Stars--Mars, instead of Mars.

    Coextensive headings such as

> GOLD, Mining, Winding, Headgear, Vertical shaft
> GOLD, Prospecting, Drilling, Mining
> COTTON, Deterioration, Fungi, Phodamine deriva-
>   tives
> COTTON, Bleaching, Hydrogen peroxide

Coates also called "summarization, the abstraction of the
overall idea embodied in the subject content of a given literary unit ... basic to most forms of subject cataloguing"
[p. 16]. But it is not basic to Cutter's specific entry, still
in far wider use in both America and Australia, and even in
Great Britain, than his alternative, not basic to some other
forms. And there is a special motive for it, not explicitly
discussed in his book, the single entry motive. In 1967
another British disciple of Ranganathan, Mills, was more
explicit in referring to

> ... the American method of subject cataloguing
> (non-specific classes with a slight degree of mul-

tiple entry to boost the exhaustivity as opposed to
the prevailing British method of single specific
entry).[21]

Coates said

> In practice, of course, the principle of a summary
> subject heading per whole document is not adhered
> to quite rigidly.   A book may be incapable of sum-
> marization because it has not unity of content; it
> may be multitopical, and require several entries
> [p. 16].

There can be books with a miscellany of subjects; ships,
and sealing wax, and cabbages and kings, and so no unity of
subject, though there may be a contrived connection.   But
what he said is confusing.   There is what he called unity in
what he called a specific subject heading such as Cotton,
Bleaching, Hydrogen peroxide, and this can be the only entry
heading for a document on this subject, supported by cross
references.   But the same document could also be on Linen,
Bleaching, Hydrogen peroxide, and this would require another
entry with supporting cross references.

In his British Technology Index (BTI), now to be considered, Coates sometimes had this multiple entry, for example an article on both, under IRON-CHROMIUM, Oxida-
tion, High temperature and under STEEL, Stainless, Oxida-
tion, High temperature.   In some cases, however, he had
what is class or generic entry in Cutter's sense, for example an article called Standards & the fluidity test on cotton & rayon, under the generic heading TEXTILES, Chemical
damage, Fluidity tests.   Generally however his headings
seem to have been specific in both Cutter's sense and his
own.   But single entry is implied for a subject which can
be expressed in a hierarchical chain such as Cotton, Bleaching, Hydrogen peroxide.

From being head cataloger for the British National
Bibliography, classified, mainly single entry, with chain
procedure indexing, Coates became editor of the later British
Technology Index of periodicals which apparently had to be
alphabetical with no basis in classification schedules.   Its
first annual volume (1962) had an introduction by Coates, in
which he said first,

There are basically two methods of constructing

an alphabetical index of this kind and their respective techniques may be illustrated by the treatment
of such a subject as 'Bleaching cotton by hydrogen
peroxide.' One method would be to make three
separate entries under

BLEACHING
COTTON
HYDROGEN PEROXIDE.

He pointed out difficulties and said,

The various mechanical methods of "coordinating"
concepts in card indexes attempt to overcome these
difficulties. They cannot, however, be applied to
printed indexes in page form.

This seems to be true whether the coordination is manual
or mechanical. Then he said,

The second basic method ... is the one used in
this index. Instead of three entries a single entry
is made with supporting references as follows

COTTON, Bleaching, Hydrogen peroxide
Hydrogen peroxide, Bleaching, Cotton
    See COTTON, Bleaching, Hydrogen peroxide
BLEACHING, COTTON
    See COTTON, Bleaching

This opposition of only two basic methods as stated will
not hold. In 1962 the Wilson Applied Science & Technology Index
gave entries under Bleaching--Cotton, with a see reference from
Cotton--Bleaching, and with entry of the same articles under
Hydrogen peroxide, with a see also reference from Bleaching
materials. In his introduction to his 1963 volume, Coates
dropped this opposition. But the rest remained, and his adopted
method, without any mention of Ranganathan or chains, is nevertheless an adaptation of chain procedure indexing of classified
files to an alphabetical file, but not according to Ranganathan's
own adaptation because there is no derivation from classifying, and see instead of see also references. Obviously classifying would not be economical if used merely to derive
alphabetical indexing; and as there are no entries under the
headings referred from, the references could not be see also.
But under some headings there is a listing of "related headings," and in these, he said, librarians would recognize the
lineaments of the decimal classifications.

It was Coates' BTI which prompted Ranganathan's 1964 article on subject heading and facet analysis. [22] He did not mention Coates, perhaps because Coates did not mention him, or use any of his terminology, a change from his 1960 book; but Coates had stuck to the cause, with ingenuity. As shown above, Ranganathan stuck to his isolate and basic subject terms and ideas; and his basic point was this:

> Some current writings disclose a misconception about Facet Analysis. They seem to imply the belief that Facet Analysis is either by itself Classification or that it is a technique designed exclusively for Classification. At any rate Facet Analysis and Classification are taken to be inseparable. This is not correct [p. 111].

After exposition of subject determination and heading assignment in terms already in his Colon Classification, [23] he gave only one example from BTI 1962, suiting his approach,

> FABRICS, Cotton, Finishing, Flameproofing, Phosphorus. Some approaches to the permanent flameproofing of cotton: systems containing phosphorus ... [p. 113].

Fabrics can be regarded as a basic subject followed by a chain of isolates. He then considered the order of components, or constituents and said five "would admit 120 different sequences" [p. 112]. He chose what he called the Forward rendering, on his Wall--Picture or dependence principle; thinking of murals, then no wall no picture, and so on; no fabrics no cotton, and so through to no Phosphorus. But with an obvious "Reverse rendering, "

> Phosphorus. Flameproofing. Finishing. Cotton. Fabrics.

After further discussion of choice of one term out of five as the entry word, he harked back to his own ideas about what he called "The School of Specific Subject Heading" which "would trace its origin to Cutter"; this would prefer the reverse rendering, so that in the particular case its entry word would be Phosphorus; but this was not Coates' choice, nor would it have been Cutter's. Coates distinguished between Cotton and Fabrics, Cotton; but though there is Bleaching under both there is no reference either way. How-

ever, Ranganathan argued for Fabrics, for "a general documentation list such as the BTI." This must take what Coates
usefully called in his book "the point of view ... of a 'neutral' catalogue without bias to a particular subject" [p. 17].

Consideration of the meaning of subject may lead too
far into consideration of IR systems, but they do produce
explicit or implied differences of definition. This is particularly so at different levels of generic and specific subject,
and this has relevance for the basic question. Cutter arrived at his specific entry too much as something which had
to be exclusive of class or generic entry. This produces
conflict with the usage principle, because inversions such as
Sheep, Merino are logically class subdivision, but are accepted and even expected usage in alphabetical indexing in
English, although the trend is now away from them. And in
French, Mouton merino is impeccable usage, which must be
used, if Cutter's idea of the usage of the public in speaking
of subject means anything.

Cutter originated or established the term "specific
entry" as early as 1876, and is followed in his definition by
very many more librarians and catalogers, speaking and
reading English, than the comparatively few members of the
regiment in step with Coates and the tune of his alternative
conception. And to avoid cuckoo in the nest confusion, worse
confounded, the term is better left to Cutter and "the American type dictionary catalogue." The coextensive heading
concept, basically required only for single entry with chain
indexing or cross reference, turns Cutter inside out, and
his specific entry above all not class or generic entry in his
terms, is stigmatized as generic. But little has so far been
said of those who use catalogs, the secret people, as Chesterton called the people of England:

> Smile at us, pay us, pass us; but do not
>   quite forget,
> For we are the people of England, that never
>   has spoken yet
> . . . .
> It may be that we shall rise the last as Frenchmen
>   rose the first,
> Our wrath come after Russia's wrath and our
>   wrath be the worst.

Little has been said here, nor will any more be said,
about coordinate indexing. It certainly seems to escape some

of the difficulties of subject expression of precoordinate indexing, because it has no problems of what the Indo-British
school calls citation order.   But it may be out of the frying
pan into the fire.   Whereas the other is pre-coordinate it
has to be post-coordinate, and its initial uncoordination has
produced the term relation problems which some of its ex-
ponents have tried to solve by their roles and links.   The
conclusion seems then to be that these, as developed in the
EJC-Battelle Institute system, are better done without, and
the noise and the slop put up with; but with amelioration by
means of precoordinated or bound terms to suit particular
subject situations.   The alternative may be an inordinate
amount of noise or slop, only to be tolerated in comparatively small and closed subject areas of operation.   And this
may mean that the question of what is a subject, and how
information is to be exactly fitted to it, has only been swept
under the carpet.

However, just before moving out to the man in the
street, microphone in hand, one or two things more may be
said of whatever is meant by specific subject.   Coates was
a classification man.   He accepted Cutter's usage principle,
but pointed out that for many enquirers subjects are generic
rather than specific.

> When there is no customary usage to follow, the
> cataloguer can best serve the enquirer by uniform-
> ity of method and decision based on a few all-em-
> bracing rules.   Upon this last point rests the whole
> justification for alphabetico-specific catalogue, for
> it is known that many enquirers use a class term
> approach in the first place.   Despite this, the
> alphabetico-specific catalogue uses specific terms,
> because of the sheer difficulty (both for the cata-
> loguer and the enquirer) of deciding ... which
> generic term? [p. 36-7].

This is not the whole justification of alphabetico-
specific entry.   With, or without, the subheadings, which
Coates may be said to have advocated to the n th degree, a
particular or isolate subject name can have a multiplicity of
relations at one point of entry.   Vickery said that "Julia
Pettee became almost lyrical on this point."

> 'Names, ' as she calls topics or specific subjects,
> 'names have a new function that transcends the
> laws of logic of the linear classification scheme....

> The parallel lines of our classification schemes are
> drawn through the flat surface of plane geometry.
> The interrelationships of a topical name demand
> another dimension. Names reach up and over the
> surface. Sugar, for example, many-handed like a
> Hindu god, reaches up a hand from Chemistry,
> from Agriculture, from Applied arts.   These hands
> clasp in the air under the single term Sugar'....[24]

Surely Ranganathan himself could not have done better
than that, but what did she mean? This passage, in her
Subject Headings: The History and Theory, is lyrical and metaphysical enough to be obscure, and has been taken by Coates
to mean cross reference in the dictionary catalog, though in
his context Vickery does not seem to have thought so.   In an
article replying to a criticism of her book she pointed out,
with water, as an example, that in what is usually understood by classification this is in various classes according
to aspect, but in the alphabetico-specific catalog it "collects
in one word all various aspects and applications" of the
object water.   And she concluded

> It is not a new theory of subject headings that is
> needed, but a better mastery by catalogers of the
> field of knowledge and a clearer insight into the
> ways patrons think. [24]

The reviewer had said that "catalogers tend to sacri-
fice both books and patrons to the logical system they have
created," and might have said, "the logical and illogical and
inconsistent systems they have created," such as that of the
Library of Congress. [25]   Books can express no thoughts,
though their authors sometimes do, when they realize how
catalogers have indexed their books.   Patrons often express
themselves, but where do they get their ideas?   And though
they don't get them from dictionaries, the only reliable
source of information seems to be dictionaries, under the
entry word subject.

It may become necessary to return to Coates' point
that "when there is no customary usage to follow, the cataloger can best serve the enquirer by uniformity of method
and decision based on a few all-embracing rules" [p. 36].
Cutter settled on the usage, "not of the cataloger but of the
public in speaking of subjects" [p. 69].   But this begs a
question, not what is the usage of the public in speaking of
subjects as already defined by the cataloger, but what do they

think is meant by subject? In 1959, John Metcalfe published a book called Information Indexing and Subject Cataloging. In 1960 Drake had a criticism of parts of it published in the Australian Library Journal under the title, "What Is a Subject?"26 And from consideration of dictionary definitions he concluded that

> the distinction between classifying subjects and classifying by subject is not sharply enough drawn ... so that it requires only to be stated without demonstration or elaboration [p. 36].

The particular issue might be a red herring here, or at least a space consuming excursion; what is of immediate interest is the evidence Drake drew from dictionaries.

He quoted the Shorter Oxford Dictionary which quotes the fuller original, to the effect that subject might mean, "III.10. the subject-matter of an art or science," a subject in the sense of a school or university subject, or discipline. This is a meaning of discipline which has been revived and used in the introduction to the DDC, 17th edition, as quoted above, to the effect that subject is secondary to this. The disciplines of learning may be considered fairly permanent, but as Drake put it, there is another sense in which subject changes according to interest. The dictionary quoted says: "13. In a specialized sense; that which forms or is chosen as the matter of thought, consideration, or enquiry, a topic, theme."

Following this there is the further definition of subject to which Drake referred: "14. the theme of a literary composition, that a book, poem, etc., is about." And finally with reference to this, there is what may not be in the Shorter Oxford: "Subject noun ... chiefly with reference to cataloguing books according to their subjects; subject catalogue, index, list, reference."

The definition of subject as the subject-matter of an art or science, or discipline brings in a question of what is meant by matter. Under this the full Oxford has

10.   The subject of a book or discourse; as theme, topic; subject or exposition

11.   The substance of a book, speech or the like; that which a spoken or written composition contains in respect of the facts or ideas ex-

pressed, often as opposed to the form of
words ('manner') in which the subject is presented.

Although 10 is said to be obsolete, it seems little different
from 11. And both 10, under Matter, and 13, under Subject,
bring in more vexed questions of what is to be meant by
topic. The word topic can be, as shown, little or nothing
more than a synonym for subject in the senses quoted. And
Cutter in his definitions gave Polytopical, treating of several
topics ... denoting works on many subjects. But he, and
Haykin, seem also to have attached a special meaning to
topic, with some support from the full Oxford dictionary.
Originally it appears to have meant commonplaces or maxims,
platitudes, or truisms, which could be used to support discussion of any theme or subject; but it came to mean "a
head under which arguments or subjects may be arranged";
for example if abstinence were a topic, or subtopic under
virtue, then continence or chastity could be arranged, or
classified under it. And so abstinence or even virtue is
then an aspect of chastity, or a class in which chastity can
be included.

Many librarians have learnt from experience and noted
that uninstructed users of specific entry catalogs look under
headings broader than that for the particular subject of immediate interest. Haykin gave the example of birds as a
subject or subject heading including canaries.[27] And as already noted Coates said that "many enquirers use a class
term approach in the first place" [p. 36]. It may then be
assumed, and has been by the present writer and others,
that classifying is innate, intuitive, instinctive. And in some
ways it may be, if it can be argued that even some animals
show some rudiments of grouping by likeness, and that man
has become superior by ability to classify and to use classification and generalization as means to knowledge, especially
by and in science. But at least in later than prehistoric
development, superiority by this means seems to have depended on minority reasoning and record rather than on unaided intuition or instinct in the masses.

As might be expected Ranganathan went to an extreme
with theory, that the classified approach is inbuilt. He wrote
of Classified Pockets in the dictionary catalog and "neural
necessity": "... classified arrangement is a neural necessity.
That is why a pure dictionary arrangement has to be adulter-
ated by some element of classified arrangement," but all this

meant was not assuming the last term in a classificatory
chain to be a specific subject as he demanded.   In his Prolegomena he wrote:

> To arrange things in a more or less helpful se-
> quence is an inherent habit of man. . . .   Perhaps
> his inherent tendency to arrange is a concomitant
> of the finiteness of the speed of nervous impulse
> within human body.   When speed is finite, structure
> is inevitable.   When structure is sensed, sequence
> is but natural.   This gets expressed extra-neurally
> also.   This arrangement is a neural necessity.   It
> is instinctive, almost bio-chemical in nature, and
> involuntary.   The result is involuntary classifica-
> tion. [28]

Looking under a generic heading for a specific subject may
however be traced much more superficially to uses of the
word "subject."

     Catalogers, indexers, documentalists, and informa-
tion retrievalists have invented or developed various means
to achieve their ends, some as panaceas or cure-alls, some
for special needs and situations, and with them their special
terms such as "isolate."   But the word "subject" has remained a convenient common term by which information retrieval instruments have been labeled.   The uninstructed,
inexperienced user of these instruments, of at least the older
do-it-yourself kind, comes to their use with an idea of subject as meaning an art or science or discipline.   The user
has got this from his school and university curricula and
syllabi; he may use or read the word differently in other
contexts, but in the library and literature catalog context it
would seem reasonable to expect the academic, teaching and
learning use.   This may help to explain a difficulty in schools
of librarianship, of teaching graduate students the sense, intention and reason of specific entry.   As one librarian put
it, he did not find difficulty in teaching specific entry, but
he had found that his students found difficulty in learning it.

     There seems then to be common assumption from
familiar uses of words, of something like Ranganathan's distinction of an isolate such as gold, and a basic subject or
class which could include it.   An outsider asked the subject
of a book particularly on gold, might say, if he had the gold
standard on his mind, that its subject could be currency or
exchange; in another context or with another interest he might

suggest metals, or metallurgy, or mining as its subject.
But if pressed, he would probably agree that the subject of
a book on gold, even with limitation to currency or metallurgy or mining, could be gold, at least "sort of"; and if
he were a user of contemporary general encyclopedias he
would probably agree that he would expect to find in them
articles under Gold and phrases beginning with the word.

There is conflict and confusion in the use of the word
"subject" both by those who compile and those who consult catalogs and indexes. There is ambiguity in its general and
special use, and also in its use for objects of information,
general and special, concrete and abstract, real and imagi-
nary, and limitations of information on them to aspects.
Objects and aspect have been formally distinguished in some
classification notations and in headings and subheadings, but
only systematically in the once obscured but by now fairly
well known concrete-process distinction of Julius Otto Kaiser
in his book Specific Indexing, published in London in 1911,
but first developed by him in the Philadelphia Commercial
Museum in 1896-7. In hierarchical classification such as
Dewey's, there is aspect division without notational distinction, and in an alphabetico-specific entry from Cutter's
phrases up into Library of Congress practice, inconsistent
use of phrases and formal subdivision. For example, DC,
16th edition, has 771.5, a simple number extension for
Photography--Chemistry indexed as Photographic chemistry;
and the LC headings list, 7th edition (1966), has Photographic
chemicals and Photographic chemistry.

After much beating about some bushes, and some
beating of josses, even his own, the writer's conclusion is
that "subject" has not proved a satisfactory term in information
retrieval because of ambiguity in its use in information retrieval at large. It is however very much in everyday language and may have to be continued in use in communication
with catalog and index users. But it is unsatisfactory as a
technical term in compilation, because of conflicts and confusions of meaning, particularly with distinctions of general
and specific, and of object and aspect. Isolate has had
some use to distinguish one of its meanings, but not without
ambiguity of what Kaiser called Concrete and Process and
what Cutter with more certain breadth of meaning called object and aspect. For himself the writer intends to go on
distinguishing object and aspect.

Notes

1. Dunkin, P.S. "Criticisms of Current Cataloging Practice," Library Quarterly, 26 (1956), 293.
2. ASLIB, 3rd Conference, 1926, 20-44.
3. Cutter, C.A. Rules for a Dictionary Catalog, 4th ed. rewritten, 1904, 68, 71-75, 123-128.
4. Cutter, C.A. Rules, 123-4.
5. Cutter, C.A. Rules, 67.
6. Dewey, M. Decimal Classification, 17th ed., vol. 1, 9-10.
7. Otlet, P. "Sur la Structure des Nombres Classificateurs," Institut International de Bibliographie, Bulletin (1895), 230-242.
8. Bradford, S.C. Documentation, 2nd ed., London, Crosby Lockwood, 1953. ASLIB Proceedings, 1926.
9. Bliss, H.E. Bibliographic Classification, New York, 1952-3, vol. 1, 15, 21, 105; Vol 3, 4-5.
10. Ranganathan, S.R. Colon Classification, 6th ed. reprinted with amendments, 1963, 1, 22-3.
11. Ranganathan, S.R. "Subject Heading and Facet Analysis," Journal of Documentation, 20 (1964), 109-119.
12. Ranganathan, S.R. "Self-Perpetuating Scheme of Classification," Journal of Documentation, 4 (1948), 232.
13. Note 11 above, Ranganathan, S.R. "Subject Heading...," 110.
14. Farradane, J.E.L. "A Scientific Theory of Classification and Indexing and Its Practical Application," Journal of Documentation, 6 (1950), 83-90. Further considerations, ibid., 8 (1952), 73-92.
15. Cf. note 6 above.
16. Coates, E.J. Subject Catalogues Headings and Structure, 1960, 12-13.
17. Ranganathan, S.R. Theory of Library Catalogue, 1938, 84-5.
18. Cf. note 12 above.
19. Coates, op. cit. 111-12, 131.
20. Coates, E.J. "The Use of B.N.B. in Dictionary Cataloguing," Library Association Record, 59 (1957), 197-202.
21. Journal of Documentation, 23 (1967), 87.
22. Cf. note 11 above.
23. Ranganathan, Colon Classification..., 1.
24. Vickery, B.C. "Structure of a Connective Index," Journal of Documentation, 6 (1950), 148. Pettee, Julia. Subject Headings (1946), reprinted 1947.

Pettee, Julia, "A New Principle in Dealing with Subject Matter Needed," Journal of Cataloging and Classification, 11 (1955), 17-19.

25. Knapp, Patricia B.   Journal of Higher Education, 18 (1947), 277-278.

26. Drake, C. L.   "What Is a Subject?" Australian Library Journal, January 1960, 34-41.

27. Haykin, D. J.   Subject headings; A Practical Guide, 1951, 10.

28. Ranganathan, S. R.   Prolegomena to Library Classification, 2nd ed., Madras, Madras Library Association, 1957, 431.

FROM PIG TO MAN

Paul S. Dunkin

This is the story of a bloodless revolution. It all began in the most unlikely place, on the most unlikely occasion. In the inner sanctum of the Harvard Faculty Club, on the evening of June 21, 1941, a bright young man, named Andrew D. Osborn, read a paper to a little band of self-anointed elite of the library establishment, self-dubbed the American Library Institute.

Dr. Osborn talked about what he called "The Crisis in Cataloging."

The Anglo-American cataloging code of 1908 had been a pamphlet of 88 pages; now, in 1941, had appeared a monstrous "preliminary American second edition" with 408 pages. Why? The legalistic theory of cataloging, that was why. Cataloging, Dr. Osborn insisted, is an "art," and its rules are "actually rather few and simple." But the legalist must have a rule for every point that could possibly come up. The legalist was, of course, wrong for at least three reasons: (1) legalistic rules try to cover "matters of taste and judgment"; and we all know how it goes ... de gustibus ...; (2) legalistic debating and rule-making go on forever; (3) legalistic codification obscures principles; and what we began doing fifty years ago for good reason we keep on doing now long after the reason is gone.

Simplification and basic principles--not the letter of the law. Simplification and basic principles; that was what we needed. Simplification and basic principles; the bright young man was a prophet, a Daniel come to judgment. What was more, he insisted: the chief problem of library administrators was the cost of elaborate, legalistic cataloging. So behind the prophet who wanted to follow principles stood the man who wanted to save cash. Revolutions make strange bedfellows.

But it caught on. The Crisis in Cataloging (1941) was

a little book with few specific facts. But the title was ar-
resting, the style was popular, and in its sweeping generalizations the simmering frustrations of a whole generation
came to boil. The Library Quarterly published "The Crisis
in Cataloging" as an article, [1] and the American Library Institute made it a pamphlet and flooded the country with it.
Everybody read it, every cataloger fretted and frothed about
it. The pamphlet gave a name and an atmosphere to a whole
era of thinking about cataloging.

As with every revolution, so with this one, there was
much that was not new.

As long ago as 1852, Charles C. Jewett had pro-
claimed that "Nothing, so far as can be avoided, should be
left to the individual taste or judgment [Osbornian phrase!]
of the cataloger." [2] Obviously it is wasteful for many catalogers to catalog different copies of the same books; Jewett
wanted to avoid this and he proposed that American libraries
join the Smithsonian in producing a single stereotype plate
for the catalog entry of each book cataloged in the country.
This would, of course, mean rigid, detailed cataloging--and
to heck with individual taste and judgment.

Jewett failed; but fifty years later the publication of
LC cards made cooperative cataloging a reality. The "Preface" of the 1908 Anglo-American Catalog Rules: Author and
Title Entries [3] tells the result. The instructions to the ALA
Committee in 1901 "called for a code of rules which should
be in accord with the system governing the compilation of
catalog entries at the Library of Congress." As a result
the needs of smaller libraries came up for immediate "consideration" and the Committee decided that "its decisions
must be guided chiefly by the requirements of larger libraries of a scholarly character."

LC cards, like Jewett's stereotype plates, meant
standardization; and standardization meant detailed rules to
comply with the setter of pace and precedent, the Library
of Congress--and nothing left to the individual taste and
judgment of the cataloger. This goal the 1908 rules had
achieved; and the 1941 draft sought only to bring catalogers
into line with the ever more detailed cataloging practice LC
had been elaborating since 1908. [4]

But there had been another trend in American cataloging. Charles A. Cutter, in 1876, had sought to "investigate

what might be called the first principles in cataloging"; he had begun his set of rules with a statement of "objects" of the catalog; and he had tried to build his rules around them.[5] Moreover, he had recognized the needs of three different kinds of catalog: "Short," "Medium," and "Full." With many rules Cutter gave full discussion of the alternatives, why he had chosen as he had, and how they would apply to the three kinds of catalog.

In the fourth and last edition of his classic (1904), however, Cutter remarked on the "great change" in cataloging produced by LC cards, suggested that the "golden age of cataloging is over," and urged the use of LC cards. His conclusion was typical: "Cataloging is an art, not a science [Osbornian phrase again]. No rules can take the place of experience and good judgment [Osbornian word once again] but some of the results of experience may be best indicated by rules."[6]

The bright young man's ideas were not new; nor were the ideas of his adversaries; nor were the facts on which each staked claims. But the revolution swept on. In the storm of controversy the Library of Congress took action and the American Library Association appointed a committee.

The LC Studies of Descriptive Cataloging appeared in 1946. The book had a statement of basic principles not unlike those for description in Cutter's "objects" and it suggested that these principles could be served adequately by brief and simple description. An experiment reported by Elizabeth C. Pierce showed that brief transcription of titles would identify books adequately; indeed, collation rather than full title transcription proved to be the most effective way to separate editions, issues, and states of the same work. Also included was Seymour Lubetzky's devastating theoretical analysis of the then current detailed practices. Scholarly analysis thus supported Dr. Osborn's attack. Practicing catalogers were then polled to find out how much of this slashing of detail they would put up with, and they agreed they could take a great deal.

All this, of course, was not new. In the 1876 edition of his rules Cutter had remarked drily: "The more careful and student-like the probable use of the library the fuller the title should be--fuller, that is, of information not of words. Many a title a yard long does not convey as much meaning as two well chosen words."[7]

The Library of Congress then drew up its new rules
for description. A preliminary edition of 1947 was followed
by a final edition in 1949: "The Green Book." The new
rules were not as drastic as the reform urged in the LC
Studies; but they had come a long way from the ALA draft
of 1941. The American Library Association adopted the
Green Book as its official substitute for Part II of the 1941
draft.

Meanwhile the ALA Committee had decided that Part
I of the 1941 draft with all its detail about entry and heading
would do for LC and the other research libraries, and a
new, rearranged edition of these rules appeared with the
blessing of the ALA also in 1949: "The Red Book."

So the first skirmish of the revolution had ended in
both victory and defeat. "The battle of the three dots has
been won," rejoiced Dr. Osborn, and he hailed the "clarification of cataloging theory and simplification of cataloging detail" in the Green Book; but he urged that the same sort of
thing be done with the Red Book.[8] Jesse Shera was not joy-
ful at all. The 88 pages of 1908 had now swollen to a total
of 406 pages in the Green Book and the Red Book; even the
Green Book was at fault, because it had ignored limited cataloging, although recent Chicago Graduate Library School
studies showed that "in both public and academic libraries
the users of the catalog are completely unaware of the meaning, to say nothing of the utility, of most of the information
... on catalog cards."[9]

The prophet who wanted to follow principles had won
only half a victory. Now the prophet's partner, the administrator who wanted to save cash, stepped into the fray. In
1052 appeared the pamphlet, Rules for Descriptive Cataloging in the Library of Congress: Supplement, 1949-51. "Supplement" sounds innocent enough; actually the little book announced two drastic LC policy decisions: (1) each new personal name entry would now be established in the Library of
Congress "in the form given in the work being cataloged
without further search, provided that" it "conforms to the
ALA rules for entry, and is not so similar to another name
previously established as to give a good basis for the suspi-
cion that both names refer to the same person"; and (2) description would be limited to information readily available in
the work being cataloged, and the Green Book would apply
in full only to basic reference books, scholarly books, rare
books, and the like; most other material would receive lim-

ited cataloging with simplified collation and notes. "No Conflict" and "Limited Cataloging" the two ideas were called.
Technically they were only LC administrative decisions, affecting only LC catalogs; but in fact the widespread use of
LC cards made them two brand new rules affecting all cataloging.

The search for cash had cut the Gordian Knot of complexity where the search for principles had failed. Thanks
to the Establishment the revolution had won after all.

But revolution breeds more revolution. Already a
new prophet was at work in the Library of Congress. In
the very next year after the Supplement came Seymour
Lubetzky's Cataloging Rules and Principles (1953). Vigor-
ously he attacked the Red Book. First, as to structure:
"Is this Rule Necessary?" For rule after rule his relent-
less logic built up a resounding "No!" The rule was not
necessary, because it dealt with a specific case rather than
with the general condition which that case represented. Then,
as to the "Corporate Complex": In the beginning Cutter and
Hanson had intended "not to distinguish between societies and
institutions as such, but rather to distinguish between corporate bodies having distinctive names ... and those having
common names which had to be identified by the name of
the place where they were located." Thus, the Red Book's
elaborate concern about institutions and societies had forgotten the real purpose of the rules, just as Dr. Osborn had
said would be the case with legalistic cataloging. Finally,
as to a "Design for a Code": As the LC Studies had done,
so now Mr. Lubetzky proposed an initial statement of principles of entry not unlike those in Cutter's "objects": "to
enable the user ... to determine readily whether ... the
catalog has the book he wants" and "to reveal to the user ...
under one form of the author's name, what works the library
has by a given author and what editions or translations of a
given work."[10] Among specific proposals Mr. Lubetzky suggested (1) form of entry often along "No Conflict" lines; (2)
greater use of pseudonyms; and (3) separate entry under successive names of corporate bodies.

Leonard Jolley greeted the Lubetzky report as a
"sign of the end of the divergence between the conservatism
of the ALA and the radicalism of the Library of Congress."
It was "the definitive expression of the destructive criticism
of a decade. No one will need to do this work again."[11]
On the whole, reaction was generally favorable, although

there were a few who suggested that Mr. Lubetzky might be somewhat too idealistic.[12]

The revolution swept on. ALA appointed a new Catalog Code Revision Committee. Wyllis Wright was chairman, and Seymour Lubetzky was appointed editor for a new code. The Committee's "Statement of Objectives and Principles" proposed to work within the framework of the Lubetzky report; to bring the rules for entry and for description together in one volume again; and to include rules for "non-book" material. One pronouncement was to become famous:

> Economy in cataloging should be emphasized as far as is possible.... However, when there is a choice between clarity in the catalog and simplicity in the cataloging process, the former, representing the convenience of the user, ... should prevail.... In preparing the revision the amount of recataloging which may be involved in changes to the rules should not be considered if the change is otherwise desirable.[13]

"Convenience of the user": here again was something old. In the fourth and last edition of his Rules Cutter had suggested that "the convenience of the public" must always come first even though it might lead to violation of "strict consistency in a rule and uniformity in its application."[14] The ALA codes of 1908 and 1949 endorsed this idea.[15] But now the Committee was suggesting that "clarity in the catalog" (presumably the result of consistency) would serve the "convenience of the user" and should prevail even if it meant a loss of "economy in cataloging." The prophet no longer marched arm in arm with the administrator.

Code revision procedure was simple, thorough, and democratic. Mr. Lubetzky submitted rules to the section heads of LC's Descriptive Cataloging Division, then to the Code Revision Steering Committee, and finally to the full Code Revision Committee. Each rule was thus progressively reviewed and revised. Finally, all catalogers were brought into the process at two institutes: Stanford 1958, and McGill 1960. For each institute, Mr. Lubetzky presented the latest draft of the code (1960 draft with an explanatory commentary); and there were elaborate, thoughtful background papers. All who wished could come (some 200 did at each institute) and question the editor, the chairman, and the authors of the papers. Prophets need more than

ideals and logic.   They must also be able to sit for long
hours on hard chairs and talk back to their critics, gently,
patiently, understandingly.   And after the ordeal of each institute there were more changes. . . .

The American cataloging code revolution was part of
an international revolt.   The Americans were working, as
with the 1908 code, with the British to produce a code for
all English-speaking peoples.   But also in Italy, France,
Germany, and elsewhere complaints about old codes and
work on new codes pushed ahead.   Mr. Ranganathan's Heading and Canons (1955) for instance, was as drastic and stimulating as Mr. Lubetzky's critique, and Mary Piggott's Cataloguing Principles and Practice: An Inquiry (1954) was as
thought provoking as the American institutes. [16]

As early as 1954 (the year after the Lubetzky report)
the IFLA council had set up an international working group
to study the international coordination of cataloging rules;
and UNESCO encouraged and assisted the IFLA.   The Council on Library Resources made it possible for IFLA to plan
and hold an International Conference on Cataloging Principles
in Paris in October 1961.   People from 53 countries and 12
international organizations attended.   The Conference worked
much like the American institutes.   There was a draft of a
proposed Statement of Principles, and there were elaborate
working papers.   Discussion of the draft statement and the
papers lasted over a week; and the final version of the statement received approval of a large majority of the delegates.

For Americans the Paris Conference was the high
point of the revolution.   The Statement of Principles had
been based almost entirely on the Lubetzky draft of 1960; in
the discussions Mr. Lubetzky, Mr. Wright, and the entire
delegation spoke with influence; finally, before the whole
world, the Conference adopted the American-based Statement
with little major change and by an overwhelming majority.
What was more, each delegation was to return home and
work to build its own nation's code about the Paris statement.   Our political Revolution of 1776 has not yet reached
every corner; in two short weeks our code revolution had
swept the world.   The American delegation left Paris in
triumph.

Home once more, they were greeted by a massive
counter-revolution.

From the outset of the Lubetzky phase of the revolution, just as in the Osborn phase, there had been disagreement on details. Even in the Code Revision Committee this was true; for instance, the rule on serials had been reversed and later reversed again. Library journals had carried much discussion. Finally, there had been the papers of the institutes and the Paris Conference; these also disagreed with details. At no time had there been unanimity; but in every instance disagreement had been resolved through discussion and then a vote by the full Committee.

Now the black bird of cost had come home to roost. The Committee's statement of 1955 had been idealistic: quality, not cost of change, should determine the shape of the rules. Actually, once work had begun, it never had turned out quite that way. Discussion in Committee and institutes had come back to costs time and again, and the rules themselves had now and then departed from logic to meet what seemed a practical need; the commentary which accompanied Mr. Lubetzky's Code of Cataloging Rules (1960)[17] had pointed out a number of such rules.

After the McGill Institute of 1960 Mr. Lubetzky joined the faculty of the University of California at Los Angeles and had little free time to continue with his work as editor. For some time work on the code had drifted; and, without new rules being constantly turned out to divert their attention, critics were free to re-examine the rules already accepted. The new ideas were in print both in Mr. Lubetzky's Code of Cataloging Rules (1960) and in the Paris statement. Big libraries looked them over and began to grumble about the cost of changing their card catalogs to conform. Somewhat to the surprise of the Committee, the Library of Congress joined the grumbling. After all, LC had issued the LC Studies of Descriptive Cataloging and the Green Book. LC had given Mr. Lubetzky time as a staff member to write his famous critique of the Red Book and later to work as editor of the new code. LC had sponsored the publication of Mr. Lubetzky's Code of Cataloging Rules (1960) and had invited the author of the commentary of that work to make his contribution. Finally, LC's Sumner Spalding had represented LC on the Steering Committee and also the full Committee; and LC section heads had always been the first to whom new rules had been submitted for criticism. Why should LC complain now?

The old alliance of the prophet who wanted to follow principles and the administrator who wanted to save money had collapsed.   The revolution was in real trouble.

There was a frantic scrambling around.   The Association of Research Libraries, something of a latter-day, no-
nonsense successor to the prestigious American Library Institute, set up a special committee to study cost of implementation of the new code.   The ALA Cataloging and Classification Section asked representatives of other parts of
ALA to advise the Code Revision Committee.   The CCS Cataloging Policy and Research Committee and many other librarians talked and wrote endlessly about the cost of revising old catalogs to meet new rules.

Finally, the Association of Research Libraries and the
Library of Congress agreed on what they wanted the new code
not to do, and at the Miami Conference in 1962 the ALA
Catalog Code Revision Committee agreed to work out a code
to suit them, which would in other respects follow the Paris
statement.   The price was high.   The major concession was
that the new code would keep the traditional "Institutions"
rule and enter many corporate bodies under place instead of
under name.   Thus, ironically, the American Committee on
whose draft code the Paris statement rested was itself unable to carry out a major feature of that statement.

At the request of CCS, the Library of Congress
granted Sumner Spalding a leave of absence to serve as editor.   Lucile Morsch replaced Mr. Spalding as LC representative on the Steering Committee and the full Committee, this
time with explicit authority to speak for LC.   Miss Morsch
also served as editor of the rules for description.   Funds to
complete the work came from the Council on Library Resources.

Anglo-American Cataloging Rules, North American
Text appeared early in 1967. [18]   It is a compromise and,
like every compromise, it is not an inspiring document.
Perhaps its greatest achievement is that it brings together,
in one document and somewhat revised, what was before to
be found in the ALA Red Book, the LC Green Book, and a
host of paperbacks of various colors on LC treatment of
"non-book" material.   (The British Text, 1967, [19] differs in
several ways, perhaps chiefly in that it follows the Paris
statement for "Institutions," and departs somewhat from the
LC Green Book for rules for description.)

Two final ironies marked publication of the North

American text. LC and ARL had insisted on compromise in
the code because of the cost it might bring in revising their
card catalogs; but at the same time they were pushing ahead
with plans for automation. Also, LC announced its "superimposition" policy: LC would apply the new rules only to
works new to the Library and only to headings for persons
and corporate bodies being established for the first time.
There would, of course, be some exceptions. Thus LC had
itself played a decisive role in code revision and the Miami
Compromise, but LC would not always conform to the results, and libraries would know when LC had conformed only
after they had seen the LC cards for a particular title.

The crisis in cataloging had at last dragged to an end.
The new rules were the old rules, changed a little, rearranged, elaborated, phrased in straight governmentese, once
more 400 pages long--this time exactly 400.

"The creatures outside looked from pig to man, and
from man to pig, and from pig to man again; but already
it was impossible to say which was which."--Final sentence
of George Orwell's Animal Farm.

Notes

1. A. D. Osborn, "The Crisis in Cataloging," Library
    Quarterly, 11 (1941), 393-411.
2. C. C. Jewett, Smithsonian Report on the Construction
    of Catalogues of Libraries, Washington, D. C., Smith-
    sonain Institution, 1853, 8.
3. Catalog Rules: Author and Title Entries. Compiled
    by ... the American Library Association and the
    [British] Library Association. American edition.
    Chicago, American Library Association, 1908, viii.
4. A. L. A. Catalog Rules: Author and Title Entries.
    Prepared by the ... American Library Association
    with the Collaboration of ... the [British] Library
    Association. Preliminary American 2nd ed. Chicago,
    American Library Association, 1941.
5. C. A. Cutter, Rules for a Printed Dictionary Catalogue,
    Washington, D. C., Government Printing Office, 1876,
    5-10.
6. C. A. Cutter, Rules for a Dictionary Catalog, 4th ed.,
    Washington, D. C., Government Printing Office, 1904,
    5-6.
7. C. A. Cutter, Rules for a Printed Dictionary Cata-
    logue..., 55.

8. A. D. Osborn, "L. C. Catalog Code," Library Journal, 75 (1950), 763-764.

9. J. H. Shera, "Review of A. L. A. Cataloging Rules for Author and Title Entries and Rules for Descriptive Cataloging in the Library of Congress," Library Quarterly, 20 (1950), 147-150.

10. S. Lubetzky, Cataloging Rules and Principles; a Critique of the A. L. A. Rules for Entry and a Proposed Design for Their Revision.... Washington, D. C., Library of Congress, 1953, 36.

11. L. Jolley, "Review of Cataloging Rules and Principles, by Seymour Lubetzky," Journal of Documentation, 10 (1954), 78-81.

12. M. F. Tauber, S. M. Haskins, et al., "ALA Rules for Entry: The Proposed Revolution!" Journal of Cataloging and Classification, 60 (1953), 123-142.

13. Committee on Catalog Code Revision, "Statement of Objectives and Principles for Catalog Code Revision," Journal of Cataloging and Classification, 12 (1956), 103-107.

14. C. A. Cutter, Rules for a Dictionary Catalog, 4th ed. ..., 6.

15. Catalog Rules: Author and Title Entries ..., 1908, ix. A. L. A. Cataloging Rules for Author and Title Entries..., 2nd edition, ed. Clara Beetle, Chicago, American Library Association, 1949, xx.

16. S. R. Ranganathan, Heading and Canons; Comparative Study of Five Catalogue Codes, Madras, S. Viswanathan, 1955. M. Piggott, Cataloguing Principles and Practice: An Inquiry, London, Library Association, 1954.

17. S. Lubetzky, Code of Cataloging Rules: Author and Title Entry, Chicago, American Library Association, 1960.

18. Anglo-American Cataloging Rules. Prepared by the American Library Association, the Library of Congress, the Library Association, and the Canadian Library Association. North American Text. Chicago, American Library Association, 1967.

19. Anglo-American Cataloguing Rules.... British Text. London, The Library Association, 1967.

BOOK CATALOGS

Maurice F. Tauber and Hilda Feinberg

> "Book catalogs, with all the advantages
> they offer to those remote from their
> collections, are once again coming into
> their own." J. H. Shera, Documenta-
> tion..., 82.

The current concern with book catalogs has resulted
to some extent from the realization that card catalogs have
not been effective in providing overall service to readers.

The emergence of new technical developments has
made it possible to re-evaluate the relationship of users to
the contents of libraries, and the application of the newer
technology has demonstrated the possibility of providing readers with information in book catalog form that has not been
available to them in the past.

In this paper we have presented (1) a brief history
and background of book catalogs; (2) methods of production;
(3) format; (4) costs; (5) advantages and disadvantages; and
(6) future possibilities.

The present interest and activity in book catalog ex-
perimentation and production indicate that libraries are approaching a period in which a revival of catalog production
in book form is current, continuing a cycle of early book
catalogs, then card catalogs, and now back to book catalogs.
The changing technology of the times in each case contributed
to a great extent to the substitution of one form for the other.

Although book catalogs appeared in Europe centuries
earlier, the first one to emerge in the United States was a
catalog issued by Harvard in 1723. This was followed in
1743 by the first Yale catalog, designed as a service to
students and faculty members of the University to disclose
the then current holdings. Princeton University issued its

first book catalog in 1760, a 36-page listing describing 1, 281 volumes. Between 1813 and 1875, Columbia College and other schools of Columbia compiled 13 different catalogs; while the University of Pennsylvania issued seven during the period between 1823 and 1875. Examples of important letterpress printed catalogs of this period are represented by the catalogs of the Boston Athenaeum, 1807-71; the Astor Library, 1857-66; the Peabody Institute in Baltimore, 1883-1905; and the Columbia University Catalogue of the Avery Architectural Library, 1895. Many such catalogs were produced in the U. S. between 1723 and 1875.

One of the most important of the late 18th- and 19th-century book catalogs was that of the British Museum, issued initially as a two-volume work in 1787. The original catalog was replaced in 1813-19 by a catalog in seven volumes. In 1849 a plan was devised for writing the entry for each book on a separate slip and pasting the slips into large folio volumes of blank leaves. In this manner 150 volumes were filled in 1850, and by 1880, the catalog had grown to nearly 2500 volumes. Printing of the catalog was begun in 1881, and when it was completed in 1900, the catalog contained nearly two and a quarter million entries.

Charles C. Jewett, in 1853, suggested a plan for the establishment of a union catalog, the institution of cooperative cataloging, and the building up of the Library of the Smithsonian Institution as the national library of the United States. His plan for producing a catalog in which he proposed to prepare stereotype plates for each book title, the plates to be stored at the Smithsonian Institution, ended in failure. Among the reasons for the failure of the project was the inadequacy of the stage of technology at that period.

The manuscript or printed book catalog, varying widely in format and quality, served until the latter part of the 19th century as the standard form of the library catalog. The catalogs of this period have been described by Hines:

> Often the listing was a single-entry one for each item. The base arrangement was frequently accidental, by such aspects as size or other shelf arrangement not reflecting the contents of the works. Subarrangement in these cases was usually by author. Sometimes the base arrangement was by author. Early catalogs tended to be rudimentary, both in the provision of access points and in

the fullness and accuracy of the information provided for each title. Indexes were sometimes provided for the base listing, complementing the base
access system. Broad class arrangement was not
unusual, whether supplemented by title and author
indexes or not. By the last quarter of the nineteenth century, all of the essential bibliographic
techniques currently available were developed and
available to compilers of book catalogs, whose
choice of catalog elements was limited only by
economic considerations of production. [1]

In the mid-19th century, the manuscript catalog of
the Library of the Surgeon General's Office was small enough
to be recopied periodically to incorporate new accessions.
However, before the turn of the century the library under-
took its first printed catalog in three volumes, A Catalogue
of Books in the Library of the Surgeon General's Office, to
be followed at a later period by the Index Catalogue. The
biweekly production of the present National Library of Medicine Current Catalog has been described by Weiss & Wiggins. [2] An historical account of the printed book catalog in
American libraries has been presented by Ranz. [3]

During the period from the beginning of the 20th century until the present, the card catalog has served as the
standard tool for revealing the holdings of libraries. Among
the factors which led to the emergence of the card catalog
and its substitution for the book catalog were the continuing
growth of library collections, the increasing cost of producing book catalogs, and the introduction of the Library of
Congress printed card service in 1901. An additional factor
was the changing technology of the times as represented by
the increased general use of the typewriter.

Recent advances in machine technology and equipment,
and the growing problems related to the card catalog have
led to a new interest in the book-form catalog. Among the
technological advances which influenced this revived interest
were such developments as the emergence in 1953 of a high-
speed sequential card camera; advances in relation to both
punch card equipment and computers; the availability in 1964
of a 120-character print chain for electronic computers, offering both upper-and lower-case type with a more legible
print-out, and refinements in offset printing methods, resulting in reduced production costs for book catalogs.

Among other factors which have contributed to the renewed interest in book catalogs are (1) the increased volume of publication; (2) the immense growth of library collections; (3) the increased demand for information, materials, and expanded services; (4) the growing size and complexity of the card catalog, containing in some cases, hundreds of thousands, and even millions of cards in some of the larger libraries; (5) the problem of maintenance and rehabilitation of the card catalog, with varying degrees of deterioration of present cards; (6) the time and effort required to interfile large quantities of new cards, and to withdraw others; (7) the increasing problem of lack of sufficient space for the growing number of large card catalog files, and the increase in the cost of such files; (8) the general problem of growing backlogs of uncataloged and unclassified materials, as well as inadequately cataloged materials, and the necessity in some cases for re-cataloging and reclassification; (9) the trend toward cooperative development and use of resources of geographically separated library units, resulting in a need for multiple copies of the catalog at each location; and (10) an increasing interest in specific library catalogs by researchers, teachers, and by other libraries, making commercial distribution of the book catalogs economically desirable.

The card catalog problems of the New York Public Library, resulting from its size, its complexity, and its physical condition, have been investigated by Matta in a study exploring future prospects for the production and maintenance of the catalog, and comparing the advantages and disadvantages of card catalogs and book catalogs.[4] The advantages and methods of conversion from the present system are discussed, the machinery required for the conversion to book catalog form is described, the costs of conversion are calculated and the annual costs of book catalog production are given. A detailed analysis of the problems of rehabilitating an old catalog is presented. It was estimated that at that time (1964) almost one-third of the 8,000,000 cards in NYPL were in need of rehabilitation. Comparing the cost of such a task with the cost involved in issuing book catalogs, Matta concluded that it would be more expensive to rehabilitate, produce and maintain the card catalog than to convert, produce and maintain book catalogs of the holdings. It was recommended that the New York Public Library Reference Department transfer its present card catalog to book catalog form, and start a new supplementary card catalog.

Henderson and Rosenthal in a subsequent study offered the following major recommendations:

> That the catalogs of the Research Libraries of the
> New York Public Library be divided chronologically
> at the earliest possible date; that the present (or
> retrospective) Public Catalog be reproduced photo-
> graphically in book form; that the future (or pro-
> spective) catalogs be produced in a combination of
> card and book form from a store of machine-read-
> able data.... [5]

A notable event in the production of printed book catalogs was the issuance by the Library of Congress in the
1940's of a depository catalog of Library of Congress cards
in book form, thereby making it generally available to all
libraries in the United States as well as abroad, and in addition relieving American libraries of the growing costs of
maintaining the depository catalogs in card form. A Catalog
of Books Represented by Library of Congress Printed Cards
Issued to July 31, 1942, produced by photographing the cards
and printing them in reduced size, 18 to a page, required
167 volumes, and reproduced approximately 1,900,000 cards.
The Library of Congress has continued the publication of
catalogs in book form. The largest single bibliographic
project in the history of the Library of Congress has been
the publication of the National Union Catalog Pre-1955 Imprints by Mansell Information/Publishing, Ltd. of London.
It is estimated that the 16 million cards that make up the
catalog will require approximately 610 volumes to be published over ten years, each standard 704-page volume containing about 21,000 entries. By removing duplicates and
consolidating entries the 16 million cards should be reduced
to about 12 3/4 million.

Monumental book catalogs of other national libraries
are the catalog of the Bibliothèque Nationale in Paris, the
Catalogue Général des Livres Imprimés: Auteurs, begun in
1897, but still unfinished; the Deutscher Gesamtkatalog, 1931-
39, which was abandoned at the letter "B," and the General
Catalogue of Printed Books held by the British Museum, to
the end of 1955, running to 263 volumes and four million
entries.

In 1963, a state-of-the-art of book catalogs was presented in a collection of papers entitled Book Catalogs, edited by Kingery and Tauber. [6] The papers in the volume,
assembled at the request of the Interdivisional Committee on

Book Catalogs of the American Library Association, included
a description of some American 20th-century book catalogs,
their purposes, format, and production techniques; an analysis of the relation of book catalogs to card catalogs; bibliographical and cataloging standards, and applications for book
catalogs. [A later state-of-the-art report, by Tauber and
Feinberg, is Book Catalogs, Scarecrow, 1971, presenting an
updated collection of papers on the subject.]

Book catalog trends in 1966, with emphasis on cooperative and centralized aspects were analyzed by David C.
Weber.[7] While he ascertained that the number of libraries
using them at that time numbered less than 50 out of over
10,000, he predicted that the impact of computers in library
applications during the next decade would increase the number of libraries producing book catalogs, and that other pioneering libraries would turn toward direct computer inquiry
in a real-time mode of operation, dispensing with the visible
catalog in card or book form. Of the continuing catalogs in
print in 1966, Weber estimated that at least 15 used the high
speed electronic computer, and had developed their own programs, all but one had used a computer available within the
institution; ten used the high-speed sequential card camera;
all but one contracted the production outside; seven used
unit record equipment; and five used variations of the Library of Congress shingling-photographic technique.

In answer to queries for information on the preparation and current use of book catalogs, the American Library
Association, through the Book Catalogs Committee of its
Resources and Technical Services Division, submitted in
1966 a questionnaire to 40 libraries which were then producing book catalogs. The Association made an attempt to
identify trends in the use of such catalogs, the methods of
production, and the structure and format of the books. The
results of the questionnaire indicated a definite trend in book
catalog production. The increase was not limited to any
particular type of library, but was apparent in public, college and university, and special libraries.

Production Methods

Several techniques have been utilized to produce book
catalogs. The Library of Congress catalogs were made by
placing catalog cards on sheets and photographing them. The
resulting book catalogs were essentially copies of the card

catalog in page form. A catalog of this type cannot be kept up-to-date except by interfiling of new cards, laying the cards out again, and re-photographing the entire catalog. Among other disadvantages of this type of book catalog are its bulkiness and the presence of excessive unused white space on the page. In an effort to reduce the bulkiness, some catalogs have been printed in reduced size. This solution has not been satisfactory, as it causes problems of legibility.

Another technique for producing book catalogs is based upon the use of IBM tabulating cards, used in conjunction with a line printer. The printout of the line printer may be reduced photographically for offset printing of the catalog. The King County Library System of Seattle, Washington used IBM punch cards for producing its early book catalogs. IBM automated equipment was also the first type used by the Los Angeles County Public Library when it initiated its book catalog. [8] A high-speed sequential camera was subsequently employed, [9] and finally a computerized catalog was introduced.

The punch card is restricted in the number of special symbols it can accommodate. Punctuation marks, diacritical marks, and abbreviations may cause difficulties. The printout resulting in all upper case letters produces a monotonous and hard-to-read page. This type of catalog also becomes excessively bulky, difficult to handle, and it may present binding problems. A further disadvantage is the necessity to store and handle repeatedly a large number of punch cards.

The sequential camera has proved to be an effective technique for some libraries. These cameras are capable of automatically photographing catalog data that have been typed on the space at the top of a punch card at high speeds ranging from 7,000 to 14,000 cards per hour. [10] The cards enter the camera through an automatic, precision-feeding device. A photographic negative is obtained which is cut and formated into pages, and then printed. Several high-speed special cameras have been used for this purpose: (1) Vari-Typer Corporation's Foto-List, used to produce the British National Bibliography; (2) Kodak's List-O-Matic camera; and (3) Lithoid's Compos-O-Line, used to produce the Free Library of Philadelphia's book catalog. [11] The photographic method offers the advantages of varied type faces and sizes, a more efficient utilization of space, smaller size, and improved ease in handling. In the photographic process, the

data can be either reduced or enlarged.   This offers an advantage in the preparation of juvenile catalogs, as they may
be prepared in an enlarged print.

    Several drawbacks have become obvious, however,
which limit the usefulness of this method.   Many manual
operations are required.   Correction of errors involves finding the proper card, removing it, retyping or correcting it,
and re-inserting the card in the file.   The creation of multiple entries from the original citation is also a manual operation, requiring that each separate entry in the catalog be
typed in its entirety.   Filing is a manual process in that
sequence numbers must be assigned to the entries.   Other
serious drawbacks include the rigidity of the system, the
difficulty in changing the format of the page, the need for
handling large quantities of cards, the lack of creation of a
machine-readable record, and the limited ability of the system to use catalog copy produced elsewhere.[12]

    Recent technological advances in computer capabilities,
the growing availability of computer systems, and the lowering of hardware and software costs make computer-aided
book catalog production increasingly practical.   Dolby, Forsyth, and Resnikoff have concluded in a recent study that the
mechanism of the cataloging function is not only necessary
and desirable, but also inevitable, the primary deterrent being the substantial cost of converting the retrospective file
to machine-readable form.   It is predicted that user cost
factors and the steadily improving situation in hardware and
software costs, together with the steadily rising cost of library personnel, will force libraries to an ever increasing
amount of automation.[13]

    It is pointed out by Dolby, et al., that present cat-
aloging practice provides sufficient information to support
numerous arrangements of the catalog and subsets of the
catalog.   In manual operations, the cost of expanding access
beyond present levels increases at least linearly with the
number of access files created, while mechanization provides
the opportunity to produce added access files at low cost,
making the contents of the library available to the user from
a number of access points.[14]

    Computer-based systems for producing book catalogs
have encountered problems in programming satisfactory rules
for filing.[15,16]   Although specific rules have been established
for library filing, modifications of standard library practice

are a common occurrence in order to operate within the
machine limitations, and to keep the costs of programming
at lower levels. Simonton has pointed out the fact that

> ... a fundamental choice must be made between
> revision of the form of certain of our entries and
> acceptance of new filing patterns, on the one hand,
> and the expenditure of considerable editing and/or
> programming time in an attempt to retain the tra-
> ditional entries and patterns, on the other hand. [17]

The computer filing code of Hines and Harris reflects the
first approach, [18] while the report by Nugent on the Library
of Congress filing rules, [19] and that of Cartwright and Shoffner, on the catalogs of the California State Library, discuss
the latter approach. [20]   It has been suggested that the library community agree upon a set of new standards for
mechanized filing.   Cartwright and Shoffner present several
advantages of a national code of rules:

> First, we feel that the advent of nationally distrib-
> uted catalog copy in machine-readable form will
> make standardization in cataloging even more at-
> tractive than it has been in the past, because the
> possibilities of achieving this standardization will
> be greater than have existed, and because the
> costs of applying non-standard methods will be
> much greater than they have been in the past.
> Secondly, the relationship between the form of the
> heading adopted and the filing rules is very close;
> therefore, the national agency which adopts a new
> set of filing rules should be in a position to in-
> fluence cataloging rules as they apply to the form
> of headings.   What must be sought is a heading
> structure which will both convey the information
> desired and be amenable to computer filing. [21]

     The system for computerized publishing of book cata-
logs may be viewed as consisting of the following components: [22]

     (1) Input Procedures and Hardware: To convert the
catalog data into machine-readable form for manipulation.
     (2) Computer Hardware and Software: The software
may include programs that can format the page, set up
columns, strip in running heads, number the pages, prevent
widows, justify margins, hyphenate, correct errors, and

update subsequent editions.[23]   These procedures reduce the
amount of human effort which has been expended in the past
in producing book catalogs.

(3) Output Hardware: Output equipment includes such
machines as photo-composition equipment, which converts
the computer output tapes to negatives or reproduction copy
for printing.

The computer will accept the catalog data only in
machine-readable form.   At the present time, various methods exist for bringing data to machine-readable form.   Input
can be accomplished with punched cards, paper tape, magnetic tape, on-line terminals, or characters read by optical
character recognition equipment (OCR).   Keypunching, paper
tape punching, and magnetic tape writing utilize keystroking
to encode machine-processable information.[24]   On-line terminals are used for keying data directly into a computer.[25]
Data are usually simultaneously typed out or displayed on a
cathode ray tube.   Previously prepared magnetic tape records, such as the Library of Congress MARC tapes, may
also be used as input.   Keying on a paper-tape typewriter
is faster than on a key-punch, and offers an advantage in
that one of the products of typing is a hard copy that can be
used for proofreading.   It is difficult, however, to correct
errors on paper tape.   Magnetic tape offers an alternative
to keypunching, and it is now possible to enter data directly
on magnetic tape from a typewriter-like keyboard.   The
magnetic tapes can be read into a computer at much higher
speeds than perforated tape--at a rate of 10,000 to 100,000
characters per second--whereas the fastest readers for perforated tape operate at less than 2,000 characters per second.   In addition, magnetic tape can be easily erased and
corrected.   A further advantage is the fact that it confines
its information to a shorter length than punched paper tape;
for example, a typical page might be contained in two inches
of magnetic tape, compared with 200 inches of paper tape.
The magnetic tape is much thinner, and when there is no
further need for the information on the tape, it can be erased
and used over again.   At the present time the least expensive
and most widely available input device is the card punch.[26]

The input to the computer is the slowest element in
the total cycle.   It requires about 16 man-hours of keypunch
and key-verifier time to keep the computer processor occupied for .075 second, demonstrating how expensive, and
how slow the keypunch input process is.[27]   It is for this
reason that interest in optical scanners, or optical character
recognition machines, has been manifested.[28-32]

The machine consists of a photoelectric device which scans the document, recognizes each character, and translates it into machine-readable language, recording it on punch cards, paper tape, or magnetic tape. The scanner eliminates key-stroking altogether by automatically scanning and reading printed or typed source data. OCR equipment falls into two classes: one consists of readers which can recognize only special fonts; the other consists of devices capable of reading a number of different fonts. The ordinary typewriter equipped with normal type font can be converted to rigid optical font. Libraries may make arrangements with service bureaus to have typewritten copy scanned and converted to magnetic tape.[33] The present costs for purchase or rental of optical page readers, paper tape readers, and keyboard equipment have been compiled by Dolby.[34]

Warheit considers a direct on-line terminal connected to the computer as the best, but most expensive means for capturing data, as information can be encoded directly into the computer via a typewriter or visual display terminals.

> Such on-line preparation of inputs can take advantage of the powerful editing capabilities of the computer. On-line operation not only permits the capture of information while the actual record is being prepared, but, in an integrated or 'total' library system, such capture begins with the first acquisitions record. Erroneous data can be 'erased' during initial typing. Changes, additions and reorganization of text can be made simply by updating the necessary portions of the original information in storage. Manual retyping of corrected draft or final text is eliminated. Information, therefore, can be captured as it is generated, eliminating the cost and time of retranscription by a keypunch operator.[35]

Electronic processing of the catalog data is effected by the computer. Its performance will be influenced by the accuracy of the input data and the input instructions, as the computer can only follow the instructions that are stored in its electronic memory. These instructions are known as the "software." Special book catalog programs usually

> ... involve the normal card-to-tape and edit modules as well as the various sort and format modules to set up the individual outputs desired: shelf

list, author catalog, and subject catalog--the
title breakdown usually being combined with the
author or subject catalog. There may be other
programs such as special cross reference print,
special merge modules to print cumulations, authority list prints, especially for catalogs which
include report literature where corporate author,
contract, and report number cross reference lists
are required.[36]

A review and survey of output printing devices has
been prepared by Sparks, et al.[37] Methods which can be
used to print book catalogs may be outlined as follows:

1. Directly by the computer line printer or terminal
as an original and carbons.
2. Directly by the line printer as above, onto offset
masters and printed from the masters.
3. Photo-reduced line printer copy printed on an
offset press.
4. Full-sized or reduced electrostatic reproduction
directly from paper copy printed by the computer printer.
5. Photocomposition.
6. Microfilm copy.
7. Electrostatic printed copy produced from microfilm input.[38]

Until recently the line printer and photocomposition
were the usual methods of printing book catalogs from machine-readable data. A technique now available is represented by the introduction of electronic composition machines
based on electronic character generation, capable of exceedingly high speeds as compared to composition machines now
on the market.

Whereas the computer line printers are limited to
single fonts, photocomposition may offer multifont capabilities, and good graphic quality output. While the cost of
creating page masters by means of photocomposition is much
higher than it is on the computer-printer, the number of
pages is lower, as photocomposition with its multiple type
fonts and variable-width characters makes it possible to
pack more entries onto a page without losing legibility. As
a result, the cost of reproducing multiple copies and binding
is reduced.[39]

Currently available machines for photocomposition

employ a tape input to control the exposure of a film negative, character by character, with precise positioning of
characters and precise control of spacing between lines.
The earlier photocomposition machines were paper-tape driv-
en, operating at the relatively slow speeds of about 10-40
characters per second. The faster magnetic tape driven
systems operate at speeds ranging from 300-500 characters
per second.

Experiences in developing electronic photocomposers
have been described in recent publications.[40-44] With this
method of typesetting, characters are merely collections of
electronic dots that have been projected onto the face of a
cathode-ray tube. An electronic matrix is set up, and a
letter is composed by placing dots at the proper position in
that grid. The characters are stored in a computer memory
that dictates in which position to write and not to write the
dots. As each letter is needed to set copy, it is brought
out of the memory and displayed on the tube where it ex-
poses either sensitized paper or film.

In spite of the progress that has been made toward
the use of high speed composition techniques, a number of
problems remain, such as a restriction on available character sets, poor legibility in many cases, a lag in programming, problems occurring with program languages, lack of
standards in the design of equipment, and the lack of compatibility of input and output devices. The principal benefits
to be derived from the employment of electronic data processing equipment in typographic composition have been identified as a reduction in the manual clerical effort, a reduction
in publication time, and the extremely important advantage
inherent in the opportunity to use each record for multiple
purposes.

The years 1968 and 1969 began the era of recognition and growth for computer output microfilming (COM).
A computer output microfilmer accepts digital output from
the computer, converts it to analog signals, and prints it
on microfilm at rates from 25,000 to 100,000 characters
per second. It is a third-generation output device that over-
comes numerous problems created by the impact printer,
and one COM unit is the equivalent of as many as 30 impact
printers operating simultaneously.[45] Whether this system
will be applicable to the production of book catalogs remains
to be seen.

Format

A lack of agreement among producers of book catalogs has been evident in relation to the format and content of the catalogs. The final decision depends upon several factors including the purpose of the catalog, the type and quantity of information which is provided, the method of production, the funds available for book catalog production, and the needs of the users.

The amount of information included in the entries varies in different book catalogs. Some include all of the information appearing on the catalog card, while others, providing the minimum elements, are designed primarily as finding lists.

Depending upon its purpose, the book catalog may contain current and/or retrospective materials; its scope may be limited or comprehensive; and it may provide one or several access points to the contents. Most libraries producing computerized book catalogs have favored the divided catalog, rather than the dictionary arrangement. Variations in column width and length, spacing between columns, indentations, margins, size of page, size of print, type face, arrangement of elements, and methods of binding may be observed. Some are perfect-bound, in buckram oversewn, wire sewn, or spiral bound form. Others are offered in loose-leaf or post binder form. [46] The most popular volume size is 8 1/2" x 11."

The influence of typography on the cost of printed catalogs has been investigated. From the cost point of view it is desirable to concentrate the greatest number of characters per square inch, while maintaining legibility, as the more characters which can be accommodated on each page, the fewer the number of pages, and the lower the cost of paper, printing, and binding. It has been concluded that "printing, binding and paper costs are primarily a function of the total amount of space taken up by the catalog material. These costs can be minimized by choosing condensed type faces in small point sizes, by restricting the use of all-caps formats, by using semibold type faces in place of bold, and by maximizing the character density per square inch."[47]

Weinstein and George, in approaching the problem of the cost of printed book catalogs from the standpoint of entry form and content, propose that entries

> ... be the shortest, physically smallest, least in-
> clusive set of bibliographic data consistent with the
> needs of real use. This is not to deny the value
> of each bibliographic element now included on li-
> brary cards, typically Library of Congress cards,
> but rather to question the necessity of their repeti-
> tion throughout the entry set.[48]

The authors propose a catalog consisting of a basic section
of complete bibliographic records, supplemented by computer-
generated indexes. By eliminating a certain repetitive mass
of bibliographic data, more efficient computer usage becomes
possible.

The book catalogs of the four science libraries at the
University of Rochester were produced as short title supplements to the card catalog for immediate bibliographic access
to the collections.[49]

Updating of the catalog is accomplished by issuing
supplements, or by producing completely new editions.
Weekly, monthly, bi-monthly, and quarterly supplements
may be issued. After the basic catalog is published, daily
card supplements may be prepared for use until the next
cumulation is scheduled. The complete catalog may be re-
issued quarterly, semi-annually, annually, or over longer
periods of time. For some types of materials frequent updating of the catalog is not required.

Costs

The cost of publishing the book catalog includes the
composition cost, the printing and binding costs, and paper
costs. As indicated by Dolby, et al., composition costs are
relatively independent of format and type size, although this
factor varies with different composition devices.[50] The
printing cost is influenced by the frequency of cumulation,
the number of pages printed, and the number of copies
printed.

The quantitative variables which are significant in
evaluating the cost of producing library catalogs in book
form have been analyzed in a publication investigating the
economics of book catalog production. These variables have

been listed by Hayes, Shoffner, and Weber as (1) the characteristics of the collections to be cataloged, (2) the characteristics of the published catalogs, and (3) the characteristics of the production method. [51]   The costs of book catalogs produced by various methods were compared.

In a study of the computer-produced book catalog being used in the Baltimore County (Maryland) Public Library, the basic and annual costs of the present book catalog were compared with the cost of maintenance of the card catalogs. Considered also was the effect of the adoption of the book catalog on the costs of rendering various services, and the functions and services that have been added or eliminated. Although the costs could not be accurately estimated, it was found that the book catalog has provided significant benefits by affording the users access to the entire library collection, as was reflected by a 51 per cent increase in intra-library loan requests during the first year after the introduction of the book catalog. [52, 53]

An effort towards evaluation of the utility and cost of computerized library catalogs has been made in which the cost to the user, the cost of programming, cost of hardware, and cost of conversion of catalog data to machine-readable form are reviewed. [54]

Both the advantages and the drawbacks encountered in the use of catalogs in book form have been cited in the literature. [55]   In order to examine the problem in perspective, it would be of value to enumerate and compare the views of others who have considered the possibility of presenting their collections in book form.

Advantages

1.   Multiple copies of the book catalogs can be issued.   It is impractical to produce multiple copies of complete card catalogs.   The catalogs in book form may be widely distributed to other libraries and to individuals, extending the usefulness of the collection.
2.   A number of simultaneous users can be accommodated at the same time.   It is awkward for many patrons to use the card catalog at the same time.   This disadvantage is minimized to an extent by the portability of the catalog trays.
3.   Book catalogs are mobile.   Copies are conven-

iently available in various areas. Users can be comfortably
seated while consulting the catalog. In open stack libraries,
volumes of the book catalog may be placed in the stack area
so that patrons can have the catalogs in the same area as
the books. Book catalogs can be consulted outside of the
library, and in other libraries.

4. In a card catalog only one card may be seen at
a time. The book catalog, on the other hand is easy to
scan. The layout of items on a printed page makes it possible for the user to view numerous entries at the same
time, and to see a full sweep of the holdings on a subject
at a glance. [56] Various editions and the relationships between volumes can be seen, and browsing is enhanced. The
use of book catalogs may be easily taught to patrons. Children have been able to use the book-form catalogs with ease.
Card catalogs have become increasingly complex, causing
difficulties for inexperienced users.

5. The book catalog is compact, occupying less
space than that needed to house bulky card catalogs, and requires no special or expensive cabinets to house it. [57]

6. Numerous problems relating to the maintenance
of the card catalog are avoided. The continuous cost of
filing represents a major disadvantage of the card catalog.
Illegal removal of cards, replacement of deteriorated cards,
and disarranged cards may be avoided with the book catalog.

7. Possible inaccuracies are more easily spotted
in a book catalog than in a card catalog. The use of book
catalogs reduces the amount of clerical and professional
work required to correct errors in the catalog. When an
error is made it may be corrected in the next issue of the
catalog. Time saved can be released for other tasks.

8. In situations where significant changes in cataloging are desirable, a new catalog may be produced in book
form rather than recataloging the old one. Old catalogs may
have many inconsistencies, need to have their subject headings updated, their author entries corrected, and may require a general overhauling as a result of policy changes
over the years, and changes in head catalogers. [58]

9. The book catalog encourages uniform cataloging,
classification, and subject headings. [59] Greater accuracy is
realized through standardization of methods and procedures.
In library systems the quality of the catalog is uniform, and
not subject to modification by branch or departmental staff
members. The control of catalog information at one point

brings out uniformity throughout the system. Book catalogs strengthen coordinated library systems by facilitating the distribution of cataloging information to branches. Branch card catalogs can be removed as an unnecessary expense. No matter in which branch the user is located, he can receive equal opportunity to use any book in the collection without having to travel to the main library to consult the card catalog. Utilization of the available resources of all the libraries in the system may be increased. Member libraries of the systems have the advantages of separate catalogs and central records.

10. The book catalog is of benefit to the library staff. Reference, inter-library loan, acquisitions, cataloging and departmental librarians, as well as faculty and other personnel have a catalog of holdings within reach of their desks for instant reference. Acquisitions policy is under better control, as holdings are more frequently reviewed. Reference librarians find it easy to use and helpful in answering telephone requests. Much time is saved in being able to consult the catalogs at the cataloger's desk without having to walk to the central catalog.

11. Bibliographic control is increased by constant revision of holdings. The publication of periodic cumulative supplements assures the maintenance of currency of the book catalog. Accurate information can be obtained about new books through the use of the cumulative supplements.

12. For closed stack libraries, the book catalog can be used for browsing. The patron can photocopy any section of the book catalog which contains the desired material.

13. Other libraries may use the book catalog as a book selection and buying guide, and as a key to scholarly resources in other libraries. It may aid them in cataloging their collections and in verifying citations for inter-library loans. The volume of inter-library loan transactions may be increased, and inter-library loan operations improved by the provision of book catalogs. The book catalog may be considered as a reference and research tool.

14. Libraries may consider the possibility of selling printed copies of their catalogs or special-purpose bibliographies produced from cataloging data to scholars, other libraries, and possibly to the public.

15. Mail-order library service may be instituted by provision of book catalogs to homes, industries, businesses, schools and other institutions.

16. In a computer-based system for book catalog

production, it is possible to obtain many more approaches
to the holdings of the library than is feasible in a card catalog system, increasing the number of access points under
which information about library items are filed. The inherent restrictions of the fixed format of the printed unit catalog
card are eliminated, making it possible to construct bibliographic tools in a variety of formats and arrangements.[60]
The facility of the computer to sort information rapidly into
a variety of sequences makes multiple uses of the machine-
readable catalog files possible. Various listings can be pro-
duced--by subject, author, title, type of material, language,
chronological order, and others. The machine-readable data
may be used for acquisitions, circulation, and information
retrieval purposes, as well as for the preparation of special
bibliographies.

Disadvantages

     1. Book catalogs are less current than card catalogs;
the book catalog may be obsolete as soon as it is produced.
Since the book catalogs are not up-to-date, a supplementary
listing must be available to assure access to the complete
collection between printings of the catalog. Problems are
created by books that are acquired after publication of the
catalog, and by books withdrawn or transferred to different
locations. The use of the book catalog with its supplements
necessitates looking into several volumes, the main catalog,
and possibly numerous supplements.
     2. The cost of production of the book catalog is
higher. The small library may find the computerized catalog beyond its financial means. When more experience is
gained in the preparation of book catalogs, when cooperative
efforts in this area are realized, and when the fringe benefits resulting from the use of book catalogs are utilized, the
cost may not be as excessive over a period of time as it
seems.

     3. Many libraries in an effort to reduce costs have
limited their cataloging when preparing book catalogs, making
it briefer, including less bibliographic information, or limiting the number of subject headings. The practice of crowd-
ing the information on the page in order to reduce the size
of the catalog has decreased legibility.
     4. The book catalog is inflexible. To make changes
or deletions requires defacing the work.[61] In the card catalog, changes and deletions are relatively easy to effect, and
new entries can be inserted without difficulty.

5. The book catalog is susceptible to wear, mutila-
tion, and theft. Pages may be removed from the catalog.
Normal wear and tear may present problems.
6. The book catalog volumes may be large and
heavy, creating problems in binding and in handling.

7. When a patron carries a volume of the book catalog to the stacks, to the photocopy area, or to other areas
in the library, he has removed a large part of the alphabet.
Using a card tray, the reader has removed only a small
portion of the catalog, and the tray is generally available in
the vicinity of the card catalog for perusal by others.
8. Changes in filing rules in computer-produced
book catalogs may cause problems for the user.
9. It is the opinion of some librarians that the book
catalog does not surpass the card catalog for use in one
place.

The final consideration in regard to the use of book
catalogs will be based upon such factors as the particular
type of library, the character and size of its collection, its
objectives, its clientele, with consideration of their present
and future needs, the library personnel; equipment and funds
available, and the relative advantage and fringe benefits provided to the users in comparison to the costs involved.
Such benefits include the wide distribution of the book catalogs representing the library's collections. The advantages
of extending services and cooperative uses of resources are
factors to be considered.

> There is great need for experimentation, with
> close attention to cost, both of present and pro-
> posed methods, in a wide variety of types and
> size of libraries, before the question of feasibility
> can be answered. In this period of experimentation,
> the precepts, patterns, and products of the past
> must be carefully scrutinized, and only those of
> firmly established and continuing validity and utility
> permitted to influence our judgment of feasibility. [62]

One of the basic decisions required in the consideration of adopting book catalogs is whether the book catalog
should supplant or supplement the card catalog. Some regional and public library systems have dispensed with card
catalogs in branch and extension divisions, but have retained
the main public card catalogs. The Free Library of Philadelphia has removed all card catalogs of their collections
from branch libraries.

R. D. Johnson described the production of a book catalog for an undergradutate library, the J. Henry Meyer Memorial Library of Stanford University. [63] Copies of the catalog
are situated at 18 locations throughout the library, replacing
the standard card catalog. In addition, copies of the catalog
have been placed at other points on the campus, such as the
main and departmental libraries, offices of academic departments, and in student dormitories.

The first book catalog to be produced specifically for
school use was the Catalog of the Junior High School Libraries, Farmingdale (N. Y.) Public Schools, produced in April,
1967, using data processing machinery. It is a catalog of
Farmingdale's three junior high school library collections,
providing separate subject, title, author, and class lists. [64]

A prolific producer of printed library catalogs over
the past few years has been the commercial firm of G. K.
Hall in Boston. Its book catalogs, primarily of special collections, are made by microfilming the catalog cards, making
electrostatic prints from the microfilm, arranging the prints
in three columns of seven cards each, and re-photographing
them at a reduction of two-thirds to make the offset plates.
The process, however, produces a bulky and costly catalog
with a considerable waste of space. The quality of reproduction depends somewhat on the condition of the card entries.

Among other commercial organizations that have been
engaged in book catalog production are Econolist, Los Angeles,
which has prepared and printed book catalogs for various Libraries in California; Alanar, a subsidiary of Bro-Dart Industries, which has produced book catalogs for NASA, California Junior College Libraries, St. Louis Junior College
District, [65] and the Mid-Hudson Library System; Documentation, Inc. (now a LEASCO firm), Bethesda, Maryland, which
produced book catalogs for the Montgomery County (Maryland)
Library System;[66] Science Press, a subsidiary of Printing
Corp. of America, producers of the Black-Gold District book
catalogs; Professional Library Service (Xerox), which has
provided book catalogs for the Rio Hondo Junior College,
Whittier, California, Fort Steilacom Community College,
Tacoma, Washington, San Diego County Library, San Diego,
California, and the Torrance Unified School District, Tor-
rance, California; Rocappi, Inc. Composition Div. of the
Lehigh Press, Inc., Pennsauken, N. J., which prepared the
Chester County (Pennsylvania) book catalog; and Compucen-
ters, Inc., Marina Del Ray California, which is producing the

Los Angeles County Public Library's present catalogs.

The Oregon State Library has issued a book-form catalog prepared on a Rhoton 910 by Sedgwick Printout Systems.[67] The Livermore Laboratory (Sandia Corp., Livermore, California) has integrated its acquisitions, cataloging, circulation, and selective dissemination of information into a single computer-oriented system. The use of the computer to compile book catalogs has been instrumental in eliminating backlogs and maintaining the flow of work on a current basis.[68] The library makes use of two separate catalogs, one for books, and one for technical reports. The two catalogs are generated weekly, and cumulated monthly, quarterly, annually, and at five-year intervals.

A computer-produced catalog in 16 mm. microfilm form has been installed in the Technical Information Center of Lockheed Missiles & Space Company. Upper case print is generated on a Stromberg Carlson 4020 and transferred to microfilm. The microfilm is loaded into 40 cartridges, each cartridge containing 100 ft. of film on which are exposed 1,800 two-column pages of computerized catalog text. Each page contains approximately 14 entries. The records, when in card form, previously occupied 720 standard library catalog drawers. Four catalogs and eight readers have been installed on library premises for use of scientist-engineers, and five catalogs and five readers for use of library staff.[69]

A book-form catalog at the London Borough of Camden Library has been produced by ICT (International Computers & Tabulators). Each computer printout is microfilmed and reproduced by Rank-Xerox to provide copies in the lending libraries.[70]

Several libraries are contemplating the design of on-line, real-time inquiry of catalog data held in computer storage. It is indicated by some that eventually the cost of mass storage and access will be so low that the need for printed catalogs will no longer exist. To this end, they envision the library user operating a console with direct access to the memory bank. Fussler and Payne have been engaged for some time in the development of an on-line, real-time bibliographic data system at the University of Chicago.[71]

The Future

Recent technological advances in computer capabilities,

along with decreasing computer costs, increase the likelihood
that libraries will venture in the future towards increased
computer-aided book catalog production.   The discussion above
clearly indicates that there has been a turn of the circle in
regard to the identification of holdings of libraries through
book catalogs as opposed to card catalogs.   It would appear
that there would be a proliferation of book catalogs with the
advantages clearly identified above.   The need for card catalogs for current records and for special listings will no doubt
continue.

It is expected that inter-library loans will increase,
the facilities for large-scale reproduction of requested materials will be expanded, and that the number of qualified
personnel must be increased to meet the growing demand for
services which can be expected to result from wide distribution of holdings.

The publication of the card catalogs of many libraries
by commercial organizations and other agencies will undoubtedly result in easier identification of the holdings of libraries
of various types.   Such information should help to achieve
one of the goals of librarians--to provide access to particular
titles for the use of scholars wherever they may be located.

Further studies to indicate how access to library collections is facilitated through use of book catalogs; to investigate user and staff reactions to the book catalog; and to observe changes in patterns of library service occurring as the
result of the introduction of book catalogs would be most valuable for the future development of the book catalog.[72]

Notes

1.   Hines, T.C., "Book Catalogs," in Kent, A. and Lan-
     cour, H. eds., Encyclopedia of Library and Informa-
     tion Science, Vol. 2, New York, Dekker, 1969, 661.
2.   Weiss, I.J., and Wiggins, E.V., "Computer-Aided Cen-
     tralized Cataloging at the National Library of Medi-
     cine," Library Resources and Technical Services, 11
     (1967), 83-96.
3.   Ranz, J., The Printed Book Catalogue in American Li-
     braries: 1723-1900, Chicago, American Library As-
     sociation, 1964.
4.   Matta, S., "The Card Catalog in a Large Research Li-
     brary: Present Conditions and Future Possibilities in

the New York Public Library," DLS Dissertation, New York, Columbia University School of Library Service, 1965.

5. Henderson, J.W., and Rosenthal, J.A., Library Catalogs: Their Preservation and Maintenance by Photographic and Automated Techniques. Cambridge, Mass., The M.I.T. Press, 1968, ix (M.I.T. Report No. 14).

6. Kingery, R.E., and Tauber, M.F., eds., Book Catalogs, New York, Scarecrow Press, 1963. [Also: Tauber and Feinberg, Book Catalogs, Metuchen, N.J., Scarecrow Press, 1971.]

7. Weber, D.C., "Book Catalog Trends in 1966," Library Trends, 16 (1967), 149-64.

8. Hewitson, T., "The Book Catalog of the Los Angeles County Public Library: Its Function and Use," Library Resources and Technical Services, 4 (1960), 228-32.

9. MacQuarrie, C., "The Metamorphosis of the Book Catalog," Library Resources and Technical Services, 8 (1964), 370-78.

10. Becker, J., "Automatic Preparation of Book Catalogs," ALA Bulletin, 58 (1964), 715-16.

11. Brown, M.C., "A Book Catalog at Work," Library Resources and Technical Services, 8 (1964), 353.

12. Cartwright, K.L., "Automated Production of Book Catalogs," in Salmon, Stephen R., ed., Library Automation: A State of the Art Review, Chicago, American Library Association, 1969, 58-59.

13. Dolby, J.L., Forsyth, V., and Resnikoff, N.L., An Evaluation of the Utility and Cost of Computerized Library Catalogs. Washington, D.C., U.S. Office of Education, Bureau of Research, 1968.

14. Ibid., 20.

15. Perreault, J.M., "The Computer and Catalog Filing Rules," Library Resources and Technical Services, 9 (1965), 325-31.

16. Popecki, J.T., "A Filing System for the Machine Age," Library Resources and Technical Services, 9 (1965), 333-37.

17. Simonton, W., "Automation of Cataloging Procedures," in Salmon, S.R., ed., Library Automation, op. cit., 47.

18. Hines, T.C., and Harris, J.L., Computer Filing of Index, Bibliographic, and Catalog Entries, Newark, N.J., Bro-Dart, 1966.

19. Nugent, W.R., "The Mechanization of the Filing Rules

for the Dictionary Catalogs of the Library of Congress," Library Resources and Technical Services, 11 (1967), 145-66.

20. Cartwright, K. L., and Shoffner, R. M., Catalogs in Book Form: A Research Study of Their Implication for the California Union Catalog, with a Design for Their Implementation, Berkeley, California, Institute of Library Research, University of California, 1967.

21. Ibid., 26.

22. Markus, J., "State of the Art of Computers in Commercial Publishing," American Documentation, 17 (1966), 76-88.

23. Library Automation--Computer Produced Book Catalog, New York, International Business Machines, Inc., 1969, 1.

24. Zuckerman, R. A., "Computerized Book Catalogs and Their Effects on Integrated Library Data Processing: Research and Progress at the Los Angeles County Public Library," in Carroll, D. E., ed., Proceedings of the 1967 Clinic on Library Applications of Data Processing, Illinois, University of Illinois Graduate School of Library Science, 1967, 72.

25. Balfour, F. M., "Conversion of Bibliographic Information to Machine Readable Form Using On-Line Computer Terminals," Journal of Library Automation, 1 (1968), 217-26.

26. Chapin, R. E., and Dale, H. P., "Comparative Costs for Converting Shelf List Records to Machine Readable Form," Journal of Library Automation 1 (1968), 66-74.

27. Lannon, E. R., "Optical Character Recognition in the U. S. Government," in Advances in Computer Typesetting. Proceedings of the 1966 International Computer Typesetting Conference, London, The Institute of Printing, 1967, 48.

28. Wishner, R., "The Role of Paper Tape and Optical Scanning Input in Textual Data Processing," in Proceedings, of the 1965 Congress, International Federation for Documentation, Vol. II, Washington, Spartan Books, 1966, 240.

29. Nadler, M., "The Perspectives for Practical Optical Character Recognition," in Advances in Computer Typesetting, Proceedings of the 1966 International Computer Typesetting Conference, London, Institute of Printing, 1967, 36.

30. Rabinow, J., "Optical Character Recognition Today," in Computer Yearbook and Directory, 1st ed., Detroit,

American Data Processing, Inc., 1966, 75-82.

31. Dyer, R., et al., Optical Scanning for the Business Man, New York, Hobbs, Dorman, 1966.

32. Wilson, R.A., Optical Page Reading Devices, New York, Reinhold, 1966.

33. Los Angeles County Public Library, An Optical Character Recognition Research and Demonstration Project, California, Los Angeles County Public Library System, 1968.

34. Dolby, et al., op. cit., 55-58.

35. Warheit, I.A., "The Computer Produced Book Catalog," Special Libraries, 60 (1969), 574.

36. Ibid., 575.

37. Sparks, D.E., et al., "Output Printing for Library Mechanization," in Markuson, B.E., Conference on Libraries and Automation, Airlie Foundation, 1963, Libraries and Automation, Proceedings, Washington, D.C., Library of Congress, 1964, 155-200.

38. Library Automation--Computer Produced Book Catalog, op. cit., 30.

39. Cartwright, K.L., "Automated Production of Book Catalogs," op. cit., 77.

40. Morre, J.K., and Cavanaugh, J.F., "A Picture Worth a Thousand Words," Electronics, 40 (1967), 113-28.

41. Corrado, V.M., "Experience in Development of an Electronic Photo-composer," in Hattery, L.H., and Bush, G., Automation and Electronics in Publishing, Washington, D.C. Spartan Books, 1965, 81-90

42. Bozman, W.R., "Computer-Aided Typesetting," in Alt, F.L., and Rubinoff, M., eds., Advances in Computers, Vol. 7, New York, Academic Press, 1966.

43. Makris, C.J., "A Special Purpose Computer for High-Speed Composition," in American Federation of Information Processing Societies, Conference Proceedings, 1966 Fall Joint Computer Conference, San Francisco, Washington, D.C., Spartan Books, 1966, 137-48.

44. Lanzendorfer, M.J., "Character-Generating Phototypesetters," Part V, Printing Magazine/National Lithographer, 91 (1967), 68-69, 94.

45. Yerkes, C.P., "Microfilm--A New Dimension for Computers," Datamation, 15 (12) (1969), 94-97.

46. Weber, op. cit., 157.

47. Dolby, et al., op. cit., 81.

48. Weinstein, E.D., and George, V., "Computer-Produced Book Catalogs: Entry Form and Content," Library Resources and Technical Services, 11 (1967), 185.

49. Richmond, P., "Book Catalogs as Supplements to Card

Catalogs," American Documentation, 16 (1965), 147.
50. Dolby, et al., op. cit., 81.
51. Hayes, R.M., Shoffner, R.M., and Weber, D.C., "The
     Economics of Book Catalog Production," Library Re-
     sources and Technical Services, 10 (1966), 57-90.
52. Childers, T., Kieffer, P., Leonard, F., and Susaki,
     S., Book Catalog and Card Catalog: A Cost and Serv-
     ice Study, Towson, Md., Baltimore County Public Li-
     brary, 1967.
53. Griffin, H.L., "Automation of Technical Processes in
     Libraries," in Cuadra, C.A., ed., Annual Review of
     Information Science and Technology, Vol. 3, Chicago,
     Encyclopaedia Britannica, Inc., 1968, 241-62.
54. Dolby, et al., op. cit., 25-60.
55. Tauber, M.F., and Stephens, I.R., "Technical Services
     in Michigan State Library," New York (typewritten
     manuscript), 1965, 101-05.
56. MacQuarrie, C., "Library Catalog, a Comparison,"
     Hawaii Library Association Journal, 21 (1965), 18.
57. Pizer, I.H., "Book Catalogs Versus Card Catalogs,"
     Medical Library Association Bulletin, 53 (1965), 225-
     38.
58. MacQuarrie, "Library Catalog, a Comparison," op. cit.,
     19.
59. Weber, op. cit., 152.
60. Library Automation--Computer Produced Book Catalog,
     op. cit., 1.
61. Pizer, op. cit., 229.
62. Simonton, W., "The Computerized Catalog: Possible,
     Feasible, Desirable?" Library Resources and Tech-
     nical Services, 8 (1964), 407.
63. Johnson, R.D., "A Book Catalog at Stanford," Journal
     of Library Automation, 1 (1968), 13-50.
64. Harris, J.L., "Programming the Library Catalog,"
     Drexel Library Quarterly, 5 (1969), 84-91.
65. Jones, R.C., "A Book Catalog for Libraries--Prepared
     by Camera and Computer," Library Resources and
     Technical Services, 9 (1965), 205-06.
66. Moreland, G., "Montgomery County (Md.) Book Catalog,"
     in IBM Mechanization Symposium, May 25-27, 1964,
     New York, IBM, 1965, 43-60.
67. Loeber, T.S., "Master Book Catalog Distributed in
     September, or Mohammed and the Catalog," PNLA
     (Pacific Northwest Library Association) Quarterly, 32
     (1967), 5-7.
68. Paxton, E.A., Bodie, E.K., and Jacob, M.E., "In-
     tegrating Major Library Functions into One Computer-

Oriented System," in American Society for Information Science Proceedings, Vol. 5, Columbus, Ohio, 1968, 141-49.

69. Kozumplik, W. A., and Lange, R. T., "Computer-produced Microfilm Library Catalog," American Documentation, 18 (1967), 67-80.

70. Maidment, W. R., "The Computer Catalogue in Camden," Library World, 67 (Aug., 1965), 40.

71. Fussler, H. H., and Payne, C. T., Annual Report 1966/67 to the National Science Foundation from the University of Chicago Library, National Science Foundation GN-566 [n. d.].

72. Cf. 1971 volume, Book Catalogs [reference no. 6]; and the discussions of automatic systems in Kolers, P. A., and Eden, M., eds., Recognizing Patterns, Cambridge, Mass., M. I. T. Press, 1968, 138-230.

V.   CONTEXTS

"We are still quite far from any real understanding of
how scientists read, why they read as they do, and the
ways in which the efficiency of their reading can be
improved. That this is true, I submit, is because the
act of reading itself, the mechanism by which we acquire information, is far more complex than has been
generally assumed. Because we are habitual readers,
whether for pleasure, for profit or for release from
boredom, we have come to take the act of reading, of
acquiring information through the medium of the printed
page, for granted, and any real understanding of reading must wait upon the researches of the neurologists,
the brain specialists, and certain battalions in that het-
erogeneous army which calls itself psychologists. To
the work of these must be added a better understanding
of how knowledge is generated and augmented, the ways
in which it is disseminated through society, and the
impact it has upon social patterns and behavior. This
is epistemology, but it is a new kind of epistemology
which seeks a deeper understanding of the role of scientific knowledge in the totality of the social milieu."

J. H. Shera, Documentation..., 153 f.

"The value system of a culture exerts a strong influence
upon the communication of knowledge within a society
and the ways in which the society utilizes knowledge.
As in the biological world one is aware of only those
mutants that survive, so in a society there is doubtless
a substantial amount of knowledge that fails in the ruth-
less competition for acceptance. ... Very little is
known about the appearance and ultimate fate of the
mutant in knowledge. At times the intellectual climate
seems right for innovation and there is no innovator;
again, there is an innovator who speaks only to deaf
ears. One dare not press historical determinism too
far; without St. Paul, the history of Christianity would
have been vastly different; Luther had to find his princes,

and Newton his Royal Society. Yet in spite of the power of chance and the mutational character of alterations in knowledge possessed by society, after considering the long course of recorded history one cannot avoid the impression that there is an orderly development in public knowledge as recorded in the transcript of successive civilizations and societies."

J. H. Shera, in The Foundations of Access..., 22 f.

HISTORIOGRAPHS, LIBRARIANSHIP,
AND THE HISTORY OF SCIENCE

Eugene Garfield

The study of the history of science has recently taken on new importance as an academic discipline. It's easy to see why. With the pace and complexity of scientific developments accelerating, the need for improved guidelines for scientific research becomes more obvious each day. As critical as today's dilemmas of pesticides, pollution, and nuclear weapons are, applications of current scientific research could produce far more serious problems in the future. For example, the work of molecular biologists could produce a happier, healthier world population or, as suggested by some, it could produce some horrible new weapon of war.[1]

Guidelines for scientific research, however, do not simply materialize from thin air. A solid understanding of past developments and the present nature of science itself is required first. Professor Derek de Solla Price claims, "We are getting to the point where there must arise a fairly hard academic discipline to help understand the machinery that makes science act the way it does and grow the way it grows."[2]

By studying the history of science in a more intensive and accurate fashion, we may obtain badly needed insight into such problems as:
a. The role of science in war and peace.
b. The use and misuse of research.
c. The inter-relations of science and technology.
d. The reciprocal responsibilities of scientists and society.
e. The funding and control of science.

f. The determination of future policies on scientific education.
g. The formulation of a public policy on science in general.

With such important questions to be answered, writing the history of science can no longer be looked on as an exercise to satisfy one's curiosity. This endeavor is too important to be fulfilled, as it has been in the past, as an avocation of scientists. What is needed, as in any other complex activity, is a highly trained specialist.

There have been some beginnings towards this objective. In 1950 there were five professional historians of science in North America, and only a handful of schools that offered Ph. D. s in this subject. There are now at least 125 scholars in the field and 25 major universities offering degree programs in the history of science.

Probably the first full-time historian of science was George Sarton of Harvard who founded ISIS, the chief journal of the field. In his early work, Sarton was primarily concerned with precise chronological reconstructions of events. In his subsequent work, he used more of a narrative approach and began to analyze and interpret cause and effect relationships. Later, Alexandre Koyré of Princeton attempted to explain the development of a new scientific concept by examining the work of the scientist against the prevailing philosophical and intellectual assumptions of his time. Koyré, however, did not regard a scientist's outer social milieu as an important factor in shaping his work. More recently, historians of science have begun to stress the relationship between new ideas and the outer social order in which they develop.[3]

Whatever the approach, the historian of science will produce useful results only in direct proportion to the investigative and evaluative tools at his disposal. The difficulty of amassing the facts of history is well known. Much human error is injected on the part of the historian despite his dedication and rigorous standards. Even with an event like the assassination of President Kennedy, which was observed by countless persons, there still remains doubt as to precisely what occurred. Writing the history of science has its own particular difficulties. The motivation and evolution of ideas are frequently omitted from scientific writings. Usually, major achievements in science are easily recognized; minor or less heralded contributions are difficult to identify and are often overlooked. Even relatively important events may be missed in the plethora of data to be evaluated. It is not surprising, therefore, that there are always numerous uncertainties in writing even a fragment of the history of science.

Historiographs

A new tool that promises to help the historian of science out of this predicament is the "historiograph," a term coined by the Institute for Scientific Information to describe a graphic display of citation data that shows key scientific events, their chronology, their inter-relationships, and their relative importance. Although the technical feasibility of this tool has been established, and a good portion of the required citation data base is available, much work remains to acquaint the historian of science with its availability and its applications. I feel that this is a role that is most properly filled by the librarian. I also feel that if librarians take advantage of this opportunity, they will be actively participating in a field of growing social significance and will have taken one more step towards achieving the dynamic professional image they desire.

As early as 1922 E. Wyndham Hulme used the term "statistical bibliography" in his lectures at the University of Cambridge. Hulme used the term to describe the process of illuminating the history of science and technology by counting documents. In later years, Pritchard used the word "bibliometrics" to describe the quantitative analysis of citations. Russian historians of science have suggested the use of the term "scientometrics" for this type of study. [4]

It was almost by accident, however, that Dr. Gordon Allen triggered the activities that led to the development of the historiograph. In a private communication to me in 1960, Dr. Allen diagrammed the relationships between the citations of a bibliography on the staining of nucleic acid as shown in Figure 1. Although Dr. Allen did not think of this diagram in the context of a historical tool, my examination of it lead me to form the hypothesis that, in most cases, a network diagram of citation relationships would, in fact, constitute a fairly reliable "outline" for writing the history of a field of science. This belief was further reinforced in discussions with Bernal, [5] Price, [6] Leake, [7] and Shryock. [8] I then published an article in American Documentation[9] in 1963 which

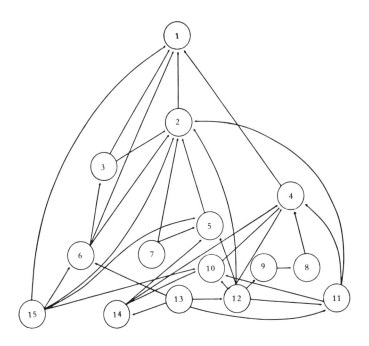

Figure 1.   Citation Relationships of a Bibliography on Staining Nucleic Acid.

Key:

1. Rabinowitch.   1941.
2. Michaelis.   1947.
3. Michaelis.   1950.
4. Zanker.   1952.
5. Northland.   1954.
6. Lawley.   1956.
7. Peacocke.   1956.
8. Appel.   1958
9. Appel.   1958.
10. Steiner.   1958.
11. Steiner.   1959.
12. Bradley.   1959.
13. Bradley.   1959.
14. Bradley.   1960.
15. Loeser.   1960.

summarized my thoughts on the subject and proposed some
specific applications.

Testing the Validity of Historiographs

In 1964, the Institute for Scientific Information began
work on Air Force Office of Scientific Research Contract
AF49(638)-1256 to verify whether citation data are useful heuristic tools for the historian.[10] Essentially, the plan of the
study was to construct two network diagrams of the history
of a field of science: one based on the traditional historical
account, and one based on a reconstruction of the same history by using citation relationships. If the two diagrams co-
incided to any significant degree, it could be concluded that
citation data was, in fact, useful in writing the history of
science.

To conduct the study it was necessary to select a recent important scientific break-through which was based on
the cumulation of years of diverse scientific achievement.
The discovery of the DNA code was selected as this event.
The basis for this choice was: (1) the publication in 1963 of
Dr. Isaac Asimov's book, The Genetic Code,[11] which describes the major scientific developments that led to the laboratory duplication of the process of protein synthesis under
control of DNA, and (2) the availability of the Genetics Citation Index and the 1961 Science Citation Index to provide the
required citation data.

In our study, Dr. Asimov's book was construed as the
historian's account of the discovery of the DNA code. The
GCI and the SCI provided most of the data by which we would
attempt to construct a history of the same topic by other than
expository accounts.

To construct the two historiographs, we proceeded as
follows: first we carefully identified the specific papers involved in the discoveries described by Asimov in his history
of DNA. These included events explicitly named by Asimov,
as well as events not explicitly named but easily identified by
his mention of such things as date or place of investigation.
Forty key events (called nodes) were identified (36 explicit,
4 implied) which spanned a period of about 140 years (1820
to 1962). The 40 nodes were then plotted chronologically
and grouped in broad subject classification such as nucleic
acid chemistry, protein chemistry, genetics, and microbiolo-

gy. Asimov's book was then examined to determine the historical relationships between these 40 nodes. The explicit and implicit relationships were then diagramed as shown in Figure 2.

An extensive literature search was then conducted to identify the specific published works related to each node described by Asimov. The strictest criteria were adopted to insure that the reference citations chosen were the ones which most definitely corresponded to the discovery in question. It turned out that 17 of the 40 nodes represented more than one paper. Thus, 65 articles were required to cover the 40 nodes.

The bibliography of each node article was examined to determine the connections between it and other node articles. The 40 nodes were then redrawn in exactly the same positions and lines drawn to show the direct and indirect citation connections as shown in Figure 3. Finally, the two diagrams were superimposed and the degree of coincidence determined. Figure 4 is a summary of the relationships observed from the superimposition of the two diagrams.

From this comparison it was determined that: (a) enough of the network diagrams were coincident so that it could be concluded that citation data could be used to develop the history of a field; and (b) significant new relationships between nodes were identified by citation linkages which did not coincide with Asimov's linkages.

Over and above these findings, it became clear that one picture was indeed worth a thousand words. The graphic displays of the history made it easier and quicker to grasp the total flow of the development of the field. Further, they made it possible to tie-in seemingly unrelated events. It was at this point that we became convinced that the historiograph would be a boon to the historian.

Need for Automatic Diagraming

It soon became obvious, however, that the manual production of historiographs would severely limit the usefulness of this tool. As the number of nodes increased in a history, it soon became almost physically impossible to draw all the connecting lines. Also, as the lines increased, the clarity of the diagram decreased. [Cont. p. 392.]

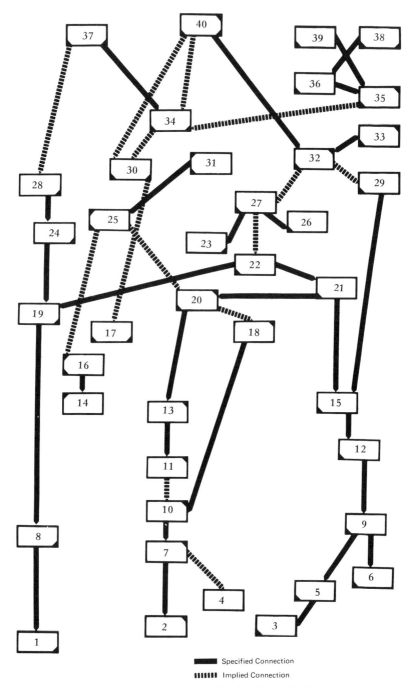

Figure 2. Asimov's Specified and Implied Relationships in the History of DNA

1. Braconnot. 1820.
2. Mendel. 1865.
3. Miescher. 1871.
4. Flemming. 1879.
5. Kossel. 1886.
6. Fischer, Piloty. 1891.
7. De Vries. 1900.
8. Fisher. 1907.
9. Levene, Jacobs. 1909.
10. Muller. 1926.
11. Griffith. 1928.
12. Levene, Mori, London. 1929.
13. Alloway. 1932.
14. Stanley. 1935.
15. Levene, Tipson. 1935.
16. Bowden, Pirie. 1936/37.
17. Caspersson, Schultz. 1938/39.
18. Beadle, Tatum. 1941.
19. Martin, Synge. 1943/44.
20. Avery, MacLead, McCarty. 1944.

21. Chargaff. 1947.
22. Chargaff. 1950.
23. Pauling, Corey. 1950/51.
24. Sanger. 1951-53.
25. Hershey, Chase. 1952.
26. Wilkins. 1953.
27. Watson, Crick. 1953.
28. Du Vigneaud. 1953.
29. Todd. 1955.
30. Palade. 1954-56.
31. Fraenkel, Conrat. 1955-57.
32. Ochoa. 1955/56.
33. Kornberg. 1956/57.
34. Hoagland. 1957/58.
35. Jacob, Monod. 1960/61.
36. Hurwitz. 1960.
37. Dintzis. 1961.
38. Novelli. 1961/62.
39. Allfrey, Mirsky. 1962.
40. Nirenberg, Matthaei. 1961/62.

Figures 2 and 3 Key

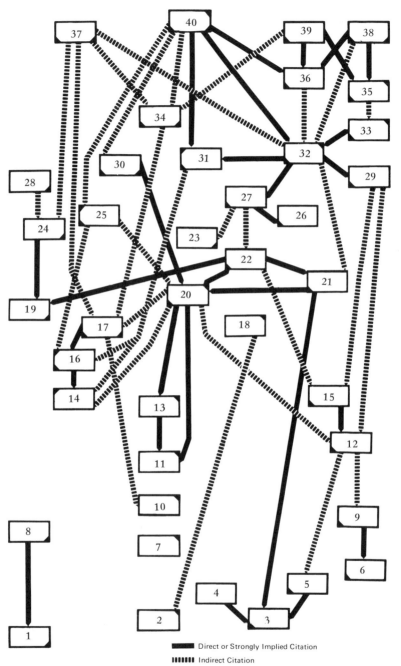

Figure 3. Direct and Indirect Citation Relationships in the History of DNA

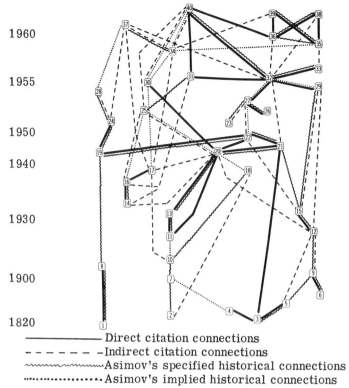

——————— Direct citation connections
– – – – – – –Indirect citation connections
〰〰〰〰〰〰Asimov's specified historical connections
·················Asimov's implied historical connections

DATE	NAME & NODE	DATE	NAME & NODE
1820	Braconnot-1	1947	Chargaff-21
1865	Mendel-2	1950	Chargaff-22
1871	Meischer-3	1950-51	Pauling, Corey-23
1879	Fleming-4	1951-53	Sanger-24
1886	Kossel-5	1952	Hershey, Chase-25
1891	Fischer, Piloty-6	1953	Wilkins-26
1900	DeVries-7	1953	Watson, Crick-27
1907	Fischer-8	1953	DuVigneaud-28
1909	Levene, Jacobs-9	1955	Todd-29
1926	Muller-10	1954-56	Palade-30
1928	Griffith-11	1955-57	Fraenkel-Conrat-31
1929	Levene, Mori, London-12	1955-56	Ochoa-32
1932	Alloway-13	1956-57	Komberg-33
1935	Stanley-14	1957-58	Hoagland-34
1935	Levene, Tipson-15	1960-61	Jacob, Monod-35
1936-37	Bawden, Pirie-16	1960	Hurwitz-36
1938-39	Caspersson, Schultz-17	1961	Dintzis-37
1941	Beadle, Tatum-18	1961-62	Novelli-38
1943-44	Martin, Synge-19	1962	Allfrey, Mirsky-39
1944	Avery, MacLeod, McCarty-20	1961-62	Nirenberg, Matthaei-40

Figure 4.

Figure 5.   Linear Display

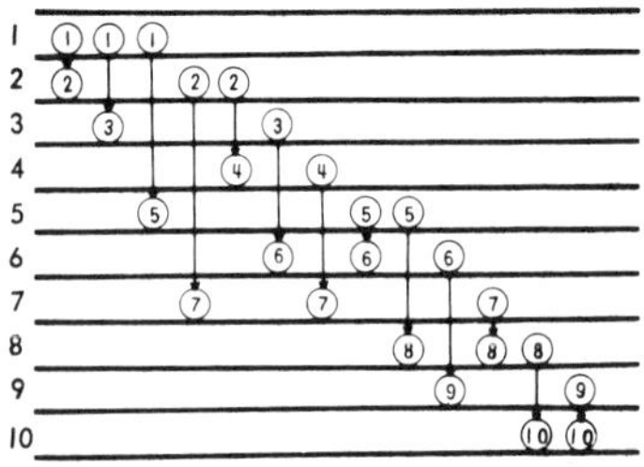

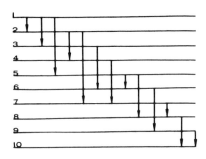

Figure 6.   Cascade Display

Figure 7.   Waterfall Display

Caption for Figure 4 (p. 389):   Comparison of History of
DNA as Derived from Asimov's Specified and Implied Rela-
tionships vs. History of DNA as Derived from Direct and
Indirect Citation Relationships.

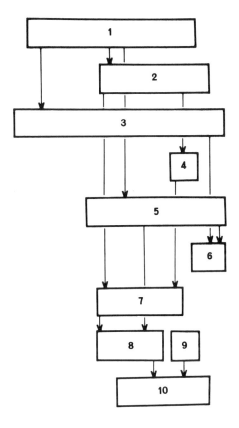

Figure 8.   Rectangular-Node Cascade Display

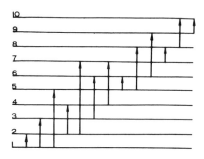

Figure 9.   Fountain Display

In 1967 ISI began an investigation of the problem of the automatic drawing of network diagrams containing nodes with many interconnections. This work was performed under Air Force Office of Scientific Research Contract AF49(638)-1547 and its objective was to identify an existing method of automatic diagraming or develop a new one that would:

    a. Allow algorithmic generation and manipulation of the diagram.

    b. Allow the display of 100 or more nodes.

    c. Allow the display of an unrestricted number of connections between nodes.

    d. Be simple to understand and aesthetically pleasing.

    e. Allow direct printout from a digital computer or plotter.

All known methods of automatic diagraming were investigated. These included methods used for:

    1. Flow charts and PERT charts[12-26]
    2. Organization charts[27]
    3. Electronic circuits[28-38]
    4. Tree systems[39, 40]
    5. Routing systems[41-44]

The investigation of previous work uncovered no method that satisfied all specified criteria. Even if all other criteria were met, the displays became inordinately complicated when more than 10 nodes were involved. It was then felt that the solution to this problem was in developing a unique way of ordering nodes and/or interconnecting lines. Some of the display formats evaluated and rejected included:

    a. Linear Array (see Figure 5)

    b. Cascade Display (see Figure 6)

    c. Waterfall Display (see Figure 7)

    d. Rectangular-Node Cascade Display (see Figure 8)

    e. Fountain Display (see Figure 9)

Diagonal Display

Finally, the concept of "Diagonal Display" was evolved and refined.[45] As shown in Figure 10, Diagonal Display involves arranging the nodes on a diagonal with interconnections shown by lines in the areas adjacent to the nodes. In this original conceptual drawing, the dots indicate a connection between nodes.

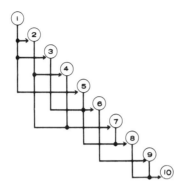

Figure 10.   Original Diagonal Display Concept.

Since the Diagonal Display concept had been entirely hand-drawn up to this point, it was now necessary to determine how this type of plot could be drawn automatically. The first attempts involved the use of a standard computer printer.   Although this was quite satisfactory for many applications, it was felt that even the addition of special characters to the printer would not give the printout the over-all visual clarity desired.

With particular concern for improving the clarity of line junctions and crossovers, we then considered several other types of output devices.   Included in these were:

    a.   Electric lamp display
    b.   Cathode ray tube (CRT) direct display
    c.   CRT plotter
    d.   Incremental pen plotter

It soon became obvious that although each device could be used in the system, the best choice for the type of printout desired would be an incremental pen plotter.   Typically, with such a device, digital signals cause the pen to move in increments in linear directions to any point on a sheet of paper.   By drawing very small, consecutive increments, the pen can also produce curved lines.

A number of commercially available incremental pen plotters were considered, and a CalComp 563 was selected

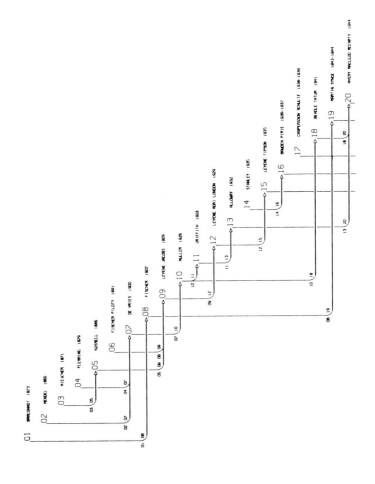

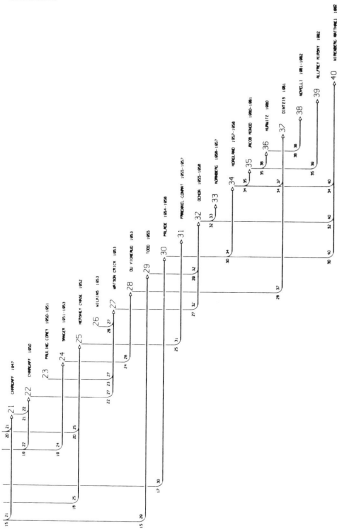

Figure 11.   Printout of Computer-Generated Diagonal Display.

as the most suitable. An appropriate program was written and several variations of the basic Diagonal Display format shown in Figure 10 were developed, with the most significant modifications being the way connections and crossovers of lines were handled. Most improvements in the selected display format involved the use of gaps in vertical lines to indicate crossovers, rounded elbows to show connections, and the addition of numbers at each elbow to show what nodes were connected at that point.

A printout was generated for the 40 nodes contained in the previously discussed history of the genetic code. This printout is shown in Figure 11. A comparison of Figure 11 with Figure 3 (the hand-drawn network of the DNA history) will make obvious the increased clarity provided by the automatic Diagonal Display.

Another test was conducted to produce a printout for a network with 80 nodes. It was concluded that this was as visually clear as the 40-node printout. In fact, it is now felt that even printouts containing 250 nodes would be equally clear.

To summarize all this, ISI's work has shown:

1. That citation relationships can be of great use in writing the history of a field of science.
2. That a graphic representation (historiograph) helps to clarify the relationships and give a quick, over-all view of the development of the field.
3. That relatively large-scale historiographs can be automatically produced on a practical basis.

Applications

Manually or automatically drawn historiographs can be used to advantage by the historian of science to:

a. Reduce a large number of seemingly unrelated events to a coherent pattern.
b. Identify classic papers.
c. Identify break-through events within the development of a field.
d. Identify the descendant of a development.
e. Keep track of how often an event influences later events.

By removing the vagaries of manual drawing, however, automatically produced historiographs provide additional depth of analysis. For example, because similar relationships will be consistently displayed in the same way, certain types of pattern analyses can be performed. The similarities or differences between the historiograph patterns of one field and those of another could lead to meaningful insights. This type of comparison could also apply to historiographs generated for sub-fields of a larger area of scientific endeavor. Pattern analysis could also be used to identify unusual chronological spacing between events and to determine how fields of science coalesce or fragment. Automatic manipulation also makes it easy to emphasize or leave out certain events in a given history. The historian can then determine if there were any alternate paths to subsequent discoveries.

Role of the Librarian

At this point, the librarian may legitimately ask, "What has all this to do with me? Of what use will historiographs be to me in my work? Where do I fit in?" Librarians should look on historiographs as tools that rightfully belong in their domain. Just as much as an index is a retrieval tool, so too is the historiograph. For example, what better way could there be for the librarian to select key papers for a newcomer to a field to read than by examining a pertinent historiograph? In the not too distant future I can envision a historian of science requesting information from the library on a specific development. The librarian will then, as he does now, compile an appropriate bibliography by manual or automatic means. However, another step will then take place that will add a new level of importance to the assistance a researcher can expect from a librarian. The librarian will then sit at a computer console (or some similar device) and use the bibliography as input data. He will ask the computer to print out or display all or part of the citation relationships existing in the input bibliography. The librarian will then assist the researcher in identifying key papers or obscure but important papers. The value of this type of service, especially with lengthy bibliographies, is self-evident.

Another important contribution that could be made by a librarian with a historiograph to analyze, would be the identification of a key paper from another field that had an impact on the field of interest. With experience, the librarian might also become skillful at recognizing certain "classic" historiograph patterns. Perhaps then, he will be able to help the historian identify the signs of declining or emerging disciplines.

The types of analyses described above can be performed by using historiographs generated from citation data currently contained in the Science Citation Index. In the near future, ISI will publish, for the first time, the Journal Citation Index. The JCI will be a statistical compilation that shows how often other journals cite each of over 2000 journals. The JCI will also show how often these 2000 journals cite any of over 25,000 other journals. With this type of data base available, it will be possible to draw historiographs that show relationships between journals rather than individual papers. This, in turn, will permit several additional types of analyses to be made.

For example, it would be possible to show the emergence and growth of a field of science by tracing the history of journals in that field. To do this, a number of journals could be used as nodes in a network. The nodes would be arranged chronologically according to when volume 1 of each particular journal appeared. The citation patterns between the journals over the years could then be drawn and the relationships observed. With this kind of display it would be possible to trace, in terms of journal development, how scientific fields branched out from older existing fields. You could literally tell which journals were the "parents" of other journals. Besides being an aid in writing the history of science, this would also be a useful tool for library science researchers.

Another use for network diagrams made from Journal Citation Index data would be to determine what disciplines make up a scientific field. For example, you could start with certain hard-core genetics journals (such as The American Journal of Human Genetics, Annals of Human Genetics, and Genetics) and have them represented as a kind of bullseye node in the center of a network diagram. Then, you could represent other journals which cite these journals or are cited by these journals as other nodes in the diagram. Those journals that had the highest number of inter-citations with the core journals would be positioned closest to the diagram bulls-eye. Those with a lesser number of inter-citations would be placed proportionately further away. Thus, with one diagram, you could get a quick, clear picture of all the disciplines involved in genetics and the extent of their involvement. Not only would this be a help to the historian of science, it would help the librarian in such things as advising the head of a science department on what journals he should receive. There is no need to emphasize the beneficial effect the ability to give such service will have on the professional status of librarians as a group.

A Project for Students

In conclusion, I would like to propose a project that would be quite appropriate for library school students. All the preceding discussion of historiographs and other types of network diagrams presupposes the existence of large-scale citation indexes to provide the data necessary to draw the historiographs. ISI has produced such indexes for all but two years of the 1960's and work is now in progress so that citation indexes for the missing years (1962 and 1963) will be available by the end of 1971. Our goal is to produce total citation index coverage for the literature of the 20th century, and steps are being taken in this direction.

ISI would like to establish a similar goal for the literature of the 19th century. In particular, we would like to start this project by creating citation indexes for the rather limited American scientific literature of that period. Unfortunately, 19th-century scientific authors had very poor citation practices--very few explicit citations were made, although implicit citations were common. Thus, before ISI's citation indexing techniques could be applied, explicit citations would have to be created from the implicit ones. It is the work of creating these explicit citations that I suggest be taken on by library students.

The value of this information to historians of science, and perhaps to civilization, would begin to approach the magnitude of the respect we all have for Jesse Shera.

Notes

1. J. Lederberg, "Essence of Life or Death?" Current Contents, 15 (April 15, 1970), M1. See also: Washington Post, March 28, 1970.
2. D. J. de Solla Price, "Measuring the Size of Science," Proceedings of the Israel Academy of Sciences and Humanities, 4 (1969), 98.

3. R. Reinhold, "Rise of History of Science Is a Reply to Technology," New York Times, Feb. 18, 1970, 51.

4. A. Pritchard, "Statistical Bibliography of Bibliometrics," Journal of Documentation, 25 (1969), 348-349.

5. J. D. Bernal, private communication, March 1962.

6. D. J. de Solla Price, private communication, March 1962.

7. C. D. Leake, private communication, August 1962.

8. R. H. Shryock, private conversation, September 1962.

9. E. Garfield, "Citation Indexes in Sociological and Historical Research," American Documentation, 14 (1963), 289-291.

10. E. Garfield, I. H. Sher, and R. J. Torpie, The Use of Citation Data in Writing the History of Science, Philadelphia, Institute for Scientific Information, 1964, 76p.

11. I. Asimov, The Genetic Code, New York, New American Library, 1962, 187p.

12. D. D. Butler and O. T. Gatto, Event-Chain Flow Charting in Autosate: A New Version, The Rand Corporation, RM-472a-PR (DDC No. AD 622744), October 1965, 69p.

13. IBM 7070/7074 Autochart Programming System, IBM Systems Reference Library File No. 7070/7074-48, February 1964, 58p.

14. 1401/1410 Autocoder Program Logic Diagrammer, IBM Program Application Library File No. 1401-01.4.128 (1964).

15. W. B. Stelwagon, Principles and Procedures for the Automatic Flow Charting Program FLOW 2, Research Department, U. S. Naval Ordnance Test Station, China Lake, California, NOTS T P 4095 (DDC No. AD 637863), August 1966, 63p.

16. System/360 FLOWCHART, IBM Systems Reference Library File No. H20-0199-0 (1950), 20p.

17. L. M. Haibt, "A Program to Draw Multi-Level Flow Charts," Proc. West. Joint Comp. Conf. (1959), 131-137.

18. C. Rain and K. Hain, An Auto-Diagrammer (NASA TMX 1317) November 1966.

19. D. E. Knuth, "Computer-Drawn Flow Charts," Comm. ACM, 6 (1963), 555-563.

20. A. E. Scott, "Automatic Preparation of Flow Chart Listings," J. ACM, 5 (1957), 57-66.

21. P. M. Sherman, "FLOWTRACE, A Computer Program for Flowcharting Programs," Comm. ACM, 9 (1966), 845-854.

22. H. E. Anderson, "Automated Plotting of Flow-Charts on a Small Computer," Comm. ACM, 8 (1965), 38-39.

23. J. F. Daly, P. E. R. T. Construction Project Network Analysis, U. S. Naval School, Civil Engineer Corps Officers, Port Hueneme, California (DDC No. AD 612 174) July 1964, 200p.

24. S. C. Parikh and W. S. Jewell, "Decomposition of Project Networks," Management Science, 11 (1965), 444-459.

25. N. B. Solomon, "Automated Methods in PERT Processing," Computers and Automation (1965), 18-55.

26. T. H. Asselin, CPM Bar Chart: A Graphic CPM Schedule Generated by Computer, School of Engineering, Massachusetts Institute of Technology, (Research Report R66-4A) February 1966, 87p.

27. M. J. Kaitz, "Acorn-Computer Generated Organizational Charts," UAIDE Proc., Sec. III 9, Space and Info. Div., North American Aviation, Douney, California (1964).

28. L. E. West and D. L. Caskey, Topographic Simulation As An Aid to Printed Circuit Board Design, Sandia Laboratory, Sandia Corporation, Albuquerque (Research Report SC-RR-66-424) August 1966, 33p.

29. P. W. Case, et al., "Solid Logic Design Automation," IBM Journal, 8 (1964), 127-140.

30. R. A. Ceshner and A. L. Rifkin, "Automating the Production of Printed Circuit Artwork," Computer Design, 5 (1966), 54-58.

31. L. L. Grigsby and W. A. Blackwell, "Design of a Linear Multiport Network by State-Space Techniques," Matrix and Tensor Quarterly, 16 (1966), 122-134.

32. S. Katz, "Method of Synthesis of Linear Networks in the Time Domain," Bull. Acad. Polon. Sci., 14 (1966), 107-111.

33. R. Waxman, et al., "Automated Logic Design Techniques Applicable to Integrated Circuitry Technology," (American Federation of Information Processing Societies), Fall Joint Computer Conference Proceedings 1966, 247-265.

34. R. M. Burstall, "Computer Design of Electricity Supply Networks by a Heuristic Method," Computer Journal, 9 (1966), 263-274.

35. I. Friedman, et al., NAP--Network Automatic Plotting, Atomics International, Los Angeles (AI-64-MEMO-15) February 1964, 118p.

36. G. G. Dodd, Principles and Applications of Unistor Graphs, Coordinated Science Laboratory, University of Illinois, Urbana (Report R-217) (DDC No. 604 095) July 1964, 47p.

37. D. M. Sheppard, et al., "A Computer-Aided Method for
     Checking and Making Monolithic Integrated Circuit
     Masks," Proc. WJCC, Los Angeles (1966), 1-7.
38. M. W. Aarons and M. J. Goldberg, "Computer Methods
     for Integrated-Circuit Design," Electro-Technology, 5
     (1965), 77-81.
39. A. J. Paul, Jr., Generation of Directed Trees, 2-Trees
     and Paths Without Duplication, Coordinated Science
     Laboratory, Univ. of Illinois, Urbana (Report R-241)
     January 1965, 45p.
40. V. E. Benes, "Programming and Control Problems
     Arising from Optional Routing in Telephone Networks,"
     Bell System Tech. J., 45 (1966), 1373-1438.
41. GE Traffic Eng. Group, Bethesda, Md., "CalComp
     Plotter Unsnarls Traffic Problems," Digital Plotting
     Newsletter, CalComp, Anaheim, California, Oct/Nov
     1964.
42. "Traffic Flow Maps Plotted Mechanically," Public Works,
     96 (1965), 117.
43. "Pipe Layouts by Computer," Mechanical Engineering,
     86 (1964), 57.
44. E. L. Rhoades and J. R. Miller, "Computer Figures
     Pipe Lengths," Plant Engineering, 19 (1965), 150-151.
45. E. Garfield and I. H. Sher, "Diagonal Display--A New
     Technique for Graphic Representation of Complex Topo-
     logical Networks," final report to U. S. Air Force,
     Office of Scientific Research under Contract AF 49
     (638)-1547, Institute for Scientific Information, Phila-
     delphia (1967), 94p. See also: E. Garfield and M. V.
     Malin, "Diagonal Display--A New Technique for Graph-
     ic Representation of Network Diagrams," 1969 Trans-
     actions of the American Association of Cost Engineers,
     13th National Meeting, Pittsburgh (1969), 222-232.

INFORMAL COMMUNICATION IN SCIENCE: ITS ADVANTAGES AND ITS FORMAL ANALOGUES*

Herbert Menzel

There is no longer any doubt about the great role played by informal, person-to-person communication in the experiences of scientific investigators--often in ways that affect their work quite vitally. (Herner, 1954; Ackoff and Halbert, 1958; Pelz, 1956; Menzel, 1959; Orr, et al., 1964, p. 33-54; Rosenbloom, McLaughlin, and Wolek, 1965; American Psychological Association, 1965; Price, 1963.) Here I would like to pay some attention to the question why this may be so--what, perhaps, are the peculiar advantages that this form of communication offers. (This is not to deny its drawbacks!) Perhaps, the answer can teach us some uses for which more formal mechanisms need to be adapted or devised; perhaps it can indicate in what respects informal communication needs to be made more effective.[1]

First, however, I would like to shield against possible misunderstanding. Formal and informal scientific communication are complementary; they must not be thought of as alternatives in the sense that, perhaps, certain messages are obtained exclusively through the printed word, the library, and the mechanized search-and-retrieval system, whereas others are obtained by the exclusive use of word-of-mouth and the telephone. The much more typical event is one in which the receipt of a single message is secured by the successive interplay of these two kinds of communication. For any given transaction between a scientist as a receiver of information and the channel that brings him that information usually has a history behind it and a future ahead of it that may be very relevant to the evaluation of the success of that

*This paper was published in 1968 by the School of Library Science, Syracuse University, in the volume, The Foundations of Access to Knowledge, ed. E.B. Montgomery (Frontiers in Librarianship, no. 8), p. 153-163, and is printed here with permission.

transaction and to the prognosis of whether this kind of transaction will happen again with similar results. Often one
channel of communication calls attention to a message to be
found in another; sometimes a third channel is required to
locate the precise document in which the message is contained; frequently one or more persons serve as relays between the source of a message and its ultimate consumer;
and contacts at each intervening step may be initiated now
by the receiver, now by the carrier of the message.   The
events which thus interplay are often distributed over a period of time. The possible relevance of a message to a
man's work may not become apparent at the time it is first
received, but only when that same message is repeated,
sometimes more than once, or when it is put together with
other information yet to be received, or when changes occur
and needs come up in the course of the scientist's own future
work.

Understanding, then, that channels of communication
often act "synergistically," we may turn to our chief ques-
tion--why should interpersonal communication play such a
great role in science?

What are the peculiar functions that account for the
continued place of these ill organized and haphazard forms
of communication in science and technology, in spite of the
existence of a vast apparatus of more formal communication
channels?   What, in other words, has interpersonal communication got that the written word and other formal means of
science communication haven't got?

In an entirely different field, an analogous question
has long since been answered. Studies of mass media campaigns have shown many times that decision-makers in the
general public (voters, buyers, blood donors, etc.) are much
more likely to be influenced by messages which reach them
through face-to-face contact than by those which reach them
through the media of mass communication.   The peculiar advantages of face-to-face communications in this context have
been summed up as follows: Personal influence about an issue is often exerted unexpectedly as a sideline or marginal
topic in a casual conversation, while mass media messages
are more often approached with an awareness of their purposefulness. Undecided persons and those opposed to the
views being transmitted are therefore more easily reached
by interpersonal communication, and are less defensive when
they are reached. Face-to-face contact is also more flexible

and provides immediate response to instantaneous feedback. A person, unlike a mass medium, is likely to raise issues and arguments of immediate personal relevance to the listener. And finally, when someone yields to personal influence in making a decision, the reward in terms of approval is immediate and personal (Lazarsfeld and Menzel, 1963).

But while some of these explanations do, as we shall see, have their analogues in the field of scientific information flow, they hardly suffice to account for the great role played by interpersonal communication in science, since the situation here differs from that of the mass media campaigns in at least two quite fundamental ways. (1) Mass media campaigns are matters of persuasion, while interpersonal communication among scientists shows its importance even in the matter of purely cognitive diffusion. (2) The target audiences of mass media campaigns are typically apathetic and lack formally institutionalized avenues of authoritative information, while scientists have a very high motivation to obtain scientific information and have a prodigious apparatus of specialized information sources available. [2]

It is therefore necessary to seek special explanations for the prevalence of interpersonal communication in science by asking what may be the peculiar functions of interpersonal communication here--the services which other forms of communication are unable or less likely to render. The following paragraphs list six such functions. Each has been brought out several times in recent studies and discussions of scientific communication.

    1. Promptness. The most obvious advantage of interpersonal communication among scientists is its speed, compared to that of the printed media, in bringing word of new scientific developments to those who are tuned in to the appropriate scientific grapevine--to the members of the "invisible college" for each scientific specialty, as Derek Price (1963) has so aptly dubbed such networks. Face-to-face conversations between scientists, telephone calls, correspondence, and the exchange of preprints bring news of recent work to the current awareness of scientific specialists many months before the same news can reach them in print. This has been most thoroughly documented for the case of psychology, where presentations at colloquia and manuscript distribution were found to precede journal publication by an average of 12-18 months (American Psychological Association, 1965, p. 130).

In recent decades this time gap has probably increased,
and the patience of scientists with such delays has certainly
decreased. The formal channels have, however, by no means
been idle. In addition to many successful efforts to speed up
the publication process in the primary journals, a variety of
speed-up current awareness and alerting services have been
instituted or suggested in various specialties and disciplines.
One may mention bulletin journals for reports of extraordinary importance, like Physical Review Letters; newsletters
of varying sorts; scientific newspapers; the listings of the
titles of manuscripts submitted to a journal, with transmission of copies on demand, as is done by Industrial and Engineering Chemistry; and, most recently, a centralized preprint exchange service, such as is currently being debated
by American physicists (Moravcsik and Pasternack, 1966).

In these diverse ways the formal communication system seeks to perform a service--prompt current awareness--
which the interpersonal network has hitherto performed more
effectively. If the formal system can perform this service,
it will probably do so more efficiently, and will reach a much
wider circle of scientists.

2. Selective Switching. In addition to promptness of
delivery, the interpersonal network appears to have a second
virtue in performing current awareness services: it routes
scientific news to the scientists to whom it is relevant. This
is especially significant for reaching those in specialties other
than the ones where the news originated. This may seem
like an odd assertion, for surely the haphazardly connected
and intermittently functioning personal network cannot improve upon the topical organization of material that is performed by the far-reaching specialization of journals, journal
sections, indexes, and formal alerting services. Nevertheless, a good deal of news of current scientific activities
reaches scientists through correspondence, visits, and cor-
ridor conversations. Much of this news proves to be of considerable significance to the receiving scientist's work.

This appears to happen most frequently among basic
researchers, and is at least in part due to the nature of
specialization among these scientists. They not only special-
ize to a high degree, but they also delineate their specialties
in highly individual and original ways; often no more than a
small handful will be specializing in precisely the same area.
All the possible ways of classifying content cannot possibly
be taken into account in the organization of journals, in the

indexing and abstracting services, or even in the selection
of titles for papers. Any given researcher is likely to find
that the way of classifying reports which would be most relevant for his purposes has not been used. Within the confines
of a narrow field, he attempts to scan everything that comes
out; but beyond that he must depend largely on friends who
work in the adjoining specialties, yet know what is of interest
to him, to flag the pertinent material for him. In the words
of an interviewed biochemist, "Everyone knows what problems
you're working on. Whenever you come across something
which might be of interest to another you make a note of it.
This way the individual is able to be acquainted with a lot
more than he would be if he didn't have the others on the
lookout too."

The interpersonal network--to the extent that it works
effectively--thus does more than can be accomplished by the
topical organization of the formal media of scientific communication: it does selective switching, matching news items
to the individual interest profile of a given scientist.

But this is precisely the goal of one of the more radical innovations in the formal information system, one which
has so far been instituted only very sporadically and that
mostly on an experimental basis: the selective dissemination
service. Thus we read in a recent announcement that

> Chemical Abstracts Service and the Organic Chem-
> icals Division of American Cyanamid Company have
> initiated a computer-based information experiment
> designed to store and retrieve abstracts of current
> technical articles and to match these abstracts
> with keyword profiles of scientist-users.
> This Selective Dissemination of Information
> (SDI) system is directed toward maximum usage of
> the modern computer capability available from
> Chemical Abstracts Service, and is intended to
> supplement the technical readers' exposure to the
> literature by including journals, and possibly other
> materials, of a general chemical nature rather
> than those pertinent to specific subject areas.
> The assumption is made that most technical
> readers constantly review specialty journals of di-
> rect interest to them.... The SDI program broadens
> each reader's scope by allowing him to scan whole
> abstracts of supplementary journals and other basic
> sources he might not have time to read in detail.[3]

Once again we find that what is new and radical in
the formal communication system is "old hat" in the interpersonal system. As always in such cases, the formal system takes on the service with deliberate planning and under
a distinct label, while the informal system performs the
same service incidentally to other activities, so that it hardly comes to the awareness of the participating individuals as
a separate function. Occasionally the switching of messages
by colleagues will transcend what can be performed by a
selective dissemination service--for a colleague may be in
a position to recognize the relevance of a message to another
scientist's work even when it does not correspond to his established interest profile. In other words, the colleague
may realize that an item of scientific news "should" be of
interest to the scientist even when the scientist himself might
not recognize its relevance at first sight--for example when
the item is clothed in a specialty terminology which is foreign to him.

3. Screening, Evaluation, and Synthesis. The advantages discussed so far--promptness and selective switch-
ing--refer chiefly to the role of interpersonal communication
in performing the current awareness function. But what of
the role of interpersonal communication in the reference
function--in the furnishing of answers to a scientist's specific
questions as they come up in his work?[4] What advantage
can there possibly be for a scientist in going to a colleague
rather than to a library, index, or other retrieval service
to find out what is known about the properties of a given
substance, or--with somewhat broader scope--what is new
in a certain field? The colleague does indeed perform certain services that traditional retrieval services do not. For
one thing, the colleague will deliver information rather than
documents. Secondly, he will, because of his own work and
interest, have gone through a large number of documents
containing relevant items of information; he will have screened
for retention in his memory those which he judged to be
worth retaining at the time that he first became acquainted
with them. In other words, he will already have performed
the operations of screening and evaluating, and perhaps of
synthesizing, not documents, but items of information, and
he will deliver to the inquiring scientist the end result of
these several operations.

But these are precisely the kinds of operations which
would be performed by the specialized information evaluation
center which has recently been proposed. To quote from a

recent comprehensive statement on communication problems in biomedical research:

> A comprehensive biomedical communication system must include not only document processing--the systematic distribution, storing, and cataloguing of documents so that they reach those likely to be interested and may be retrieved readily on demand-- but also the collection, evaluation, digestion, synthesis, dissemination, and retrieval of items of information selected from documents and other sources. This information processing begins where the processing of documents leaves off and requires a different type of processor. Compendia, critical tables, and review articles represent traditional types of information processing.... Recently a number of services have been established that provide users, on a continuing or demand basis, with items of information in a narrowly defined field. These services have come to be known as Specialized Information Centers. Those services that also undertake to provide expert evaluation of the quality, validity, and significance of the information proffered qualify as Specialized Information Evaluation Centers.... In general the greatest promise seems to be in centers that process information rather than documents, and that make possible true information retrieval, by providing scientists with the specific items of information they want rather than referring to documents that may contain the desired information [Orr et al., 1964, p. 1122-23 and 1126].

Colleagues, at their best, do all this when they answer a fellow-scientist's search question. To be sure, "colleagues at their best" are not available at all times to all scientists who would need them, in all the desired specialties.

4. Extraction of Action Implications. Another service of colleague-to-colleague communication applies more to the practitioners of applied professions than to the research scientists. This is the translation into applied or action terms of information originally reported in the language of the research laboratory or of basic-science theory. There is sometimes a considerable gap between these languages. Often, too, the information requisite for decisions on any one practical step is reported in separate articles and jour-

nals, each devoted to a different basic-science sub-specialty.

Furthermore, communication from a colleague, unlike most communication through more formal means, can add to the scientific knowledge transmitted a sense of judgment as to its significance in given practical situations and as to the stringency with which the newly acquired knowledge should be followed. In the field of medicine, in particular, one of the practitioner's most pressing information needs is one for a sense of the judgment used by the best men in the field, after the proper balancing of the often conflicting demands of the scientifically most satisfactory diagnostic procedure, of the pressures to administer therapy quickly in acute situations, and of various practical considerations (cost of or access to services; patient cooperation; time available for care; and so on). It may very well be that one of the practitioner's greatest needs is not so much to find out what the scientific precept on any question of medical care is, as to have some guidance in knowing how scientific to be and when.

Certain handbooks, manuals, and practically oriented review books perform, to some extent, the functions of collating basic-science information and translating it into action terms. These media are less successful in imparting the "sense of judgment" just alluded to. One institutionalized form of the transmission of knowledge which does incorporate all these functions is the case method of instruction and its medical equivalent--actual or simulated bedside teaching. This is, no doubt, why these methods are held in such high esteem by practitioners of the applied professions.

5. Transmitting the Ineffable. Messages with certain types of content are transmitted through direct scientist-to-scientist communication differentially often. Although data are not yet sufficient to identify all the information contents for which this is true, a certain level of know-how information is prominent among them: unpublished minor details of already published findings; information about the use of techniques, the adaptation of apparatus, or the availability of materials; generally the fruits of experience and know-how (Menzel, 1959; American Psychological Association, 1965, Report no. 11; Rosenbloom, McLaughlin, and Wolek, 1965). Information of this kind often fails to find its way into the literature; and even if published, it is difficult to track down.

One may speculate about the reasons why information of this kind remains frequently unpublished, unnoticed, or hard to spot. Authors and editors may believe--sometimes falsely--that few scientists would utilize the information. Standards of publication, more appropriate in the reporting of scientific findings, may make the communicating of know-how information unduly lengthy and laborious. The information may be regarded as trivial in some inherent, almost aesthetic, sense. Suitable and generally familiar categories for cataloging such information may not exist. And last, but not least, information of this sort may be difficult to verbalize economically, and may be much more easily "shown" than told.

Some of these impediments can be alleviated by the creation of special media for the exclusive publication of know-how information. Information which, at present, is correctly regarded as needing to be "shown," may call for the creation of an adequate, standardized, and generally recognized vocabulary. After all, many special skills and professions, once regarded as untransferrable except through apprenticeship, are now transmitted didactically; this has become possible because the steps involved have been properly conceptualized and symbols created for them. "Programmed instruction" has more recently reinforced this lesson of history.

6. Instantaneous Feedback. One of the most obvious advantages of face-to-face communication of any kind is the instantaneous feedback and the continuous exchange of messages. This applies in the exchange of scientific information as well. Interpersonal communication furnishes scientists responses to their own statements and enables them, in that way, to obtain useful criticism of their work and ideas. Through the same mechanism, it also becomes an important part of the reward system in the sciences. Conversely, a message obtained face-to-face often carries with it clues to the soundness of the speaker's mode of reasoning. (Compare the trial lawyer's principle of "voir dire," or, "they must be seen to be heard.")

But feedback also plays an important role in controlling and facilitating the information exchange of which it is a part. If one transmits a message to a colleague, one may see from his expression that it has not "come across," and add explanations. If one asks a colleague for information and he does not understand what he is being asked for, he can ask for clarification. By the judicious insertion of remarks like, "No, that isn't what I meant to ask," or "I don't need any more detail," or "Can you be more specific?," inquiries which are about to go off the track can be brought back in line before too much time and effort is wasted.

Here surely, one would think, is a peculiar advantage of interpersonal communication that the formal channels cannot duplicate.   And yet we may read in a recent announcement:

> To bring information resources ever closer to the ultimate user, computers and communications consoles are being combined in an exploratory study recently initiated by the Scientific and Technical Information Division of the National Aeronautics and Space Administration.   The purpose of the prototype study is to determine the cost effectiveness, efficiency, and user acceptability of a retrieval system which literally keeps information available at the potential user's fingertips.
> Under a contract with the Bunker-Ramo Corporation, consoles will be installed in users' immediate working areas, hooked-up by telephone lines with a central computer-search keyboard with a viewing screen.   The user 'types' topical terms, authors' names, or similar identifying data which he believes are pertinent to his query.   Within seconds, corresponding citations begin to appear on the viewing screen, according to NASA.   If the user likes what he sees, the pressing of other buttons will record his interests so that the cited documents may be sent to him.   If not, he can modify his search until relevant citations do appear.   Thus, NASA adds, this direct linking of the user with the store of information can be a real-time dialog in which the user's search question is specified and refined. [5]

Notes

1.   The best general source book to behavioral studies of the flow of information among scientists is Paisley, 1965. A more detailed review, concentrating on the years 1964-65, is Menzel, 1966(a).   An overview of certain sociological aspects is Menzel, 1966(b).
2.   For a more extensive discussion of scientists and practitioners as publics, see Menzel, 1966(c).

3. Science Information Notes, 8:2 (1966), 12.
4. For a general discussion of the multiple functions of
   science information systems, see Menzel, 1964.
5. Science Information Notes, op. cit., 13. Compare also
   Don Swanson's earlier suggestions of "Dialogues with
   a Catalogue," (1964).

References

Ackoff, R. L. and Halbert, M. M. , An Operations Research
   Study of the Scientific Activity of Chemists. Cleve-
   land: Case Institute of Technology, Operations Re-
   search Group, 1958 (mimeo.).
American Psychological Association. Reports of the American Psychological Association's Project on Scientific
   Information Exchange in Psychology, Washington,
   D. C. , American Psychological Association, vol. 1,
   1963; vol. 2, 1965; vol. 3, 1966.
Herner, S. "Information-Gathering Habits of Workers in
   Pure and Applied Science." Industrial and Engineering Chemistry 46 (1954), 228-236.
Lazarsfeld, P. F. , and Menzel, H. "Mass Media and Per-
   sonal Influence." In W. Schramm, ed. , The Science
   of Human Communication, New York: Basic Books,
   1963, 94-115.
Menzel, H. "Planned and Unplanned Scientific Communica-
   tion." In Proceedings of the International Conference
   on Scientific Information, Washington, D. C. , National
   Academy of Sciences, 1959, 199-243.
Menzel, H. "The Information Needs of Current Scientific
   Research." The Library Quarterly 34 (1964), 4-19.
Menzel, H. "Information Needs and Uses in Science and
   Technology." In C. Cuadra, ed. , Annual Review of
   Information Science and Technology, vol. 1, New York:
   John Wiley, 1966. (a)
Menzel, H. "Scientific Communication: Five Sociological
   Themes." American Psychologist, November 1966.
   (b)
Menzel, H. "Sociological Perspectives on the Information-Gath-
   ering Practices of the Scientific Investigator and the
   Medical Practitioner." In D. McCord, ed. , Bibliotheca
   Medica: Dedication of the Countway Library of Medicine,
   Boston, Harvard Medical School, 1966. (c)

Moravcsik, M. J. and Pasternack, S. "A Debate on Preprint
   Exchange." Physics Today, June 1966, 60-73.

Orr, R., et al., "Communication Problems in Biomedical
    Research." Federation Proceedings, 23 (1964), 1117-
    1176 and 1297-1331.
Paisley, W. J.   The Flow of (Behavioral) Science Information
    --A Review of the Research Literature, Stanford,
    Calif., Institute for Communication Research, Stanford
    University, 1965 (mimeo.).
Pelz, R. C.   "Social Factors Related to Performance in a
    Research Organization." Administrative Science Quar-
    terly, 1 (1956), 310-325.
Price, D. J. deSolla.   Little Science, Big Science.   New
    York: Columbia University Press, 1963.
Rosenbloom, R. S., McLaughlin, C. P. and Wolek, F. W.
    Technology Transfer and the Flow of Technical Infor-
    mation in a Large Industrial Corporation.   2 volumes.
    Cambridge, Mass., Graduate School of Business Ad-
    ministration, Harvard University, 1965 (mimeo.).
Science Information Notes.   Washington, D. C., National Sci-
    ence Foundation.   Volume 8, 1966.
Swanson, D.   "Dialogues with a Catalogue."   In R. F. Strout,
    ed., Library Catalogue--Changing Dimensions.   Chi-
    cago: University of Chicago Press, 1964.

See also D. Crane, "Information Needs and Uses" in Annual
    Review of Information Science and Technology, vol. 6,
    ed. C. Cuadra and A. W. Luke, Chicago, Encyclopae-
    dia Britannica, 1971, 2-39, and the literature cited
    there.   (Ed.)

WRITING-SYSTEM: A DATUM IN
BIBLIOGRAPHICAL DESCRIPTION

John Mountford

A problem, at first sight peripheral, occurs in the description of books or documents that are printed or hand-written in something other than the ordinary orthography of English (or of any other language, but English will be the example in the discussion which follows). In 1962, for instance, appeared <u>Androcles and the lion. An old fable renovated by B. Shaw. With a parallel text in Shaw's alphabet to be read in conjunction showing its economies in writing and reading.</u>[1] Here the extended title supplies the special information. Where the title fails to do this, a note can be added, as in the following, from the British Museum <u>General Catalogue of Printed Books</u>:

> —— [The Deseret First Book. By the Regents of the Deseret University.] pp. 36. [Salt Lake City,] 1868. 8°.
>
> Printed in characters of the "Deseret Alphabet."

The problem is not important practically; a special note satisfies the needs of descriptive bibliographer and cataloger. But theoretically this small door opens on to linguistic territory of some interest to the librarian -- at least during that period, however long it lasts in the course of training or in later life, when he is concerned about the nature of the literacy which makes libraries possible and important.

In this offering to an educator of librarians, we shall, like Alice, peer through the small door, and ask ourselves whether what we see is worth further exploration by librarians in training.[2]

Two Variables: Language and Writing-System

        The practical problem is solved by a special note.
But what is the note about? To answer this we must draw
on the science of linguistics.

        Books are written in languages, and the full descrip-
tion of a book must indicate the languages used in it.   This
dimension of description we might call "lingualism."[3]   It
consists of at least three sets of data: (1) the number of
languages used in a book; (2) their individual specification;
(3) their distribution within the book.   The simplest, and
commonest, "language profile" of an English book is: (1)
one language/(2) English/(3) used throughout.   In cataloging
practice language profiles are sometimes left implicit in the
language of the title, sometimes indicated explicitly by the
title, extended title or printing history, etc., and sometimes
made the subject of a special note.   Manuals of cataloging
regularly deal with this dimension of description, and the
identification of languages is catered to by works of reference
such as Von Ostermann's Manual of Foreign Languages.   The
information is important if only because the identity of the
language or languages of a book or any other piece of writing
determines the range of readers to whom the contents are
accessible at first hand.

        The language, then, of a book is a variable.   But once
that variable is specified we have, within it, a further variable, one which is not regularly dealt with in the manuals or
systematically handled by works of reference.   This sub-vari-
able is the "writing-system," to use the term most widely
current in linguistics.   Our description, "one language/Eng-
lish/used throughout," applies equally to the Bible printed in
the ordinary orthography and to the Bible printed in shorthand,[4] and fails to distinguish between them.   To make this
distinction further information is required about the writing-
system or writing-systems used.   This information is usually
left to be inferred in the case of orthographic variance, and
is usually supplied by a special note in the case of a shorthand version.

        It is easy to see that we have here a sub-dimension,
operating within the dimension of "lingualism," to which the
same considerations apply.   This sub-dimension contains,
for any one language specified in a language profile, at least
three sets of data: (1) the number of writing-systems used
for that language in the book; (2) their individual specifica-

tion; (3) their distribution (within that language) within the book. Our two Bibles are the same as regards lingualism, and they are alike in having a single writing-system used for the main text. But their bibliographical descriptions differ as regards writing-system on all three counts. The ordinary Bible has a simple profile: one writing-system/standard orthography/used throughout; the other Bible has: two writing-systems/standard orthography and Pitman's shorthand/title-page in standard orthography, rest of matter in shorthand.

As with lingualism, the writing-system profiles of books are in cataloging practice sometimes left implicit and sometimes indicated explicitly by the title or extended title (as in the case of Androcles and the lion), or perhaps by the printing history, etc., or made the subject of a special note.[5] There does not, however, appear to be, on the evidence of cataloging manuals and guides, systematic provision for the identification and naming of all the writing-systems, including non-orthographic or non-standard writing-systems, which may be encountered in printed or handwritten books and documents. Yet, as with lingualism, the identity of the writing-system (or -systems) of a book or other piece of writing determines the range of readers to whom the contents are linguistically accessible at first hand. The Authorized Version in Pitman's shorthand may nonplus the devout; the historian may be baffled by stenographic MSS from some 17th-century Member of Parliament or 18th-century missionary.

Kinds of Writing-Systems

We have, then, to explore an unfamiliar multiplicity of writing-systems for English, and to reconcile it with the familiar unity of writing-system presented by the overwhelming bulk of books and documents in English. For there is no denying that in ordinary usage the statement that something is written in English is taken to indicate both the language and the writing-system. (The same is true with regard to other languages.) It is taken to mean that it is written in the ordinary orthography of English--which is that single, uniform writing-system used for books of all sorts, newspapers, other periodicals, documents, correspondence, signs, notices, tickets, jottings, scrawls, graffiti, and so on, throughout the English-speaking world. This writing-system goes under a variety of names among printers, publishers, librarians, educators, and other professionally concerned with

it, and among people in general. [6]   We shall give reasons
for selecting the term "orthography" in due course.

There are two dimensions to this multiplicity of writing-systems for English.

As regards the first, we have pointed to the existence
beside the ordinary orthography of another species of writing-
system, shorthand, which serves a specialized purpose.   It
is easy for people unacquainted with shorthand to underrate
the role it plays in modern society.   We need to be aware
that it is used every day (particularly weekdays) by many
tens of thousands of people in pursuit of ends which affect
us all: commerce, government, the press, the law.   The
course of growth of all these institutions has always depended,
in part, upon written communication; and as an ancillary
means to this, since the 17th century shorthand has had an
important role--in the transcript of proceedings, in other
verbatim reporting, and in the process of correspondence.
As a species of writing-system designed to meet these special purposes, shorthand is constructed for fast writing (usually handwriting), short-term preservation, and limited readership (often only the writer himself).   Its special purpose
gives it special characteristics as a writing-system.   Thus
we have, on the first of our two dimensions, a multiplicity
of species of writing-systems for English, consisting of at
least ordinary orthography and shorthand.

But, of course, shorthand is not a single system.
Since 1588, when Timothy Bright published "the first printed
manual of shorthand in any language,"[7] some 400 systems of
shorthand for English have been published in Britain alone.
Each of these is a writing-system for English, regardless of
whether it died with its designer (as many of them did) or
expanded successfully like Pitman's, most familiar in Britain, or Gregg, most familiar in the U.S.A., both of which
date from the last century.

This, then, is the second dimension of multiplicity:
multiplicity of members of a given species of writing-system.

There is no limit to this second multiplicity: the
flow of newly designed shorthand systems for English, though
not perhaps as abundant as in the heyday of the last century,
has certainly not dried up.   Anyone is free to design a shorthand, and we must bear in mind that the figure given above
relates to published systems only.   Once we accept that the

number of potential writing-systems for English is infinite, the actual phenomena become more tractable. [8] Since there is no limit to the number of shorthands a language may have, there is no limit to the number of writing-systems a language may have. We shift our starting-point, with a vengeance, from apparent unity.

Let us reserve the term "multiplicity" for this more numerous dimension, and return to the first, less numerous, dimension, for which we may more appropriately use the term "plurality."

Whatever the potential range may be, the actual range today is quite small, though greater now than at any earlier epoch of history. As a first venture into this territory, let us tentatively list five species:

Genus: Writing-system

Species: (1) Orthography
           (2) Stenography
           (3) Cryptography
           (4) Paedography (système d'apprentissage)
           (5) Technography (système de métier)

The basis of this classification is the purpose for which the writing-system is used or for which it is designed to be used. It is a classification by function, and we shall refer to its species as "functional kinds," or as "kinds," for short. As we shall see later, this classification cuts across other, more familiar, classifications. The four kinds (2) to (5) have specialized functions, and in this they contrast with kind (1) which has a general function. We shall say a little about these four in turn in this section before returning to orthography in the next section.

The special function of shorthands, or stenographies, has been described above. Giving this kind of writing-system its more technical name, "stenography," will, with "orthography," provide a pattern for a systematic nomenclature.

In accordance with this pattern, the word "cryptography" can be used as a linguistic term to designate those writing-systems which have as their purpose not speed but secrecy. This function makes them slower as a class than orthographies. The typical form taken by cryptographies is that of an orthography plus a cipher--a cipher being a set

of transposition and/or substitution rules which act upon the
sequential symbols (the letters, particularly) of messages in
the orthography. Ciphers can be of any degree of complexity. In recent years institutional cryptology[9] has reached
new levels of complexity following the advent of the electronic computer, together with new levels of rapidity in the three
main processes of cryptology, viz., encipherment, decipher-
ment, and cryptanalysis. But ciphers, though characteristic
of institutional cryptology, are not the only form cryptographies can take. Anyone is free to invent his own cryptography, and it need not be purely parasitic upon the orthography. It may have a direct phonetic element in its structure, as did the elementary system used by the young Bertrand Russell in his private journal. [9] Russell used Greek
characters, but any shapes will do; so that personal cryptographies may be dual-purpose and serve speed and secrecy
at the same time. Obviously any writing-system can act as
a cryptography in appropriate circumstances; but cryptographies, as such, are designed to limit readership to a minimum (which may be one). This is the crucial point of contrast between them and orthographies, which, at least in
modern times, are designed to invite the widest readership.

As to multiplicity, this has always been at a premium
with cryptographies, and contemporary procedures are infinitely productive of different ciphers. In this respect cryptographies are set apart from all the other kinds of writing-
system enumerated above: all are equally capable of multiplicity, but only cryptographies exploit this multiplicity for
its own sake.

With "paedographies" and "technographies" we reach
kinds of writing-system which by and large have evolved
more recently than stenographies and cryptographies. The
two terms provide a tentative analysis (and an even more
tentative nomenclature) of the writing-systems sometimes
referred to as en bloc as "transcriptions," but which serve two
distinct purposes, pedagogical and technical, respectively.

Writing-systems for pedagogical purposes ("paedographies" or "systèmes d'apprentissage") are used in language-
teaching. Language-teaching is either mother-tongue teaching or foreign-language teaching, and paedographies are used
in both. Taking the teaching of English as our example, we
find special writing-systems for English being used in the
teaching of reading. The most notable instance, in the 1960s,
has been "i.t.a.," based on the Initial Teaching Alphabet;[11]

but others exist, and in fact this variety of writing-system
has quite a long history in the teaching of initial literacy in
English, on both sides of the Atlantic. [12] At a later stage in
the mastery of the mother tongue, the spelling of a word may
be known but not its pronunciation, and a characteristic feature of English-language dictionaries is a "key to pronunciation." Such a notation, whether crudely (kroodlee) or expertly designed (/kru:dli/), is a writing-system for English;
and since its purpose is instruction, we class it as a paedography. For foreign learners, pedagogical writing-systems
for English abound, varying from pronunciation notations,
which may be used only for isolated words, to advanced
transcriptions suitable for continuous conversational texts.
In recent years students have become increasingly familiar
with systems which represent English intonation by various
graphic devices modifying either a "phonetic transcription"
or the ordinary orthography.

    Paedographies must suit the literacy of the learner.
The "krood" pronunciation notation is suited, sensibly, to
readers who know only English orthography. A notation
suited to their French counterparts will exploit the sound-
symbol relationships of French orthography (leadership:
"lideurchip"). Where a higher level of bilingualism is expected, notations that are less language-bound are used,
based, for example, on the alphabet of the International Phonetic Association[13]--familiar to many English speakers from
"phonetic transcriptions" of French. The principle of suiting
the literacy of the learner is especially clear in the use of
romanizations in textbooks of "exotic" languages--exotic, that
is, from the point of view of languages whose ordinary orthographies are based on the Roman alphabet. We shall take up
the terms "transliteration," "transcription," and "romanization" in a later section. Here we need only note that it is
common for paedographies to be more easily readable, to the
intended readership, than the corresponding orthography.

    This is not characteristic of our last kind of writing-
system, which we called "technographies" or "systèmes de
métier." Linguists use a great variety of writing-systems
in the analysis and comparison of particular languages and
in the development of general linguistic theory. These range
from impressionistic records of informants' utterances (e.g.,
in unanalyzed languages, or in dialectology), through figure-
substitutions for written characters (in archaeological deci-
pherment, e.g., of Mycenean Greek Linear B), to notations
devised for representing linguistic information not usually

represented in other kinds of writing-system, e.g., the representation of certain grammatical structures and relationships, or of phonological or phonetic constituents, both of
which may require multilinear displays or other graphic devices not found in orthographies.

        Specialist notations of the last sort occur only frag-
mentarily in the literature of linguistics.[14] Technographies
used in scholarly publications, especially where continuous
texts are concerned, are more orthographic in appearance,
and one and the same writing-system may serve both as
technography and as paedography (e.g., romanized Sanskrit).
For, as we have seen already in the case of stenographies
and cryptographies, the five kinds of writing-system do not
constitute five mutually exclusive classes.

        Nor, in conclusion, must the five kinds which we have
listed be taken to be exhaustive. Computers, for instance,
use substitution systems for storage and transmission. Their
purpose is not cryptographic, any more than in the case of
other transmission "codes," such as Morse, which can be
written. Perhaps another functional kind of writing-system
calls for exploration here (to which the name "technography"
might be more appropriately applied?). But this does not
affect the main point of this section, which is that for any
one language there may be any number of writing-systems.
There is first a plurality of species (or kinds) of writing-
systems. The number of members in this plurality is low:
we have enumerated five. Secondly, there is no limit to the
number of members of any of the species. It is obvious
that cryptographies, paedographies, and technographies share
with stenographies this feature of unlimited multiplicity. The
same would certainly be true of the sixth possible kind of
writing-system just mentioned. It is no less true of the
first kind, orthographies, and to this consideration we must
now turn.

Orthographic Multiplicity

        In the last section, as regards orthographies, two
steps were taken: a classificatory one, by which a distinct
species of writing-system which serves the general purposes
of literacy was contrasted with other species which have
more specialized functions: and a terminological one, by
which "orthography" was adopted to designate this species.
Certain implications of the classificatory step will be made

apparent in a later section, when the concept of a writing-system will be described more fully. As to the terminological step, it is enough to point out that this application of the word "orthography" does not conflict with normal usage. If it does not fully coincide with normal usage, this is simply because of its greater precision. Normal usage does not operate with a well-defined general concept of "writing-system" from which various linguistic classifications can flow, but instead jumbles all sorts of writing-systems together--like a cutlery-drawer where the householders haven't decided whether to sort by function, size, source, value, design, or whatever. Nevertheless, normal usage, whatever it means by it, does apply the word "orthography" to those writing-systems which we are here classing as orthographies. For in general it applies the word to the traditional or standard or accepted orthography of a language--doing so easily with orthographies that are comfortably alphabetic, like English or Russian, a little less easily with more exotic ones which may or may not be alphabetic but which certainly have "letters," like Arabic or Sanskrit, and uneasily with ones which are known to be not alphabetic and which don't have "letters," like Chinese.[15] Normal usage is here taking account of internal or structural criteria which we shall look at briefly in the next section. In the meantime we will pursue our external or functional definition of "orthography."

Multiplicity of orthographies exists not only in theory but in practice. Indeed, orthographic multiplicity is the normal state of affairs leading up, in the printing era, to standardization. In the underdeveloped parts of the world, competing orthographies for the same language have been a common phenomenon where European missionary educators, of different (sometimes competing) churches, have been responsible for the the introduction of literacy. Such differences are now being widely resolved with the establishment of national systems of education, which require standardization; but orthographic allegiances can be as strong (cf. British versus American spelling!) as other forms of linguistic loyalty, and recognition of this has been an important factor in orthography design in these countries. In New Guinea, Lutheran and Catholic orthographies for Neo-Melanesian, a pidgin language used for education, were reconciled in the 1950s. A case still awaiting resolution in the 1960s was that of the Somali language, for which several orthographies, some Roman-based, some Arabic-based, were in use, and standardization was the subject of a UNESCO enquiry.[16] Standardization does not always settle for a single uniform

writing-system for a national language. In Yugoslavia we
have the example of Cyrillic and Roman forms of the orthography of Serbo-Croatian used side by side for different social/
geographic groups. In Japan we have the case of two related
writing-systems co-existing for different social purposes;
both these purposes are orthographic rather than belonging
to any other functional kind.[17] These last two examples
demonstrate concurrent multiplicity of standard orthographies.
Where orthographic reform takes place we have successive
multiplicity of standard orthographies--the most famous instance of this being the replacement, for Turkish, of an orthography based on Arabic script by one based on Roman
script. Examples of successive and/or concurrent multiplicity, with varying degrees of standardization, could be multiplied, especially among the linguistic minorities of the
U.S.S.R., where Arabic, Roman, Cyrillic, and other scripts
have served as bases for multiplicity.

It is the process of standardization (especially, but
by no means exclusively, within national states) which produces the unity of which we spoke earlier; and the standardization of the orthography is one part of linguistic standard-
ization--the evolution, by informal or formal procedures, of
a standard language. General literacy demands such standardization of language and of writing-systems. The social
role of standard orthographies is a profoundly important one,
and we shall touch on it again.[18]

The notion of competing orthographies does not apply
to the English language community. This community has
both an extension through the world (embracing many national
states) and a degree of literacy unprecedented in history: it
has been served for over a century and a half, by an orthography to all intents and purposes uniform, stable, and without serious rival throughout that time. Yet, in those same
150 years, probably more orthographies have been designed
for English than for any other language in history. This is
the orthographic multiplicity for English which the librarian
may encounter in the form of Androcles and the lion or of
less exotic systems of what is usually referred to as "spelling reform."

Shaw stood outside the organized spelling reform
movement which developed in the last century and survives
today on both sides of the Atlantic. Shakespeare appeared
in non-standard orthography (not for the first time) in the
Simplified Spelling Society's Hamlet (1946), which continues

in print.[19]   But the heyday of the spelling reform societies
lay on either side of the turn of the century, when interest
and involvement in the movement extended high into the world
of scholarship.   For a time in the 1880s and 1890s the
transactions and proceedings of both the Philological Society
in London and the American Philological Association were
published, in part (at one time the A. P. A. Treasurer's Cash
Account), in non-standard orthographies.   And to this era
belongs that remarkable example of an orthographic proposal
for English which still haunts, in pious survival, the otherwise robust pages of the Decimal Classification and Relative
Index.   Remarkable, that is, in its place, at the heart of
librarianship (and in its duration--that non-orthodox title-
page lasted a whole professional life and more); but not remarkable in its design, which was well in line with that of
the reformers whose cause Melvil Dui (to whom we shall return) espoused.

This is not the place to trace the history of the spelling reform movement in English.   Its impact on the standard
orthography has been virtually nil, yet the notion of spelling
reform is part of the confused stock of ideas about our orthography and spelling (two vaguely interchangeable words)
and indeed about our language (not clearly separated from the
writing-system) which every English literate picks up, at
least in the Anglo-Saxon countries.   All that needs to be said
here is that, as with the other functional kinds of writing-
systems for English, anyone is free to design his own, and
there is no limit to the number of orthographies which the
English language may have designed for it.   There is however a limit, in practice, to the number of orthographies
which the English language community will use, and that limit, for a long time, has been one.   In this respect our language community is typical of language communities in general; and the reduction to one is a process of standardization
normal with any communal artifact, linguistic or non-linguistic.

Orthographies, then, share multiplicity with the other
kinds of writing-system.   But they differ from the others,
socio-linguistically, in two ways: their function is to serve
the general purposes of literacy in a language community--
this characterizes them as orthographies in contrast to the
specialized, sociologically subordinate, functions of the other
kinds; and this function is usually best fulfilled by the establishment of a single standard orthography (whereas with the
other kinds, multiplicity may be tolerable, or desirable, or
even necessary).

In a later section of this paper we shall return to the
role of standard orthographies and their socio-linguistic importance. Before this is done, a number of matters alluded
to but not so far treated, must be briefly dealt with.

Writing-Systems: Typology and Script

The classification of writing-systems into functional
kinds which we have just attempted is only one such linguistic
classification. It is probably the one which, on general theoretical grounds, most concerns the librarian--this is because it is a socio-linguistic classification and it throws into
relief the function of standard orthographies in literate so-
cieties--literacy and standard orthography being part of the
air we all breathe as educated people--but a part which calls
for more analysis than it has yet received either from sociologists or from linguists.

This is not the classification, however, with which
the librarian is likely to be most familiar. He is much more
likely to think of writing-systems in terms only of standard
orthographies (the subset mentioned in the last section), and
to classify these in two ways. The first is by script, the
most obvious visual feature of a writing-system. The second
is by structure, a most unobvious feature visually, though it
may be known from association with script; the script of
Chinese character is easily recognizable (the vertical axis
of the writing may be sufficient clue), and the peculiar structural nature of it is also known under such terms as "pictographic" or "ideographic" or "logographic." We will deal
with script later in this section, after a brief look now at
structural classification.

This is the "alphabetic, query-alphabetic, non-alpha-
betic" classification referred to earlier as structural or internal. It is a "purely linguistic" classification concerning
the relations between the basic symbols of the writing-system
and the basic grammatical-and-lexical units of the language.
The traditional division has been a threefold one, into alphabetic (English, Italian, Russian, Anglo-Saxon, Hawaiian,
Hausa, and a host of others), syllabic (Amharic, Japanese
kana, Sequoiya's Cherokee, Mycencan Linear B, etc.), and
ideographic (Chinese, Japanese kanji, Egyptian hieroglyphic).
The contemporary typology of writing-systems, however, sets
up two main classes, non-phonological and phonological. Chinese is the great example of the first class, in which the

symbols indicate not the pronunciation (phonology) but the basic grammatical and lexical units of the language. This type of structural relation between writing-system and language is sometimes called "morphemic," because the fixed value of each symbol is not a phoneme (or any other phonological unit) but a morpheme. [20] "Non-phonological," though cumbrous, is better ("ideographic" is somewhat frowned upon in this connection and "pictographic" even more so). Writing-systems of the second class also indicate morphemes (as they must if they are to represent language at all), but do so by representing more or less of the phonological form of the morphemes. This is a complicated business because phonologies are complicated; but broadly speaking one basic symbol in the writing-system will represent at the maximum a syllable in the phonology, and at the minimum a phoneme in the phonology. [21] It is this range which gives rise to the traditional division of phonological writing-systems into syllabic and alphabetic (where "alphabetic" means nearly, or not so nearly, phonemic). This traditional typology is based on orthographies and these are rarely, if ever, neatly phonemic. Orthographies keep the morphemes in mind, hence the division of the string of morphemes into words, which aids the identification of the morphemes themselves and of their relations to each other; and hence such features as steel/steal, steal/stealth in English. "Phonetic transcriptions," on the other hand, often aim to be neatly phonemic, although to be readable they usually take over the word-spaces and some other punctuational devices of orthography.

The complexities of the typology of writing-systems concern the linguist engaged in his traditional task of describing languages, the structure of their grammar, semantics, lexis and phonology, and of their writing-systems. We need to note only two points about this classification into structural "types": first that it is independent of the classification into functional kinds and second, that it is independent of "script."

By "independent" we mean "theoretically in free variation." Writing-systems of any kind (functional) can be of any type (structural). Naturally, non-phonological writing-systems are more restricted in their application than phonological ones: hence the vast expansion--part of an evolutionary trend--of phonological writing-systems and the decline of non-phonological ones. But the very first English shorthand, Timothy Bright's, mentioned earlier, was in fact basically non-phonological. Since then, however, English

shorthands have been phonological, though this embraces a
very wide range of designs, from systems modelled on the
standard orthography to systems like Pitman's involving an
original phonological analysis. The advanced style of Pitman's (apart from other devices) omits most vowels--a non-
"neatly phonemic" feature characteristic of Semitic orthographies such as those of Arabic and Hebrew. [22] Orthographies designed in modern times are universally phonological; yet anyone is free to design a non-phonological one,
and Dauzat discovered such an attempt for French. [23] This
freak (and rudimentary) writing-system, like many proposed
orthographies for English, had no social success whatever.
But in describing internal structure we are not concerned
with social success: the two aspects are theoretically independent, though they may be historically related.

The same is true of "script." This word is sometimes used in the sense of "writing-system," but we are
using it more precisely to designate one part of a writing-
system, viz. , the class of physical shapes used for the basic
symbols of a writing-system, e.g. (to take the scripts of
some classical orthographies) Chinese, Devanagari, Arabic,
Hebrew, Greek, Cyrillic, Latin. This is the most easily
recognized feature of any writing-system; it is also the least
important from a structural point of view, since any set of
two-dimensional shapes will do for any writing-system as
long as it furnishes enough distinctive visual contrasts. Thus
one might substitute Chinese character shapes for the simple
geometric shapes in Pitman's shorthand. The writing-system
would not cease to be phonological in type; as to kind, it
would cease to be a very efficient shorthand for English
(though it might serve as a personal cryptography!). Substituting geometric shapes or permutations of alphabetical letters for all the characters of Chinese would likewise not
alter the non-phonological nature of that writing-system
(though some distortion in internal structure would doubtless
occur). This is not to say that scripts do not have enormous
social and practical importance: they do, and a measure of
their importance is the number of disciplines closely concerned with them, e.g. epigraphy, paleography, papyrology,
forensic handwriting analysis, calligraphy, typography, and
in part, descriptive bibliography. As Diringer, Gelb, [24] and
others have pointed out, the study of writing is for the most
part compartmentalized into these various specialized disciplines and requires a unifying theory. Unless the linguistic
nature of writing is recognized, there can be no unifying
theory. And script, for all its importance and its fascina-
tion, is the least linguistic aspect of writing.

Obviously there are close historical associations between families of scripts and families of writing-systems
(just as there are between families of writing-systems and
families of languages). These are social aspects extended
in time, and are, as we have said, independent of internal
structure. During its long history, the cuneiform script
(the product of the particular writing materials, clay and the
reed stylus) was used for non-phonological, semi-phonologi-
cal, and syllabic systems, and finally for an alphabetic one.
The same process of adaptation lies behind the symbols of
our own alphabet, but whereas cuneiform remained unmistake-
ably cuneiform throughout its history because of the constan-
cy of writing materials, successive changes in the technology
of writing have wrought great changes in our script. These
changes were not unconnected with internal changes in successive systems of writing, nor are they unconnected with the
division of disciplines mentioned above.

Writing-Systems: Total Description

A merit of "writing-system" as a general term is
that it is neutral with regard to function (as against, say,
"orthography") and also with regard to typology (as against,
say, "alphabet"). It has the further merit of being abstract--
of being well away from the marks on the paper (as against
"script")--but at the same time embracing both those marks
(writing) and the abstract rules (system) by which they are
related to language. We shall say a little more about abstractness, especially in a later section when we embody
"writing-system" in graphology and graphology in linguistics.
But in this section it is the all-embracingness of the term
which calls for attention.

People speak readily of "the spelling and punctuation
of English." The spelling and punctuation referred to belong,
of course, not to the language as such but to a particular
writing-system, the Standard Orthography of English, which
we will call for short "SOE." "English" indicates the language, "orthography" indicates the functional kind of writing-
system, and "standard" specifies the particular member--the
conventionally/officially accepted one.[25] But the word "orthography" is often used in a narrower sense meaning more
or less the same as "spelling." We must notice that it cannot bear that meaning here. Both spelling and punctuation
belong to orthography. We can usefully desynonymize "orthography" and "spelling," making "orthography" a higher order
term, designating a species of writing-system.[26]

We have now to follow up the implications of this.   If spelling and punctuation are two component parts of our orthography, what other component parts are there (if any)?   In calling SOE a writing-system, what have we committed ourselves to in terms of the totality of features which that term embraces ?

This question bears on a number of practical problems, including that of bibliographical transcribing.   Every written mark is the result of a decision.   Most of the decisions are unconscious ones, taken in accordance with a long-assimilated, smoothly working body of rules; a very small number of them are conscious ones, taken because a problem crops up and has to be dealt with consciously--in accordance with, in defiance of, in ignorance of, or occasionally in the absence of, ready-formulated rules.   Rules of one sort or another govern everything, from the orientation (i.e., the axis and direction) of the writing to the use and misuse of hyphens.   The question is: what is "everything" ?

The only full answer lies presumably in a general theory of writing-systems, which would provide a framework for describing orthographic writing-systems.   In describing SOE, for example, we have at least to include the following potpourri of functions, resources and devices: (1) Spelling: as part (a) of the representation of morphemes, some of which are represented in whole or in part by non-letter elements, and (b) of the concatenation of morphemes into words. (2) Punctuation: as part (a) of a hierarchy of constituent units extending from the highest whole (the book or work) down to the lowest whole (the letters and non-letter elements), and (b) of the marking of grammatical boundaries.   (3) Layout: as a mode of representing the relations between different portions of writing (and between writing and non-linguistic matter).   (4) Serialization devices (numerical, alphabetical). (5) Referral devices (e.g., the asterisk).   (6) Abbreviation devices (acronymic).   (7) Differentiation devices (italics, bold, caps., etc.).   (8) Distinguishing devices (capitalization). (9) Continuity devices (word-break sign, catchwords).   (10) Script: the inventory of elements, details of shapes and shape-variations, and aspects of orientation, giving visual realization to the features in groups (1) to (9).

Of course, there is nothing unfamiliar about these features.   There is nothing unfamiliar about English spelling, yet some of the rules underlying it remain unfamiliar to people highly literate in English. [27]   Nor is the notion of total description itself unfamiliar, since various codifications of SOE, in manuals, grammars, and dictionaries, point in that direction. What is unfamiliar is the idea (and ideal) of a description as something more than a codification--a description being an application of a general theory of writing-systems.

A description, for example, distinguishes between hyphenation and word-breaking, though in printed English, as in handwritten, the same mark is usually (not always) used for both functions. In normal SOE, hyphenation is linguistic; it serves a grammatical purpose, joining items which are grammatically related, and the hyphen-sign occurs only at grammatical boundaries. Word-breaking, on the other hand, has no grammatical purpose; it is not linguistically determined, and whether the wordbreak-sign coincides with a grammatical boundary or not is a matter of typographic, or manuscript, convention, not of meaning. Changes are taking place today in both features. In hyphenation we are prepared to pack what appears between two word-spaces more densely than in the past, making solid what would have been hyphenated and hyphenating what would have been spaced. In word-breaking, the exacting tradition of literacy which demanded the complex British or American printer's rules is giving way to a more pragmatic habit (suited to computer-setting) of breaking words wherever it is physically most convenient. These changes cannot be charted (still less regulated) unless hyphenation and word-breaking are kept distinct;[28] but current discussions perpetuate the terminological confusion which has its origin (like other confusions in this field) in an undue dominance of printer's terminology.

This present discussion of hyphens has application to bibliographical transcribing, mentioned in passing above.

Bibliographical transcribing is one instance of a pervasive activity of literacy, the copying of one piece of writing by means of another. Let us call this activity "copying," for short. A text may start life in handwriting, be typed and then printed, and from the printed version passages may be taken again in handwriting. Between each of these three writing-media lies an act of copying. In this general sense of the word, the printer, the secretary, the clerk, the student, and a host of others including the librarian and the bibliographer (whether analytical or systematic), are constantly engaged in copying. There are three important general variables: writing-medium, writing-system, degree of pre-

cision. The three writing-media mentioned differ from each
other in their resources and constraints: typewriting, for
example, lacks the Roman/italics contrast of print, and the
cursive/non-cursive contrast of handwriting. Acts of copying tend to be conversions from one writing-medium to another, but source and target media may sometimes be the
same. As for the writing-system, this tends to be the same
in source and target; but some copying is complicated by a
change of writing-system. This happens (a) when there are
two distinct writing-systems involved, e. g. , a cataloger ro-
manizing a Russian title page or rendering into SOE some
spelling-reform titles, or the publisher rendering an SOE
text into, say, i.t.a.; and (b) where different stages of the
same historical writing-system are involved, e. g. , the editorial problem of orthographic modernization. Lastly, degree
of precision: copying may be wholesale, as in printing, or
selective, as in note-taking by quotations. In either case
(assuming only SOE is involved) there are two kinds of precision, verbal and orthographic. In rough note-taking, we
select, shorten, simplify, verbally and orthographically, as
we go along, according to ready-made (or readily-made)
rules which we hardly bother to formulate. In printing, the
printer, and in typing, the typist, follow well-formulated
rules, which must work smoothly if speed is to be achieved.
Let us call any such set of rules a "copying system." Full
bibliographical transcribing (the quasi-facsimile treatment
of title pages, for example) is an extreme form of copying,
in which, to full verbal precision, is added a special degree
of orthographic precision. Its purpose is to enable the reader to recover the orthographic form of the original in considerable detail. The copying system must therefore be explicitly known and not left to inference, as Bowers in his
discussion of quasi-facsimile transcription rightly insists. [29]
It must, moreover, be automatic (one might say algorithmic),
within its own stated degree of precision. Selecting that
degree of precision, stating it, and achieving it require, ultimately, as part of their rationale, a total description of
the writing-system of the sort suggested above.

Hyphens are one of the snags of bibliographical transcribing. At least two acts of copying and three versions
of the writing-system are usually involved in making a quasi-
facsimile transcript and seeing it into print. In keeping track
of the hyphens, description of the writing-system (or of a
specific version of it) of the original will decide whether hyphenation and word-breaking are distinguished--whether, for
instance, there are any significant contrasts between single

and double, between long and short, or between slanting and horizontal hyphen-marks. Description of the writing-system (version) to be used in the transcript will help to determine the copying system of the bibliographer, and description of the writing-system (version) to be used by the printer will help, in turn, to determine his copying system. It is this second copying system, part of the instructions to the printer, which must regulate against what Bowers calls "false hyphens."[30]

The problem of knowing whether a hyphen was present in the original is not confined to bibliographical transcripts; it can crop up in any text where the same mark is used for hyphenation and for word-breaking. The general principle by which high typographic quality (and, with it, the authoritative transmission of text) is maintained is that the original orthographic form of a word or item should always be recoverable from any copy. This is not always the case with hyphens; and it is interesting to note that two spelling reformers of the last century were orthographic reformers in this respect. Both A. J. Ellis and R. G. Latham published texts in which, where an item was broken at a hyphenated boundary, two hyphen-marks were printed, one at the end of the first line, and one at the beginning of the second line.[31] It was presumably the hyphenation sign which was carried over.

Writing-systems are made up of minutiae, linguistic minutiae. The description of writing-systems, of how they work internally, as systems, is one task for the linguist; another is the investigation of how such systems work externally, in society. Although language description has always been the central discipline of linguistics, it has never been the only one. Perhaps, in what follows, it may be seen that more than one branch of linguistic science is of interest to library science.

Orthographic Unity

After exploring the unfamiliar multiplicity of writing-systems, we come to the familiar unity, the all-pervasiveness of SOE in the English-language community. For most English literates, the language and its orthography are so indissolubly linked as to be identified; the orthodox orthography has no name; it is "English." And a high value is set on orthodoxy, too; spelling and punctuation matter.

This socio-linguistic dominance of the standard orthography is not peculiar to the English language community.
Orthographic standardization is one aspect of language standardization, and language standardization underlies the creation of the modern mass-society with mass-literacy. It is
the function of a standard orthography, as of the standard
language it serves, to work smoothly for millions of people
in the multitudinous uses to which they put language and writing. Not all such uses, because a tiny proportion of them
require special writing-systems ancillary to the orthography;
but the development, discussion, and dissemination of these
is carried on in the orthography, as is the development, discussion, and dissemination of every other institution, instrument or skill that a literate society needs, and which is not
passed on by purely oral or physical means. In short, the
orthography serves the general purposes of literacy. The
special functions of the "paradoxical" writing-systems are
so specialized that the quantity of "paradoxical" writing to
be stored is infinitesimal in comparison with the quantity
stored in "orthodox" writing. Except for libraries and collections specially concerned with such things as spelling reform, shorthand, cryptology, and language-study, the problem from which this paper started is a quite peripheral one.

Yet, if from our discussion the standard orthography
emerges as something saisissable, with limits definable between it and the language on the one hand, and between it
and other writing-systems on the other, and as a system
having its own totality of features which need charting, then
our exploration will not have been in vain.

In considering the unity of SOE--the existence of a
single orthography throughout the English-speaking world--
we must note also its uniformity. Variations exist within
it, but, as in the case of British versus American spelling,
uniformity utterly outweighs variety. And this is true of all
the other features which go to make up the total orthography.
Where variations appear to abound in respect of, say, differentiation or abbreviation or capitalization (see any collection of house style manuals), one can be fairly certain that
uniformity is in fact growing. As the core of uniformity
expands, of course, the periphery of variety expands with it;
but one must not let the flickering edge distract one's view
from the steady massive center.

Let us illustrate orthographic unity and uniformity
with one feature from the steady center, a feature which

pervades modern life, making mass administration possible not only of books, but also of people. This feature is the alphabet of SOE. The alphabet is the letter inventory, with the elements arranged in a fixed order known to every English literate. There are other serialization devices in the orthography (the numbers, par excellence), but this is the device which matters for ordering and storing the ordinary names of things--people, places, everything. In combination with standard names and standard spellings of these names, the alphabet is the backbone of information storage and retrieval. [32] This is one of the functions of a standard orthography. And yet, as we shall see before we end, it has at times been curiously overlooked.

Graphology: A Linguistic Summary

It is perhaps opportune to present, in this section, a condensed summary of the linguistic approach to the phenomenon of writing which has been utilized in this paper.

Writing is one of the two normal media of language, the other being speech, with which we are not at present concerned. As a word, "writing" has two drawbacks: it has a wide range of meanings, and it lacks a derivative adjective. To remedy both defects and to provide a parallel to phonology (the study of language in the medium of speech), let us now bring in the term "graphology" (the study of language in the medium of writing), which we have been groping for in the earlier sections. [33] The linguistic study of writing warrants its own technical name, for writing is a medium of language in its own right. The notion of writing as a "mirror of speech," while it may have some figurative meaning with reference to certain kinds of transcription, is highly misleading with reference to orthographies. It is no compliment or conceptual help to librarians to suggest that they spend their lives among second-rate objects, surrogates for speech. The medium of writing is used in situations and for purposes for which speech will not do; and speech will not do, on its own, to organize civilization.

The key term within graphology is "writing-system." A writing-system for a language L is essentially a system of rules by which sentences of L can be expressed in writing. Two points need to be noted. First, that a writing-system really is as abstract as that. Writing is meaningful; and the rules which link the printed text of a Bible to its meaning

are the same as those which link the label DRINK ME to its
meaning: if they are not known, the writing is not understood. Secondly, writing-systems are language-particular:
a writing-system for language L cannot be a writing-system
for language M. Two writing-systems, WSL for L, and
WSM for M, may have all sorts of resemblances (script,
alphabet, values of letters, patterning of groups of letters,
etc.), but they cannot be the same, for the system of rules
constituting WSL start from the morphemes of L, and the
system of rules constituting WSM start from the morphemes
of M. Many of the rules may be similar, and it would be
absurd to discount the high degree of resemblance existing
between the standard orthographies of, for example, the languages of Western Europe. Such resemblance is an important cultural phenomenon. But a separate term is needed to
designate this collectivity (perhaps "system of writing"?) in
order not to erode the precision of "writing-system."

The graphology of a language L may include any number of writing-systems. But graphology is only one part of
linguistics--that is, of the scientific study of language--and
it is appropriate now, as we have already discussed writing-
systems, to place the study of graphology in relation to the
rest of linguistics.

For convenience, let us divide contemporary linguistics
into three main branches, with the more recently established
and named branches, socio-linguistics and psycho-linguistics,
flanking the traditional discipline of linguistics, which we will
distinguish, for the nonce, as "centro-linguistics." The two
axes of scientific inquiry, synchronic (descriptive) and diachronic (historical), exist for all three branches, as do the
two levels of scientific activity, the pure and the applied.

Socio-linguistics is the study of language in society.
One aspect of it is the construction of socio-linguistic profiles for social units such as nations, showing the number
of languages used, their distribution in the population, and
the purposes for which they are used (administration, religion, ethnic groups, etc.). An important (though neglected)
facet of such profiles is literacy, a vital determinant in
cultural development. From this aspect of socio-linguistics
we have derived the notions of "linguistic profile" and of
"lingualism," of which more will be said in the rest of this
section. The historical study of literacy as a social phenomenon includes its growth within societies (especially the historically recent phenomenon of universal literacy promoted

and maintained by education systems), its diffusion from society to society, and its evolution (the relating of changes in literacy to other cultural changes, e.g., urbanization and industrialization). The development of the library, as a central institution of literacy, belongs here, in socio-linguistics, where sociology and linguistics meet.

Literacy is made possible by the existence of writing as a medium of language. There are two (socio-linguistically) normal media of language: speech and writing. The use of language in the medium of speech is acquired spontaneously; in writing, non-spontaneously (all education systems begin with literacy teaching).

The central discipline of linguistics ("centro-linguistics") studies language and its media in general and languages and their spoken and written forms in particular. A common division into "levels" of linguistic analysis is: semantics, grammar (syntax and lexis), phonology and phonetics--to which must be added, unless literacy (and libraries) are to be left out of account, graphology and graphetics.[34] Phonology studies the sound-structure of languages, phonetics the physical sounds. This is the basis of the distinction just introduced between graphology, the study of writing-systems in terms of their structure, and graphetics, the study of the physical marks of writing. Just as phonetics studies a particular class of sounds because they are phonologically structured, so graphetics studies a particular class of visible marks because they are graphologically structured. Graphetics brings together all manifestations of writing, whatever the mode of production (manual, mechanical) and whatever the materials (marks on paper, polyvinylchloride, stone or baked clay). The intensive study these marks have received in paleography and typography (and associated disciplines) derives from their linguistic nature. The reflex of this is that non-linguistic marks are excluded from graphetics. Not all the graphic content of a book is linguistic: the proportion of linguistic to non-linguistic is a variable, which we may think of as "linguacy." This adds a fundamental dimension to the notion of "linguistic profile." In the centro-linguistic application of this notion to a unit such as a book, the dimension of linguacy will distinguish between linguistic and non-linguistic contents (as a bibliographical description must do; some books, of course, may have zero-linguacy), and the dimension of lingualism will apply only to the former. The language-medium of a book is (by definition) writing and the "writing-system profile" dis-

cussed near the beginning of this paper is the first and
broadest application of graphology in a bibliographical description; it may be followed by detail about the individual
writing-system(s) at the graphological level, and that in turn,
by detail at the graphetic level.   This is the fully explicit
theoretical sequence, which in practice is condensed.

    Graphology, then, belongs to "centro-linguistics."
Its place there simply follows upon the recognition of writing
as a medium of language.   The importance assigned to it,
on the other hand, follows upon the importance which people
attach to literacy.   Under its sociological aspect, literacy is
now receiving increasing attention from economic and educational historians and planners.   But it is perhaps the recognition of its psychological importance in the individual that will
set the study of literacy on its proper footing.   Psycho-linguistics, where psychology and linguistics meet, is a young
science and has not yet given much attention to literacy; but
it is this branch of linguistics (or of psychology, depending
on one's direction of approach) which will make the greatest
contribution to our understanding of man's faculty of lan-
guage--how much of his intellectual or cognitive development
is mediated by language, and how much of his linguistic development is mediated by literacy.

    Whereas "centro-linguistics" is concerned with lan-
guage-media, psycho-linguistics is concerned with language
skills.   The notion of linguistic profile can be applied here,
too, to the individual.   Linguacy covers the language-media
and the degree of language-ability in each medium; lingualism
covers specification of languages; a graphological profile covers specification of writing-systems.   The basic skills of
literacy are reading and writing--the taking in and the giving
out of language in the medium of writing.   Asymmetry often
exists between the two skills: a person may be able to read
other writing-systems for English, besides SOE, without being able to write them, just as one may acquire a "reading
knowledge" of a second language--unaccompanied by any comparable ability in that language in the medium of speech, but
unaccompanied also (hence skill-asymmetry) by any comparable ability to write it.   The degree of such reading ability
may be highly restricted--to the language of title pages, for
example--yet still constitute a highly serviceable form of
bilingualism.   The expression "reading knowledge" reminds
us that language skills are cognitive as well as physical:
normal literacy requires knowledge of a standard language,
knowledge of its standard orthography, and knowledge of the

technical concepts of literacy (such as, in English, "letter," "alphabet," "spelling"). [35] The first two of them, at least, must be components of the linguistic competence which operates alike in reading and in writing.

Socio-linguistic factors determine the need to transfer title-page information with or without change of language, with or without change of writing-system. Psycho-linguistic factors determine a person's ability to perform this operation. But as the main theme of this contribution has been "centrolinguistic," we will end this summary with our postponed graphological question: what are transliteration, transcription, and romanization?

None of these words appeared as the name of a functional kind or structural type, yet all three are predicated of writing-systems and are of considerable importance. They have in common a flavor of secondariness which accounts for their juxtaposition, "transliteration" being coupled with "transcription"[36] on the one hand and with "romanization" on the other. But "romanization" contains an intrinsic specification of script which is absent from the meaning of the other two. Both a transliteration and a transcription may use Roman script; or they may not--they may be Cyrillicizations or Hebraicizations or whatever. Conversely, to indicate the script of a writing-system by calling it a romanization is to say nothing about its status as a transliteration or transcription.

The common distinction between these two--transliterations are based on symbols, transcriptions on sounds--is sustained by the linguist's use of the latter term. This can be summed up as follows. Transcriptions have to do with sounds: typologically they are always phonological writing-systems, functionally they are paedographies or technographies which have as one of their objects to exhibit phonological structure in some particular way. The standard orthography of English, though it belongs to the phonological type of writing-system in respect of its structure, notoriously fails as a straightforward indicator of pronunciation. Hence the many transcriptions of English, referred to earlier, which analyze the phonology of the language independently of the orthography. Phonological independence of orthographies is the keynote of transcriptions. A transcription of English exhibits the phonology of English in a different way from the way the orthography exhibits it; a transcription of Chinese exhibits the phonology of Chinese, whereas the orthography of Chinese, the traditional character, does not exhibit it at all; and a tran-

scription of an "unwritten" language exhibits the phonology of
that language in the absence of any orthography whatever.

A transliteration, in contrast to a transcription, contains no independent structural features; its relation to orthography is one of derivation not of independence. As a writing-
system, a transliteration consists of an underlying writing-
system plus a system of symbol-substitution. Such changes
of script, as is well known, are not always simple one-to-one
affairs, but script-change is the essential object of a transliteration.

The flavor of secondariness which all three terms considered here have in common arises from their application
to ancillary kinds of writing-system as opposed to orthographies. It is intensified in the case of "romanizations" (and
parallel terms for other script-changes) because this implies
the prior existence of another writing-system, normally an
orthography, and because it relates only to the level of script.
"Transliteration" adds to this the low structural status of being derivative. But structural (centro-) factors and functional
(socio-) factors are independent of each other. A writing-
system can start life as a transcription and be adopted as an
orthography fitted out with all the orthographical trappings of
differentiation, abbreviations, fixed alphabetical order, and
so on; in the right socio-linguistic conditions the same could
happen to a transliteration, which is often already equipped
with some of the trappings. We have, after all, still to ask
ourselves the obvious question: to which of the five functional kinds does a bibliographical transliteration belong? It is
not a linguist's technography, nor a language-teacher's paedography, nor a secretary's stenography; and although it may
resemble in its derivativeness a diplomatic cipher, it cannot
be a cryptography because its purpose is not frustration but
facilitation in reading. We may conclude, giving a new twist
to orthographic multiplicity, that bibliographical transliterations are secondary orthographies, designed to suit the literacy of non-native users of a language.

The flavor of derivativeness, then, rightly belongs
only to transliterations, which are essentially parasitic writing-systems like cipher cryptographies. If "transcription"
ever has a derivative flavor, it is possibly by contamination
with "transcription" in the purely bibliographical ("copying")
sense. Transcriptions in the linguistic sense are structural-
ly independent like the second sort of cryptographies mentioned earlier. Here as elsewhere, bibliographical and lin-

guistic terminologies are, with a little care, separable and reconcilable, to the benefit of both disciplines. 37

Conclusion

> And for ther is so greet diversitee
> In English and in wryting of our tongue,... 38

From the cataloger's point of view, the problem we began with was a peripheral one. Most libraries contain no material in non-orthodox writing-systems; and few contain it in any but trifling quantity. A very few specialized libraries must deal with non-orthodox as a matter of course; some libraries, in some parts of the world, must be coping with orthographic diversity while awaiting the standardization which nowadays hangs on governmental decisions of language policy. From this last socio-linguistic situation--so greet diversitee-- librarianship in the English-speaking world has been happily free, for it came of age in the Dewey era, SOE already thoroughly standardized, several centuries after Chaucer. For the cataloger in this situation, non-orthodox material represents a very tiny leak in the system. One can envisage a reference compendium of Writing-Systems for English (WSEs) in which, at least, published stenographies, paedographies and proposed orthographies were collected, classified by kind, and individually identified and described. But this might be taking a tank to a trickle. A special note does, and will continue to do.

But from the classifier's point of view, the question we posed--what is the special note about?--is, we hope, at least a pregnant one. In this contribution, it prompted an exploration into the linguistic concept of "writing-system." This led (not surprisingly) to a piece of classification, to a piece (again not surprisingly) of interdisciplinary classification, namely, the socio-linguistic classification of writing-systems by function. This, in turn, provided a contrastive background against which standard orthography and its role in society could be seen and studied.

The concept of standard orthography is not peripheral to librarianship but absolutely central. Melvil Dewey failed to grasp it. If one reads Dewey's article "Simpler speling reazons and rules," which first appeared in the 12th edition of the famous Classification (1927), one finds bad psycholinguistics about how we learn and how we operate mentally

with SOE, worse centro-linguistics about how the spelling system of SOE works, and, worst of all, an attempt to assimi-
late orthography to transcription, as though their socio-linguistic functions were not distinct. It is not only orthography
which Dewey misconceived but standardization. When one
understands the force of standardization (and Dewey did, with
one part of his mind), one can see why "reform" made so
little headway in the Index, where standard spelling and alpha-
betization really mattered. One can see, too, why the article bore so little relation to the pioneering Introduction which
it followed, apart from the superficial resemblance of being
printed in the same non-orthodox orthography.

To the documentalist we have offered very little.
"There is more to the intellectual content of librarianship
than was dreamed of by Melvil Dewey." We have illustrated
the truth of these words of Dean Shera in one facet only.
Librarianship is concerned with "graphic records," and we
have concentrated on the word "graphic" to the exclusion of
the word "record." Yet linguistics is about messages as
well as media, for it is about the mind of man no less than
about the noises he makes with his mouth and the marks he
makes with his hands. The structure of language tells us
something about the structure of man's mind. The structure
of meaning tells us something about the structure of man's
knowledge. Contemporary work in general linguistic theory,
especially in semantic theory, is of much more fundamental
significance than the mainly graphological offering which we
have been able to make.

Alice, after her long vertical fall, had some difficulty
with the horizontal movement required by the small door.
So it may be with the education of librarians. The horizontal
mode takes some adjusting to. No one knows better than
Dean Shera that over the general sciences of man semantics
is an arch wherethrough knowledge meets knowledge.

Notes

1. Harmondsworth, Middlesex, Penguin Books, 1962.
2. As a non-librarian, privileged to contribute to this
    volume, my sense of privilege is equalled only by
    my sense of apprehension. My thanks are due to
    Professor Conrad Rawski, editor of this volume, Dr.
    Merald Wrolstad, editor of Visible Language, and
    Mr. John Farrell, sub-librarian of the University

of Bristol Library, for much help and encouragement.

3. A back-formation, for the nonce, from "bilingualism,
multilingualism."

4. The Holy Bible containing the Old and New Testaments.
Authorised Version. Lithographed in the Easy Reporting Style of Pitman's Shorthand. "Twentieth Century
Edition." (London, Sir Isaac Pitman & Sons, Ltd.;
Bath, N.Y., no date). The title page is in the standard orthography. Had it been in the writing-system
of the main text, it would not have been readable by
the ordinary literate. Contrast The Holy Bible containing the Old and New Testaments: According to
the Authorised Version, Arranged in paragraphs and
parallelisms, and printed phonetically. (London,
Fred Pitman, Phonetic Depot, 20 Paternoster Row,
1850), where the whole of the title page, just quoted,
appears in a non-orthodox but readable orthography.

5. The British Museum has a valuable holding of non-orthodox material, and it is interesting to take as an
example of a cataloging code the Rules for Compiling
the Catalogues of Printed Books, Maps and Music in
the British Museum (London, British Museum, 1936,
reprinted 1960). Provision is made in Rule 29, entitled "Minor Points Noted in the Description," for
noting "The language or languages in which the book
is written, if necessary," but no mention is made of
the writing-system or writing-systems either in Rule
29 or in Rule 32 which deals with Notes "concerning
points not already dealt with in Rules 25-29." Writing-systems are, of course, made the subject of
Notes, as we have seen already in connection with
The Deseret First Book. Mention is made, in Rule
29, of Black Letter and Gothic Letter; and it is perhaps advisable, in view of the natural interest of the
descriptive bibliographer in type fonts and faces, to
stress that one writing-system (as we shall use the
term in this paper) can be realized in any number of
typographic variants or manuscript variants. We use
the same standard orthography of English in handwriting, typewriting, and printing.

6. "Orthography, script, alphabet, spelling, writing, print"
qualified by "conventional, ordinary, standard, traditional," etc.

7. Characterie. / An Arte / of shorte, swifte, / and
secrete wri- / ting by Charac- / ter. / Jnvented by
Timothe / Bright, Doctor of / Phisike. / [Ornament]

/ Jmprinted at London by / I. Windet, the Assigne /
of Tim. Bright. / 1588. / Cum priuilegio Regiæ
Maiestatis. / Forbidding all other to print / the
same.
       For Timothy Bright and his Characterie, see
W. J. Carlton's Bibliotheca Pepysiana volume, from
which the transcript and the quotation are taken (p. 1
and p. 2 respectively): A Descriptive Catalogue of the
Library of Samuel Pepys. Part IV. Shorthand Books.
With biographical and bibliographical notes by William
J. Carlton (London, Sidgwick & Jackson, Ltd., 1940).
       A chronological list of English shorthand sys-
tems published in the United Kingdom from 1588 to
1950 will be found in the Appendix (p. 231-42) to
E. H. Butler's The Story of British Shorthand, London,
Pitman, 1951. See also R. C. Alston, A Bibliography
of the English Language from the Invention of Printing
to the Year 1800, Volume VIII: Treatises on Short-
hand, Leeds, England, printed for the author by E. J.
Arnold & Son, Ltd., 1966; this was reviewed by W. J.
Carlton in The Journal of Typographic Research, 1
(July 1967), 331-35.

8.   This is not uncommon in linguistics: compare grammar,
     where there is no limit to the length of sentences, and
     hence an infinite number of sentences in any language.
     Recognition of this fact, especially since Chomsky's
     Syntactic Structures (1957), has made the approach to
     syntax more realistic.

9.   The vast institutional proportions attained by modern
     cryptology are described in David Kahn, The Code-
     breakers: The Story of Secret Writing, London,
     Weidenfeld and Nicholson, 1966.

10. The Autobiography of Bertrand Russell. 1872-1914,
     London, Allen & Unwin, 1967, 41. The young Beatrix
     Potter also kept a journal in a personal cryptography:
     see The Journal of Beatrix Potter, Transcribed from
     Her Code Writing by Leslie Linder, London, F.
     Warne, 1966. Pepys wrote his Diary in Shelton's
     tachygraphy (1635), which, like Bright's charactery,
     claimed the merits of both speed and secrecy. The
     daughter of a friend of the present writer uses "Shaw's
     alphabet" for cryptographic purposes at school.

11. Several of Beatrix Potter's stories have been published
     in i. t. a., including The Tale of Peter Rabbit, London,
     Frederick Warne, i. t. a. Edition, 1965, title page
     partly in non-orthodox writing-system. The extent of
     publication in this writing-system can be gauged from

the National Book League's exhibition booklet, The
Initial Teaching Alphabet: Books for the Teacher and
Child, selected by John Downing, London, National
Book League, 1965.

12. For a survey, see John Downing, Evaluating the Initial
Teaching Alphabet: A Study of the Influence of Eng-
lish Orthography on Learning to Read and Write,
London, Cassell, 1967, and more recently, by the
designer of i.t.a., Alphabets and Reading: the Initial
Teaching Alphabet by Sir James Pitman, K.B.E., and
John St. John, London, Pitman, 1969.

13. The organ of the International Phonetic Association, entitled since 1886 Le Maître Phonétique, provides an
example of a periodical publication in a non-orthographic writing-system. The common abbreviation of
the title is m.f., derived from the "phonetic" form.
(Note also the absence of capitalization.)

14. See, for example, Chomsky and Halle, The Sound Pattern of English, New York, Harper & Row, 1968.

15. A reference to the traditional writing-system of Chinese
as "Chinese orthography" occurs in one of Sir Isaac
Pitman's Spelling Reform pamphlets, "Report of a
Public Meeting on Spelling Reform" held at the Adelphi
Rooms, May 29, 1877, 3.

16. B.W. Andrzejewski, S. Strelcyn, J. Tubiana, Somalia:
The Writing of Somali, Paris, UNESCO, 1966 (reproduced from typescript).

17. The number of orthographic writing-systems in use in
Japan is variously reckoned; it is often given as four.
But two is sufficient for our illustration: the traditional literary orthography in which non-phonological lexical symbols (kanji) are supplemented by phonological
syntactic symbols, and a less literary orthography in
which phonological symbols function alone. Japanese
ciphers, highly developed in World War II, were based
on the phonological syllabary (kana) or on romanizations (see Kahn, op. cit.).

18. A good survey will be found in Paul L. Garvin, "The
Standard Language Problem: Concepts and Methods,"
in Dell Hymes, ed., Language in Culture and Society:
A Reader in Linguistics and Anthropology, New York,
Harper & Row, 1964, 521-526; and for an illuminating
case-history of orthographic standardization in minia-
ture (for the language of Ponape, Eastern Carolines),
see Garvin's "Literacy as a Problem in Language and
Culture" in Report of the 5th Annual Round Table
Meeting on Linguistics and Language Teaching, ed.

H. J. Mueller, Washington, D. C.: Georgetown University Press, 1954, 117-129. For a valuable reappraisal of an established orthography and its rôle, see R. Thimonnier, Le Système Graphique du Français: Introduction à une Pédagogie Rationelle de l'Orthographe (Paris, Plon, 1967).

19. Shakspeer'z Hamlet: A Vurshon in Nue Speling. Edited bie P. A. D. MacCarthy, M. A. Publisht on behaaf ov dhe Simplified Speling Sosiëty bie Sur Iezak Pitman & Sunz, Ltd., Lundon, 1946. (Title page in Nue Speling).

20. The general meaning of this key-term in linguistics can be illustrated from English. The item "home-truths" consists of four morphemes: home - true - th - s. Home and true are lexical morphemes (one finds them in the dictionary); th and s are grammatical morphemes (one finds them in a grammar)--th as in warmth, growth, death, and s as in cats, dogs, horses (corresponding, be it noted, to three different sounds in the phonology). It is easy to visualize arbitrary, nonphonological characters (such as "&" for and, used on the title page of the Nue Speling Hamlet, quoted in the last note) for the grammatical morphemes, which are limited in number. It is less easy to visualize a whole corpus of such characters for the thousands of lexical morphemes in a language. But such morpheme symbolization works extremely well in the case of the traditional Chinese orthography.

21. In the phonology, syllables are analyzed into vowel phonemes and consonant phonemes. The simplest view of "phoneme," then, is that it is the general term for the class constituted by these two familiar sub-classes. Cat has three phonemes, cats has four; death, likewise, has three phonemes, deaths has four.

22. A Hebrew paedography may differ from the standard orthography in just this respect: it may have the vowels fully represented.

23. A. Dauzat, "Une Curiosité Graphique: Un Alphabet Hiéroglyphique Français sous Louis-Phillippe," Le Français Moderne,   (1947), 215-216.

24. D. Diringer, Writing, London, Thames and Hudson, 1962; I. J. Gelb, A Study of Writing, rev. ed., Chicago, University of Chicago Press, 1963.

25. What, incidentally, is its legal status?

26. We must notice also that "spelling" is not a suitable candidate for the wider sense of "orthography," since it can hardly be stretched to include punctuation in its meaning.

27. Take for example the spelling of "their." This is an instance of the widespread rule whereby i replaces y before a suffix (they-r, cf. you-r). The i/y interchange is itself an instance of the rule which runs right through the spelling system of SOE that at a morpheme boundary, the morpheme on the left is susceptible to change, not the morpheme on the right. Knowing how to spell is like other aspects of linguistic knowledge: the knowledge need not be conscious knowledge. In this sense we operate rules which are unfamiliar to us.

28. No distinction is made, for example, in Arthur H. Phillips, Computer Peripherals and Typesetting, London, H.M.S.O., 1968, 25-28, where the heading "Hyphenation" introduces a (nonetheless) useful account of efforts to overcome "the difficulty of writing adequate word-breaking programs for the English language" [p. 25], cf. "Means of Machine Hyphenation." There are two different approaches which have been explored to develop computer word-breaking; one is a dictionary look-up in which all the acceptable break points have been recorded and the other is to formulate a set of rules based on word structure. This second method is said to use a 'hyphenation algorithm.' The algorithmic method encounters several difficulties in dealing with the English language. The most simple algorithm for word breaking is based on the occurrence of vowels and consonants" [p. 26]. It may be the case that a distinction is being maintained between the two terms within typesetting terminology; linguistically, however, only the problem of word-breaking is under consideration. The problem of hyphenation in SOE is aptly illustrated, as it happens, by the treatment of the item "word-breaking" itself in the sentence just quoted; the same discrepancy with the same item, with no grammatical justification, appears towards the bottom of p. 25.

29. F. Bowers, Principles of Bibliographical Description, Princeton, N.J., Princeton University Press, 1949, chap. 4.

30. F. Bowers, op. cit., p. 179.

31. A.J. Ellis, A Plea for Phonetic Spelling, 2nd ed., London, F. Pitman, 1848; R.G. Latham, A Defence of Phonetic Spelling, London, Fred. Pitman; Bath, Isaac Pitman, 1872. It is worth remembering that both Ellis and Latham were considerable linguistic scholars. The linguistic problem is the same as that which Bow-

ers mentions as a special case of the "false hyphen" in bibliographical quasi-facsimile transcripts. The problem is not confined to copying, of course: it is one of comprehension. For an example of a recently proposed solution, see Carl Dair, Design with Type (London, Benn, 1968), and his "fracture," a mark for wordbreak distinct from the hyphen-mark. The reviewer of this book in the Times Literary Supplement (Aug. 15, 1968), acknowledging the problem as a real one, did not himself wholly escape the ambiguity which crops up, occasionally crucially, with the traditional hyphen--is it a hyphen-hyphen or a wordbreak-hyphen?

32.   See J. Metcalfe, Alphabetical Subject Indication of Information, New Brunswick, N.J., Rutgers University Press, 1965.

33.   The linguistic use of "graphology" will be found in A. McIntosh, " 'Graphology' and Meaning," Archivum Linguisticum, 13 (1961), 107-120; M.A.K. Halliday, A. McIntosh, and P. Strevens, The Linguistic Sciences and Language Teaching, London; Longmans, 1964; W.N. Francis, The English Language: An Introduction, New York; W.W. Norton, 1963; and elsewhere.

34.   "Graphetic and graphological categories and terminology, at least as developed as those of phonetics and phonology, are clearly needed, if we do not consider any 'representational' relationship to be essential between speech and writing." T.F. Mitchell, "Syntagmatic Relations in Linguistic Analysis," Transactions of the Philological Society, 1958, 102, n. 1.

35.   For a delightful revelation of the importance of these elementary concepts, see J.F. Reid, "Learning to Think about Reading," Educational Research, 9 (Nov. 1966), 56-62.

36.   We are using "transcription" only in the "writing-system" sense and not in the "text" sense or the "act" sense. This is why we were obliged earlier to speak of a transcribed text as a "transcript," the product of an act of transcribing.

37.   The general linguistic point of view we have been putting forward should be congenial to the increasingly international outlook and practice of librarians. A straw in the wind is the change in the terminology of the Anglo-American Cataloguing code: "transliteration tables--or romanization tables as they are now called...." T.E. Allen & D.A. Dickman, eds., New Rules for an Old Game, Vancouver, University of British Columbia, 1967, 94.

38. Chaucer, <u>Troilus and Criseyde</u>, as quoted in Shera's notes, <u>Documentation</u>..., viii.

VI.   FORECAST

"But much more would be gained if memory were not
the only source of knowledge."

J. H. Shera, <u>Historians...</u>, 101.

"The librarian, like Shelley's West Wind, is both 'destroyer and preserver'; or to use Grayson Kirk's
phrase, 'critic and architect.' Preserver he has always been; it is in the role of destroyer that he feels
less secure. 'To serve society is a noble calling,'
say the librarians; but society must constantly change,
reshape itself, struggle with new problems. 'Here
below to live is to change,' wrote Cardinal Newman,
and that which once served society may no longer be
useful. In a world of mingled menace and promise,
the winds of change blow as surely through the library
stacks as they do through the corridors of the United
Nations or the chambers at No. 10 Downing Street.
The librarian, therefore, must be both critic and ar-
chitect--destroyer of that which is obsolete and builder
of his own future. If he is not, his responsibilities,
the opportunity to serve society in which he takes so
much pride, will pass to other more competent hands."

J. H. Shera, <u>Documentation...</u>, 95 f.

INNOVATION IN LIBRARIES:
EFFECT ON FUNCTION AND ORGANIZATION*

Robert S. Taylor

"But it is notorious that adopting new means

---

*Work on this paper was supported in part by the U. S.
Office of Education under Grant No. OEG 1-7-071180-4351 and
by a grant from the Educational Facilities Laboratory.

in order to better accomplish old ends very
often results in the substitution of new ends
for old ones."
                    E.G. Mesthene, "How Technology
                    Will Shape the Future," Science,
                    161 (July 12, 1968), 141.

The quotation above illustrates the dilemma that libraries will soon face--the break with a long tradition and a
redefinition of objectives.   This will not happen suddenly.
It is happening, and one year the profession will realize that
its purpose is no longer "the theory and practice of bibliographical control."[1]   Rather, the librarian will find that he
has a different kind of institution, with different kinds of
demands on it, with different kinds of processes in it--an
institution he may not be prepared to deal with.   It is a bit
like the story of the railroad magnate who was approaching
bankruptcy until one day he suddenly realized he was not in
the railroad business, but in the transportation business.
This changed his whole approach and his conception of the
kinds of problems he had to solve.   It may be that librarians
are no longer in the "book business" but in the communication
business.

It is neither daring nor unconventional--in fact it is
rather banal--to assert that libraries have changed, are
changing, and will change.   The point is that most such assertions stop when this has been said, except for those
flights of fancy that tell us what the library will be like some
time in the future.   And by the way these imaginative flights
closely resemble today's libraries, which makes such fancies
rather suspect.   Neither these assertions nor future fancies
tell us anything about the road between "here" and "there."

This paper, then, is an exploration of the kinds of
questions we should ask and of the options open or closed to
the profession as the institutional base changes.   We cannot
expect solid answers, for at present there are too many undefined economic, educational, and cultural variables for any
high degree of confidence.   Our problem, then, becomes one
of defining the pertinent questions, and of formulating the
framework of those questions and of the kinds of answers we
can anticipate; what we know with reasonable assurance and
what we do not know, because this is the only basis upon
which we can plan future libraries and present education.
As Bertrand de Jouvenel has said in his extremely pertinent
work on conjecture:

The reason why we give forecasts is not that we know how to predict: decision-makers mislead the public if they suggest to it, or even so much as allow it to think, that this is so. We do not make forecasts out of presumption, but because we recognize that they are a necessity of modern society. And for my part, I would willingly say that forecasting would be an absurd enterprise were it not inevitable. We have to make wagers about the future; we have no choice in the matter. We are forever making forecasts--with scanty data, no awareness of method, no criticism, and no cooperation. It is urgent that we make this natural and individual activity into a cooperative and organic endeavor, subject to greater exigencies of intellectual rigor. [2]

What kinds of changes can we anticipate in the next one or two decades? What will be the rate of those changes? What factors influence the rate of change? Can the library adapt meaningfully to those changes? What effect will change have on the traditional goals of libraries? on their physical structure? on their organization and function? What effect will those changes have on user demands?

Can we predict change in libraries? Or are we dealing with too small a unit and too short a time? It is indicative of the problem that we can say with fair assurance that most of the technology is available for large scale innovation in information disseminating institutions, such as libraries. The problem is not one of invention and availability, but rather of acceptance, suitability, and adaptation. And these factors in turn are based not only on professional attitudes, but also on economics, professional capabilities, and in changes taking place in the larger context of publishing, education, telecommunications, and computing technology.

Acceptance of innovation strikes at some very deep roots of book-based libraries and of the process of reading. One may argue as Benjamin DeMott does so eloquently, when writing about reading: "I commit myself both to a sense of my own essential unity as a human being and also to a conviction of the uses of consciousness--my capacity to discern my needs, my situation, and to satisfy the need to transform the situation by my own efforts."[3]

Within the aura of change, libraries, and in fact the whole culture, will, at least pay lip service, if not subscribe

to this commitment, perhaps however in a much broader
sense. We must also remember that, in the past, very few
people have been able, or had the opportunity, to read in
Mr. DeMott's sense. Reading has been an accepted base
of our civilization for centuries, an unconscious assumption
until very recently. As our culture begins to examine the
bases of education and the uses of literacy, we may wish to
see the assumptions of reading in a different context. It
does not answer some questions we are beginning to ask: is
literacy based only on the written work? Reuel Denney has
asked the significant question in the following statement in
which he discusses a particular critic:

> He sees little good in communications development
> in which the mass media reach the people in a his-
> torical sequence different from the sequence in
> which they reached us--that is print first, movies,
> and radio-TV last. Why the particular sequence
> in which we developed our industrialized communica-
> tions system should be the better one remains more
> or less unstated. Could not the ... leap, from
> oral to audio-visual, be just as good?[4]

Mr. DeMott's and Mr. Denney's statements represent
two ends of one of the spectrums of literacy. They also
represent varying implications toward the acceptance of change
in libraries, changes in the type of library publics, in education, and, without being McLuhanesque, in forms and patterns
of communications which will force librarians, or their institutionalized equivalents, to alter their response to their
publics. The question is whether acceptance will be grudging,
enthusiastic, or rational. We hope it is the latter.

We are, for example, building information retrieval
systems on top of library systems, when instead we should
be asking what kind of communication system does this particular institution require--and building a communications
system in support of those requirements. The sometimes
dead hand of the library is imposing very real constraints
on the options open to the profession.

Certainly most users want to use the codex form for
most of the tasks they have used it for in the past. But
"most of the tasks" are really a very minor part of their
total information requirements. That means, the library as
presently constituted satisfies only a minor part of their requirements.

In considering the suitability of various kinds of changes, we should do this within the framework of Mesthene's statement at the beginning of this paper. Will innovation in present-day libraries change their objectives? Even though we have no positive answer to this question we can explore some of the current trends and their implications.

Automation of library processes, for example, may, during the next decade, reverse the trend of the past half-century toward more and better information, reference, and reader services. This reversal, however, may be tempered by other factors to be discussed below. Libraries will be forced to place a larger portion of their budgets into automated processing development and into library networks. However, if the profession can maintain balance and an awareness that this is only a temporary state, then it will have the experience and the positive base upon which to build truly interactive systems. The purely data processing aspects of automation are a necessary first step toward a major change in objectives. Automation itself is not a change, because it operates within the conventional framework of library processes. It is merely a refinement of current practice.

Libraries must automate, and librarians themselves must be able to analyze and to decide rationally the rate and design of the process. Overconcern with the automation of routine processes may cut the librarian off from the user, just as the concern with the technique of cataloging of the past 80 years has tended to alienate the user.* For above all, the user does not care about the intricacies of cataloging, of main entries, or of bibliographical control. He wants that bit of information or that book or paper or tape or film: items, in many cases, he can only describe in the vaguest of terms. It is this "vaguest of terms" that provides the context for the breadth of system design basic to library adaptation, which will follow the automation of routine processes.

The smaller library, unable to invest in total automa-

---

*Don't misunderstand this statement. The librarian must become far more aware of the problems of programming and of automated system design, for he must ask intelligent questions and make decisions based on a thorough knowledge of computing systems. But, he must not in this process lose sight of the fact that he is operating a service that must continue to function.

tion, will be assisted by the growth of commercial processing
and cooperative processing agreements.   Both of these take
advantage of high volume and assembly line processing, offering the smaller library materials at a lower cost than each
library alone could obtain.   For long-term decision-making
and rational prediction, however, the profession badly needs
analytic studies of the costs and labor skills involved in all
the processing options.   For the small library, an additional
advantage will be compatibility with national and regional
systems, and, more importantly, an eventual shift of effort
to user services.   There will be a price for this, however,
principally in some loss of local autonomy and in the need
for librarians familiar with systems design, able to make
informal decisions within a cooperative framework.

A second major impact on libraries will result from
the radical broadening of the communications spectrum from
print to sound and image.   However, mere shift in emphasis
from books to non-print forms will not, in itself, cause a
change from a book-based to a communications-oriented institution.   Non-print also comes in packages and, like books,
can be handled and warehoused.   Because of the nature of libraries, this element will at first only cause an extension in
the variety of packages handled.   But, like automation, the
seeds for change in basic objectives are built into this process.   The culture surrounding the newer media will tend to
emphasize a different concept of content and communication.

The last 20 years have witnessed a remarkable rise
in media centers on campus, with a similar development in
secondary school systems.   However, until recently, these
centers have grown with little relation to the conventional library.   Nor for that matter has the conventional library had
much interest.   This rise and separate development of media
centers may make it politically impossible for any physical
or organizational convergence to take place, except as it may
be imposed from above.   Unless the library takes the initiative in this process, it will result in a lessening of the relative position of the library within its institutional or community framework.

DeMott's argument quoted earlier, that it is only
through reading that one can commit oneself to the uses of
consciousness, implies that no other form allows us to do
this.   This is a highly restrictive formula, however flatter-
ing it may be to book-based librarians.   Indeed another article by the same author[5] implies that one may enjoy the the-

ater in much the same way.   Therefore it may not be a matter of form, i.e., different media, but rather of the receptivity of those who interact with the form and surrounding
culture.

Either as part of the library or as something closely
allied to it, other media will have permanent effect on the
library.   As we learn more about their attributes, books and
other media will tend to extend each other.   They are competitive only to those who wish to take sides in an argument
that will become increasingly sterile.   The major problems,
and they exist with print as well, will be those of maintaining quality, or at least qualitative relevance to the various
publics of particular libraries.

The changes in the background and cultural experiences
of the publics who require information and knowledge, be it
visual, audio, or print, provide a second form of pressure
on libraries to move toward assumptions based on communication.   Though one can easily argue with the McLuhan statements, the plethora of messages and pseudo-messages in all
forms gives substancy to the prophecy.   Without attempting
to destroy the incredible richness of portions of this varied
and incandescent media culture, some form of filtering and
structuring is necessary.   If it cares to make the effort and
if it can make what may be a quantum leap, the library may
be the only present institution that can accomplish this.   The
children's sections of public libraries, for example, have for
some time brought together the oral and visual aspects of
their wares.   New pressures on library branches serving inner city populations have opened up a broad spectrum of non-
print services and happenings inconceivable a decade ago.
Whether such pressures will have an influence on academic
libraries depends in part on the continuing demands from the
student culture.   But the demand for change will continue
and whether, or rather how soon, it affects the academic library rests, in good part, on the capabilities and attitudes
of the profession.

Three other interrelated factors will have a major
impact on libraries: the paperback book, the growth of inexpensive copying, and individually customized services for
scientific and technical information.   The paperback has had,
and will have, a tremendous effect on readers who for the
first time have many more inexpensive options than books on
library shelves.   The airport terminal, the supermarket, the
drugstore become extensions of the library.   This is not to

argue for the quality of much of what appears in such stores
and newsstands. It is merely to point out that these options
exist and are part of the communications culture, and therefore of the library.

     In the last decade the growth of copying has, of course,
been phenomenal. Its effect has been principally on libraries
serving education and research. Depending on the approach
to copyright, now under debate in Congress, and on the development of cheaper copy costs, the implications for libraries are large. Copying, under either a liberal or a restrictive law, is here to stay. Increasingly, the growth of copying offers the user the option of borrowing an item or having
it copied inexpensively. Eventually we can foresee a return
to the noncirculating library of the 19th century. This will
restrict borrowing, with the concomitant effects on circulation staffs and systems, and eventually on the organization
of the book stacks.

     The third element, customized services, is a result
of two factors. First, the nature of science and technology,
particularly in the last half-century, has supported the growth
of "invisible colleges," groups who communicate constantly
among themselves, developing their own networks and sources
of new knowledge and information. Secondly, libraries, organized around the concept of the book and its permanency,
have not been able to provide the kinds of services required,
particularly for technology. Hence these commercial services have grown, which filter, according to personal interest
profile, material going to an individual, or supply bibliography and hard copy in answer to a specific question, or provide instant information on demand such as in poison control
centers, or tell an inquirer of others who are working on
his specific problem.

     The past growth and probable future growth of all
three of these services will tend to disperse, even more
widely than is now the case, information and book resources
required by potential library patrons. Compared to 20 years
ago, the reader, the researcher, the browser, and the student are offered many more options today to fulfill his needs
regardless of definition or medium.

     Miniaturization will in time have a strong effect on
buildings and on service to users. As participants in the
Educational Facilities Laboratories Conference on the Impact
of Technology on the Library Building pointed out, "the long-

range effect of microfilm technology on the book and library building will be greater than that of the computer."[6] The development of microforms is an almost perfect example of the apparent slowness of an innovative technology with high potential. The microfilm has been available in libraries since the mid-thirties; but, despite its great promise, it has had almost no significant effect. Why? We can point with a good deal of truth to a fragmented industry, a lack of standardization, a rather small market for the development and marketing effort necessary, and the ever-present copyright problem. The awkward readers, the lack of suitable reader-printers, and a commitment to the codex form have discouraged both users and librarians to foster its exploitation.

In summary, there are many factors, some obvious and some not so obvious, forcing change on the library. Their effect will be the result less of formally planned change, such as automation, than as influences changing the culture of the library. More immediately, the unforeseen necessities of innovation will cause changes in the structure and relative importance of parts of the organization. The costs of automation during the next decade will, for example, probably draw support away from user services and from resource development in the individual library. To reduce the effect of these costs, the library, particularly smaller ones, will move toward commercial processing and cooperative processing, with a resultant loss in local autonomy. The increase in non-print media in libraries will provide an additional burden of "bibliographical" control and handling. However, because of the culture surrounding such media, libraries may become more communications conscious. Some types of libraries, particularly children's sections and those serving the inner city, have begun to move in this direction already. This in turn may counter the necessary emphasis of data processing on technique.

The growth of paperback books, copying systems, and customized information services will tend to disperse and diversify the options open to all types of readers; as a result the library may increasingly become a less important resource. However, the complexities and variety of these options, together with the cost, both in money and time to the individual, will offer the library an opportunity to combine these services and resources into a single set of services. The effects of microforms will not be felt for at least ten more years, but, when certain developmental and economic problems have been met, they will have a significant effect on library facilities and services.

The impact of all of these and other as yet unknown
factors on the institution of libraries defines the context of
change. The rate of that change is, in good part, still in
the hands of the profession. The danger is that a new technique such as automation, superimposed on an old system,
seldom continues according to original plan and is frequently
abandoned after the "experimental period," with sometimes
drastic effects on morale and future planning. This has happened several times in the past decade. Richard Evans, in
his studies of resistance to innovation, points out that university "administrators and faculty members alike find it difficult, if not impossible, to evaluate the merits and demerits
of a new idea prior to or even after its adoption." Hence,
most, if not all, innovations are adopted on an experimental
basis, "with a built-in mechanism for abandoning such an innovation."[7] Libraries badly need to develop evaluative procedures for measuring the "success" of their accomplishments
within the context of their objectives. Until this is done the
library can only react. It cannot initiate a rationally planned
program with built-in evaluation at certain levels.

There appear to be three major choices for libraries
within this context, with a whole range of variations. First,
the library can become a warehouse with seating. There
are many of these now. This means that all efforts will be
directed toward the acquisition, handling, storing, and control of physical objects. If this is the road chosen, no matter how tinted the glass or how fine the carpets, the library
will be a supply depot. In some cases this may be a desirable solution. It will certainly be a less expensive solution
for the costs will be shifted to the user.

A second option is that the library might become a
switching system to connect the user with other people, other
places, other systems, acting primarily as a filter and nego-
tiator in the process. Within limits, and on an undefined
and informal basis, many good special libraries and technical
information centers at present operate this way. A memorandum for a meeting on library research and development
held at Yale University in 1967 states the eventualities of this
option most succinctly:

> ... those institutions which today are willing to
> undertake significant long-range research efforts
> are likely to be those which in 1990 can boast to
> prospective faculty and students that they have one
> of the nation's leading information systems. In

1990, the fact that a university once had one of the
nation's leading research libraries may no longer
be interesting except for antiquarians. [8]

The third option is related to the one just described,
but with certain important differences.   Whereas the former
is based principally on the computer and information processing, this option attempts a symbiosis of man and the diversity
of communication systems.   It draws upon the symbolism of
print, that "second chain of human inheritance."   It utilizes
the computer to produce, to control, and to manipulate records.   It uses the new media experience to expand and extend the linearity of print.

At present these media and computer systems are
inchoate and unorganized, but as they become formalized (and
they will), the conventional book library will occupy an increasingly smaller corner within the information transfer and
communications processes.   It may be appropriate to pose
the question (but not to answer) whether the library should
really be a fixed place or system, whether it should not be
a process--a mediator between user and knowledge, some of
which is stored on shelves in a variety of forms, some available from distant people and places.   These options are still
open to libraries--but they will not remain forever open.

There are obvious implications for staff and organization in the second and third options.   The librarian must become a modern generalist, concerned and knowledgeable about
print, sound, and image, about automation and computer technology, and about formal and informal communication systems.   In short, he must become much more sophisticated
about the processes of communication, in contrast to the artifacts of communication.

The changes are already reflected in the organization
of a few libraries, with a shift from the traditional catalog
department to a computer and processing division.   There is
a higher ratio of clerical to professional staff and, despite
the arguments, a better definition of professional tasks.
Such a change also implies an extensive investment in equipment and, particularly in the beginning, considerable developmental costs for programming, computer time and storage.
The third option in particular implies extensive investment
and skills in communication systems.

In this review the author has by no means been unbiased. He has faced, but not solved, the dilemma put so beautifully by de Jouvenel:

> ... Thus the wish to predict and the wish to persuade conspire to impress on the minds of men the idea of a line of the future, and to dissuade the forecaster ... from opening the fan of possible futures. [9]

This has not been unintentional, for it has been an attempt at self-education in a field we know little about, that of prediction. It is hoped that this brief review will stimulate others to concern themselves with this most critical problem for the profession and for the institution of libraries, so that we can have a more rational understanding of the options and constraints that we face.

Notes

1. Smith, E. "Do Libraries Need Managers?" Library Journal, 94 (1969), 502.
2. Jouvenel, B. de, The Art of Conjecture, New York, Basic Books, 1967, 277.
3. DeMott, B. "Reading: A Commitment to Consciousness," Wilson Library Bulletin, 42 (1967), 74.
4. Denney, R. "The Cultural Context of Print in the Communications Revolution," Library Quarterly, 25 (1955), 378.
5. DeMott, B. "Can't I Just Watch?" New York Times, Mar. 2, 1969, Sect. III, 1, 7.
6. Educational Facilities Laboratories, The Impact of Technology on the Library Building, New York, 1967, 13.
7. Evans, R. I., and Leppmann, P. K., Resistance to Innovation in Higher Education, San Francisco, Jossey-Bass, 1967, 135.
8. Yale University Library, Faculty Advisory Committee on Research and Development, Memorandum (10 October 1967), 3 (mimeo).
9. Jouvenel, op. cit., 103.

THE LIBRARY IN THE FUTURE OF HIGHER EDUCATION

Neal Harlow

Documenting the future is an uncertain game. "No one can predict the political future," a scientist (and science-fiction writer) recently said, "but it is possible to map technological change." Or, to take the word of a sociologist, "predicting the social future is relatively easy." And a noted physicist has recently declared that we cannot look backward for guidance, since "the future is not a prolongation of the past."[1] Whatever the possibilities of prediction may be, when the future no longer grows out of the past, change will have become instantaneous, and we can discard the evolutionary process and return to a belief in creation.

Tentatively, let us argue that the academic library in 1990 will look more as it does now than different from it, since its environment has been shaped during a long period of development. Academic libraries in America have evolved from small, often fortuitous collections of printed books which held a very tenuous relationship even to the limited educational objective of the early classical colleges--to discipline the mind through the study of Greek, Latin, and dialectic. These educational conditions came to be gradually transformed under pressure from the scientific method, new subject disciplines, the influence of evolutionary thought upon all intellectual areas, and the democratic tendency in the rising state universities to regard all studies and students as eligible for admission.[2] As a result of such radical changes, academic libraries (at first for faculty and then also for students) began to grow in size to accommodate the new content, the flood of publication, and the increasing urgency of information. In time, some of them grew to gigantic proportions.

Other educational and sociological forces have had their effect: large masses of students, a growing emphasis upon reading and independent study, specialization on one hand and interdisciplinary studies on the other, more advanced degree programs, a massive growth of research, cooperative

measures to promote library utilization, mechanized and computer-based technology, expanding federal, state, and local
sources of financial support, and recent expressions of student "power" and of dissatisfaction with a variety of campus
conditions.[3] These have all been widely influential.

And some of the most urgent and familiar problems
of the academic library will likely remain: how to become
a comprehensive source of information for the whole campus,
to develop forms of service which are suitable and acceptable
to all levels of users, to plan local resources with recourse
to a wider network, to utilize machines and manpower to best
advantage, and to do all of these things and live within the
sometimes inhibiting fiscal, educational, and social constraints
of an institution.

Technological innovation--both foreseen and unpredicted
--will improve intellectual and administrative organization,
make electronic information networks feasible, speed up the
handling and transfer of data, and separate routine and repetitive operations from those requiring judgment and decision.
But the basic requirements of the system will be the same.
New technology will not diminish the librarian's responsibility
as planner, organizer, and interpreter to identify, control,
and evaluate materials and information, to perceive the need
of the user, and to stand between him and the total store of
information in and beyond the local outlet. An increasing
understanding of processes and the utilization of systems and
machines will improve access to knowledge, better enabling
the librarian to focus the system upon where the people are.

Although the fundamental nature of the academic library's responsibility may remain much the same, there is
reason to believe that beneath that brick and bibliographic
facade a more dynamic influence upon the community may
begin to take shape. Today, in many places, the academic
library exists as a repository mainly, although having information stored somewhere is no longer good enough. Often
it does not play an active role in the learning process but
fulfills a kind of stand-by function in case curiosity or a
teacher's deadline provides pressing motivation. Librarians
(and their faculty colleagues) are largely unaware of the distinction being made in the literature of higher education between "acquiry" and "inquiry" (the acquisition and examination
of information) as reciprocal elements in the teaching and
learning process.[4] The responsibility of librarians to manage the acquiry phase (with teachers directing inquiry) is

therefore unfulfilled. They may be insensible to the existence
in the academic community of several kinds and "levels of
need" for library service and proffer a standard issue (of
"loan" and "reference") to all. [5] They are vague or limited
in their view of what the functions of the library should be
in supporting independent intellectual growth and research
and what accessibility really means.   Their orientation may
be more toward the institution than the user (operations, not
output), and their measure of effectiveness may not be related
to user benefits.   Cost-effectiveness as a criterion by which
the user judges accessibility in a competitive complex of library and non-library services may not have come to their
attention. [6] Librarians, in their uncertainty, may even aspire
to identify with another profession--the faculty--rather than
develop their own unique contribution and status.

Even great libraries may therefore exist more in a
state of being than of doing. Neither the student (whose education is at stake) nor the faculty (engaged in teaching and
research) is relevantly served. Such libraries may be described as high voltage sources with a minimum of current
flowing through the system; any man may plug in his own
lamp, but little power is generated, little intellectual force
felt.

Many who thus criticize the academic library put their
faith in machines. But whatever the development of the computer may eventually be in handling information, libraries in
education cannot be reduced wholly to the push-button level.
The library in this context is not a source of information
only; it is a tool for learning, and even when "instant" data
can be mechanically produced, the inquirer must first be
able to determine what he needs to know--based upon a realization of what his state of knowledge already is--understand
the structure of the subject and of the information system
with which he must cope, be able to accept new evidence and
integrate it with the old, and carry on from "acquiry" to "inquiry" and back and forth again.

The objective, to develop a student's capacity to pursue
learning independently, "whether stated or not, is inherent in
the idea of a liberal education in the modern world."   The
student must come to recognize that the function of information in inquiry is not to provide "the answer to a question"
but to serve as evidence to be examined.   He must learn to
identify, locate, and use information in the immediate quest
for understanding so that his capacity for inquiry becomes a

normal learning process for all graduates, not only for those
who go on to master a field of specialization. He must use
the question (inquiry) to shape the course of the search for
information (acquiry) and then use the information to direct
further inquiry. While the teacher "teaches" (stimulates and
guides inquiry), it is the librarian's responsibility both to
"manage acquiry," so that retrieving information will be in
itself a genuine learning experience, and to "instruct," that
is, to accommodate learning to the individual students' differences and levels of need. [7]

With such joint action by faculty and librarian, competence in independent study can be developed through the library
by teaching the student how to make a series of relevant
judgments relating to material and bibliographic approach and
acquainting him with the patterns which exist in the bibliographical system (knowledge not being an intellectual anarchy).
Whereupon, the individual may take advantage of whatever
manual or mechanical aids for acquiring pertinent data may be
current. Then, having mastered the underlying principles,
he need not each time thereafter be required to repeat labo-
riously the routine searching procedure but, at a higher level
of need, be provided with information in whatever forms it is
most useful. The library has seldom attempted an educational
role on this plane of action and responsibility.

"While the future will have to choose between many
competing superlatives," let us pick one of the possibilities
for the academic library. A range of needs and means are
available for exploration.

The beginning college student, engaged in general education as preparation for future living and study, will have a
special kind of library (much or little automated) which dis-
penses, with maximum accessibility and the least amount of
discomfort and vexation, a diversity of materials which an
above average young student requires for free and required
reading, looking, and listening, in cooperation with the teaching staff. The primary objectives at this educational level
will be to develop a basis of common knowledge and of skills
and an initial capacity for independent learning as a habit
which will persist after he leaves the campus behind (and
been "cut off," as Henry Wriston says, "from the source of
supply"). In teaching the process of independent study--the
only permanent form of learning--the library will acquaint
him with the function of information in inquiry (as evidence,
not answers) and familiarize him with informational sources.

It will teach him to recognize and evaluate content and to understand the organization of the scholarly disciplines, the arrangement of material in libraries, and the pattern and utility of bibliographic structure and method. The students' library, by accepting responsibility to manage the acquiry portion of the learning cycle, will become part of the educational process and place the library where the action is.

For the second level of user, the maturing, normally specializing student (upper division subject "majors," honors people, and those making the transition to advanced study), the general academic library will offer opportunity for a greater depth of understanding and occasion to observe the relationships among a number of subject fields as bases for maturing judgment and specialization. The student must now learn the attitudes and techniques of investigation, the bibliographic structure of knowledge in a chosen field (as it differs from its organization in libraries), and the use of libraries as a system of bibliographic organization. He should be offered information instead of guidance when its use becomes more important to his education than the intellectual exercise in finding it. He must use information so that his growing capacity for inquiry will enable him not only to become master of a field of specialization but to establish a normal learning process for a lifetime. Academic librarians, by becoming colleagues of the faculty in the teaching process, providing ready access to collections, sophisticated bibliographic direction and guidance, and assistance in "acquiry," and by teaching the use of the library as a "system of ways" from one stage of the learning process to the next, can educate a generation of college graduates to depend upon intellect instead of impulse in forming judgments.

The third category of user in a university--the faculty, advanced students, and staff in their research capacity--will receive as much attention from the public service departments as they now do from acquisitions. (Many faculty are indeed quite unaware or skeptical of the library's capacity to assist them--although they may hire less qualified people in research positions--and both librarians and faculty will require repeated demonstrations and persuasion.) Librarians, in supporting the process of discovery, will be in many subject areas not only collectors and transporters of information (i.e., delivering it to the user in the exact form in which it is received) but transformers, processors, and analyzers, [8] calling upon both bibliographic and subject knowledge in needed proportions. Studies indicate that accessibility is the single most important factor governing the use of resources; and the cost-benefit ratio to the user (what it costs him in time, effort, or money in relation to the benefits received and to competing services) is a prime factor to be considered in upgrading service. Providing documents, citations, answers, work space and facilities, instruction and consultation, and such adjunct services as translation, editing, and state-of-the-art reviews[9] will make available to academic research the intellectual support now being successfully modeled by commerce and government. While the "real future is not logically foreseeable," because many of the variables may be unknown or unrecognized, the academic library is more certain to persist if it adopts an active role. It may indeed be that the library in the future of higher education cannot survive in a passive, introverted state, offering a minimum level of service to all comers. A library is not a building, books, people, or even a computer (when the time comes) but a complex system of ways to connect users with recorded knowledge; and the range of needs in a university, from beginner to scientist and scholar is enormously wide.

Among the games people will play in our increasingly crowded and complex future will be making decisions based upon some knowledge of what the choices are. The library will continue to be a chief source of pertinent data, providing evidence, not answers. The product of higher education who has learned to find and use information in the quest for understanding will be one-up on his less well educated playmate. And in the United States of tomorrow, this could happily be a high percentage of the population.

Notes

1. Arthur C. Clarke, Daniel Bell, and I. I. Rabi.
2. G. P. Schmidt, The Liberal Arts College, New Brunswick, N. J., Rutgers University Press, 1957, particularly p. 44-45, 68, 71-72, 146-149, and 158-161.
3. Contemporary points of view, reflecting anti-intellectualism and "student power" on the campus, are represented in Students and Society; Report of Conference, Santa Barbara, Calif., Center for the Study of Democracy, 1967.
4. For a summary of the literature relating to "acquiry" and "inquiry," see W. R. Hatch, What Standards Do We Raise? (New Dimensions in Higher Education, No. 12), Washington, D. C., Government Printing Office,

1964, OE-53019; particularly p. 20-22. Note also especially the "Standards" numbered 1, 2, 4, 6, 10, 11, and 12 in preceding text. Patricia Knapp relates "acquiry" and "inquiry" to teaching library use in references cited under footnote 7, below.

5. N. Harlow, "Levels of Need for Library Service in Academic Institutions," College and Research Libraries, 24 (Sept. 1963), 359-364; and "An Open Skies System of Academic Library Service," Journal of Education for Librarianship, 2 (Spring 1962), 183-190.

6. Cost-effectiveness as a user's criterion for assessing library services is discussed briefly in R. H. Orr, "Development of Methodologic Tools for Planning and Managing Library Services: Part I," Bulletin of the Medical Library Association 56 (July 1968), 235-240. For a brief discussion of "supplier-oriented" vs. "user-oriented" objectives; supposed objectives and real and imputed ones; and what objectives may justify public support, see R. W. Conant, ed., The Public Library and the City, Cambridge, Mass., M. I. T. Press, 1965, p. 67-73, 102-109, 112-113.

7. P. B. Knapp, "Independent Study and the Academic Library," in The Monteith College Library Experiment, New York, Scarecrow Press, 1966, p. 275-285. In the main body of the text, see particularly chapters VII (Conclusions), V (Teaching the College Student To Find His "Way" in the Library), and III (Library Assignments in the Pilot Project); a useful sociological study of the relationships between librarian and faculty will be found in chapter II. Knapp's study is undoubtedly the most important one yet to be done in respect to integrating the academic library with the educational process.

8. A description of these "types of communicators" will be found in F. Machlup, The Production and Distribution of Knowledge in the United States, Princeton, N. J., Princeton University Press, 1962, p. 32-33.

9. For an analysis of a "Functional Classification of Library Services," based upon what the user receives, see R. H. Orr, "Development of Methodologic Tools," cited in note 6, above.

VII. LIBRARY EDUCATION

"Of all the forms of education, professional education is
perhaps the most inherently paradoxical, for it is at
once important and trivial.... This paradox of professional education arises from the need to reconcile, within its educational program, the pragmatism of a John
Dewey with the self-sufficient search for intellectual excellence of a Cardinal Newman, and the reconciliation
of this duality must be effected in the absence of any
real understanding of the mysteries of the learning process. Yet, despite his ignorance of how man learns,
the educator must bring together into a harmonious relationship the theoretical and the practical, the philosophical and the technological, the pragmatism of the
presence and the perspective of the future. The development of the intellect must go hand-in-hand with a
thorough training that has authentic practical ends. However rightly and tenaciously one may cling to a firm
belief that the first concern of education is the training
of the intellect, he must acknowledge that in professional
education there is inevitably an irreducible minimum of
the vocational.... In America today the primary value
of knowledge is its utility; thus the useful arts are
equated with democracy because they are believed to
contribute to the comfort and improved living standards
of all the people.... But the tidal wave of vocationalism
that today imperils education for librarianship may only
in part be attributed to the 'spirit of the times' and the
seeming inability of education to define its goal. Librarianship itself must assume a full measure of responsibility for its failure to erect a theoretical frame of
reference for the profession, within which its educational program can be viewed.... Because librarianship is
much more than a bundle of tricks for finding a particular book, on a particular shelf, for a particular person,
with a particular need, education for librarianship should
not be merely the assimilation of facts, the mastery of
specialized skills, or even the comprehension of a machine's modus operandi. The end of education is wis-

dom, where wisdom is the ability to relate means to
goals, and it proceeds toward this end through the
training of the intellect."

J. H. Shera, Libraries..., 174-177.

"Because librarianship is facing some very critical
years which may well decide its future course, we hope
that those responsible for the professional education of
tomorrow's librarians will learn from the mistakes of
the past, and prepare the student to understand a world
in which everything that he has learned about the how
of librarianship may be overthrown before he has lived
out his professional life, a world in which only the why
is the eternal verity."

J. H. Shera, "On the Importance...,"
Wilson Library Bulletin, 42 (1968), 174.

THE LIBRARY AS A COMPLEX ORGANIZATION: IMPLICATIONS FOR LIBRARY EDUCATION

Patricia B. Knapp

The proposition central to this paper is that librarianship
is always practiced in the context of the complex organization.
If it is large enough, the library itself may be such an organization; if it is a one- or two-man village, school, college, or special library, it is a unit within the organization
of the community, the school, the college, the business, the
plant, or whatever. Furthermore, with increasing emphasis
on library systems, whether these be merely bibliographical
networks or actual consolidations, the significance of the organizational context becomes ever more apparent.

Librarianship, of course, is not the only occupation
practiced in an organizational setting. Ours is an organizational society and the occupations which were once truly individual and independent, such as farming, domestic service,
shopkeeping, repair service, are either shrinking in numbers
or are being brought together into service, collective bargain-
ing, or entrepreneurial organizations. Even the oldline established professions of medicine and law, which were once
almost defined by the one-to-one relationship between the doc-

tor and his patient or between the lawyer and his client, are increasingly practiced in and through organizations.

These trends have led sociologists to devote considerable attention to patterns of interaction among occupational and organizational groups. That part of their work which is particularly concerned with the role of the professional in the organization has, it seems to me, useful implications for our understanding of librarianship and, therefore, for library education and research. (The question of the extent to which librarianship qualifies as a profession is, as we shall see, integrally related to occupational-organizational interaction.)

The paper draws upon sources in sociology and education which are concerned with organizations, with occupations, and with professional education, but it should not be considered in any sense a review of these bodies of literature. Its purpose, rather, is to develop an argument which can be summarized as follows:

Whenever professionals work in the context of an organization, there is an inevitable tension between the authority inherent in the formal structure and procedures (i.e., the "rationality") of the organization and the authority of specialized knowledge and training (the expertise) inherent in the professional role. This tension has potential for creative as well as harmful effects. In order to prepare librarians to deal creatively with this crucial source of strain or conflict, library education should consider ways of helping students understand the organizational content in which they must work and at the same time preserve their sense of professional mission and identity.

As a basis for this argument, the paper first sketches briefly some of the models used by sociologists for the analysis of complex organizations. And, finally, it attempts to use this organizational-professional perspective as a kind of lens to bring into focus certain problems and dilemmas in librarianship today.

The Rational Model.[1] The classic model of the formal organization, as developed by Weber and as applied in the Scientific Management Movement, founded by F. W. Taylor, is symbolized by the organization chart. This model assumes division of labor among workers whose competence is diverse and narrowly specialized. Coordination is achieved through supervision carried out in accordance with a hierarchical pat-

tern of authority and responsibility. Authority is reflected in
position in the hierarchy and is based on power, that is,
right and responsibility to direct the activities of subordinates.
It is, however, usually "legitimated" on the basis of knowledge. The assumption is that the closer one is to the apex
of the hierarchy the greater is one's knowledge of the goals
of the organization and the extent of their achievement, and
the total workings of the organization, that is, the means
through which the goals are achieved. The organization functions on the basis of a rational analysis of ends and means;
implementation is through formal, impersonal rules and procedures. Achievement of organizational goals depends on
compliance of members, and this compliance is motivated by
loyalty to the organization and by incentives consisting of
economic rewards and promotions.

The Natural System Model. Organization theorists
of the rational persuasion recognize, of course, that behavior
in actual organizations often does not conform to this rational
model, but they are inclined to see such variation as devia-
tions or aberrations to be solved by adjustments in incentive
programs, by improvements in working conditions, or by
"better communication," that is, by more precise and specific
formulation of rules and procedures or by internal public relations efforts designed to stimulate pride in the organization.

Adherents of the "natural system" model, on the other
hand, argue that the rational model is, itself, inadequate as
a basis for inquiry into the nature of organizations. The
famous Hawthorn studies, demonstrating the significance of
peer group relationship and of satisfactions unrelated to wages
and promotions, were instrumental in the development of the
Human Relations school of administration. Management was
advised to concern itself with worker morale, with the composition of worker groups, with methods of giving workers a
sense of participation in decision-making and in the formulation of goals. In the "natural system" model, the goal of
the organization becomes not the publicly stated aim of the
organization, but the equilibrium of the system itself, the
maintenance of stability in the interrelationship of its parts.

Synthesis and the Structuralist Model. Many organizational sociologists have pointed to weaknesses in both the rational model and the natural system model. Gouldner notes
that studies based on the former tend to assume the administrative viewpoint and to underestimate irrational elements in
management, while those based on the latter tend to under-

estimate the very real impact of formal organizational structures and procedures at the same time that they overlook
quite rational motivations on the part of the workers. [2] He
calls for

> ... a single and synthesized model which will at
> once aid in analyzing the distinctive characteristics
> of the modern organization as a rational bureaucra-
> cy, the characteristics which it shares with other
> kinds of social systems, and the relationship of
> these characteristics to one another. [3]

Etzioni indicates that a synthesis has emerged in the
work of the Structuralists:

> It is in exploring the 'harmony' view of the Human
> Relations writers that the Structuralist writers rec-
> ognize fully the organizational dilemma: the inevit-
> able strains--which can be reduced but not elimi-
> nated--between organizational needs and personal
> needs; between rationality and non-rationality; be-
> tween discipline and autonomy; between formal and
> informal relations; between management and work-
> ers, or, more generically, between ranks and divi-
> sions. [4]

He indicates that the current analysis of organizations
pays attention to groups both within and without the organization, to the relationship between the organization and its environment, and to articulation between formal and informal
elements of the organization. [5]

The Organization Professional

The profession is a social system which shares some
of the characteristics of rational bureaucracy: it is one of
the groups which exists both within and without the organization; it is an element in the environment in which the organization functions. And the trend toward organization in our
society is matched by an accelerating trend toward professionalization of occupations.

The professions rest upon a division of labor which
is different from that assumed in the rational bureaucracy.
In this pattern, the practitioners are all trained in the skills
required as a basis for their work; they are expected to de-

velop internalized standards of performance; they are largely unsupervised; they are controlled, instead, by peer group approval or disapproval in accordance with norms accepted by the group.

> The true professional, according to the traditional ideology of professions, is never hired. He is retained, engaged, consulted, etc., by some one who has need of his services. He, the professional, has or should have almost complete control over what he does for the client. [6]

Hughes, along with other writers on the sociology of occupations, points out that in our modern world, not even the long-established professions of law and medicine practice in accordance with this traditional ideology. And yet, with the older professions, the idealized image from the past of the doctor and his patient, the lawyer and his client, the pastor and his parishioner remains as a touchstone defining professional goals even when they must be realized within the context of an organization. The fact that payment for services comes in the form of a salary from an organization rather than from the clients' fees is less significant than the existence of an internalized standard of professional-client relationship, acquired as a part of a professional "culture."

The claim of the professional to autonomy, however, rests upon more than tradition. It is justified on the basis of an authority of knowledge quite different from that of the administrator in the bureaucratic hierarchy. The professional's authority of knowledge comes from his long training prior to his association with the organization, from his continuing association with professional colleagues, and from his participation in the goal-setting activities of his profession. It is, in short, knowledge which is unrelated to the professional's position in the hierarchy.

The likelihood of conflict between these two systems of authority is obvious. One writer discussed areas of conflict under headings which are revealing: "(1) the professional's resistance to bureaucratic rules; (2) the professional's rejection of bureaucratic standards; (3) the professional's resistance to bureaucratic supervision; and (4) the professional's conditional loyalty to the bureaucracy."[7] But various kinds of adjustment have also been observed. Professionals sometimes simply accommodate themselves to the constraints of the bureaucracy, in a sense, submitting their professional goals to the goals of the organization, their authority to the authority of the hierarchy. Often the "line" authority of the organizational chart is supplemented by boxes designating "staff" units which have responsibility for advising line officers, but no power to command subordinates. [8] Vollmer, studying the activities of research scientists in organizations, identifies what he calls "research" entrepreneurship" as one of the "adaptation mechanisms ... which permit professionals to live in more or less bureaucratic environments and yet retain their professional integrity and independence."[9] He found that ability and opportunity to sell research ideas were associated with professional autonomy and productivity.

In an analysis which is particularly useful for our purpose, Etzioni discusses the relationship between "administrative authority," that is, what we have called the authority related to position in the hierarchy, with "professional authority," which we have called the authority of knowledge, as they occur in three types of organizations.[10] In non-professional organizations, such as business and industry, administrative authority largely determines goals and exercises control. In professional organizations, such as hospitals and universities, "administrators are in charge of secondary activities; they administer means to the major activity carried out by professionals."[11] In semi-professional organizations, for which Etzioni's examples are the primary school, the social work agency, and the nursing service of the hospital, administrative authority is in control, but it rests with professionals who have been promoted to administrative positions.

Although Etzioni distinguishes between the full-fledged professions and the semi-professions on the basis of the length of training required for each and on the significance of the questions with which they are entrusted, the major thrust of his distinction is concerned with authority in the organization.

> First, professional work here has less autonomy;
> that is, it is more controlled by those higher in
> rank and less subject to the discretion of the pro-
> fessional than in full-fledged professional organiza-
> tions, though it is still characterized by greater
> autonomy than blue- or white-collar work. Second,
> the semi-professionals often have skills and person-
> ality traits more compatible with administration,
> especially since the qualities required for communi-
> cation of knowledge are more like those needed for

the creation and, to a degree, application of knowledge. Hence, these organizations are run much
more frequently by the semi-professionals themselves than by others.[12]

The work of semi-professionals is governed by schedules and regulations. They are fairly closely supervised, or,
in situations not conducive to direct observation, they are
required to report in detail. Most significant is the fact that
while the full-fledged professional looks down on administrators and prefers to avoid administrative responsibility (except
perhaps for the eminence of the top job), the semi-professional is likely to regard the administrative hierarchy as the
normal career ladder to professional recognition and achievement.

There has been considerable discussion in library literature of the question of librarianship as a profession, some
of it concerned with analysis of the extent to which the field
measures up to the "marks of a profession," some of it
proposing ways in which our professional status could be enhanced. Matters of professional status, recognition, and
prestige, for their own sake, are not germane to the present
discussion. What is to the point is those attributes of professional status which have particular significance in the organizational contexts in which librarians work.

The Rational Model and the Authority of Knowledge.
As we have seen, the professional's authority-of-knowledge
is a source of conflict in the rational model of the complex
organization because (a) it is acquired through long years of
training outside the organization (where the trainee is subject
to non-organizational sources of influence); (b) it is a generalized knowledge basic to the whole field of professional practice (so that it does not require detailed coordination); (c) it
is assumed to encompass its own norms and standards of
performance (so that the professional expects to work auton-
omously, free from organizational regulations and supervision); and (d) it is unrelated to position in the organizational
hierarchy (so that the professional looks to his peers rather
than his superiors for appraisal of his performance).

What, in this context, is the knowledge of the librarian?
The realistic view is that librarianship in practice is essentially a craft or, at best, an art. The knowledge on which it
is based is in the main derived from experience with what
makes sense, what works. Although the curriculum in library

schools pays some attention to information theory, to systems analysis, and to the psychology and sociology of reading and communication, the emphasis is still on concrete and practical aspects of traditional library activities. We have not developed a coherent framework of general principles on which to base our professional practice. And what little library research there is is similarly directed toward the solution of immediate practical problems.[13]

Within librarianship, no one has devoted more attention to the question of what the librarian's body of knowledge should be than Jesse Shera. He has written lucidly and persuasively in support of what he calls "social epistemology" as a new discipline upon which librarianship should be based.

> The focus of this new discipline will be upon the production, flow, integration, and consumption of all forms of communicated though through the entire social pattern. From such a discipline should emerge a new body of knowledge about, and a new synthesis of, the interaction between knowledge and social activity.[14]

But the new discipline has yet to be developed, and

> In large measure librarianship has based its claims to professionalism and the right to be described as a science upon the technology that over the years its practitioners have developed and which its initiates must master ... but a technology is a means not an end. Lacking theory to give it direction and purpose, it drifts aimlessly. If it reaches its goal, it does so only by fortuitous circumstances. ... To condemn library techniques as little more than clerical routines does not diminish the importance of such routines to the practicing librarian, or deny that their mastery by the competent librarian should not be taken for granted. They simply are not indices of the librarian's professional position.[15]

Small wonder, then, that the librarian's "professional" authority-of-knowledge carries little weight in opposition to the authority-of-position in the rational bureaucracy.

In the semi-professional organization, as Etzioni describes it, the potentiality for conflict between the two kinds of authority might appear to be virtually eliminated, in any case, since administrators are recruited from the ranks of the professionals. If one accepts the avoidance of such conflict as an overriding goal, one might argue as did Munn in 1949 that the major emphasis in library education should be on administration.[16] Carried to its logical conclusion, this argument reinforces the rational model of the organization. One difficulty with Munn's proposal, of course, is that not all librarians turn out to be administrators. More importance for the present discussion, however, lies in the possibility that if librarianship is redefined as library administration it will in the process lose all claim to being professional knowledge. Goode, commenting on Munn's point, remarks:

> Nevertheless, much of this administration is not specific to librarianship. I would venture to say that a good chief librarian could transfer most of the skills he uses daily to a high-level managerial position in any corporation. That is, most of his work is not either pushing back the frontiers of knowledge in his field or applying the general principles of his field, but simply integrating human beings in a corporate enterprise.[17]

That this outcome is probably more theoretical than actual is indicated by the inadequacy of the rational bureaucratic model of the organization. Before examining librarianship in the light of other models, however, let us consider another source of conflict within that model.

The Rational Model and the Determination of Goals. In the classic bureaucratic model, the organization is a means for attaining desired ends. The responsibility for deciding what those ends should be and how they should be defined rests with those who are at the top of the pyramid of authority. In the classic model of the profession, on the other hand, the goal of service to society overrides all and the profession itself carries the right and responsibility for determining the specific goals within this context.

Through education controlled by the profession, the new professional is expected to acquire a clear understanding of profession's goals, the capacity to make judgments in the light of such goals, and a set of internalized standards of performance which are regarded as the appropriate means to attain them.

In the semi-professions, again, where administrators are promoted from the ranks, ideally there should be complete agreement about goals among all levels of the organization. And since the professional members of the organization at all ranks will have acquired the same internalized standards as to appropriate means, there should be no conflict between professional compliance (based on internalized standards) and bureaucratic compliance (based on the authority structure and organizational loyalty).

This harmonious picture is far from reality, of course, in all occupations falling into the semi-professional category. For librarianship the discrepancy may be greater than in other fields because the goals of our service are diffuse and because we cannot clearly define the client for whom we perform it. And yet among librarians the service motivation is very strong. The case on either side of every controversial issue within the field is buttressed by arguments having to do with the information service requirements of different client groups. Is the university sacrificing the educational needs of the undergraduate to the research needs of the faculty? If the public library focuses its attention on the inner-city, will it neglect the needs of its traditional middle-class clientele? Is access to information a more or less important service for us to provide than guidance in its use? Librarians in all kinds of libraries and at all levels of organizational hierarchies have strong convictions on these issues. Their convictions, however, do not necessarily coincide with stated policy, if such there be, of the organizations in which they work, and they may be supported and reinforced by peer groups within the organization or by official or unofficial reference groups in the profession.

Because we are accustomed to the rational model of the organization and inclined to accept uncritically the assumption that its effectiveness must be evaluated on the basis of the extent to which all its activities are directed toward the achievement of its recognized goals, our initial reaction to the observation of such sources of ambivalence or conflict is to call for clarity and consensus. We urge administrators to see to it that organizational goals are clearly formulated, that policies are established in conformity with them, that members of the organization are fully informed (often that they be given "a sense of participation") so that their understanding and acceptance of both goals and means will be full and without question. Or, on the other side of the fence, we exhort the profession to come to grips with the ambiguities and conflicts in its aims, we insist upon the responsibility of the profession's educators to produce graduates instilled with a professional philosophy, presumably also without ambiguity or conflict.

The work of organization theorists suggests, however, that such proposals are not likely to be seriously heeded, because of the limitations of the rational model of the organization from which they stem. Etzioni calls for a "system model" instead of a "goal model" for analysis and evaluation of organizations:

> The starting point for this approach is not the goal itself but a working model of a social unit which is capable of achieving a goal. Unlike a goal, or a set of goal activities, it is a model of a multifunctional unit. It is assumed a priori that some means have to be devoted to such nongoal functions as service and custodial activities, including means employed for the maintenance of the unit itself. From the viewpoint of the system model, such activities are functional and increase the organizational effectiveness. It follows that a social unit that devotes all of its efforts to fulfilling one functional requirement, even if it is that of performing goal activities, will undermine the fulfillment of this very functional requirement, because recruitment of means, maintenance of tools, and the social integration of the unit will be neglected.[18]

One of the organization's functions, for example, is to exist (and survive) in an environment, even though that environment may tend to impose goals which are contrary to those of the organization itself.[19]

Another function of the organization is the allocation of resources among a variety of activities. The effectiveness with which it does so is to be measured, in the system model, not by the proportion of resources allocated to activities which are directly goal-serving but by a balance leading to maximum goal achievement of the total organization. A measure of this sort may justify time spent by employees on nonproductive but morale-building activities. It may even justify the proliferation of administrative positions which rank-and-file professionals constantly deplore.

The Natural System Model and Peer Group Relation-

ships. The focus of attention on the work group in the natural system model of the organization is complicated by the
presence of professional workers, since professional status
may be the basis for a peer group relationship which cuts
across the groupings based on involvement in a common task.
In business organizations, for specialists engaged in activities
such as accounting, advertising, or research, the two groupings often coincide. In organizations such as the hospital,
where the status of doctors is high, clear-cut, and generally
recognized, primary identification is likely to be with the
professional peer group. In organizations of semi-professionals, one would expect to see ambivalent if not actually
contradictory tendencies. The long struggle to differentiate
clearly between professional and non-professional tasks in the
library represents a striving toward professional identification. The common conflict between technical services and
readers services divisions represents a tendency to identify
with the work group. The effort of academic librarians to
achieve faculty status offers a more striking example of our
problem in deciding what peer group we want to identify with.
Goode observes:

> By defining much of their task as "teaching," these
> [academic] librarians can make a fair case for
> their claim to faculty status. On the other hand,
> if their definition of core professional problems
> were unique and special to the tasks of a library,
> they could gain all of the material advantages--
> which figure so prominently in their argument--
> without demanding the title of another profession.
> One might indeed ask in this connection whether
> such professionals would prefer to belong to an as-
> sociation of academics, or an association of librar-
> ians. [20]

But material advantages are not all. In the academic
world membership in a peer group with the status and power
of the faculty is attraction enough, though admittedly it is not
to be attained automatically as a concomitant of professional
titles and perquisites. Similarly, those who regard public
librarians who unionize or school librarians who join teachers' unions as selling out their professional status for financial gain underestimate the power of such "non-rational"
motivations as peer group identification and loyalty. In opposition to bureaucratic authority, moreover, the union may
be the most powerful instrument available to protect or enhance the worker's control over his job or, in this case, his
"professional autonomy."

The Natural System Model and Client Relationships.
A typology developed by Blau and Scott classifies formal organizations on the basis of their "prime beneficiary," as follows:

> Four types of organizations result from the applica-
> tion of our cui bono criterion: (1) 'mutual-benefit
> associations,' where the prime beneficiary is the
> membership; (2) 'business concerns,' where the
> owners are prime beneficiary; (3) 'service organ-
> izations,' where the client group is the primary
> beneficiary; and (4) 'commonweal organizations,'
> where the prime beneficiary is the public-at-large.[21]

In this classification the library would obviously be considered a service organization and yet we should note that many
of the functions performed by it are justified as directed toward a public good defined in terms of the hypothetical needs
of the "larger" society or the anticipated needs of the future
rather than in terms of the expressed needs of its immediate
patrons.

The client is also the prime beneficiary of the service
of professional practice and in organizations controlled by
full-fledged professionals, as we have seen, the classic face-
to-face client-professional relationship is still dominant, at
least as a powerful tradition.   This relationship, moreover,
is characterized by the professional's duty to decide what
service the client needs, whether or not it is what he wants,
while the client has the freedom only to accept the service
prescribed or seek help elsewhere.   In organizations of the
semi-professions, however, the administration tends to have
the power to determine what services shall be provided and
often, in fact, what clients shall be served.

The variety of organizational contexts in which librarians work makes this matter of client relationship a most
difficult one.   In the public library, for instance, the long-
standing battle over "quality" versus "demand" as the criterion for book selection reflects one of the major dilemmas
of the service organization.   Rigid adherence to the prescription of "quality" may simply bar a large number of potential
clients from the service; subservience to "demand" may turn
the service organization in the direction of the business concern, whose motto is caveat emptor.   The current conflict
over service to inner-city residents, who do not want library
service but are presumed to need it, versus service to mid-

dle-class patrons, who have always used the library but may
not actually need it as much, is another case in point. These
are examples of situations which require decisions involving
the whole organization rather than just the librarian-client relationship. Bundy and Wasserman are probably right in de-
ploring librarians' unwillingness to exercise their right to
prescribe for their patrons, that is,

> ... the essential timidity of practitioners, clearly
> reflected in the widespread, deep-seated, and
> trained incapacity or high degree of reluctance to
> assume responsibility for solving informational prob-
> lems and providing unequivocal answers. [22]

But the reluctance of the rank-and-file librarian to take on
the professional's responsibility to determine what the client
needs is of minor significance in the context of an organization whose total resources are involved in serving that need.
Books of high quality cannot be prescribed if they have not
been acquired. Similarly, the organization in which the administrator is expected to carry the role of an enlightened
statesman with a vision broad enough to encompass the needs
of the total community determines whether or not someone is
assigned or, indeed, permitted to serve the inner-city.

The organizational context in which the school librarian works creates different problems of client relationship.
For one thing, the school itself is a type of service organization in which the pupil, who is the prime beneficiary does not
have the right, inherent in the classic client-professional relationship, of rejecting the service. In essence, school children are a captive clientele of teachers, but only occasionally, or in second-hand fashion, of the librarian. This suggests that the librarian advising the teacher about library
materials for a given learning experience (whether the teacher accepts or rejects the advice) is involved in a relationship
closer to the professional model than he is in his relationship
with the pupils who actually use the resources.

The school, moreover, is a type of organization which
has no control over admission to its service, so that its primary goal of education may be displaced by such secondary
goals as the maintenance of institutional order and control.
It is deplorable but not surprising that the teacher often ex-
ploits the school library in seeking relief from such distract-
ing responsibilities. [23] In short, Bundy and Wasserman are
quite right in pointing to "some fundamental question and am-

biguity about who the client really is--the school, the teacher, or the student. "[24]

    The organizational context of the college or university
shares some of the client relationship ambiguities of the
school but it presents some additional ones as well.   Here,
again, there is the likelihood that service to the student can
be best achieved through service to the faculty mediator.
Furthermore, in the university at least, the faculty member
is a primary beneficiary to the extent that he is engaged in
advanced study, research, or community service.   But the
academic librarian has almost never succeeded in establishing himself in a professional-client relationship with the faculty.   Bundy and Wasserman suggest that the remedy lies in
subject specialization for the librarian, but their reasoning
is extremely dubious--at least in the academic context.
Their characterization of the professional role emphasizes
the prescriptive responsibility of the professional:

> The professional, by virtue of his training, experi-
> ence, and specialized knowledge, offers the client
> the counsel, service, or prescription which he
> views to be appropriate whether or not this is pre-
> cisely what the client wants or thinks he wants.
> The professional's guidance may not always be fol-
> lowed, but the judgment and recommendation of the
> professional are not open to question or debate by
> the layman.   The professional knows. [25]

Later, on the matter of subject specialization, they say:

> Granted the need for organizational skill, the serv-
> ice ideal, and technical grounding in information
> handling, it will only be when the client can respect
> the subject competence of the librarian that he will
> accept him and respect him for his professional
> competence in the meaning employed here. [26]

    The flaw in this argument, it seems to me, lies in
the fact that it is precisely in his own subject specialization
that the college or university professor is not a layman.   As
a patient he will accept his doctor's prescription because he
is confident the doctor has knowledge he does not have.   As
a legal client he will accept his attorney's advice on the same
basis.   It would follow, then, that although specialized subject competence on the part of the librarian might win him
respect, esteem, or even a colleague relationship, it would

never win him acceptance in a professional role. His only claim to act as a professional with the faculty member as his client rests upon that "technical grounding in information handling" which is so easily granted in the passage quoted and which, in the present state of the art, hardly deserves to be called anything more impressive. The weakness of this claim is perhaps nowhere so apparent and so painful as it is in the academic world. For the institution of higher education is heavily committed to the philosophy of authority based on knowledge, to the pattern of organization which concedes to administration only enough bureaucratic authority to keep the machinery going. Without a theoretical and scientifically-based body of knowledge of its own, librarians will continue to be evaluated by the faculty primarily on the basis of how efficiently they manage their part of the machinery.

The Structuralist Model and Professionalization. Organizational analysis based on the structuralist model makes use of the concept of the "functional autonomy," or degree of interdependence of the various parts of the organizational system.[27] These "parts" consist of both individuals and units, work groups, peer groups, hierarchies, or any other such formal or informal members of the organization, but they also include non-members of the organization such as clients, occupational or professional groups, and sources of community or financial support. From this perspective, the academic librarian's desire for faculty status or the school librarian's participation in the teachers' union, in the examples given earlier, appears not as rejection of his own profession as a peer group in favor of one with greater prestige or power, but instead as recognition of his functional dependence upon others for the achievement of his own professional objectives.

Leonard Riessman, in a study of civil service employees, sheds light on the pulling power of professional versus institutional identification. He identifies four types of civil servant: (1) the "functional bureaucrat," who identifies with his professional specialization, looking to it for recognition and success; (2) the "specialist bureaucrat," who maintains contact with his profession but looks toward the bureaucratic promotion system as the path to success; (3) the "service bureaucrat," who sees the bureaucracy as a necessary vehicle for serving the group whose recognition constitutes the success he seeks; and (4) the "job bureaucrat," whose orientation is entirely toward the organization and who defines success in terms of financial rewards and promotions

within its structure.[28] Theoretically, the functional bureaucrat, whose reference group is the profession, and the service bureaucrat, whose reference group is the clientele, would
have greater functional autonomy than the other two groups.
In librarianship, however, other factors enter the picture.

First, because our professional associations are dominated by administrators, for the librarians who work in
large libraries, professional recognition is likely to follow,
if not actually depend upon, success in climbing the organizational ladder. Second, because so much library work is done
behind the scenes, a large proportion of librarians who consider themselves as service-oriented have no visible client
reference group. And third is the fact that most librarians
are women. Etzioni maintains (without producing evidence
on the point) that "women on the average are more amenable
to administrative control than men."[29] Whether or not this
is true, they are undoubtedly less mobile than men and therefore more likely to be "locals" than "cosmopolitans," that is,
more committed to the local organization than to the larger
profession.[30] In this connection, it may be worth noting that
a local orientation is not necessarily incompatible with a
commitment to a client reference group. But such a commitment may nevertheless conflict with professional values,
as, for instance, when the small-town librarian resists participation in a library system for fear of its effect upon his
relationship to his present patrons.

The picture of librarianship which emerges from this
discussion of its organizational context may seem to some
readers exceedingly gloomy. My own position is that it offers a fresh perspective of great promise for helping us understand our field and, specifically, for library research and
education. This perspective calls, first, for a re-examination of some of the assumptions behind our current thinking.

Our view of the organization is dominated by the rational-bureaucratic model, modified somewhat by certain
"democratic" values which are part of our general culture,
values to which we adhere in what is often a sentimental
rather than a realistic fashion. Thus, a "good" administration is one in which matters of authority and responsibility
are clear-cut and well-defined, activities are performed in
accordance with uniform standards, procedures are codified,
performance is evaluated by means of objective measures of
cost and efficiency. The "good" administrator achieves all
this, of course, with due regard for the individual rights and

"human" feelings of the personnel.

On the other hand, our view of the profession is dominated by the classic model of the profession, usually with the high-status professions of law and medicine as our examples. We look to our professional association for the promulgation and enforcement of standards and a code of ethics, for strict control over entry to the profession, for recognition of the individual librarian's right to be regarded as "professionally" qualified to speak with authority on all matters pertaining to the library needs of the patron, the organization, the community, or, indeed, the society he serves. In seeking solutions to some of our problems, we usually try to draw a parallel with medicine rather than with occupations similar to our own.

The potential for conflict between these two models is evident. But what is more important, as I have tried to demonstrate, is that both models are out-of-date and inadequate not only for our own immediate purposes but also as theoretical bases for understanding what goes on in a society which is more and more organized and, at the same time, more and more "expert." A more sophisticated view, perhaps synthesizing these two trends, could lead to promising developments in library research and education.

Organization Theory as a Component in Social Epistemology. Recognition of the increasingly organizational character of our society requires, almost by definition, that the new discipline of social epistemology proposed by Shera take into account the organizational context in which knowledge is acquired, communicated, and used. And if the task of librarianship is, again in Shera's phrase, "the management of knowledge," we must see to it that the methods we use to accomplish that task are compatible with the social structures we deal with. This suggests that significant studies in organizational sociology should be drawn upon for such courses as in "the library in society," "library and information systems," and "bibliographic organization." It suggests, furthermore, a rich field for research, particularly at a time when all kinds of organizations and associations have become alerted to, if not thoroughly alarmed about, their dependence upon information in their work. Librarians and information scientists have done some investigating of information needs and communication patterns, but the work has barely begun and so far it is mostly limited to studies concerned with highly specialized groups, particularly in the sciences. There ap-

pears to be ample room for research on the interaction between information and organization. (What kind of information is communicated, through what channels, to whom, how,
with what effect upon organizational relationships and performance?) And of course libraries themselves, because of
their variety and because their organization is complex and
often ambiguous, would be promising subjects for investigation.

Organization Theory in Type-of-Library Courses. The
current overemphasis in type of library and in administration
courses on organization charts, standards, recommended procedures and other such features of the rational-bureaucratic
model should be modified to present a more balanced picture,
one which would take into account other organizational models
and emphasize the variations among libraries. The school librarian, for example, should understand the school as a fore-
shortened hierarchy, one in which administrative officers are
not numerous but are relatively powerful. In this situation,
the school librarian is the peer of the classroom teacher in
the formal structure, but is functionally dependent upon the
teacher in the performance of his job.

The public library should be understood as one of those
public service institutions which has difficulty defining its
clientele or, in Blau's terms, its "prime beneficiary." This
difficulty can lead to conflicts within the organization or to
displacement of the "service" goal by the goal of organizational survival.

The academic librarian, caught in the middle of the
faculty-administration conflict, should recognize this conflict
as one between the authority-of-knowledge and the authority-
of-position. The academic library itself is, and probably
must be, an administratively-oriented organization, but it
exists in a larger organizational milieu which is professional-
ly-oriented. This difference is, in itself, a source of misunderstanding and, potentially, of conflict.

Organization Theory in "Function" Courses. Standard
textbooks for courses in technical processes and reference
usually pay some attention to the interrelationships between
these two functional divisions in the library. But the treatment is superficial. It fails to take into account the stresses
which arise from the fact that performance in the technical
services is directed toward production while in reference work
it is directed toward client service. In the large library,

moreover, efficient operation in the technical services calls
for division of labor, specialization of knowledge and skills,
interdependence among workers at all levels, and, thus, for
coordination and supervision through centralized authority.
In contrast, even if a library is large enough to organize its
reference services on the basis of subject specializations,
each reference librarian within a given unit is expected to
be in command of the total reference process (though the
process may include referral). His work is relatively independent, hard to supervise, hard to control.

The Organizational Context of Field Experience. One
serious consequence of our current reliance upon the over-
simplified and anachronistic models of the rational bureaucracy and the classic profession is that the new professional,
in his first exposure to the "real" world on the job, often
undergoes an adjustment which may be traumatic. The most
frequent complaints have to do with assignment to "unprofessional" tasks. Sometimes these complaints mean merely that
the tasks are routine and tedious, but often enough they sig-
nify a lack of professional autonomy. Many students who
leave library school with a high sense of mission feel frus-
trated by bureaucratic restrictions in the large library, or
blocked, if they work, for instance, in a school, by their
dependence upon other elements in the organization. Some
adjust by embracing the organizational values and pattern,
promptly setting their sights on the administrative ladder to
be climbed. Others settle for a redefinition of their professional aims into the comfort and security of a circumscribed
"job." And still others retreat into an embittered sense of
disillusionment with "the system."

One possibility for reducing such unproductive adjustments, borrowed from social work education, [31] lies in a
carefully planned and administered field work experience. In
a very real sense, it is the business of the professional
school to present the student with an ideal world, one in
which theory and principles are supreme, the "best practice"
is always followed, and judgments are suspended until all
the evidence has been examined. It is just as clearly the
business of the professional in practice to deal with a real
world in which the goals and methods of the organization are
powerful, resources are limited, habits are strong, and decisions must be faced, often before all the facts are in.

Like the social workers, we might use a field work
experience to bridge the gap between these two worlds, help-

ing the student to move from an over-dependence on the professional school (without a too-ready rejection of it as "ivory tower") toward appreciation and understanding of the organization's advantages and limitations (without a too-ready shift to dependence on its authority). The goal would be professional autonomy within the organizational framework.

Organization Theory in Professional Acculturation. Many studies have shown that the student in the professional school acquires a cluster of values, attitudes, opinions, and patterns of behavior which may not be recognized explicitly in terms of instructional objectives or course content,[32] but which are widely accepted as crucial for gaining admission to the brotherhood of the profession. We know little if anything about what happens to library school students in this process of professional acculturation--here is another promising area for research--and, almost by definition, the process is one which resists deliberate manipulation. Nevertheless, if librarians and, especially, library educators were to re-examine their preconceptions about librarianship as a profession and about the library as an organization, they might be able to develop a new and more sophisticated model of the field, one which would be a pervasive component in the culture transmitted to the students. In such a model, the service goal of the profession and the service goal of the organization would be continually reconciled. There would be a constant movement toward equilibrium between the organization as the means to achieve professional objectives and professional service as the means to achieve organizational objectives. What we need is a dynamic model, in tune with our society and appropriate for our time.

Notes

1. The terms "rational model" and "natural system model" are used by Alvin Gouldner, "Organizational Analysis," in Sociology Today: Problems and Prospects, ed. by R. K. Merton, L. Broom, and L. S. Cottrell, Jr., New York: Harper & Row, 1959 ("Harper Torchbooks") II, 400-428. Elements of the models presented are discussed by several of the writers referred to herein.
2. Ibid., 407-410.
3. Ibid., 426.
4. A. Etzioni, Modern Organizations, Englewood Cliffs, N. J., Prentice-Hall, 1964, 41.

5. Ibid., 49.
6. E. C. Hughes, "Professions," in The Professions in America, ed. by K. S. Lynn and the editors of Daedalus, Boston, Houghton Mifflin, 1965, 9.
7. W. R. Scott, "Professionals in Bureaucracies--Areas of Conflict," in Professionalization, ed. by H. M. Vollmer and D. L. Mills, Englewood Cliffs, N. J., Prentice-Hall, 1966, 269.
8. V. A. Thompson, "The Organizational Dimension," Wilson Library Bulletin, 42 (March 1968), 697.
9. H. Vollmer and D. L. Mills, eds., Professionalization, Englewood Cliffs, N. J., Prentice-Hall, 1966, 276.
10. Etzioni, op. cit., 75-93.
11. Ibid., 81.
12. Ibid., 87.
13. Cf. W. Goode, "The Librarian: From Occupation to Profession?", Library Quarterly, 31 (1961), 306-18.
14. J. H. Shera, Libraries and the Organization of Knowledge, Hamden, Conn., Archon Books, 1965, 16.
15. Ibid., 163.
16. R. Munn, "Education for Public Librarianship," in Education for Librarianship, ed. by B. Berelson, Chicago, American Library Association, 1949, 22. A more recent proposal of the same sort is made by R. M. Dougherty ("Manpower Utilization in Technical Services," Library Resources and Technical Services, 12 [Winter 1968], 82): "to what extent the present personnel shortage could be alleviated with proper manpower utilization is moot, but I feel strongly that the results would be far more productive if the profession were to concentrate on educating systems analysts, rather than trying to recruit 100,000 additional librarians."
17. Goode, op. cit., 314-15.
18. A. Etzioni, "Two Approaches to Organizational Analysis: A Critique and a Suggestion," Administrative Science Quarterly, 5 (1960), 261.
19. Etzioni's example is the institution of the mental hospital or prison, where the goals of therapy and rehabilitation conflict with the community's demand for custodial measures. Ours might be the public library in a community dominated by proponents of censorship. In neither instance is there the implication that the organization must adjust to its environment merely to survive. Obviously it can, indeed, it must, undertake to change that environment. But in doing so its efforts are at least partially diverted from its primary goal.

20. Goode, op. cit., 315.
21. P. M. Blau and W. R. Scott, Formal Organizations: A Comparative Approach, San Francisco, Chandler, 1962, 43.
22. M. L. Bundy and P. Wasserman, "Professionalism Reconsidered," College & Research Libraries, 29 (1968), 8.
23. The typology of service organizations based on organization selection of clients and client control over participation is presented in R. O. Carlson's "Environmental Constraints and Organizational Consequences: The Public School and Its Clients," in Behavioral Science and Educational Administration, ed. by D. E. Griffiths. National Society for the Study of Education Sixty-Fourth Yearbook, Part II, Chicago, University of Chicago Press, 1964, 262-276.
24. Op. cit., 13.
25. Ibid., 8.
26. Ibid., 10.
27. Gouldner, op. cit., 419.
28. L. Riessman, "A Study of Role Conceptions in Bureaucracy," Social Forces, 27 (1949), 308-9.
29. Etzioni, Modern Organization, 89.
30. A. W. Gouldner, "Cosmopolitans and Locals: Toward an Analysis of Latent Social Roles--I," Administrative Science Quarterly, 2 (1957), 281-306.
31. Cf., for example, R. Gilpin, Theory and Practice as a Single Reality, Chapel Hill, N. C., University of North Carolina Press, 1963.
32. A notable example is H. S. Becker, et al., Boys in White, Chicago, University of Chicago Press, 1961.

WHAT AND HOW OF DOCUMENTATION TRAINING

S. R. Ranganathan

0   Purpose of Education

01   Induction into the Culture of the Group

It is an inherent instinct in man to transmit his knowledge and practices from generation to generation. There is a pretty Chinese legend about it. The king was sitting in the evening sun. One of his technical advisers was talking to him about the new agricultural method just invented in the country. At that moment the king's eyes happened to fall on his grandchildren playing at some distance. A look of sadness suddenly appeared on the face of the king. Those around him felt concerned. They elicited from him the cause of his sadness. "The new agricultural method is quite good," he said. "These new methods will disappear with us. How can my grandchildren have the benefit of the knowledge of these?" The courtiers reassured him, saying in effect, "Education will transmit these new methods to the new generation." In fact, education does induct the new generation into the culture of the group. This is almost a primitive purpose of education. We find this primitive purpose prevailing even among animals. Witness, for example, the hen educating the chicken in picking up grains and worms from the street and from the dust-heap.

02   Development of Personality

The purpose of education is much richer than mere transmission of information and knowledge. Its whole purpose is the development of the whole personality of the student towards its fullness--the bodily sheath, the sheath of lower emotions, the mental sheath, the sheath of sublimated emotions, and the innermost sheath--the soul--characterized by intuition. [1]

03   Dominant Purpose in Documentation Training

A person seeking education to become a documentalist

would have normally completed his university education and
would have taken a primary degree and perhaps even a post-
graduate degree in some one of the traditional subjects.
While going through that course, he would have already acquired competence for further self-education in respect of the
physical and the lower emotional sheaths. The development
of these sheaths need not therefore figure directly in the professional training of a documentalist. At the other end, the
continuous refinement of the sublimated emotions and the release of the intuition can only be helped by an adept in spiritual attainment; these are out of bound in a professional
course. At any rate, these cannot figure directly in the professional training of a documentalist. The only sheath that
would figure directly in his training would be the mental
sheath, though the higher order of mental education in documentation training may happen to contribute incidentally and
indirectly to the development of the other four sheaths; this
will depend on the personality of the teacher.

1   Factors in Mental Education

11   Three Factors

Mental education involves:

1. Increasing acuteness in experiment and observation;
2. Enrichment of memory; and
3. Sharpening of intellect.

These three elements cannot be separated though they are
mentally recognizable as distinct. In the education for certain professions, training in experiment and observation is
dominant; it is so in professions such as Engineering and
Agriculture, whose fields of practice are predominantly material. Enrichment of memory may be dominant in the education for some other professions.

12   Dominant Factor in Documentation Training

The documentation profession is concerned with the
intellectual output of the specialists in diverse subject-fields.
It should comprehend, organize, and serve the records of
all such intellectual output. It should serve them to each
specialist in the measure of his needs at the moment.

     1. He should bring nascent micro documents into active use to satisfy Law 1 of Library Science;

     2. He should serve them pinpointedly to every reader to satisfy Law 2;

     3. He should serve all the relevant documents exhaustively to satisfy Law 3;

     4. He should serve them expeditiously to satisfy Law 4;[2] and

     5. He should do so in spite of the continuing downpour, of perhaps 100 nascent micro documents per day.

This description of the purpose of the documentation profession makes it clear that the sharpening of the intellect should be the dominant factor in documentation training.

13   Two Other Factors

     To single out the sharpening of the intellect as the dominant factor does not imply the neglect of the two other factors. Memory, particularly associative memory, should be cultivated and steadily enriched by every documentalist. Formal training cannot achieve this. It can be achieved only be continuing practice and deep interest all through life. Experiment and observation too are now and then necessary to improve the intellectual performance of the documentalist and, for this purpose, to improve the techniques of documentation work and service. Occasions should be created in the course of the period of training to enable the student to see the inadequacy of the current techniques in documentation work. The need for improving the methods of eliciting the requirement of a specialist reader in precise terms and for correlating them to the entries in the documentation list should be brought home while doing reference service, which is called Documentation Service when applied to the service of nascent micro documents to the specialist reader. Experiments will have to be made on these; and they can be made only while on floor duty helping readers. In other words, something like the clinical method in vogue in the training of medical students should be followed in the training of a documentation student.

2   Curriculum in Documentation

21   Subjects in Umbral Region

     The following subjects form the umbral region of documentation work and services:

1.   Development and structure of the universe of subjects;
2.   Advanced classification denoted by the term "Depth Classification" (theory and practice);
3.   Advanced cataloging including abstracting work (theory and practice);
4.   Organization of documentation; and
5.   Documentation service.

These are the major subjects needing great attention in documentation training. [3]

211   Universe of Subjects

A good grasp of the development and structure of the universe of subjects, a knowledge of the outstanding epochs in its development, and familiarity with the outstanding contributors and their contributions are necessary to get a whole view of the problems of documentation. These are particularly necessary to make the student recognize the happenings in the wavefront in the universe of subjects and develop sensitiveness to the need for dynamism in the documentation techniques. This subject will overload beyond measure the curriculum for the course for B. Lib. Sc. --the first degree in library science. It can be taken up only in a later course for documentation training.

212   Depth Classification

Unless the millions of nascent micro documents are helpfully organized in the documentation lists, retrieval work will not be efficient. It will be marred by leakage and noise. Their organization needs depth classification. It should be a self-perpetuating one, as new proliferations in the universe of subjects take place overnight, as it were. This makes it necessary for the documentalist to learn a dynamic penetrating theory of classification and also the methodology for designing depth schedules for the classification of the micro subjects going with a Basic Subject. This cannot be taught in the course for B. Lib. Sc. It can be taken up only in a later course for documentation training.

213   Advanced Cataloging

Advanced cataloging includes abstracting, preparation

of abstracting and indexing periodicals, trend reports in anticipation of demand, and ad hoc documentation lists on demand.   This cannot be taught in the B. Lib. Sc. course, though
preparation of a simple bibliography should be.   Advanced
cataloging can be taken up only in a later course for documentation training.

214 Organization

The organization for documentation is not the same as
that for general library service.   The selection, acquisition,
routine of technical treatment, and the circulation of the micro documents, which are mostly without independent physical
existence, are quite different from those of books.   Further,
the organization of the rational system of documentation centers will have to be done on a basis quite different from that
of the national library system of libraries.   The B. Lib. Sc.
course cannot cover these adequately.   These would increase
the curricular load beyond the capacity of the students and
that of the duration of the course.   They can be taken up
only in a later course for documentation training.

215 Documentation Service

A precise formulation of the requirement of a reader
is far more difficult in the case of a specialist than in the
case of a generalist reader.   Even to get a good approximation to it, the documentalist should, with the immediate help
of the specialist reader, make a deep facet analysis of his
requirements--deeper than in the case of a generalist reader.
While making this facet analysis with the reader, one part
of the mind of the documentalist should be scanning the documentation list of micro documents and their scatter among
the host documents.   This work requires deep experience and
familiarity with micro documents.   These cannot be got in
the B. Lib. Sc. course.   This can be begun only in a later
course for documentation training.   Of course, this knowledge
will have to be continuously deepened throughout the career of
a documentalist.

22 Translation Service (Fringe Subject 1)

At the depth of micro subjects, important documents
will be found to be widely scattered in many languages.   It
will be wasteful, if not impossible, for each specialist reader to learn many languages in order to read the relevant documents in all the languages.   National and international econ-

omy demands the supply, to specialist readers, of translations of the relevant documents in languages alien to him.
Translation requires a technique different from that for documentation work and service, in addition to the knowledge of
the languages concerned. It needs an independent course of
its own. This load cannot be included in the course for documentation training. Further, it is uneconomical for the documentalist himself to function as translator. It will surely
take away from his time and thought, the whole of which is
needed for work in the umbral region of documentation. This
has been well established by now in almost every country,
though about half a century ago competence in translation
work was deemed to be an essential qualification; and competence in library techniques was mentioned only as a desirable additional qualification to those to be put in charge of
specialist libraries. But it is necessary and it will also be
sufficient, if a documentalist is trained to organize and to
supervise the translation service to be got out of professional
translators--full-time or part-time, as the case may be.
Translation service can thus be only a fringe subject in the
course for documentation training.

23   Reprography Service (Fringe Subject 2)

A micro document does not have an independent physical existence. Its host macro document may not be available in the library or even in the country. It may also be
irreplaceable. Therefore, it may be risky to transport the
whole of the host document from one library to another, or
from one country to another, for the use of only one of its
many micro contents and that too for a short while only.
Further, a specialist reader would often wish to own a copy
of the micro document. These two factors indicate the advantage of making reprographs of the micro documents in
such cases. Reprography is severely a technician's job,
needing its own training and also involving full-time work.
Therefore, it is not proper to add its load to the course for
documentation training. But it is necessary and it will be
sufficient if a documentalist is trained to organize and supervise the reprography service, entrusted to the technicians in
reprography. Reprography service can thus be only a fringe
subject in the course for documentation training.

24   Machine Retrieval (Fringe Subject 3)

Machine retrieval is a new subject claiming the attention of documentalists. The construction, maintenance, and

servicing of the retrieval machine belong to the engineering profession. It is economical to leave the programming work also to a specially trained technician. Therefore, it is not proper to add the load of machine retrieval to the course for documentation training. But it is necessary and it will be sufficient if a documentalist is trained to organize and supervise the machine retrieval work. Machine retrieval, with punched card at one end and computer at the other end, can thus be only a fringe subject in the course for documentation training.

25 Confusion Caused by Wrong Emphasis on Fringe Subjects

Unfortunately, the old law "Distance breeds enchantment" appears to have taken possession of some documentalists. Of course, these are often persons who had apparently never made a deep study or application of the advanced reaches of the subjects in the umbral region of documentation. Driven by these factors, they get easily fascinated by the "wonder working" quality of the computer and the reprographic methods. These lend themselves to be used as showpieces while taking the higher authorities round. These authorities too sometimes get mesmerized by these spectacular things, while they could not at all sense the relatively invisible but necessary and far more basic work done behind the screen in the umbral region of documentation. Free printing or reprographic service offered by a documentation center to the higher authorities--often even at the cost of its legitimate use for the benefit of the specialist readers--touch a weak point in man; and this leads some of the higher authorities to step up their estimate of the efficiency of the documentation center, without taking into consideration its legitimate service of top priority to specialist readers.

For the time being, a myth gets circulated equating documentation with the fringe subjects in it. Such mishaps form part of the infantile ailments of any new profession or subject. For example, about 50 years ago there was no library profession in India. In the public mind only attendants (janitors) were associated with the library. When a professional post was created in the Madras University Library, the term "Librarian" was used to denote that post. This term caught the imagination of the people. The janitors in that library used to get letters addressed as "Librarian." Thus, janitorship and librarianship were equated for some time! Today, the computer has not yet come into the documentation field in India. But reprography has. The tech-

nicians in reprography style themselves as documentalists.
Even big institutions are unable to see the difference between
the qualifications and the functions of the documentalist on
the one hand and of the reprographer on the other. This
misleads them to appoint a technician in reprography to the
post of a documentalist. One can imagine the disastrous consequences. A few years ago, a translator was appointed
documentalist in a national documentation center. He was
even asked to conduct a regional seminar on documentation!
This kind of confusion caused by wrong emphasis should be
eliminated as quickly as possible. It is for the documentation profession to eliminate it.

26   Confusion Even in Training Centers

I have seen in some countries the documentation training center giving a course largely in punch-card technique,
reprography, and thesaurus-building. The teachers had never
seriously taken the subjects in the umbral region of documentation. The general education of the students was too low to
enable them to understand the subjects in the umbral region.
Since this happens in some countries of the West, some of
the newly developing countries imitate them in their low interpretation of "documentation training." A university was
approached to adopt a curriculum heavily loaded with the
fringe subjects of retrieval by punched card and other mechanical means, reprography, and translation for the master's
degree in documentation. Fortunately, the proposal was not
accepted. This confusion even in the training centers must
be stopped. It is for the documentation profession to stop it.

3   Methods for Education in Documentation

31   Lecture Method

In the course for documentation training, there should
be a few provoking lectures once in a week or two, to ex-
pose the students to new problems to be pursued. There
should also be a few inspiring lectures at intervals to sum
up and clinch the ideas developed from time to time. Certainly, the first lecture of the course and the last one should
be tuned to a very high pitch. The first should rouse curiosity in abundance about the what, the why, and the how of
documentation. The last lecture should give the students a
momentum that will carry them forward for long after leav-
ing the course. It must have a message which will inspire

and guide them throughout their career.   This alone is the
right use of lecture as a method in training. [4]

32   Discussion Method

The most effective way to keep all the students in the
class mentally alert, active, and attentive is to adopt the
discussion method of teaching.   In this method the one-way
talk of the teacher will disappear.   Each student will soon
shed his shyness.   His mind will open.   All students will
soon vie with one another to make their own contribution in
developing the subject.   In the discussion method, the teacher's part will be arduous.   He should have a good grasp of
the subject.   He should know the psychology of the students.
He should know how to direct the discussions along profitable
lines, in a participative way.   He should be prompt to bring
back the discussions on the right lines without inhibiting any
student, whenever it goes along the tangent.

One of the possible illusions in a discussion arises
out of failure to distinguish between idea plane and verbal
plane.   Very often brief statement of a proposition in new
words and recasting the sentences in diverse ways are taken
to be equivalent to forward movement in the idea plane.   But
in reality they only amount to rolling within the verbal plane.
Again, synonyms and homonyms, infesting a natural language,
distract thought.   They also lead to aberration and confusion
in thinking.   The discussion method offers a splendid opportunity to make the students sensitive to these faults and to
train them in the use of precise, homonym-free, and syno-
nym-free technical terminology of documentation.   The teacher should broadly plan his work a few days ahead.   He
should be agile enough to change the plan whenever necessary.
He should prescribe books and articles for preparatory study
by the students.   He should also suggest in the course of
discussion books and articles for parallel study and follow-up
work.   He should thus incidentally accustom the students to
the use of bibliography.   This is the most rewarding method
for daily class room use in developing the theory of documentation and its techniques. [5]

33   Practical Work

A mere theoretical knowledge and a verbal understanding of the techniques of documentation will not be of
avail in the day to day work of the documentalist.   Therefore, the method of documentation training should include a

great amount of grind in practical work and in observation
work.   Practical work should loom large in classification and
cataloging.   Observation work should loom large in the study
of organization and administration.   As stated in section 13,
clinical observation should loom large in documentation service.   The records of experience gained in the practical, observational, and clinical work should form the concrete basis
for discussion in the theory classes.

34 Self-Study

Self-study is essential to give to student-documentalist
the opportunity to have the joy of exploring for himself.   He
should be encouraged to go beyond what is listed in bibliography given by the teacher for preparatory, parallel, and
follow-up studies.   The student should be encouraged to have
recourse to self-study in familiarizing himself with the reference books, bibliographies, and documentation periodicals
in diverse subjects.

35 Group Study

The study to be done for the course in the "Universe
of Subjects: Its structure and development" is too vast to
be done fully by each student.   This is a fit field for accus-
toming the documentalist to group study and team work.   The
field should be divided among the students.   They should all
share the findings of all of them.

36 Essay Work

The course of documentation training should not lose
sight of the fact that the student should be trained in precise
expression and presentation of ideas.   This is no doubt done
in the discussion method, but as Bacon said, "Writing maketh
a man perfect."   The student should be given opportunity to
write essays on some specified topics covered in the theory
class from time to time.   An average of one essay a week
should be possible.

37 Tutorial Work

Effective training in documentation requires tutorial
work.   It brings the method of training closest to the ideal
of individual instruction.   The practical work done, notes of
the observations made in the organizational and administrative work, the notes on the clinical work in documentation

service, and the essays written should be reviewed intimately with each student during the weekly tutorial hour. [6]

4 Wrong Methods

41 Dictation of Notes

The make-believe method of dictating notes can have no place in the professional training in documentation--and in fact, in education of any kind. Instead of sharpening the intellect, this method inhibits it. In a country making a fetish of examinations, cramming the words in the notes is both necessary and sufficient to qualify as a documentalist. As a measure of self-protection, the teacher may even be tempted not only to abstain from mentioning to the students the names of the books available on the subject, but even keep them out of their reach! This is an inheritance of the practice that developed in schools and colleges in examination infested countries. This method blesseth neither the teacher nor the taught. To practice dictation of notes in documentation training is antisocial.

42 Illusion of Lectures

Another wrong method inherited from the mass-method of teaching practiced in schools and colleges is the lecture method--lecture from hour to hour, from day to day, from week to week. [7] In this connection an amusing experience comes to my mind. About 30 years ago, the District Board (County Council) of Malabar invited me to take part in giving a refresher course to the members of the teaching profession. I went towards the end of the course. I was put down for the very first hour, 8 a.m. The faded faces of the teachers attracted my attention. After introducing my subject in about the first ten minutes, I began my usual method of developing the subject through questions and answers. But even before the expiry of the first ten minutes, some of the teachers were already struggling with their heavy eyelids. My first two questions were answered with some liveliness by some wakeful teachers. Some wit and humor developed. I mentioned that continuous lecturing, with the students thrown into a passive condition, is an effective method of inducing sleep in them. This elicited an uproarious laughter. The near-sleeping teachers woke up and heard my repeating the sentence. They all stood up thinking that I had asked all the sleeping teachers to stand up! ... The teachers said in chorus, "Exit Lecture, Exit One-Way Talk."

5   Extra-Mural Method of Training

51   Field Experience under Guidance

Theoretical knowledge and practical work done as an auxiliary to the course on theory are necessary; but they are not sufficient by themselves. A student with such a training alone should not be sent out as a trustworthy documentalist. He should be made to prepare a long documentation list with abstracts all by himself on the basis of specified periodicals on a specified subject. Such a field work is best done as a pilot project even before the student leaves the course. In this in-course project, the teacher can keep a watch over the student's progress and help him out of any difficulty that he may come across. I would call this Field Experience under Guidance. [8]

52   Field Experience Without Guidance

Even field experience during term time under guidance will not prove sufficient. The student should be made to build up field experience for a specified period, quite unaided and by himself. This is best done as a post-course project. The work should come even closer to reality than in the in-course project. The subject field for the post-course project may be the same--it is better that it is the same--as the one chosen for the in-course project. The difference between the two projects will be in the periodicals forming the basis and in the presentation of the documentation list. The post-course project should be turned on preparing a trend report; and the period to be covered by the report should be pre-scribed; it may conveniently be three years. There should be no restriction on the periodicals to be scanned; the ideal should be to reach exhaustiveness. The entries used should be given in an appendix, as an alphabetical indexing bibliography. The text of the trend report should give a coherent picture of the development of the subject. Naturally, the presentation should be in a classified sequence in order to secure coherence. Perhaps, a period of six months may be necessary to complete this post-course project. The training center should evaluate the trend report. Unless it is satisfactory, the student should not be certified to be fit to practice as documentalist. [9]

53   Weekly Colloquium

531 Collective Study of a Specific Subject

The weekly colloquium is a multipurpose institution
in a documentation training center. To understand the subjects developed in the lessons--be they theoretical or practical, observational or tutorial--with insight and precision, it
is helpful to train the intellect to discuss a specified subject
collectively in a colloquium. This is the first purpose of the
weekly colloquium.

532 Training in the Method of Debate

Such discussions will form a necessary means of developing the subject of documentation in the coming years of
the students. Therefore, the weekly colloquium should also
train the students in the correct and profitable methods of
debate. To gain this end, it is found helpful to have a rehearsal before each colloquium begins. At the colloquium itself the local librarians and others interested should be invited to attend. And they should also be allowed to take part
in the discussion sparingly. This will help the student to
shed his shyness and harden himself to face an audience.
The debate itself should be conducted according to the normal
rules. The expression should be precise. Wherever possible each point made should be supported by citation of authority. It is helpful to center the debate round one or two
definite propositions. Training in finding out the "truth" of
the subject by debate among peers is the second purpose of
the weekly colloquium.

533 Preparation for Scientific Debate

To make the debate run along exhaustive and right
lines, to make the necessary citations possible, each student
should be made to study all the relevant documents bearing
on the topic for discussion to qualify himself for participation in the weekly colloquium. This is a quality very often
neglected in scientific debates--let alone political debates,
where "fireworks" is more often the aim than arriving at
"truth." To cultivate the right habit of preparing in full
measure for taking part in a debate on documentation is the
third purpose of the weekly colloquium.

534 Self Documentation Service

The preparation for a debate on any topic on documentation should include studying intensively the published docu-

ments on the topic. They will be mostly micro documents.
They may be found in sections of books and in articles in
periodicals. The cultivation of the habit of thus doing documentation service to oneself and knowing what has been already recorded on the topic is the fourth purpose of the weekly colloquium.

535   Collective Preparation of Documentation List

A prior requirement for documentation service--even
if it be for self-documentation service--is the preparation of
a documentation list. The following is a sample organization
for the collective preparation of the documentation list needed
for the debate in a particular colloquium. For definiteness
in description, we shall take Wednesdays as the colloquium
days. We shall also count the weeks from Wednesday to
Wednesday.

1. The collection in the library is divided into groups
such that the scanning of the volume in each group will take
more or less the same time as that in any other group; this
is done permanently for the whole course; each student is
assigned a group for scanning; the group is changed each
week in cyclical permutation.
2. In each colloquium there is a leader, an opposition leader, a rapporteur, a documentalist, and the other
participants. These offices go round among the students in
cyclical permutation from colloquium to colloquium;
3. Wednesday 1: In the colloquium of this day, the
topic for the colloquium for Wednesday 4 is determined and
announced;
4. Week 1: During Week 1, each student scans the
volumes in his group with the announced topic in view and
prepares his documentation list in 12.5 x 7.5 cm slips; he
hands it over to the documentalist on the Monday of the week,
the documentalist prepares a consolidated list, makes copies
of it, and distributes them to all the students on Wednesday
2;
5. Week 2: During Week 2, each student studies
the relevant literature with the aid of the documentation list;
6. On the Tuesday of Week 2 the leader, the opposition leader, and the rapporteur for the concerned colloquium
meet under the guidance of the teacher and frame one or
two propositions to be discussed at the colloquium;
7. Wednesday 3: The proposition framed is announced at the colloquium on Wednesday 3; at the end of the
colloquium of Wednesday 3, the participants divide them-

selves into two groups--one for the support and the other for the opposition of the proposition;

8. Week 3: During Week 3, each student studies the documents again purposively in order to play his part in the colloquium;

9. Sunday of Week 3: Rehearsal under the guidance of the teacher;

10. Wednesday 4: Colloquium; and

11. Thursday of Week 4: The minutes of the colloquium are finalized and circulated among the students.

536 Coverage of the Library Collection

The organization mentioned in section 535 incidentally makes each student become thoroughly familiar with all the volumes in the collection of the library bearing on library science. This is the sixth purpose of the colloquium. [10]

54 Annual Seminar

Full-fledged documentation service is of recent origin. The discipline of documentation is taking shape only just now. Most of the techniques used in the service and taught in the training centers are only provisional and elemental. It will take at least a generation to reach maturity and a state of steady growth. Certainly, till then, the documentation training center should continue to keep in close touch with the alumni. It is best for it to do so even after then. It should promote exchange of thought among them and with the center itself. The alumni should be assigned problems for pursuit in the discipline of documentation. There should be an annual seminar for the collective examination of the findings of the different alumni. In our experience, about a week is found necessary for the annual seminar. It is best for each seminar to suggest the problems for pursuit in the succeeding year. This will secure some continuity in the ideas pursued in the successive seminars. The proceedings of the seminar should be published promptly. The seminar system for the alumni will promote coordinated team-research in documentation.

6 Humanism and Training in Documentation

Humanism stands for the improvement of each individual as well as of the society as a whole. A training course in documentation outlined as above has every chance to serve the cause of humanism.

61 Improvement of the Individual

In the first place each student will get work satisfaction in the measure of his own capacity. Any student with the capacity, industry, and will to do research will also be helped by the documentation training center to discover and develop his research capacity. At least the training center should throw the ferment, as it were, which will make such a student continue to do and to derive joy from research in his later life. There is no special method for this. Each of the methods described in sections 3 and 5 will prove effective in the hands of an earnest teacher with personality and resourcefulness. Whenever opportunity lends itself, he will lift the horizon of the field of documentation as it were and give the students a glimpse of the problems in documentation lying beyond and awaiting pursuit.

62 Improvement of the Society

The documentation training center should engage itself in research through its staff and through research students. This is necessary for the documentation techniques to keep step with the new proliferations in the universe of micro subjects forming incessantly in the wavefront of knowledge. This in turn is necessary to feed the research workers in diverse subject fields to the full satisfaction of the Five Laws of Library Science. The research worker should be fed in this way in order to prevent the dissipation of the research potential in the world by being wasted on unintended and unwanted duplication of one and the same investigation. The research potential should be conserved in that way as the whole of it is wanted to set right the imbalance between population on the one hand and natural and near-natural commodities on the other. Such a research is necessary to improve the technology so as to increase the yield of natural commodities and natural raw materials by intensive methods of cultivation and exploitation. Research will also have to find out technological methods for the production of consumable commodities out of non-consumable raw materials -- such as artificial textile, building, and packing materials, and even food. Research will also have to find quick means of communication and transport so as to distribute the total resources of the world equitably among all the people of the world, in spite of the non-correlated distribution of materials and men on the face of the earth. Thus, research in the discipline of documentation has a definite place as a link in the chain leading to social betterment. This is the justifica-

tion for asking a documentation training center to function
also as the apex of the documentation research centers of
the community.

7   Testimony of Experience

The above description of the what and the how of documentation training is not based on speculation; but it is the
result of actual experience.

71   DRTC: 1962 Onwards

The latest and the fullest experience is in the Documentation Research and Training Center (= DRTC) in Bangalore.   DRTC is making a fairly good approach towards the
ideal.

72   Delhi University: 1947-1955

Long before DRTC was established in 1962, most but
not all of these methods were developed in the Department
of Library Science of the University of Delhi from 1947 on-
wards.   Sir Maurice Gwyer, the then vice-chancellor, gave
the opportunity and the facilities for this by establishing a
Department of Library Science, teaching the subject from
the B. Lib. Sc. course, through the M. Lib. Sc. course,
right up to doctorate work.   There was no annual seminar
there, but the Biennial Indian Library Conference served the
purpose, though in a lower key.

73   Madras and Benares Universities: 1929-1946

Long before work was started in Delhi, a course in
library science in general along the lines described here was
begun in 1929 in the University of Madras.   Documentation
figures in that course only in a feeble incipient form; for documentation, as it is understood today, had not then come into
practice.   However, the methodology was the same except
for the extra-mural methods of projects, colloquia, and seminars.

74   Arts Colleges: 1917-1923

The rest of the methodology of training students had
been practiced by me even from 9 July 1917, when I started
teaching, to 4 January 1924, when I began work as university

librarian. It was used in teaching not library science or documentation but physics and mathematics. Totally unconscious of my future changeover to the library profession, even then I made education library-centered. This was the result of my dislike of text-books and notes-centered teaching to which I had been exposed as a student from 1897-1917.

75 Experience Through Half-a-Century

Thus the testimony of experience through half-a-century goes in support of what has been described in this paper.

8 Felicitations to Dr. Shera

This paper is to be woven into the garland to be presented to our good friend Dr. Jesse Hauk Shera. He is a leading educator of U.S.A. in the field of library science in general and documentation in particular. Through his many writings, he has enhanced the status of the subject during the last two decades. He was one of the first in U.S.A. to understand and appreciate the work in the field being done in India. He is a founder-member of the American Study Group of Classification promoting the spread of the Indian school of thought in that hemisphere. Under his guidance the School of Library Science of Case Western Reserve University has become, since 1952, an eminent center "for the exploration of the new horizon in education for librarianship" in general and documentation in particular. As one marching about ten years ahead of Dr. Shera along the same road of life, I greet him with the assurance: "Come along Jesse. The farther we go the more enchanting and the more rewarding is the experience. It is ever-increasing joy. I wish you a splendid progress along this road for many many years to come."

Notes

1. Library Book Selection. 2nd ed., 1966. Chap DN. (Note: The term "sublimated emotions" has been wrongly printed in the diagram as "stimulated emotions.")

2. [Reference is made to the Five Laws of Library Science: (1) Books are for use; (2) Every reader his book; (3) Every book its reader; (4) Save the time of the reader; and (5) A library is a growing organism.

Library Education   513

Cf. S. R. Ranganathan, The Five Laws of Library Science, Madras, Madras Library Association, 1931 and later. --Editor.]

3. "Course of Training in Documentation," Annals of Library Science 6 (1959), Paper N. Also published in S. R. Ranganathan, ed., Documentation and Its Facets (1963), chap. D5.

4. Ranganathan, S. R. "Lecture vs. tutorial," Training in Library Science 5. An. Lib. Sci. 1 (1954), 252-56.

5. Neelameghan, A. "Structure of the Main Entry in an Advanced Documentation List," Teaching in Library Science 5 (Lib. Sc., 3; 1966; Paper E);----and Bhattacharyya, G. "Discussion Technique in Teaching Library Science," Teaching in Library Science 10 (Lib. Sc., 3; 1966; Paper U);----and Ranganathan, S. R. "Use of Symbolic Language in Teaching. Case Study," Training in Library Science 9 (An. Lib. Sc. 9; 1962; Paper R). Ranganathan, S. R. "Array Change or Level Change?" Teaching in Library Science 2 (Lib. Sc., 2; 1965; Paper F);----. "Classification of Linguistics," Teaching in Library Science 1 (Lib. Sc. 1; 1964; Paper K);----. "Development in Notational Plane Up to Primitive Faceted Notation," Teaching in Library Science 6 (Lib. Sc. 3; 1966; Paper M);----. "Documentalist and Subject Specialist," Training in Library Science 11 (An. Lib. Sc. 10; 1963; Paper K);----. "Evolution of Reference and Documentation Service," Teaching in Library Science 3 (Lib. Sc. 2; 1965; Paper Q);----. "Special Library vs. Specialist Library," Teaching in Library Science 19 (Lib. Sc. 4; 1967; Paper N);----and Neelameghan, A. "Design of a classification schedule," Training in Library Science 10 (An. Lib. Sc. 10; 1963; Paper B); and "Effective Decade," Training in Library Science 8 (An. Lib. Sc. 9; 1962; Paper Q).

6. Ranganathan, S. R. "Lecture vs. Tutorial," Training in Library Science, cited in note 4, above.

7. Ibid.

8, 9. Bhattacharyya, G. and Neelameghan, A. "Project Technique in Teaching Library Science," Teaching in Library Science 11 (Lib. Sc. 3; 1966; Paper V).

10. Gopinath, M. A. and Neelameghan, A. "Colloquium in Teaching Library Science," Teaching in Library Science 12 (Lib. Sc. 3; 1966; Paper W).

General References

Ranganathan, S. R.   "Education for Documentalists" (Lib. Sc.
3; 1966; Paper C);----. Vitalising the University Education of Librarians, Teaching in Library Science 7
(Lib. Sc. 3; 1966; Sec. R7).

ON THE PROFESSIONAL IMAGE AND
THE EDUCATION OF THE LIBRARIAN*

Horst Kunze

Libraries are old; the librarian's image as an independent professional is relatively young. The function of libraries as well as the professional image of the librarian is determined by society and its scientific and educational needs. During the more than two thousand years of library history the librarian appears most of the time as a scholar without special bibliothecal training. In this lengthy epoch he acted primarily as knowledgeable keeper, collector, and guardian of the treasures entrusted to his office. Concerning his education as a librarian there was but little reflection. The idea of the scholar librarian was still maintained by Friedrich Adolf Ebert, who stated in 1820, wholly in keeping with the views of 18th-century encyclopedism:

> As in any other field, the ability to fulfill the specific duties of the librarian depends on a thorough background, which differs from that of other scholars only in respect to its comprehensiveness and breadth. [1]

The history of libraries in Europe, which for a long span of time is identical with international library history, permits us to observe the emergence of new concepts of the librarian's task, brought about by social change. This is clearly illustrated by two famous works of European library literature, Gabriel Naudé's Advis pour Dresser une Bibliothèque (Paris, 1627)[2] and Christian Molbech's Über Bibliothekswissenschaft oder Einrichtung und Verwaltung öffentlicher Bibliotheken (Leipzig, 1833).[3]

Who turns to Naudé's Advis with modern ideas, and expects "dresser une bibliothèque" to imply practical advice on establishing a library, is bound to be disappointed. Of the

---

*Translated from the German by C. H. Rawski.

122 octavo pages in the original edition of the Advis, only
pages 91 to 106 contain a few pointers regarding the practical
activities of the librarian.   These are the two chapters on the
"Lieu qu'il Faut Choisir pour Dresser et Establir une Bibliothèque" and the "Ordre et la Disposition que Doivent Garder
les Livres dans une Bibliothèque."[4]   On the other hand, the
modern reader of the Advis will encounter Naudé the student
and connoisseur of literature, who comments on the important
trends of man's intellectual heritage.   In this respect Naudé
is a typical representative of the century-old bibliothecal tradition that accepted the scholar librarian as a matter of course.

In the 18th century, which was the cradle of modernity
for all European countries, we find beginnings which the 19th
century cultivated and brought to fruition.   For the libraries
this meant far-reaching change and, occasionally, upheaval.
Mass problems arose and had to be coped with.   The causes
are well known: steadily increasing literary production; the
rise of periodical literature; acquisition of older collections
(manuscripts and printed books) due to secularization; inunda-
tion of libraries with books of all kinds deposited in accordance with acts of legislation.   Simultaneously, the tremendous
upsurge of the arts and sciences, and of technology, and the
rapidly increasing number of scholarly and scientific workers,
posed the question of use with a new urgency.   The great
European collections of manuscripts and printed books, which
prior to 1800 reflected in intent and arrangement the old disciplinary structure, gradually change into service libraries in
which users expect not only the retrospective stock of books,
but also materials concerning recent, and, increasingly, current investigations and findings in all fields of knowledge.

These, in brief, are the reasons for the rise in the
19th century of a literature which addressed Naudé's
subject in a different manner and with a different purpose:
the handbooks and compendia of Bibliothekswissenschaft,
written by librarians for non-librarians or on-going practitioners, which stressed the organization and administration
of libraries.   Here belong beside the Saxon Friedrich Adolf
Ebert and the Bavarian Martin Schrettinger, the Dane Christian Molbech,[5] and many others.   The concept of Bibliothekswissenschaft, a bibliothecal science, was first introduced in
the new literature by Martin Schrettinger;[6] after him, and
still before Molbech, it was adopted in Germany by Friedrich
Adolf Ebert.   The new library literature reflected the changing professional image of the librarian, who is now also responsible for the "Brauchbarkeit,"[7] the usefulness, of his

treasures. He is still expected to be a good scholar, but he
must also be versed in the "Lehre über die Einrichtung und
die Verwaltung einer Bibliothek in wissenschaftlicher Form"--
doctrine of library organization and administration in a scientific manner. 8 From these manuals on the establishment
and operation of a library leads a direct line to the textbooks
on library administration and fundamentals of librarianship,
as they exist today in all countries with modern library service. 9

It should be noted that the bibliothecal science developed in the early 19th century was not identical with modern
library science, but was clearly limited to that segment of
our field which we designate as "library administration," "library economy," "Bibliothekslehre," "Bibliothekonomie," etc.
The new stress on activities peculiar to librarianship had to
lead to the development of a library profession. Librarians
recognized the advantage of specialized personnel with documented competency. At the time, the most feasible goal was
the Certificate, an official proof of accomplishment which had
to be earned by examination. In the bureaucratic states of
Europe recognition of specialized occupational expertise in libraries meant social and economic recognition of the librarian
(as a civil servant). It is this social and economic recognition which the initiators of professional librarianship had foremost in mind, and not an academic curriculum of professional
education. This is borne out by the first act concerning the
education of academic librarians, the "Ordnung zur Ausbildung
akademisch gebildeter Bibliothekare in Deutschland" issued for
Prussia in 1893, which regulates the admission to education
for librarianship, but leaves the task of obtaining the necessary knowledge and skills largely to the admitted candidate.

Any form of library education has to be aimed at a
specific kind of librarianship, which, in turn, is determined
by nationwide library development. Any professional image
of the librarian, which mirrors the needs and aspirations of
a specific professional situation, must make use of certain
generalizations.

Let us stay with the facts of history. In Germany and
in other European countries, bibliothecal activities were dominated up to the end of the 19th century by the large scholarly
and scientific libraries and their inclusive subject collections.
These were mostly national, university, or state libraries.
They also had the greatest need for academically educated
professional librarians. These libraries functioned in support

of scholarship, and it was in the course of their activities
that the main problem areas of modern librarianship became
clearly articulated: acquisition (book selection and preparation); access (lists of new acquisitions, bibliographies, exhibits, union catalogs, information service); and use (service
and loan transactions).   The new quantitative methods, necessitated by the task of controlling large numbers of books, became also particularly significant in the large research libraries.   These great polymath institutions determine the
professional image of the European librarian in the 19th century and, in large measure, continue to do so even in our
days.

The most important changes affecting the library situation of all leading library countries, hence internationally
generalizable, are (1) the rise of a large number of special
libraries, designed to meet the demands of a discipline or an
area of research; and (2) the establishment and growth of a
network of general public libraries.10   In accordance with
national factors and trends, the development of special libraries has taken a different direction in various countries.   However, sooner or later, it has occurred everywhere, dictated,
as it were, by the requirements of modern science and education.   The support of general public library systems is a
politicum of the first order and depends, just as the bibliothecal content--knowledge--upon varying, and contrasting, national goals and tendencies.

How should library education respond to the needs of
the large general research libraries as they adjust to social
change; the special libraries which assert themselves in all
fields of scientific endeavor; and the public libraries, serving
children, young people, and adults alike? It has become evident that education for librarianship cannot ignore these widely
differing tasks.   Yet the possibilities of solving the resulting
educational problems are limited and depend upon the size of
the various countries.

In very large and populous library countries with relatively great demand for all kinds of specialized personnel, it
is not difficult to introduce additional special subject training
in the course of study.   But, even so, it is impossible to do
this for all fields of knowledge and all their respective educational needs.   Specific areas that are judged important (such
as technology, science, history, and social sciences) have to
be singled out.   Such additional areas of specialization, of
course, are also subject to the natural confines of a profes-

sional curriculum. A cardinal problem of modern society is
shortening the time required for professional education--which
is difficult, and not to extend it--which would be easy.

In small library countries only a few selected areas
of specialization can be appended to the curriculum. However, I think that, as far as special subject courses are concerned, the determining factor lies elsewhere. Today, there
exists a different reason for questioning seriously the race to
satisfy special demands on library education, namely, the
rapidity of change in the disciplines themselves, which ren-
ders parts of their content obsolete at a fast, and, often
surprisingly fast pace. Professional education without provision for subsequent continuation is becoming clearly inadequate. In the future, we will have to provide for two phases
of study: one given to acquiring the fundamentals; and one
of intermittent continuing education to repair the cracking
foundations, which proceeds more flexibly and aims at greater
differentiation.

If this is so, and we consider the fact that the large
research libraries, likewise, are at the crossroads of traditional concepts and methods, and utilization of modern information technology, then it can be easily seen that it is unrealistic to expect the library curricula to produce, today or
tomorrow, competent specialists for all branches of library
service.

It follows that the best preparation for the multifaceted
demands of library practice is obtained through serious study
of the fundamentals of librarianship, paralleled by a practi-
cum or several separate excursions into the service, in application of what has been studied. Thus it is essential to
determine what constitutes the fundamentals of librarianship
today. The quasi-sophisticated assertion that the modern librarian need not know anything save where to find knowledge,
should not be bandied about thoughtlessly. It implies only
the partial truth that it is not the sum total of all learned
facts that produces a librarian, but, rather, an understanding
of bibliothecal activities and an appreciation of the goals and
concerns they are intended to serve. Both require a very
particular aggregate of active knowledge and the ability to
comprehend the content and the purpose of librarianship. It
is in this sense that I interpret the basics of library education: foundations of librarianship as a special field, its purposes, grounds, and methods; elements of book selection and
preparation, including problems of cataloging and classifica-

tion; elements of library technology and administration; and, as a matter of course, general aspects of documentation and information services, and of sociology of librarianship.[11]

It goes without saying that all these subjects require the how-it-came-about of historical perspective, and that, with an eye on the student's professional choice, the history of librarianship should be traced, in detail for the country concerned, and in summary for all leading library countries. This is a matter of professional ethics as far as the career librarian is concerned. For quite some time now it has not been enough to discuss these fundamentals within the contexts of a given national library situation. We have to proceed internationally and utilize all available sources of professional knowledge. This requires foreign language skills which, for this reason, must also be considered as basic for library education. For most students the natural limits of their capacity hold this language requirement to just two or three foreign languages; these, however, should be obligatory. Furthermore, if library science is a discipline like any other discipline, familiarity with the methodology of reflective inquiry is needed. Learning to master, theoretically and in practical application, the ground rules of research, creates the best foundation for continuing growth in a profession. As we have said, today depends on these fundamentals; tomorrow will also depend on them, only much more so. The object is to familiarize the student with the activities of librarianship, and to help him form his own sound judgment as to their place and function in library practice. For he will be expected to be both able and willing to use imaginatively and change boldly and constructively the working methods and patterns of the library.

The graduate library schools can offer to their students merely the prerequisites for professional competence. It is the practice of librarianship which produces a librarian, who is useful to society. But this may be accomplished within a shorter period of time with the aid of an educational armamentarium sufficient for continued study and learning after graduation.

Who has become old and grey in this profession and has had an opportunity to experience or to study the diverse programs and procedures of library education, knows for sure that our curricula, better or worse, do not turn a student (who has followed good or bad advice in choosing the library profession) into a good professional librarian. In this respect librarianship is truly a profession. No one has felt and expressed this more clearly than Friedrich Adolf Ebert, who, a scholar himself, stressed for anyone desiring to qualify as a librarian the motto, "aliis in serviendo consumor." Ebert was justified to stipulate also "a special and very particular love for his field and his course of activities,"[12] which, incidentally, led him to believe that, in essence, the librarian "non fit sed nascitur." Today, the scholar-librarian has ceased to be a matter of course. We need him, but we can afford him only as a specialist within selected subject areas. Nevertheless, a librarian without a love of books, of their content, and their shape and form as objects, is hard to imagine. Professional expertise, no matter how specialized and sophisticated, still does not make a librarian, if the spark fails to kindle a love for the profession: thus it appears also from this vantage point that an education stressing the fundamentals, an education which imparts what, in the last analysis, makes up and holds together the librarian's world, is the most promising condition for the flame.

One of the librarians with such a burning love for the profession, Jesse H. Shera, has searched for the essential problems of librarianship and has courageously attacked them in his writings. To him, I dedicate these aphoristic thoughts.

Notes

1. "Die Tauglichkeit zur Erfüllung der besonderen und eigenthümlichen Pflichten seines Berufes gründet sich bei dem Bibliothekar, wie in jedem anderen Fache, auf gründliche Vorkenntnisse, und er unterscheidedt sich nur darinn von Gelehrten anderer Fächer, dasz diese Vorkenntnisse zugleich möglichst umfassend und mannichfaltig seyn müssen." F. A. Ebert, Die Bildung des Bibliothekars (2nd edition, 1820), ed. H. Kunze, "Neudrucke aus dem Buch und Bibliothekswesen," Leipzig, Harrassowitz, 1958, 10-11.
2. G. Naudé, Advis pour Dresser une Bibliothêque (1627), ed. H. Kunze, "Neudrucke aus dem Buch und Bibliothekswesen," Leipzig, Edition, 1963.
3. The original edition, Om offentlige Bibliotheker, Bibliothekarer, og det, Man Har Kaldet Bibliotheksvidenskab, was published in 1829 in Copenhagen. The German edition, translated by H. Ratjen from the second edition of the Danish text, appeared in Leipzig in 1833.

4. "The Building and Its Location" and "Arranging the Books" in A. Taylor's English translation of Naudé, Advice on Establishing a Library Berkeley, University of California Press, 1950, 59-70.

5. I have purposely singled out Christian Molbech (1783-1857) as prototype of the new literature of Bibliothekswissenschaft in the 19th century, in order to show that this development which originated in Germany spread also to other European countries in which similar social conditions obtained.

6. M. Schrettinger, Versuch eines vollständigen Lehrbuchs der Bibliothekswissenschaft, 2 vols., Munich, Lindauer, 1808-1829.

7. Molbech, op. cit., 17.

8. Molbech, op. cit., 18.

9. The expression Bibliotheksländer is henceforth rendered as library countries.

10. The German text lists "Volksbibliotheken, Öffentliche beziehungsweise Allgemeine öffentliche Bibliotheken."

11. "Bibliothekssoziologie."

12. "Eine besondere und ganz eigenthümliche Liebe für sein Fach und seinen Arbeitskreis," Ebert, op. cit., 56.

THE CONTRIBUTORS

BOOTH, Andrew Donald. Ph. D., D. Sc. President, Lake-head University, Thunder Bay, Ontario, and visiting professor of library science, Case Western Reserve University. Author of numerous books and scientific papers on machine translation and quantitative properties of language and other aspects of information storage and retrieval.

CLAPP, Verner W. A.B. (Trinity College); graduate study, Harvard University. Consultant and past president, Council on Library Resources. Among his many contributions to the professional literature are The Future of the Research Library (1964); and Copyright : A Librarian's View (1968). Mr. Clapp died in June 1972.

DeVLEESCHAUWER, Herman J. Ph. D., Litt. D., Dr. h. c. (Glasgow). Professor emeritus, University of South Africa, Pretoria. His publications are listed in D. Rausche, The Bibliography of Professor H. J. deVlee-schauwer (Pretoria, S. A., 1957, 1966).

DITZION, Sidney. Ph. D. Associate professor and acting chairman, Department of History, City University of New York. His books and articles on libraries and librarians include Arsenals of Democratic Culture: A Social History of the American Public Library Movement 1850-1900 (Chicago, A. L. A., 1947, 1966).

DUNKIN, Paul S. Ph. D. Professor in the Graduate School of Library Service, Rutgers, The State University. Author of Cataloging U. S. A. (Chicago, A. L. A., 1969). Former editor of Library Resources and Technical Services.

FAIRTHORNE, Robert A. B. Sc. Senior principal scientific officer in the Royal Aircraft Establishment, Farnborough. Many publications on technical and documentation topics, among them Towards Information Retriev-

al (1961, 1968) and "Progress in Documentation,"
Journal of Documentation, 25 (December, 1969).

FEINBERG, Hilda.   M. S. L. S.   Head librarian, Revlon Re-
    search Center Library, New York.   Author of "Lit-
    erature Resources for the Cosmetics Industry," in
    Literature of Chemical Technology (ed. R. F. Gould,
    1968); Book Catalogs (with M. F. Tauber, 1971).

FOSKETT, Douglas J.   M. A.   Fellow of the Library As-
    sociation, London.   Librarian, University of London
    Institute of Education and Lecturer, School of Librar-
    ianship, University College, London.   Author of books
    and papers in the field of classification, information
    retrieval, and the social function of libraries.   Editor
    of J. H. Shera's Libraries and the Organization of
    Knowledge and Documentation and the Organization of
    Knowledge (see "A Bibliography..." above in this
    book, nos. 8 and 9.)

GARFIELD, Eugene.   Ph. D.   President, Institute for Sci-
    entific Information, Philadelphia, which issues the
    Science Citation Index.   Special lecturer on informa-
    tion retrieval, University of Pennsylvania.   Author of
    over 50 articles on librarianship and information sci-
    ence.

GOFFMAN, William.   Ph. D.   Dean and professor, School
    of Library Science, Case Western Reserve University.
    Author of scientific papers on mathematical theory of
    communication and its application to design and opera-
    tion of information systems, and on bibliometric and
    cybernetic subjects.   Cooperated with V. Newill in
    studies of the application of epidemic theory to the
    transmission of ideas and the growth of knowledge.

HARLOW, Neal.   M. A., L. H. D. (Moravian College).   Dean
    and professor emeritus, Graduate School of Library
    Service, Rutgers, The State University.   Past presi-
    dent, Canadian Library Association, and Association
    of College and Research Libraries (ACRL).   Author
    of papers on librarianship and library education.

HARMON, Glyn.   Ph. D.   Associate professor, Graduate
    School of Library Science, University of Texas.   Au-
    thor of "Research Problem Sensitivity: A Professional
    Recruitment Criterion," College and Research Librar-

ies (November, 1967); and "On Integration of the Integrative Disciplines" in Research Designs in General
Semantics, Conference Proceedings, 1969.

ISARD, Gretchen M. Administrative aide, Case Western Reserve University, has served as secretary and general
assistant to Dr. Shera during the last ten years of his
tenure as dean.

KNAPP, Patricia B. Ph. D. Associate professor, Depart-
ment of Library Science, Wayne State University.
Among her publications are College Teaching and the
College Library, ACRL Monograph 23 (1959) and The
Monteith College Library Experiment (1966).

KOCHEN, Manfred. Ph. D. Associate professor, Departments of Library Science and Psychiatry; research
scientist, Mental Health Research Institute, University
of Michigan. Among his numerous publications are
Some Problems in Information Science (1965), and The
Growth of Knowledge (1967). He is co-author of Automation and the Library of Congress. (1963).

KUNZE, Horst. Ph. D. Director general, Deutsche Staats-
bibliothek and Professor für Bibliothekswissenschaft,
Humboldt University, East Berlin. Received the Na-
tionalpreis der Deutschen Demokratischen Republik in
1961. Author of numerous books and articles, among
them, Grundzüge der Bibliothekslehre (1966) and
Schatzbehalter vom Besten aus der älteren deutschen
Kinderliteratur (1969). He is co-editor of the Lexikon
des Bibliothekswesens (1969).

MENZEL, Herbert. Ph. D. Professor of sociology, New
York University. Numerous publications in the field
of communication and communication in specialized
publics, among them "The Medical Television Audience
of the New York Academy of Medicine after Four
Years" (Bulletin of the New York Academy of Medicine, 1968), and "Planning the Consequence of Unplanned Action in Scientific Communication" in Ciba
Foundation Symposium on Communication in Science:
Documentation and Automation (1967).

METCALFE, John W. B.A. Fellow of the Library Association, London; fellow, Library Association of Australia.
Past director, School of Librarianship, University of

New South Wales (1959-1968). Among his publications
are Subject Classifying and Indexing of Libraries and
Literature (1959) and Alphabetical Subject Indication of
Information (1965).

MORSE, Philip M. Ph. D., Sc. D. (Case Institute of Technology). Professor of physics, and director, M. I. T.
Operations Research Center, Massachusetts Institute
of Technology. Author of Library Effectiveness (1968),
five other books, papers, and articles on physics,
operations research, and search theory. Editor, Annals of Physics.

MOUNTFORD, John D. M. A. (Oxford). Senior lecturer,
La Sainte Union College of Education, Southampton,
England. Research officer (linguistics), Reading Research Unit, University of London Institute of Education. Contributed "Writing" in Encyclopaedia of Linguistics, Information, and Control (ed. A. R. Meetham,
1969).

RANGANATHAN, Shiyali Ramamrita. M. A., L. T., D. Litt.
(University of Delhi), D. Litt. (University of Pittsburgh). National research professor in library science (India) and honorary professor in documentation,
Research and Training Centre, Bangalore. Among his
60 books and more than 1, 200 papers and articles on
classification and many other aspects of librarianship
Professor Ranganathan regards as most important The
Five Laws of Library Science (1931); Colon Classification (1933-); Classified Catalogue Code (1934); and
Prolegomena to Library Classification (1937; 1957; 1967).

RAWSKI, Conrad H. Ph. D. Professor of library science
and coordinator of the Ph. D. program in library and
information science, Case Western Reserve University.
Author of a number of publications on the scientific
study of subject literatures, their properties and structure, among them "Subject Literatures and Librarianship" in Library School Teaching Methods: Courses
in the Selection of Adult Materials (ed. L. E. Bone,
1969).   His Petrarch: Four Dialogues for Scholars
appeared in 1967.

RICHMOND, Phyllis A. Ph. D. Professor of library science,
Case Western Reserve University. Author of many
papers on topics of classification, information science,

and library education, among them "Contribution Toward a New Generalized Theory of Classification" in Classification Research (ed. P. Atherton, 1965).

SINCLAIR, Dorothy M. Ph. D. Associate professor of library science, Case Western Reserve University. Author of professional articles, reports, and library surveys. Her Administration of the Small Public Library (Chicago. A. L. A.) appeared in 1965.

TAUBER, Maurice F. Ph. D. Melvil Dewey Professor, Columbia University. His many contributions to library literature include Technical Services in Libraries (1952); The University Library (with L. R. Wilson, 1956); Book Catalogs (with Hilda Feinberg, 1971); Louis Round Wilson: Librarian and Administrator (1967); and Library Surveys (with I. R. Stephens, 1968). Edited with J. Orne, Education and Libraries: Papers of Louis R. Wilson (1967).

TAYLOR, Robert S. M. A., M. S. L. S. Dean, School of Library Science, Syracuse University. Among his publications are "Towards an Educational Base for the Information Sciences and Information Engineering" in Symposium on Education for Information Science (ed. L. B. Heilprin et al., 1965); "Professional Aspects of Information Science and Technology," Annual Review of Information Science and Technology, 1966; and "Question-Negotiation and Information Seeking in Libraries," College and Research Libraries, 29 (May, 1968).

VICKERY, Brian C. M. A. (Oxford). Fellow of the Library Association, London. Head of the Research Department, ASLIB. Founding member of the Classification Research Group (1952). His work includes several specialized faceted classification schemes. His recent books are Faceted Classification: A Guide to Construction and Use of Special Schemes (1961, 1968), and Techniques of Information Retrieval (1970).

WRIGHT, H. Curtis. Ph. D. Associate professor, Graduate Department of Library and Information Sciences, Brigham Young University. His "Metallic Documents of Antiquity" appeared in the Summer 1970 issue of the Brigham Young University Studies.

INDEX: Names, Subjects, and Titles†

* preceding page number indicates an entire paper in this book
: preceding page number indicates quotation
f after page number indicates the following page

Aarons, M. W. 402 n. 3
Aboutness 264-67
   extensional 264-66
   intensional 265f
   relation 264f
Abstracting 407, 498f
Abstraction 170
Academic libraries 457, 468, 486f
   future 463, 466-68
   problems 464
   & Public library systems 83
   relevance 465
   research level 467f
Accession list 192
Accounting Index 225
Accretion and assimilation 222
Acculturation, professional 492
Ackoff, R. L. :127, :142 n. 35, 143 n. 46, 145 n. 64, n. 65, 166, 403, 413
Acquiry and inquiry 464-67, 468 n. 4
Action
   gratuitous 137

& information 409f
   professional 42, 409f
   reconstruction 42
   required knowledge 43
Activities
   bibliothecal 127f, 519f
   goal-intended 43, 127-29, 135-37, *403-14 passim, 473f, 480
   see also Interdependence; Interdisciplinarity
Administration 474f, 478, 480, 487-89
Advis pour Dresser une Bibliothèque (1627) 515f
Affirmation and denial 265f
Agriculture 496
ALA see American Library Association
Alanar 370
Alexander, the Great 89, 91-93, 94f, 97, 99f, 107
   campaigns 92f
   Nearchos voyage 96
   Panhellenism 92f, 97, 99
Alexandria 96
   Aristotelian philosophy in 102

---

†I am grateful to my wife Helen and to my daughter, Judith E. Kleen, who helped with making this index. --Editor.

Alexandria. Mouseion *87-113
  academic institution 97f
  catalog 104f
  conferences 98
  Greek thesis 95-100, 102, 107
  Platonism 101
  Ptolemaic thesis 90, 107
  public relations 98
  research 97f, 102, 104, 107
  shelf list 107
  translations 98f
Alexandria. Serapeion 100, 112 n. 6
Alexandrian libraries *87-113
  bibliography on 109-11
  manuscript search 105
Alice (L. Carroll) 415, 442
"All about" book 318
Allen, G. 382
Allen, T. E. 448 n. 37
Alphabet 415, 421, 434f
Alphabetical order see Order, alphabetical
Alston, R. C. 444 n. 7
Ambiguity *268-301 passim, 268, 275
America, 18th century 61
American Cyanamid Co. 407
American Documentation 382
American Documentation Institute (1964) 176
American Journal of Human Genetics 398
American librarianship
  historical documentation of 63; see also Library history
American libraries
  printed book catalogs 352
American Library Association 341f, 347f
  book catalog committees 354f
  Catalog Code Revision Committee 344, 347

Catalog Rules (1908) 344, 348 n. 3, 349 n. 15
  (1941--) ·344, 348 n. 4
Cataloging and Classification Section 343, 347
  Glossary 217 n. 3
  Red Book 342, 346f
  Rules for entry 342
American Library Institute 339f, 347
American Petroleum Institute 274
American Philological Association 425
American Psychological Association 403, 405, 410, 413
Analet 318f
Analogy 223f
Analysis
  critical 41, 43-47, 50, 124-26, 132-37
  epistemic 121-23, 137
  semantic 272
  structural 474f
Anderson, H. E. 400 n. 22
Androcles and the Lion 415, 417, 424
Andrzejewski, B. W. 445 n. 16
Anglo-American Cataloging Rules (1967)
  British 347, 349 n. 19, 448 n. 37
  North American 347, 349 n. 18
Animal Farm (1945) 348
Annals of Human Genetics 398
Annals of Library Science (1958) :316
Anticipation 170
Antipater 92, 100
Apostel, L. :225, 230 n. 16
Applied Science and Technology Index 224, 328
Apprenticeship 411
Area, scientific 406f; see

also Specialization
Aristophanes 109
Aristotle 89, 91f, 95-100,
    102f, 107, 224
  influence in Egypt 101
  library of 96, 101
  Lyceum in Athens 89f, 95,
    97, 99-102
Armarium 106
Arrowgraphs 273
Arsinoe 89
Asimov, I. 384f, 400 n. 11
Aslib Conference (1926) 314,
    337 n. 2
Aspect 309f, 312, 317, 322,
    324, 336
Aspness, G. 218
Asselin, T. H. 401 n. 26
Assimilation and accretion
    22; see also Acquiry
    and inquiry
Association of Research Li-
    braries 347
Assurance 131
Assurbanipal 94f, 102f
Assyria 93f
  cultural policy 103
  libraries 102f
  scribes 103
Astor Library
  book catalog 1857-66 351
Astronomy 116
Asymmetry 122, 438
Athens, ancient 89, 91, 96,
    101
  cultural policy 99
  Peripatos 89f
  propaganda 97
  see also Aristotle; Greece
Atherton, P. 184
Attention span 155
Audience 152
Auerbach, E. 120
Australian Library Journal
    333
Author 175, 263, 410f
Authority 474, 476
  administrative 477

knowledge 479, 487, 490
  organizational 473, 477
  pattern 473f
  position 479, 490
  professional 473, 477
Automation 169, 268, 270,
    348, 455f, 465, 500f
  cost factor 357
Autonomy 475, 477f
  functional 487
  of inquiry 119f
  professional 483, 492
Auto-posting 274f
Awareness, current 406

Babylonia 93f, 98f, 103
Bacon, F. :504
Balfour, F. M. 374 n. 25
Ballston Spa, N. Y. 65
Baltimore. Peabody Institute
  book catalog 1883-1905
    351
Baltimore County, Md., Pub-
    lic Library 365
Bar-Hillel, Y. 150f, 166
Base, institutional 452
Basic subject see Class,
    basic
Beard, C. A. 56f
Becker, H. S. 494 n. 32
Becker, J. 373 n. 10
Bell, D. :463, 468 n. 1
Benes, V. E. 402 n. 40
Berelson, B. 154, 166
Bergen, D. 182, 184, 231
    n. 26
Bernal, J. D. 382, 400 n. 5
Bertalanffy, L. von :182,
    :228, 231 n. 25
Berul, L. H. 164f, 167
Bhattacharyya, G. 513 n. 5,
    n. 8, n. 9
Bible :116, 417, 435f
  phonetic 443 n. 4
  Pitman 416, 443 n. 4
  Septuagint 90
Bibliographic Classification
    (1952-53) 314

Bibliographic control see
     Control, bibliographic
Bibliographic data system 371
Bibliographic difficulties 264
Bibliographies 499
     ancient 104f
     descriptive 428
     statistical 382
     student use of 503
Bibliometrics 382
Bibliothecal activities 128-30
Bibliothekonomie 517
Bibliothekslehre 517
Bibliothekswissenschaft 516f
Bigelow, J. 133, 145 n. 64
Biological Abstracts 224
Biology, molecular 380
Black, M. 139 n. 12, 143
     n. 43
Blackwell, W. A. 401 n. 31
Blanshard, B. 138 n. 2
Blau, P. M. :484, 490, 494
     n. 21
B. Lib. Sci. see India, Bach-
     elor of Library Science
Bliss, H. E. 314, 318, 337
     n. 9
Bodie, E. K. 376 n. 68
Bohanan, P. :41, 50 n. 2
Bohr, N. 224, 227
Book 437
     language profile 416
Book catalogs 303, *350-77
     adoption 369
     advantages 365-68
     bibliographic data 364,
        368
     binding 363
     & browsing 366f
     & card catalog 353, 369f
     centralized 355
     compactness 366
     conversion to 353f
     cooperative 355
     costs 364f, 368
     disadvantages 368f
     distribution 353
     format 363f, 366, 369

future 371f
history 350-52
legibility 362f, 368
maintenance 365f, 368f
mobility 365, 369
monumental 354
producers 370f
production 355-62
     in school libraries 370
     selection tool 367
     in special libraries 371
     in undergraduate libraries
        370
     use 365f, 368-70
Book Catalogs
     Tauber-Feinberg (1971)
        355, 373 n. 6, 377 n. 72
     Tauber-Kingery (1963)
        354f, 373 n. 6
Book potential 254
Book preparation 519f
Book selection see Library
     materials, selection
Bookmobile 74, 80
Books
     ancient 106
     arrangement of 253-61,
        256f, 303
     description 471
     & government 92, 97,
        518
     & micro documents 499
Booth, A. D. *243-45, 523
Booth, W. C. 52 n. 25
Boston Athenaeum
     catalog 325, 351
Boston Public Library 62,
     65
Boulding, K. 115, 120,
     140 n. 20, :222, :227,
     :228, 229 n. 3, 231
     n. 22, n. 26
Bowers, F. 432f, 447 n. 29,
     n. 30
Bozman, W. R. 375 n. 42
Bradford, S. C. 314, 337
     n. 8
Brain, as magic loom 233

Braithwaite, A. B. 144 n. 52
Brauchbarkeit 516
Brenner, E. H. 274, 277 n. 9
Bridgman, P. W. :137, 145
  n. 73
Bright, T. 418, 427
British Museum. General
  Catalogue of Printed
  Books 354, 415
British Museum. Rules for
  Compiling the Catalogues
  ... 443 n. 5
British Museum catalogs
  (1787--) 351
British National Bibliography
  321, 324f, 327, 356
British Technology Index 327,
  329
Broadfield, A. 143 n. 43
Bronfenbrenner, M. 145 n. 65
Bronowski, J. :170, 184
Brooks, B. 188, 218
Bross, I. D. J. 230 n. 17,
  n. 18
Brown, J. D. 313f
Brown, M. C. 373 n. 11
Brown, R. 50 n. 10
Browser 253f, 256
  generalist 256-61, 261
    n. 8
  interest span 253
  specialist 256, 258-61,
    261 n. 8
Browsing *246-61
  & librarian 252-61
  as search 246
  search coverage 248
  search rate 248
  time 250-52
Bruner, J. S. 174
Buchanan, J. M. 145 n. 65
Buck-passing 190, 195f,
  197-201, 204-06, 208f,
  214
  diagram 199
Bulletin journals 406
Bundy, M. L. 217 n. 8, 218,

:485f, 494 n. 22, n. 24,
  n. 25, n. 26
Bunge, M. 51 n. 19
Bunker-Ramo Corp. 412
Bureaucracy 487f
  model of 480
  & professional 475-78
  rational 475
Bureaucrats 487f
Burstall, R. M. 401 n. 34
Business Periodicals Index
  224
Busiris 91
Butler, D. D. 400 n. 12
Butler, E. H. 444 n. 7
Butler, P. :42, 50 n. 5,
  :127, 143 n. 43, :170,
  184
Byzantium 91

California State Library 358
Calligraphy 426
Callimachus 105, 107
Callisthenes 100
Cambridge University 382
Campbell, N. R. 213 n. 14,
  224
Carbon 14, radioactive 124
Card camera, sequential
  352, 355f
Card catalog 253, 353,
  369f
  & browsing 253
  interest potential 253f
  rehabilitation 353
  search rate 253
Carlson, R. O. 494 n. 23
Carlton, W. J. 444 n. 7
Carnap, R. 231 n. 30
Carnegie, A. 66
Carter, L. F. 160, 167
Cartwright, D. 52 n. 23
Cartwright, K. L. :358,
  373 n. 12, 374 n. 20,
  375 n. 39
Case, P. W. 401 n. 29
Case method 410

Case Western Reserve Univ.
  School of Library Science
    70, 179f, 512
Caskey, D. L. 401 n. 28
Cassander 91, 101
Cassiodorus 303
Catalog 303, 320
  alphabetico-classed 318
  book or card 350; and re-
    spective entries
  classified 303, 313, 318
  computerized 355, 360f,
    367f; & browsing 253
  dictionary 303, 313, 326,
    330, 363
  divided 363
  juvenile 357
  kinds (Cutter) 341
  neutral 329f
  union 351
  use 334
Catalog of Books Represented
  by Library of Congress
  Printed Cards... 354
Catalog topics 303-77
Catalogica, ancient oriental
  104
Cataloging 270, 307, 441,
    455, 519f
  advanced 498f
  an art 339, 341
  cooperative 340, 351
  costs 339, 346-48
  descriptive 341, 416
  legalistic 339, 343
  principles 339, 343
  rules 339f, 343-45
  simplified 339
  subject 326f
Cataloging codes *339-49
  Miami Conference (1962)
    347
  Institutes: McGill (1960)
    344, 346 Stanford (1958)
    344
Cataloging Rules and Principles (1953) 343
Catalogue of Books in the Li-

brary of the Surgeon
  General's Office 352
Cataloguing Principles and
  Practices (1954) 345
Catchword method 307
  ancient 106
Categorization 174
Cathode ray tube 359, 362,
    393
Causation, historical 62f
Cavanaugh, J. F. 375 n. 40
Caws, P. 50 n. 12
Centro-linguistics 436-39,
    441f
C-field 44-47
Chain 319f
Chain organization 195-201
Chain procedure 319-24,
    328
  symbiosis by 320-22
  see also Classification
Change 139 n. 11, 452f,
    457, 459, 463
  acceptance 454
  prediction 453
Channel 154f, 159f, 161-63,
    403f
  formal 406
  language 158
  type 157f
Chapanis, A. 230 n. 13
Chapin, R. E. 374 n. 26
Character recognition 233,
    359f
Characterie... (1588) 443
  n. 7
Chaucer, G. :441, 449 n. 38
Chemical Abstract Service
    407
Chernoff, H. 261 n. 3
Chesterton, G. K. :330
Chicago Public Library 61
Childers, T. 376 n. 52
Chinese language 439f
Chomsky, N. 444 n. 8, 445
  n. 14
Chronology of events 382
Churchman, C. W. 145 n. 64,

n. 65, 222, 229 n. 6

Cicero :116, 138 n. 4

Cipher 419f, 440, 445 n. 17

Circulation 254-56

Citation data 382, 384, 399
  analysis 382
  graphic display 382
  heuristic tool 384
  network 382-85
  order 331
  patterns 397

Citation index 399

Clapp, V. *7-9, 523

Clarke, A. C. 229, :463, 468 n. 1

Class
  anterior 318
  basic 315, 336
  compound 315
  definition 305
  posterior 318

Classification *169-86, 172, 233, 268n, 519f
  American Study Group 583
  concealed 275
  depth 315, 498
  of entities 148, 181-83
  expansive 307
  facet analysis 329; see also Facet analysis
  generic 173f
  glossaries see Terms, glossaries of
  hierarchical 173f, 269, 273, 295-300, 318f, 336
  interdisciplinary 441
  involuntary 334f
  main classes 180
  micro subjects 498
  multiplicative 174f
  scheme 176f, 179f, 183
  socio-linguistic 483
  single place 346f
  synthetic 314
  term 268n, 270-72, 275f
  theory 183, 498f
  see also Subject

Classification as artificial lan-

guage 176

Classification Research Group 180, 183f

Classified Catalogue Code (1958) 321

Classified order see Order, classified

Classified pockets 322, 334

Classing, human 116, 335

Clausius, R. 120

Clay tablets 94, 105f

Cleverdon, C. W. 158, 167f

Client 476, 481, 484-87

Client and professional see Client relationship

Client relationship 476, 484-87
  academic library 486f
  public library 484f
  school library 485f

Cliometrics 64

Coates, E. J. :320, 321, 323, :324-26, :327f, 328-30, :331, :332, :334, 337 n. 16, n. 19, n. 20

Code 238f

Code of Cataloging Rules (1960) 346

Coding 151f, 262

Cognition 151

Collection
  fluid 74
  organization and housing 127, 467
  quality and demand 188, 484
  subject 517f
  see also Library materials

College, invisible 405, 458

Colloquium 506-09
  collection coverage 509
  debate 507
  documentation list 508f
  group study 507
  preparation 507
  self-documentation 507f

Colon classification 176, 315, 321-23, 329
Colophon 106
Columbia College
book catalogs 351
The Columbia Encyclopedia (1963) 140 n. 21
Columbia University
Avery Architectural Library Catalog (1895) 351
Conference on Reference (1966) 189
COM see Computer output microfilming
Committee on Catalog Revision, Statement (1956) 349 n. 13
Committee on Scientific and Technical Information 269, 276 n. 3
Common sense 42, 50 n. 9, 174
Communication 150f, 175f
artifacts 461
formal 407f
individual 154f
informal 162, 192, *403-14
informative 150-52, 160, 163
instructional 150
internally generated 214f; see also Buck-passing
interpersonal 403-05, 405-12
key aspects 154
organizational 154-56
patterns 489f
process 234, 461
psychology of 478f
sociology of 478f
structure 154-56, 161-63
technology 151
theory 154-56, 242, *403-14
Communication systems
biomedical 408f
complex 461

Communications culture 457f
Complex organizations see Organizations, complex
Compos-O-Line 356
Compucenters Inc. 370
Computer *243-45 passim, 355, 422, 459, 500f
memory 193f, 233, 362
output microfilming 362
print chain 352
programs 203f, 207, 500f
search 412
systems 207, 412, 461
Computing machine see Computer
Conant, R. W. 469 n. 6
Concept formation 174f
Concepts 44, 138, 144 n. 62, . 148, 156, 172, 314
coordination 327f
corresponding 267
in information studies 156, 163-66
ordering 174
pattern 172
primitive 49
scalar 158f
scientific 175
spontaneous 175
Conceptual structure 175
Concrete, notion of 307-11, 336
Conduct of inquiry see Inquiry
Confirmation, empirical 44, 47, 49, 138
Conflict 473, 476, 479f, 483
Conjecture 47, 453
Connective notions 46f, 124, 126, 135
Connectivity, logical 44-47
Constant, G. 44, 45
Constructs 44-47
Consultant, referential see Referential consultant
Contact, effective 236, 239f, 242

Content 129f
  .linguistic 437
  non-linguistic 437
  organizational 473
Context 265-67, 270
  definition 274
  organizational 472f, 478-
    87, 491f
  see also Environment
Control
  administrative 473f, 488
  bibliographic 187, 452,
    459
  bibliothecal 129f
Conversation 405f
Coombs, C. H. 52 n. 27
Coordinate indexing see Indexing, coordinate
Copying 431, 440, 458
  acts of 431f
  & circulation 458
  general variables 431
  precision 431
  system 431-33
  writing-medium 431
  writing-system 431
  see also Reprography;
    Transcription, biblio-
    graphic
Copyright 456f
Corrado, V. M. 375 n. 41
COSATI see Committee on
  Scientific and Technical
  Information
Cost-effectiveness 465, 468,
  469 n. 6
Cost-measures 213f
Council on Library Resources
  345, 347
Crane, D. 414
Credibility 42f, 137f, 142
  n. 38
  see also Why-questions
CRG see Classification Research Group
The Crisis in Cataloging (1941)
  339f
Criminology 120

Crombie, A. C. 139 n. 13
Cross-reference 176, 269f
CRT see Cathode ray tube
Cryptography 419f, 440
  & orthography 420
  personal 420, 428
Cryptology 420, 434
C-Systems see Systems,
  causative
Cuadra, C. A. :147, 167
Current awareness see
  Awareness, current
Curti, M. 57, 67 n. 4, 68
  n. 11
Custer, B. A. :313, 319
Cutter, C. A. 304, :305f,
  :307, 310, :311, 313,
  320-22, :324, 325f,
  329-32, 334, 336, 337
  n. 3-n. 5, :340f, 343f,
  :344, 348 n. 5-n. 7, 349
  n. 14
  no name problem :312
  object and aspect 306f
  phythydraulics :312f
Cybernetics 120

Dair, C. 448 n. 31
Dale, H. P. 374 n. 26
Daly, J. F. 401 n. 23
Danto, A. C. 140 n. 24, 141
  n. 29
Data 43
  diagnostic 42f, 47, 240f
  natural history 44-48
  see also Citation data
Dauzat, A. 428, 446 n. 23
Davis, W. 222, 230 n. 7
Debate 507
Decision making 404, 409,
  474
Decision theory 249
Decoding 151f
Deduction 131, 138, 144
  n. 62
Definition 144 n. 62
  operational 47
  parenthetical 270, 276

Definition (Cont.)
  n. 5
  verbal 274
De Grazia, A. 222, 230 n. 7
Delphi. Library 95
Demetrius of Phaleron 89-91,
  95f, 99-102, 105-07
DeMott, B. :453, 454, 456f,
  462 n. 3, n. 5
Denial and affirmation 265f
Denison, B. 14 item 32, 15
  item 38, 18 item 61,
  21 item 101
Denney, R. :454, 462 n. 4
Dennis, D. 217 n. 4
Dependency modes 121-23,
  135
Depression era 57, 65
Depth Classification (1953)
  315
Descartes, R. 224
Description, bibliographic
  428, 437
Descriptor 266, 274
Deseret alphabet 415, 443
  n. 5
Destination 154, 234, 262,
  404f
  see also Receiver; Target
Destouches, J. L. 230 n. 19
Detroit Public Library 67
Deutsch, K. 219, 222, 230
  n. 8
Deutscher Gesamtkatalog 354
DeVleeschauwer, H. J. *87-
  113, 108, 112 n. 2, 523
Dewey, J. 119, 471
Dewey, M. 173f, 254f, 304f,
  313, 324, 336, 337 n. 6,
  n. 15, 425, 441f
  Decimal Classification and
  Relative Index for Li-
  braries (1876--) 173f,
  176f, 253f, 304, 313f,
  333, 425, 441f
Diachronicity 119, 122
Diadochi 91, 93, 96f, 103,
  108

document acquisition 103
  policies 99
Diagnosis, empirical 47,
  240f
Diagram 273, 385-96
  algorithmic generation
  392
  algorithmic manipulation
  392
  automatic 392f
  display formats 390-96
  as historian's tool 382
Dickman, D. A. 448 n. 37
Dictionary 268, 274, 333
Diringer, D. 428, 446 n. 24
Disciplinary sortcrossing
  118f, 124, 138
Disciplines 116, 179f, 398f,
  467, 475
  causative 121-23
  definition 117f
  dependency modes 121-23
  epistemic processes 121-
  23
  growth 138, 227
  implicative 121-23
  interdependence 119f
  levels 121-23
  objectives 117-19
  & professions 41
  quadrants 121-23
  state of 119
  subject matter 117-19,
  121-23
  unity 117f
Discourse 138, 263, 266f
Discovery 172, 467f
Disney, R. 218
Display 385, 393
Dissemination 127
Distance, diagrammatic 398f
Ditzion, S. *55-69, 67, 67
  n. 4, 68 n. 7, n. 9, n. 15,
  523
Dix, W. S. 261 n. 9
DNA code 384f
  historiograph 384-89
  see also Watson-Crick

model
Document 127, 173, 264, 404, 408, 415
  host document 499f
  macro document 500
  micro document 497-500
  see also Knowledge records
Documentation 147, 150f, 314, 497, 499-502, 520
  curriculum 497-502
  education methods 496f, 502-05
  fringe subjects 499-502
  organization of 499
  social benefits 509-11
  terminology 503
  training *495-514, 497f, 501-04
  & translation 499f
  umbral subjects 497-502
Documentation Inc. 370
Documentation list 499, 506, 508f
Dodd, G.G. 401 n.36
Doing 132f
Dolby, J.L. 357, 360, :363, 364, 373 n.13, 375 n.34, n.47, 376 n.50, n.54
Dorking Conference see International Study Conference on Classification... (1957)
Dougherty, R.M. :493 n.16
Downing, J. 445 n.12
Drake, C.L. :333, 338 n.26
Drott, C. 216
DRTC see India. Bangalore Documentation Research and Training Centre
Duggan, M. 86 n.8
Duhem, P. 224, 230 n.14
Dui, M. see Dewey, M.
Dunkin, P.S. 305f, 337 n.1, *339-49, 523
Dyer, R. 374 n.31
Dynamics, theoretical 144 n.62

Ebert, F.A. :515, 516f, :521, 521 n.1
Ecology 120
Econolist 370
Eden, M. 377 n.72
Education 170, 471f, 496
  continuing 519
  & library *463-69
  professional 471
  purpose 471, 496
  vocational 471
Education Facilities Laboratories Conference (1967) 458f, 525 n.6
Education Index 225
Effective contact see Contact, effective
Effectiveness 239f
Efficiency 239f
Egan, M.E. 8, 11 items 2, 4; 12 item 16, 13 item 19, 17 item 57, 20 items 86, 87, 89, 91; 21 item 96, 34 items 307, 308; 165, 167, :188, 218, :303
Egypt, Ptolemaic 89, 92f, 95-99
  scribes 103
Eiconics 222
EJC see Engineers Joint Council
EJC-Battelle Institute system 331
EJC Thesaurus (1964) *268-301 passim, 272-74, 276 n.2, 301 (1967) 275f
Element
  quintessential 48f
  rational 44
  sensory 44
Elkind, D. 140 n.22
Ellis, A.J. 433, 447 n.31
Elsinore Conference see Study Conference on Classification Research (1964)

Emerson, R. W. 63
Encounter, interdisciplinary
122-26, 131f, 135-37
Encyclopaedia Britannica 265
Encyclopedia of the Social Sci-
ences (1933-35) 230
n. 15
"Energy" 176f, 317, 324
Engineering 120, 496
Engineers Joint Council 269,
276 n. 2
England. National Physics
Laboratory 243
English-speaking world
orthography 417f
writing-system 417f
Entity 138, 148
Entropy 120
Entry
alphabetico-specific 331
class 306, 312
corporate 347
direct 326
indirect 326
single 319f, 326
specific 306, 312, 320,
322, 325f, 330, 335
Environment 151, 154, 156,
162f, 170, 237, 264f
see also Context
Epigoni 91, 97
Epigraphy 428
Epistemic levels 135
Epistemology 147, 151
genetic 120
social see Social episte-
mology
ERIC see U. S. Office of
Education. Educational
Research Information
Center
Error control 47
Etzioni, A. :475, :477f,
479f, :482, 488, 492
n. 4, 493 n. 5, n. 10-12,
n. 18, n. 19, 494 n. 29
Evans, R. I. :460, 462 n. 7
Events, patterns of 43, 396

Everett, E. 62
Excellence, intellectual 471,
497
Expansive Classification
(1891-93 & later) 305f,
307, 311-13, 324, 340f,
344, *303-38 passim
Experience 44, 410f, 497
Expertise 193f, 521
Explanation 43, 124-26,
132f, 138, 142 n. 38
Ezra 98

Facet analysis 176, 314f,
317, 324, 329, 499
fundamental categories
176f, 181f, 317; see
also "Energy"; "Mat-
ter"; "Personality";
"Space"; "Time"
isolate focus 315
Facts, relevant 52 n. 21,
n. 24, 124
Fairthorne, R. A. 143 n. 48,
*262-67, 264, 523f
Fairthorne's folly 263-65
False drop 271f, 304
False hyphen see Hyphen,
false
False negative 240
positive 240
Farmingdale, N. Y. Catalog
of Jr. High School Li-
braries 370
Farradane, J. E. L. 316,
:318f, 337 n. 14
analet 318f
isolates 318f
operators 318f
Farrell, J. 442 n. 1
Federal Council for Science
and Technology, COSA-
TI see Committee on
Scientific and Technical
Information
Feedback 154, 239, 411f
Feibleman, J. K. 145 n. 63,
180, 184

Feinberg, H. *350-77, 355, 524
FID see International Federation for Documentation
Field work 491f, 503f, 506-09, 519f
Five laws of library science 170, 497, 510, 512 n. 2
Fonts 360f
Ford, A. B. 143 n. 40
Forecast 451-69
see also Prediction
Forsyth, V. 357, 373 n. 13, 375 n. 34, n. 47, 376 n. 50, n. 54
Foskett, D. J. 11 item 8, 12 item 9, *169-86, 184f, 524
Foto-List 356
Foundations of the Unity of Science (1969) 229, 231 n. 30
Fovea 247
"Fracture" 448 n. 31
Francis, W. N. 448 n. 33
Frank, P. 52 n. 21, 140 n. 16
Frankl, P. 139 n. 11
Franklin, B. 61
Frantz, R. W. 68 n. 12
Freiser, L. 217 n. 5, 219
Freudenthal, H. 230 n. 16, 231 n. 24
Friedman, I. 401 n. 35
Fussler, H. H. 371, 377 n. 71

Gallio's Principle 262, 266f
Gardin, J. C. :228, 231 n. 28
Garfield, E. *380-402, 382f, 400 n. 9, n. 10, 402 n. 45, 524
Garvin, P. L. 445 n. 18
Gatto, O. T. 400 n. 12
GCI see Genetics Citation Index
Gelb, I. J. 428, 446 n. 24
General System Theory (1968)

182
Generalization 173, 175
The Genetic Code (1963) 384
Genetics 398
Genetics 398
Genetics Citation Index 384
Geneva, Switzerland 174
Geometry 116
Geophysics 120
George, V. :363f, 375 n. 48
Geshner, R. A. 401 n. 30
Gillispie, C. C. 140 n. 15
Gilpin, R. 494 n. 31
G. K. Hall & Co. 370
Glimpse 246f, 252
probability 247
rate 247
Goal-intended activities see Activities, goal-intended; Interdependence; Interdisciplinarity
Goals
& models 480-82
organizational 481
professional 480f
service 492
see also Librarianship, goals
Goffman, W. *234-42, 242 n. 3, 524
Goldberg, M. J. 402 n. 38
Gombrich, E. H. 51 n. 18
Goode, W. :480, :483, 493 n. 13, n. 17, 494 n. 20
Goodman, N. 50 n. 9, 51 n. 17, 52 n. 30
Gopinath, M. A. 513 n. 10
Gouldner, A. 474, :475, 492 n. 1-3, 494 n. 27, n. 30
Grammar 116, 437
Graphetics 437, 448 n. 34
Graphic records 188f, *415-49 passim, 442; see also Document; Knowledge records
Graphology 429, 435-42, 448 n. 34

Graphology (Cont.)
  centro-linguistic 438
  definition 435
  profile 438
  & writing-system 436
Grasp, synoptic 121-23, 137
Greece, ancient 91, 97, 99,
    100-04
  bibliographical activity 105f
  language 97, 99
  libraries 95, 99f
  papyrus books 94, 105f
  Polis constitution 105
  preservation of texts 104
Greek Linear B, Mycenean
    421f
Griffin, H. L. 376 n. 53
Grigsby, L. L. 453 n. 31
Grogan, D. 217 n. 1, 219
Groups 473, 481
Gwyer, M. 511

Hagstrom, W. 164, 167
Haibt, L. M. 400 n. 17
Hain, C. 400 n. 18
Hain, K. 400 n. 18
Halbert, M. M. 403, 413
Halle, M. 445 n. 14
Halliday, M. A. K. 448 n. 33
Hamburger, H. 216
Hamilton, D. R. L. 159, 163-
    66, 168
Hamlet 424f, 446 n. 19, n. 20
Handbooks 410
Handwriting analysis 428
Hanson, N. R. :43, :44, 50
    n. 6, 51 n. 16, n. 17
Harary, F. 52 n. 23
Harlow, N. *463-69, 469 n. 5,
    524
Harmon, G. *221-31, 524f
Harris, J. L. 358, 373 n. 18,
    376 n. 64
Harvard College 61
Harvard University 350, 381
  Faculty Club 339
Harvey, W. 224
Haskins, S. M. 349 n. 12

Hatch, O. W. 68 n. 13
Hatch, W. R. 468 n. 4
Hattusa 104
  library 93f, 102f
Hawthorne studies 474
Hayes, R. M. 365, 376 n. 51
Haykin, D. J. :306, 334,
    338 n. 27
Heading and Canons (1955)
    345
Hebrews, ancient 98f
Hecht, S. 246
Hempel, C. G. 42, 59 n. 8,
    n. 13, 52 n. 21, 141
    n. 31, :142 n. 28, 144
    n. 55
Henderson, J. W. :353f,
    373 n. 5
Henderson, M. M. 268, 276
    n. 1
Henkle, H. H. 165, 167
Herner, S. 403, 413
Hesse, M. B. 231 n. 24
Hessel, A. 108, 112 n. 11,
    n. 12
Hewitson, T. 373 n. 8
Hierarchy
  administrative 478
  organizational 473, 475f,
    478
  structured 148, 174-76,
    270-74, 319-27
Hines, T. C. 18 item 64,
    :351f, 358, 372 n. 1,
    373 n. 18
Historiographs 382-99
  analysis 396f
  development 382-84
  nodes 385, 392, 396,
    398f
  patterns 396-98
  production 385f, 396
  retrieval tool 397
  validity 384f
History 55-113 passim, 55-
    58, 60f, 70, 120
  prediction 70
  term 276 n. 4

History of science 380f, 384
  key events 385, 396-98
Hittites 93f, 102, 107
Hjelmslev, L. 175
Holton, G. 140 n.17
Homans, G.C. 51 n.15
Homer 109, 112 n.8
Homestead, Pa. 66
Homographs 273
Houston, Texas 63
Hugh of St. Victor :116f,
  138 n.5, n.6
Hughes, E.C. :476, 493 n.6
Hulme, E.W. 382
Hume, D. :266, 267 n.1
Hume's Principle 266
Husserl, E. :117f, 118f,
  124, 138, 139 n.8, n.9
Hyphen 430, 432f
  false 433, 447 n.31
Hyphenation 431, 432f
  algorithm 447 n.28

IBM equipment 356
Ideas, spread of 61
IFLA see International Fed-
  eration of Library As-
  sociations
Ignorance 262-64
  symmetries of *262-67
Iliad 92
Illinois library law 61
Incremental pen plotter 393f
Index Medicus 177f, 224
Index terms see Terms
Index to Legal Periodicals
  225
Indexes 176, 264, 326-30
Indexing 172f, 268n, 304f,
  307, 323, 406f, 498f
  alphabetical 307, 311, 327f
  classified 307
  coordinate 265-68, 274,
  305, 330f
  systematic see Systemat-
  ic indexing
Indexing systems 267-69
India 96

arts colleges (1917-23)
  511f
Bachelor of Library Sci-
  ence 498f, 511
Banares University 511
Bangalore. Documenta-
  tion Research and
  Training Centre 511
Delhi. Biennial Indian
  Library Conference
  511
Delhi University 511
documentation centers,
  national 499, 501
documentation training
  *495-514
  examinations 505
  library profession 501
  Madras University 501,
  511
  Malabar 505
  Master of Library Sci-
  ence 511
Indian Standard Glossary of
  Classification Terms
  (1963) 316f
Indicator tablets, ancient
  106, 112 n.10
Indo-British school of classification 330f
Indus 92
Industrial and Engineering
  Chemistry 406
Informatics 184
Information 160, 234, 458
  assessment 183
  categorization 155
  channel see Channel
  concepts and relations
  156-59
  destination see Destination; Target
  & documents 408
  environment see Environment
  evaluation 408-10
  exchange of 411f
  flow 156, 160, 405

Information (Cont.)
 focus 155
 generation 151
 items 243f
 & literature 308
 message see Message
 need 169f, 190f, 454, 489f
 & organization 489f
 processing 461
 & professional action 409f
 receiver see Destination;
  Receiver; Target
 representation 151, *415-
  49 passim
 response 154
 screening 408-10
 source see Source
 standardization 155
 synthesis 408-10
 transmission see Information transfer
 value system 192
Information centers 192, 409,
  460
Information Indexing and Subject Cataloging (1959)
  333
Information officer see Referential consultant
Information retrieval 233-301
  passim, 266f, 303f, 435
 computerized *243-45,
  268, 412, 500f
 & ignorance 265-67
 process 236
 shadow land of 305-07
Information retrieval systems
  151, *234-42, 262, 264
 components 239
 function 236
 language 238
 performance measure 239-
  42
 sensitivity 241f
 specificity 241f
 tutorial 222
 use 236, 265-67
 see also Systems

Information science 115f,
  *147-68, 171, 263f
 field of 147, 153f, 160
 fundamental concerns 234
 & information theory 175f
 as system 160-62
 & technology 147, 160-63
 terminology 273
Information service 175f,
  497, 500f
 customized 457-59
 design 158f
 filter function 458
Information systems see
  Information retrieval
  systems
Information technology 147,
  151, 158, 355-64
 & information science
  160-63
Information theory *234-42,
  478f
 & information science
  175f
Information transfer 147,
  150-52, 154, 156, 160-
  62, 165, 171, 234,
  410f, 461; *187-220,
  *380-402, *403-414
  passim
 direction 154
 feedback 154, 411f
Inhelder, B. 174, 185
Initial Teaching Alphabet
  420f, 444 n. 11
Innovation 156, 453, 460
 in libraries *451-62
Inquiry 43, 136-38, 436,
  465f
 & acquiry 464-67, 468
  n. 4
 autonomy 119f
 conduct 119, 122-26,
  165, 520
 & question answering 465
 see also Research
Institute for Scientific Information 382, 384, 392,

396, 398f
Institutions 58-60, 347, 453, 518
Instruction methods 411, 502-09
Integrative levels 180
Intellect and education 464-66, 471f, 496f, 509f
Intelligibility 117, 137f, 142 n. 38
see also Why-questions
Interdependence 119-21, 136f
Interdisciplinarity *116-36, 179, 184, 463f
asymmetric 122
condition 116-19, 135
encounter 122-26, 131f
situation 119-22, 124-26
symmetric 122
Interdisciplines (Boulding) 120
Interest potential 250-53, 256
Interest profile 407, 458
Intermediary 160
International Aerospace Abstracts 234
International Encyclopedia of the Social Sciences (1967) 229, 230 n. 15
International Encyclopedia of Unified Science see Foundations of the Unity of Science
International Federation for Documentation 229, 314
World Science Information System 229
International Federation of Library Associations 345
International Conference on Cataloging Principles, Paris (1961) 345, 347
International Phonetic Association 421, 445 n. 13
International Study Conference on Classification for Information Retrieval, Dorking (1957) 174
Interpersonal communication

see Communication, interpersonal
Interstate compact legislation 83
Introspection 41, 48, 473, 520
Invisible college see College, invisible
Irwin, R. 143 n. 43
Isard, G. M. 8, *11-40, 525
ISI see Institute for Scientific Information
Isis 381
Isolates 310, 315-19, 335f
I-Systems see Systems, implicative
i. t. a. see Initial Teaching Alphabet

Jacob, M. E. 376 n. 68
James, W. :116, 138 n. 1
Japan 424
JCI see Journal Citation Index
Jewell, W. S. 401 n. 24
Jewett, C. C. :340, 348 n. 2, 351
Johnson, R. D. 376 n. 63
Johnson, S. C. 174, 185
Jolley, L. :343, 349 n. 11
Jones, R. C. 376 n. 65
Journal Citation Index 398
Journal of Documentation issue for B. Kyle 176
Journals 398f, 406f
Jouvenel, B. de :452f, :462, 462 n. 2, n. 9

Kahn, A. 219
Kahn, D. 444 n. 9, 445 n. 17
Kaiser, J. O. :307-11 passim, 314, 324, 336
Kaitz, M. J. 401 n. 27
Kana 424, 445 n. 17
Kanji 424, 445 n. 17
Kaplan, A. 52 n. 29, :119f,

Kaplan, A. (Cont.)
140 n. 14, 141 n. 34,
:143 n. 41, 144 n. 57,
227, 231 n. 21, n. 24
Katz, S. 401 n. 32
Kelly, G. A. :179, 185
Kelsen, H. 141 n. 29
Kelvin, Lord 224
Kennedy, President J. F. 381
Kent, A. 11 items 5, 6, 7;
18 item 73
Key papers 396f
Keypunching 359
Keyword 267, 407
Khinchin, A. I. 239, 242 n. 1
Kieffer, P. 376 n. 52
Kilgour, F. 188f, 218f
Kimball, G. E. 261 n. 1
King, L. S. 50 n. 10
Kingery, R. E. 354, 373 n. 6
Kirk, G. 451
The Kiss 44f
Knapp, P. B. :332, 338 n. 25,
468 n. 4, 469 n. 7, *472-
94, 525
Know-how 42, 410f
Knowing 132f, 464-68
Knowledge 135, 187-89
access to 127, 518f
bibliographic structure 467,
498
common sense 42, 50 n. 9,
174
consistency 263f
development 498
evaluation 222, 265
fields 116, 498; see also
Subject fields
future 131
linguistic 447 n. 27
management 489
map 117
observational 131; see
also Data
organization of 121-23,
183, 227-29
preservation 170f, 495
production *380-414 pas-

sim, 451-69 passim,
496f
professional 42f, 131,
476, 478f
public 188f, 379f
rational 47
synthesis *221-31 passim
theoretical 47
use 188f; see also Use
and user
wavefront 498, 510
Knowledge authority 476,
478-80, 486f, 490
Knowledge industry 189
"Knowledge most worth having" 47, 222, 396f
Knowledge records 41, 127,
143 n. 44, 171f, 496f;
see also Document;
Graphic records
access to 127, 172
properties 129f, 171
Knuth, D. E. 400 n. 19
Kochen, M. *187-220, 188,
219f, :222f, 230 n. 9,
525
Kolers, P. A. 377 n. 72
Koopman, B. O. 261 n. 2
Koson, D. 216
Koyré, A. 381
Kozumplik, W. A. 377 n. 69
Kuhn, T. S. 119, 139 n. 10,
n. 13, 140 n. 15
Kunze, H. *515-22, 525
Kyle, B. 176, 180

Labor, Division of 473,
475
Lagides 89, 91
Lakatos, I. 139 n. 13
La Mettrie, J. de 224
Lange, R. T. 377 n. 69
Language 175, 238, 416f
artificial 238
media 438
natural 238, 503
profile 416
reading knowledge 438

representation 238f, *415-49 passim
standardization 151, 424, 434f, 441
structure 442
study 434
teaching 420
use 437f
& writing-system 416f, 426
Language of
professional use 409f
research 409f
theory 409f
Languages
distribution & specification 416
exotic 421
Western European 436
Lannon, E. R. 374 n. 27
Lanzendorfer, M. J. 375 n. 44
Lasswell, H. D. 154, 167, 222, 229
Latham, R. G. 433, 447 n. 31
Lattice 174, 176
Law 472f, 476, 486, 489
Law of diminishing return 248f
Lazarsfeld, P. F. 405, 413
Leake, C. D. 382, 400 n. 7
Learning 174, 464-66, 471, *495-514 passim
Lederberg, J. 399 n. 1
Lee, R. E. 67, 68 n. 10, 69 n. 19
Lehmann, W. 216
Leigh, R. D. 86 n. 7
Leonard, F. 376 n. 52
Leppmann, P. K. 462 n. 7
Letters 423, 443 n. 5
Levi, I. 51 n. 18
Levins, R. 231 n. 27
Lewis, D. J. 145 n. 64
Liberal arts 116f
Librarian 85, 442
beginner 491f
book-based 456f

certificate 517
as civil servant 517
client relationship 484f
as critic 451
dedication 521; see also 43
& discourse 253
education *515-22
& faculty 465f, 486f
generalist 461; see also Referential consultant
& ignorance 263-65
information handling 486f
professional associations 488
professional status 397, 399, 465, 483, *515-22
scholar 515f, 521
subject specialization 486f; see also Specialization
task 127-31, 263-65, 267, 515
& writing-system *415-49 passim, 426
Librarianship 147, 151, 169
activities 43, 127, 135f
basic issues 115-231 passim, 519f
bibliothecal activities 127-30
contexts 379-449 passim
European 516-18
forecast 451-69 passim
goals 43, 127, 135f, 452, 469 n. 6
& history 55-113, 520
how and why 472
interdisciplinarity *116-46
interdisciplinary requirements 131-35
& janitorship 501
knowledge on and about 43, 48f, 131, 478f
language of 49
model 48f, 492

Librarianship (Cont.)
  & organization 472f, 478-
    89
  practice 132-35, 520f
  preconceptions 492
  principal concerns 43, 115·
    231 passim, 127-31,
    135f
  problem area 43, 48f, 127-
    36
  profession 41, 132, 452,
    472f, 478, 488f, 517,
    520f
  properties 43, 135f
  quintessential element 49
  relationships 43, 127
  research in 127, 133, 135-
    37, 479, 488f
  responsibility 41
  service activities 129-31,
    483
  as social science 184
  sociology of 520
  structure and function 127,
    133
  supportive activities 130f
  system 127
  & technology 169-72, *452-
    62 passim; see also
    Technology
  texts and handbooks 516f
  theory of 41-53 passim,
    132-35, *169-86, 216,
    471f, 487
  tools 183
Libraries 437, 441, 455f
  academic see Academic
    libraries
  agency function 67
  ancient *87-113 passim,
    90, 94f, 102f, 104-07
  & bibliographic organiza-
    tion 467f
  & communications culture
    457-59
  cooperation 76, 83, 85;
    see also Public librar-
    ies

  early New England 59f
  European 516-18
  function 451-62
  future 453
  & literacy 436f
  organization 451-62
  public see Public librar-
    ies
  school see School li-
    braries
  special see Special li-
    braries
  tax-supported see Public
    libraries
  term 269f, 275, 277-94,
    295-300
  use 246-67 passim, 454;
    see also Use and user
Library
  as complex organization
    *472-94
  & conflict 483; see also
    Conflict
  departments 461, 479
  & educational process
    *463-69 passim, 467f
  functions 187-89, 215f,
    460
  instruction 466
  services 467f, 469 n. 9,
    484f
  switching system 460
  tasks 483
  technology see Technol-
    ogy
  as warehouse 460
  see also Use and user
Library administration 480,
  516f, 520
  see also Administration
Library Association Record
  (1967) 315
Library classification see
  Classification
Library countries 518f,
  522 n. 9
Library education 471-522
  passim

courses & curricula 478f, 490f, 519-21
  field experience 491f, 519f
  fundamentals 519f
  language requirement 520
  phases of 519f
  research 520
  students 491f
  & type of library 518f
Library history 55-113, 70f, 515
  American 55-69
  new 56f, 66f
  19th century 516f
Library Literature 67
Library materials 152, 252-61
  selection 127, 187, 484, 519f
  see also Collection
Library networks *70-86 passim, 455, 518
Library of Congress 183, 188, 195, 325, 341, 346f
  cards 340, 352, 364
  cataloging practices 340f
  catalogs 354-56
  classification 176, 253f, 332
  Descriptive Cataloging Division 344
  filing rules 358
  Green Book 342f, 346f
  machine-readable catalog 359
  National Union Catalog. Pre-1956 Imprints 354
  "radicalism" 343
  Rules for Descriptive Cataloging... Supplement 1949-51 342
  Studies of Descriptive Cataloging (1946) 341, 343, 346
  Subject Headings (1966) 313, 336
  Superimposition policy 348

Library profession see Librarianship, profession
Library Quarterly 340
Library science 115, 516-18, 520
Library Science Abstracts 225
Library science, five laws of see Five laws of library science
Library scientist 189f
Library Services Act 78
Library Services and Construction Act 80-83
'Life', term 272, 276
Linderman, W. 219
Line, M.B. 168
Line printer 356, 361
Linguacy 437f
Lingualism 416f, 436-38
Linguistic competence 438f, difficulties 264, notation 421f, profile 436-38, theory 442
Linguistics 147, 151, 416, 429, 436, 442
Links and roles 322, 331
Lipetz, B. 188, 219
List-O-Matic 356
Liston, D.M. 160, 167
Literacy 415, 423f, 434-40, 448 n.35, 454
Literature and information 308
Literature search 195, 385
Literatures, ancient 90, 92-96, 98f, 103
Livermore Laboratory. Library 371
Livingston, H.H. 144 n.58, n.60, 145 n.62
Lockheed Missiles & Space Co. Technical Information Center 371
Loeber, T.S. 376 n.67
Logic 141, 147, 176
London. Borough of Camden

Library 356
Lubetzky, S. 341, 343-46, 349 n.10, n.17
Luce, R.D. :135, 145 n.66
Luther, M. 379

MacCarthy, P.A.D. 446 n.19
Macedonia 93f, 96, 100
McFarland, A.S. 17 item 52
Machine 171-73, 357f, 465
Machine-readable record 357, 359
Machlup, F. 143 n.44, 469 n.8
McIntosh, A. 448 n.33
McLaughlin, C.P. 403, 410, 414
McLuhan, M. 454, 457
McMullen, H. 64, 68 n.14
MacQuarrie, C. 373 n.9, 376 n.56, n.58
Magraw, R.M. 140 n.18, 144 n.51
Maidment, W.R. 377 n.70
Le Maître Phonétique 445 n.13
Makris, C.J. 375 n.43
Malin, M.V. 402 n.45
Manual of Foreign Languages... (1952) 416
MARC see Library of Congress, Machine-Readable Catalog
March, J.G. 140 n.19, 154f, 167
Margenau, H. 44, 50 n.12, 51 n.20, 52 n.24, 143 n.47
Markus, J. 374 n.22
Marrou, H-I. :136, :145 n.68
Martyn, J. 158, 167
Massachusetts Bay Colony 61
Matching problems 262
Mathematics 147, 151, 182
Matrix 267, 362
Matta, S. 353, 372 n.4
"Matter" 176f, 317, 324

Maurer, F. 120
Maxwell, J.C. 224
Media 442, 457
  centers 456
  mass- 404f
Medical Literature Analysis and Retrieval System 192, 217 n.4
Medical Subject Headings (MESH) 177-80
Medicine, field of 410, 472f, 476, 486, 489
Medium
  primary 158, 161
  secondary 158, 161
MEDLARS see Medical Literature Analysis and Retrieval System
Memory 451, 497
Memphis 91
Menninger, K. 144 n.50
Mention 264, 265f
Menzel, H. 156, 163f, 167, *403-14, 403, 405, 410, 412 n.1, n.2, 413 n.4, 525
MESH see under Medical Literature Analysis and Retrieval System
Message 154, 156f, 159-63, 165f, 175f, 403, 411f, 442
Mesthene, E.G. :451f, 455
Metaphor 223f, 273
Metcalfe, J.W. *303-38, 333, 448 n.32, 525f
Method 43
  bibliographic 467
  clinical 497, 504
  historical 56-59
  quantitative 518
  scientific 142 n.35; see also Inquiry
Microfilm and forms 458f
Mikhailov, A.I. 184f
Milkau, F. 87, 97, 104, 107, 112 n.3, n.7, n.9

Mill, J.S. 138 n.2
Miller, J.G. 142 n.36
Miller, J.R. 402 n.44
Mills, D.L. 493 n.9
Mills, J. :326f, 337 n.21
Milne, A.A. 42
Mitchell, T.F. 448 n.34
M. Lib. Sci. see India. Master of Library Science
Moby Dick 264
Model 217 n.9, *221-31 passim, 222, 230 n.15
  in biology 228
  bureaucratic 480, 490; see also Model of organizations
  doctor-patient 126
  & goal determination 480-82
  mathematical 224, 230 n.15
  of organizations *472-94 passim
  physical 224
  planetary 227
  tool-for-optimal-action 42
  use of 224f, 227f
Molbech, C. 515-17, 521 n.3, 522 n.5, n.7, n.8
Montague, B.A. 176, 185
Monypenny, P. 86 n.3
Mooers, C. 267, :274, 277 n.8
Moravcsik, M.J. 376 n.66, 406, 413
Morgenstern, O. :136, 145 n.67
Morison, E.E. :137, 145 n.71
Morpheme 427, 430f, 446 n.20
Morre, J.K. 375 n.40
Morris, C. 231 n.30
Morsch, L. 347
Morse, P.M. *246-61, 261 n.1, n.5, n.6, n.7, 526
Morse code 175, 422
Moses, L. 261 n.3

Mote, L.J.B. 164, 167
Mountford, J.D. *415-49, 526
Muenchhausen, Baron von 183
Mulvihill, E.H. 274, 277 n.9
Munn, R. 480, 493 n.16
Murdock, J.W. 160, 167
Murray, J.A.H. 230 n.12
Musgrave, A. 139 n.13
Music 116

Nadel, S.F. 51 n.19
Nadler, M. 374 n.29
Nagel, E. 142 n.34, 144 n.59, :182, :184, 185
NASA see National Aeronautics and Space Administration
National Aeronautics and Space Administration 412
National Book League 445 n.11
National Library of Medicine 177, 352
National Science Foundation 166f
Nationalism, cultural 62
Naudé, G. 515f, 521 n.2
Neelameghan, A. 513 n.5, n.8, n.9, n.10
Neleus, library of 101f
Nelson Associates 86 n.1, n.4
Neo-Melanesian language 423
Network
  interpersonal 407
  referential *187-220 passim
  theoretical 44-47
Network diagram 384-96, 398f
Neurath, O. 231 n.30
Neurophysiology 147, 151

Nevins, A. 141 n. 29
New Deal period 56
New York City 83
  Three R's program 83,
    86 n. 5
New York Public Library 353
Newill, V. A. 242 n. 3
Newman, J. H. 451, 471
Newsletters 406
Newspapers, scientific 406
Newton, I. 224, 227, 380
Nineveh, library 94, 102-04
  shelf list 107
NLM see National Library
  of Medicine
Noise 154, 268, 304, 331
Non-print materials 344, 347,
    456f, 459
Normal science 119
Norman, R. Z. 52 n. 23
Northrop, F. S. C. 44, :48,
    52 n. 26, 53 n. 32, 138,
    144 n. 58, n. 60, :n. 62,
    227, 230 n. 20
Notched cards 262
Note-taking 432, 505
Notion 175, 314
  connective 46f, 124, 126,
    135; see also Rules of
    correspondence
NSF see National Science
  Foundation
Nue speling 446 n. 19
Nugent, W. R. 358, 373 n. 19
Nyquist, E. B. 86 n. 5

Object 127, 129f
  Cutter's 309f, 312, 322,
    324, 336, 343, 351
Occupations, sociology of
    *472-94 passim
OCR see Optical Character
  Recognition
Oettinger, A. G. 142 n. 37
Offset printing 352, 356
Ong, W. J. :117, 139 n. 7
Operators 318f

Optical Character Recogni-
    tion 359f
Optimization 239, *243-45,
    *246-61 passim
Order 116, 172, 174, 303
  alphabetical 305, 310,
    440
  classified 334f
Ordnung zur Ausbildung...
    (1893) 517
Oregon State Library 371
Organization chart 473
Organization models and li-
    brarianship 478-89
Organization theory
  & library education 490-
    92
  in library education
    courses 489-91
  in professional accultura-
    tion 491
  & social epistemology
    489f
Organizational context see
    Context, organizational
Organizational design 207f,
    210
Organizations *472-92 pas-
    sim
  analysis of 473-75
  authority 477
  function 482
  goals and means 474,
    492
  & librarianship *472-92
    passim
  multi-unit 85f
  nature 473-75
  non-professional 477
  prime beneficiary 484
  & profession 473, 475-78
  professional 475-78
  semi-professional 477,
    479f, 484
  stability 474
  types of 477f, 484
  see also Model of organ-

izations
Oriental libraries, ancient
93-96, 102-06
see also Alexandrian libraries; Libraries, ancient
Orientation 155
Orr, R.H. 160, 167, 403,
:409, 414, 469 n.6, n.9
Orthographies 415-19, 422-
24, 435, 440, 442, 446
n.26
& cryptography 420
multiplicity 422-26, 440f
non-standard 425
phonological independence
439f
proposed 441
reform 424
secondary 440
Semitic 428
socio-linguistic dominance
434
& spelling 429
standardization 423, 434f
uniformity 433-35
& writing-systems 425
Orwell, G. :348
Osborn, A.D. 339, 341-43,
346, 348 n.1, 349 n.8
Ostermann, G.F. von 416
Otlet, P. :314, 337 n.7

Paedographies 419-21, 439-
41
Hebrew 446 n.22
Paisley, W.J. 156, 163, 167,
412 n.1, 414
Paleography 428, 437
Palmer, R. 188, 216, 219
Paperback book 457-59
Papers, classic see Key
papers
Papyrology 428
Paré, G. 138 n.6
Pargellis, S. 63
Parikh, S.C. 401 n.24

Paris. Bibliothèque Nationale. Catalogue
Général... 354
Paris Conference (1961) see
International Federation of Library Associations
Parkinson, C. 219 n.16
Parkinson's law 214
Parsons, E.A. 87, 90, 97,
107, 109, 112 n.4, 113
n.19
Parsons, T. 120, 140 n.17
Pasternack, S. 406, 413
Pastorate 476
Patron see Client; Client
relationship; Use and
user
Pattern 172, 233
analysis 397
conceptual 43f, 172, 233
theoretical 43-47
Patterns of communication
*187-220 passim, 380-
414 passim, 489f
Paul, A.J. 402 n.39
Paxton, E.A. 376 n.68
Payne, C.T. 371, 377 n.71
Peer group 474, 481-83
Peirce, C.S. :48, 52 n.29,
:133, 144 n.61, 145
n.63
Peisistratos 96, 98, 107
Pella 97
Pelz, R.C. 403, 414
Pepys, S. 444 n.10
Pergamus 97
Peripatos 97, 101f, 107
Perrault, J.M. 373 n.15
Perry, J.W. 11 items 5,
6, 7
Persians, ancient 92-94
"Personality" 176f, 317,
324
Personality development 495f
Peters, R.S. 170, 185
Petrarch :138, n.6

Petrof, B.G.   50 n. 4
Pettee, J.   275, 277 n. 10,
   :331f, :332, 337 n. 24
Philadelphia, Pa.   61
Philadelphia Commercial Mu-
   seum   307, 336
Philadelphia Free Library
   356, 369
Philip of Macedon   89, 91
Phillips, A.H.   447 n. 28
Philosophical Society (London)
   425
Philosophy   116
Phoenicians   98f
Phoneme   427, 446 n. 21
Phonetics   437, 448 n. 34
Phonology   426f, 435, 437,
   439, 446 n. 21, 448 n. 34
Photocomposition   361f
Physical Review Letters   406
Piaget, J.   120, 121-23, 137,
   140 n. 22, n. 25, n. 27,
   n. 28, 141 n. 29, :n. 30,
   174, 185
Piaget's system of sciences
   121-23
Pierce, E.G.   341
Piggott, M.   345, 349 n. 16
Pinakes   105, 107
Pitman, I.   445 n. 15
Pitman, J.   445 n. 12
Pitman's stenography   417,
   428
Pizer, I.H.   376 n. 57, n. 61
Planck, M.   224
Plato   99, 263
   Academy   98
Platthy, J.   112 n. 5
Plotters   393f
Polanyi, M.   182, 185
Pollack, L.   174, 185
Polycrates   96
Pool, I. DeS.   187f, 219
Popecki, J.T.   373 n. 16
Popper, K.R.   52 n. 21, n. 22,
   142 n. 35
Positivism, on mathematics

182
Postulates   144 n. 62
Potter, B.   444 n. 10, n. 11
P-plane   see   Protocol data
Practice and theory   132-35,
   471f, 491
Pragmatism   471
Prediction   43, 132f, 138,
   158, 160, 170, 172f,
   463
Preprints   405f
Price, D.J. DeS.   :122, 141
   n. 33, 168, :380, 382,
   399 n. 2, 400 n. 6, 403,
   405, 414
Princeton University   381
   book catalog (1760)   350f
Printing   431, 443 n. 5
Print-out   352, 356
Pritchard, A.   382, 400 n. 4
Probability   *187-220 passim,
   *246-61 passim,   246-49
Problem of inquiry   47, 119,
   124-26, 135-37;   see
   also   Inquiry
Problem solving   155, 160
Process   119, 148, 234,
   307-11, 336, 461
Processing   76, 455f, 459
Profession   42, 410, 475-78
   autonomy   476
   & bureaucracy   475-78
   culture   476
   goals   473f, 480
   image   *515-22 passim
   intellectual content   41
   knowledge authority   478-
   80
   model   48f, 480, 492
   & organizations   473, 475-
   78
   performance   48f, 127-31,
   263-65, 267, 480, 515
   practitioners   409f
   productivity   477
   quintessential element   41,
   49

responsibility 41, 485
role 473
self knowledge 41, 48,
473, 520
service goals 452, 469
n. 6, 481, 492
as social system 475
status 478, 483, *515-22
passim
supportive disciplines 50
n. 11
technology 41
see also Client relationship
Professional Library Service
(Xerox) 370
Professionalization 475f, 487-
89
Profiles of the Future (1962)
229
Program routine 155, 160
Progress 171
Prolegomena to Library Classification (1937, 1957,
1967) 314f
Pronunciation 439
Propositions
basic 117f, 138, 144 n. 62
relational 148, 156-58,
160, 163-66
see also Concepts
Protocol data 44-47
Prussia 517
Psycho-linguistics 436, 438f,
441f
Psychological Abstracts 224
Psychology 147, 151
of communication 478f
Ptolemaic thesis 102f, 107
Ptolemy I, Soter 89-92, 95-
97, 100f, 103, 107f
Ptolemy II, Philadelphos 90f,
101, 105
Public libraries 518, *55-69,
*70-86
as agency 58, 61
architecture 64
A/V service 81

children's section 457,
459
client relationship 484f
& community 65-67
consultants 76, 81
cost sharing 74
county 71, 74, 76
distribution of resources
74
funds 59, 64, 76-83
growth patterns 70-86
inner city branches 457,
459
large 80f
local option pattern 80
multi-library systems 70f,
74-76, 78
municipal 74n
networks 71, 518
prime beneficiary 490
processing centers 81
public relations 81
& public schools 62
quality vs. demand 484
resources 76-83
rural service 72-74, 78-
80
in service training 76
small, local 71, 72-74,
76
surveys 80
systems 71f, 78-80
teletype 81
Public library history *55-
69
Public library movement 60-
62
Public relations, internal
474
Publications
intermediary 152f
primary 152f
secondary 152f
standards 410f
Publishing, computerized
358f
see also Book catalogs,

Publishing (Cont.)
production
Punch card 262, 352, 356, 359, 501
Punctuation 429f, 433, 446 n. 26

Quenemoen, H. 216
Question
answering 190-95, 465
categories 209, 211-13
negotiation 193, 208
reinforcement 208-10
well formulated 208f

Rabi, I.I. :463, 468 n. 1
Rabinow, J. 374 n. 30
'Radio receivers', term 271f, 276
Raiffa, H. :135, 145 n. 66
Randall, J.H. :139 n. 11
Ranganathan, S.R. 170, 176f, 180f, 185, 314-22, :315, :317, :318, :320, :321, 324, 328f, 332, :334f, 337 n. 10, n. 11, n. 12, n. 13, n. 17, n. 18, n. 22, n. 23, 338 n. 28, 345, 349 n. 16, *495-514, 512 n. 1, n. 2, 513 n. 3-7, 514, 526
Ranz, J. 352, 372 n. 3
Rapaport, D. 174
Rawski, C.H. 7, 25 item 157, 26 item 159, *41-53, 51 n. 18, 53 n. 31, *116-46, 138 n. 6, 504 n. 1, 515, 526
Reader see Use and user
Reader-printers 459
Reading 379, 454, 478f
Reality 47, 175f
Reason 138, 142 n. 38
Recataloging 344
Receiver 156, 160-65, 234-39, 403-05
Reconstruction, conceptual 43

Records see Knowledge records
Reductionism 182
Redundancy 154
Rees, A.M. 217 n. 5, 219 n. 18
Reference 187, 497
answers--samples 191f
concept 187, 190
function 189-95, 408
groups 481
librarian 215, 233; see also Referential consultant
questions--samples 190f
& technical processes 490f
theory of 189f
see also Buck-passing; Referral
Referential consultant 190, 192-95, 212, 215f, 404
Referential consulting networks *187-220
model 195-208
Referral 189f, 192, 195, 207-11, 214
Refutation 47
Reichenbach, H. :131, 144 n. 54
Reid, J.F. 448 n. 35
Reinhold, R. 400 n. 3
Reiser, O.L. 180f, 185
Relational propositions see Propositions, relational
Relations
fundamental 138, 173-75
human 474f
logico-mathematical 46
peer group 474f
Relevance 124, 175f, 234, 236, 239f, 406-08, 410, 457
explanatory 126
see also Contact, effective
Reporting, scientific 380-

556

414 passim, 410f
Representation 275, 448 n. 34
Reprography 457, 459, 500-
02
see also Copying
Research 380, 462, 477, 510
520
ad hoc 132-34, 436
basic 133f, 406f, 436
see also Inquiry
Research libraries 467f, 516-
18
Resnikoff, N. L. 357, 373
n. 13, 375 n. 34, n. 47,
376 n. 50, n. 54
Responsibility *472-94 pas-
sim, 474, 485
Retrieval see Information re-
trieval; Information re-
trieval systems
Review books 410
Rhoades, E. L. 454 n. 44
Rhodes 99
Richards, E. M. 68 n. 7
Richardson, E. C. 314
Richmond, P. A. 180f, 185,
*268-301, 276 n. 4, 375
n. 49, 526f
Riessman, L. 487f, 494 n. 28
Rifkin, A. L. 401 n. 30
Robinson, J. H. 56
Rocappi Inc. 370
Rogers, E. M. 156, 165, 167
Roget, P. M. 177
Roles and links 331
Romanization 421, 439f, 445
n. 17
Rosenbloom, R. S. 164, 166f,
403, 410, 414
Rosenblueth, A. 133, 145
n. 64
Rosenthal, J. A. :353f, 420
n. 5
Royal Society 380
Royce, J. R. 229 n. 3
Rules 474, 478
of correspondence 46f, 50
n. 12

Rules for a Dictionary Catalogue (1875-76) 304-
07, 341
Russell, B. 420, 444 n. 10
Rutherford, E. 224, 227
Ryle, G. :48, 50 n. 7, 52
n. 28, n. 30, 143 n. 43,
145 n. 65

Saint Paul 379
Sanskrit, romanized 422
Sarton, G. 381
Saussure, F. de 175
Scanner, optical 359
Scheffler, I. 139 n. 13, 144
n. 53
Scheler, M. :139 n. 12
Schenk, G. K. 86 n. 2
Schlatter, R. :140 n. 23
Schlesinger, A. M. 57
Schmidt, G. P. 468 n. 2
Scholar librarian see Li-
brarian, scholar
School libraries 83, 458f,
490
School-district libraries 62
Schools 485
Schrettinger, M. 516f, 522
n. 6
SCI see Science Citation
Index
Science 121-23, 148f, 412
history of 380-82
Science Citation Index 384,
398
Science Information Notes
414
Science Press 370
Scientific literature, 19th
century American 399
Scientific Management Move-
ment (1911) 473
Scientometrics 382
Scope note 270, 276
Scott, A. E. 400 n. 20
Scott, W. R. :476, :484,
493 n. 7, 494 n. 21
Screening test 240

Scribal cultures, ancient 93-
95, 102-04, 107
Script 426-28, 430, 440
changes 440
cuneiform 429
SDI see Selective Dissemination of Information
Search 152, 155-58, *246-61
passim
advantage 257, 260
allocation 249-52
pragmatic 132f, 153
prediction 158
& probability 246-49
procedure 239
purpose 157f, 161f
purposiveness 162
success 162
techniques 244-46
theory *246-61 passim,
250
time 243-45
visual 246f
volume 161-63
see also Browsing
Seattle, Wash. King County
Library System 356
Segur, B. 216
Selection see Library ma-
terials, selection
Selective Dissemination of Information 407
Seleukos 97
Selye, H. 52 n.24, :143 n.39
Semantic confusion 268
Semantics 272, 437, 442
Semi-professions 477f, 481
see also Profession
Semites, ancient 93, 97-99
Sense data 174
Sensitivity 240-42
measure 241f
Serapis 100
Service activities 129f
Service libraries, rise of
*55-69 passim, 516
Service organization 484

see also Organizations
Shakespeare, W. 424f, 446
n.19, n.20
Shannon, C. 238f
Shaw, G.B. 415, 424
Shaw's alphabet 415, 444
n.10
Sheffer, H.M. :132, :133
Sheffield (England). Free
Public Library System
217 n.6
Sheffield City Libraries 1856-
1956 219
Shelf order 254f
see also Books, arrange-
ment of
Shelley, P.B. 451
Shelton's tachygraphy (1635)
444 n.10
Sheppard, D.M. 402 n.37
Sher, I.H. 400 n.10, 402
n.45
Shera, J.H. 7-9, :41, 42,
48, :50, 50 n.1, 51
n.14, n.18, :55, 56,
:57, 58f, 64, 67, 67
n.1, n.2, n.4, 68 n.6,
n.14, 70, 89, :115f,
116, :127, :132, :136,
138 n.3, 143 n.42,
144 n.56, 145 n.70,
n.71, 169f, 174, 185f,
:188, :223, 230 n.10,
n.11, :233f, 246, 261
n.4, 262, :303, :342,
349 n.9, :350, :379f,
399, :442, :451, :471f,
:479, :489, 493 n.14,
n.15, 512, 521
writings of *11-40
Shera's fallacy 43
Sherman, P.M. 400 n.21
Sherrington, C. 233
Shoffner, R.M. :358, 365,
374 n.20, 376 n.51
Shorter Oxford Dictionary
:333

Shorthands see Stenographies
Shryock, R. H. 382, 400 n. 8
'Signal generators', term
    271f, 276
Signals 151, 175
Simon, H. A. 154f, 167
Simonton, W. :358, :369,
    373 n. 17, 376 n. 62
"Simpler speling reezons and
    rules" (1927) 441f
Simplified Spelling Society
    424f
Simulation 235
Sinclair, D. M. *70-86, 527
Situation, bibliothecal 127-30
Situation, interdisciplinary
    119-22, 124-26, 131f,
    135f
Skepsis 101
Slater, M. 158, 167f
Slavens, T. 216
Slop 304, 331
Smith, E. 143 n. 43, :452,
    462 n. 1
Smithsonian Institution 340,
    351
Social epistemology 169f, 179,
    184, 379, 479
    & organization theory 489f
Social Planetarium 222
Social Science and Humanities
    Index 224f
Social sense 170
Social utilization, effective
    188f
Social Work Abstracts 225
Social work education 491f
Socio-linguistics 436, 439-42
Sociological Abstracts 225
Sociology 147, 151f, 154
    of communication 478f
    organizational 489f
    of reading 478f
Socratic myth 98
SOE see Standard Orthog-
    raphy of English
Solberg, J. J. 218

Solomon, N. B. 401 n. 25
Somali language 423
Sophists 98
Sorge, R. 189, 217
Sortcrossing, disciplinary
    118f, 124, 138
Sorting problems 262
Source 154, 156, 160, 166,
    234, 239, 404f, 458
"Space" 176f, 317, 324
Spalding, S. 346f
Sparks, D. E. 361, 375
    n. 37
Special libraries 212, 460,
    518
Specialization 155, 406f,
    463f, 486f, 518f
Specificity 240-42
    measure 241f
Spelling 424, 429-31, 433f,
    446 n. 26, 447 n. 27
Spencer, C. 52 n. 25
Spencer, G. 61, 67, 68
    n. 8
Spencer, H. 47, 59
Spencer, S. 67 n. 4
Spitzer, L. 120
Sprott, W. J. H. 168
Stalin, J. V. 217 n. 2
Standard Orthography of Eng-
    lish 429f, 432-35,
    439, 441, 447 n. 27
Standardization 340, 442
Stanford University. J.
    Henry Meyer Memorial
    Library 370
Stangl, P. 188, 219
Starbuck, W. H. 143 n. 39
State (condition) 119, 148,
    *234-42 passim
    function 144 n. 62
State libraries 71, 76, 81-
    83, *515-22 passim
State universities 463
Statements 148, 263-65,
    308, 319
Statics, theoretical 144 n. 62

Steiner, G. A. 154, 166
Stelwagon, W. B. 400 n. 15
Stenographies 416, 418f,
    427f, 434, 440f
Stephens, I. R. 376 n. 55
Stereotype plates 340, 351
Stimulus, environmental 155
Stoics 97
Storage *243-45
Strabo 87, :111 n. 1
Straton 101f
Strelcyn, S. 445 n. 16
Strevens, P. 446 n. 33
Structure 116, 172
    administrative 85, *472-
        94 passim
    conceptual 172f, 175, 440
    disciplinary 116-19, 442
    language 442
    meaning 272, 442
    phonological 439
Student power 464, 468 n. 3
Studies, interdisciplinary
    *116-46 passim, 463f
Study, independent 465-67,
    496, 504
Study Conference on Classifi-
    cation Research, Elsi-
    nore 1964 180
Subject *268-301 passim,
    *303-38 passim, 268f,
    303f, 309, 315f, 318f,
    330-34, 349-51
    see also Class; Classifica-
        tion; Statements
Subject Catalogue Headings
    and Structure (1960)
    324
Subject Classification (1906)
    313
Subject fields 116-19, 135,
    151, 268f, 333, 398,
    518f
Subject heading *268-301 pas-
    sim, *303-38 passim,
    269f, 275, 320, 329-31
Subject Headings (1946) 332

Subject Headings: A Practi-
    cal Guide (1951) 306
Subject scan 157, 161f
Subjects, umbral 497f
Submarines 246, 250
Subscription libraries 60,
    63f
Sumer 103
Supervision *472-94 passim,
    478
Supportive activities 130f
Surgeon General's Office.
    Library
    manuscript catalog 352
Susaki, S. 376 n. 52
Swanson, D. 188, 220, 413
    n. 5, 414
Switching, selective 406-08,
    458-61
Symbol 151, 440
Symmetry 122, *262-67
Synergistic function 404
Synonyms 273
Synoptic grasp 46, 121-23,
    137
Syntagmatic Organization Lan-
    guage 228
Synthesis, organizational
    474f
SYNTOL see Syntagmatic
    Organization Language
System of sciences (Piaget)
    121-23
Systematic indexing 307-11,
    314
Systematic Indexing (1911)
    307, 336
Systèmes d'apprentissage
    see Paedographies
Systèmes de métier see
    Technographies
Systems 182, 234, 461,
    478f
    artificial 235
    causative (C-systems)
    121-23
    components 235, 239

deductive 144 n. 62
definition 235
design 236-39
effectiveness 239f
efficiency 239f
error adjusting 239
evaluation 235
function 235
implicative (I-systems)
121-23
model *221-31 passim,
482
natural 235
optimization 235f
organizational 86 n. 1,
487
performance 235f
purpose 235f
self-organizing 239
structured 174-76
theory 182, *234-42 pas-
sim, 235
see also Information re-
trieval systems
Szilard, L. 125

Tagliacozzo, R. 188, 216,
220
Tape *243-45 passim, 359
Target *234-42 passim, 403-
05
see also Destination; Re-
ceiver
Tars, A. 216
Tauber, M. F. 349 n. 12,
*350-77, 354f, 373 n. 6,
376 n. 55, 527
Taxonomy 43, 173, *268-
301 passim
Taylor, A. 522 n. 4
Taylor, F. W. 473
Taylor, R. 145 n. 64
Taylor, R. S. 147, 168, 218
n. 12, 220 n. 22, *451-
62, 527
Teacher 486, 490
Technical processes 483,
490f

Techniques 142 n. 35, 355-
64, 460
Technographies 419, 421f,
439f
Technology 41, 147, 151,
158, 160-63, 355-64,
412, *452-62 passim,
464, 479, 520
Temperance movement 65f
Terminologies
bibliographic 439-41
general 269
linguistic 439-41
specific 269
Terms *268-301 passim,
270f, 304, 318
bound 331
broad 269, 273, 334
definition 273f
distinctness 273
glossaries of 304, 315-
18
isolated 308
main 271f
narrow 269
related 269-73, 297-99,
308, 318, 331
technical 304
Thall, M. 216
Thebes 89, 91
Theophrastos 89, 99-102
library of 101
Theorem 138, 144 n. 62
Theorizing 48f
Theory 42f, 47, *169-86
& facts 52 n. 21, n. 24
function 43-47, 49f
linguistic 442
network 44-47
& practice 132-35, 471f
propositional character
43
semantic 442
Theory of Library Catalogue
(1938) :320, 321
Therapy, musical 120
Thesaurus 177-80, 268f,
268n, 502

Thesaurus (Cont.)
combined 268f
& facet analysis 177-79
inner 269f, 274, 277-94,
295-300
for subject libraries 277-
94
within thesaurus *268-301
Thesaurus of Engineering and
Scientific Terms (1967)
275
Thesaurus of Engineering
Terms (1964) 269-75
Thesaurus of English Words
and Phrases (1852--)
177
Thimmonier, R. 446 n.18
Thompson, V.A. 493 n.8
Ticknor, G. 62
"Time" 176f, 317, 324
Title page information 438
Titles of papers 407
Titulus 106
Tool, scientific 142 n.35,
171
Topic 305f, 334f
see also Subject; Subject
fields
Torpie, R.J. 400 n.10
Torrey, J. :65f, 68 n.17
Trade-offs 237
Tradition 42
Transcription 420f, 439f,
442, 448 n.36
bibliographic 430f; see
also Copying
phonetic 421, 427
quasi-facsimile 432
Translator 499f, 501f
Transliteration 421, 439-41
bibliographic 432, 440
as parasitic writing-system
440
as secondary orthography
440
Transmission 151, *187-220
passim, *234-42 passim,

*262-67 passim, 495
Trial solutions 236f
Troilus and Criseyde 448
n.38
Truth 42, 117, 119, 263f
Tubiana, J. 445 n.16
Tullock, G. 145 n.63, n.65
Turkish language 424
Typing 431, 443 n.5
Typography 428, 437

UDC see Universal Deci-
mal Classification
Ueber Bibliothekswissen-
schaft... (1833) 515
Understanding 137, 152,
174f
United Nations 86
UNESCO 345, 423
U.S. Library of Congress
see Library of Con-
gress
U.S. National Library of
Medicine see National
Library of Medicine
U.S. Office of Education.
Educational Research
Information Center
179f
Universal Decimal Classifica-
tion (1895) 314
University of California.
Los Angeles 346
University of Chicago
bibliographic data system
371
Graduate Library School
57f, 176, 342
University of Pennsylvania
book catalog 1832-75 351
University of Rochester,
N.Y.
book catalog 365
Urquhart, D.J. 9
Use and user 129f, 151-54,
175, 180, 187-89, 211,
235-37, 239, 246, 252,

254, 263-67, 331f, 350,
412, 454f, 458, 463-65,
466-68, 499, 501, 518
see also Client; Client relationship
User groups 180, *246-61
passim, 464f, 468, 484-
87, 499-501
Utility measures 213f

Vale, M. R. 86 n. 6
Values 170, 192f
Van Loo, W. 216
Variables 144 n. 62, 148,
156, 162f
Vavrek, B. 220
Verbalizing 152
Vickery, B. C. *147-68, 315,
:331f, 337 n. 24, 527
VINITI 184
Vitruvius :138 n. 5
Vocationalism 41, 471
Vollmer, H. :477, 493 n. 9
Vygotsky, L. S. 172, 175,
186

Walker, R. D. :136, 145
n. 69
Warheit, I. A. :360f, 422
n. 35, 423 n. 36
Wasserman, P. 217 n. 8,
218, :485f, 494 n. 22,
n. 24-26
Watson, J. D. 141 n. 32
Watson-Crick model 227
see also DNA code
Waxman, R. 453 n. 33
Weber, D. C. 355, 365, 373
n. 7, 375 n. 46, 376
n. 51, n. 59
Weber, M. 473
Weinberg, A. M. :127, 143
n. 45, 144 n. 49, :227,
231 n. 23
Weinstein, E. D. :363f, 375
n. 48
Weisbrod, B. :137, 145 n. 72

Weiss, I. J. 352, 372 n. 2
Weiss, P. 222, 229 n. 5
Wells, A. J. 321
Wells, H. G. 193, 220,
:221, 222, 229 n. 1,
n. 2
West, L. E. 401 n. 28
Western Reserve University
179f
White, C. M. :143 n. 43
White, M. 140 n. 24
Whitehead, A. N. 170
Whitehill, W. M. 68 n. 7,
n. 16
Why-questions 133, 142
n. 38
see also Credibility; In-
telligibility
Wiener, N. 133, 145 n. 64
Wiggins, E. V. 352, 372
n. 2
Wilson, L. R. 67 n. 4, 143
n. 43, 374 n. 32
Wingfield, A. 174, 186
Wisdom 195, 472
Wishner, R. 374 n. 28
Wolek, F. W. 164, 166f,
403, 410, 414
Wolfowitz, J. 239, 242 n. 2
Wood, D. N. 159, 163-66,
168
Woodford, F. 66f, 69 n. 18
Woodger, J. H. :142 n. 34
Word-break sign 431, 433,
447 n. 28
Word meanings 175
Words in limbo 273
Work 155
World Brain 222, 229
World encyclopedia 221f,
223, 228f
concept *221-31 passim
World Information Center
222
World machine, Newtonian
224
World Reference System 222

World Science Information
     System 229
World War I 221
World War II 246
Wright, H. C. *87-113, 527
Wright, W. 344f
Wriston, H. :466
Writing 428, 430f, 434-36,
     443 n. 5
  see also Graphology
Writing media 431f, 437
Writing-system 416, 425,
     432f, 435f, 440, 443
     n. 5, 448 n. 36
  & bibliographic description
     *415-49
  change of 431
  & graphology 436
  & language 416f, 426
  & librarian 426
  linguistic concept 441
  profile 417, 437f
  purpose 419
  types 417-22, 426-29;
     see also Paedographies;
     Technographies
Writing-systems 416f, 419,
     429, 441
  & orthographies 425, 429f
  parasitic 440
  theory 430
  total description 429-33
Writing-Systems for English
     441
Wrolstad, M. E. 442 n. 1
WSEs see Writing-Systems
     for English
Wynar, B. :189, 220

Yale University. Library
     460
  book catalog (1743) 350
  Faculty Advisory Memoran-
     dum (1967) 462 n. 8
Yerkes, C. P. 375 n. 45
Yugoslavia 424

Zetterberg, H. L. 50 n. 10
Zuckerman, R. A. 374 n. 24